# U.S. History
## Making a New Nation

RESEARCH COMPANION

## Program Authors

**James Banks, Ph.D.**
University of Washington
Seattle, Washington

**Kevin P. Colleary, Ed.D.**
Fordham University
New York, New York

**William Deverell, Ph.D.**
University of Southern California
Los Angeles, California

**Daniel Lewis, Ph.D.**
The Huntington Library
Los Angeles, California

**Elizabeth Logan Ph.D., J.D.**
USC Institute on California and the West
Los Angeles, California

**Walter C. Parker, Ph.D.**
University of Washington
Seattle, Washington

**Emily M. Schell, Ed.D.**
San Diego State University
San Diego, California

mheducation.com/prek-12

Send all inquiries to:
McGraw-Hill Education
120 S. Riverside Plaza, Suite 1200
Chicago, IL 60606

ISBN: 978-0-07-692875-0
MHID: 0-07-692875-6

Printed in the United States of America.

4 5 6 7 8 9 LWI 23 22 21 20 C

## Program Consultants

**Tahira DuPree Chase, Ed.D.**
Greenburgh Central School District
Hartsdale, New York

**Jana Echevarria, Ph.D.**
California State University
Long Beach, California

**Douglas Fisher, Ph.D.**
San Diego State University
San Diego, California

**Nafees Khan, Ph.D.**
Clemson University
Clemson, South Carolina

**Jay McTighe**
McTighe & Associates Consulting
Columbia, Maryland

**Carlos Ulloa, Ed.D.**
Escondido Union School District
Escondido, California

**Rebecca Valbuena, M.Ed.**
Glendora Unified School District
Glendora, California

## Program Reviewers

**Gary Clayton, Ph.D.**
Northern Kentucky University
Highland Heights, Kentucky

**Lorri Glover, Ph.D.**
Saint Louis University
St. Louis, Missouri

**Thomas Herman, Ph.D.**
San Diego State University
San Diego, California

**Clifford Trafzer, Ph.D.**
University of California
Riverside, California

# Letter From the Authors

Dear Social Studies Detective,

Think about the United States of America. Why did different groups of people decide to settle in the territory that would become the United States? When the nation was formed, how did the economy, the politics, and groups of people change? In this book, you will find out more about how a territory became a nation. You will think about what it meant to become an independent United States—and what it means to be an American.

As you read, take on the role of a detective. As questions come to your mind, write them down. Then analyze the text to find the answers. What grabs your interest? Take notes as you read. You will use your notes as you share what you learned with your classmates. Look closely at all of the text—photos, maps, time lines, and historical documents will bring the history of the United States to life!

Enjoy your investigation into the world of social studies where you will explore how a group of territories became the United States, a place full of women, men, and children who came from many places to form a growing and diverse country!

Sincerely,

The IMPACT Social Studies Authors

IN CONGRESS, JULY 4, 1776.

# The unanimous Declaration of the thirteen united States of America,

When in the Course of human events, it becomes necessary for one people to dissolve the political bands which have connected them with another, and to assume among the powers of the earth, the separate and equal station to which the Laws of Nature and of Nature's God entitle them, a decent respect to the opinions of mankind requires that they should declare the causes which impel them to the separation. —— We hold these truths to be self-evident, that all men are created equal, that they are endowed by their Creator with certain unalienable Rights, that among these are Life, Liberty and the pursuit of Happiness. — That to secure these rights, Governments are instituted among Men, deriving their just powers from the consent of the governed, — That whenever any Form of Government becomes destructive of these ends, it is the Right of the People to alter or to abolish it, and to institute new Government, laying its foundation on such principles and organizing its powers in such form, as to them shall seem most likely to effect their Safety and Happiness. Prudence, indeed, will dictate that Governments long established should not be changed for light and transient causes; and accordingly all experience hath shewn, that mankind are more disposed to suffer, while evils are sufferable, than to right themselves by abolishing the forms to which they are accustomed. But when a long train of abuses and usurpations, pursuing invariably the same Object evinces a design to reduce them under absolute Despotism, it is their right, it is their duty, to throw off such Government, and to provide new Guards for their future security. — Such has been the patient sufferance of these Colonies; and such is now the necessity which constrains them to alter their former Systems of Government. The history of the present King of Great Britain is a history of repeated injuries and usurpations, all having in direct object the establishment of an absolute Tyranny over these States. To prove this, let Facts be submitted to a candid world. —— He has refused his Assent to Laws, the most wholesome and necessary for the public good. —— He has forbidden his Governors to pass Laws of immediate and pressing importance, unless suspended in their operation till his Assent should be obtained; and when so suspended, he has utterly neglected to attend to them. —— He has refused to pass other Laws for the accommodation of large districts of people, unless those people would relinquish the right of Representation in the Legislature, a right inestimable to them and formidable to tyrants only. —— He has called together legislative bodies at places unusual, uncomfortable, and distant from the depository of their Public Records, for the sole purpose of fatiguing them into compliance with his measures. —— He has dissolved Representative Houses repeatedly, for opposing with manly firmness his invasions on the rights of the people. —— He has refused for a long time, after such dissolutions, to cause others to be elected; whereby the Legislative powers, incapable of Annihilation, have returned to the People at large for their exercise; the State remaining in the mean time exposed to all the dangers of invasion from without, and convulsions within. —— He has endeavoured to prevent the population of these States; for that purpose obstructing the Laws for Naturalization of Foreigners; refusing to pass others to encourage their migrations hither, and raising the conditions of new Appropriations of Lands. —— He has obstructed the Administration of Justice, by refusing his Assent to Laws for establishing Judiciary powers. —— He has made Judges dependent on his Will alone, for the tenure of their offices, and the amount and payment of their salaries. —— He has erected a multitude of New Offices, and sent hither swarms of Officers to harrass our people, and eat out their substance. —— He has kept among us, in times of peace, Standing Armies without the Consent of our legislatures. —— He has affected to render the Military independent of and superior to the Civil power. —— He has combined with others to subject us to a jurisdiction foreign to our constitution, and unacknowledged by our laws; giving his Assent to their Acts of pretended Legislation: — For Quartering large bodies of armed troops among us: — For protecting them, by a mock Trial, from punishment for any Murders which they should commit on the Inhabitants of these States: — For cutting off our Trade with all parts of the world: — For imposing Taxes on us without our Consent: — For depriving us in many cases, of the benefits of Trial by Jury: — For transporting us beyond Seas to be tried for pretended offences — For abolishing the free System of English Laws in a neighbouring Province, establishing therein an Arbitrary government, and enlarging its Boundaries so as to render it at once an example and fit instrument for introducing the same absolute rule into these Colonies: — For taking away our Charters, abolishing our most valuable Laws, and altering fundamentally the Forms of our Governments: — For suspending our own Legislatures, and declaring themselves invested with power to legislate for us in all cases whatsoever. — He has abdicated Government here, by declaring us out of his Protection and waging War against us. —— He has plundered our seas, ravaged our Coasts, burnt our towns, and destroyed the lives of our people. —— He is at this time transporting large Armies of foreign Mercenaries to compleat the works of death, desolation and tyranny, already begun with circumstances of Cruelty & perfidy scarcely paralleled in the most barbarous ages, and totally unworthy the Head of a civilized nation. —— He has constrained our fellow Citizens taken Captive on the high Seas to bear Arms against their Country, to become the executioners of their friends and Brethren, or to fall themselves by their Hands. —— He has excited domestic insurrections amongst us, and has endeavoured to bring on the inhabitants of our frontiers, the merciless Indian Savages, whose known rule of warfare, is an undistinguished destruction of all ages, sexes and conditions. In every stage of these Oppressions We have Petitioned for Redress in the most humble terms: Our repeated Petitions have been answered only by repeated injury. A Prince, whose character is thus marked by every act which may define a Tyrant, is unfit to be the ruler of a free people. Nor have We been wanting in attentions to our Brittish brethren. We have warned them from time to time of attempts by their legislature to extend an unwarrantable jurisdiction over us. We have reminded them of the circumstances of our emigration and settlement here. We have appealed to their native justice and magnanimity, and we have conjured them by the ties of our common kindred to disavow these usurpations, which, would inevitably interrupt our connections and correspondence. They too have been deaf to the voice of justice and of consanguinity. We must, therefore, acquiesce in the necessity, which denounces our Separation, and hold them, as we hold the rest of mankind, Enemies in War, in Peace Friends. ——

We, therefore, the Representatives of the united States of America, in General Congress, Assembled, appealing to the Supreme Judge of the world for the rectitude of our intentions, do, in the Name, and by Authority of the good People of these Colonies, solemnly publish and declare, That these United Colonies are, and of Right ought to be Free and Independent States; that they are Absolved from all Allegiance to the British Crown, and that all political connection between them and the State of Great Britain, is and ought to be totally dissolved; and that as Free and Independent States, they have full Power to levy War, conclude Peace, contract Alliances, establish Commerce, and to do all other Acts and Things which Independent States may of right do. —— And for the support of this Declaration, with a firm reliance on the protection of divine Providence, we mutually pledge to each other our Lives, our Fortunes and our sacred Honor.

John Hancock

Button Gwinnett
Lyman Hall
Geo Walton

Wm Hooper
Joseph Hewes,
John Penn

Edward Rutledge

Thos Heyward Junr.
Thomas Lynch Junr.
Arthur Middleton

Samuel Chase
Wm Paca
Thos Stone
Charles Carroll of Carrollton

George Wythe
Richard Henry Lee
Th Jefferson
Benja Harrison
Thos Nelson jr.
Francis Lightfoot Lee
Carter Braxton

Robt Morris
Benjamin Rush
Benja Franklin
John Morton
Geo Clymer
Jas Smith
Geo Taylor
James Wilson
Geo Ross

Caesar Rodney
Geo Read
Tho M:Kean

Wm Floyd
Phil Livingston
Frans Lewis
Lewis Morris

Richd Stockton
Jno Witherspoon
Fras Hopkinson
John Hart
Abra Clark

Josiah Bartlett
Wm Whipple
Saml Adams
John Adams
Robt Treat Paine
Elbridge Gerry
Step Hopkins
William Ellery
Roger Sherman
Samel Huntington
Wm Williams
Oliver Wolcott
Matthew Thornton

The Declaration of Independence

# Contents



# Reference Sources

Chapter 1

# The Land and Native Peoples of North America

## How Were the Lives of Native Peoples Influenced by Where They Lived?

# Chapter 2

# The Age of Exploration

## What Happened When Diverse Cultures Crossed Paths?

Chapter 3

# A Changing Continent

## What Is the Impact of People Settling in a New Place?

# The Road to War

## Why Would a Nation Want to Become Independent?

# The American Revolution

## What Does the Revolutionary Era Tell Us About Our Nation Today?

Chapter 6

# Forming a New Government

## How Does the Constitution Help Us Understand What It Means to Be an American?

Chapter 7

# A Growing Nation

## What Do the Early Years of the United States Reveal About the Character of the Nation?

Chapter 8

# The Civil War and Reconstruction

## What Was the Effect of the Civil War on U.S. Society?

# Skills and Features

## Then and Now



## Around the World



## Primary Source



## Literature



## Map and Globe Skills

## Field Trips



## InfoGraphics



## Did You Know?



## Citizenship



## Perspectives



## Biographies

## Time Lines



## Charts, Graphs, and Diagrams



## Maps

## Primary Source Quotations

### Chapter 1



### Chapter 2



### Chapter 3



### Chapter 4

## Chapter 5



## Chapter 6

**George Mason.** "Federalists and Antifederalists Debate a Bill of Rights," by Gordon Lloyd. http://teaching americanhistory.org/bor/fed-antifed-debate . . . . . . . . . . . . . . . . . . . . . . . . . . . . . . . . . . . . . . . . 312

**Elbridge Gerry.** "Elbridge Gerry's Reasons for Not Signing the Federal Constitution." http://www.loc.gov/teachers/classroommaterials/presentations andactivities/presentations/timeline/newnatn/usconst/egerry.html. . . . . . . . . . . . . . . . . . . . . . . . . . . . . . 312

**Patrick Henry,** speaking before the Virginia Ratifying Convention, June 1788. . . . . . . . . . . . . . . . . . . . . . . . . . . 312

**William Tyler Page.** "'American's Creed' by Future Clerk of the House William Tyler Page." http://history.house.gov/HistoricalHighlight/Detail/35813?ret=True . . . . . . 318

## Chapter 7

**Louisiana Purchase:** Treaty between the United States of America and the French Republic, art. 3. April 30, 1803. National Archives and Records Administration . . . . . . . . . . . . . . . . . . . . . . . . . . . . . . . . . .340

**Dolley Madison** to her sister, Anna Cutts, August 23, 1814. In *Dolly Madison,* by Maud Wilder Goodwin, pp. 173–175. New York: C. Scribner's Sons, 1896. . . . . . . .343

**Samuel F. B. Morse.** "Today in History—May 24." Library of Congress. https://www.loc.gov/item/today-in-history/ may-24/. . . . . . . . . . . . . . . . . . . . . . . . . . . . . .352

**Daniel Boone.** *Missouri: A Guide to the "Show Me" State.* Works Progress Administration. New York: Duell, Sloan and Pearce, 1941 . . . . . . . . . . . . . . . . . . . . .356

**A Treaty of Peace** between the United States of America and the Tribes of Indians..., art. 3. In The Public Statutes at Large of the United States of America, Vol. 7, edited by Richard Peters, 49. Boston: Charles C. Little and James Brown, 1848. . . .357

**Tecumseh.** In a speech to William Henry Harrison. Vincennes, Indiana Territory. 12 August 1810 . . . . . . . .358

**Sarah L. Byrd,** interview by Sara B. Wrenn, March 1, 1939, Portland, Oregon. Library of Congress, Manuscript Division, WPA Federal Writers' Project Collection, Folklore Project, Life Histories, 1936-39, MSS55715: BOX A729 . . . . . . . . . . . . . . . . . . . . . . . . . . .370

**"Resistance in the Courts."** Digital History, University of Houston. http://www.digitalhistory.uh.edu/disp_textbook.cfm?smtID=3&psid=691 . . . . . . . . . . . . . . . . . .374

**Chief John Ross.** "The Papers of Chief John Ross, vol 1, 1807-1839." Translated by Gary E. Moulton Norman OK: University of Oklahoma Press, 1985 . . . . . . . . . . .374

**Worcester v. Georgia,** 31 U.S. 515 (1832). https://www.law.cornell.edu/supremecourt/text/31/515 . . . . . . . . . .375

**Frederick Douglass.** http://www.pbs.org/wgbh/aia/part4/4h2927.html . . . . . . . . . . . . . . . . . . . . . . . . . . . . . . .383

**Abraham Lincoln.** https://www.britannica.com/topic/Uncle-Toms-Cabin . . . . . . . . . . . . . . . . . . . . . . . . . . . . . . .383

## Chapter 8

**Frederick Douglass**, "John Brown: An Address," Harpers Ferry, West Virginia, May 30, 1881, reprinted in The Colored Orator, 1891. https://books.google.com/books?id=Ic3TAAAAMAAJ&printsec=frontcover&dq=the+colored+orator&hl=en&sa=X&ved=0ahUKEwjnmpukp43aAhUD0oMKHWIuBs4Q6AEIKTAA#v=onepage&q=taper&f=false . . . . . . . . . . . . . . . . . . . . . . . . . . . .411

**Daniel W. Voorhees**, Addresses of Hon. Daniel W. Voorhees, of Indiana, Richmond, Virginia, 1861. http://www.wvculture.org/history/jbexhibit/voorhees.html . . . . . . . . . . . . . . . . . . . . . . . . . . . . . . . . . . . . . . . . . . .411

**Charleston Mercury**, *The Union is Dissolved* Broadside https://www.gilderlehrman.org/sites/default/files/content-images/02688p1.jpg , https://amhistory.si.edu/militaryhistory/collection/object.asp?ID=87. . . . . . . . . . . . . . . . . . . . . . . . . . . . . . . . . . . . . 416

**Henry Morton Stanley**, from Stanley, Henry M., *The Autobiography of Henry M. Stanley* (1909) . . . . . . . . .426

**Lieutenant Samuel Dana Green**, from Copy of letter written by the late Lieutenant Samuel Dana Green, U. S. Navy. https://www.history.navy.mil/research/library/online-reading-room/title-list-alphabetically/e/eye-witness-account-of-the-battle-between-the-u-s-s-monitor-and-the-c-s-s-virginia-mar-9-1862.html . . . . .429

**Alexander Hunter,** letter, September 21, 1862. https://www.nps.gov/anti/learn/education/upload/letters%20and%20diaries%20of%20soldiers%20and%20civilians.pdf Southern Historical Society Papers, Volume 10 By Southern Historical Society, 1882, accessed on Google Books . . . . . . . . . . . . . . . . . . . . . . . . . . . . . . . . .435

**John W. Fields,** from an interview conducted on September 17, 1937, Born in Slavery: Slave Narratives from the Federal Writers' Project, 1936 to 1938 https://www.loc.gov/resource/mesn.050/?sp=83 . . . . . . . . . . 441

**William T. Sherman.** Lewis, Lloyd. *Sherman: Fighting Prophet*, p. 488 par. 4 https://books.google.com/books?id=MtQwfz8uFfgC&pg=PA488&lpg=PA488#v=onepage&q&f=false http://www.sonofthesouth.net/union-generals/sherman/sherman-quotes.htm . . . . . . . . . . . . . . . . . . . . . . . . . . . . . . . . . . . .452

# Getting Started

You have two social studies books that you will use together to explore and analyze important Social Studies issues.

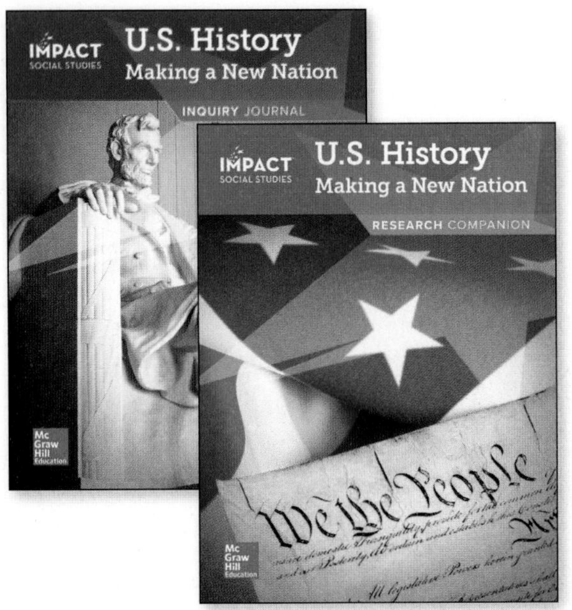

IMPACT SOCIAL STUDIES
U.S. History
Making a New Nation
INQUIRY JOURNAL
IMPACT SOCIAL STUDIES
U.S. History
Making a New Nation
RESEARCH COMPANION
Mc Graw Hill Education


### The Inquiry Journal

is your reporter's notebook where you will ask questions, analyze sources, and record information.

### The Research Companion

is where you'll read nonfiction and literature selections, examine primary source materials, and look for answers to your questions.

# Every Chapter

Chapter opener pages help you see the big picture. Each chapter begins with an **Essential Question**. This **EQ** guides research and inquiry.

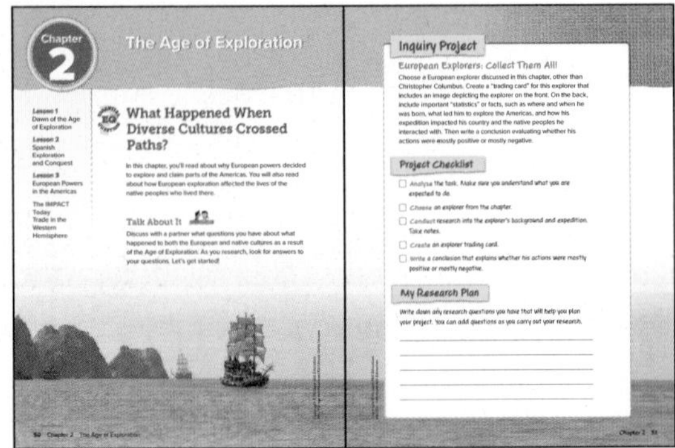

Chapter 2
The Age of Exploration
What Happened When Diverse Cultures Crossed Paths?
Talk About It
Inquiry Project
Project Checklist
My Research Plan


In the **Inquiry Journal,** you'll talk about the **EQ** and find out about the EQ Inquiry Project for the chapter.

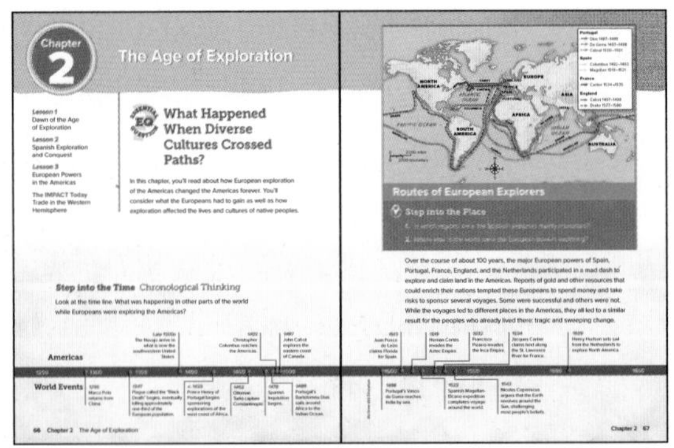


In the **Research Companion**, you'll explore the **EQ** and use a time line and map to establish the lesson's time and place.

StasKhom/iStock/Getty Images

## Explore Words

Find out what you know about the chapter's academic and domain-specific vocabulary.

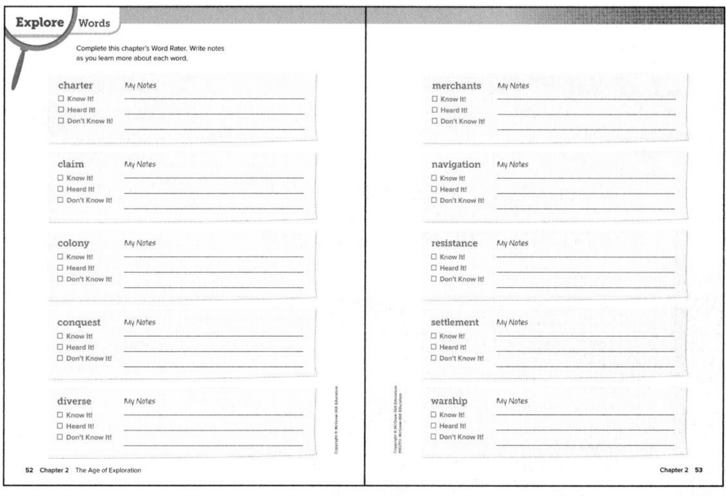

Explore Words

Complete this chapter's Word Rater. Write notes as you learn more about each word.

charter — My Notes
☐ Know It!
☐ Heard It!
☐ Don't Know It!

claim — My Notes
☐ Know It!
☐ Heard It!
☐ Don't Know It!

colony — My Notes
☐ Know It!
☐ Heard It!
☐ Don't Know It!

conquest — My Notes
☐ Know It!
☐ Heard It!
☐ Don't Know It!

diverse — My Notes
☐ Know It!
☐ Heard It!
☐ Don't Know It!

52 Chapter 2 The Age of Exploration

merchants — My Notes
☐ Know It!
☐ Heard It!
☐ Don't Know It!

navigation — My Notes
☐ Know It!
☐ Heard It!
☐ Don't Know It!

resistance — My Notes
☐ Know It!
☐ Heard It!
☐ Don't Know It!

settlement — My Notes
☐ Know It!
☐ Heard It!
☐ Don't Know It!

warship — My Notes
☐ Know It!
☐ Heard It!
☐ Don't Know It!

Chapter 2 53

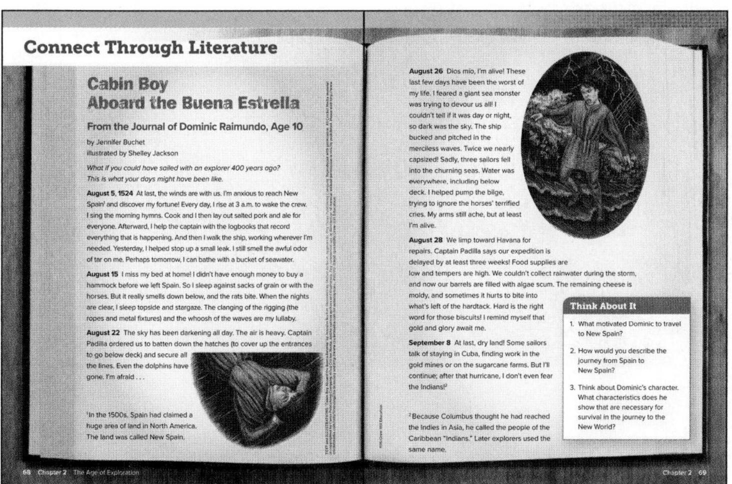

Connect Through Literature

Cabin Boy Aboard the Buena Estrella

From the Journal of Dominic Raimundo, Age 10

by Jennifer Buchet
illustrated by Shelley Jackson

*What if you could have sailed with an explorer 400 years ago? This is what your days might have been like.*

**August 5, 1524** At last, the winds are with us. I'm anxious to reach New Spain[1] and discover my fortune! Every day, I rise at 3 a.m. to wake the crew. I sing the morning hymns. Cook and I then lay out salted pork and ale for everyone. Afterward, I help the captain with the logbooks that record everything that is happening. And then I walk the ship, working wherever I'm needed. Yesterday, I helped stop up a small leak. I still smell the awful odor of tar on me. Perhaps tomorrow, I can bathe with a bucket of seawater.

**August 15** I miss my bed at home! I didn't have enough money to buy a hammock before we left Spain. So I sleep against sacks of grain or with the horses. But it really smells down below, and the rats bite. When the nights are clear, I sleep topside and stargaze. The clanging of the rigging (the ropes and metal fixtures) and the whoosh of the waves are my lullaby.

**August 22** The sky has been darkening all day. The air is heavy. Captain Padilla ordered us to batten down the hatches (to cover up the entrances to go below deck) and secure all the lines. Even the dolphins have gone. I'm afraid . . .

[1]In the 1500s, Spain had claimed a huge area of land in North America. The land was called New Spain.

68 Chapter 2 The Age of Exploration

**August 26** Dios mío, I'm alive! These last few days have been the worst of my life. I feared a giant sea monster was trying to devour us all! I couldn't tell if it was day or night, so dark was the sky. The ship bucked and pitched in the merciless waves. Twice we nearly capsized! Sadly, three sailors fell into the churning seas. Water was everywhere, including below deck. I helped pump the bilge, trying to ignore the horses' terrified cries. My arms still ache, but at least I'm alive.

**August 28** We limp toward Havana for repairs. Captain Padilla says our expedition is delayed by at least three weeks! Food supplies are low and tempers are high. We couldn't collect rainwater during the storm, and now our barrels are filled with algae scum. The remaining cheese is moldy, and sometimes it hurts to bite into what's left of the hardtack. Hard is the right word for those biscuits! I remind myself that gold and glory await me.

**September 8** At last, dry land! Some sailors talk of staying in Cuba, finding work in the gold mines or on the sugarcane farms. But I'll continue; after that hurricane, I don't even fear the Indians![2]

[2]Because Columbus thought he had reached the Indies in Asia, he called the people of the Caribbean "Indians." Later explorers used the same name.

Think About It

1. What motivated Dominic to travel to New Spain?
2. How would you describe the journey from Spain to New Spain?
3. Think about Dominic's character. What characteristics does he show that are necessary for survival in the journey to the New World?

Chapter 2 69

## Connect Through Literature

Explore the chapter topic through fiction, informational text, and poetry.

## People You Should Know

Learn about the lives of people who have made an impact in history.

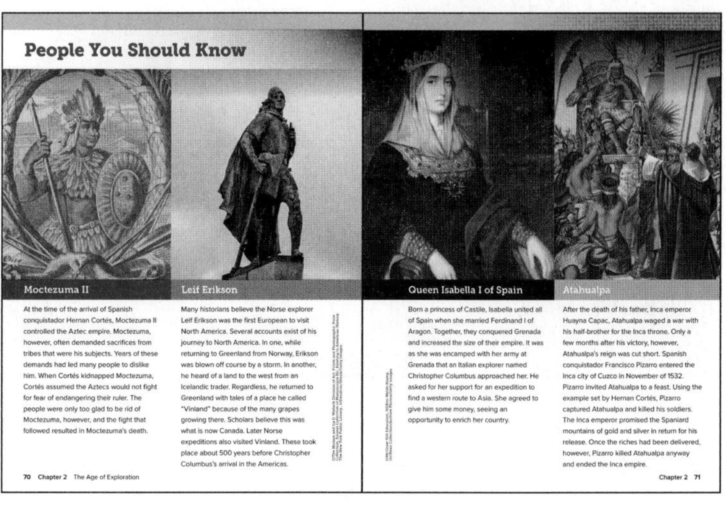

People You Should Know

Moctezuma II

At the time of the arrival of Spanish conquistador Hernan Cortés, Moctezuma II controlled the Aztec empire. Moctezuma, however, often demanded sacrifices from tribes that were his subjects. Years of these demands had led many people to dislike him. When Cortés kidnapped Moctezuma, Cortés assumed the Aztecs would not fight for fear of endangering their ruler. The people were only too glad to be rid of Moctezuma, however, and the fight that followed resulted in Moctezuma's death.

Leif Erikson

Many historians believe the Norse explorer Leif Erikson was the first European to visit North America. Several accounts exist of his journey to North America. In one, while returning to Greenland from Norway, Erikson was blown off course by a storm. In another, he heard of a land to the west from an Icelandic trader. Regardless, he returned to Greenland with tales of a place he called "Vinland" because of the many grapes growing there. Scholars believe this was what is now Canada. Later Norse expeditions also visited Vinland. These took place about 500 years before Christopher Columbus's arrival in the Americas.

70 Chapter 2 The Age of Exploration

Queen Isabella I of Spain

Born a princess of Castile, Isabella united all of Spain when she married Ferdinand I of Aragon. Together, they conquered Grenada and increased the size of their empire. It was as she was encamped with her army at Grenada that an Italian explorer named Christopher Columbus approached her. He asked for her support for an expedition to find a western route to Asia. She agreed to give him some money, seeing an opportunity to enrich her country.

Atahualpa

After the death of his father, Inca emperor Huayna Capac, Atahualpa waged a war with his half-brother for the Inca throne. Only a few months after his victory, however, Atahualpa's reign was cut short. Spanish conquistador Francisco Pizarro entered the Inca city of Cuzco in November of 1532. Pizarro invited Atahualpa to a feast. Using the example set by Hernan Cortés, Pizarro captured Atahualpa and killed his soldiers. The Inca emperor promised the Spaniard mountains of gold and silver in return for his release. Once the riches had been delivered, however, Pizarro killed Atahualpa anyway and ended the Inca empire.

Chapter 2 71

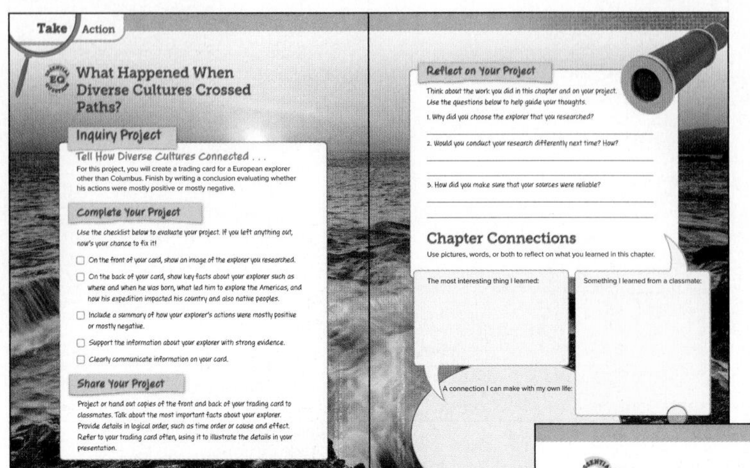
Take Action

What Happened When Diverse Cultures Crossed Paths?

Inquiry Project

Tell How Diverse Cultures Connected . . .

For this project, you will create a trading card for a European explorer other than Columbus. Finish by writing a conclusion evaluating whether his actions were mostly positive or mostly negative.

Complete Your Project

Use the checklist below to evaluate your project. If you left anything out, now's your chance to fix it!

- On the front of your card, show an image of the explorer you researched.
- On the back of your card, show key facts about your explorer such as where and when he was born, what led him to explore the Americas, and how his expedition impacted his country and also native peoples.
- Include a summary of how your explorer's actions were mostly positive or mostly negative.
- Support the information about your explorer with strong evidence.
- Clearly communicate information on your card.

Share Your Project

Project or hand out copies of the front and back of your trading card to classmates. Talk about the most important facts about your explorer. Provide details in logical order, such as time order or cause and effect. Refer to your trading card often, using it to illustrate the details in your presentation.

78 Chapter 2 The Age of Exploration

Reflect on Your Project

Think about the work you did in this chapter and on your project. Use the questions below to help guide your thoughts.

1. Why did you choose the explorer that you researched?
2. Would you conduct your research differently next time? How?
3. How did you make sure that your sources were reliable?

Chapter Connections

Use pictures, words, or both to reflect on what you learned in this chapter.

The most interesting thing I learned:

Something I learned from a classmate:

A connection I can make with my own life:

## Take Action

Complete your Inquiry Project and share it with your class. Then take time to discuss and reflect on your project. What did you learn?

Connections in Action!

Back to the EQ

**Think** about the Chapter EQ, **"What Happened When Diverse Cultures Crossed Paths?"**

- **Talk** with a partner about what you learned in the chapter. Choose a group of native people who encountered Europeans. Make a list of ways these encounters affected your group and its area.
- What was your group's relationship with the Europeans? Did that relationship change over time? If so, how?
- **Share** your ideas with the class; then have a class discussion about the overall effects of exploration on native peoples in the Americas.

104 Chapter 2 The Age of Exploration

More to Explore

How Can You Make an IMPACT?

**Job Interview**

Work with a partner to choose an explorer. One person will play the part of that explorer. The other person will play the part of the European king or queen the explorer wants to have sponsor an expedition to the Americas. Use evidence from your research to conduct a job interview for the expedition. The monarch should try to determine why the journey is a good idea and whether the explorer is the right candidate for the job. The explorer should try to convince the monarch that the monarch's country will benefit from the journey and that the explorer is the right person to lead the expedition.

**Letter to the Editor**

Imagine that you are a citizen of an Aztec or Inca city and that the city has a newspaper. Write a letter to the editor of the newspaper that argues for or against building a relationship with the Europeans. Use evidence from the text to support your opinion.

**Crossword Puzzle**

Create a crossword puzzle using all ten words from the chapter Word Bank. Write an appropriate clue for each word. Exchange puzzles with a partner, and solve your partner's puzzle.

Chapter 2 105

## Connections in Action

Think about the people, places, and events you read about in the chapter. Discuss with a partner how this gives you a deeper understanding of the chapter EQ.

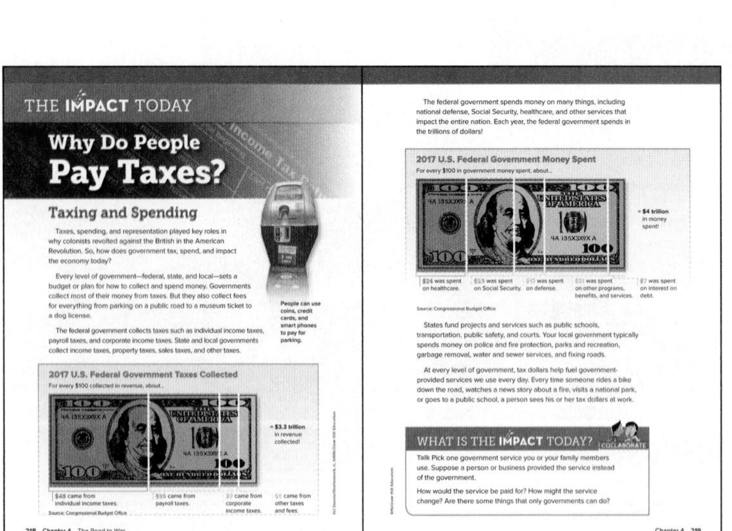
THE IMPACT TODAY

Why Do People Pay Taxes?

Taxing and Spending

Taxes, spending, and representation played key roles in why colonists revolted against the British in the American Revolution. So, how does government tax, spend, and impact the economy today?

Every level of government—federal, state, and local—sets a budget or plan for how to collect and spend money. Governments collect most of their money from taxes. But they also collect fees for everything from parking on a public road to a museum ticket to a dog license.

The federal government collects taxes such as individual income taxes, payroll taxes, and corporate income taxes. State and local governments collect income taxes, property taxes, sales taxes, and other taxes.

People can use coins, credit cards, and smart phones to pay for parking.

2017 U.S. Federal Government Taxes Collected

For every $100 collected in revenue, about...

= $3.3 trillion in revenue collected!

$48 came from individual income taxes. $35 came from payroll taxes. $9 came from corporate income taxes. $8 came from other taxes and fees.

Source: Congressional Budget Office

218 Chapter 4 The Road to War

The federal government spends money on many things, including national defense, Social Security, healthcare, and other services that impact the entire nation. Each year, the federal government spends in the trillions of dollars!

2017 U.S. Federal Government Money Spent

For every $100 in government money spent, about...

= $4 trillion in money spent!

$26 was spent on healthcare. $23 was spent on Social Security. $15 was spent on defense. $31 was spent on other programs, benefits, and services. $7 was spent on interest on debt.

Source: Congressional Budget Office

States fund projects and services such as public schools, transportation, public safety, and courts. Your local government typically spends money on police and fire protection, parks and recreation, garbage removal, water and sewer services, and fixing roads.

At every level of government, tax dollars help fuel government-provided services we use every day. Every time someone rides a bike down the road, watches a news story about a fire, visits a national park, or goes to a public school, a person sees his or her tax dollars at work.

WHAT IS THE IMPACT TODAY?

Talk Pick one government service you or your family members use. Suppose a person or business provided the service instead of the government.

How would the service be paid for? How might the service change? Are there some things that only governments can do?

Chapter 4 219

## The IMPACT Today

Take what you have learned in the chapter and tie it to today's world. Consider how key questions related to geography, economics, and citizenship impact us today.

# Every Lesson

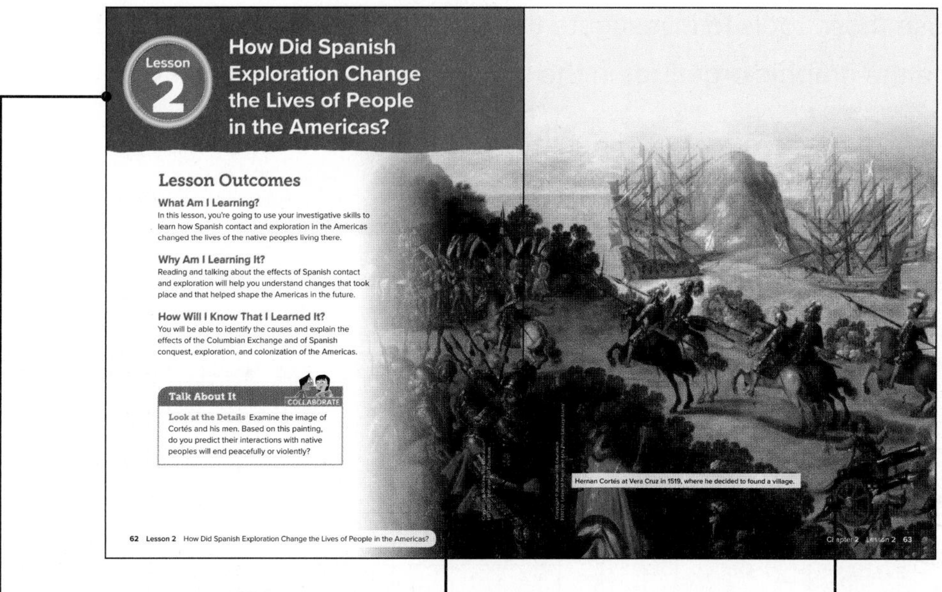

Lesson 2

How Did Spanish Exploration Change the Lives of People in the Americas?

Lesson Outcomes

What Am I Learning?

In this lesson, you're going to use your investigative skills to learn how Spanish contact and exploration in the Americas changed the lives of the native peoples living there.

Why Am I Learning It?

Reading and talking about the effects of Spanish contact and exploration will help you understand changes that took place and that helped shape the Americas in the future.

How Will I Know That I Learned It?

You will be able to identify the causes and explain the effects of the Columbian Exchange and of Spanish conquest, exploration, and colonization of the Americas.

Talk About It — COLLABORATE

Look at the Details Examine the image of Cortés and his men. Based on this painting, do you predict their interactions with native peoples will end peacefully or violently?

Hernan Cortés at Vera Cruz in 1519, where he decided to found a village.

62 Lesson 2 How Did Spanish Exploration Change the Lives of People in the Americas?

Chapter 2 Lesson 2 63

**Lesson Question** lets you think about how the lesson connects to the chapter EQ.

**Lesson Outcomes** help you to think about what you will be learning and how it applies to the EQ.

**Images and text** provide opportunities to explore the lesson topic.

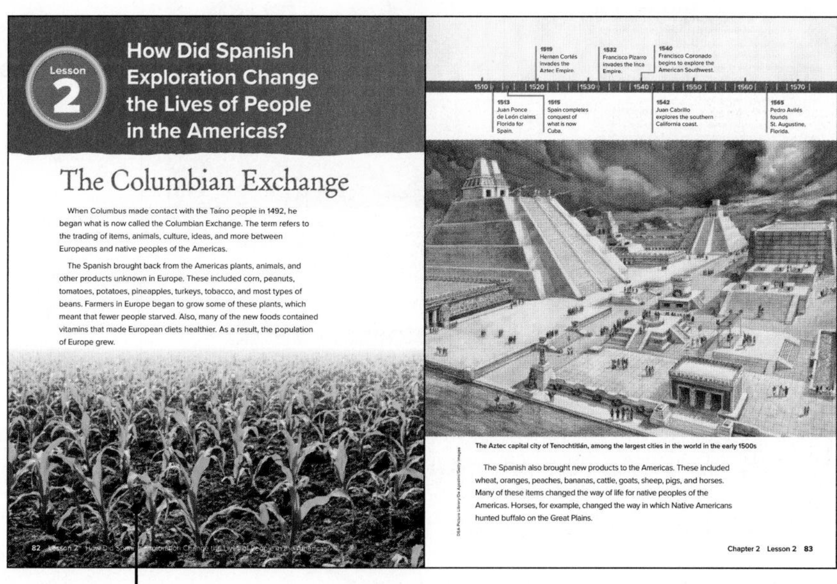

Lesson 2

How Did Spanish Exploration Change the Lives of People in the Americas?

The Columbian Exchange

When Columbus made contact with the Taíno people in 1492, he began what is now called the Columbian Exchange. The term refers to the trading of items, animals, culture, ideas, and more between Europeans and native peoples of the Americas.

The Spanish brought back from the Americas plants, animals, and other products unknown in Europe. These included corn, peanuts, tomatoes, potatoes, pineapples, turkeys, tobacco, and most types of beans. Farmers in Europe began to grow some of these plants, which meant that fewer people starved. Also, many of the new foods contained vitamins that made European diets healthier. As a result, the population of Europe grew.



The Aztec capital city of Tenochtitlán, among the largest cities in the world in the early 1500s

DEA Picture Library/De Agostini/Getty Images

The Spanish also brought new products to the Americas. These included wheat, oranges, peaches, bananas, cattle, goats, sheep, pigs, and horses. Many of these items changed the way of life for native peoples of the Americas. Horses, for example, changed the way in which Native Americans hunted buffalo on the Great Plains.

82 Lesson 2 How Did Spanish Exploration Change the Lives of People in the Americas?

Chapter 2 Lesson 2 83

**Lesson selections** deepen your understanding of the lesson topic and its connection to the EQ.

# Analyze and Inquire

The Inquiry Journal provides the tools you need to analyze a source. You'll use those tools to investigate the texts in the Research Companion and use the graphic organizer in the Inquiry Journal to organize your findings.

**Inquiry Tools** assist with analysis and exploration.

**Graphic Organizers** help you organize information as you read.

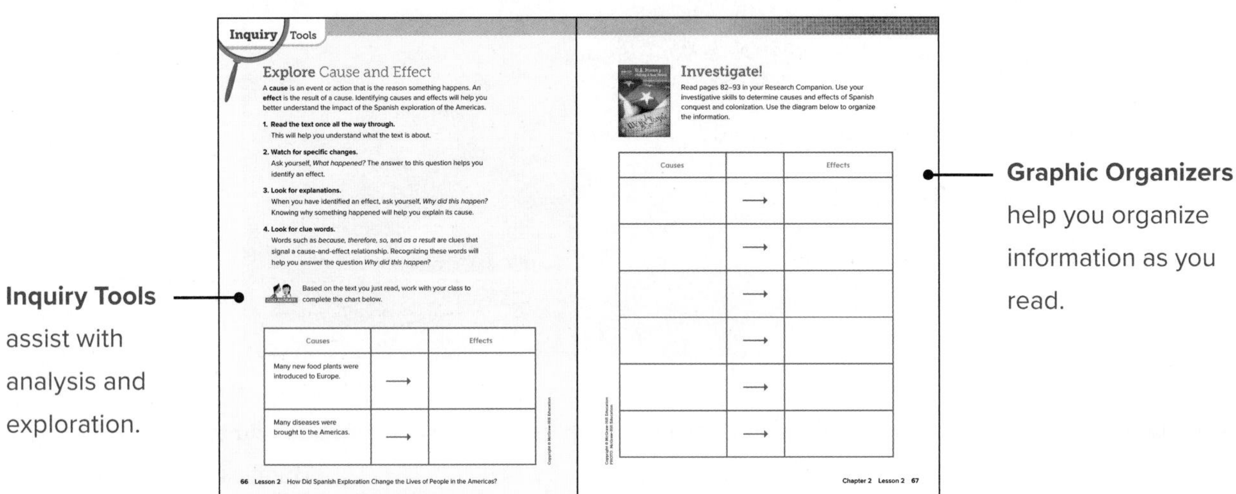

Inquiry Tools

## Explore Cause and Effect

A **cause** is an event or action that is the reason something happens. An **effect** is the result of a cause. Identifying causes and effects will help you better understand the impact of the Spanish exploration of the Americas.

1. **Read the text once all the way through.** This will help you understand what the text is about.
2. **Watch for specific changes.** Ask yourself, *What happened?* The answer to this question helps you identify an effect.
3. **Look for explanations.** When you have identified an effect, ask yourself, *Why did this happen?* Knowing why something happened will help you explain its cause.
4. **Look for clue words.** Words such as *because, therefore, so,* and *as a result* are clues that signal a cause-and-effect relationship. Recognizing these words will help you answer the question *Why did this happen?*

COLLABORATE Based on the text you just read, work with your class to complete the chart below.

| Causes | | Effects |
|---|---|---|
| Many new food plants were introduced to Europe. | → | |
| Many diseases were brought to the Americas. | → | |

Copyright © McGraw-Hill Education

66 Lesson 2 How Did Spanish Exploration Change the Lives of People in the Americas?

## Investigate!

Read pages 82–93 in your Research Companion. Use your investigative skills to determine causes and effects of Spanish conquest and colonization. Use the diagram below to organize the information.

| Causes | | Effects |
|---|---|---|
| | → | |
| | → | |
| | → | |
| | → | |
| | → | |
| | → | |

Copyright © McGraw-Hill Education PHOTO: McGraw-Hill Education

Chapter 2 Lesson 2 67

**Primary Sources** let you read the words and study the artifacts of people from the past and present.

**Maps** show where events happened.

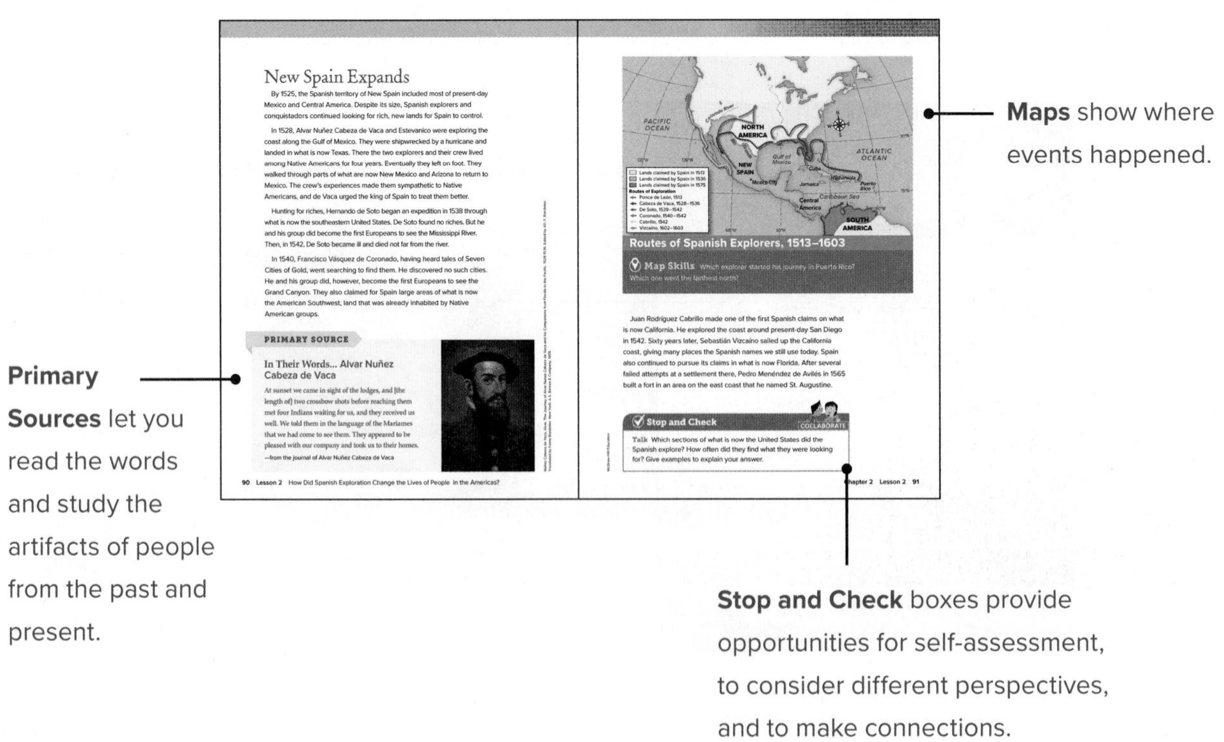

## New Spain Expands

By 1525, the Spanish territory of New Spain included most of present-day Mexico and Central America. Despite its size, Spanish explorers and conquistadors continued looking for rich, new lands for Spain to control.

In 1528, Alvar Nuñez Cabeza de Vaca and Estevanico were exploring the coast along the Gulf of Mexico. They were shipwrecked by a hurricane and landed in what is now Texas. There the two explorers and their crew lived among Native Americans for four years. Eventually they left on foot. They walked through parts of what are now New Mexico and Arizona to return to Mexico. The crew's experiences made them sympathetic to Native Americans, and de Vaca urged the king of Spain to treat them better.

Hunting for riches, Hernando de Soto began an expedition in 1538 through what is now the southeastern United States. De Soto found no riches. But he and his group did become the first Europeans to see the Mississippi River. Then, in 1542, De Soto became ill and died not far from the river.

In 1540, Francisco Vásquez de Coronado, having heard tales of Seven Cities of Gold, went searching to find them. He discovered no such cities. He and his group did, however, become the first Europeans to see the Grand Canyon. They also claimed for Spain large areas of what is now the American Southwest, land that was already inhabited by Native American groups.

PRIMARY SOURCE

### In Their Words... Alvar Nuñez Cabeza de Vaca

At sunset we came in sight of the lodges, and [the length of] two crossbow shots before reaching them met four Indians waiting for us, and they received us well. We told them in the language of the Mariames that we had come to see them. They appeared to be pleased with our company and took us to their homes.

—from the journal of Alvar Nuñez Cabeza de Vaca

90 Lesson 2 How Did Spanish Exploration Change the Lives of People in the Americas?

PACIFIC OCEAN
NORTH AMERICA
Colorado River
NEW SPAIN
Mexico City
Gulf of Mexico
Cuba
Hispaniola
Jamaica
Puerto Rico
Caribbean Sea
Central America
ATLANTIC OCEAN
SOUTH AMERICA
Lands claimed by Spain in 1513
Lands claimed by Spain in 1536
Lands claimed by Spain in 1575
Routes of Exploration
Ponce de León, 1513
Cabeza de Vaca, 1528–1536
De Soto, 1539–1542
Coronado, 1540–1542
Cabrillo, 1542
Vizcaíno, 1602–1603

**Routes of Spanish Explorers, 1513–1603**

**Map Skills** Which explorer started his journey in Puerto Rico? Which one went the farthest north?

Juan Rodríguez Cabrillo made one of the first Spanish claims on what is now California. He explored the coast around present-day San Diego in 1542. Sixty years later, Sebastián Vizcaíno sailed up the California coast, giving many places the Spanish names we still use today. Spain also continued to pursue its claims in what is now Florida. After several failed attempts at a settlement there, Pedro Menéndez de Avilés in 1565 built a fort in an area on the east coast that he named St. Augustine.

**Stop and Check** COLLABORATE

**Talk** Which sections of what is now the United States did the Spanish explore? How often did they find what they were looking for? Give examples to explain your answer.

Chapter 2 Lesson 2 91

**Stop and Check** boxes provide opportunities for self-assessment, to consider different perspectives, and to make connections.

# Report Your Findings

At the end of each lesson, you have an opportunity in the Inquiry Journal to report your findings and connect back to the EQ. In the Research Companion, you'll reconsider the lesson focus question based on what you've learned.

**Think** about what you have learned.

**Write About It** using text evidence to support your ideas.

**Connect** to the EQ.

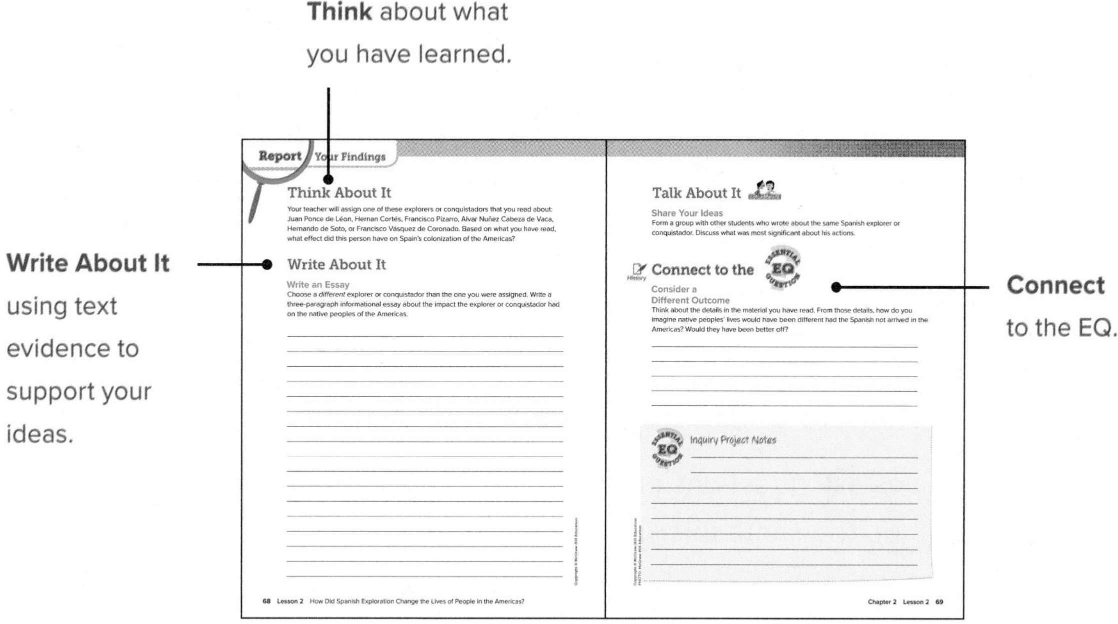

Report Your Findings

### Think About It

Your teacher will assign one of these explorers or conquistadors that you read about: Juan Ponce de Léon, Hernan Cortés, Francisco Pizarro, Alvar Nuñez Cabeza de Vaca, Hernando de Soto, or Francisco Vásquez de Coronado. Based on what you have read, what effect did this person have on Spain's colonization of the Americas?

### Write About It

Write an Essay

Choose a *different* explorer or conquistador than the one you were assigned. Write a three-paragraph informational essay about the impact the explorer or conquistador had on the native peoples of the Americas.

68 Lesson 2 How Did Spanish Exploration Change the Lives of People in the Americas?

### Talk About It

Share Your Ideas

Form a group with other students who wrote about the same Spanish explorer or conquistador. Discuss what was most significant about his actions.

### Connect to the EQ

History

Consider a Different Outcome

Think about the details in the material you have read. From those details, how do you imagine native peoples' lives would have been different had the Spanish not arrived in the Americas? Would they have been better off?

Inquiry Project Notes

Chapter 2 Lesson 2 69

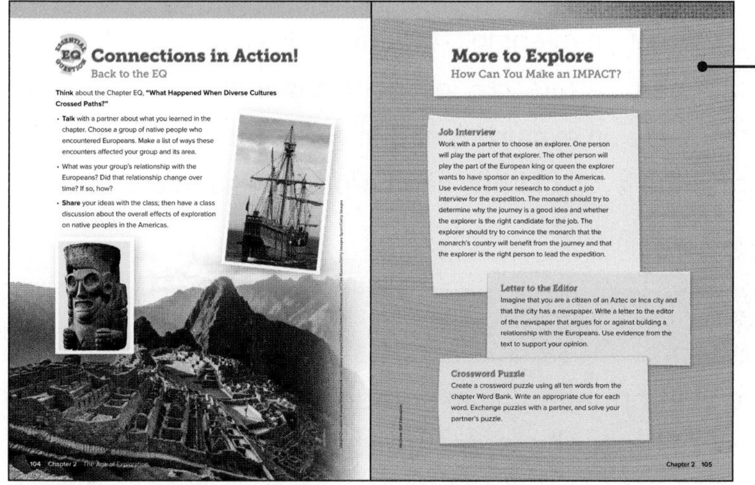

### Connections in Action!

Back to the EQ

**Think** about the Chapter EQ, **"What Happened When Diverse Cultures Crossed Paths?"**

- **Talk** with a partner about what you learned in the chapter. Choose a group of native people who encountered Europeans. Make a list of ways these encounters affected your group and its area.
- What was your group's relationship with the Europeans? Did that relationship change over time? If so, how?
- **Share** your ideas with the class; then have a class discussion about the overall effects of exploration on native peoples in the Americas.

104 Chapter 2 The Age of Exploration

### More to Explore

How Can You Make an IMPACT?

**Job Interview**

Work with a partner to choose an explorer. One person will play the part of that explorer. The other person will play the part of the European king or queen the explorer wants to have sponsor an expedition to the Americas. Use evidence from your research to conduct a job interview for the expedition. The monarch should try to determine why the journey is a good idea and whether the explorer is the right candidate for the job. The explorer should try to convince the monarch that the monarch's country will benefit from the journey and that the explorer is the right person to lead the expedition.

**Letter to the Editor**

Imagine that you are a citizen of an Aztec or Inca city and that the city has a newspaper. Write a letter to the editor of the newspaper that argues for or against building a relationship with the Europeans. Use evidence from the text to support your opinion.

**Crossword Puzzle**

Create a crossword puzzle using all ten words from the chapter Word Bank. Write an appropriate clue for each word. Exchange puzzles with a partner, and solve your partner's puzzle.

Chapter 2 105

**Think about** what you read in the lesson. How does this give you a new understanding about the lesson focus question?

# Be a Social Studies Detective

How do you learn about people, places, and events in the present or in the past and the impact they had on history? Become a Social Studies Detective!

## Explore, investigate, report, and make an impact!

### Investigate Primary Sources

Detectives ask questions and use clues to help them solve mysteries. You can do the same thing by examining primary sources.

### What's a Primary Source?

A **primary source** is a record of an event by someone who was present at the event when it happened. Letters, diaries, newspaper articles, photographs, and drawings are all examples of primary sources. Birth certificates, bank records, and even clothes can be primary sources.

### Did You Know?

A **secondary source** is information from someone who was not present at the event he or she is describing. Secondary sources are based on primary sources.

StasKhom/iStock/Getty Images

PRIMARY SOURCE

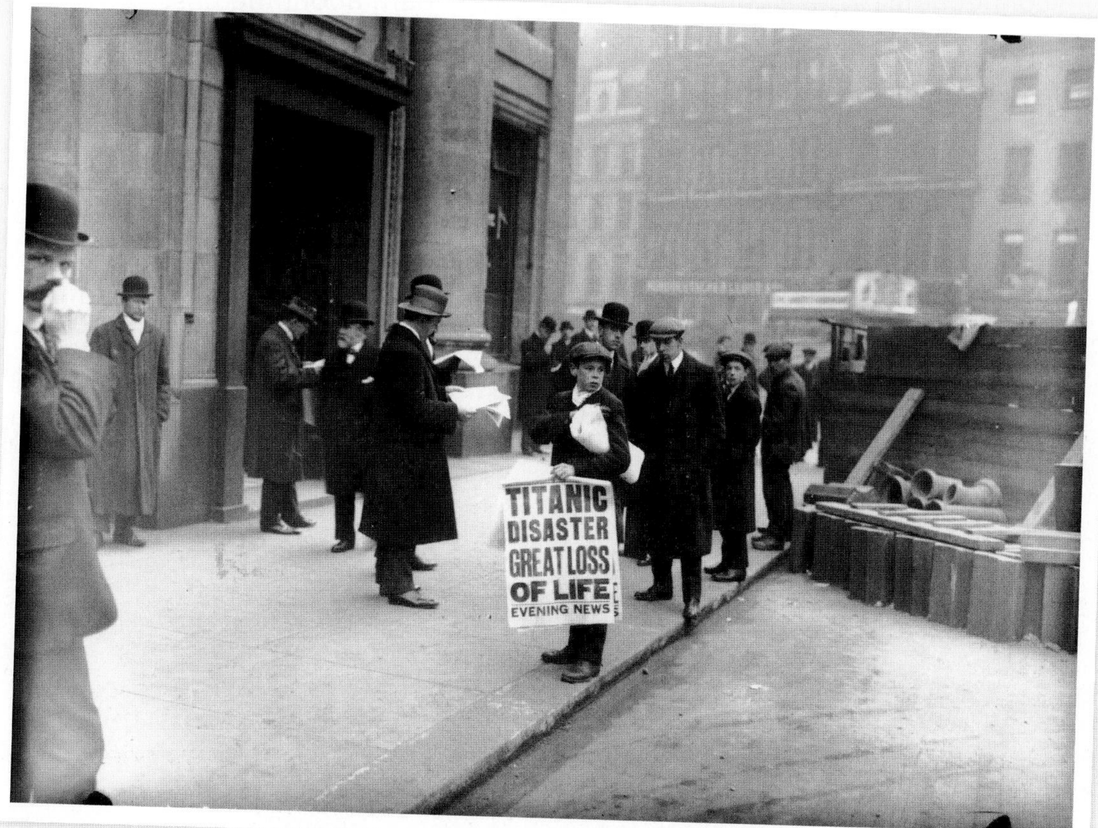


## Social Studies Detective Strategies

### Inspect

- Look closely at the source.
- Who or what is it?
- How would you describe it?

### Find Evidence

- Where did the event take place?
- When did it happen?
- What are the most important details?

### Make Connections

- Is this source like others you found?
- Are there other perspectives that you need to consider?
- What information supports your idea?

Social Studies Detectives examine primary sources to make connections. These connections help them learn about the past and understand the present. Use the Social Studies Detective Strategy to analyze the image below.

PRIMARY SOURCE

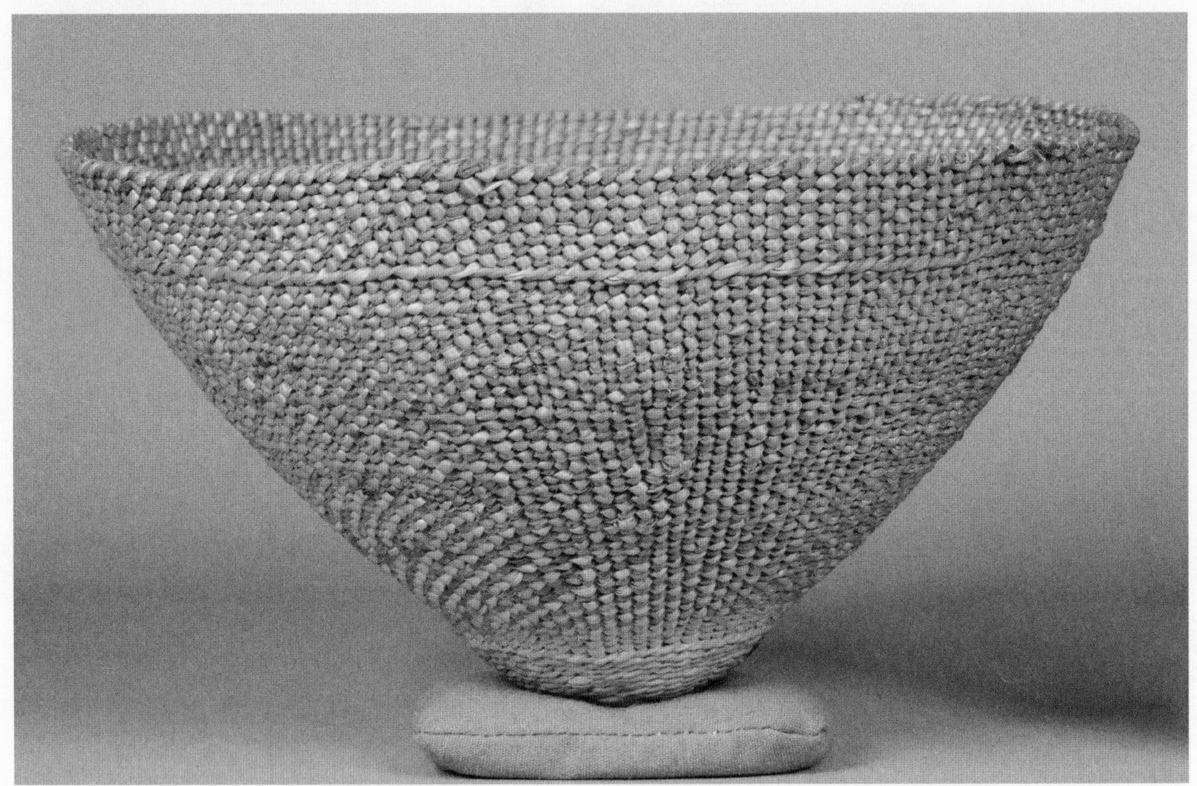

## Social Studies Detective Strategies

1. Inspect
2. Find Evidence
3. Make Connections

Inspect the primary source below. Ask questions. Who wrote the diary? When did they write it? Why do you think they wrote it? Look for clues to answer your questions.

**June 3d, Sunday.** We left El Paso at eight this morning, and rode until ten, when we reached a deserted rancho, and with some trouble encamped near a river bed with waterholes along it. A beautiful lagoon with water holes a hundred yards long enabled us all to take refreshing baths, and I watched with pleasure the languid flight of the great blue heron, changing his position as he was approached. Two Mexicans, hunting cattle, came to us here, and Lieut. Browning bought a wild mule, for which he gave a few dollars and a broken down mule. (p.94)

**September 2d.** Two days out from Ures we came to some Pimos Indians washing gold from black ore, which they said produced well; we found some lumps of ore in the dust, all of irregular shapes. The value is only about one real (about ten cents) for each bushel of dirt. Each man made about two dollars a day.
We had fine grass and pond water here, and are off for Altar. (P.143)

from *Audubon's Western Journal: 1849-1850*

TEXT: Audubon, John W. Audubon's Western Journal: 1849-1850. Cleveland: The Arthur H. Clark Company, 1906.; PHOTO: McGraw-Hill Education

# Explore Geography

Geographers are detectives who understand how our world is connected by studying the earth's surface and digging for clues about how people have shaped our planet. This section gives you the tools that you'll need as you explore geography.



## Reading a Map

Maps are drawings of places on Earth. Most maps have standard features to help you read the map.

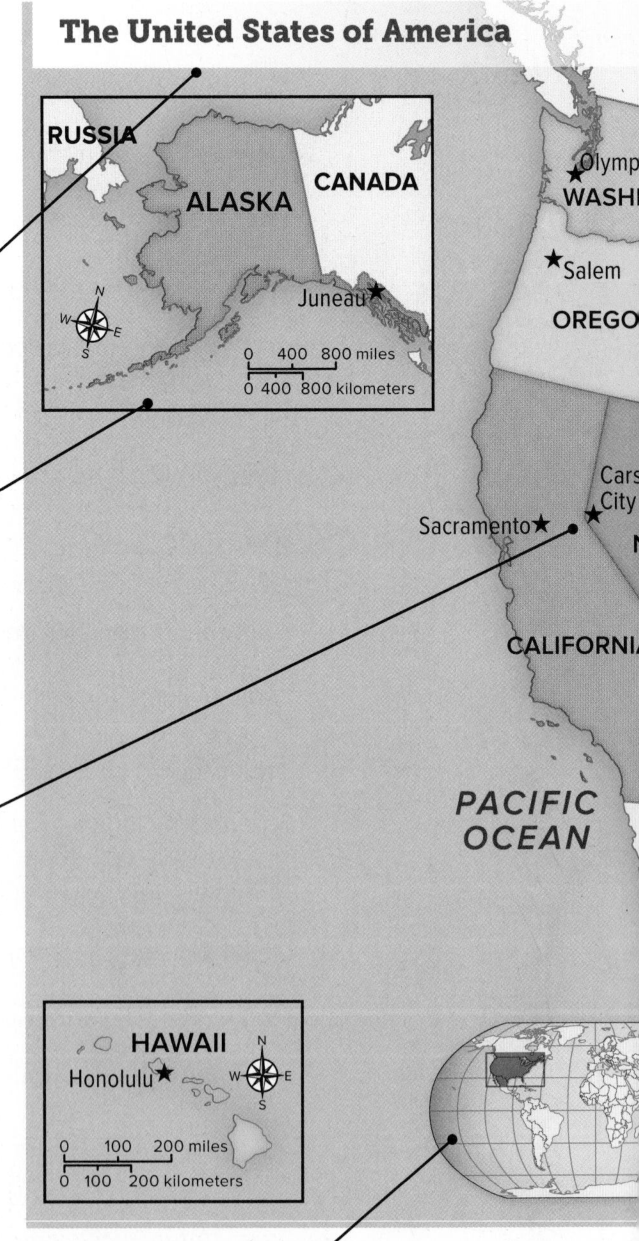


**Map Title** The map title tells you what information is on the map.

**Inset Map** An inset map is a small map included on a larger map. The inset map might show an area that is too large, too small, or too far away to be included on the main map.

**Boundary Lines** Boundary lines are political. The boundaries between states usually are drawn differently from the boundaries between nations.

**Locator** A locator map is a small map set into the main map. It shows the area of the map in a larger region.

**Scale** The scale shows the relationship between distances on a map and real distances. The line on this map scale covers 300 miles. One inch on the map is equal to 300 miles.

**Compass Rose** The compass rose shows where north, south, east, and west are on a map.

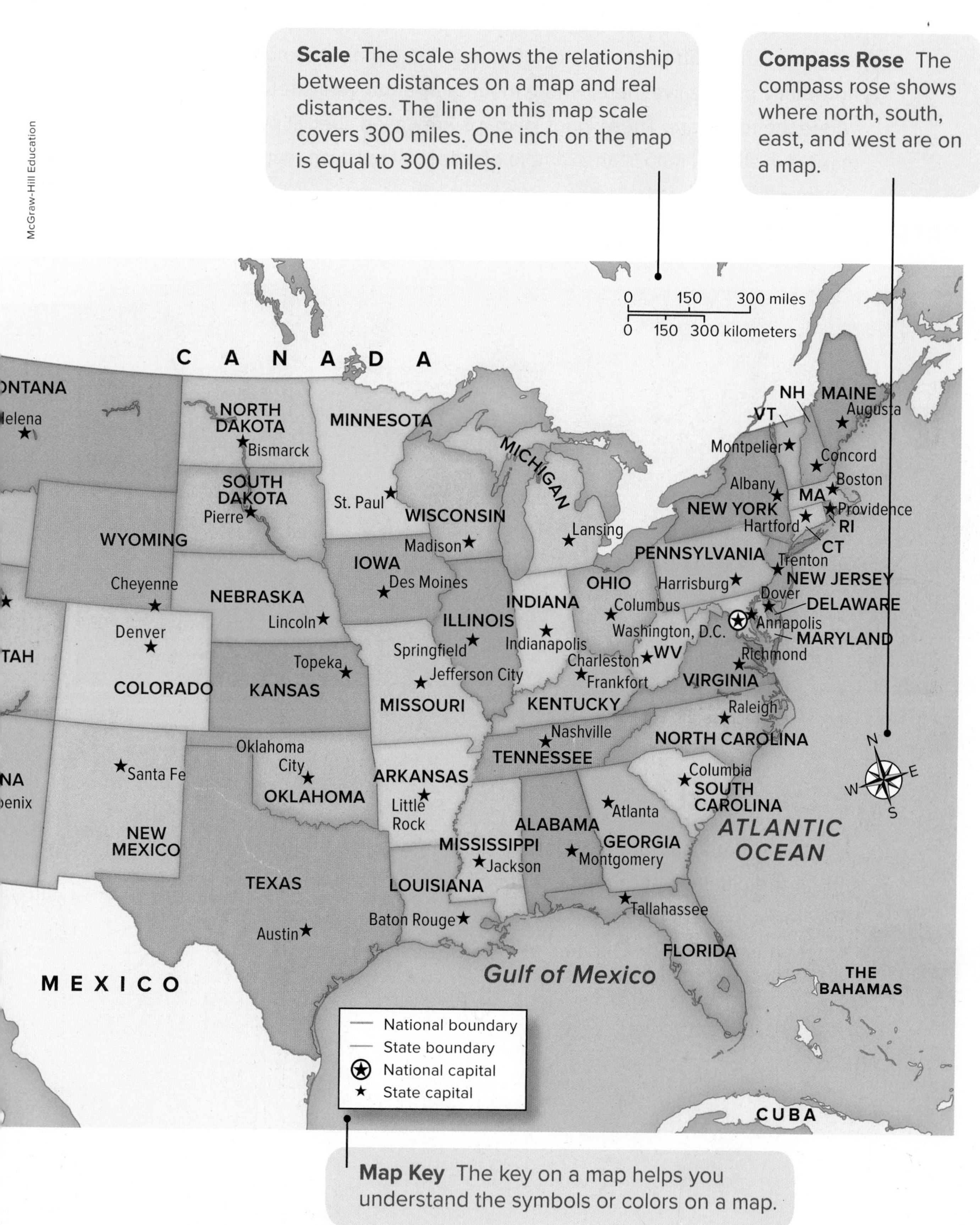


**Map Key** The key on a map helps you understand the symbols or colors on a map.

# Special Purpose Maps

Maps can show different kinds of information about an area such as how many people live there, where mountains and rivers stretch, and where the roads are. These kinds of maps are called special purpose maps. A historical map is an example of a special purpose map.

**PRIMARY SOURCE**

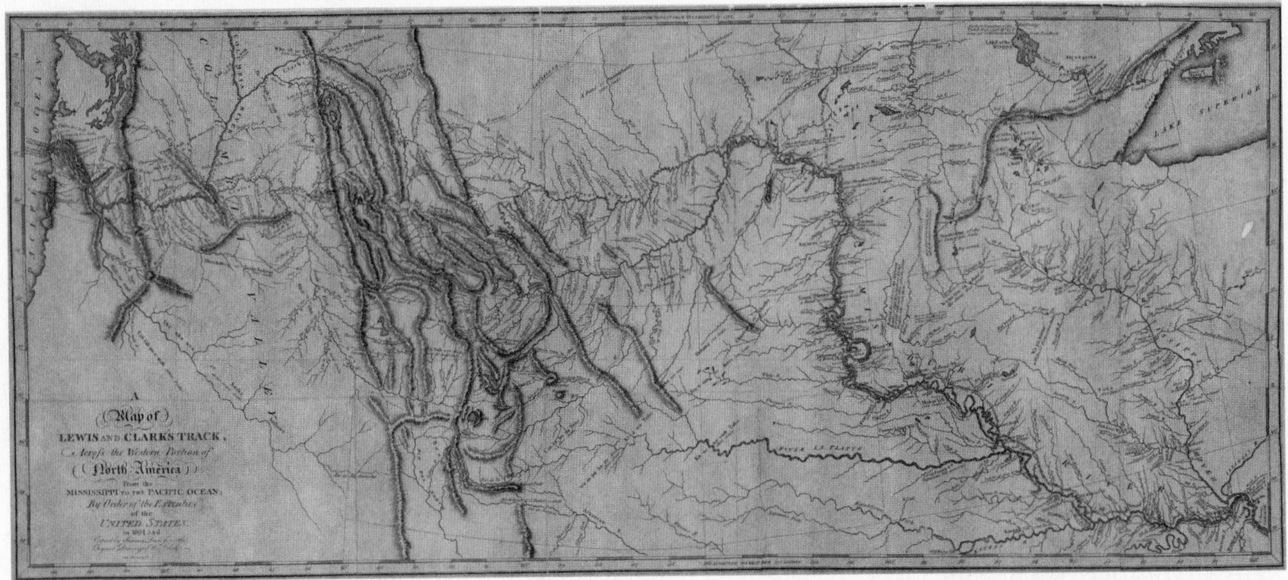


Lewis and Clark's route across the Louisiana Territory

## Historical Maps

Historical maps capture a period in time. They show information about the places where past events occurred. The map above shows how the explorers Lewis and Clark found their way across North America to the Pacific Ocean.

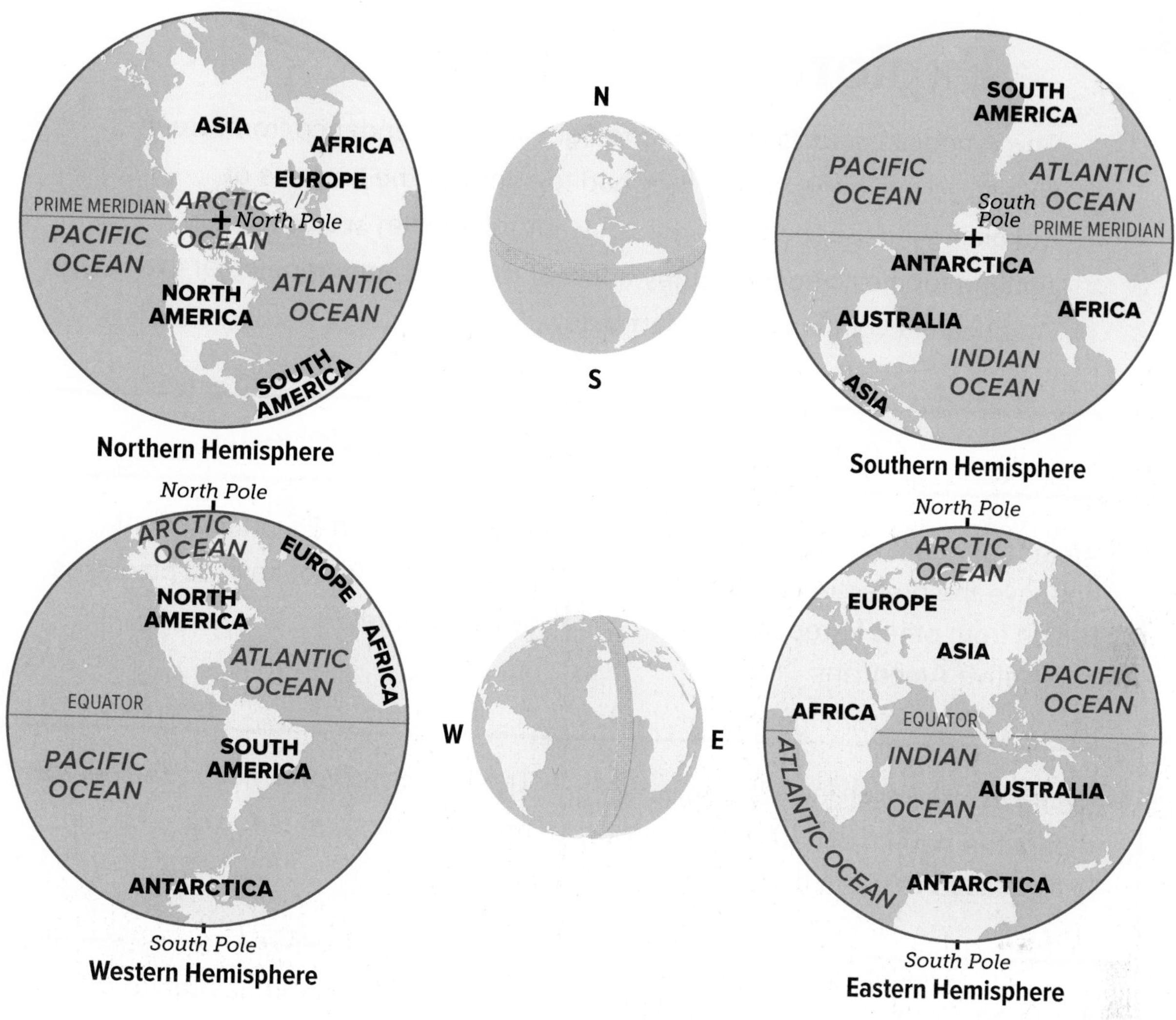


## Looking at Earth

Another way to look at the earth is by using a globe. Geographers have divided the Earth into northern and southern hemispheres at the Equator. The area north of the Equator is called the Northern Hemisphere. The area south of the Equator is called the Southern Hemisphere. The Prime Meridian runs from north to south around the Earth. The hemisphere east of the Prime Meridian is the Eastern Hemisphere. The hemisphere west of the Prime Meridian is the Western Hemisphere.

# Explore Economics

The American colonists decided to fight for independence from Great Britain. To make this choice they had to consider the benefits of becoming independent and the costs, or things they would lose, in fighting for their freedom. Study a few of the costs and benefits of the American Revolution in the chart below.

| Costs | Benefits |
|---|---|
| An independent new nation would not have the protection of Great Britain from other European powers and Native Americans. | The colonists in an independent America would not have to pay taxes to Great Britain. |
| Going to war against Great Britain meant the people could be charged with treason or die in battle. | The colonists would get to decide how their new government would be run. |
| A war against Great Britain would be expensive and the colonists didn't have a lot of money to support the war effort. | The colonists would be able to trade goods and make deals with other countries. |

(t)StasKhom/iStock/Getty Images, (b)D. Hurst/Alamy

## Talk About It

If you were a colonist at the time of the American Revolution, would you have wanted to stay a part of Great Britain or fight to become an independent new nation? Use evidence to support your answer.

**PRIMARY SOURCE**

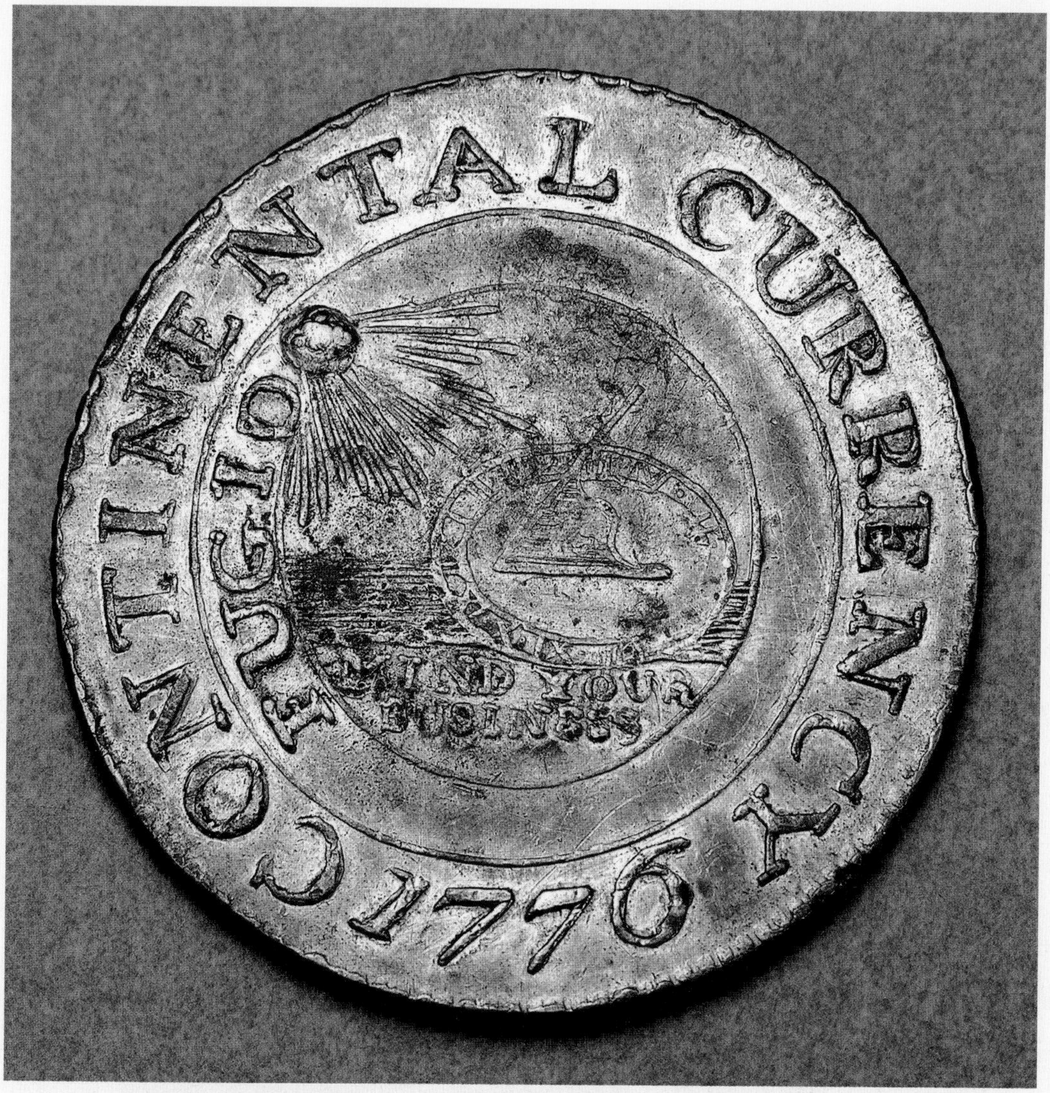

Currency from the period of the American Revolution

# Explore Citizenship

You can learn to make an impact by being a good citizen. Some important words that define what it means to be a good citizen are listed on page 19a. They help us understand how to be better citizens in our home, neighborhood, school, community, country, and world.

# Take Action!

You have learned to be a Social Studies detective by digging for clues and you practiced exploring and investigating geography, economics, and civics. Now it's time to explore the lessons in this book and make an impact!

**PRIMARY SOURCE**

President Lincoln at Antietam, Maryland, in 1862

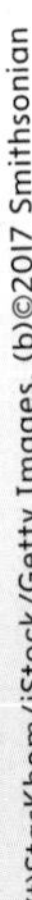

# Be a Good Citizen

**COURAGE**
Being brave in the face of difficulty

**FREEDOM**
Making choices and holding beliefs of one's own

**HONESTY**
Telling the truth

**JUSTICE**
Working toward fair treatment for everyone

**LEADERSHIP**
Showing good behavior worth following through example

**LOYALTY**
Showing support for people and one's country

**RESPECT**
Treating others as you would like to be treated

**RESPONSIBILITY**
Being worthy of trust

(t)McGraw-Hill Education, (b)C Squared Studios/Getty Images, (inset)Daniel Kaesler/EyeEm/GettyImages

# The Land and Native Peoples of North America



ESSENTIAL QUESTION EQ

## How Were the Lives of Native Peoples Influenced by Where They Lived?

In this chapter, you'll read about groups who lived in the Americas before the arrival of Christopher Columbus and other European explorers. You'll think about how native peoples' locations influenced their daily lives. You'll also learn more about their cultures and heritage.

## Step into the Time Chronological Thinking

Look at the time line. What was happening in other parts of the world while different civilizations were emerging in the Americas?

**Americas**

**c. 12,000 B.C.** Early humans may have crossed land bridge from Asia to North America.

**c. 9000 B.C.** Clovis hunter-gatherers roam North America.

**c. 1200 B.C.** Olmec civilization begins in Mexico.

**c. 100 B.C.** Inuit people settle the Arctic.

c.120,000 B.C.

**World Events**

**c. 120,000 B.C. to 80,000 B.C.** Modern humans evolve in Africa.

**c. 7000 B.C.** Chinese build first Great Wall of China.

**c. 2500 B.C.** Sailors navigate trade route between Greece and Egypt.

**c. 27 B.C.** The Roman Empire begins.

**A.D. 712** The Japanese people compile their first written history.

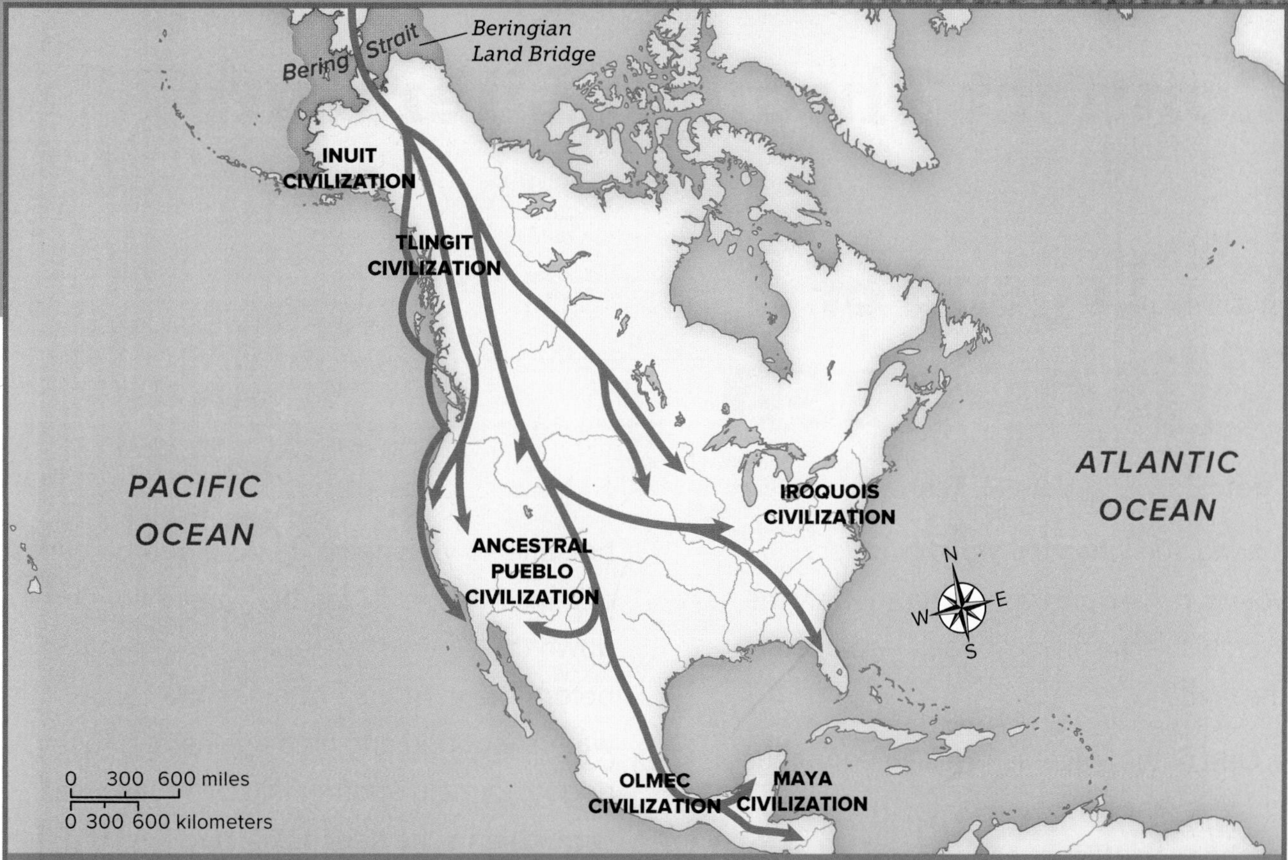

Bering Strait
Beringian Land Bridge
INUIT CIVILIZATION
TLINGIT CIVILIZATION
PACIFIC OCEAN
ANCESTRAL PUEBLO CIVILIZATION
IROQUOIS CIVILIZATION
ATLANTIC OCEAN
N
W
E
S
0 300 600 miles
0 300 600 kilometers
OLMEC CIVILIZATION
MAYA CIVILIZATION

## Migrations of Early Humans in North and Central America

### Step into the Place

1. Where were some of the major civilizations of early America?
2. What do you think led early humans to migrate and settle where they did?

Human settlement of the Americas began as long as 14,000 years ago when early humans crossed the Bering Land Bridge from Asia to modern-day Alaska. People migrated across the Western Hemisphere, creating civilizations as they went.

**c. A.D. 900** Maya civilization declines in Central America and Mexico.

**A.D. 1100–1300** Chinese, Arab, and European sailors use a magnetic compass.

**c. A.D. 1150** Hopi civilization is at its height in desert Southwest.

**c. late A.D. 1300s** Navajo civilization begins in desert Southwest.

**A.D. 1492** King Ferdinand and Queen Isabella of Spain send Christopher Columbus to find a trade route to Asia.

**A.D. 1519–1522** Magellan-Elcano expedition sails around Earth, proving Earth is round.

**A.D. 1540** Spanish explorer Francisco Vásquez de Coronado begins battle with Zuni people.

**c. A.D. 1570** Iroquois Confederacy forms in Eastern Woodlands.

**c. A.D. 1700** Tlingit people govern territory of Pacific Northwest.

A.D. 1700

# Connect Through Literature

## The Legend of Wishpoosh

retold by Elizabeth M. Tenney

Long ago when the world was very young, no people lived on earth. Only the Watetash—the animal people—roamed the land.

One of the Watetash was an enormous king-beaver who went by the name of Wishpoosh. Wishpoosh resided in Lake Keechelus[1] high in the snow-capped Cascade Mountains.

Now Wishpoosh was a very destructive beaver. He had a great appetite and ate absolutely everything that came his way. Soon he had eaten all the smaller creatures in the lovely mountain lake, as well as those that lived on the shore. Then he began devouring all the trees and the plants which surrounded the lake.

Wishpoosh was destroying so many creatures and so much vegetation that Speelyei, the coyote god of the mid-Columbia region, decided that he must do something to stop Wishpoosh.

Speelyei jumped into Lake Keechelus and struggled with Wishpoosh. They rolled and twisted and fought each other, causing the waters of the lake to boil. Wishpoosh became so violent that he tore out the banks of Lake Keechelus and the waters flooded down the canyon, sweeping everything before them. At the bottom of the canyon the waters stopped and held against the rocky ridges, forming another lake. This lake was larger than Lake Keechelus, and covered the Kittitas[2] Valley.

But the struggle between Wishpoosh and Speelyei was not over yet. Wishpoosh continued to thrash about madly, eating everything that he could find, growing larger and larger as he ate.

For a while, the rocky ridges restrained the flood, but Wishpoosh had become so large and so strong that at last even the ridges gave way and the loosened waters swept down to fill the great basins of Cowiche, Naches, and Ahtanum.

Yet even these basins, surrounded by their hills, could not hold the monster beaver. Before long they, too, gave way, and the waters flooded down in a torrent through the Yakima area. The waters cut a passage through barren hills and filled the level plains of what are now Simcoe and Toppenish.

(bkgd)McGraw-Hill Education

For a long time this water was dammed by the Umatilla highlands, but Wishpoosh did not give up. As before, he continued to thrash about, eating everything he could find in the waters and everything he could find on the lands. Finally, again he broke the rocky hills that kept the waters in, and the water flooded to form the greatest lake of all between the Umatilla on the east and the Cascade Mountains on the west. The entire area was under water.

Yet even this huge lake could not hold the frenzied beaver. After a time, the mighty Cascades gave way before his onslaughts. The water then flowed to the sea, draining all the valleys behind.

But even that was not the end of Wishpoosh. Once in the ocean, Wishpoosh laid about himself with such fury that he devoured all the fish, even the whales! He threatened all creation.

Speelyei saw that he must bring an end to Wishpoosh or the world would be lost. Transforming himself into a floating branch, he drifted to Wishpoosh and was soon swallowed up.

Once inside the beaver, Speelyei turned back into himself, drew out his knife, and began to cut out all of the giant beaver's vital organs.

At last this was too much even for Wishpoosh. His life ceased. His huge carcass was cast up by the tide onto the beach at Clatsop near the mouth of the Great River.

Speelyei stood looking at the carcass. What should be done with it? The coyote god took his knife and cut off the beaver's head. From it, he fashioned a group of people—the Nez Perce—who were great in council and great in oratory. From the beaver's arms he made another people—the Cayuse—who were powerful with the bow and war-club. The beaver's legs became the Klickitats, a people who were swift runners. The belly of the beaver became the Chinooks whose lands offered much to eat. Finally there remained the hide and the insides. Speelyei picked these up and, turning toward the east, hurled them as far as he could. These became the Snake River Indians.

Thus were formed the various peoples who lived in the northwest corner of the land.

---

[1] Lake Keechelus (spelled "Kichelos" in the early literature) still exists as a mountain lake. It is situated near the summit of the Snoqualimie Pass, the main east-west highway (#90) which crosses the state of Washington, leading to Seattle. Lake Keechelus can be clearly seen from the highway which skirts its shores for several miles.

[2] Kittitas is a well-known valley in Central Washington which surrounds present-day Ellensburg. Kittitas was once the territory of the Kittitas people.



## Think About It

1. How are Speelyei and Wishpoosh alike? How are they different?
2. Why did the two characters fight?
3. What conclusions about Native American civilization can you draw from this story?

# People You Should Know

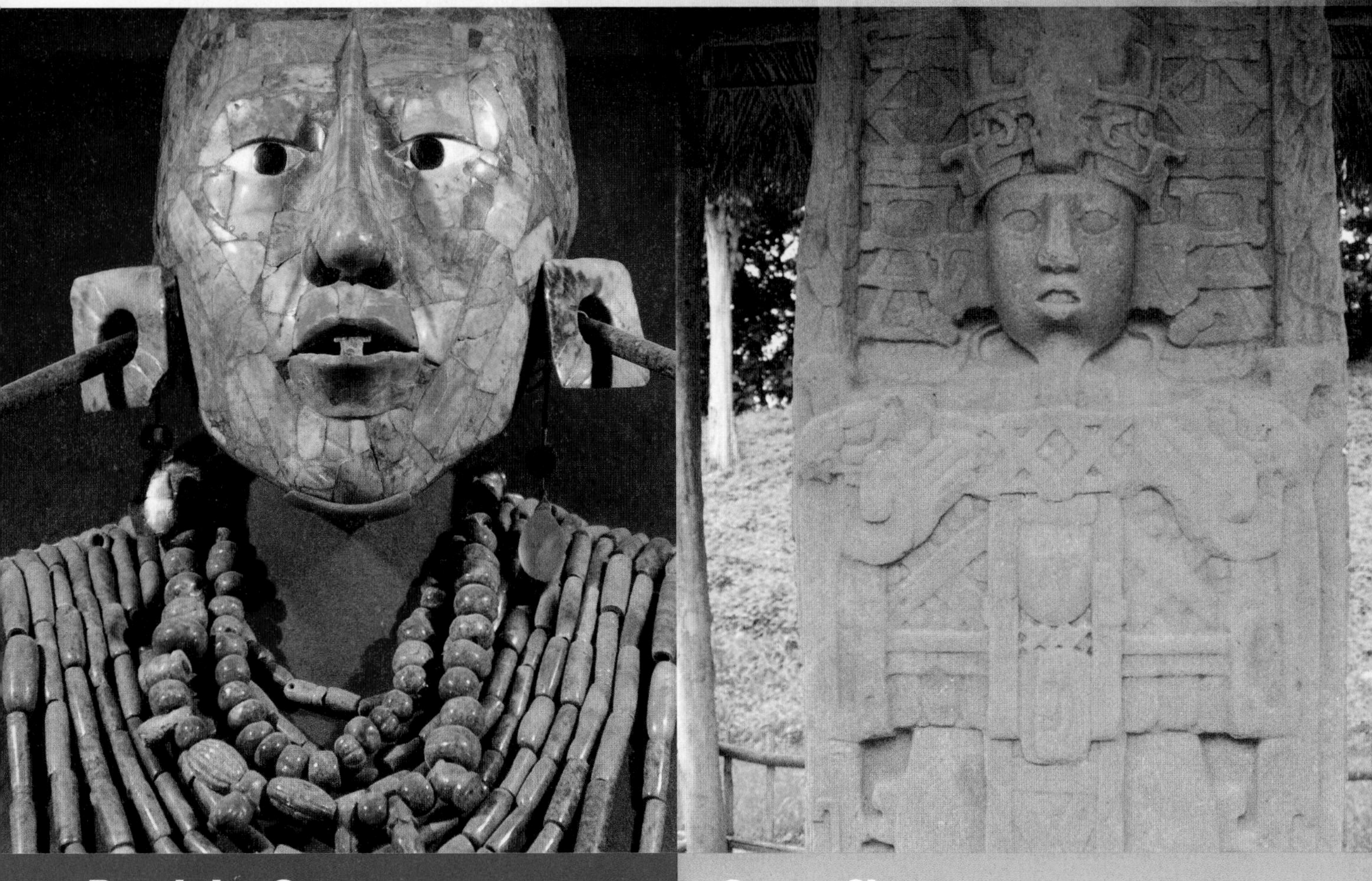

## Pacal the Great

K'inich Janaab Pakal, also known as Pacal the Great, ruled the ancient Maya city of Palanque, located in what is now Chiapas, Mexico. Pacal ruled Palanque for almost 70 years and made it into a very powerful city. He is known for his many building projects, particularly the pyramid-shaped Temple of Inscriptions. This pyramid had a building at the top with walls inscribed entirely with Maya text. Archaeologists later discovered the remains of Pacal, wearing an elaborate jade mask, inside the pyramid.

## Cauac Sky

K'ak' Tiliw Chan Yopaat, also known as Cauac Sky, ruled the ancient Maya city of Quiriguá, located in a tropical forest south of present day Lago de Izabal in southeastern Guatemala. Cauac Sky claimed independence from the much larger neighboring city-state of Copán in A.D. 738 after defeating Copán's great leader, Waxaklajun Ub'ah K'awil or 18-Rabbit. Cauac Sky ruled Quiriguá for 60 years and had stone monuments built to honor him. You can see these stone monuments today, including the one of Cauac Sky above, by visiting the Quiriguá Archaeological Park and Ruins in Guatemala.

## John Herrington

John Herrington became the first Native American to fly in outer space. He is a member of the Chickasaw Nation. The Chickasaw are a group of native people that lived in the American Southeast before being forcibly moved in the 1830s to what is now Oklahoma. In 2002, during a space shuttle mission, he performed a spacewalk. During the walk, he honored his Native American heritage by carrying six eagle feathers, two arrowheads, a braid of sweet grass, and the flag of the Chickasaw Nation.

## Wilma Mankiller

Wilma Mankiller descended from the Cherokee of the Southeast Woodlands. She was born in Oklahoma, but moved with her family to San Francisco, California. There she was inspired by a Native American protest on the island of Alcatraz, which Native Americans believed belonged to them. She returned to Oklahoma and became active in the government of the Cherokee Nation. She became the first female chief of the Cherokee Nation in 1985. She served as chief for ten years, working to improve healthcare and job opportunities for her people.

(t)McGraw-Hill Education, (bl)David DeHoyos/NASA, (br)Peter Turnley/Corbis Historical/Getty Images

# How Did the Characteristics of Early Native American Groups Develop?

## The First Hunter-Gatherers

The first humans to settle the Western Hemisphere were probably **hunter-gatherers** from Asia. These early humans lived by gathering wild plants and hunting animals. Many scientists today believe they reached North America by crossing a land bridge from Asia that formed when sea levels dropped during the last Ice Age.

For thousands of years this land bridge, which scientists call Beringia, linked what is now Siberia to Alaska. Herds of Ice Age animals crossed Beringia. The early humans hunted these animals, which included elephant-like wooly mammoths and mastodons.

An Ice Age mastodon was nearly as large as a modern elephant. It had short, powerful legs and long, sharp tusks. Its tough hide was covered with long, reddish brown hair. To hunt such a dangerous animal, early humans would have needed effective weapons and teamwork.

**c. 9000 B.C**
Clovis people hunt Ice Age animals.

**c. 1200 B.C.**
Olmec civilization begins in Mexico.

**c. A.D. 200**
Hohokam settle in American Southwest.

**c. A.D. 700**
Mississippian people first occupy Cahokia.

**c. A.D. 900**
Maya civilization declines in Central America and Mexico.

000 | 8000 | 7000 | 6000 | 5000 | 4000 | 3000 | 2000 | A.D. 1 | 900

Ice Age hunters followed woolly mammoths across a land bridge from Asia.

Archaeologists are people who study the tools and other artifacts of people who lived long ago. Using such evidence, they reach conclusions about how ancient people lived. Archaeologists have different views about exactly when early humans first reached North America. They have evidence that these people had migrated all the way to the southern tip of South America by about 10,500 B.C. The people's migrations must have taken place over a long time. So their arrival in North America likely occurred centuries earlier.

Archaeologists also have different views about which route (or routes) these early Native American groups might have used in their migrations throughout North and South America. Some scientists think they used an ice-free inland route. Others think early humans traveled by boat along the Pacific Coast.

## Did You Know?

Beginning in the 1930s, archaeologists started to find evidence that early Native Americans may have hunted large Ice Age animals. Scientists found slim, beautifully crafted stone spear points mixed in with the bones of extinct animals, such as mammoths. The first site where these spear points were found was near present-day Clovis, New Mexico. Spear points discovered recently along Buttermilk Creek in Texas date from between 13,500 and 15,500 years ago.

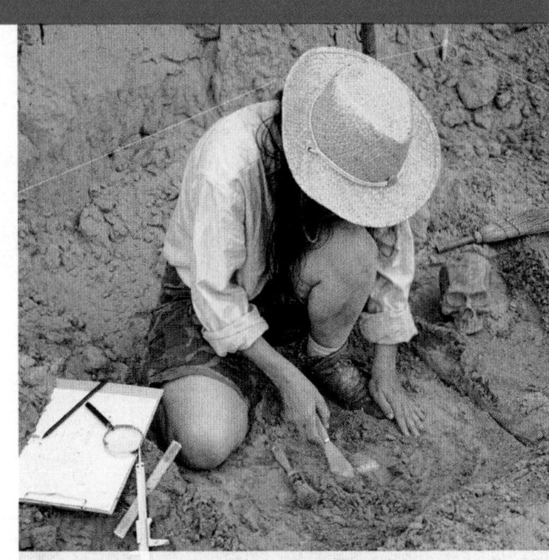

Archaeologists use special tools when uncovering artifacts.

microgen/Getty Images

## Stop and Check

**Think** Consider the routes that archaeologists believe early humans took when migrating into North America. What probably caused these people to select these routes?

**Find Details** As you read, add additional information to the graphic organizer on page 11 in your Inquiry Journal.

# The Olmec

About 11,500 years ago, the last Ice Age ended. The climate of the Western Hemisphere slowly grew warmer and drier. Many of the Ice Age animals that the early Native Americans had hunted became extinct. These hunter-gatherer cultures had to adapt to survive. Instead of gathering wild plants, they began to grow their own food. By about 4000 B.C., farmers in Mexico and Central America were raising three crops: maize (also called corn), beans, and squash.

One of the most important effects of farming is that a community can raise more food than it needs to feed itself. This food surplus allows members of a community to focus on civic and cultural developments in the arts, society, and government that help build an advanced civilization.

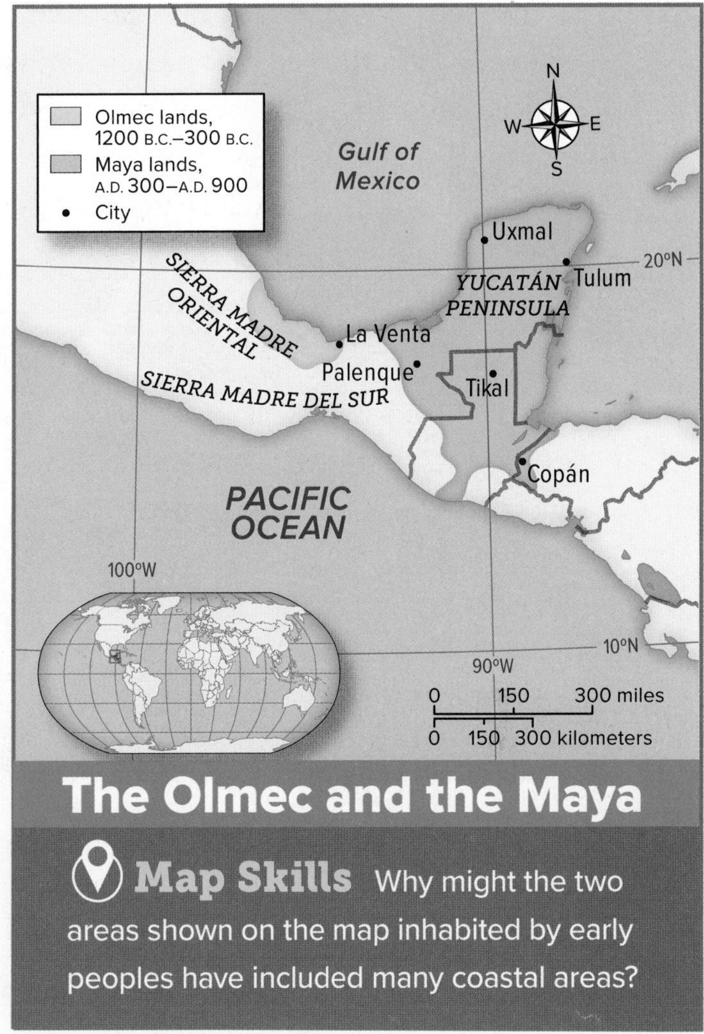


**The Olmec and the Maya**

**Map Skills** Why might the two areas shown on the map inhabited by early peoples have included many coastal areas?

The first civilization to develop in the Western Hemisphere was started by the Olmec people. It developed in the hot rain forests of southern Mexico about 1200 B.C. The Olmec built temples, carved huge stone statues, played ball games, and created a calendar and a writing system. They spread their culture across Mexico and Central America through an effective trade network.

**Stop and Check**

**Think** Why is a food surplus so important to the growth of a civilization?

Called "The Temple of the Inscriptions," this structure is more than one thousand years old and rises almost 90 feet above the Maya city of Palenque in present-day Mexico.

# The Maya

The Maya developed their culture in the same part of Mexico as the Olmec. They traded with their Olmec neighbors and were influenced by their culture. Between about A.D. 250 and 900, Maya culture reached its peak. Archaeologists call this the "Classic Period" of Maya civilization.

During the Classic Period, the Maya world grew to more than 40 cities, each with a population between 5,000 and 50,000. In cities such as Uxmal, Tikal, and Copán, the Maya built great palaces for their rulers and huge pyramid temples to honor their gods. These structures were covered with elaborate carvings and inscriptions in their system of picture writing. Scholars often refer to such inscriptions as **hieroglyphs**. The meaning of these inscriptions was unknown for centuries after Maya civilization collapsed. Thorough translations appeared in the mid-1900s.

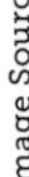

## Did You Know?

The Maya were fascinated with time. They created a 365-day calendar. The year was divided into 18 months of 20 days each. The remaining five days were not shown in any month and the Maya believed those days were unlucky. To show when historical events took place, they used a system of dating called the "Long Count." Translated to today's calendar, the Maya's Long Count suggests the world was created about 3114 B.C.

Mayan influence is seen in the design of this Aztec stone calendar.

Maya cities were ruled by kings who claimed that Maya gods had chosen them. These rulers directed huge building projects and commanded the army. To form alliances and strengthen trade, Maya rulers often married members of the royal families of other cities.

Maya civilization declined rapidly after A.D. 900. Archaeologists have looked for explanations in the environment. They think that as time passed, the population of the Maya cities outgrew their food supply. Rulers fought over farmland. People began to abandon the Maya cities in search of food. Drought may also have led to their decline. However, the Maya did not disappear. Today, more than six million descendants of the ancient Maya still live in Mexico, Belize, and Guatemala.

## Stop and Check

COLLABORATE

**Talk** How did cultural characteristics spread from one early Native American group to another?

# Early Desert Peoples

The early Native American groups of the Southwest developed in an environment very different from the rain forests of Mexico and Central America. About A.D. 200, a group known as the Hohokam moved from a part of the Sonoran Desert in northern Mexico to present-day Arizona, between the Salt River and Gila River. At that time, the area received only about three inches of rain a year. Yet the settlers discovered ways to turn the desert into fields of corn, beans, squash, and cotton.

The Hohokam built a complex irrigation system to bring water to their fields. With simple tools such as sharpened sticks and stone blades, they dug shallow canals that stretched for hundreds of miles. Hohokam farmers used small gates to direct water from these canals into their fields. The Hohokam irrigation canals were built so well that some of them are still used today.

Hohokam farmers lived in small villages. They built their houses by digging a shallow pit and covering it with a wooden frame, roofed with plant material called thatch. Building underground helped to keep Hohokam houses cool during the day and warm at night. The Hohokam wove cotton into cloth for clothing. They made baskets and pottery for storage. Hohokam jewelry was crafted from turquoise mined in the desert and from shells. Shell jewelry was especially prized. Hohokam traders traveled long distances to trade cotton cloth and pottery for shells gathered by people on the Gulf of California and the Pacific Coast.

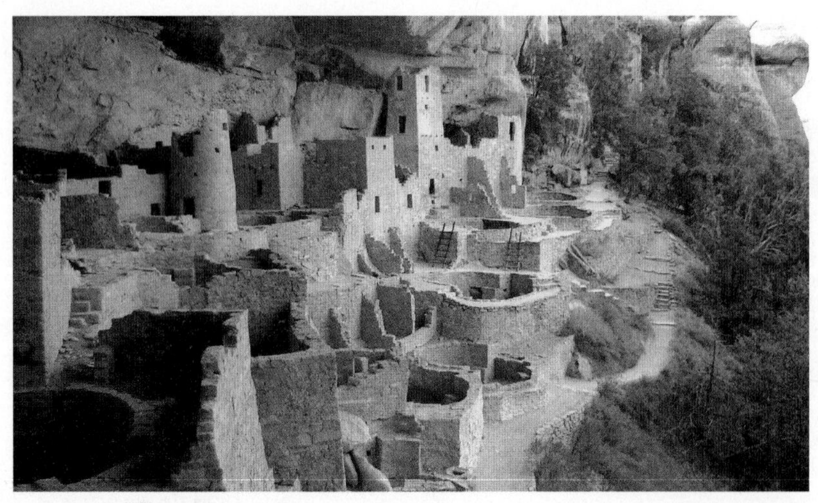

**The Ancestral Pueblo people built the Cliff Palace at Mesa Verde, in what is now Colorado.**

The Ancestral Pueblo were another of the Native American groups to settle in the deserts of the Southwest. In about A.D. 700, the Ancestral Pueblo people settled in the "Four Corners" area where Utah, Colorado, Arizona, and New Mexico meet today. Like the Hohokam, the Ancestral Pueblo planted squash, corn, and beans. The high desert plateaus where they lived were not suited to the use of canals for irrigation, however. Instead, the Ancestral Pueblo developed a method called dry farming. They channeled rainwater and snowmelt into catch basins. Then this water was slowly released into narrow, pebbled-lined drains to the crops.

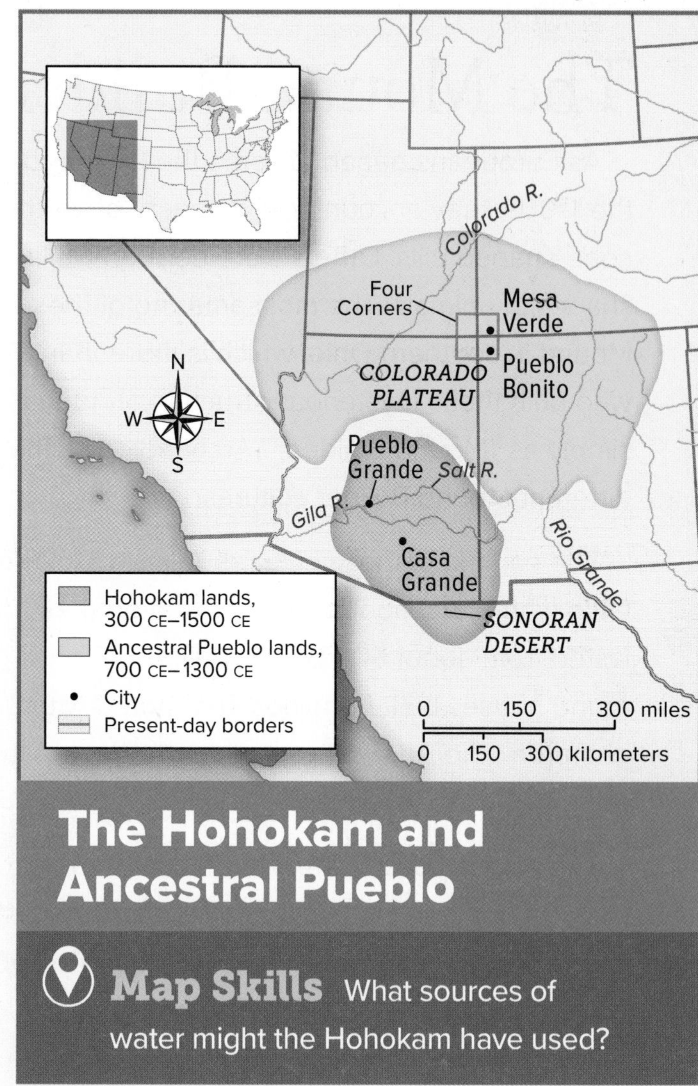


## The Hohokam and Ancestral Pueblo

**Map Skills** What sources of water might the Hohokam have used?

The Ancestral Pueblo are known as the first "cliff dwellers." They lived in huge apartment-like dwellings built along the steep sides of the cliffs. Living in cliff dwellings, such as Mesa Verde, made it easier for the Ancestral Pueblo to defend themselves against enemies. These dwellings were made of finely carved stone and logs that were plastered with adobe. Adobe is a mixture of mud and straw that dries into a hard clay. An adobe house stays cool during the heat of the day and warm during cold desert nights.

### Stop and Check

COLLABORATE

**Connect to Now** Which features and practices of societies of the early desert people might be helpful to modern American society? Discuss your opinion with a partner.

# The Mound Builders

As Europeans began to settle the Ohio and Mississippi river valleys in the 1700s, they encountered a variety of earthen mounds. Some were cone-shaped hills. Others were earthen walls. A few even had the shapes of animals. The most amazing of these is the Great Serpent Mound in southern Ohio, which is more than 1,300 feet long. The people who built these mysterious structures and then left were once referred to simply as "Mound Builders." Archaeologists have identified several different Mound Builder cultures.

The earliest of these cultures is known as the Adena, after a site in Ohio where archaeologists first studied their mounds. The Adena culture lasted from about 500 B.C. to A.D. 100. These people lived in villages of round houses built from logs and roofed with bark. Originally hunter-gatherers, the Adena people later began to farm. Their crops included gourds and sunflowers.

The Adena used stone to craft both simple tools and complex objects such as smoking pipes used in rituals. They fashioned ornaments from copper, mica, and shells—materials that they obtained through trade with distant peoples. What is known about Adena culture comes from such objects, which the Adena people placed in the burial mounds they built for their dead.

Between about 200 B.C. and A.D. 500, another mound-building culture called the Hopewell occupied the same region as the Adena culture. The Hopewell people were also named for a site in southern Ohio where archaeologists first studied their culture. The Hopewell people shared many features of the Adena culture. Hopewell artists created objects from copper, mica, and obsidian, a volcanic glass. Like the Adena people, the Hopewell obtained these materials through a far-flung trade network.

The Adena people built the Great Serpent Mound.

Tony Linck/SuperStock

## Then and Now

Archaeologists have been studying the Cahokia mounds since the late 1800s, but only a small part of the site has been excavated. Seventy of the original 120 mounds are preserved today in Illinois's Cahokia Mounds State Historic Site (established in 1979). Cahokia was named a World Heritage Site in 1982, meaning it deserves special protection.

An artist's depiction of Cahokia about A.D. 1100

One of the last major Native American groups to develop before the arrival of Europeans was the Mississippian culture. Mississippian culture developed in the Mississippi River valley between A.D. 700 and 900.

Large-scale farming of corn, beans, squash, and other crops produced food surpluses. This encouraged the growth of large populations in Mississippian towns and cities. Priest-kings ruled Mississippian society. Each town or city controlled a group of outlying villages. High fences of sharpened logs defended these villages from attack. Warfare seems to have been frequent.

The greatest Mississippian city is the site known today as Cahokia. Built in what is now southern Illinois, Cahokia at its peak was home to more than 20,000 people. A plaza for holding ceremonies was the center of a Mississippian city. Around this plaza were groups of mounds on top of which might have been a temple or a chief's dwelling. Monk's Mound at Cahokia was 100 feet high and covered 14 acres. It was the largest pre-Columbian earthen structure in the Western Hemisphere.

## Stop and Check

COLLABORATE

**Talk** Which characteristics did the Adena, Hopewell, and Mississippian cultures share?

# How Did the People of the Desert Southwest Meet Their Needs?

## The Pueblo People

The Pueblo peoples of the American Southwest have inhabited the area for more than a thousand years. They mostly farmed crops such as corn and beans, and they built permanent homes out of stone and adobe clay. The Spanish word for these homes is *pueblo*, and that is how these people got their name.

Pueblo homes were modeled after the cliff dwellings of the Ancestral Pueblo. They are cube-like rooms stacked on top of each other. The largest rooms are at the bottom, while the smaller rooms are near the top. There are also fewer rooms near the top. So the entire house does not look like a big square or rectangle but more like a small, stepped pyramid. Wooden ladders outside of the rooms were usually used to get from one floor to another. Sometimes the bottom floor would have no doors or windows, and a person could get in only by climbing a ladder. This made the structure easy to defend because the ladder could be pulled up.

Pueblo buildings were usually home to several families and had connecting shared rooms. They also contained *kivas*, special below-ground rooms used for rituals and ceremonies.

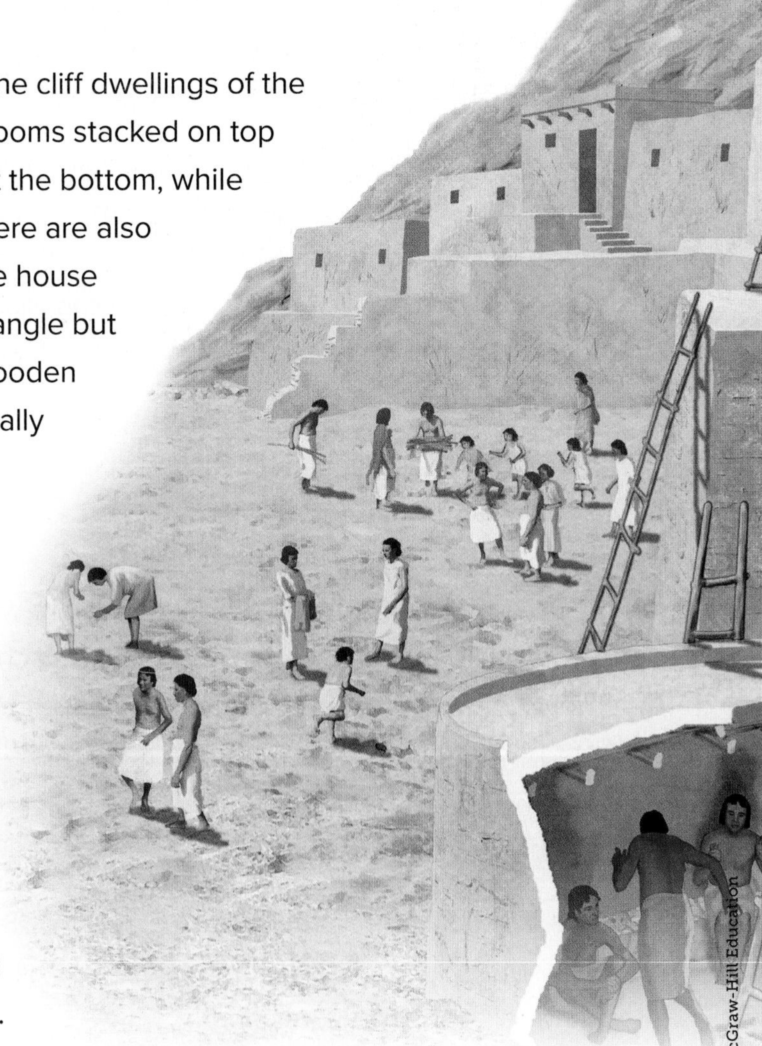
McGraw-Hill Education

**1150**
The Hopi build Oraibi, the oldest continuously occupied settlement in the United States.

**1276–1299**
The Great Drought causes cultural shift in Ancestral Pueblo peoples.

**Late 1300s**
The Navajo arrive in the Southwest.

**1540**
Spanish explorer Francisco Vásquez de Coronado interrupts a sacred Zuni ceremony and causes a battle.

50 | 1300 | 1540

A Southwest pueblo

There are many groups that make up the Pueblo people. Two of these are the Zuni and the Hopi.

The Zuni occupy their ancestral land in the Zuni River valley, though their territory is not as large as it was in the past. Attacks by Spanish treasure hunters and, later, settlers from the United States caused the Zuni to abandon some of their villages. They gathered into a single village to better protect themselves. This village was called Halona and is now called Zuni.

Another Pueblo group is the Hopi. The Hopi people are believed to be one of the oldest desert peoples. Their village of Oraibi is believed to be nearly nine hundred years old. They used dams and irrigation to grow crops such as corn, cotton, beans, and squash. They also took advantage of the sand dunes that formed against the sides of **mesas**. These dunes would trap moisture, and so the Hopi would plant crops in them.

Hopi men and women had different jobs. The men farmed and hunted. They also wove cloth from cotton. The women gathered food like nuts and berries. They also made baskets and pottery to store their food. The Hopi were among the first people to fire, or strengthen by heating, their pottery, using coal.

**Kachina dolls**

Chuck Place/Alamy Stock Photo

Important parts of Hopi culture include *kachinas*. According to Hopi beliefs, kachinas are spirits who live in sacred places for half of the year. During the other half, they live near the Hopi villages and bring with them rain and the growing season. The kachinas are represented by masked dancers who perform in the villages when the kachinas visit. There are hundreds of kachinas, so the dancers often give small, carved kachina dolls to children to help them learn about the spirits.

North Platte River
Colorado River
Navajo
Navajo
Hopi
Old Oraibi
Zuni
Apache
Rio Grande
Pecos River
Apache
Gila River
Apache
Papago
0 100 200 miles
0 100 200 kilometers
Pueblo lands
Non-Pueblo lands
Present-day boundaries
• Town

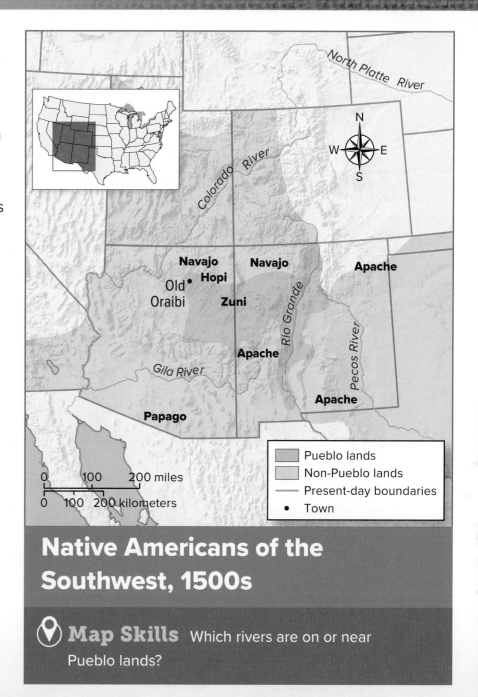

## Native Americans of the Southwest, 1500s

**Map Skills** Which rivers are on or near Pueblo lands?

### Stop and Check

**Talk** With a small group, list the advantages of the pueblo buildings. What makes them ideal for the Hopi and Zuni lifestyles?

**Find Details** As you read, add additional information to the graphic organizer on page 19 in your Inquiry Journal.

# The Navajo

The Navajo were neighbors to the Pueblo and borrowed some of their ideas. They used irrigation to grow crops, made clothes with cotton, and were skilled in making jewelry and pottery. Despite these similarities, the Navajo were not related to the Pueblo. The Navajo were related to the Athabascans of Alaska and Canada. Scholars think the Navajo migrated from the northern tundra to the southwestern deserts in the late 1200s.

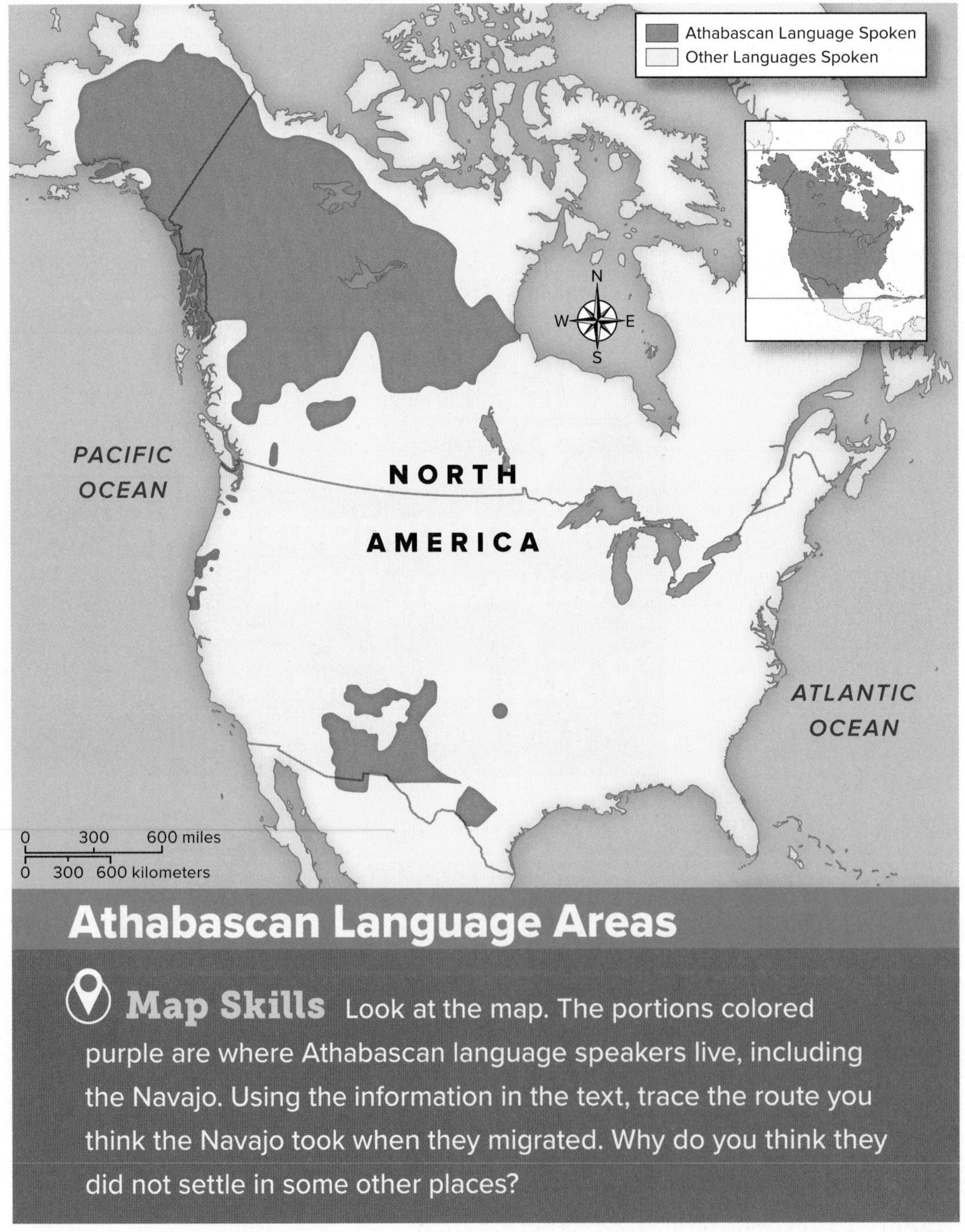


## Athabascan Language Areas

**Map Skills** Look at the map. The portions colored purple are where Athabascan language speakers live, including the Navajo. Using the information in the text, trace the route you think the Navajo took when they migrated. Why do you think they did not settle in some other places?

The Navajo were originally hunter-gatherers but quickly adopted new techniques for surviving in the desert. In addition to learning farming from the Pueblo, the Navajo also learned from Spanish settlers when they arrived in the 1500s. They were interested in the animals the Spanish brought with them. The Navajo soon became skilled at herding sheep and cattle, as well as at riding horses. Their relationship with the Spanish was otherwise hostile. The Spanish clashed with several of the Native American groups. The Navajo became close allies with the Pueblo and the Apache in fighting the Spanish.

The Navajo lived in *hogans*, large dome-shaped buildings. Hogans were made of logs or stone and covered in mud and dirt. They had one entrance, usually facing east and covered with a blanket. Hogans had no windows, only a hole in the roof so that smoke from the fire could escape.

A hogan

Traditionally, the Navajo believe in *hozho*, or "walking in beauty." This means maintaining balance with the Earth. They believe that being out of harmony with the Earth is the cause of illness and suffering. In order to restore harmony, they still take part in long ceremonies involving singing and dancing. Many of these ceremonies are still practiced today.

## Stop and Check

**Think** What changes did the Navajo have to make when they moved from the North to the South?

**Find Details** As you read, add additional information to the graphic organizer on page 19 in your Inquiry Journal.

(t)McGraw-Hill Education, (b)B.A.E. Inc./Alamy Stock Photo

# The Apache

The Apache language, like Navajo, is in the Athabascan family. Therefore, many historians believe the Apache also migrated from Canada. Apache **oral history**, on the other hand, claims it was the opposite. According to the oral history, the Athabascans to the north are descendants of the Apache in the south. Whatever their origins, the Apache are quite different from the Navajo and Pueblo peoples.

The Apache were not farmers, but hunter-gatherers. They hunted buffalo, deer, cougar, and other animals. The Apache were very skilled hunters and had tricks such as rubbing themselves with animal fat to hide their scent. They also gathered agave, cactus, nuts, and berries. Sometimes they would get food and supplies by trading with their Pueblo neighbors. Other times, they would conduct raids against Pueblo villages, earning them a reputation of being fierce and warlike. The name *Apache*, in fact, comes from the Zuni word for "enemy."

**An Apache basket**

Chuck Place/Alamy Stock Photo

## InfoGraphic

### How to Build a Wickiup

**Step 1** The Apache made poles from green and flexible tree branches.

**Step 2** Holes were dug in a circle for the poles.

**Step 3** The poles were bent and tied with strips of animal skin to create a dome.

Although fearsome to enemies, the Apache were gentle and affectionate to their children and relatives. Like many Native American groups, the Apache trace their ancestors through their mothers, rather than their fathers. They traditionally lived in relatively small groups made up of their extended family. These groups were independent, and it was not until recent times that the Apache unified under a single government.

The Apache lived in *wickiups*. These houses were dome-shaped, like the Navajo hogans, but did not use earth or clay as building materials. Instead, they were covered in skins, reed mats, brush, or grass. Although the wikiups were not as strong as the pueblos or hogans, they could be easily taken apart and moved. This was helpful for the Apache, who moved from place to place.

**Step 4** Smaller willow poles were tied around the sides and top.

**Step 6** They finished the wikiup with a fire pit and smoke hole for a chimney.

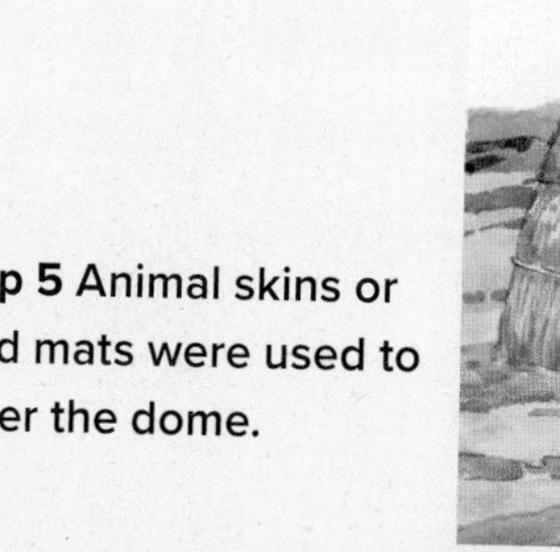

**Step 5** Animal skins or reed mats were used to cover the dome.

## Stop and Check

COLLABORATE

**Write** What made the Apache unique among Southwestern Native Americans?

# How Were Native Peoples of the Pacific Coast Shaped by Their Surroundings?

## A Variety of Landscapes

Native Americans settled in a number of vastly different natural environments in the American West. Native Americans established settlements in the snowy Arctic regions of Alaska, the forested coasts of Oregon and Washington, and the arid deserts of southern California. Surviving in each of these climates required very specific skills, and, as a result, Native Americans across the American West developed unique ways of life.

Ancestors of the Navajo and Apache people may have reached the Pacific Northwest about 5000 B.C. Eventually, some of the descendants of these people migrated south, but others remained in the region. The Tlingit people belong to the same language family as the Navajo and Apache—meaning the groups share a common ancestor—but their surroundings have caused them to develop a very different way of life.

Hand-woven baskets were an important tool in Pomo life.

**c. 100 B.C.**
Inuit settle the Arctic.

**c. A.D. 1700**
Tlingit people govern a large territory in the Pacific Northwest.

**A.D. 1855**
Chief Seattle and other Pacific Northwest Indian chiefs sign the Port Elliott Treaty, granting their land to the U.S. government.

100 B.C. A.D. 1 1700 1800

**A.D. 1**
Miwok begin occupying lowlands of California.

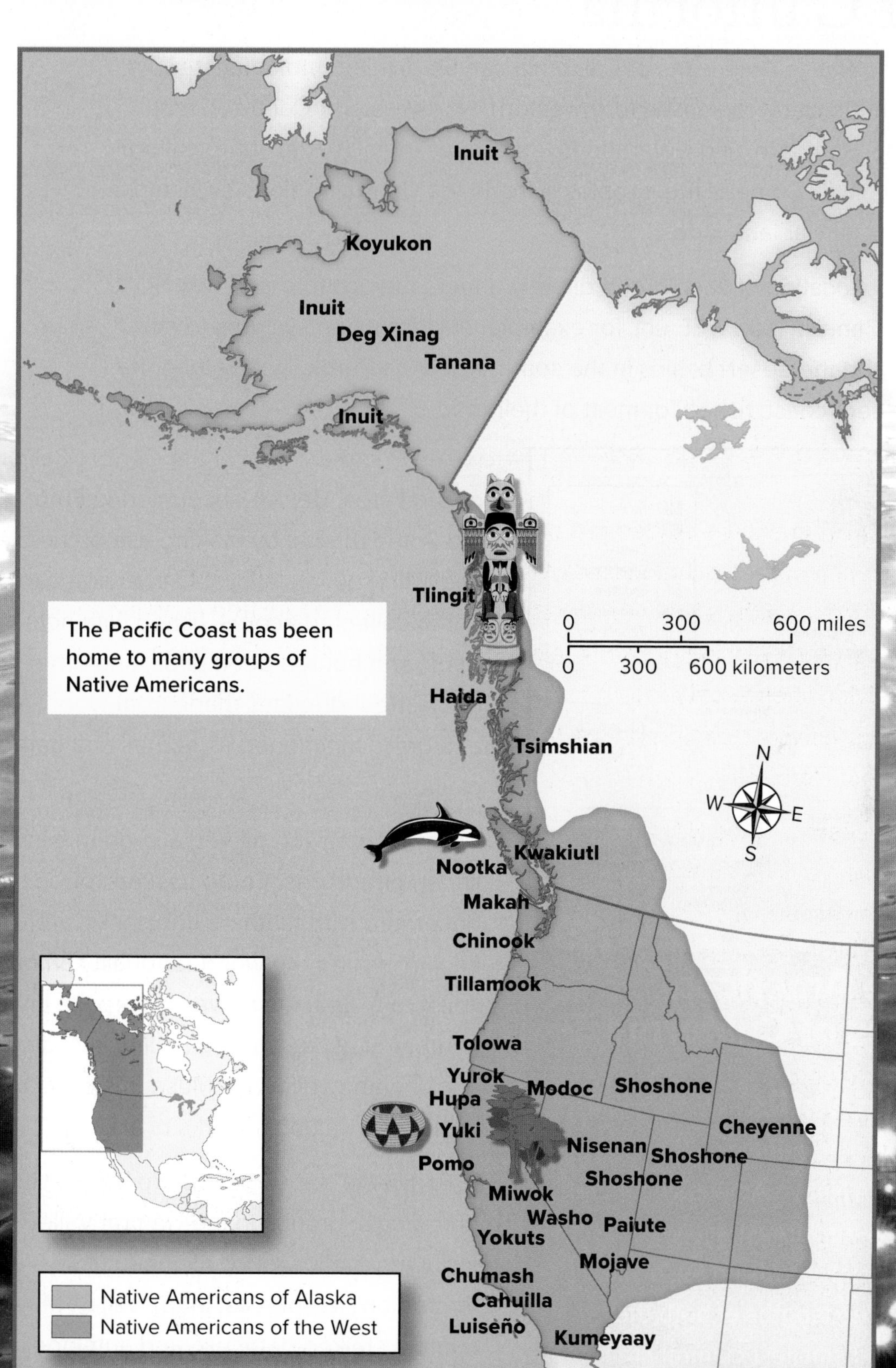


The Pacific Coast has been home to many groups of Native Americans.

# Native Americans of California

The Native Americans of California can be divided into at least six distinct cultural regions—Northwestern, Northeastern, Central, Great Basin, Southern, and Colorado River. Groups in each area share cultural similarities. Some of the peoples living in the Central region, for instance, speak similar languages.

The location of each group directly affects their culture and way of life. The Cahuilla (kuh WEE uh), for example, built irrigation systems to raise crops in the desert basins in the south, while the Yurok, living along the northern coast, fished for most of their food.

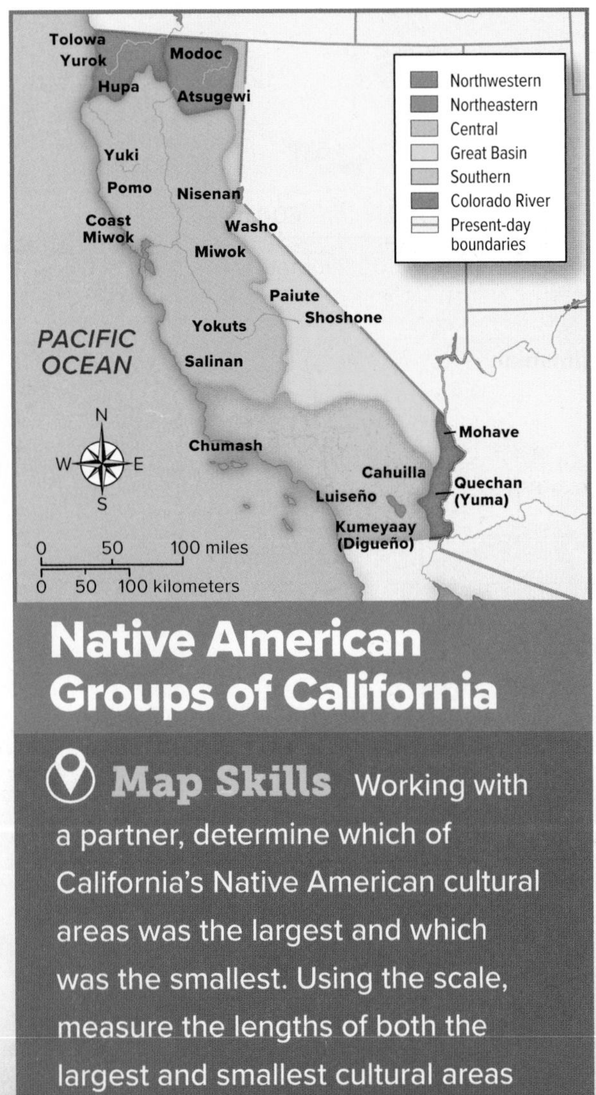


## Native American Groups of California

**Map Skills** Working with a partner, determine which of California's Native American cultural areas was the largest and which was the smallest. Using the scale, measure the lengths of both the largest and smallest cultural areas from north to south.

The Pomo are part of the Central California cultural area. Before encountering Europeans, the Pomo thrived by making use of the plentiful natural resources available in their region. The Pomo collected acorns, fished with nets and traps, and hunted deer, birds, and other small game. Roundhouses made from wood, earth, and grass functioned as homes and gathering places.

Basket weaving played a large role in Pomo life and traditions. Pomo baskets, often decorated with feathers and shells, are well known around the world for quality among art collectors. Baskets served a purpose in a number of aspects of Pomo life, including cooking and childcare. Museums collect Pomo baskets as valuable works of art.

Farther to the south, before the arrival of Europeans, groups in the Central Valley, including the Miwok, built their cultures around the region's resources. In the valley, Miwok hunters stalked deer, elk, and antelope. In the marshes, they set traps for otters and beavers.

Forests may have been the most pivotal source of the Miwok way of life. Oak trees provided the Miwok with their staple product, the acorn. Children would shake loose acorns from the oaks' upper branches, while women collected the fallen acorns in large baskets. The Miwok women ground the acorns into flour to make bread, biscuits, and soup.

Southern California's deserts do not have this same wealth of resources. There, groups such as the Cahuilla, the Serrano, and the Chemehuevi (cheh mih HWEY vee) adapted to use the few plants that grow in the desert. The Cahuilla also developed irrigation systems to raise crops including corn, squash, beans, and melons. By digging ditches to feed into small lakes, the Cahuilla made use of the limited precipitation to sustain a vibrant culture.

**PRIMARY SOURCE**

## How the World Grew... Miwok Legend

**In the beginning the world was rock. Every year the rains came and fell on the rock and washed off a little; this made earth. By and by plants grew on the earth and their leaves fell and made more earth. Then pine trees grew and their needles and cones fell every year and with the other leaves and bark made more earth and covered more of the rock.**

**If you look closely at the ground in the woods you will see how the top is leaves and bark and pine needles and cones, and how a little below the top these are matted together, and a little deeper are rotting and breaking up into earth. This is the way the world grew—and it is growing still.**

— translation of a Northern Miwok legend by C. Hart Merriam, published in 1910

### Stop and Check

COLLABORATE

**Talk** Why are the Miwok not known for building irrigation systems like the Cahuilla?

**Find Details** As you read, add additional information to your graphic organizer on page 27 in your Inquiry Journal.

TEXT: Merriam, C. Hart, ed. The Dawn of the World. Cleveland: The Arthur H. Clark Company, 1910.; PHOTO: McGraw-Hill Education

# Native Americans of the Pacific Northwest

Native peoples of this region reside in communities along the Pacific Coast from what is now British Columbia to northern California. The ocean supplies seafood and plants for the groups of Native Americans living in the Pacific Northwest.

Long ago, wood from the area's forests allowed these people to construct homes, carve canoes and masks, and fashion household items including dishes and spoons. The Pacific Northwest peoples believed that all living things, including plants and animals, had rights that should be respected. They were careful to cut down only as many trees as they needed to continue their way of life.

## Did You Know?

Chief Seattle (c. 1786–1866) was the leader of the Suquamish and Duwamish people who lived in what is now northwestern Washington state. Seattle wanted to work with European settlers to coexist with the groups of Native Americans living in the area. In 1855, Seattle agreed to give over his people's land to the U.S. government and move to a reservation. European settlers changed the name of their village to Seattle to honor Chief Seattle. When groups of Native Americans tried to take back their land by force, Chief Seattle kept his warriors out of the battle. He thought that facing the much larger force of settlers was not a good idea. He wanted to retain other lands for his people.

Chief Seattle

Pacific Northwest groups such as the Tlingit carved **totem poles** as a way of chronicling their clan and family histories. Totem poles are made from long logs that are carved and decorated to represent people or animals. Each totem pole is made up of a series of these symbols, called totems. The totems and their order often reflect the stories of the clans and families of a village.

Tlingit and Chinook families often marked major life events, such as a wedding or a change of leader, with a ceremony known as a **potlatch**. At a potlatch, guests of the family receive gifts and enjoy feasting and music. The host is responsible for gift giving and sometimes can offer more than a hundred presents at a single potlatch. The host receives respect and standing among the community as a result of his or her wisdom and appropriate generosity. Pacific Northwest peoples still hold potlatches today, and they are an important source of cultural identity for many people who live in the region.

The Makah people made their home on the shores of the Pacific Ocean and the Strait of Juan de Fuca. Though the Makah hunted many kinds of sea animals, including seals, porpoises, and sea otters, whale hunting held a special place in Makah life.

A modern-day potlatch ceremony

Makah canoes carrying as many as sixty hunters at a time would set out in search of whales. After a successful hunt, the Makah gave thanks for their triumph. Every part of a whale was used in different Makah activities.

## Stop and Check

**Write** Reread the text and make a list of all of the ways that Native Americans of the Pacific Northwest used wood. Is there a material that is as important to Americans today as wood was to these groups of Native Americans?

# Subarctic Peoples

The Subarctic region of North America stretches from Alaska on the Pacific Ocean to Newfoundland and Labrador on the Atlantic Coast. A northern forest and marshland known as the taiga covers large parts of the Subarctic.

Many Subarctic peoples hunted by following the seasonal movements of moose and caribou and also fished for salmon. Hunters often used bows and arrows or set up traps to capture their prey. To protect from the cold, people made leggings, moccasins, and parkas from animal skins. Some groups set up temporary hunting and fishing camps of lean-to structures with sloped walls for shelter. During the long and snowy winter, some groups built more permanent structures. The Deg Xinag in the western Subarctic built partially below-ground houses from wood and sod.

Some Subarctic groups along the Pacific Coast had permanent villages run by a council of elders, but the groups farther inland were organized in smaller bands of family members.

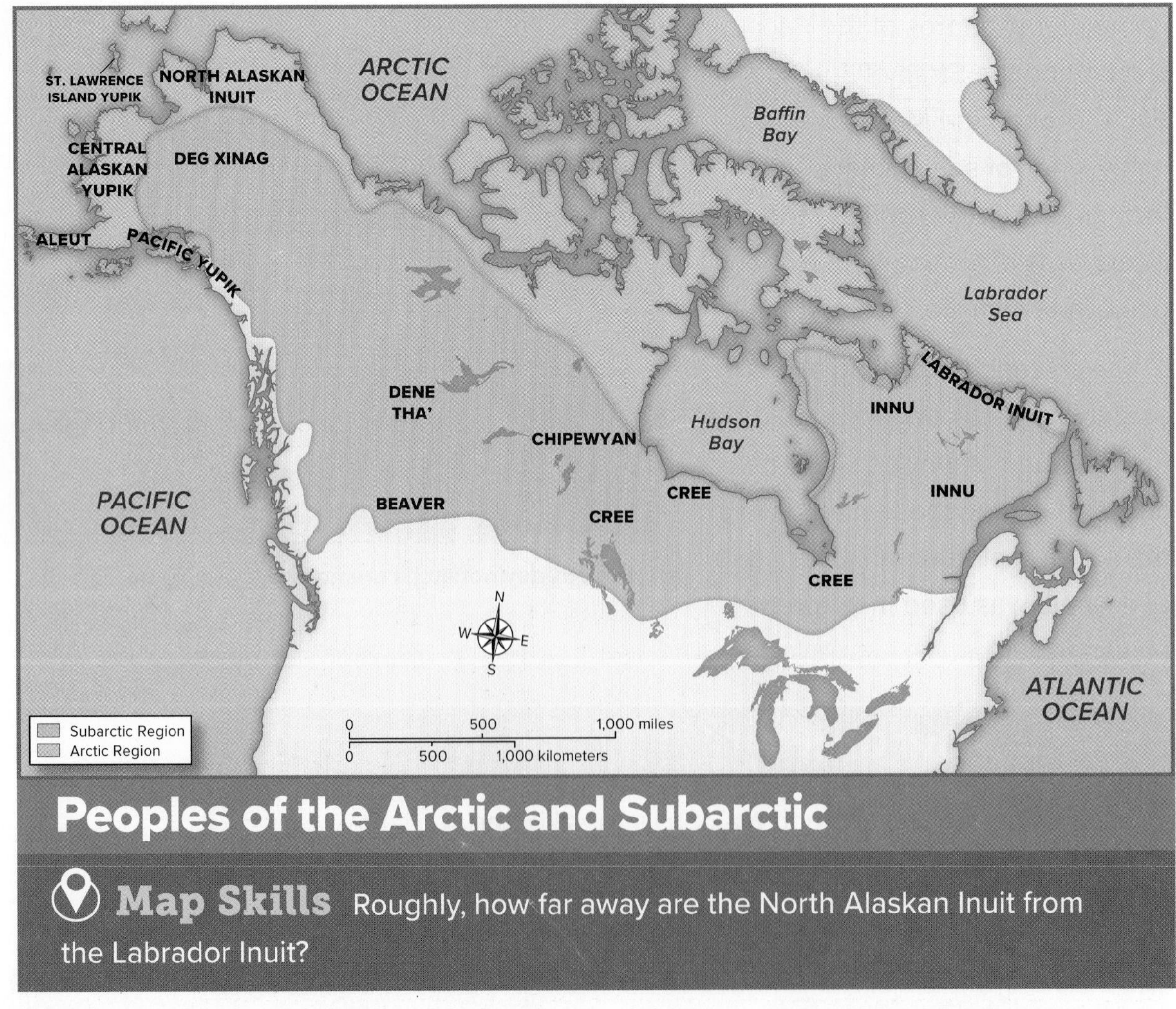


## Peoples of the Arctic and Subarctic

**Map Skills** Roughly, how far away are the North Alaskan Inuit from the Labrador Inuit?

# Arctic Peoples

Some Deg Xinag, Aleut, and Inuit families lived in partially below-ground homes.

Beyond the tree-covered taiga is a treeless zone of rocky soil and low-growing shrubs called the tundra. For most of the year, the arctic region is covered in ice and snow. The native peoples of the Arctic—such as the Inuit, Yupik, and Aleut—adapted to the extreme cold, making clothes from caribou furs and other animal hides. The winters are severe with only a few hours of sunlight per day. During this time, many Arctic peoples constructed below-ground houses or snow-block homes called igloos. They hunted seal, walruses, and whales along the coast. Many Inuit hunted with long spears called harpoons.

The brief summers bring with them very long days of sunlight in which streams of water from snow melt attract migratory animals such as caribou and musk oxen. These animals were the primary hunting targets of arctic peoples in the summer.

Among some Inuit, the senior male was considered the clan chief. The chief of the strongest clan was the village chief. Some groups had no chief.

## Then and Now

### The Inuit Economy

The early Inuit did not exchange money for goods and services. Instead, they produced their own food, clothing, and other necessities. Because clan members had different skills, sharing and cooperation were essential for the early Inuit's way of life. Sharing is still a key element of Inuit society, but many Inuit today take part in a wage economy. An Inuit person might earn income working for the local government or through some other profession. Hunting of caribou and seal still occurs, but growing industries include tourism and real estate. Some Inuit earn money from selling sculptures, carvings, and prints.

## Stop and Check

**Talk** How did climate and wildlife affect the daily lives of Arctic and Subarctic peoples?

# How Did the Great Plains Influence the Traditions of the People Living There?

## Grass and Sky for Miles

The Great Plains region covers a huge area of land that spreads from Canada south to Texas, and from the Rocky Mountains east to North Dakota, South Dakota, Nebraska, Kansas, and Oklahoma. It is mainly made up of hills and flat, grassy stretches of land called **prairies**. Except near rivers, it is difficult to grow crops in the Great Plains. Most Native American peoples who lived there could not depend on farming for food. Instead, they followed and hunted the huge herds of buffalo that roamed the prairies. (These animals were first called "buffalo" by early American settlers. The name stuck, but these large, cattle-like animals are actually bison.)

Plains peoples depended on the buffalo for more than just food. Buffalo hides were used to make clothes and shelter. Plains peoples made ropes, bowls, needles, thread, and tools from other parts of the buffalo. In fact, they had a use for every part of the buffalo.

Buffalo were part of the spiritual practice of the Plains peoples. These peoples prepared for each hunt with special ceremonies, and they believed they needed the support of the spirit of the buffalo for the hunt to be successful. Buffalo roamed from place to place, so many Plains peoples developed a lifestyle that allowed them to follow the herds.

**c. 1300**
Native Americans settle the Plains.

**1500s**
Horses first come to North America.

**1600s**
The Lakota are pushed westward by competing groups.

1300 | 1400 | 1500 | 1600 | 1700

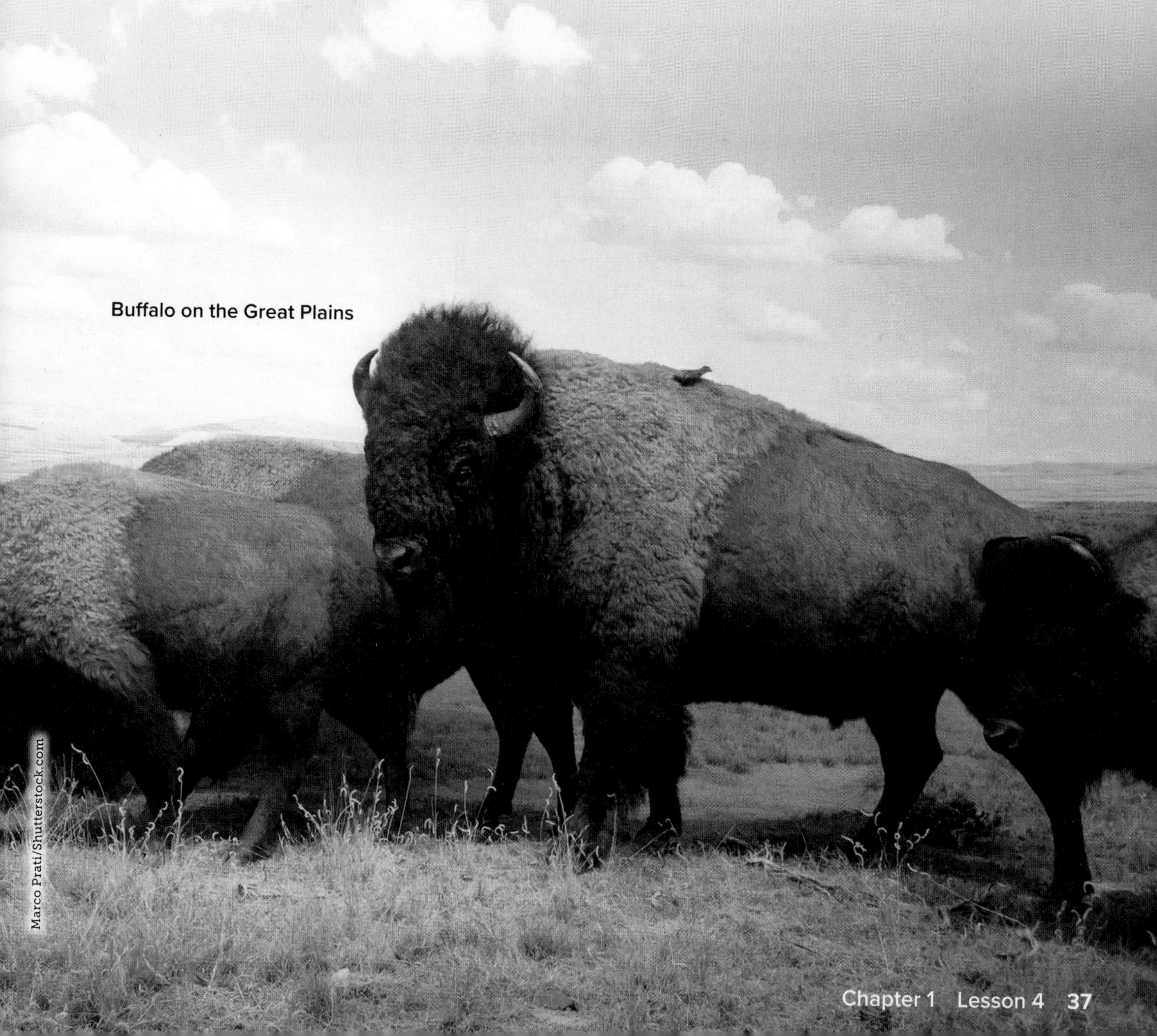

**Buffalo on the Great Plains**

Marco Prati/Shutterstock.com

# Peoples of the Plains

Native Americans began settling the Great Plains as early as A.D. 1300. By the 1700s, groups included the Lakota, Dakota, and Nakota Sioux as well as the Pawnee, Cheyenne, Crow, Kiowa, and several others. Some people moved to the region because of drought, or a long period without rain, in the place where they used to live. Many people lived near rivers, which provided fertile land for them to farm. Others who followed the buffalo were nomads, or people who move from place to place with no fixed residence.

Plains peoples who traveled usually lived in cone-shaped homes called teepees. These structures consisted of buffalo hide spread across long poles. When the buffalo moved, women collapsed the teepees and set them back up in a new place. Those who lived near rivers set up more permanent homes called lodges made of logs, grasses, and dirt. But they also used teepees when they needed to travel to hunt.

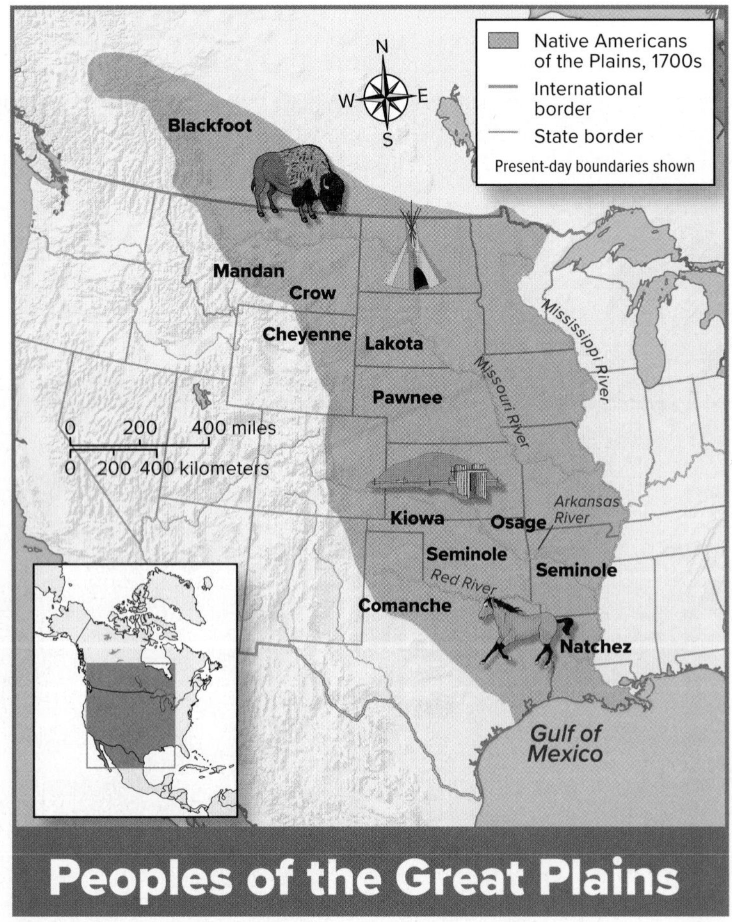


Peoples of the Great Plains

The peoples of the Great Plains made their clothing mostly out of buffalo and deer hide. Men of the northern plains wore a shirt, leggings that reached their hips, and moccasins with hard bottoms that would protect their feet on rocky terrain. They also wore a breechcloth, which was a short apron worn around the waist. When the weather grew cold, they would wear high boots and a robe made from buffalo hide. The inside of the robe was covered with fur of the buffalo. In the warmer southern plains, men would leave their upper bodies bare. Some decorated their upper bodies with tattoos.

Teepees in Wyoming



## Did You Know?

**Horses**

You may have thought that people in the Great Plains region have been riding horses for thousands of years. Before the 1500s, however, nobody had ridden a horse in North America. Explorers from Spain brought horses to the Americas, and some of the horses escaped. After about one hundred years, the horses had traveled up to the Great Plains. There the Lakota caught and tamed them. After another hundred years, most Native Americans on the Plains were using horses to help them hunt buffalo and move their camps.

The introduction of horses completely changed the way of life for the Plains people. Before they had horses, Plains people followed the buffalo on foot. They trained dogs to pull belongings on a special sled called a *hupak'in*. After the introduction of horses, a person's wealth was measured by the number of horses owned.

Plains women wore long dresses, leggings to the knee, and moccasins. They used the eye-teeth of elk to decorate their dresses. Eye-teeth are canine teeth on the upper jaw, below the eyes. Because each elk had only two eye-teeth, a dress decorated by a number of eye-teeth demonstrated the ability of the hunters in the woman's family. Men and women would wear billed caps or fur hats to protect them from both the sun and the cold. More elaborate headdress was used for ceremonial occasions. It sometimes contained eagle feathers.

Most of the trade among different plains groups occurred between hunting nomads and agricultural villagers. They traded items such as dried meat and buffalo robes for corn and squash. Trades could take place in two places. Nomads sometimes visited villages. Sometimes trade took place at trade fairs.

Trade fairs were events held away from villages where villagers and nomads would meet to trade. Members of different groups would ceremonially adopt each other during trades. Because family played such an important role in life on the plains, when people from different groups thought of each other as brothers and sisters, trade went more smoothly. Plains people also developed a form of sign language so that members of groups who did not speak the same language could trade.

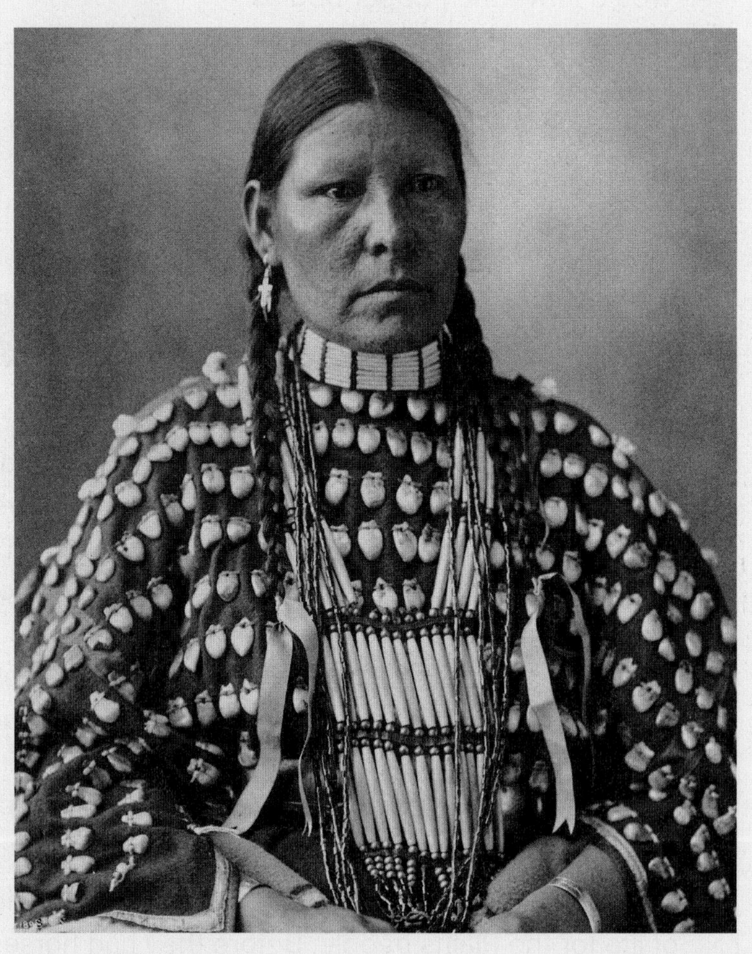

This woman's dress is decorated with elk teeth.

Large quantities of trade goods were transported on bullboats, which were round boats made from buffalo hide and willow reeds. These boats allowed large trade networks to develop. In addition to food and clothing, other traded goods included arrowheads, bowls, and other tools made of fiber, bone, antler, or stone.

Before Europeans brought horses to the Americas, large-scale warfare was rare. However, small raiding parties between different groups were common. They sought to steal goods from each other and gain glory by proving their fighting skill. The greatest glory someone could gain in battle was called "counting coup." This meant getting close enough to an enemy during battle to touch him without killing him. It was considered a great feat of bravery. After the arrival of Europeans, large battles between groups became more common as they clashed over resources, especially horses.

A bullboat

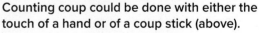

Counting coup could be done with either the touch of a hand or of a coup stick (above).

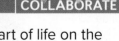

## Stop and Check

COLLABORATE

**Talk** What do you think was the most interesting part of life on the plains? Why?

**Find Evidence** As you read, add additional information to the graphic organizer on page 35 in your Inquiry Journal.

InfoGraphic

# Life on the Plains

What was life like if you were a Native American on the Plains? Your daily activities greatly depended on whether you were a man or a woman.

**Men**

- Were responsible for boys' education.
- Could serve as keeper of the people's history and stories.
- Hunted buffalo and other game.
- Fought in wars.

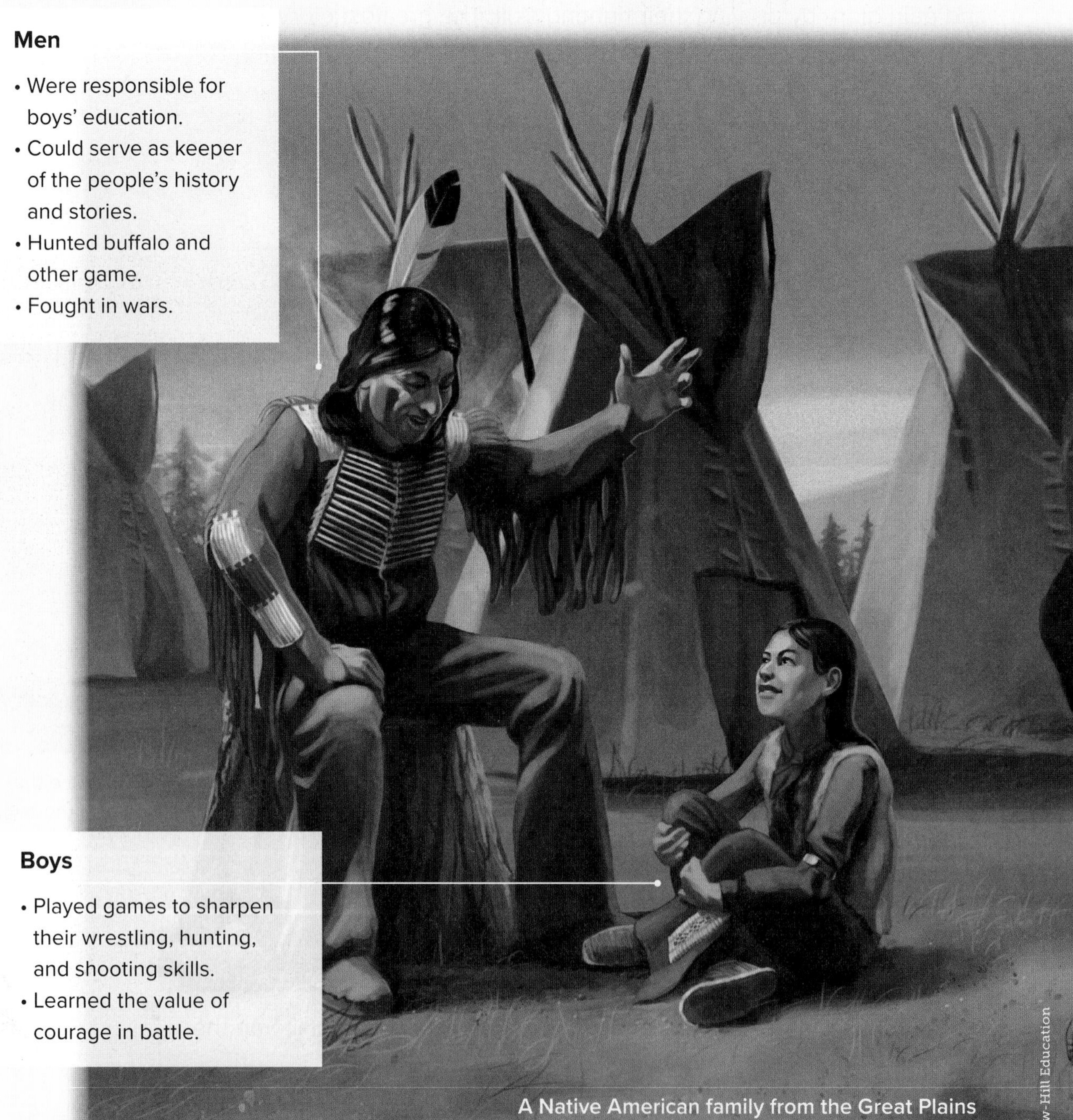

**Boys**

- Played games to sharpen their wrestling, hunting, and shooting skills.
- Learned the value of courage in battle.

A Native American family from the Great Plains

Boys and girls who grew up in native cultures on the Great Plains also had specific roles. For all children, education started early. Usually it consisted of listening to stories and learning songs.

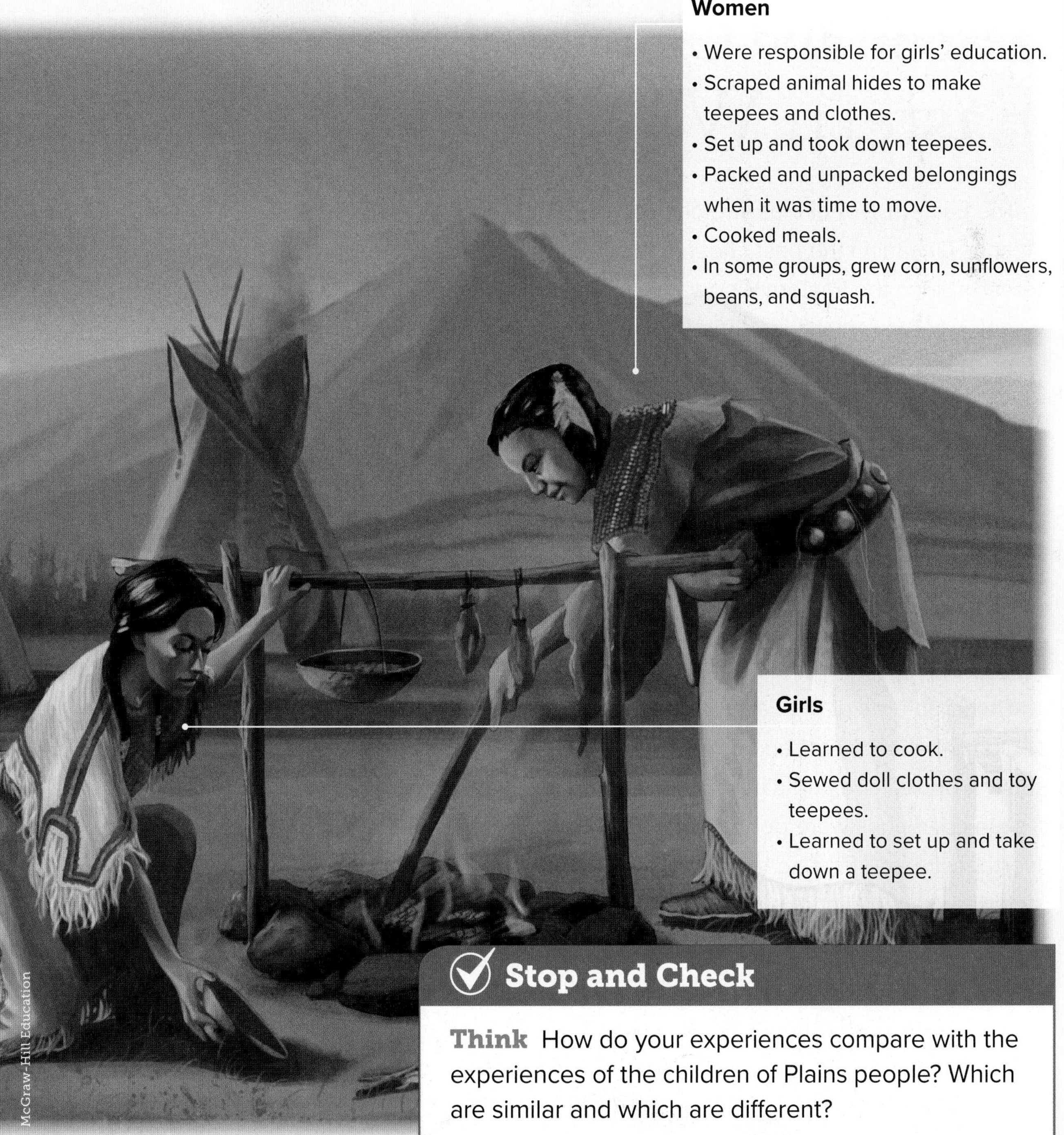

**Women**

- Were responsible for girls' education.
- Scraped animal hides to make teepees and clothes.
- Set up and took down teepees.
- Packed and unpacked belongings when it was time to move.
- Cooked meals.
- In some groups, grew corn, sunflowers, beans, and squash.

**Girls**

- Learned to cook.
- Sewed doll clothes and toy teepees.
- Learned to set up and take down a teepee.




## Stop and Check

**Think** How do your experiences compare with the experiences of the children of Plains people? Which are similar and which are different?

# How Did the Eastern Woodlands Impact the Lives of Early People?

## Terrain and Climate of the Eastern Woodlands

The Eastern Woodlands stretch from the Mississippi River to the Atlantic Ocean. In the past, most of this area was covered in thick forests. Since the Eastern Woodlands cover a large area, the early peoples of the region were often very different from one another.

The seasons often guided how the people of the Eastern Woodlands lived. During the winter, men hunted game such as deer, bear, rabbits, beavers, and wild turkeys. During spring, the soil was ideal for growing crops. In summer, men fished, carved canoes, and built homes while women gathered berries and wild plants. In autumn, the people gathered, dried, and stored the crops for the winter. After the **harvest**, they let the land rest for several years before replanting the crops. They used different land the next year.

The large area of the Eastern Woodlands can be divided into two regions: the Northeast and the Southeast. The Southeast was more thinly wooded and had a mild climate and a long growing season. These conditions were good for farming. The thicker forests of the Northeast made farming more challenging. There, many early peoples practiced a type of farming called **slash-and-burn**. They cut down and burned the trees in the forest, and ash from the burned vegetation helped make the soil fertile.

**c. A.D. 700**
The Mississippian culture arises in the Southeast Woodlands.

**c. 1570**
The Iroquois Confederacy is formed.

**c. 1722**
Tuscarora join the Iroquois Confederacy.

700 | 1000 | 1600 | 1700

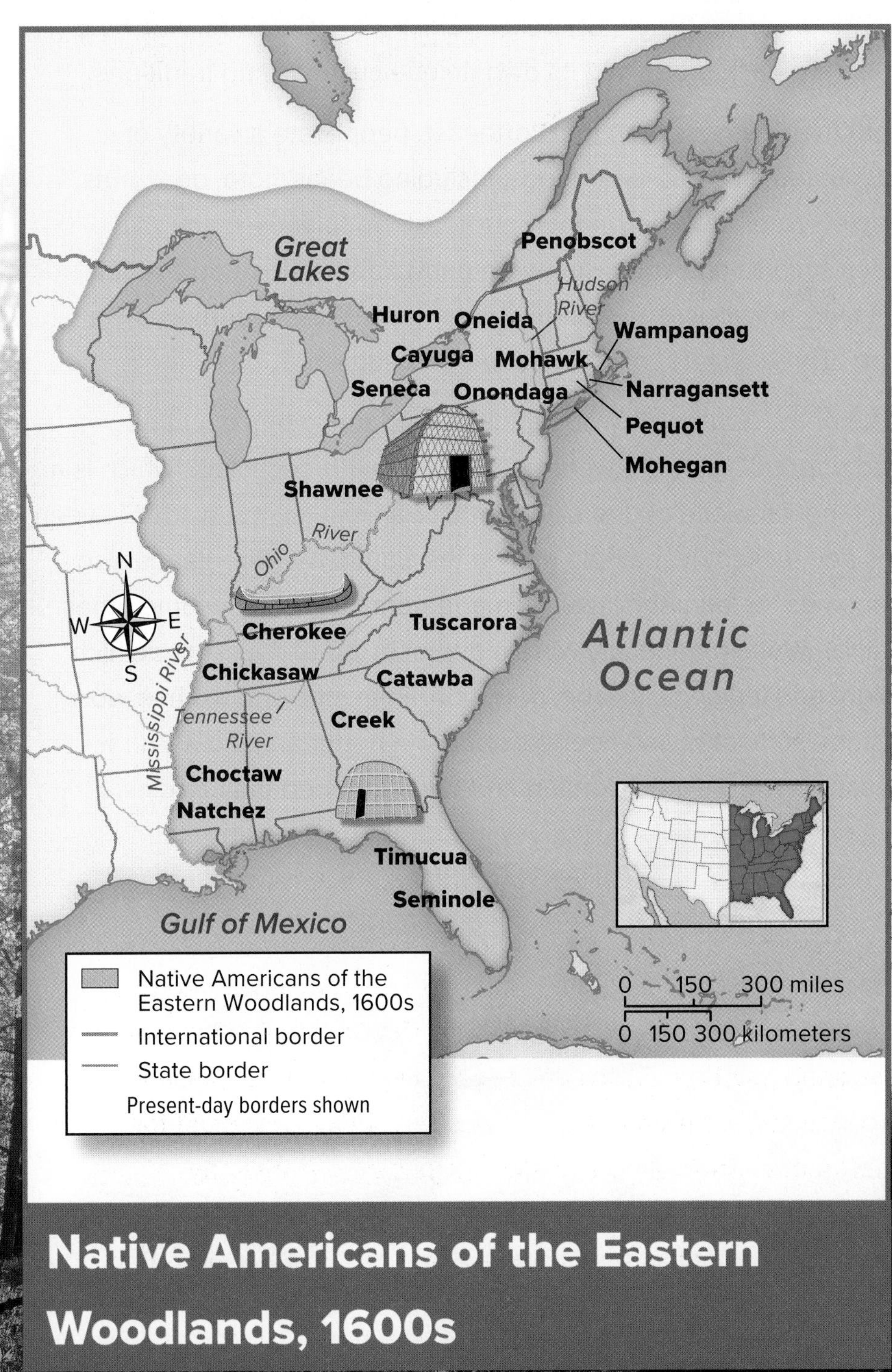


## Native Americans of the Eastern Woodlands, 1600s

Adam Aczel/EyeEm/Getty Images

# People of the Southeast Woodlands

Among the Native American groups that lived in the Southeast Woodlands were the Creek, Cherokee, Chickasaw, Catawba, Natchez, and Choctaw. Each group had its own unique customs and traditions.

In both the Southeast and the Northeast, people ate a variety of farmed, hunted, and gathered foods, including beans, corn, deer, nuts, and maple syrup. However, in the Southeast Woodlands, many wild resources such as rice and bison were unavailable. The people relied more heavily on crops. The Cherokee in the Southeast, for example, grew the "Three Sisters" of corn, beans, and squash.

People of the Southeast Woodlands wore clothing that could be adjusted depending on the weather. Men wore a breechcloth, which is a long rectangular piece of deerskin, cloth, or animal fur. It is worn between the legs and tucked over a belt. Men in the Southeast Woodlands also wore leggings, or leg pants, usually made from buckskin or some other soft leather. Women generally wore a deerskin top and a skirt to which they might add leggings, a cape, or a robe. Both men and women wore moccasins—soft-soled and heelless shoes. In hotter areas of the Southeast, men wore little clothing and often tattooed their bodies.

**Moccasins—soft-soled, heelless shoes—made by Native Americans of the Eastern Woodlands**

Ways of life varied from group to group in the Southeast. The Cherokee, who lived mainly in what is now Tennessee and Georgia, constructed fairly large villages, with each having 20 to 60 houses and a large meeting building. Cherokee homes were usually made of wattle—twigs and branches woven together to make the house's frame—and daub, which is a sticky substance like mud or clay. The Cherokee covered the wattle frame with daub, which held it all together. This created the look of an upside-down basket. The Cherokee also placed fences around their villages for protection against enemies. Each Cherokee village had its own leaders and made its own decisions. However, during times of celebration or war, villages came together. One celebration, called the Green Corn Festival, honored the summer's first corn crop with dances and games.

Like the Cherokee, the Natchez built homes from wattle and daub. The Natchez lived in permanent villages in what today is Mississippi. They were successful farmers, but they also hunted, fished, and gathered food from plants. Like the Hopewell and Mississippian people before them, the Natchez built ceremonial mounds.

The Creek arranged their towns around a central town plaza, used for religious ceremonies and games. Surrounding the plaza were family homes built out of poles and covered with grass, mud, or thatch. Like the Cherokee, the Creek relied on the "Three Sisters" of corn, beans, and squash for food. In addition, they hunted small animals and gathered plants.

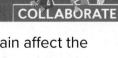

The "Three Sisters" crops: corn, squash, and beans

## Stop and Check

COLLABORATE

**Talk** How did climate and terrain affect the diet and clothing of the Native Americans in the Southeast Woodlands?

**Find Details** As you read, add additional information to the graphic organizer on page 43 in your Inquiry Journal.

# People of the Northeast Woodlands

Like the Southeast Woodlands, the Northeast Woodlands area was populated by different groups each with their unique customs and traditions. The Mohawk, Onondaga, Cayuga, Oneida, Seneca, Narragansett, and Pequot groups lived in the Northeast Woodlands.

Because of differences in climate and terrain, people in the Northeast ate food unavailable to people in the Southeast. Rivers in the Northeast, for example, had annual runs of fish, like salmon, that moved up rivers from the sea. In the North, people often had to rely more on fish than on crops because frost frequently destroyed crops. On the Atlantic coast and along major rivers, shellfish were plentiful and provided a major source of food for the people living there.

Because of the colder climate, the clothing worn by people in the Northeast differed from what people in the Southeast wore. While the basics—breechcloth and leggings for men and deerskin tops and skirts for women—remained the same, people in the Northeast wore heavier and warmer leggings and various furs. Northeast groups also used snowshoes for walking in the snow. Snowshoes work by distributing a person's weight over a larger area so that the person does not sink in the snow.

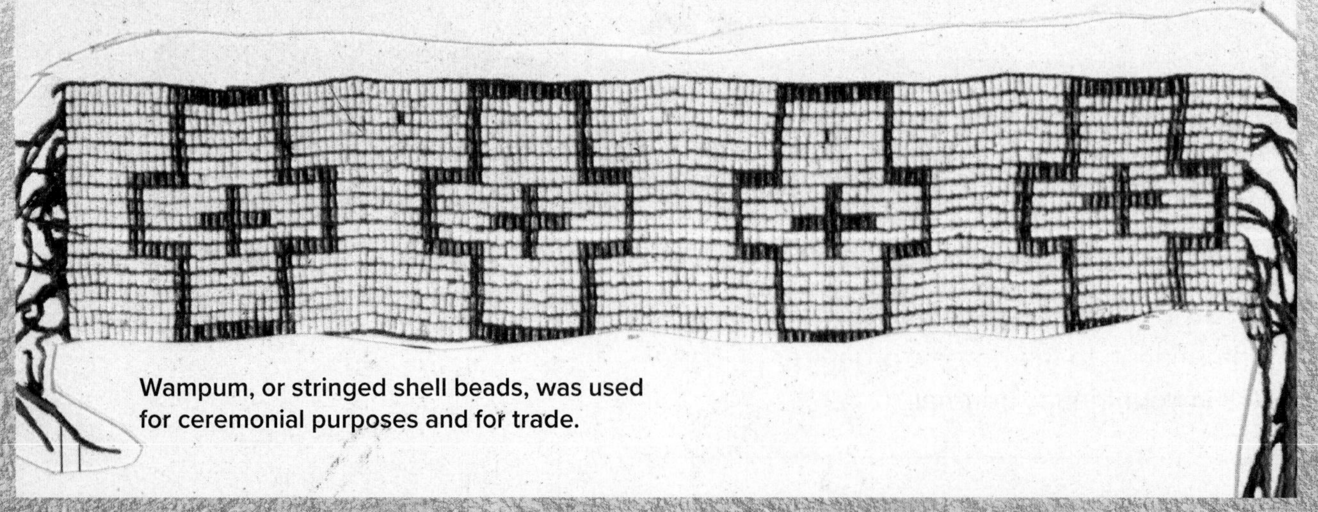

**Wampum, or stringed shell beads, was used for ceremonial purposes and for trade.**

In the 1500s, the Iroquois lived mostly in what is now upstate New York. Historians call this group the Iroquois because they spoke languages in the Iroquoian language family. However, the Iroquois call themselves Haudenosaunee (hoe dee noh SHOH nee). In Iroquoian, this means "people of the longhouse."

For housing, the Iroquois depended on wigwams and longhouses. The Iroquois made wigwams by bending young trees to form the round shape of a dome. Then, over this basic shape, they wrapped pieces of tree bark to protect against bad weather. Over the bark layer they added thatch, or dried grass. A small hole at the top allowed smoke from the fire to escape.

Longhouses were long, rectangular homes. The Iroquois made their longhouses by building a frame from saplings, or young trees. They covered the frame with bark sewn together. Inside, they built a long hallway with rooms on both sides. Then they lined the walls with sleeping platforms, covered with deerskin. They also built in shelves for storing baskets, pots, and pelts (the skins of animals with the fur attached). Several families lived in the same longhouse.

Almost all Iroquois property was controlled by clans—groups of families who shared the same ancestor. Women were the leaders of their clans. Among the Iroquois, it was women who decided how the land would be used and who would use it. When a man married, he moved into his wife's longhouse and lived with her family. Children took their clan name from their mother. No important decision could be made without the approval of the clan mother. Although the leaders of each village were men, it was the clan mother who chose them.

## Stop and Check

COLLABORATE

**Talk** Native American groups found different ways to organize themselves and their members. Why was it important that the groups organized themselves?

# Government in the Woodlands

To help protect themselves, the Creek formed a confederacy. A confederacy is a group of people formed for a common purpose. The Creek Confederacy divided its towns into peace (white) towns and war (red) towns. Red towns declared war, planned military actions, and met with enemies. White towns passed laws and held conquered groups. However, during war, people in peace towns joined in the fighting.

Farther north, the Iroquois also had a system of government. When they were a small group, they cooperated on many matters. By about A.D. 1300, their numbers had grown, and their communities were crowded. Arguments arose and fighting broke out. The Iroquois believed that if one person was wronged, it hurt the whole clan. For this reason, wrongs had to be punished. The Iroquois also fought with other Eastern Woodlands peoples, often over hunting grounds. Warfare soon became a constant problem for the Iroquois.

According to Iroquois history, two Iroquois leaders, Deganawida and Hiawatha, saw that fighting was destroying their people. In the 1500s, these two leaders urged the Iroquois to join together to make peace. In about 1570, five separate Iroquois groups joined together to form the Iroquois Confederacy, also known as the Iroquois League. The Confederacy is still active today.

**PRIMARY SOURCE**

## In Their Words... Constitution of the Iroquois Nations

If a nation, part of a nation, or more than one nation within the Five Nations should in any way endeavor to destroy the Great Peace by neglect or violating its laws and resolve to dissolve the Confederacy, such a nation or such nations shall be deemed guilty of treason and called enemies of the Confederacy and the Great Peace.

They [the offending people] shall be warned once and if a second warning is necessary they shall be driven from the territory of the Confederacy. . . .

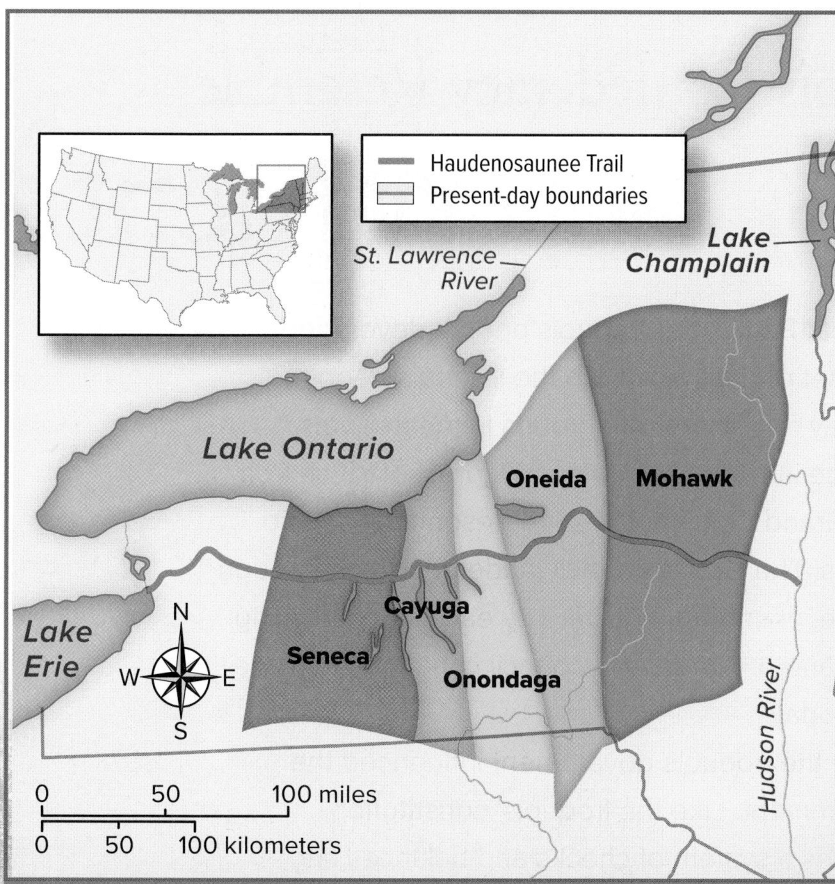


## The Iroquois Confederacy, 1600

**Map Skills** Which group of Iroquois lived the farthest east?

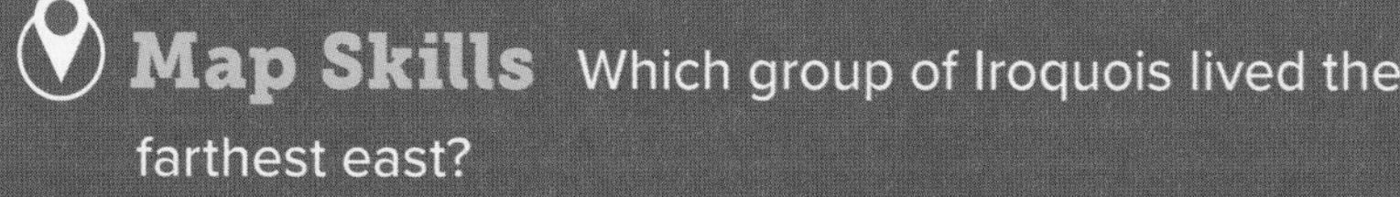

## Stop and Check

COLLABORATE

**Talk** What was the major reason the Iroquois formed a confederacy?

**Find Details** As you read, add additional information to the graphic organizer on page 43 of your Inquiry Journal.

**What Do You Think?** How did climate and surroundings impact early peoples of the Eastern Woodlands?

# Does the Iroquois Confederacy Resemble the U.S. Government?

In order to keep the Great Peace, the Iroquois people developed the Great Law. This was a set of rules by which the Iroquois people lived. They also set up a way for each of the groups in the Iroquois Confederacy to have a voice in making decisions. Representatives from all of the clans met at the Grand Council. These representatives were chosen by the clan mothers. The Grand Council made decisions through discussion and compromise, or settled a dispute by each side agreeing to give up part of what it wanted. The Grand Council continues to make decisions for the Iroquois today.

Some historians believe the Iroquois government influenced the plan of the American government. Like the Iroquois' constitution, the U.S. constitution includes a system of checks and balances and separation of powers. In fact, in 1988 the U.S. Senate passed a resolution acknowledging the influence of the Iroquois Confederacy on the U.S. Constitution. But just how much did the Iroquois Confederacy influence our government? How democratic was the Iroquois Confederacy?

**PRIMARY SOURCE**

## In Their Words... Concurrent Resolution 331

**To acknowledge the contribution of the Iroquois Confederacy of Nations to the development of the United States Constitution and to reaffirm the continuing government-to-government relationship between Indian tribes and the United States established in the Constitution.**

**Whereas the original framers of the Constitution, including, most notably, George Washington and Benjamin Franklin, are known to have greatly admired the concepts of the Six Nations of the Iroquois Confederacy . . .**

—U.S. Senate, October 21, 1988

TEXT: U.S. Congress. House. A Concurrent Resolution to Acknowledge the Contribution of the Iroquois Confederacy of Nations to the Development of the United States Constitution and to Reaffirm the Continuing Government-to-Government Relationship between Indian tribes and the United States Established in the Constitution. HR 331. 100th Cong., 2nd sess. (October 4, 1988): H.Rept 100-1031.; PHOTO: McGraw-Hill Education

## Build Citizenship

**Justice**

1. List ways the American government is like the Iroquois Confederacy.
2. List ways the American government is different from the Iroquois Confederacy.
3. Do you think the Iroquois Confederacy had more similarities or more differences with our government?

## Think About It

**Perspectives**

1. Find a classmate that answered the question differently than you.
2. Take turns giving your perspective and supporting it with reasons and evidence.
3. Discuss with your classmate whether or not you think the Iroquois Confederacy was a democracy.

An 18th century French engraving of Deganawida meeting with the Iroquois Confederacy



### Talk About It

Think about how you described the Iroquois government. Discuss the following questions with a partner. What makes a government a democracy? Is it the way leaders are chosen, or is it the way the government makes decisions?

# Connections in Action!

## Back to the EQ

**Think** about the Chapter EQ, **"How Were the Lives of Native Peoples Influenced by Where They Lived?"**

- **Talk** with a partner about each group you learned about in the chapter. Which civilization did you find the most interesting, and why? Consider how that group's location affected its way of life. Create a graphic organizer that lists or compares and contrasts interesting facts about the groups you and your partner chose.
- What do you think will change about these Native Americans' ways of life once Europeans arrive?
- **Share** your ideas with the class.

# More to Explore

## How Can You Make an IMPACT?

### Q and A

Work with a partner. Each of you will play the part of a member of an early Native American group. Write three to five questions for your partner to answer about the culture and civilization of his or her chosen group. You will answer your partner's questions about the group you chose.

### Travel Guide

Write a blog post for a travel website that will persuade early humans to migrate to a specific region of the Americas. Include information about the location's soil, rivers, or weather. Make suggestions about what kind of civilization the early humans could build in your chosen location. Draw a picture of the area to illustrate your blog post.

### Picture It!

Choose three words from the Chapter Word Bank. Create an illustration or series of illustrations, such as a comic strip, that provides context for each word you chose. Share your images with the class, and tell how each one gives context to the vocabulary word.

THE IMPACT TODAY

# How Does Where We Live IMPACT US?

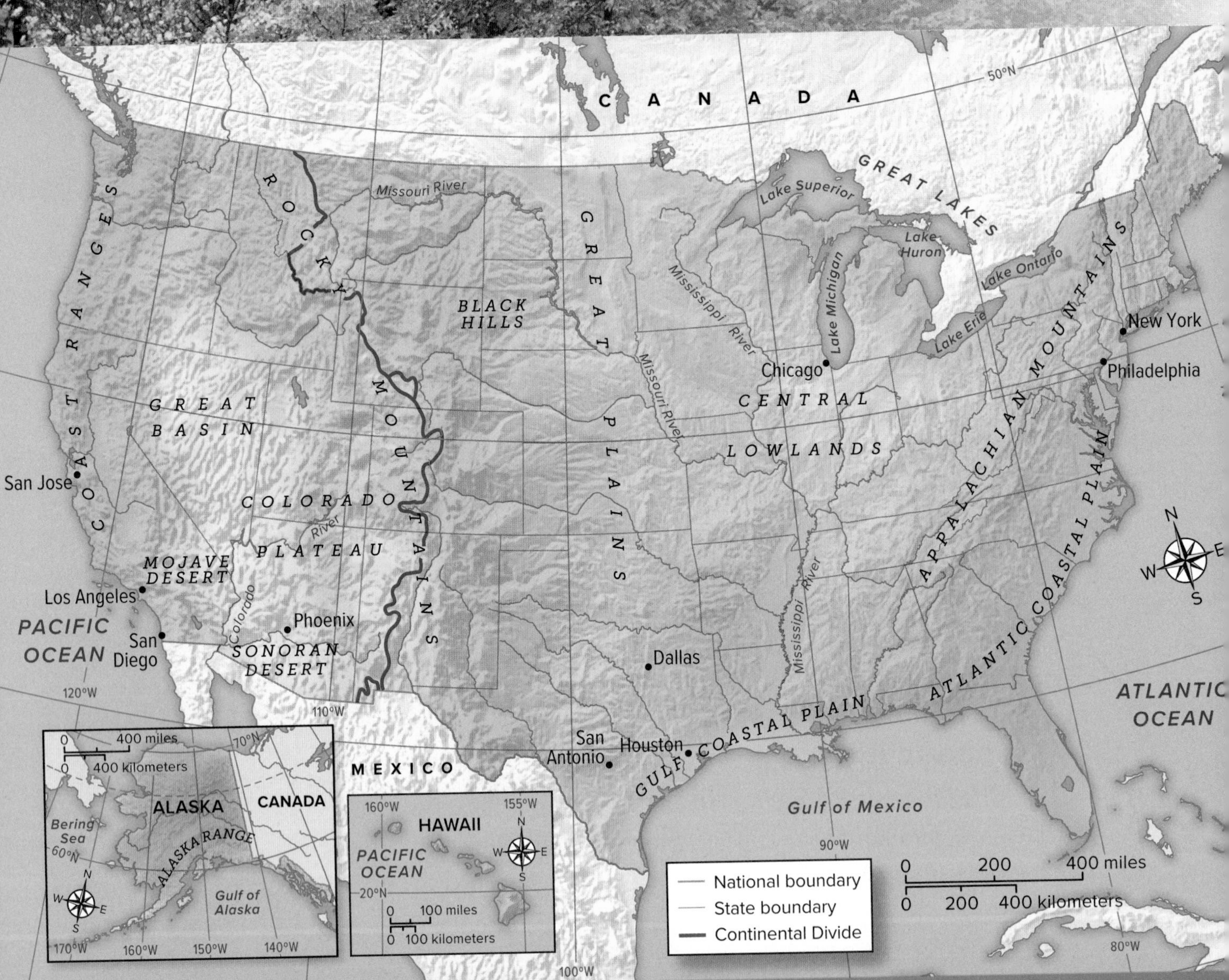


## United States Physical Map

**Map Skills** What landforms are near where you live? How close are you to the Great Plains? What direction are the Rocky Mountains from where you live?

PHOTO 24/Getty Images

# Physical Regions of the United States

A physical map shows **landforms**, which are natural features of Earth's surface. The United States is home to many different landforms, including mountains, plains, valleys, plateaus, and canyons.

The Atlantic Coastal Plain is a lowland area through the East Coast of the United States. In the north, this region is rocky, but to the south the land is good for farming. The Appalachian Mountains run along the eastern part of the United States from Maine south to Alabama.

The Gulf Coastal Plain has rich soil that is good for farming. Cotton is a major crop in this area. The Central Lowlands consists of grassy hills, rolling flatlands, forests, and rich farmland. The Central Lowlands includes the area known as the Midwest. Important crops there include corn and soybeans.

The region known as the Great Plains consists of prairies, flat land that is covered in tall grasses. Farmers there raise crops, including corn and wheat, and graze cattle. The region is also rich in resources such as coal, oil, and natural gas.

Great Plains

The western mountain ranges rise up to the west of the Great Plains. The Rocky Mountains are the most well-known of the western ranges. The Pacific Coast ranges to the west of the Rockies include the Cascades and the Sierra Nevada.

The Continental Divide runs along the Rocky Mountains and extends all the way to Alaska. It separates the flow of water in North America. Rivers to the east of the Continental Divide drain into the Arctic Ocean, the Atlantic Ocean, and the Gulf of Mexico. West of the Continental Divide, rivers flow into the Pacific Ocean and the Gulf of California.

Continental Divide

Plateaus and canyons lie between the Rocky Mountains and the Pacific Ocean. This area includes the Mojave Desert, which covers parts of California, Utah, Nevada, and Arizona. It also includes the Grand Canyon.

## WHAT IS THE IMPACT TODAY?

COLLABORATE

**Talk** Think about the region where you live. What kinds of geographic features, such as hills, mountains, lakes or rivers, are there in the area? How do you think the physical environment impacts the way people live in your region?

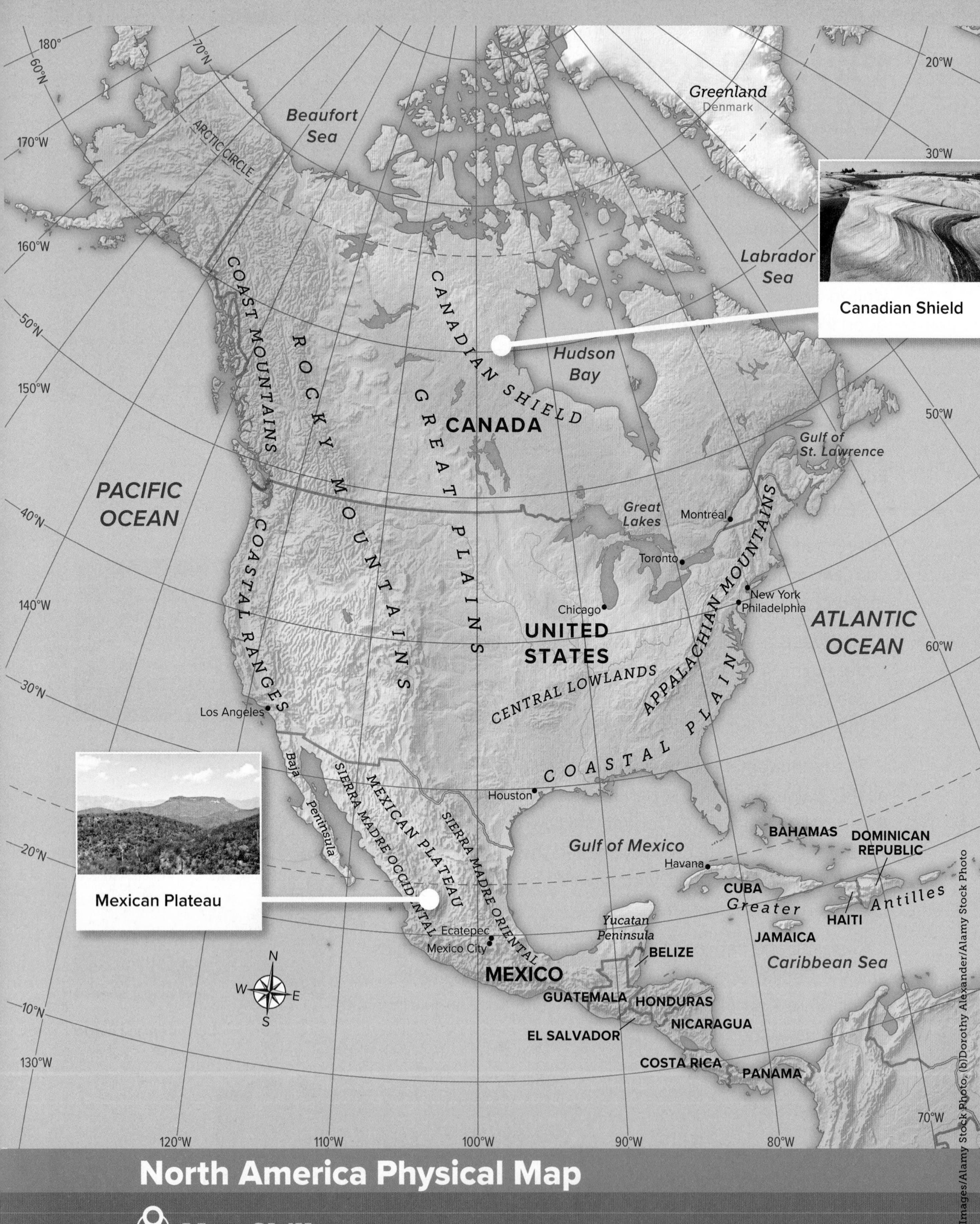




## North America Physical Map

**Map Skills** Where are the Canadian Shield and Mexican Plateau on the map?

# Physical Regions of North America

North America is the third largest continent in the world in terms of area. All of North America is in the Northern Hemisphere, north of the equator. Southern Mexico and the countries of Central America are sometimes referred to as Mesoamerica. Island nations such as Cuba, Puerto Rico, and the Bahamas are referred to as being part of the Caribbean because they are in the Caribbean Sea.

The map on page 58 shows the physical regions of North America. The Canadian Shield and the Mexican Plateau play a starring role in the physical features of our neighbors.

## The Canadian Shield

The Canadian Shield is an enormous, horseshoe-shaped region that covers half of Canada and parts of the northern United States, including sections of Minnesota, Wisconsin, and New York. The Canadian Shield extends for about 3 million square miles. This region is made up of some of the oldest rock on Earth and is covered by a relatively thin layer of soil. Because it is made up of rock, the Canadian Shield is not the best farmland. This area is used for mining.

## The Mexican Plateau

A plateau is an area of land that is higher than the surrounding land and has a pretty flat surface. The Mexican Plateau extends south from the United States border to central Mexico. This plateau is about 700 miles long and 200 miles wide and covers about forty percent of Mexico. It averages about 4,000 feet above sea level. The northern part of the plateau is dry and not many people live there. The central and southern parts of the plateau have fertile soil and good rainfall. These areas are home to rich farmland. Many of Mexico's major cities are also located in this region.

## WHAT IS THE IMPACT TODAY?

COLLABORATE

**Talk** Choose a city from the map on page 58. Look at the physical features in the area around the city. Talk with a partner about why you think the physical features were important to the development of the city. How do you think these physical features might impact the city and its residents today?

## South America Physical Map

**Map Skills** Where are the Andes Mountains and Amazon River Basin on the map?

# Physical Regions of South America

South America is the fourth largest of the seven continents in area. South America is mostly in the Southern Hemisphere. Like its neighbor to the north, South America has a variety of landforms, including mountains, grasslands, river basins, and plateaus. Mountains line the western edge of the continent, and river basins cover millions of square miles of land in the interior of the continent. Dry coastal plains run along the Atlantic and Pacific coasts, and grasslands cover large areas in the northern and southern sections of the continent. The map on page 60 shows the physical regions of South America. Two of the largest regions are the Andes Mountains and the Amazon River Basin.

## The Andes Mountains

The Andes Mountains run along the western coast of South America and extend along the top of the continent to the Caribbean Sea. At 5,500 miles long, the Andes form the longest mountain range in the world. The Andes consists of a variety of landforms, including high peaks and plateaus. Farming is difficult on the Andes, although coffee, corn, and potatoes grow in some areas. The major industries in the mountains are gold, silver, copper, lead, and zinc mining and raising livestock, including sheep, goats, llamas, and alpacas.

## The Amazon River Basin

The Amazon River is about 4,000 miles long and is one of the world's longest rivers. The Amazon River Basin is the area that is drained by the Amazon River and all the rivers that flow into the Amazon. This area covers almost 3 million square miles and is home to the Amazon Rain Forest, the largest rain forest in the world. The widest range of life forms on Earth, including millions of kinds of insects, animals, and plants, live in the Amazon Rain Forest. In the twentieth century, people began settling large areas of the rain forest. The forests were cleared for farming, grazing, and mining. Logging became an important industry. Many people are concerned that continued clearing of the rain forest could create global environmental problems. Countries and organizations around the world are working together to find solutions for this shrinking forest.

## WHAT IS THE IMPACT TODAY?

COLLABORATE

**Talk** How do you think the physical environment impacts people who live in the Andes Mountains and the Amazon River Basin? In which of these places would you most like to live?

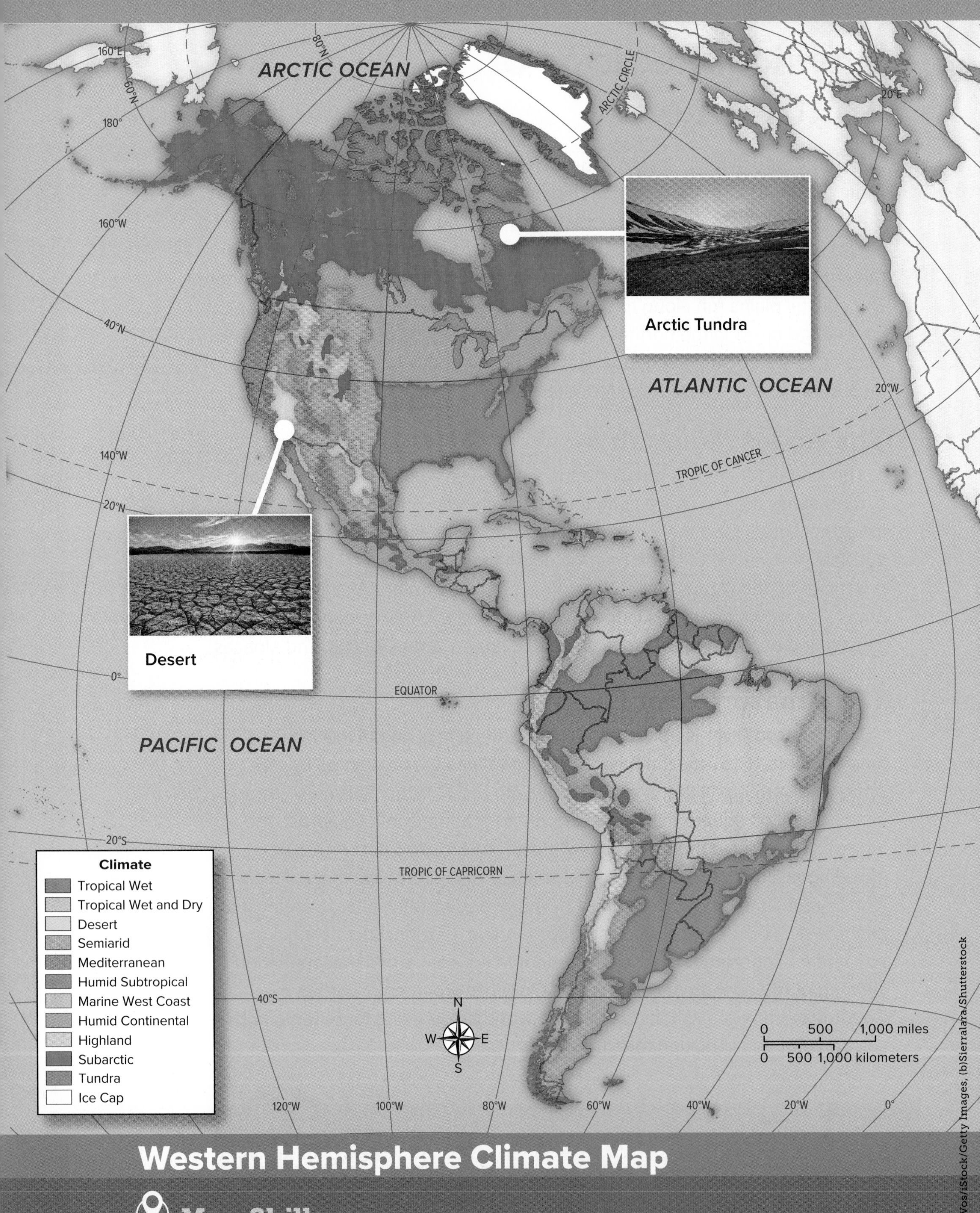


(t)JenDeVos/iStock/Getty Images, (b)Sierralara/Shutterstock

## Western Hemisphere Climate Map

**Map Skills** What type of climate do you live in according to the map key?

# Climate Regions in the Western Hemisphere

A **climate map** shows the dominant weather patterns for a region. Let's examine three climate regions in the Western Hemisphere from the map on page 62—Arctic Tundra, Desert, and Humid Continental.

## Arctic Tundra

The tundra is a vast, flat, treeless plain north of the Arctic Circle. Trees don't grow in the tundra because the subsoil, the layer of soil six to ten inches below the surface, is always frozen. This is called permafrost. Tundra vegetation includes mosses and small shrubs. The tundra has a very long, cold winter and a short summer. The average winter temperature is −20° Fahrenheit. The average summer temperature is about 50° Fahrenheit. When the frozen soil melts in the summer, the land becomes marshy. The tundra is also windy and dry, getting only about six to ten inches of precipitation a year.

## Desert

Most people think of deserts as hot, dry expanses of sand covered with different kinds of cacti and brush. But there are also rocky deserts along coasts, such as the Atacama Desert in northern Chile. The Mojave Desert is hot and dry. It gets less than thirteen inches of rainfall each year, and the temperature in parts of the Mojave can reach 120° Fahrenheit during the day. Most mammals that live in these deserts are small and search for food at night when it's cooler. Hot and dry deserts are also home to some insects, reptiles, and birds. All of these animals and insects have adapted to survive in the hot, dry climate.

## Humid Continental

The Humid Continental region has extreme weather changes, with warm summers and brisk, cold winters. The region covers a large area of the United States, stretching from New England west all the way to the Great Plains. Regular rainfall makes this region ideal for farming. Snowfall is common in the winter. A large variety of animals live in this region, including deer, rabbits, raccoons, coyotes, and thousands of kinds of birds. Many of these animals migrate as the temperatures change with the seasons.

## WHAT IS THE IMPACT TODAY?

COLLABORATE

**Talk** Choose one of the three regions you read about—the Tundra, the Desert, and Humid Continental regions. Imagine living there. How do you think climate would affect your daily life if you lived in that region?

ARCTIC OCEAN

PACIFIC OCEAN

ATLANTIC OCEAN

180°
0°N
20°W
160°W
40°W
40°N
140°W
60°W
20°N
120°W
100°W
80°W
ARCTIC CIRCLE
TROPIC OF CANCER

**Vegetation**

- Tropical rain forest
- Tropical grassland (savanna)
- Desert scrub and desert waste
- Temperate grassland
- Mediterranean scrub
- Deciduous forest
- Coniferous forest
- Mixed forest (deciduous and coniferous)
- Tundra
- Ice cap

0 250 500 miles
0 250 500 kilometers

N
E
S
W

Mixed Forests

PHOTO 24/Getty Images

# North America Vegetation Map

**Map Skills** Look back at the North America Physical Map on page 58. What type of vegetation do you see in the Canadian Shield and the Mexican Plateau?

# Vegetation in North America

North America is home to many different types of **vegetation**. There are evergreen and deciduous forests, grasslands, deserts, and tundra. The type of climate a region has helps determine the kind of vegetation that will grow in that region. Think about how the vegetation zones below connect to the climate of the region.

## Mixed Forests

The eastern half of the United States and southern Canada is home to mixed forests, meaning they have deciduous and conifer tree forests. These are two distinct types of forest. A deciduous forest has trees that lose their leaves in the winter. The kinds of trees in a deciduous forest include maple, birch, oak, aspen, and dogwood. Conifers are evergreen trees. Pine, cedar, cypress, spruce, and fir are all types of conifers. Mixed forests survive in areas that have four seasons, with warm summers and cold winters.

## Temperate Grasslands

The largest expanse of temperate grasslands in North America runs through the Great Plains of the United States and into southern Canada. In the United States, these grasslands are known as prairies. There are very few trees and shrubs on the prairie because events such as drought and prairie fires make it difficult for them to grow. Prairie vegetation consists of several types of grasses, including purple needlegrass, foxtail, and wild oats. Wildflowers, such as asters and goldenrod also thrive on the prairie. These grasses and wildflowers are able to survive the cold winters and hot summers of the prairie.

## Desert Scrub and Waste

With little rainfall, there isn't much vegetation in the desert. Plants that do grow include shrubs that hug the ground and short, woody trees. Taller saguaro cacti grow in the Sonoran Desert in Arizona. Desert plants have adapted to the harsh environment. These plants store the nutrients they need to survive in their leaves. They also have deep root systems that store water for long periods of time. Plants that live in the hot and dry desert climate include Joshua tree, prickly pear, creosote, and cholla.

## WHAT IS THE IMPACT TODAY?

COLLABORATE

**Talk** The early Hohokam adapted to meet their needs in the desert. How do you think people today use or adapt to the vegetation in their regions?

Chapter
2

# The Age of Exploration

ESSENTIAL
EQ
QUESTION

## What Happened When Diverse Cultures Crossed Paths?

In this chapter, you'll read about how European exploration of the Americas changed the Americas forever. You'll consider what the Europeans had to gain as well as how exploration affected the lives and cultures of native peoples.

## Step into the Time Chronological Thinking

Look at the time line. What was happening in other parts of the world while Europeans were exploring the Americas?

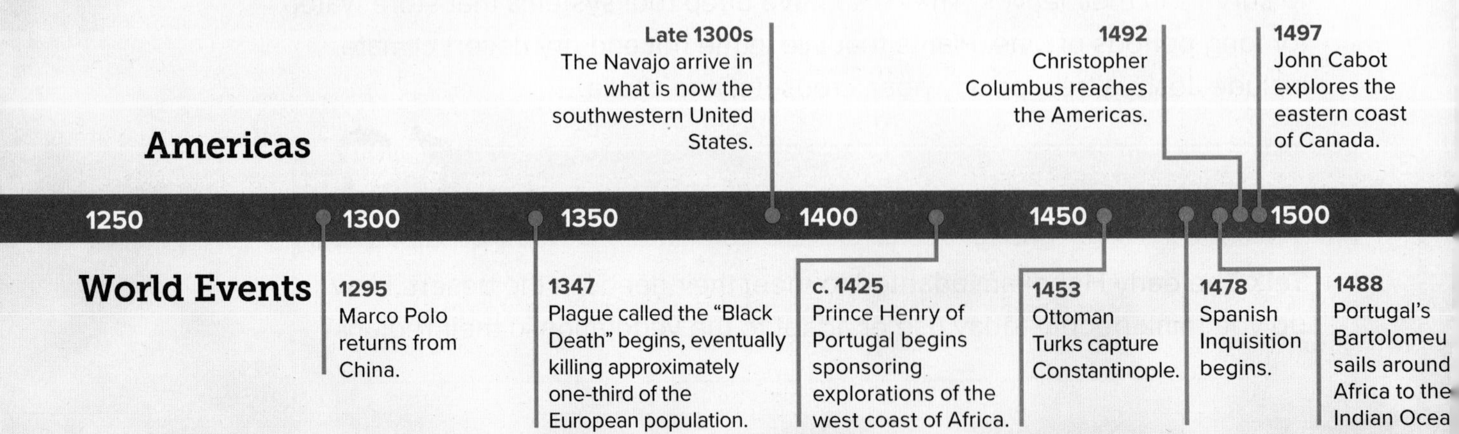
Americas
Late 1300s The Navajo arrive in what is now the southwestern United States.
1492 Christopher Columbus reaches the Americas.
1497 John Cabot explores the eastern coast of Canada.
1250
1300
1350
1400
1450
1500
World Events
1295 Marco Polo returns from China.
1347 Plague called the "Black Death" begins, eventually killing approximately one-third of the European population.
c. 1425 Prince Henry of Portugal begins sponsoring explorations of the west coast of Africa.
1453 Ottoman Turks capture Constantinople.
1478 Spanish Inquisition begins.
1488 Portugal's Bartolomeu sails around Africa to the Indian Ocea

Portugal
Dias 1487–1488
Da Gama 1497–1498
Cabral 1500–1501
Spain
Columbus 1492–1493
Magellan 1519–1521
France
Cartier 1534–1535
England
Cabot 1497–1498
Drake 1577–1580

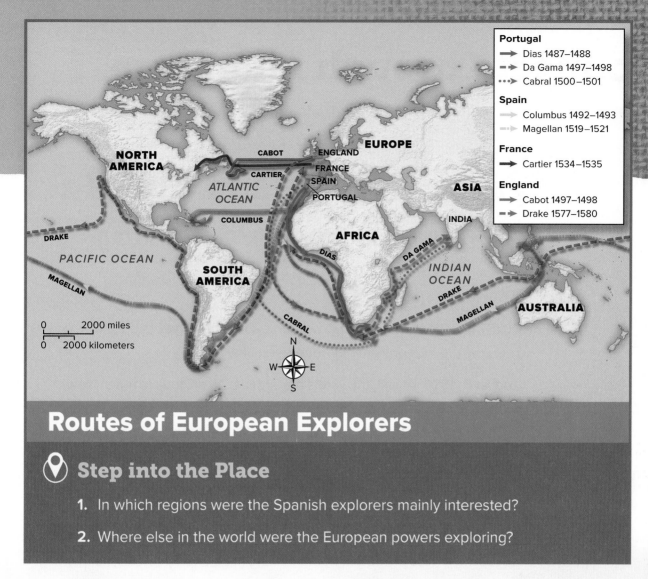

# Routes of European Explorers

## Step into the Place

1. In which regions were the Spanish explorers mainly interested?
2. Where else in the world were the European powers exploring?

Over the course of about 100 years, the major European powers of Spain, Portugal, France, England, and the Netherlands participated in a mad dash to explore and claim land in the Americas. Reports of gold and other resources that could enrich their nations tempted these Europeans to spend money and take risks to sponsor several voyages. Some were successful and others were not. While the voyages led to different places in the Americas, they all led to a similar result for the peoples who already lived there: tragic and sweeping change.

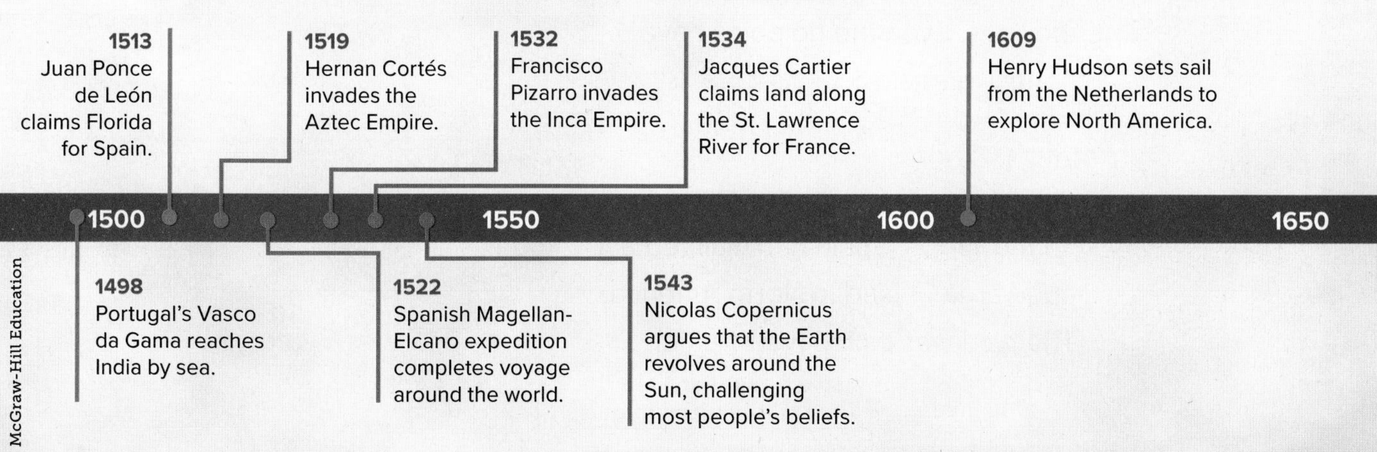

1498 Portugal's Vasco da Gama reaches India by sea.
1522 Spanish Magellan-Elcano expedition completes voyage around the world.
1543 Nicolas Copernicus argues that the Earth revolves around the Sun, challenging most people's beliefs.

# Connect Through Literature

## Cabin Boy Aboard the Buena Estrella

### From the Journal of Dominic Raimundo, Age 10

by Jennifer Buchet
illustrated by Shelley Jackson

*What if you could have sailed with an explorer 400 years ago? This is what your days might have been like.*

**August 5, 1524** At last, the winds are with us. I'm anxious to reach New Spain[1] and discover my fortune! Every day, I rise at 3 a.m. to wake the crew. I sing the morning hymns. Cook and I then lay out salted pork and ale for everyone. Afterward, I help the captain with the logbooks that record everything that is happening. And then I walk the ship, working wherever I'm needed. Yesterday, I helped stop up a small leak. I still smell the awful odor of tar on me. Perhaps tomorrow, I can bathe with a bucket of seawater.

**August 15** I miss my bed at home! I didn't have enough money to buy a hammock before we left Spain. So I sleep against sacks of grain or with the horses. But it really smells down below, and the rats bite. When the nights are clear, I sleep topside and stargaze. The clanging of the rigging (the ropes and metal fixtures) and the whoosh of the waves are my lullaby.

**August 22** The sky has been darkening all day. The air is heavy. Captain Padilla ordered us to batten down the hatches (to cover up the entrances to go below deck) and secure all the lines. Even the dolphins have gone. I'm afraid . . .

[1] In the 1500s, Spain had claimed a huge area of land in North America. The land was called New Spain.

**August 26** Dios mío, I'm alive! These last few days have been the worst of my life. I feared a giant sea monster was trying to devour us all! I couldn't tell if it was day or night, so dark was the sky. The ship bucked and pitched in the merciless waves. Twice we nearly capsized! Sadly, three sailors fell into the churning seas. Water was everywhere, including below deck. I helped pump the bilge, trying to ignore the horses' terrified cries. My arms still ache, but at least I'm alive.

**August 28** We limp toward Havana for repairs. Captain Padilla says our expedition is delayed by at least three weeks! Food supplies are low and tempers are high. We couldn't collect rainwater during the storm, and now our barrels are filled with algae scum. The remaining cheese is moldy, and sometimes it hurts to bite into what's left of the hardtack. Hard is the right word for those biscuits! I remind myself that gold and glory await me.

**September 8** At last, dry land! Some sailors talk of staying in Cuba, finding work in the gold mines or on the sugarcane farms. But I'll continue; after that hurricane, I don't even fear the Indians![2]

[2] Because Columbus thought he had reached the Indies in Asia, he called the people of the Caribbean "Indians." Later explorers used the same name.

## Think About It

1. What motivated Dominic to travel to New Spain?
2. How would you describe the journey from Spain to New Spain?
3. Think about Dominic's character. What characteristics does he show that are necessary for survival in the journey to the Americas?

# People You Should Know

## Moctezuma II

At the time of the arrival of Spanish conquistador Hernan Cortés, Moctezuma II controlled the Aztec empire. Moctezuma, however, often demanded sacrifices from tribes that were his subjects. Years of these demands had led many people to dislike him. When Cortés kidnapped Moctezuma, Cortés assumed the Aztecs would not fight for fear of endangering their ruler. The people were only too glad to be rid of Moctezuma, however, and the fight that followed resulted in Moctezuma's death.

## Leif Erikson

Many historians believe the Norse explorer Leif Erikson was the first European to visit North America. Several accounts exist of his journey to North America. In one, while returning to Greenland from Norway, Erikson was blown off course by a storm. In another, he heard of a land to the west from an Icelandic trader. Regardless, he returned to Greenland with tales of a place he called "Vinland" because of the many grapes growing there. Scholars believe this was what is now Canada. Later Norse expeditions also visited Vinland. These took place about 500 years before Christopher Columbus's arrival in the Americas.

## Queen Isabella I of Spain

Born a princess of Castile, Isabella united all of Spain when she married Ferdinand I of Aragon. Together, they conquered Grenada and increased the size of their empire. It was as she was encamped with her army at Grenada that an Italian explorer named Christopher Columbus approached her. He asked for her support for an expedition to find a western route to Asia. She agreed to give him some money, seeing an opportunity to enrich her country.

## Atahualpa

After the death of his father, Inca emperor Huayna Capac, Atahualpa waged a war with his half-brother for the Inca throne. Only a few months after his victory, however, Atahualpa's reign was cut short. Spanish conquistador Francisco Pizarro entered the Inca city of Cuzco in November of 1532. Pizarro invited Atahualpa to a feast. Using the example set by Hernan Cortés, Pizarro captured Atahualpa and killed his soldiers. The Inca emperor promised the Spaniard mountains of gold and silver in return for his release. Once the riches had been delivered, however, Pizarro killed Atahualpa anyway and ended the Inca empire.

# Lesson 1 Why Did the Spanish Explore the Americas?

## A Time of Change in Europe

During the Middle Ages—the period between ancient and modern times—most Europeans rarely traveled. However, toward the end of the period they began making pilgrimages, or religious journeys, to Christian holy sites. Some went as far away as areas in the Middle East considered the "Holy Land" by Jews, Christians, and Muslims. The contact with new regions made Europeans desire goods from foreign lands.

Soon, a new class of Europeans developed, **merchants** who made their living by buying and selling goods. They prospered especially in Italian port cities like Venice. They traded for the gems, silks, and spices of China and the East Indies, the islands off Southeast Asia. Members of one Venetian family, the Polos, actually traveled to China themselves and met with the great ruler Kublai Khan. On a second journey, they took 17-year-old Marco Polo. He returned to Italy years later and told of the wonders he had seen. His impressions were recorded in a book now called *The Travels of Marco Polo*, which further stirred people's imaginations. Another person who encouraged Europeans to travel to new lands was Prince Henry of Portugal, whose sailors explored the west coast of Africa in the early 1400s.

1295
Marco Polo returns from China.
c. 1425
Prince Henry of Portugal begins sponsoring explorations of the west coast of Africa.
1453
Ottoman Turks capture Constantinople.
1492
Christopher Columbus reaches the Americas.
1522
Spanish Magellan-Elcano expedition completes voyage around the world.
1300
1400
1500
1600
1700
1488
Portugal's Bartolomeu Dias sails around Africa to the Indian Ocean.
1498
Portugal's Vasco da Gama reaches India by sea.

This historical map, circa 1700, shows the east and west hemispheres of the Earth.

Trade with Asia usually moved along a route called the Silk Road. It was named for a product much in demand—Chinese silk. Sometimes, goods from China came by sea, because the Chinese had made many advances in sailing. Goods from the East Indies also came partly by sea. But whether entirely or only partly over land, the trade from Asia had to pass through the Middle East to reach the Mediterranean Sea and Italy.

In 1453, the Ottoman Turks captured Constantinople (now Istanbul, Turkey). They cut off most European trade through the Middle East. European leaders began to sponsor, or pay for, voyages of exploration. They hoped to make their countries rich by finding new trade routes that did not go through the Middle East. Important advances in **navigation**, or the science of guiding a boat, made this possible.

During the Age of Exploration, Europe was bursting with religious conflict and change. Spain wished to become an even more powerful country after recapturing land it had lost to invading peoples from North Africa. Spaniards called this violent recapturing of territory the *Reconquista.* The Protestant Reformation caused many people who were upset with the Roman Catholic Church to break away and form new churches. Some people wished to stay and improve the Catholic Church—an effort called the Counter-Reformation. Competing religions, ideas, and countries would become key drivers of the Age of Exploration.

**Merchants trading in Venice, Italy**

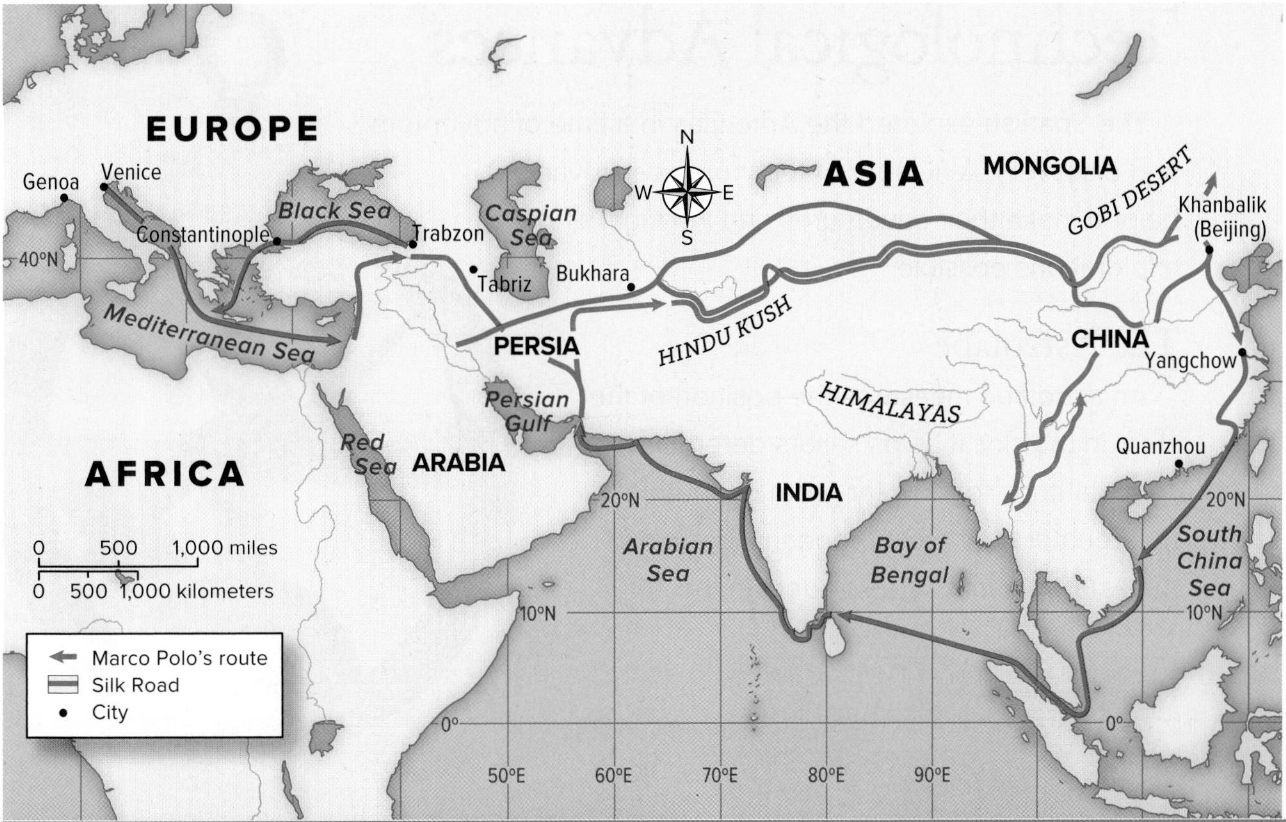

## The Travels of Marco Polo, 1271–1295

**Map Skills** With a classmate, trace the different routes between Venice and Khanbalik, China. Which go entirely over land in Asia? Which go partly by sea?

### Stop and Check

**Talk** How did Marco Polo and Prince Henry of Portugal each help encourage the growth of trade?

**Find Details** As you read, add additional information to the graphic organizer on page 59 in your Inquiry Journal.

# Technological Advances

The Spanish explored the Americas in a time of adventure and discovery. A number of technological advances helped make their adventures and Portugal's explorations possible.

## The Astrolabe

An astrolabe measures the position of the stars in the sky. It helps sailors determine a ship's latitude, or how far north or south of the Equator they are. Europeans learned of the astrolabe from Arab traders in the 1100s.

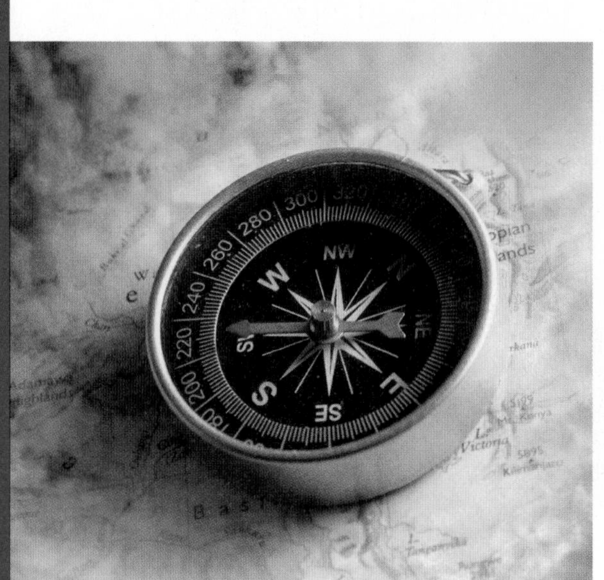


## The Compass

A compass has a magnetic arrow that points north so that people can figure out in which direction they are going. The compass was invented in China and introduced to Europeans in the 1200s, probably by Arab sailors.

## The Stern Rudder

Chinese sailors used an oar that hung off the stern, or back of the boat, to help control the direction in which the boat sailed. This evolved into the stern-mounted rudder, which directed the flow of water passing over it to help steer a ship. By the 1400s, European shipbuilders had adopted and improved the stern-mounted rudder.

## The Printing Press

Around 1450, German inventor Johannes Gutenberg built Europe's first printing press that used movable type to print the text. Printed materials could be mass-produced far more easily and cheaply than handwritten documents. They helped spread news about explorers' discoveries and encouraged others to take to the seas.

## The Carrack

The carrack was a three- or four-masted sailing ship developed in the Italian city of Genoa in the late 1400s. It was very strong and useful on long voyages. The *Santa Maria*, the ship on which Columbus sailed to the Americas, was a carrack.

## Sextant and Chronometer

In 1759, John Bird invented the sextant. This tool uses two mirrors and a movable arm to measure the angles of stars in the sky. Also invented in the middle of the 18th century, the chronometer is a device that helps keep accurate time at sea. These two devices finally allowed sailors to determine longitude, or the distance east or west of the Prime Meridian. Measuring longitude as well as latitude made navigation and mapmaking more accurate.

### Stop and Check

COLLABORATE

**Talk** Based on what you've just read, how important do you think technology was in encouraging the explorers of the day? Discuss your opinion with a partner.

# A Sea Route to the Indies

By the late 1400s, Europeans knew that China and the islands off Southeast Asia held great riches. Explorers from Portugal, such as Bartolomeu Dias and Vasco da Gama, were trying to reach these lands. They wanted to sail around the southern tip of Africa and then across the Indian Ocean. Christopher Columbus, a sailor from Genoa, Italy, had a different idea. He believed that he could reach the East Indies more quickly by sailing west across the Atlantic Ocean, known then as the Ocean Sea. He did not know the North and South American continents would get in the way. He persuaded King Ferdinand and Queen Isabella of Spain, Portugal's neighbor and rival, to pay for his voyage. In return, he would **claim** lands and open valuable trade for Spain.

On August 3, 1492, Columbus sailed from Spain with three ships—the *Niña,* the *Pinta*, and the *Santa Maria*. For weeks, the ships traveled across unknown waters. Finally, on October 12, a member of the crew, called the lookout, spotted land. Columbus would call the island he had reached San Salvador. Today, we know it as part of the Bahama Islands. A native people called the Taíno warmly greeted his crew. The two groups exchanged gifts.

**PRIMARY SOURCE**

## In Their Words... Christopher Columbus

"... to some of them I gave red caps, and glass beads which they put on their chests, and many other things of small value, in which they took much pleasure and became so much our friends that it was a marvel. Later they came swimming to the ships' launches where we were and brought us parrots and cotton thread in balls and javelins and many other things, and they traded them to us for other things which we gave them, such as small glass beads and bells. In sum, they took everything and gave of what they had very willingly."

—from the journal of Christopher Columbus, October 12, 1492

TEXT: Olson, Julius E., and Edward Gaylord Bourne, eds. The Northmen, Columbus and Cabot, 985-1503. New York: Charles Scribner's Sons, 1906.; PHOTO: GL Archive/Alamy

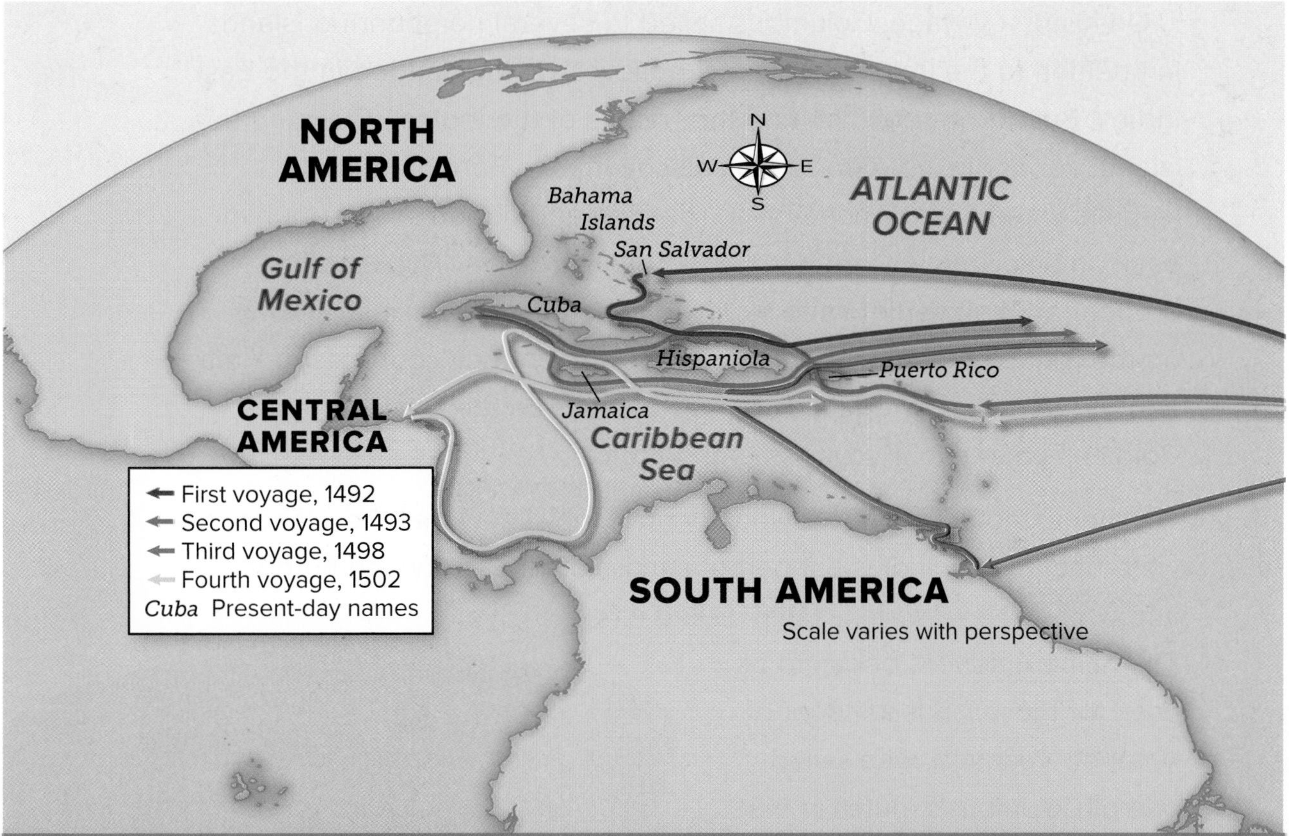

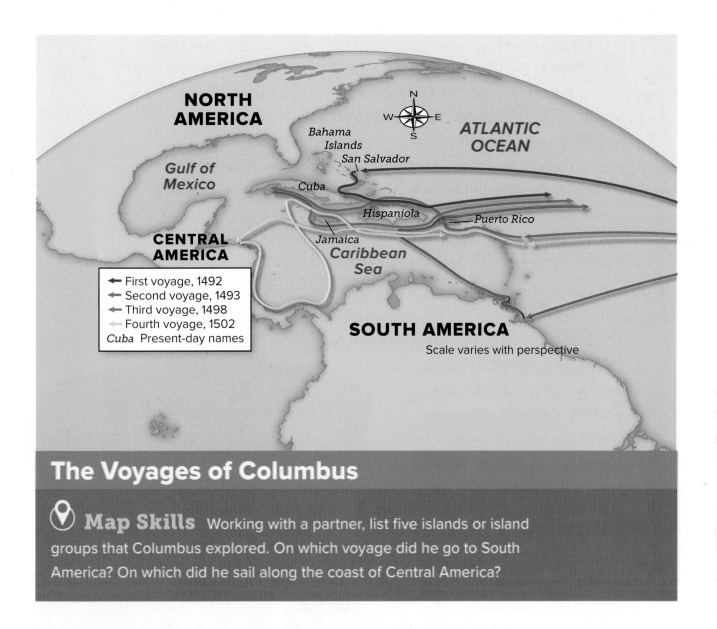

## The Voyages of Columbus

**Map Skills** Working with a partner, list five islands or island groups that Columbus explored. On which voyage did he go to South America? On which did he sail along the coast of Central America?

### Did You Know?

Because he thought he had reached the East Indies, Columbus called the people he encountered *Indios*, Spanish for *Indians*. The name stuck, even though it was an error. The people Columbus actually met, the Taíno, did not survive long after the coming of the Spanish. This was due to diseases introduced by the Spanish, as well as harsh treatment, enslavement, starvation, and warfare. However, some of their culture is still evident in certain English and Spanish words such as *barbecue* and *hurricane*.

On his first voyage, Columbus sailed to several neighboring islands in addition to the Bahamas. He still believed he had landed in the East Indies. But nowhere did he find the "riches of the Indies." Claiming the islands for Spain, he reported his discoveries to Ferdinand and Isabella when he returned home. The king and queen soon sent him back on a second voyage to extend Spanish claims. This time he brought enough settlers and supplies to establish a Spanish **colony** on the island he named Hispaniola. The present-day countries of Haiti and the Dominican Republic are now located on the island. In all, Columbus made four voyages to the area.

Other explorers soon followed. By now, they knew that the islands were not the East Indies but part of a mass of lands between Europe and Asia—a New World, as they called it. The name *Americas* began to be used for these lands in honor of Amerigo Vespucci, who sailed one of Columbus's routes in 1499. In 1513, Vasco Núñez de Balboa became the first Spanish explorer to record seeing the great waters to the west of these lands. Another explorer, Ferdinand Magellan, named those waters the Pacific Ocean. Magellan died as he attempted to sail around the world. His voyage was completed in 1522 by his crew under the command of Juan Sebastián Elcano. The voyage took three years.

A Taíno artifact

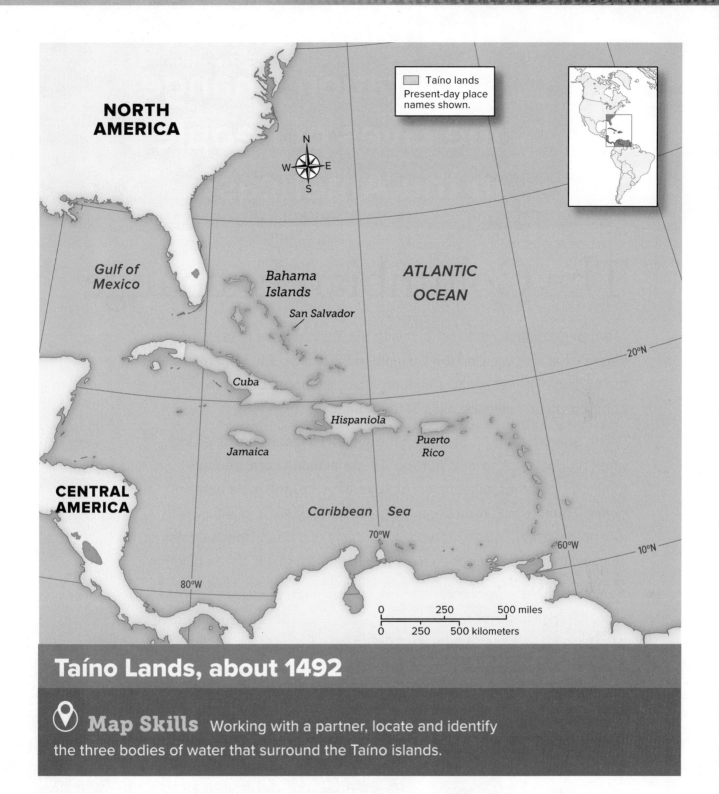

## Taíno Lands, about 1492

**Map Skills** Working with a partner, locate and identify the three bodies of water that surround the Taíno islands.

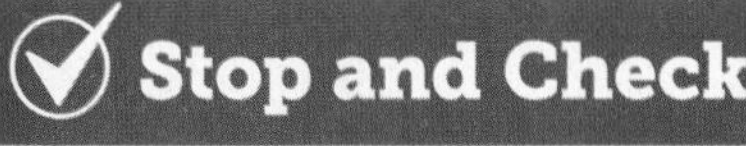

### Stop and Check

**Think** What did the Magellan-Elcano voyage prove that Columbus was right about? How did it prove that he was wrong about some things?

Lesson 2

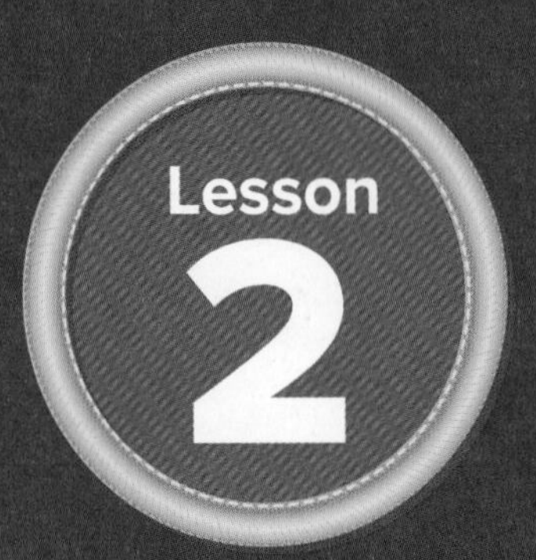

# How Did Spanish Exploration Change the Lives of People in the Americas?

## The Columbian Exchange

When Columbus made contact with the Taíno people in 1492, he began what is now called the Columbian Exchange. The term refers to the trading of items, animals, culture, ideas, and more between Europeans and native peoples of the Americas.

The Spanish brought back from the Americas plants, animals, and other products unknown in Europe. These included corn, peanuts, tomatoes, potatoes, pineapples, turkeys, tobacco, and most types of beans. Farmers in Europe began to grow some of these plants, which meant that fewer people starved. Also, many of the new foods contained vitamins that made European diets healthier. As a result, the population of Europe grew.

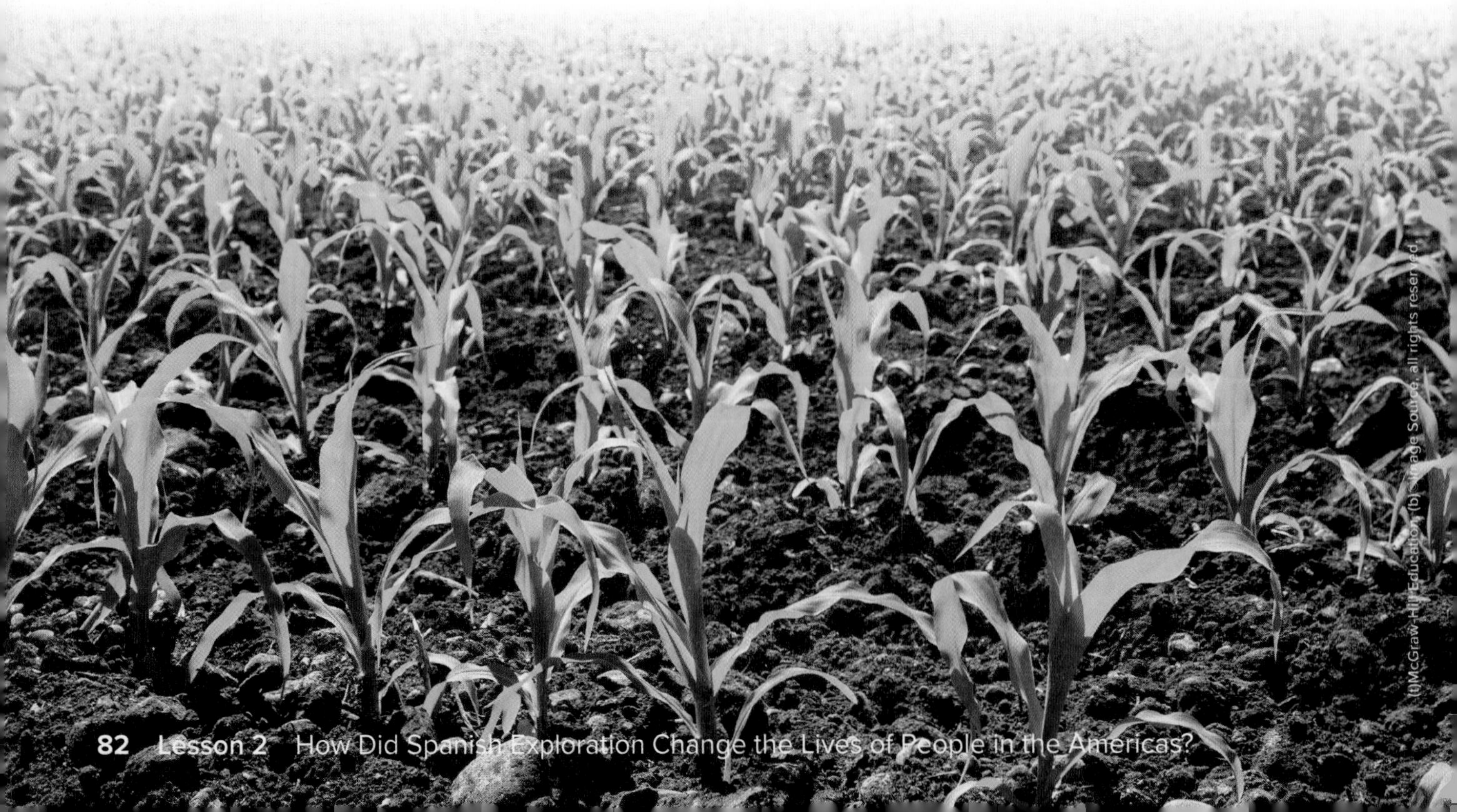

1510 | 1520 | 1530 | 1540 | 1550 | 1560 | 1570

**1513**
Juan Ponce de León claims Florida for Spain.

**1515**
Spain completes conquest of what is now Cuba.

**1519**
Hernan Cortés invades the Aztec Empire.

**1532**
Francisco Pizarro invades the Inca Empire.

**1540**
Francisco Coronado begins to explore the American Southwest.

**1542**
Juan Cabrillo explores the southern California coast.

**1565**
Pedro Avilés founds St. Augustine, Florida.

**The Aztec capital city of Tenochtitlán, among the largest cities in the world in the early 1500s**



The Spanish also brought new products to the Americas. These included wheat, oranges, peaches, bananas, cattle, goats, sheep, pigs, and horses. Many of these items changed the way of life for native peoples of the Americas. Horses, for example, changed the way in which Native Americans hunted buffalo on the Great Plains.

The Columbian Exchange did not involve just Europe and the Americas. It transformed the whole planet. Some of the plants Europeans brought to the Americas originally came from Asia and Africa. Many plants from the Americas traveled around the world as well. Chili peppers, for instance, were brought to Asia by European sailors and became popular ingredients in many Asian dishes.

The Spanish introduced sugar to the Americas. Sugar cane, which originated in Southeast Asia, was a precious commodity in Europe because it grows only in warm, rainy climates. Brazil and islands in the Caribbean proved to be ideal for growing the crop. The demand for sugar would make it one of the most valuable crops grown in the Americas.

Not all things traded in the Columbian Exchange were useful. The Europeans also brought diseases such as smallpox and measles to the Americas. Because these diseases were new to the natives, they had not developed any **resistance** to them. As a result, they died in very large numbers.

The Spanish also forced many natives to work as enslaved persons and even shipped some back to Spain on voyages during which many died. By 1550, few Taíno survived. Enslaved Africans were brought to the islands to replace them. This forced relocation of peoples was also part of the Columbian Exchange.

## Stop and Check

**Talk** What positive effects did the Columbian Exchange have on people native to the Americas? What negative effects did the Columbian Exchange have on them and on others?

**Find Details** As you read, add additional information to the graphic organizer on page 67 in your Inquiry Journal.

# Spanish Exploration and Conquest in the Americas

By 1515, Spain had spread its control to several islands in the Caribbean Sea. Spain's **conquests** gave them land to settle and people to enslave, but they did not bring the riches the Spanish sought. Sometimes they saw bits of gold in the hands of the island natives. The Spanish wondered, *Where did this gold come from?*

Juan Ponce de León was a Spanish explorer who came to the Americas on Columbus's second voyage. Later he was governor of the island that would come to be known as Puerto Rico. In 1513, Ponce de León landed in what is now the state of Florida. He called the area *La Florida* (Spanish for "full of flowers") and claimed it for Spain. He was looking for gold, although legend says that he was also seeking a Fountain of Youth—a place where magical waters could restore one's youth. But Ponce de León found no gold in Florida, and no Fountain of Youth either. When he returned there in 1521 to establish a Spanish **settlement**, he was wounded in fighting with the Calusa people of the area. He traveled to Cuba and died there of his wounds.

Hernan Cortés, another Spanish explorer, was more successful in his search for riches. In fact, he is called a *conquistador*, Spanish for "conqueror." Like Ponce de León, Cortés was very interested in finding gold. Having heard stories from the native people, he decided there must be a great empire rich in gold to the west of the Caribbean islands. He was right.

Ponce de León was among the first Spanish explorers to claim land in what is now the United States.

An empire is a large area in which different groups are controlled by one ruler. Since the 1430s, the Aztec Empire had ruled over several native groups in what is now central Mexico. The Aztecs built a magnificent capital, Tenochtitlán, where more than 300,000 people lived. In 1502, Moctezuma II became the emperor, or ruler of the empire. However, many native peoples under his rule had started to rebel against the Aztecs.

**Statue of an Aztec eagle knight warrior found at the main temple in Tenochtitlán**

In 1519, Hernan Cortés left Cuba seeking the great riches he had heard about. After landing in what is today the coastal city of Veracruz, Mexico, he and his soldiers moved inland. When he arrived at Tenochtitlán, Moctezuma met with him. He offered Cortés gifts of gold and precious jewels. These were not enough for Cortés, however. He took Moctezuma prisoner, causing a riot in which the emperor was killed.

## Did You Know?

Tenochtitlán was built on watery, swampy land. The Aztecs developed floating gardens called *chinampas*. They stuck rows of thick posts into the swamp. Then, they filled spaces between the posts with mud.

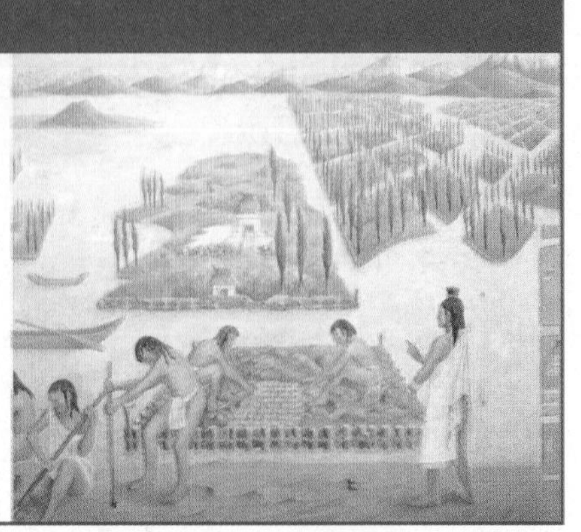

The Aztecs then drove Cortés and his troops from the city. They battled on the plains of Otumba, where Cortés and his troops killed the Aztec commander. The Spanish then retreated to a friendlier area.

A few months later, Cortés returned with a larger force to fight the Aztecs. Along the way, his army was joined by a number of native fighters unhappy with Aztec rule.

This help from native allies was just one reason the Spanish were able to defeat the Aztecs. The Spanish soldiers also had two things that the Aztecs did not: fine swords and horses. These gave the Spanish a clear fighting advantage. In fact, even when outnumbered, forces with swords and lances fighting on horseback usually won the day.

After 75 days of battle, Cortés and his army destroyed the Aztec capital. On its ruins, the Spanish built Mexico City. It would be the capital of a colony the Spanish called *Nueva España*, or New Spain.

**Spanish and Aztec warriors fighting at the Battle of Otumba**

In 1531, Francisco Pizarro, another Spanish conquistador, sailed to the west coast of South America with a small army. Like Cortés, he was following rumors he had heard of an empire rich in treasures. From the coast, he traveled with his troops to the mighty Inca Empire high in the Andes Mountains.

The Incas ruled an empire of 12 million people. Because they lived in thick stone cities high in the mountains, they did not fear the Spanish attack. The Spanish, however, had new weapons the Incas had never seen. Gunpowder had come to Europe from China centuries before. The troops Pizarro brought with him were armed with a type of gun called the *harquebus*. Incan weapons were no match for this.

**The walls of Machu Picchu show the skill of Inca builders.**

Pizarro's army captured Atahualpa, the Inca emperor, and killed 1,500 of his followers. When Atahualpa offered a roomful of gold in return for his freedom, Pizarro agreed. From all over the empire, valuable gold objects poured in. Yet, after the treasure was delivered, Pizarro had Atahualpa killed anyway. In 1533, the Spanish completed their conquest of the Inca Empire by capturing its capital of Cuzco.

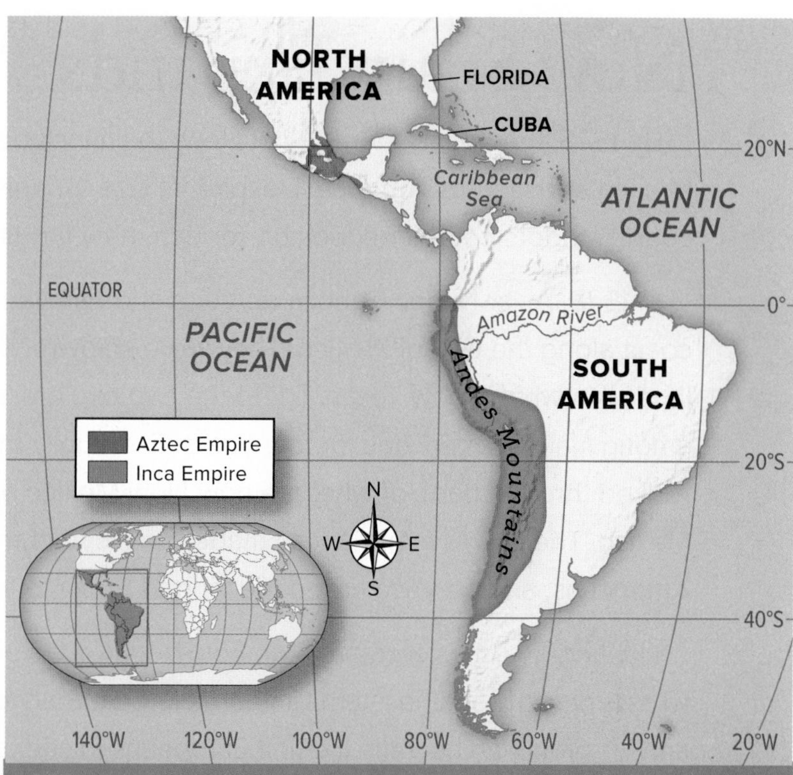


## The Aztec and Inca Empires

**Map Skills** Using the information in the text and the labels on the map, identify the Aztec Empire and Inca Empire on the map. How many Aztec Empires could fit inside the territory of the Inca Empire?

### Stop and Check

**Talk** What seems to have been the strongest motive, or reason, for Spanish exploration and conquest? What advantages did the Spanish have to help them conquer the Aztecs and Incas?

# New Spain Expands

By 1525, the Spanish territory of New Spain included most of present-day Mexico and Central America. Despite its size, Spanish explorers and conquistadors continued looking for rich, new lands for Spain to control.

In 1528, Alvar Nuñez Cabeza de Vaca and Estevanico were exploring the coast along the Gulf of Mexico. They were shipwrecked by a hurricane and landed in what is now Texas. There the two explorers and their crew lived among Native Americans for four years. Eventually they left on foot. They walked through parts of what are now New Mexico and Arizona to return to Mexico. The crew's experiences made them sympathetic to Native Americans, and de Vaca urged the king of Spain to treat them better.

Hunting for riches, Hernando de Soto began an expedition in 1538 through what is now the southeastern United States. De Soto found no riches. But he and his group did become the first Europeans to see the Mississippi River. Then, in 1542, De Soto became ill and died not far from the river.

In 1540, Francisco Vásquez de Coronado, having heard tales of Seven Cities of Gold, went searching to find them. He discovered no such cities. He and his group did, however, become the first Europeans to see the Grand Canyon. They also claimed for Spain large areas of what is now the American Southwest, land that was already inhabited by Native American groups.

**PRIMARY SOURCE**

## In Their Words... Alvar Nuñez Cabeza de Vaca

At sunset we came in sight of the lodges, and [the length of] two crossbow shots before reaching them met four Indians waiting for us, and they received us well. We told them in the language of the Mariames that we had come to see them. They appeared to be pleased with our company and took us to their homes.

—from the journal of Alvar Nuñez Cabeza de Vaca

Nuñez Cabeza de Vaca, Alvar. The Journey of Alvar Nunez Cabeza de Vaca and his Companions from Florida to the Pacific, 1528-1536. Edited by AD. F. Bandelier. Translated by Fanny Bandelier. New York: A.S. Barnes & Company, 1905.

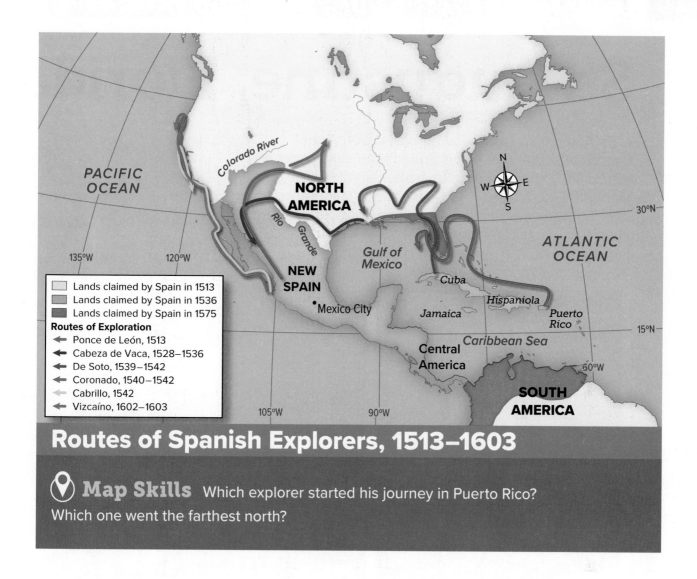

## Routes of Spanish Explorers, 1513–1603

Lands claimed by Spain in 1513
Lands claimed by Spain in 1536
Lands claimed by Spain in 1575

**Routes of Exploration**

- Ponce de León, 1513
- Cabeza de Vaca, 1528–1536
- De Soto, 1539–1542
- Coronado, 1540–1542
- Cabrillo, 1542
- Vizcaíno, 1602–1603

**Map Skills** Which explorer started his journey in Puerto Rico? Which one went the farthest north?

Juan Rodríguez Cabrillo made one of the first Spanish claims on what is now California. He explored the coast around present-day San Diego in 1542. Sixty years later, Sebastián Vizcaíno sailed up the California coast, giving many places the Spanish names we still use today. Spain also continued to pursue its claims in what is now Florida. After several failed attempts at a settlement there, Pedro Menéndez de Avilés in 1565 built a fort in an area on the east coast that he named St. Augustine.

### Stop and Check

COLLABORATE

**Talk** Which sections of what is now the United States did the Spanish explore? How often did they find what they were looking for? Give examples to explain your answer.

Field Trip

# St. Augustine, Florida

St. Augustine, Florida, is the oldest permanent European settlement in the United States. After coming ashore in August of 1565, Spanish admiral Pedro Menéndez de Avilés turned the site into a fort and named it St. Augustine. It remained a Spanish city for more than 200 years. Today, you can see the Spanish influence in the city's historic district.

Grace United Methodist Church

**Castillo de San Marcos**
This fort was built by the Spanish between 1672 and 1695 to protect the city from naval attacks by the British and the French. It was constructed from blocks of coquina, a combination of limestone and seashells. When you tour the two levels of the fort, you can see how carefully it was built. It was never captured by military force.

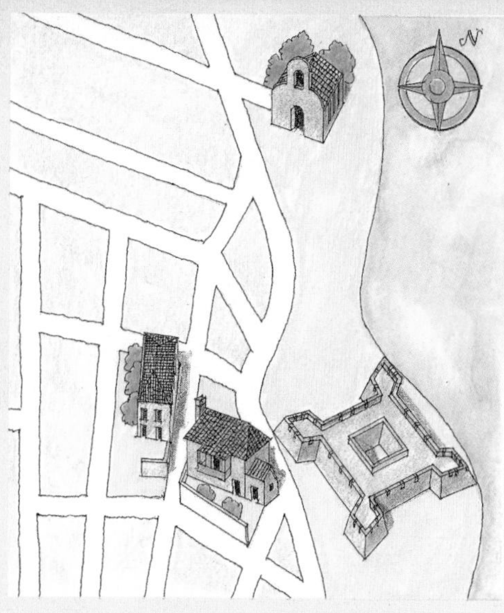

A map of Old St. Augustine, Florida

## Stop and Check

**Write** Compose a speech for a tour guide in St. Augustine. Your speech should describe the sights of the old city.

**What Do You Think?** Do you think you would like to visit St. Augustine? Why or why not?

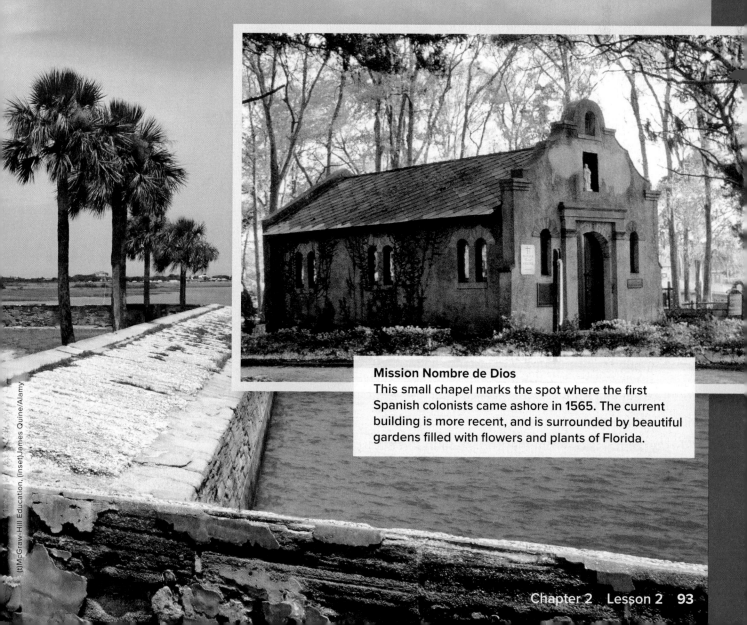

**Mission Nombre de Dios**
This small chapel marks the spot where the first Spanish colonists came ashore in 1565. The current building is more recent, and is surrounded by beautiful gardens filled with flowers and plants of Florida.

# How Did European Exploration Affect the Americas?

## The Search for a Northwest Passage

Spain was not the only European country that sailed west to look for a shorter route to Asia. England, France, the Netherlands, Portugal, and Sweden also sent explorers across the Atlantic Ocean. While Spain focused on exploring South America and the southern part of North America, the other nations explored the east coast of North America. They were trying to find a route to Asia through North America by using waterways, such as bays and straits. This supposed route was called the Northwest Passage.

In 1497, just five years after Columbus's first voyage, John Cabot set sail on a voyage across the Atlantic. Cabot, an Italian, had received permission from the English king to sail west to explore unknown lands. Cabot took along goods from merchants in the port of Bristol, England. He hoped to trade for Asian goods.

1497
John Cabot explores the eastern coast of what is now Canada while searching for the Northwest Passage.
1524
Giovanni da Verrazzano reaches an area now known as New York Harbor.
1534
Jacques Cartier claims land along the St. Lawrence River for France.
1584
Queen Elizabeth I of England grants a charter allowing Sir Walter Raleigh to send a group of colonists to Roanoke Island.
00
1450
1500
1550
1600
1650
1608
Samuel de Champlain establishes the colony of Quebec for France.
1623
The Dutch West India Company establishes the colony of New Netherland.
1638
The Swedish South Company forms a colony along the Delaware River.


Henry Hudson's ship, the *Half Moon*

An oil painting of John and Sebastian Cabot

Cabot reached the North American coast somewhere in the region of what is now Newfoundland, an area in Canada. He could not find any people to trade with. What he did find were huge quantities of fish in the coastal waters. The English merchants were interested in this discovery. Dried fish was an important source of food at the time. Unfortunately, Cabot disappeared during his next voyage, probably the victim of a huge storm. Following Cabot's lead, Portugal sent sailors to the Newfoundland area. It established a small colony there as a base for fishing ships.

Another Italian, Giovanni da Verrazzano, obtained the support of the king of France. Verrazzano traveled up the Atlantic Coast. He explored areas including what are now New York Harbor and the mouth of the Hudson River. He had friendly encounters with Native Americans on this voyage.

Giovanni da Verrazzano

Verrazzano's next voyage was to Brazil, where he found a type of wood that is valuable in creating dyes for textiles. Verrazzano's voyages were overlooked in Europe, however. They occurred during the same decade that Spain conquered the Aztec Empire and brought large amounts of gold home to Europe.

The Hudson River, named for the English explorer Henry Hudson

(bkgd spread)ctraixaxu/iStock/Getty Images, (t)Time Life Pictures/The LIFE Picture Collection/Getty Images, (b)North Wind Picture Archives

Henry Hudson's voyages to the area that is now New York occurred in the early 1600s. Hudson was from England, but he worked for both England and the Netherlands. The Dutch East India Company hired Hudson in 1608 to try to find a shorter route to Asia. This company had been set up to increase Dutch trade with what is now Indonesia.

In 1609, Hudson's ships reached the same area near New York that Verrazzano had visited. Hudson sailed far up a river that was later named after him, the Hudson River. He concluded that it did not lead to a Northwest Passage because it became shallow as he moved north; also, it contained fresh water, not salt water.

Hudson returned to Europe and then began exploring for England in 1610. This time his effort to find the Northwest Passage ended in disaster. He sailed into a bay in northern Canada now called Hudson Bay. He became stuck in the ice and spent the winter there. He and his crew had to eat spoiled food. When spring came and the ice melted, the crew took over the ship and put Hudson and his son in a rowboat with a few other crew members. They were never heard from again. The crew was arrested when it returned to England.

During his second voyage to North America, Henry Hudson, his son, and others were abandoned in a rowboat after most of his crew rebelled.

## Stop and Check

COLLABORATE

**Talk** Why did European explorers want to find a Northwest Passage?

**Find Details** As you read, add additional information to the graphic organizer on page 75 in your Inquiry Journal.

**What Do You Think?** In your opinion, why were the explorers unable to find a Northwest Passage?

# New Netherland

In 1621, a group of Dutch merchants formed the Dutch West India Company. This company established the colony of New Netherland in 1623. This colony was the earliest European settlement in what is now New York state. The Dutch West India Company established the colony in that location because Henry Hudson had claimed the land for the Netherlands in 1609.

The first settlements in New Netherland were established along the Hudson River. The Dutch colonists benefited from the rich resources in the area, particularly fur obtained by trading with native peoples. In 1626, Peter Minuit became the colony's governor. Some Dutch settlers established a profitable trading post on the southern tip of Manhattan Island. Minuit negotiated with native peoples there to recognize and accept the Dutch settlement, called New Amsterdam.

Minuit offered the native peoples weapons, tools, and other supplies as part of the agreement. These goods were worth about 60 guilders, or about 700 dollars in today's money. But the native peoples did not believe that they were selling Manhattan. Because of communication difficulties, they thought they were agreeing only to share the land.

New Netherland was one of the most **diverse** European colonies in North America. People of different religious and ethnic backgrounds were allowed to settle there. However, New Netherland was also one of the first colonies to bring enslaved Africans to North America. Fighting occurred between the colonists and native peoples in the early 1640s. The governor of New Netherland, Willem Kieft, was unhappy that native peoples were moving into the northern part of New Netherland.

The Dutch West India House was built in the Netherlands in 1623.

Ger Bosma/Alamy

These peoples were trying to escape attacks by other Northeast Woodlands groups that were seeking to expand their territories. Against the advice of other colonial leaders, Kieft sent Dutch soldiers to attack native villages. The result was a series of attacks by both sides that left hundreds dead. Many Dutch settlers returned to Europe because of the violence.

In 1647, Peter Stuyvesant became the leader of New Netherland. He had a conflict with a Swedish colony along the Delaware River. He believed the colony was on Dutch territory. He had a fort built in the area. When the Swedes took over the fort, Stuyvesant sent a force to take over the Swedish colony, which had log cabins that were later widely copied.

As English colonies in North America grew, some English leaders became interested in New Netherland. England and the Netherlands fought wars in Europe in the 1600s. In 1664, the brother of the King of England sent four **warships** to New Amsterdam harbor. His troops demanded that Stuyvesant surrender the entire Dutch colony. Stuyvesant wanted to fight, but his colonists instead surrendered. Most stayed in North America, living under British rule.

## Then and Now

### The Northwest Passage

Although there is a Northwest Passage from the Atlantic Ocean to the Pacific Ocean, it was nearly impossible to pass through during the age of European exploration. This is because the passage lies far to the north and was usually covered by Arctic ice. The illustration at the upper right shows a Dutch explorer stuck in this ice in the 1500s.

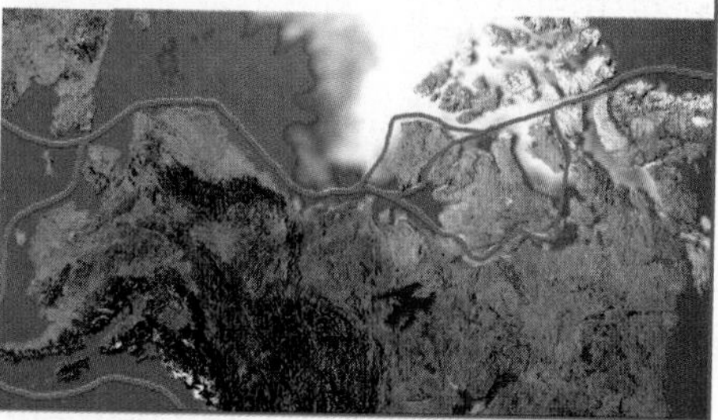

But with the gradual melting of the Arctic ice cap in recent years, the Northwest Passage is now nearly ice-free during the summer. Ships are able to travel through the passage in warmer months. The photograph at the lower right shows the Northwest Passage in August 2016.

## Stop and Check

**Think** Why did Dutch settlers choose to settle in what is now New York state?

(t)McGraw-Hill Education, (c)North Wind Picture Archives/Alamy, (b)NASA/Goddard Space Flight Center Scientific Visualization Studio

# The Founding of New France

After Giovanni da Verrazzano failed to find the Northwest Passage for France, the king of France sent Jacques Cartier in 1534 to continue the search. Cartier explored what is now Canada, sailing up the St. Lawrence River. The French adapted the name *Canada* from the Huron group of native peoples. In the Huron language, *kanata* means "village."

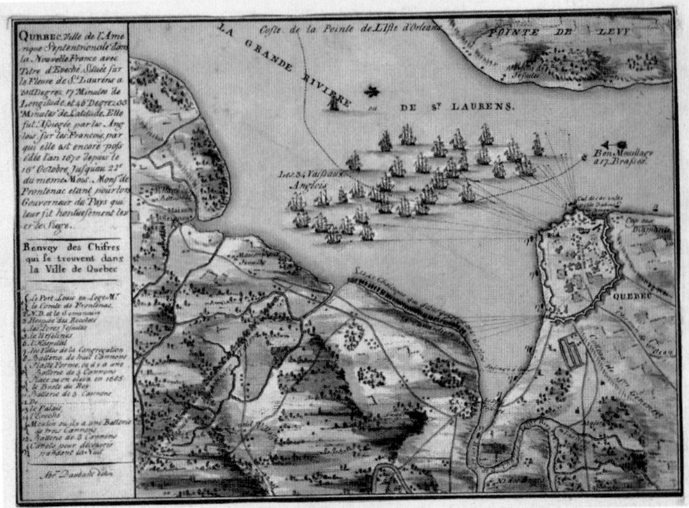


This map shows France's first fort in Quebec, Canada.

**PRIMARY SOURCE**

## In Their Words... Jacques Cartier

July 24 – We had a cross made thirty feet high, which was put together in the presence of a number of savages on the point at the entrance to this harbor, [and on it] was written LONG LIVE THE KING OF FRANCE. When we had returned to our ships, the chief, dressed in an old black bearskin, arrived in a canoe with three of his sons and his brother ... And pointing to the cross he made us a long harangue, making the sign of the cross with two of his fingers, and then he pointed to the land all around about, as if he wished to say that all this region belonged to him, and that we ought not to have set up the cross without his permission.

—from the journal of Jacques Cartier, 1534

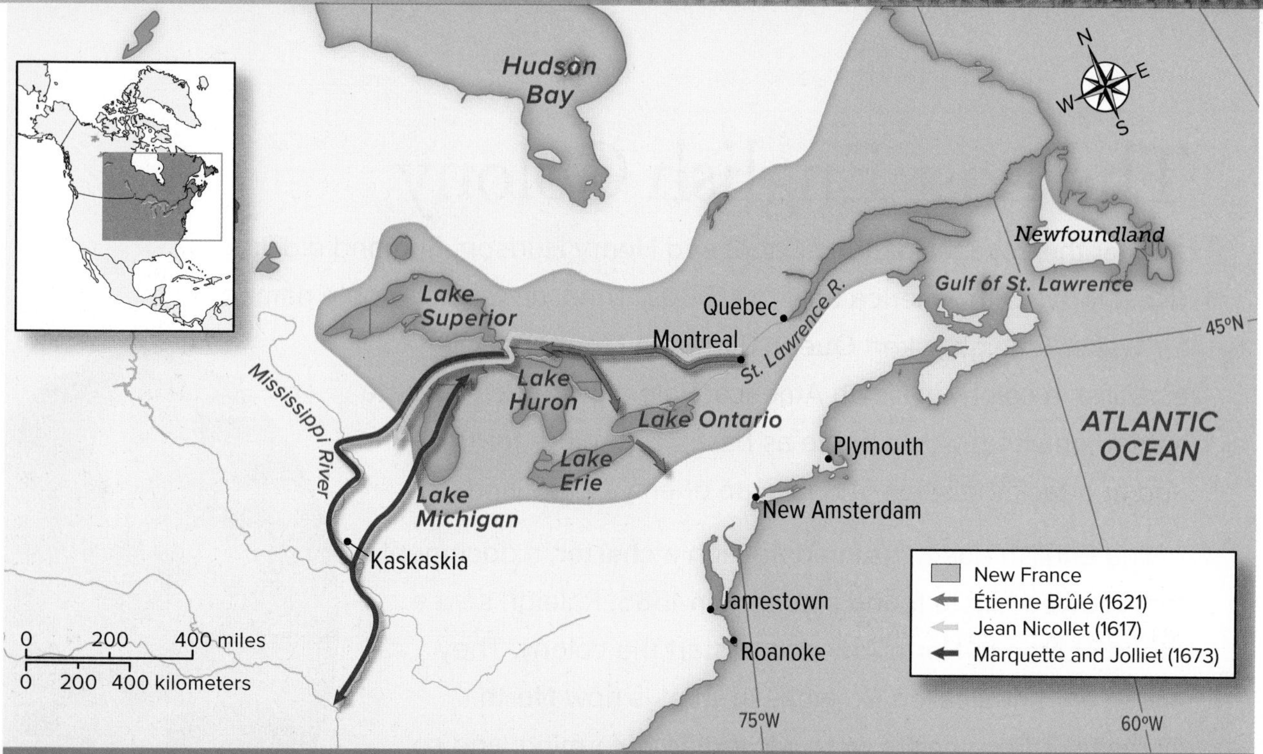

## The French Explore New France, 1617–1673

**Map Skills** The map shows the routes of French explorers. Which lakes did Étienne Brûlé explore?

The next important French explorer in Canada was Samuel de Champlain. King Henry VI of France appointed him governor of French settlements in North America, called New France. Champlain made four voyages to North America. On one voyage, he established a colony in what is now Quebec City. Champlain was on friendly terms with native peoples. This allowed the French to expand their fur trade.

On another voyage, Champlain brought along a young explorer named Étienne Brûlé. In 1615, he sent Brûlé to continue the search for a passage to Asia. Brûlé was unable to find it, but he did explore what are now Lake Ontario, Lake Erie, and Lake Superior. In 1634, a French explorer named Jean Nicollet explored what is now Lake Michigan.

Although some French people moved to Canada, growth was slow. French rulers were disappointed that Cartier could find neither gold nor a Northwest Passage. The focus of New France's economy continued to be the fur trade, and only a few large settlements thrived.

### Stop and Check

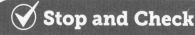

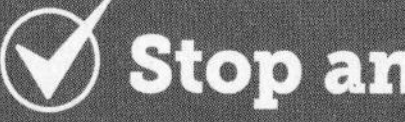

**Think** In your opinion, why did French rulers not make a greater effort to expand the size of the colonies in New France?

# The Lost English Colony

After the voyages of John Cabot and Henry Hudson, England did little to explore North America until the 1580s. Then, an English noble named Sir Walter Raleigh asked Queen Elizabeth I for permission to establish a colony in North America. Raleigh wanted to create settlements that would serve as bases to explore for treasure and to attack the ships of Spain, an enemy of England.

Sir Walter Raleigh

The English queen granted Raleigh a **charter**, a document that allowed him to found a colony. In 1585, Raleigh sent a group of men to North America to start the colony. They chose an island called Roanoke in what is now North Carolina. The colonists were not skilled at farming, and so they tried to get goods by trading with native peoples. The native peoples lost interest in trading, and the colonists decided they had to steal food from them. This led to fighting. After a difficult winter, the colonists returned to England in 1586.

John White arrives in Roanoke to find the colony abandoned.

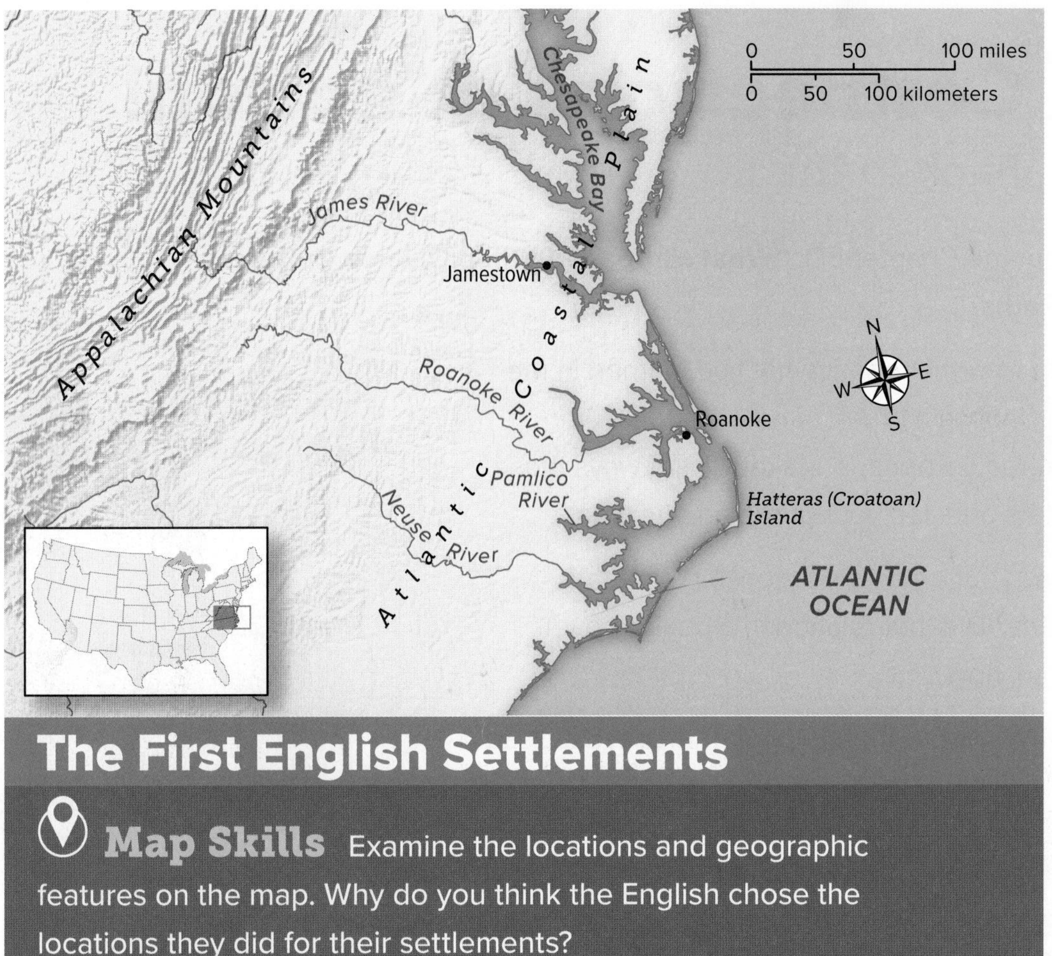


## The First English Settlements

**Map Skills** Examine the locations and geographic features on the map. Why do you think the English chose the locations they did for their settlements?

In 1587, another group of colonists led by John White returned to Roanoke. This time the group included women and children. The colony again had difficulty finding enough food. White sailed back to England to get supplies. But while he was there, war broke out between England and Spain. England needed all of its ships for the war. By the time White returned to the colony three years later, it had been abandoned. The only clue was the word *Croatoan* carved on a tree. The Croatoan were a native people in the area. What happened to the English settlers has never been determined.

### Stop and Check

COLLABORATE

**Talk** In your opinion, why did the Roanoke Colony fail?

**What Do You Think?** What do you think happened to the people in the "lost colony"?

# Connections in Action!

## Back to the EQ

**Think** about the Chapter EQ, **"What Happened When Diverse Cultures Crossed Paths?"**

- **Talk** with a partner about what you learned in the chapter. Choose a group of native people who encountered Europeans. Make a list of ways these encounters affected your group and its area.
- What was your group's relationship with the Europeans? Did that relationship change over time? If so, how?
- **Share** your ideas with the class; then have a class discussion about the overall effects of exploration on native peoples in the Americas.

(bkgd)Christian Vinces/Shutterstock.com, (l)akg-images/CDA/Guillemot/Newscom, (tr)Clive Mason/Getty Images Sport/Getty Images

# More to Explore

## How Can You Make an IMPACT?

### Job Interview

Work with a partner to choose an explorer. One person will play the part of that explorer. The other person will play the part of the European king or queen the explorer wants to have sponsor an expedition to the Americas. Use evidence from your research to conduct a job interview for the expedition. The monarch should try to determine why the journey is a good idea and whether the explorer is the right candidate for the job. The explorer should try to convince the monarch that the monarch's country will benefit from the journey and that the explorer is the right person to lead the expedition.

### Letter to the Editor

Imagine that you are a citizen of an Aztec or Inca city and that the city has a newspaper. Write a letter to the editor of the newspaper that argues for or against building a relationship with the Europeans. Use evidence from the text to support your opinion.

### Crossword Puzzle

Create a crossword puzzle using all ten words from the chapter Word Bank. Write an appropriate clue for each word. Exchange puzzles with a partner, and solve your partner's puzzle.

THE IMPACT TODAY

# Why Do Products and Ideas Move From Place to Place?

## Markets and Resources

European explorers in the 1400s wanted to find new markets where they could trade and find goods that Europeans needed or wanted, such as gems, silk, and spices. When they arrived in the Western Hemisphere, they found raw materials such as crops, minerals, and lumber as well as gold and other riches. Today, lack of resources and demand for specific products and services continue to drive trade between countries.

The tropical climate and rich soils of Central America are ideal for growing coffee beans.

In a market economy, people are allowed to buy and sell goods and services with little control by the government. Trade flourishes in a market economy because people can trade almost anything they want. Buyers seek to purchase the highest-quality goods and services with the money they have available. Sellers of goods and services seek to make high profits. Profit is the difference between the cost of making the good or delivering the service and what it is sold for.

The most important goods in a nation's economy often depend on what resources the nation has available. For example, a country with plenty of fertile soil and regular rainfall can raise large amounts of valuable crops. A country with plentiful mineral resources can manufacture metals, such as steel. Large forests can provide the resources for a lumber industry. An outstanding educational system would be a helpful resource for a technology industry.

In the Western Hemisphere, there are many regions well suited to growing grain and soybeans, especially in the Great Plains region of the United States and Canada. In both North and South America, much of these crops are used to feed cattle, pigs, and chickens. In the tropical regions of Latin America and the Caribbean, the climate creates ideal conditions for growing coffee beans and sugar cane.

The Spanish explorers who first arrived in the Western Hemisphere grew wealthy from the region's gold and silver. Today, gold is still an important mineral in Peru and in North America. But the most important mineral resource is petroleum. Nations with large oil reserves include Canada, Venezuela, the United States, Brazil, and Ecuador. Other important mineral resources include iron ore and coal.

The combination of natural resources, human resources, education, and technology can help countries grow key industries. The aerospace industry plays a key role in the economies of the United States and Brazil. The United States produces many of the largest jet airplanes, and Brazil produces many mid-sized jet airplanes.

Embraer 120ER from Brazil

Boeing 777 jet from the United States

## WHAT IS THE IMPACT TODAY?

**Talk** Think about an important product or service made or delivered in your city or state. Discuss how this product or service benefits the people in your city and state.

What characteristics of your city or state help create this product or service? Think about the natural resources, human resources, and education systems where you live.

(t)McGraw-Hill Education, (c)mikvivi/iStock/Getty Images, (b)Mayskyphoto/Shutterstock

# Trade

Because the United States economy is so large, and foreign trade plays a key role in its success. U.S. goods are shipped to all parts of the world, and dozens of nations ship goods to the United States. The goods and services sent to other countries are called exports, and the goods and services received from other countries are called imports.

U.S. exported goods include both manufactured products and raw materials. Electronic goods and transportation equipment are important categories of manufactured exports. Among the raw materials and agricultural products exported are petroleum and soybeans.

Multinational corporations handle much of the world's foreign trade. These companies have offices in more than one country. Countries examine imported goods for quality. They also may charge a fee called a tariff on imported goods. Multinational corporations must understand manufacturing and trade rules of different countries to be successful.

Services also play an important part in foreign trade. Saving money in banks and flying foreign airlines are examples of services people use from different countries.

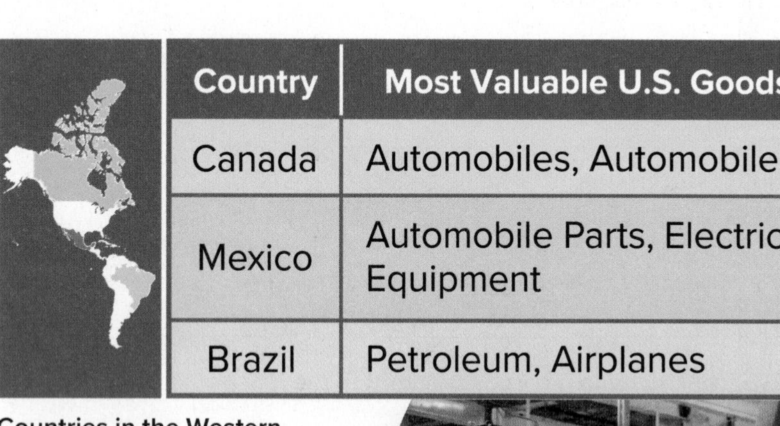

| Country | Most Valuable U.S. Goods Imported |
| --- | --- |
| Canada | Automobiles, Automobile Parts |
| Mexico | Automobile Parts, Electrical Equipment |
| Brazil | Petroleum, Airplanes |

**Countries in the Western Hemisphere That Import the Most U.S. Goods**

# Interdependence

Nations depend on one another when it comes to goods and services. Some nations, like Japan, lack many raw materials. Other nations lack the technology needed to manufacture computers and other complex products. Trade helps nations obtain the goods and services they are unable to produce themselves. When countries rely on each other for goods and services, they are **interdependent** with each other.

The United States relies heavily on countries in the Western Hemisphere for its foreign trade. Two of its top three trading partners, Mexico and Canada, are in the Western Hemisphere. The other top trading partner is China. Some U.S. companies have factories in Canada and Mexico and in other countries because of resources available there. Often, U.S. companies make products in other countries because of lower costs. Among the products made in Canadian and Mexican factories are automobiles and appliances.

All nations have trade agreements with each other, but sometimes disagreements arise. When this happens, the World Trade Organization, based in Switzerland, helps resolve these disagreements. The World Trade Organization cannot force a solution, but it can hold hearings and make recommendations to help resolve the dispute.

Nongovernmental organizations also are involved in trade. They often will focus on a particular issue. For example, the World Wildlife Fund monitors trade involving endangered species.

**Automobiles are one of the most important goods in U.S. foreign trade. These cars are being made in Canada for export to the United States.**

## WHAT IS THE IMPACT TODAY?

**Talk** Choose a product that your family uses every day that comes from another country.

Do research to find the country the product comes from and why the country might make that product. Why do you think we import the product from that country?

Chapter
3

# A Changing Continent

Lesson 1
The Jamestown Colony

Lesson 2
Cooperation and Conflict in North America

Lesson 3
The New England Colonies

Lesson 4
The Middle Colonies

Lesson 5
The Southern Colonies

The IMPACT Today
Culture in the Western Hemisphere

ESSENTIAL
EQ
QUESTION

## What Is the Impact of People Settling in a New Place?

In this chapter, you'll read about how European settlements developed across the East Coast of North America. You'll learn how those settlements affected the lives of Native Americans who lived in those areas.

### Step into the Time Chronological Thinking

Look at the time line. What was happening in other parts of the world while Europeans were settling North America?

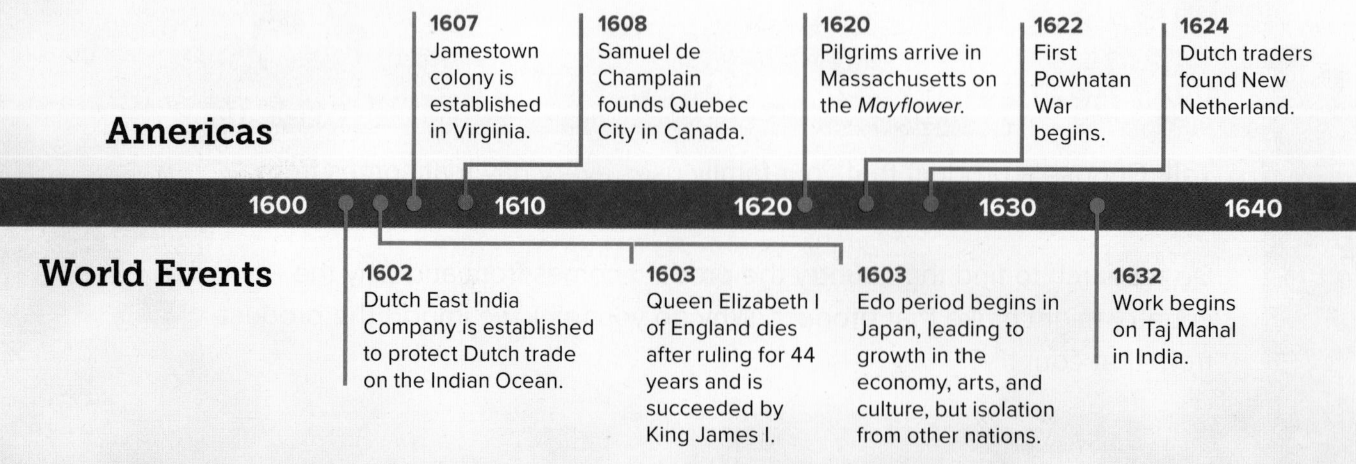
Americas
1607
Jamestown colony is established in Virginia.
1608
Samuel de Champlain founds Quebec City in Canada.
1620
Pilgrims arrive in Massachusetts on the *Mayflower.*
1622
First Powhatan War begins.
1624
Dutch traders found New Netherland.
1600
1610
1620
1630
1640
World Events
1602
Dutch East India Company is established to protect Dutch trade on the Indian Ocean.
1603
Queen Elizabeth I of England dies after ruling for 44 years and is succeeded by King James I.
1603
Edo period begins in Japan, leading to growth in the economy, arts, and culture, but isolation from other nations.
1632
Work begins on Taj Mahal in India.

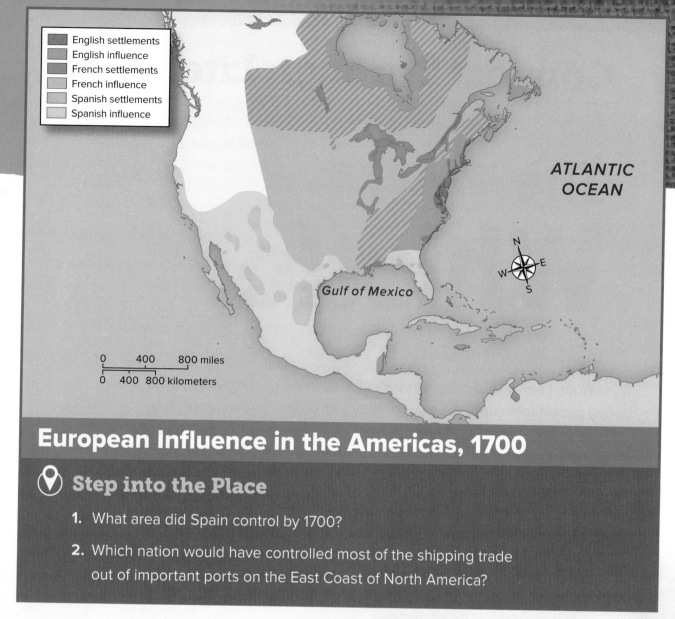

English settlements
English influence
French settlements
French influence
Spanish settlements
Spanish influence

ATLANTIC OCEAN

Gulf of Mexico

N E S W

0 400 800 miles
0 400 800 kilometers

## European Influence in the Americas, 1700

### Step into the Place

1. What area did Spain control by 1700?
2. Which nation would have controlled most of the shipping trade out of important ports on the East Coast of North America?

Between 1600 and 1700, three major powers fought for control of territory in North America. England, Spain, and France created settlements across the East Coast. Most coastal territory ultimately belonged to England, but Spain kept control of the area that is now Florida. France gained control of much of the interior areas of what is now the United States and Canada.

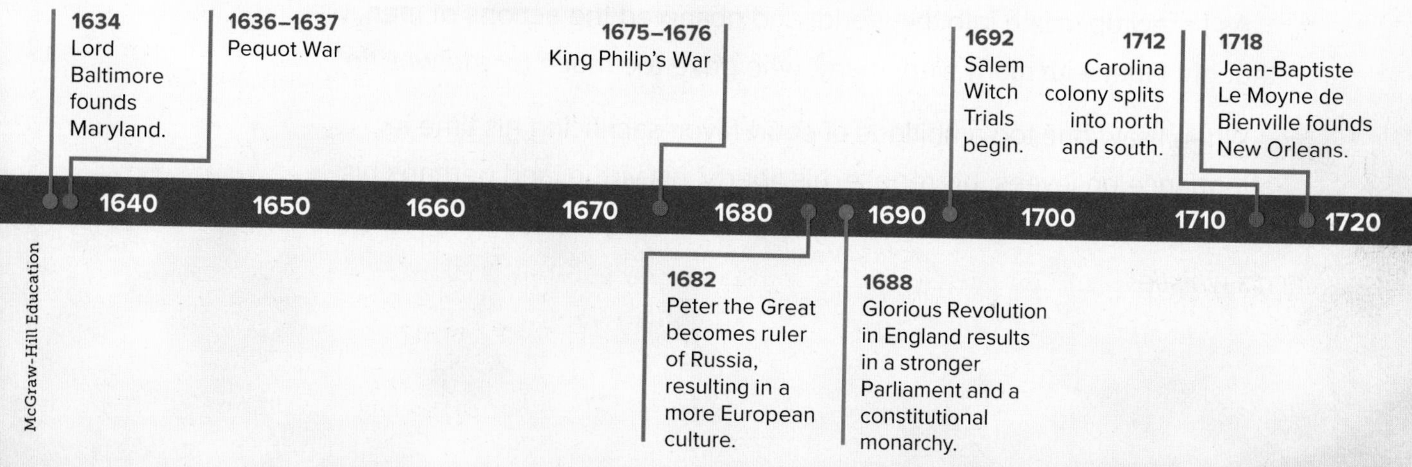

1634 Lord Baltimore founds Maryland.

1712 Carolina colony splits into north and south.

1682 Peter the Great becomes ruler of Russia, resulting in a more European culture.
1688 Glorious Revolution in England results in a stronger Parliament and a constitutional monarchy.

# Connect Through Literature

# The Whistle

by Benjamin Franklin

When I was a child of seven years old, my friends, on a holiday, filled my pocket with coppers. I went directly to a shop where they sold toys for children; and being charmed with the sound of a *whistle*, that I met by the way in the hands of another boy, I voluntarily offered and gave all my money for one. I then came home, and went whistling all over the house, much pleased with my *whistle*, but disturbing all the family. My brothers, and sisters, and cousins, understanding the bargain I had made, told me I had given four times as much for it as it was worth; put me in mind what good things I might have bought with the rest of the money; and laughed at me so much for my folly, that I cried with vexation; and the reflection gave me more chagrin than the *whistle* gave me pleasure.

This, however, was afterwards of use to me, the impression continuing on my mind; so that often, when I was tempted to buy some unnecessary thing, I said to myself, *Don't give too much for the whistle*; and I saved my money.

As I grew up, came into the world, and observed the actions of men, I thought I met with many, very many, *who gave too much for the whistle*.

When I saw one too ambitious of court favor, sacrificing his time in attendance on levees, his repose, his liberty, his virtue, and perhaps his friends, to attain it, I have said to myself, *This man gives too much for his whistle*.

Franklin, Benjamin. *The Whistle*. Boston: Brad Stephens & Company, 1921.

When I saw another fond of popularity, constantly employing himself in political bustles, neglecting his own affairs, and ruining them by that neglect, *He pays, indeed*, said I, *too much for his whistle*.

If I knew a miser, who gave up every kind of comfortable living, all the pleasure of doing good to others, all the esteem of his fellow-citizens, and the joys of benevolent friendship, for the sake of accumulating wealth, *Poor man*, said I, *you pay too much for your whistle*.

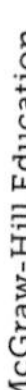

When I met with a man of pleasure, sacrificing every laudable improvement of the mind, or of his fortune, to mere corporeal sensations, and ruining his health in their pursuit, *Mistaken man*, said I, *you are providing pain for yourself, instead of pleasure; you give too much for your whistle.*

If I see one fond of appearance, or fine clothes, fine houses, fine furniture, fine equipages, all above his fortune, for which he contracts debts, and ends his career in a prison, *Alas!* say I, *he has paid dear, very dear, for his whistle.*

Old Paper Studios/Alamy

When I see a beautiful sweet-tempered girl married to an ill-natured brute of a husband, *What a pity,* say I, *that she should pay so much for a whistle!*

In short, I conceive that great part of the miseries of mankind are brought upon them by the false estimates they have made of the value of things, and by their *giving too much for their whistles.*

Yet I ought to have charity for these unhappy people, when I consider that, with all this wisdom of which I am boasting, there are certain things in the world so tempting, for example, the apples of King John, which happily are not to be bought; for if they were put to sale by auction, I might very easily be led to ruin myself in the purchase, and find that I had once more given too much for the *whistle*.

## Think About It

1. Based on the text on page 112, what does the word *levee* mean?
2. What does Ben Franklin mean when he says that someone pays too much for a whistle?
3. What are some situations today that you think cause people to "give too much for their whistle"?

# People You Should Know

## Olaudah Equiano

Kidnapped from his home in Nigeria at the age of 11 in 1756, Olaudah Equiano was sold into slavery. He was eventually purchased by a sea captain, and he sailed the world before purchasing his own freedom. After he settled in England, he wrote the story of his life: *The Interesting Narrative of the Life of Olaudah Equiano*. The book helped to persuade many people of the evils of the slave trade.

## Anne Hutchinson

The well-educated daughter of an Anglican church leader in London, Anne Hutchinson was vocal about her religious beliefs. After emigrating to Boston at the age of 43, she spoke out against the Puritans' strict rules about how people should worship. Many people in the Massachusetts Bay Colony agreed with her and attended the discussions she hosted. Governor John Winthrop disagreed with her, however, and she was ultimately banished from the colony. She started her own settlement in what is now Rhode Island in 1638.

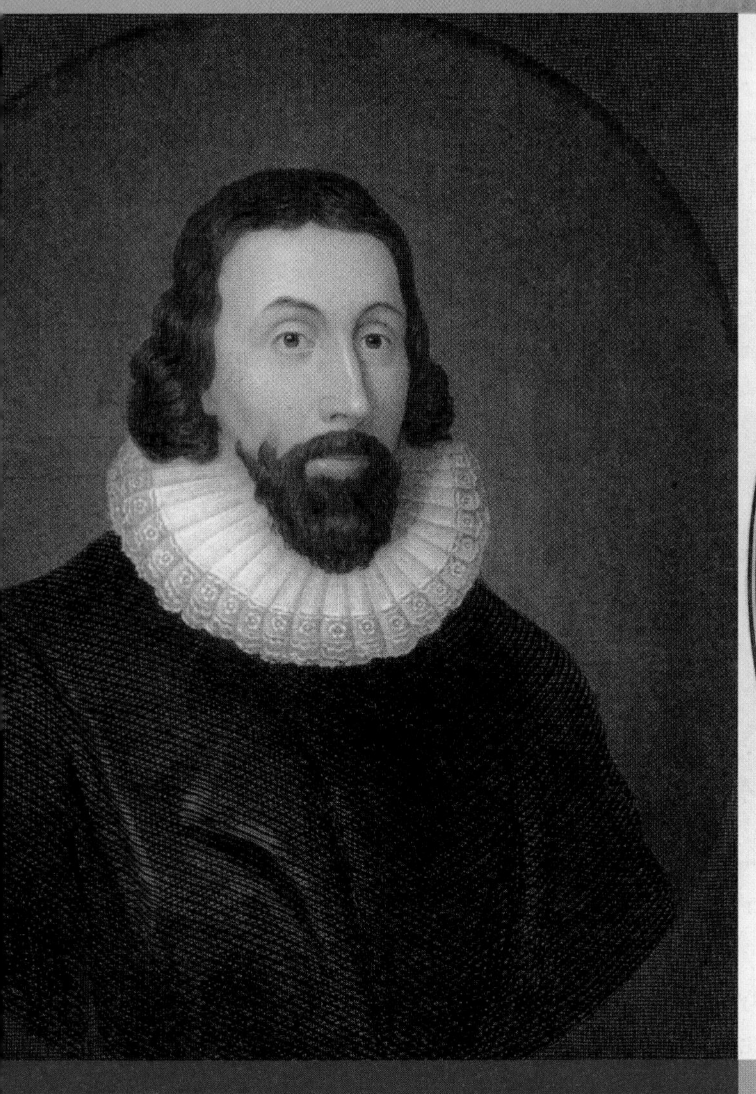

## John Winthrop

As the governor of the Massachusetts Bay Colony for parts of the 1630s and 1640s, John Winthrop believed the new Puritan settlement should be a "city on a hill," a model of perfect morals and social behavior. He wanted everyone to sign a covenant, or sacred agreement, with the Puritan faith. He also worked to make sure that anyone who disagreed with his strict rules was removed from the colony.

## Benjamin Franklin

Most people know about Benjamin Franklin as one of the authors the Declaration of Independence and as a scientist and ambassador. But his career began at the age of 16 in 1722 when he started writing essays in his brother's newspaper. He convinced his brother and the readers of the paper that his essays were written by a middle-aged woman named Silence Dogood. Later, Franklin earned fame and fortune as a newspaper printer in his own right.

# How Did Early English Settlers Cooperate and Clash with Native Americans?

## England's First Permanent Colony in North America

After the failure of the Roanoke colony, England did not attempt another colony until Queen Elizabeth's successor, King James I, came to power. In 1606, he granted a group of merchants called the Virginia Company a charter to establish another colony. In December 1606, the Virginia Company sent 144 men and boys to establish the colony of Jamestown near the mouth of Chesapeake Bay in what is now the state of Virginia. It was England's first permanent North American colony.

Jamestown nearly failed from the start. The location was poorly chosen. The settlers wanted a place that they could easily defend. They also wanted a place with water deep enough to allow ships to anchor near the shore. What they did not consider, however, was that the land was swampy and the water from that part of the James River was salty and dangerous to drink.

**1612**
John Rolfe introduces tobacco to the colony.

**1614**
Pocahontas marries John Rolfe.

**1619**
The House of Burgesses meets for the first time; enslaved Africans are brought to Jamestown.

**1622**
The Second Powhatan War begins.

00 | 1605 | 1610 | 1615 | 1620 | 1625 | 1630 | 1635

**1607**
Jamestown is established.

North Wind Picture Archives/Alamy

Settlers building Jamestown

Many of the colonists were not prepared for the challenges of Jamestown. Many came from the upper class and were interested in finding treasure. They had little experience or desire to do hard outdoor work, such as building or farming. They did not plan to stay permanently but wanted to find gold and return to England. Their participation did little to help. Also, the seven men on the council selected to lead the colony were distrustful of one another and did not cooperate well.

The poor conditions at Jamestown led to starvation and disease. After two-thirds of the colony had died, Captain John Smith took over as leader. He understood the importance of hard work, especially in a survival situation. He required every person to work four to six hours every day. According to some sources, he told the colonists, "Those who don't work, don't eat." His firm leadership saved the colony, but its troubles weren't over yet.

The Virginia Company continued to support the colony. It would send supply ships with food, tools, goods for trading, and additional settlers. These ships did not come often, however. The "First Supply" arrived in January 1608. It carried about 100 new settlers. It was also an all-male colony. The "Second Supply" did not come until October of that year. It carried 70 new settlers, including the first two women of the colony, Martha Forest and her maid, Anne Burras. Even after women began to arrive, the gender ratio remained skewed throughout most of the seventeenth century. This social structure posed significant challenges for a society that saw family as a main center of social order, economy, and survival.

**Jamestown men wore chest plates in battle.**

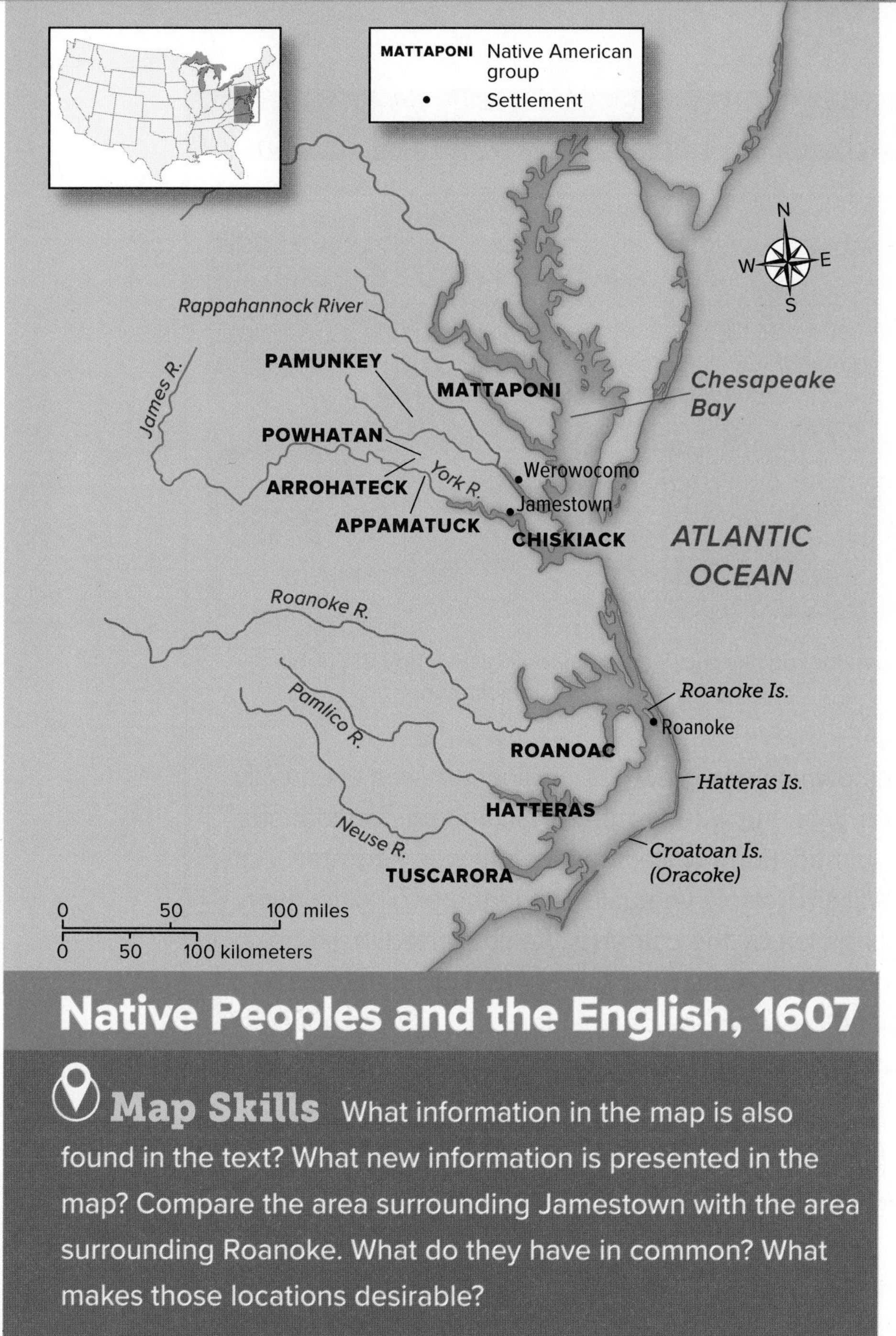


## Native Peoples and the English, 1607

**Map Skills** What information in the map is also found in the text? What new information is presented in the map? Compare the area surrounding Jamestown with the area surrounding Roanoke. What do they have in common? What makes those locations desirable?

The "Starving Time" occurred when Captain John Smith left the colony in 1609 and it nearly collapsed. Tensions with the Powhatan people and lack of leadership caused the majority of the colonists to die of starvation and disease. When the group of settlers who had been shipwrecked in Bermuda reached Jamestown in May 1610, they found the colony in such poor condition that they considered abandoning it. They received news that more ships bringing supplies and people would be arriving, so they stayed and rebuilt the colony with the survivors. Among the shipwrecked settlers was John Rolfe, who would end up helping to save the colony.

## Then and Now

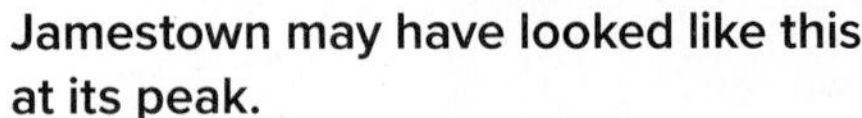

Jamestown may have looked like this at its peak.

Archaeologists study the remains of old Jamestown.

As the Jamestown colony grew, the original fort was eventually abandoned. Over time, the wood rotted away and the foundations became buried in mud. For a while, the location was forgotten. An archaeologist, William Kelso, eventually found the original location by studying writings left by the colonists. Kelso started the Jamestown Rediscovery Project in 1994. He and others began to uncover, study, and preserve the original fort. Visitors can now visit the site of Jamestown.

## Stop and Check

**Write** What problems did the Jamestown colony face? What recommendations would you give to solve these problems?

**Find Details** As you read, add additional information to the graphic organizer on page 91 in your Inquiry Journal.

# Relations Between the Powhatan and the Colonists

In addition to being a salty swamp, the location of Jamestown was also in Powhatan territory. The Powhatan Confederacy was an alliance of about thirty groups. They were led by Chief Wahunsonacock (wah hun SAHN uh kahk), also called Chief Powhatan. He was an intelligent leader who had been successfully increasing the strength and territory of his people when the colonists arrived. Historians are not sure exactly how many groups Chief Powhatan ruled, but he had thousands of warriors at his command. For the struggling Jamestown colony, the Powhatan could be much-needed allies or dangerous enemies.

As an experienced soldier, Captain John Smith knew Jamestown could not survive a full-force attack from the Powhatan, so he wisely chose to avoid conflict as much as possible. He and Chief Powhatan respected one another. Although there were a few conflicts, the relationship was mostly peaceful, and the Jamestown colony was able to get food through trade with the Powhatan.

Unfortunately, Smith was injured in a gunpowder accident. His injury forced him to return to England. Then, in 1618, Chief Powhatan died. Power passed to one of his brothers, who ruled briefly before passing the title again to another brother, named Opechancanough (ohp CHAN kuh nawf). He was angry about the growth of the Jamestown colony into native lands, and he waged wars against the colony for the next several decades.

Colonists traded with the Powhatan for food.

**Stop and Check**

**Think** What made it possible for the colonists to trade with the Powhatan?

# The Real Story of Pocahontas

The most famous story about Jamestown and the Powhatan is the story about Chief Powhatan's daughter, Pocahontas. Her real name was Matoaka; Pocahontas was her nickname and meant "the playful one." According to legend, when she was around 13 years old, her father captured Captain John Smith and planned to execute him. Pocahontas saved Smith's life by convincing Powhatan to let him go.

Pocahontas saving John Smith

Historians are uncertain if these events happened at all. Captain Smith was known to exaggerate stories. Some historians suggest that the incident was not an attempted execution and that Smith misunderstood a ceremony making him a sub-chief under Powhatan. What is more certain is that Pocahontas was curious and friendly toward the colonists. This improved relations between the two groups. She later married John Rolfe, a successful Jamestown farmer. This marriage brought peace between the settlers and the Powhatan, who had been growing more hostile since Captain Smith returned to England. Pocahontas died of illness in 1617 while visiting England with her husband.

Pocahontas

## Stop and Check

COLLABORATE

**List** Make a list of facts and myths about Pocahontas. Compare your list with a partner's list.

**Find Details** As you read, add additional information to the graphic organizer on page 91 in your Inquiry Journal.

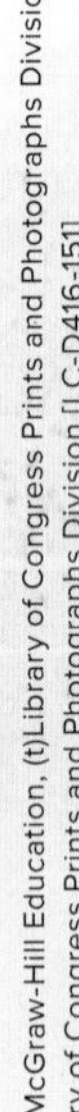

# The Legacy of the Colony

In 1612, John Rolfe introduced a new form of tobacco to the colony. It grew well in Virginia and quickly became a **cash crop**. The colony would grow in population and size due to the wealth gained from the new crop. Unfortunately, tobacco is hard on the soil, and so the colonists needed more and more land to grow it. This caused conflicts with the Powhatan and was one of the reasons for the Powhatan Wars. The value of tobacco, however, made the colony strong and the colonists wealthy enough to protect themselves.

Tobacco required a lot of labor, so indentured servants were brought from England to work. Their employers paid for them to travel there, and the indentured servants worked under contract for five to seven years until they repaid their debt. The colonists wanted even more expansion, however, and eventually began purchasing enslaved Africans to work on tobacco farms.

**Tobacco farming**

Slavery in the English colonies began in the early 1600s.

This means that the cruel practice of slavery in North America has its roots in England's first permanent colony. The slave trade had already been established by other countries, and in 1619, a Dutch ship entered the port of Jamestown carrying enslaved Africans. Twenty of them were exchanged for food. Since slavery had not yet been established in the colony, these first Africans may have been treated more like indentured servants. Records at the time listed them as servants, not slaves. Some apparently gained freedom after working a certain number of years.

This situation would not last. As the contracts on indentured servants ended and the **demand** for tobacco and other crops grew, planters needed more workers. Some planters attempted to enslave Native Americans, since the relationship had become much worse after the departure of Captain John Smith and the death of Chief Powhatan. The Native Americans knew the land well and had friends and family to help them, so attempts to enslave them were unsuccessful. Enslaved Africans, however, did not have the same networks of friends or family in the unfamiliar land of North America. Escaping was more difficult. By 1650, the number of enslaved Africans in the Virginia colony had grown to about 300.

Another important legacy of Jamestown was the first representative government set up by Europeans in the Americas. In 1619, the Virginia Company had the colonists establish their own government, the House of Burgesses. By this time, the Virginia colony had expanded into eleven settlements. Each was allowed to elect two representatives, or burgesses, to speak for them when the House met in Jamestown. Since most of the burgesses were wealthy tobacco growers, one of their first laws was simply to settle the price of tobacco.

The House of Burgesses, Williamsburg, Virginia

The House of Burgesses had been around for only five years when King James took control of the colony from the Virginia Company. The company had been losing money, and the increasing attacks by the Powhatan, led by Chief Opechancanough, made King James think the colony needed more direct control. He sent royal governors to represent him in leading the colony. Despite this, the House of Burgesses continued to meet every year. Even if the burgesses were no longer in control, they liked being able to discuss what needed to be done and to be united when dealing with the royal government.

Jamestown remained the capital of the Virginia colony until 1699, after the statehouse burned down. By this time, many of the people had moved to other settlements, so they decided to rebuild in a better location. Williamsburg became the new capital, and Jamestown was eventually abandoned.

## Stop and Check

**Think** Aside from being the first successful English colony in America, what other "firsts" can be traced back to Jamestown?

**What Do You Think?** If you had been in charge of Jamestown, what would you have done differently?

# How Did Early European Settlers Compete with One Another and Native Americans?

## Competition Among European Nations

Spain, France, and England had different approaches to colonizing North America. Each nation's monarchy hoped that the North American colonies would bring wealth and greater global power. The three major empires employed different economic and governmental systems. The colonies of New Spain and New France appointed governors who reported back to the controlling government in Europe and carried out the king's and queen's orders. The English colony at Jamestown, on the other hand, was governed in its early years by a group of people who were elected to represent each settlement in the colony. The three nations competed for land and trade. Spain and France also sought to convert native peoples to Catholicism, the primary religion in those countries.

**1545**
Spain finds the largest silver deposits yet discovered in the Americas.

**1649**
The Iroquois Confederacy defeats the Huron Confederacy in the Beaver Wars.

**1718**
Jean-Baptiste Le Moyne de Bienville founds the city of New Orleans.

1550 | 1600 | 1650 | 1700 | 1750

**1608**
Samuel de Champlain founds Quebec City.

anada .

F

G

K

H

Laurent

An early map of Quebec City in modern-day Canada

Spain established territories in South America, the Caribbean, Central America and Mexico, as well as the southern and western parts of North America. Spanish settlers quickly learned to use the resources of their new colony to increase the wealth of Spain. The Spanish did not want land in the Americas to be taken by the French or the English. So, to further expand, Spanish rulers offered large portions of land to those willing to move to New Spain. These areas, called **encomiendas**, included any Native American villages on the land. The Native Americans living in an encomienda were forced to work for its owner in exchange for housing and food.

While the early English relationship with the Powhatan in the Jamestown colony involved some instances of cooperation, Spain's relationship with the Native Americans was based on conquest. The Spanish also wanted to convert all native peoples to Catholicism.

New Spain's wealth and power came in part from its gold and silver mines. Spanish settlers also built ranches and sugar cane plantations. Many of the workers in the mines and on the plantations were Native Americans. Disease, mistreatment, and dangerous working conditions resulted in the deaths of about 24 million Native Americans in just one hundred years. To replace the shrinking workforce, the Spanish brought enslaved Africans to New Spain. By 1570, more than 200,000 Africans were enslaved on the plantations of New Spain.

A mission was a common type of settlement in New Spain.

One Spanish colonist named Bartolomé de Las Casas was so upset at how colonists were treating the native people that he decided to help them. He became a **missionary**, or a person who teaches his or her religious beliefs to people with different beliefs.

Eventually, many more missionaries from Spain came to the Americas to teach the native peoples about Catholicism. Although the missionaries believed they were doing good, they forced the native peoples to work and give up their own religion. These native peoples and Spanish missionaries lived in settlements called missions. As Spain began claiming the West Coast, these missions became part of their strategy to prevent Russia and England from settling land in present-day California.

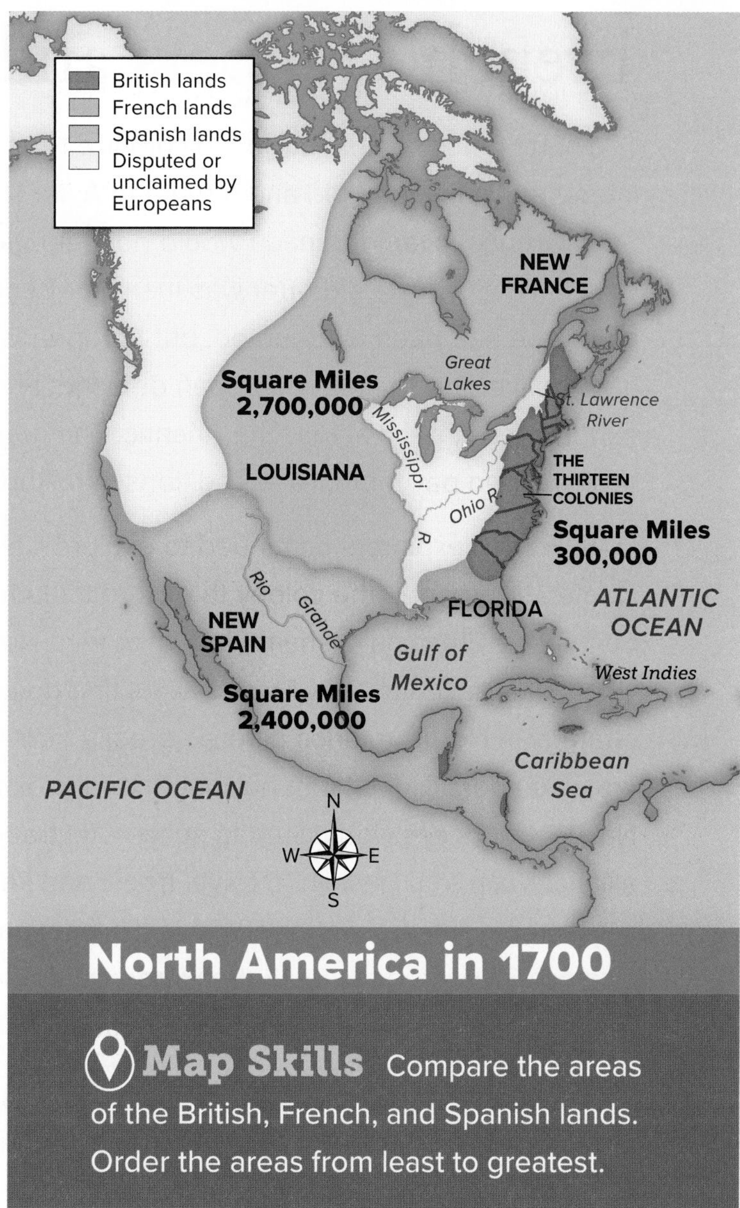


## North America in 1700

**Map Skills** Compare the areas of the British, French, and Spanish lands. Order the areas from least to greatest.

### Stop and Check

**Think** How did New Spain treat native people?

**Find Details** As you read, add new information to the graphic organizer on page 99 in your Inquiry Journal.

# French Trappers and Traders

When French settlers began to colonize North America, they were interested in finding gold and a route to Asia. Their settlements along the St. Lawrence River in Canada would not help them with either of those goals. What Canada did offer was many fur-bearing animals. The forests of Europe had been overhunted, but Europeans still desired hats made from beaver fur. To meet European demand, French settlers began to export beaver pelts across the Atlantic. The money raised through the fur trade helped pay for more expeditions into North America.

As French explorers continued to explore Canada, the king of France wanted to organize the colony to ensure it made money. He chose Samuel de Champlain (sham PLAYN) to lead New France. In 1604, Champlain sailed to New France as its first governor. Champlain's strategy in North America differed greatly from that of the Spanish conquistadors. He felt that building friendly relationships with groups of Native Americans would lead to successful trade. He believed these alliances would allow him to travel freely and keep the French settlements safe from attack. Within his first year in New France, Champlain learned to speak the Huron language. New France and the nearby Huron and Algonquin groups traded with each other and maintained friendly relations.

**PRIMARY SOURCE**

## In Their Words... Samuel de Champlain

**We departed on the following day, pursuing our way up the river as far as the entrance to the lake. In it are many beautiful low islands covered with very fine woods and meadows with much wild fowl and animals to hunt, such as stags, fallow deer, fawns, roebucks, bears, and other kinds of animals which come from the mainland to these islands.**

—from a diary entry of Samuel de Champlain, 1609

## Marquette and Jolliet

French explorers' efforts to find the Northwest Passage led them to further explore North America's waterways. In 1673, Jacques Marquette and Louis Jolliet headed south in a canoe on the Mississippi River, a river unfamiliar to them. They encountered many groups of Native Americans living on the banks of the Mississippi. While some Native Americans resisted when the colonists settled on their lands, the Illinois and other groups helped Marquette and Jolliet.

Marquette and Jolliet claimed the land drained by the Mississippi River for France. Marquette later set up a mission in present-day Illinois, and Jolliet continued to explore North America.

## La Salle and Louisiana

In 1682, René-Robert Cavelier Sieur de La Salle led an expedition down the Mississippi River. La Salle claimed the Mississippi and its tributaries, or smaller branching rivers and streams, for France. He named the region *Louisiana* after the French king, Louis XIV. La Salle wanted to build a fort at the mouth of the Mississippi and attack the Spanish in northern Mexico. La Salle and several hundred settlers, however, got lost and ended up in present-day Texas. By 1687, only 36 of La Salle's settlers remained alive.

Bark canoes were sturdy enough to withstand ocean waves and light enough to be carried.

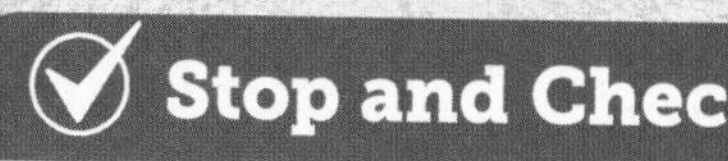

**Talk** Why did Champlain develop friendly relationships with Native Americans he encountered in New France?

## New Orleans

French colonists slowly began to settle parts of the Louisiana Territory. They built forts in strategic locations to protect new settlements from the Spanish and English. Louis XIV instructed a Canadian naval officer, Pierre Le Moyne Sieur d'Iberville, to build forts at the mouth of the Mississippi. The series of forts he built in present-day Mississippi and Louisiana further established Louisiana as a French possession. One such fort, Fort La Boulaye, lay just south of the future site of the city of New Orleans. When Iberville died of yellow fever, his younger brother, Jean-Baptiste Le Moyne Sieur de Bienville, continued his work.

Ships anchored at the Port of New Orleans, about 1800

**PRIMARY SOURCE**

## In Their Words... Pierre Le Moyne Sieur d'Iberville

If France does not take possession of this part of America, which is the finest, to have a colony strong enough to resist those that England possesses...these colonies which are becoming very extensive, will increase to such an extent that in less than a century, they will be strong enough to seize upon the whole continent of America, and to expel all other nations.

—from *The Argument to Settle Louisiana*, 1698

In 1701, Bienville became governor of Louisiana at the age of 21. He built Fort Louis on Mobile Bay and lived there until 1711. In 1718, Bienville founded New Orleans. The Louisiana Territory was much easier to farm than the rest of New France. Settlers built plantations on the fertile soil and grew indigo, rice, and tobacco. Successful plantations brought in more money from trade with Native Americans, which allowed the farmers to increase the size of the plantations. The growing plantations required more and more workers. In 1720, a ship carrying about 200 enslaved Africans landed in New Orleans. In the decade that followed, the colony imported more than six thousand enslaved Africans. Eventually, more than half of the people of New Orleans were enslaved Africans.

### Stop and Check

COLLABORATE

**Talk** Why was it important that France built forts in Mississippi and Louisiana?

TEXT: Pierre le Moyne Sieur d'Iberville. 1669. Quoted in Parliamentary Debates on the Subject of the Confederation of the British North American Provinces, 3rd Session, 8th Provincial Parliament of Canada (Quebec: Hunter, Rose & Company, parliamentary printers, 1865), 324.; PHOTO: (t)McGraw-Hill Education, (b)North Wind Picture Archives/Alamy

# New Alliances, New Conflict

As European colonial powers sought to rapidly expand in North America, they came into contact with more and more native peoples. Reactions to the Europeans varied. Some groups of Native Americans were friendly, and some were not friendly. Before the Europeans arrived, the people living in North America already traded with one another, had military agreements, and shared cultures. The settlers' arrival often complicated the existing relationships between groups of Native Americans.

In 1609, Huron and Algonquin leaders approached Samuel de Champlain asking to form a military alliance. The Huron and Algonquin had long been enemies of the Iroquois. Eventually, Algonquin commanders convinced Champlain to lend them French troops in their fight with the Iroquois.

Iroquois armies did not yet have guns and gunpowder. As a result, Champlain's men easily defeated the Iroquois. To thank the French, the Huron and Algonquin helped grow French fur traders' business in the region. After the battle with the Iroquois, France formed a permanent alliance with the Huron and Algonquin. The Iroquois confederacy, meanwhile, sought revenge.

**A colonial trading post**

The Iroquois wanted to expand their territory and regain control of the fur trade in eastern North America. The fur trade was important to the economy of the region, especially beaver fur. To achieve this goal, they engaged in a series of conflicts with the Huron, Algonquin, and French beginning in about 1640 and ending 1701. Because of a severe decline in the beaver population, these conflicts became known as the Beaver Wars.

French soldiers fight alongside Huron warriors.

In 1642, the Iroquois blocked the Huron from accessing the rivers they used to trade with the French and other native peoples. The Huron economy had become dependent on trade. The Huron nearly starved as a result of the Iroquois blockade. By 1649, the Iroquois had defeated the Huron. The Iroquois' conflicts with the French and Algonquin would continue well into the 18th century.

## Stop and Check

COLLABORATE

**Talk** Why did the Huron and the Algonquin side with Champlain in 1609?

**What Do You Think?** Did the relationships France and Spain had with the Native Americans they encountered make a difference in the outcomes of their settlements?

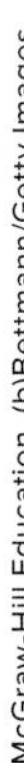

# Resources From the Americas Enrich Europe

Though many French explorers were disappointed not to find gold in Canada, they did discover another valuable resource. People across Europe were fond of hats made from pelts, or the skins of animals with the fur still on it. Unlike North America, parts of Europe were overpopulated. Some of the continent's forests had been cleared to expand cities. The larger animals that lived there became rare.

Meanwhile, large animals thrived in North America. The French colony made money by hunting and trapping mammals such as moose, elk, deer, and caribou. Beaver fur held special value. European clothing makers used the beaver's thick fur to make felt, which is a smooth, leathery fabric. Beaver hats were especially popular in the cold winters of Northern Europe. An oil naturally produced by beavers was even used to make perfumes. Hat makers had long used the fur of the European beaver to make hats, but overhunting and habitat destruction caused that species to become scarce by the 17th century. French traders were able to replace European beaver fur with an American version.

Just as in Europe, American beaver numbers decreased significantly as a result of overhunting. The animal was eventually saved by a change in fashion trends. Silk prices dropped at the beginning of the 19th century, and Europeans exchanged their beaver hats for silk ones. This allowed the beaver population to make a comeback. Today, beavers are one of the most important national symbols of Canada.

European clothes makers regarded beaver fur as a fashionable and useful material.

In the 1500s, Spain rose to become one of the world's most powerful empires. Its American colonies were key to the empire's growth. Spanish colonists mined large amounts of silver and gold in South America and Mexico. In 1545, Spanish colonists exploring in the mountains of Peru found the largest silver deposit yet discovered in the Americas. From the gold and silver, the Spanish made coins. Silver and gold coins were important to Spain's economic success because Spain produced very few goods that could be sold to other countries. Spanish traders exchanged coins for foreign goods. With this new wealth, the Spanish built ships and armies to further expand the Spanish Empire.

Spain used profits from the colonies to fund an armada, a large fleet of warships.

Other European powers tried to prevent the growth of Spain's territories. French leaders hired private sea captains to attack Spanish treasure ships as they returned to Spain. Eventually, Spain's dominance came to an end. The value of gold and silver was based on the fact that these metals were very rare. As more and more gold became available, Spanish coins were not as valuable as before. Nations that produced goods began to catch up with Spain economically. Without the ability to buy armies to protect and expand its empire, Spain's influence in the world shrank. In the 1700s, England, France, and the Netherlands fought to take Spain's place as Europe's most powerful nation.

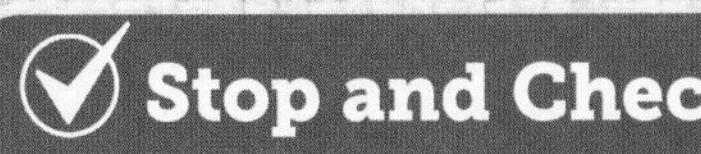

COLLABORATE

**Talk** What caused Spain's power to decrease?

# Lesson 3 What Was Life Like for People in New England?

## Seeking Religious Freedom

In England in the 1600s, it was a crime to belong to any church other than the Church of England. Members of the church called Separatists, however, wanted to set up their own churches and make their own rules. As a consequence, many members of the church were arrested and fined.

In the early 1600s, a group of Separatists decided to move to the Netherlands to escape persecution. This group later became known as the Pilgrims. The Pilgrims found religious tolerance in the Netherlands, but they eventually decided to leave. Some historians believe that they left because they were concerned about losing their English identity. The Pilgrims also found it difficult to make a living there.

The Pilgrims decided to venture to North America for both religious and economic reasons. They asked the English government permission to settle in Virginia, and the London Company agreed to pay for their passage. In return, the Pilgrims had to send resources such as timber, fish, and furs back to the company.

**Pilgrims departing on the *Mayflower* in 1620**

**1620**
Pilgrims on the *Mayflower* arrive at Plymouth in what is now Massachusetts.

**1630**
Puritans establish settlement at Boston.

**1636**
Providence colony is established in what is now Rhode Island.

**1675-1676**
King Philip's War

**1692**
Salem Witch Trials begin.

1620 | 1640 | 1660 | 1680 | 1700

**1636–1637**
Pequot War

**1700s**
First Great Awakening

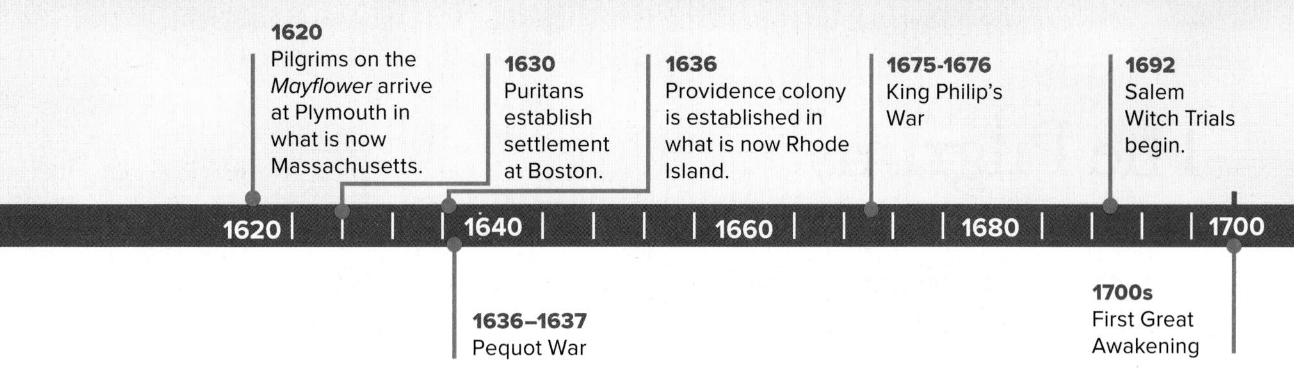

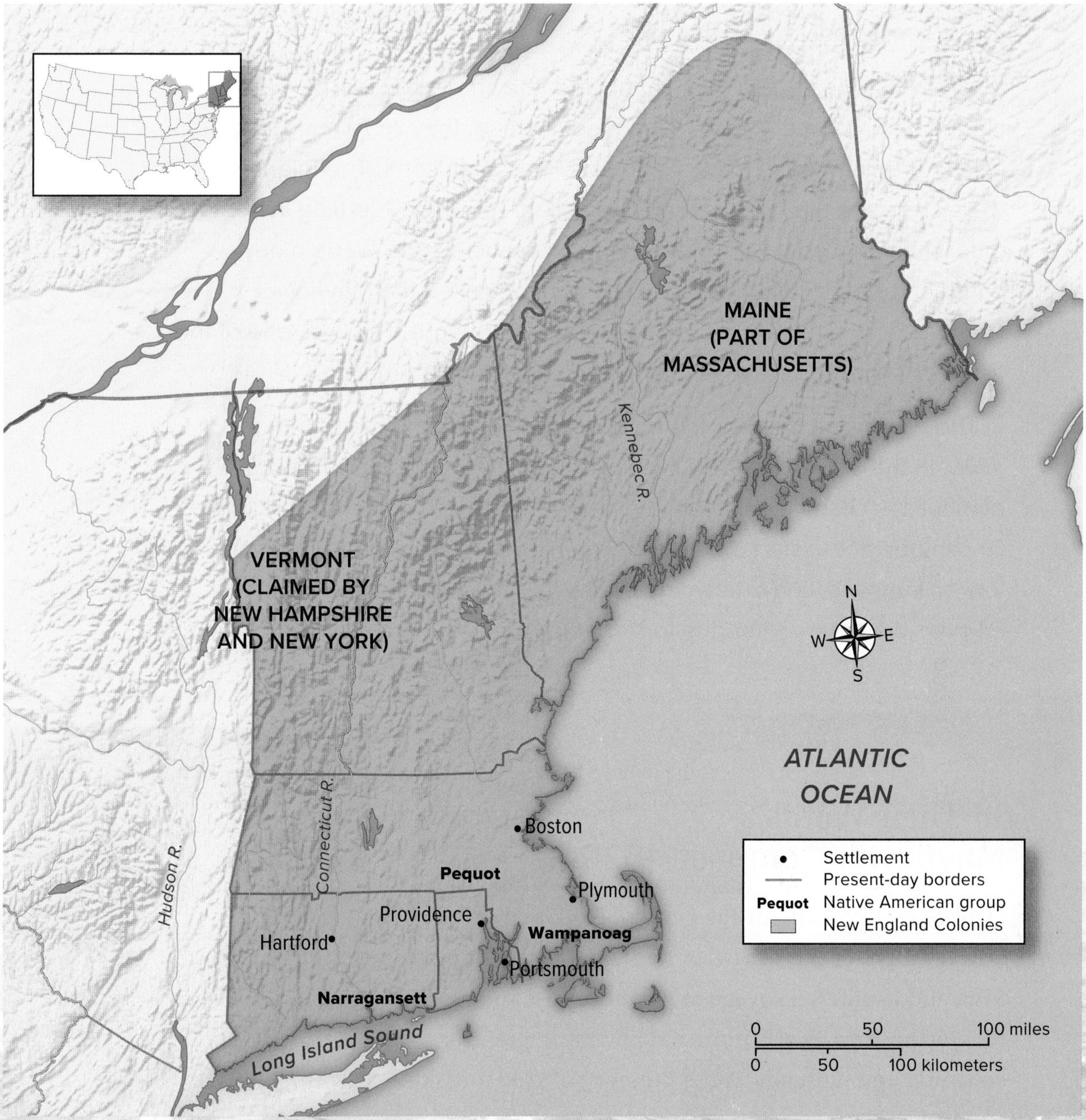

The New England Colonies were the northernmost English colonies.

# The Pilgrims

In September of 1620, 102 men, women, and children set sail from Plymouth, England, on a ship named the *Mayflower*. About 40 of the 102 passengers were Pilgrims. These Pilgrims faced a number of hardships on their 66-day voyage across the Atlantic Ocean, including storms and rough seas, disease, and hunger.

When they finally caught sight of land, they realized that they had not landed in Virginia as they had planned. Instead, they were hundreds of miles north, at what is today Cape Cod, Massachusetts. The Pilgrims were changing the rules of their original agreement by settling in a different area. Led by William Bradford, the colonists drew up a new contract for their community. This document, called the Mayflower Compact, provided the outline of a new government. This was one of the first steps toward self-government in colonial North America.

The Pilgrims did not decide on a location for their settlement right away. In the early days, they lived on board the *Mayflower*. They eventually chose a settlement they called Plymouth. They arrived in late December, at the start of a brutal winter. They were without experience, low on supplies, and utterly unprepared for the weather. Half of the Pilgrims died that winter due to starvation, disease, and the cold.

**PRIMARY SOURCE**

## In Their Words...
## Mayflower Compact, 1620

Having undertaken, for the glory of God, and advancement of the Christian faith, and honor of our king and country, a voyage to plant the first colony in the northern parts of Virginia, do by these presents solemnly and mutually in the presence of God and one of another . . . [we] combine ourselves together . . . for the general good of the colony: unto which we promise all due submission and obedience. . . .

William Bradford

The new colony seemed doomed. But in the spring, they befriended a Pawtuxet man named Squanto, who had been living with the Wampanoag people. Squanto spoke English and taught the Pilgrims how to survive. He showed them how to plant corn and use fish to fertilize the soil. He taught them how to trap animals, catch fish, and find oysters. William Bradford called Squanto "a special instrument sent from God." The Pilgrim settlement thrived and grew.

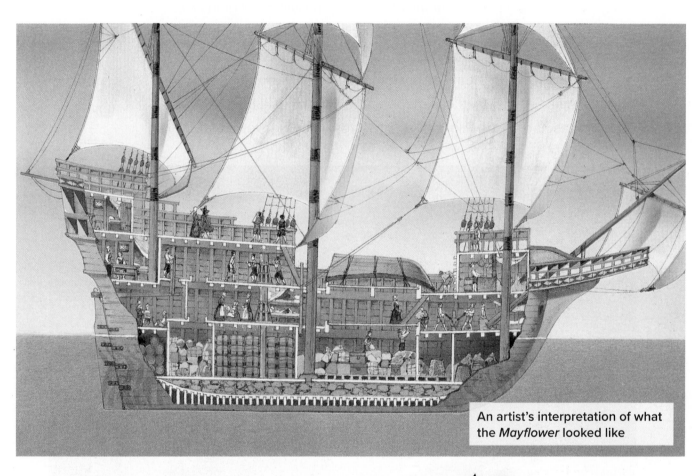

An artist's interpretation of what the *Mayflower* looked like

**Talk** Why did the Pilgrims draft a new formal agreement about how their colony would be run?

**Find Details** As you read, add new information to the graphic organizer on page 107 in your Inquiry Journal.

# The Mayflower Compact

When the Pilgrims wrote the Mayflower Compact, it was the first government framework written in the land that is now the United States. It was signed by only some of the colonists—the men. At the time, women rarely held positions of authority in civic or religious life. As a result, they did not have the opportunity to sign such important documents. The purpose of the document was to bind the Pilgrims together. However, the Mayflower Compact did not include any laws. Instead, those who signed it were pledging to follow the laws that would later be enacted by the Pilgrims' small system of self-government.

**The Pilgrims signing the Mayflower Compact**

## You Decide

Working in small groups, you will establish a new settlement.

- Give your settlement a name.
- Tell the location of your settlement.
- Indicate why you are moving to the settlement.

Work together to develop a system of laws for the settlement.

- Consider what principles are most important to your group.
- Think about the kinds of rights and protections you need.
- Write your new laws as a compact, and give the document an official title.
- Sign the compact.

## Reflect

What did developing a plan for your new community teach you about the importance of self-government?

- Who helped make the decisions about the settlement's laws and rules?
- How did you come to an agreement about the laws?
- How did you resolve conflicts with other members of your group?

## Make Connections

Consider how the development of your settlement compares with the development of the Plymouth settlement. What was similar, and what was different?

### Stop and Check

COLLABORATE

**Talk** Do you think the Pilgrims would have written a different compact if women had been included in the drafting? Would this have been better for the colony as a whole?

# The Puritans

The Pilgrims were not the only group to flee religious persecution in England. A group of Puritans made their own journey to North America in 1629. Unlike the Pilgrims, the Puritans planned to land in Massachusetts. When they arrived in 1630, they founded the Massachusetts Bay Colony. They named their first settlement Boston. Another difference between the Pilgrims and the Puritans was that the Puritans had not separated from the Church of England.

The Puritans believed God had chosen them to create a religious community that was purer than the ones in England. The Puritans worked hard to show that their community was a success. They also worked hard just to survive. Most Puritans were farmers, and made many of the things they needed by hand, such as barrels, horseshoes, cabinets, saddles, and shoes.

Because of the abundance of good lumber in New England, shipbuilding eventually became an important part of the economy. The industry was successful in part because of slave labor. Enslaved people were also put to work in shops and on farms. Massachusetts was the first colony to legalize slavery in 1641. By 1750, it was legal across all of the original thirteen colonies. Massachusetts did not outlaw slavery until 1783.

**The Puritans organized their villages so that each one had a school and a common building that served as both meeting house and church.**

A saltbox house was a common type of home in Puritan villages.

Puritan leaders wanted each settlement to be "a city upon a hill," which meant its residents had to live up to high moral standards. In an effort to enforce their rules, Puritan leaders required each family to sign a covenant with the church. If a family broke the **covenant**, it had to leave the settlement.

Puritan children were taught the value of hard work from an early age. Young children were expected to work around the house. They also learned to read, because the Puritans believed everyone should be able to read the Bible.

By age twelve, girls did the same chores as women, such as churning butter, spinning and dyeing cloth, and making soap and candles. Girls usually did not get any additional schooling.

Boys helped with the farm animals, chopped wood, and picked vegetables before going to school. At school, some had the chance to learn another language, such as Latin or Greek. Boys also began to learn a trade, such as blacksmithing or printing.

Life for Puritan women consisted mostly of managing the home and raising children. Most women were not allowed to own property, and they were supposed to be obedient to men. They were not allowed to participate in town government. Only men could vote in town meetings, in which they decided issues and made laws.

The Puritans founded the Massachusetts Bay Colony, so they would be free to practice their own religion. However, they were not tolerant of political or religious **dissension** among their own members. Roger Williams dissented, telling leaders that they should not take land that belonged to Native Americans and that they should allow the practice of other religions. Believing Williams's ideas were dangerous, Puritan leaders banished him. In 1636, Williams founded Providence, now the capital of Rhode Island.

In 1637, Anne Hutchinson was put on trial for arguing that people should be allowed to interpret the Bible themselves. Hutchinson was forced to leave Massachusetts. She founded a new settlement, now Portsmouth, Rhode Island.

Anne Hutchinson on trial

In 1692, the Puritans' strict moral codes led to one of the darkest episodes in their history. Three girls in Salem fell mysteriously ill. They blamed three women for using witchcraft on them, and other accusations soon followed. From June to September, the Puritans tried and hanged 19 people for witchcraft. Finally, a higher court stepped in to stop the trials.

Events like these left some Puritans yearning for more independence from the church. In the 1700s, ministers like John Wesley, Jonathan Edwards, and George Whitefield began to preach in a dramatic, emotional style. They emphasized the importance of faith over actions. They and their followers created the Baptist and Methodist churches, which focused on ordinary people who had not been attending church regularly. This movement, called the First Great Awakening, led many away from Puritanism.

## Stop and Check

COLLABORATE

**Talk** If the Puritans left England because people were intolerant of their religion, why didn't the Puritans tolerate other religious views in their colony?

North Wind Picture Archives/Alamy

# Native American Relations

The New England colonists had both positive and negative encounters with local Native Americans. The Pilgrims' relationship with Squanto and the Wampanoag people made the difference between the survival and extinction of their new colony.

**Squanto teaches the Pilgrims to farm.**

To give thanks for their survival, the Pilgrims and Wampanoag had a three-day festival to celebrate the good harvest. This feast would later be called the first "thanksgiving." The Wampanoag brought deer, and the Pilgrims brought turkey, goose, duck, and a variety of vegetables and fruits.

Not all relationships between New England colonists and local Native Americans were friendly, however. In 1637, the Pequot people of Connecticut and the English settlers went to war over trade disputes. The settlers were allied with the Narragansett and Mohegan people. These two peoples disliked the Pequot for their strict control of trade in the previous decades. At first, the two sides seemed evenly matched in what came to be called the Pequot War. The English had superior weapons, but the Pequot had knowledge of the land. In the end, however, the English defeated the Pequot. Many of the Pequot people taken prisoner by the English were sold into slavery.

Despite the promising beginning to the Pilgrims' relationship with the Wampanoag, Narragansett, and Mohegan peoples, the colonists soon became enemies with these groups. The Native Americans were angered by the increasing number of new colonists who were settling on their lands. By 1675, these tensions resulted in a bloody conflict called King Philip's War.

"King Philip" was the name that English settlers gave to the Wampanoag leader, Metacomet. Metacomet's father, Massasoit, had helped the Pilgrims survive their first harsh winters. However, the colonists' desire for more and more territory changed their relationship with the Wampanoag for the worse.

Thousands of people died in King Philip's War. Metacomet was eventually killed, and his family was sold into slavery. In their brutal conquest of the Native Americans, the English showed they were capable of seizing land and maintaining power. The war marked the end of any resistance to English colonization of New England.

Metacomet, also called King Philip, of the Wampanoag people

## Did You Know?

You might have thought that the English Pilgrims and the Wampanoag celebrated the first Thanksgiving in Plymouth, Massachusetts. Many historians, however, believe that it was actually French settlers who began this tradition. The French had colonized the area that is now Jacksonville, Florida. They held a Thanksgiving service in 1564, which was 57 years before the Pilgrims arrived. Spanish colonists in El Paso, Texas, also celebrated Thanksgiving services in 1598. In 1619, English colonists first held the feast we know best today.

## Stop and Check

COLLABORATE

**Talk** What caused the tensions that led to King Philip's War?

**What Do You Think?** Why did King Philip's War mark the end of resistance to English settlement of New England?

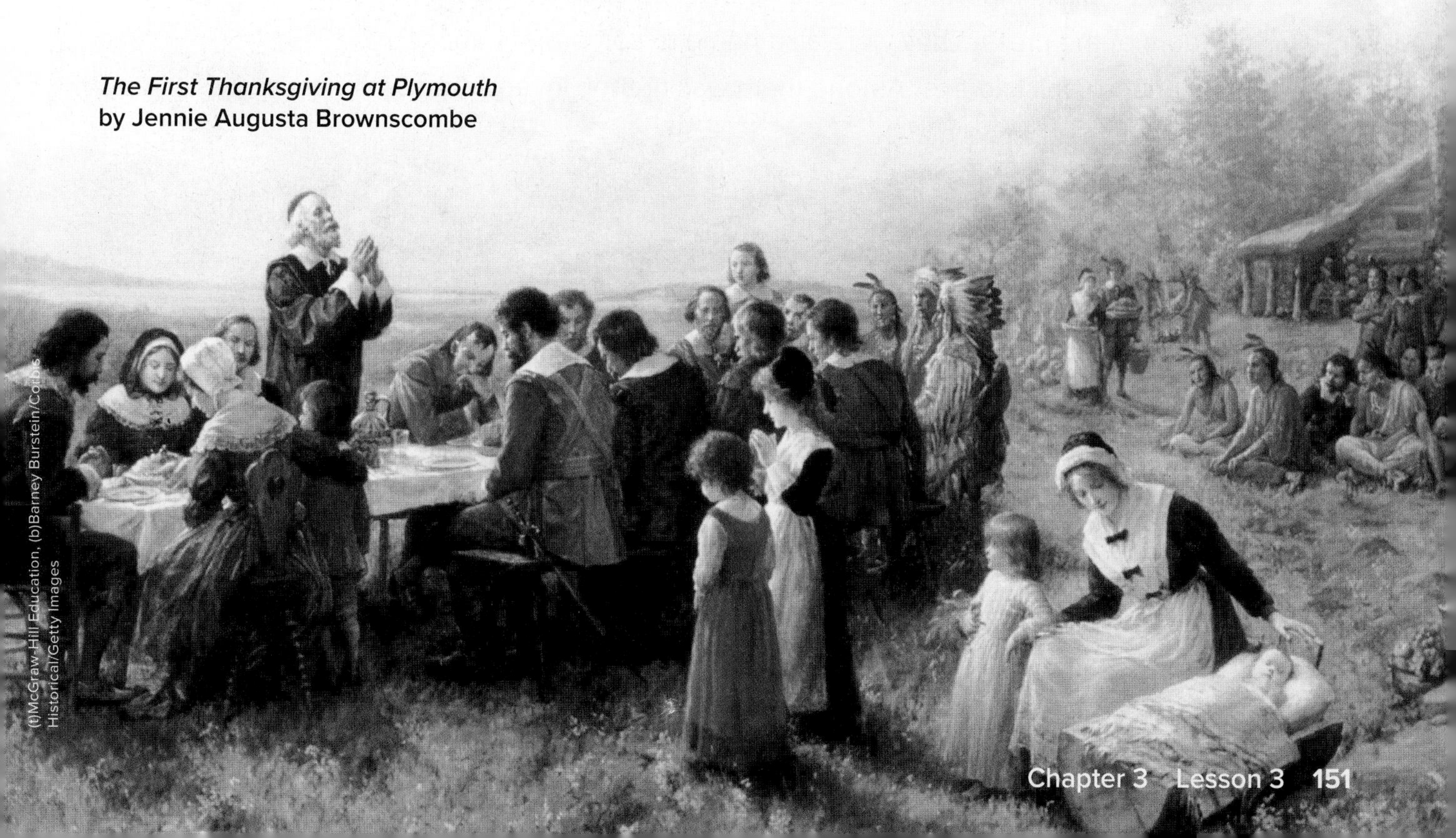

*The First Thanksgiving at Plymouth*
by Jennie Augusta Brownscombe

Lesson 4

# What Shaped Life In the Middle Colonies?

## A Region of Diversity

The English Middle Colonies—New York, New Jersey, Pennsylvania, and Delaware—were quite diverse, or varied. These colonies were home to people of many different ethnic backgrounds and religions. They became known for tolerance of these differences. They also became known as centers of **commerce**. Their central location and fine ports made them ideal for trading and distributing goods both north and south. Outside the port cities, fertile soil and a mild climate encouraged farming of wheat, corn, and other grains. Farming was so successful that growers were usually able to produce a surplus, or more than they needed. They could sell the surplus to the other colonies. For this reason, the Middle Colonies were sometimes called the "breadbasket" of colonial America.

A crossroads of ideas as well as trade, these successful colonies helped establish important American principles such as trial by jury and freedom of the press. They were also home to some of the most influential colonial figures. Among them was author, inventor, and thinker Benjamin Franklin.

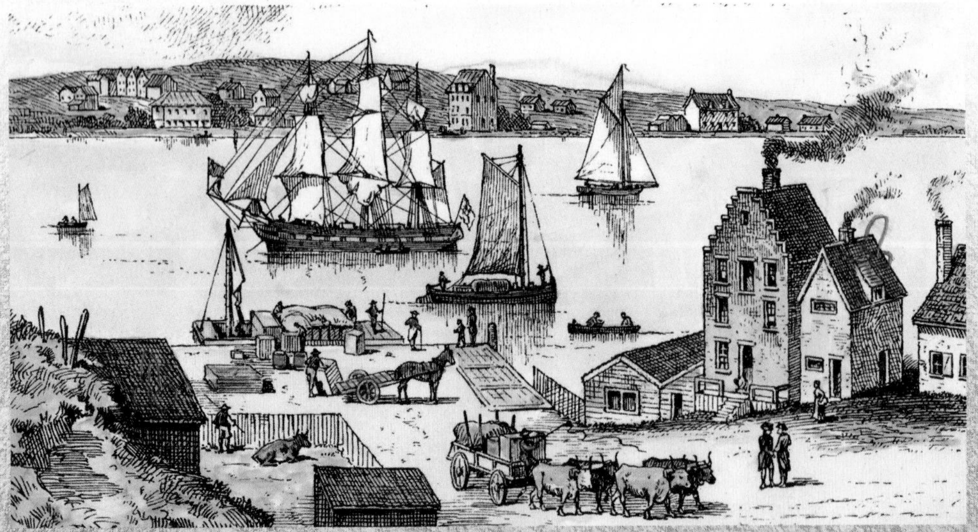

(bkgd spread)McGraw-Hill Education, (inset)North Wind Picture Archives/Alamy Stock Photo

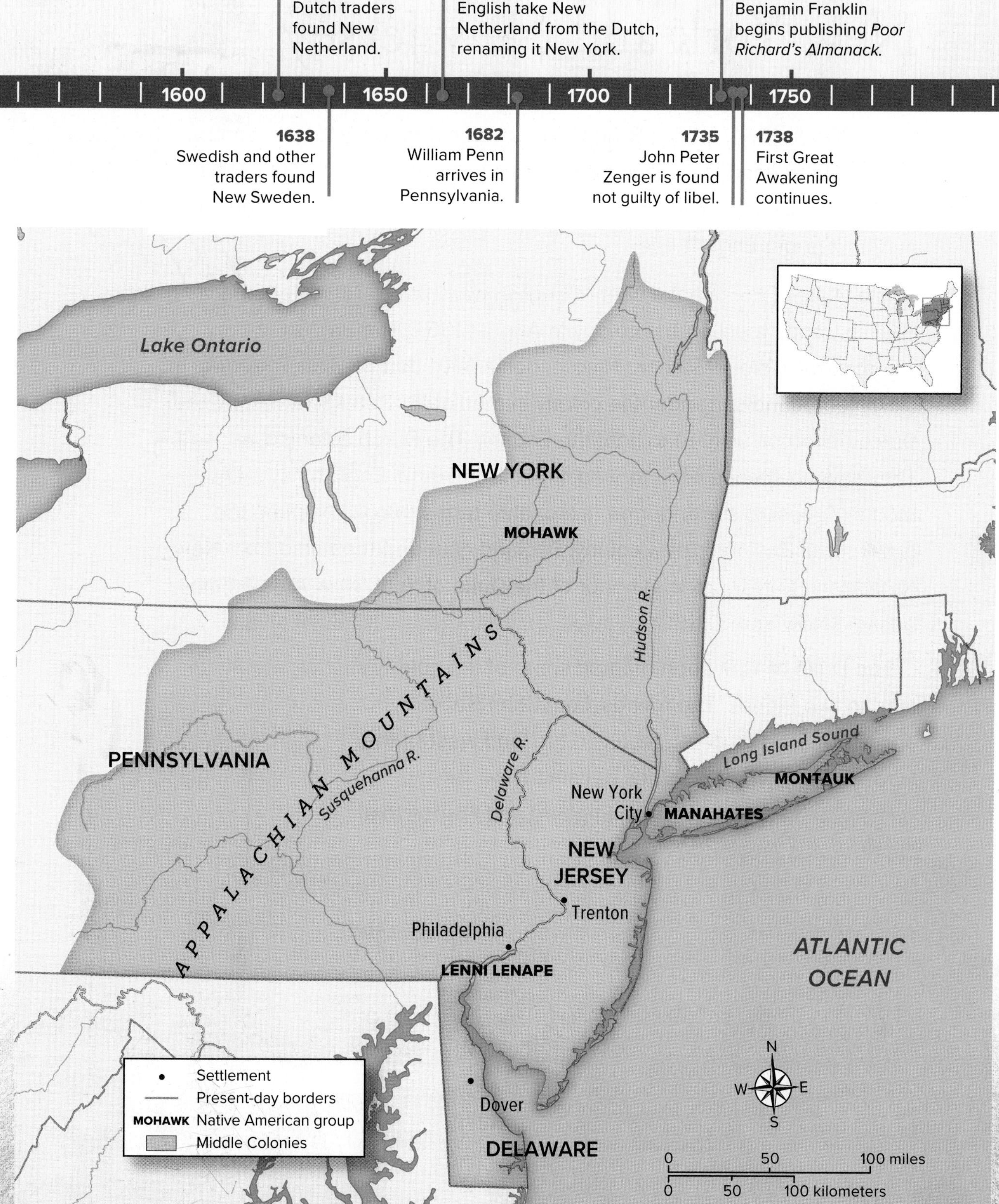


**Located between New England and the Southern Colonies, the Middle Colonies became the commercial center of colonial America.**

# New York and New Jersey

England and the Netherlands were at war in Europe for much of the late 1600s. In 1664, English King Charles II decided to try to gain control of New Netherland to expand his colonies in North America. He put his brother, the Duke of York, in charge of seizing the Dutch colony and putting it under English rule.

The Duke of York sent a fleet of English warships to New Netherland. English troops reached the colony in August 1664. The English commander, Colonel Richard Nicolls, demanded that the Dutch leaders in New Netherland surrender the colony immediately. Peter Stuyvesant, the Dutch governor, wanted to fight the English. The Dutch colonists refused. They saw no chance of victory against the powerful English navy. They thought it best to surrender on reasonable terms. Nicolls became the governor of England's new colony. England changed the name from New Netherland to New York, in honor of the Duke of York. New Amsterdam became New York City.

The Duke of York soon granted some of the colony's land to two friends. The friends, Lord John Berkeley and Sir George Carteret, received the land west of the Hudson River. Their holdings became New Jersey, named for an island between England and France that Carteret had previously governed.

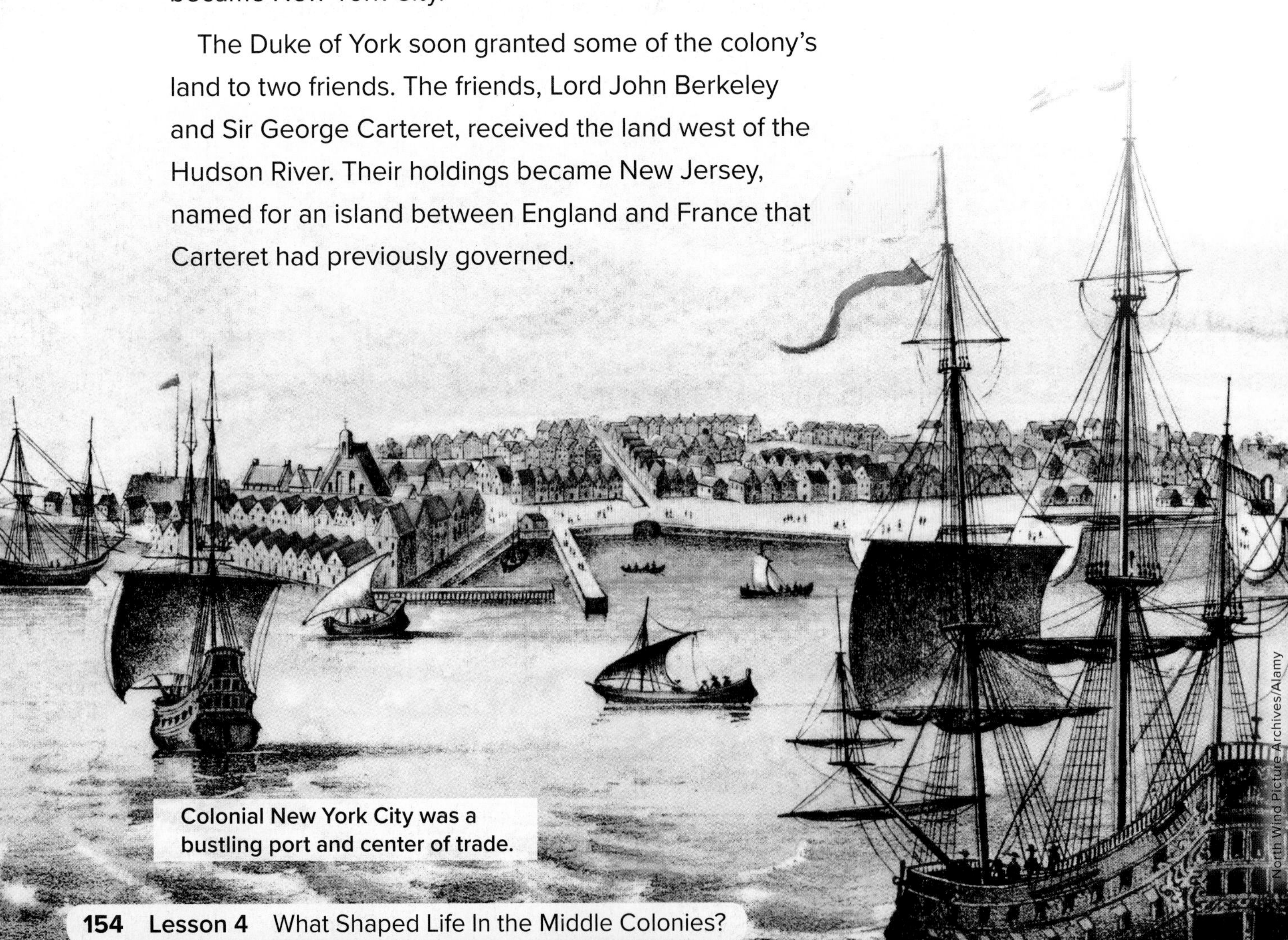

North Wind Picture Archives/Alamy

Colonial New York City was a bustling port and center of trade.

**Dutch governor Peter Stuyvesant (in the yellow sash) surrenders New Netherland to the English.**

Under English rule, the colonists in what had been New Netherland were allowed to live much as before. People continued to speak Dutch, particularly north of New York City. They could continue worshipping in their own churches. Most of those who held land were allowed to keep it. The practice of granting farmland to settlers continued. The English also agreed not to place troops in people's houses without paying for them.

People had come to the colony from all over Europe because the colony was, for the most part, tolerant of religious and ethnic differences. Women, too, had more rights here than elsewhere. They could own property, keep shops, and engage in the fur trade. The Dutch had also been active in the slave trade and brought enslaved Africans to the colony to build the settlements or to help farm the land. Though enslaved people had few rights, under the Dutch they did have a path through which many could become free. Those working directly for the Dutch West India Company could gain what was called "half-freedom," supplying slave labor only at certain times of the year.

One way in which the English differed from the Dutch was in their treatment of enslaved people. This was partly because English authorities feared rebellion from the growing number of enslaved people. They passed a law preventing enslaved people from gathering in groups of more than two. They also made it more difficult for enslaved people to win freedom and much easier to force freed Africans back into slavery.

English authorities also feared criticism, which they said might lead to unrest. In 1733, a colonist named John Peter Zenger printed newspaper articles that strongly criticized the governor of New York. Arrested and put on trial, Zenger was defended by a well-known lawyer named Andrew Hamilton. Hamilton insisted on a trial by jury, which is a group of peers who decide if someone is innocent or guilty. He then argued that newspapers must have the freedom to print material critical of the government. The judge disagreed, but the jury did not, and Zenger was found not guilty. The trial helped establish two important American principles: the right to a trial by jury and freedom of the press.

**PRIMARY SOURCE**

## In Their Words... Andrew Hamilton

**The question before the Court and you, Gentlemen of the jury, is not of small or private concern. It is not the cause of one poor printer, nor of New York alone, which you are now trying. No! . . . It is the cause of liberty.**

—from his Summation at the trial of John Peter Zenger, 1735

## Stop and Check

**Talk** What main characteristics of the Middle Colonies dated back to the Dutch and continued after the colony became English? Discuss your ideas with a partner.

**Find Details** As you read, add additional information to the graphic organizer on page 115 in your Inquiry Journal.

Zenger, John Peter. The Tryal of John Peter Zenger, of New-York, Printer, Who was Lately Try'd and Acquitted for Printing and Publishing a Libel Against the Government : With the Pleadings and Arguments on Both Sides. London: Printed for J. Wilford, 1738.

# Pennsylvania and Delaware

William Penn came from a wealthy English family. His father had even lent the King of England a large sum of money. In 1681, the king repaid the debt by granting land in North America to Penn. The land was called Pennsylvania in his father's honor.

Some years before, Penn had joined the Society of Friends, or Quakers. Some of the members of this Christian group had been jailed and even killed for their beliefs. They believed that each person could have a direct relationship with God. They also thought that all people should be treated fairly. They believed women were equal to men in God's eyes and allowed them to take on roles much larger than those in other religions. Quakers were against war and refused to join the military. In time, they would become strong opponents of slavery.

Penn himself had been jailed more than once for his beliefs. He wanted a place where Quakers and others could worship without fear. He called his colony a "Holy Experiment" to prove that people of many faiths and backgrounds could live together peacefully. Penn explained his plans in his publication *Frame of Government* and made them part of the Charter of Privileges under which the Pennsylvania colony was governed. In addition to freedom of religion and trial by jury, the charter set up an elected **assembly** that could propose and pass laws. However, not all colonists had the right to vote. In addition, a strict moral code limited some personal activities; for example, the performance of plays was banned.

William Penn

When the king gave Penn the land for his colony, a native people called the Lenape were living on it. Penn insisted on paying the Lenape for the land. He believed that Native Americans should be treated justly. His sons, however, did not share those views. After he died in 1737, they used a false document to claim that the colony was entitled to a "Walking Purchase" of more Lenape land—the distance a man could walk in one-and-a-half days. They then hired the fastest runners in the colony to cover twice as much land as the Lenape had thought they would.

When Penn founded Pennsylvania, he planned its main "towne," or capital city. He called it *Philadelphia*, Greek for "city of brotherly love." He located it where the Schuylkill (pronounced SKOOL kil) River and Delaware River meet. This seemed like a good spot for a trading port, since ships could sail down the Delaware into the Atlantic Ocean or northwest on the Schuylkill to the interior part of the colony. Penn had lived through some terrible disasters in London, and so he wanted a city where disease and fire could not spread so easily. He created a grid of wide, tree-lined streets with many small parks and gardens. On them, he planned brick and stone buildings that would not burn.

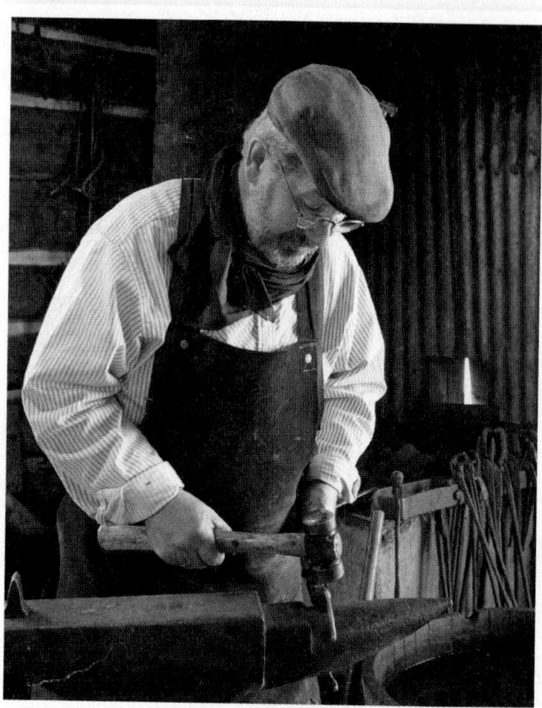

**A man dressed as a colonial-era blacksmith**

People from all over Europe came to Philadelphia. Many came because they could earn a living much more easily than in their native lands. They also appreciated the rights they could enjoy there. As trade grew, the city prospered. People who specialized in different goods and crafts—butchers, bakers, silversmiths, cabinetmakers, and blacksmiths—opened busy shops.

Outside Philadelphia, many immigrants came to farm the land. Among them were German settlers who practiced the Mennonite religion. Some belonged to a strict group of Mennonites called the Amish. These people dressed plainly and lived very simple lives. Their descendants are sometimes called the Pennsylvania Dutch, but that does not mean they are from the Netherlands. It refers to their German background and the language they spoke; *deutsch* (pronounced DOYCH) is the German word for "German."

South of Philadelphia along the Atlantic coast was the area known as Delaware. Swedish traders had come there in 1638 and claimed it as part of their colony of New Sweden. They built a settlement called Fort Christina near what is now the city of Wilmington, Delaware. Insisting that the Swedes took Dutch lands, Peter Stuyvesant had captured New Sweden in 1654 and made it part of New Netherland. Ten years later, it became an English possession along with the rest of New Netherland.

When the English king granted Pennsylvania to William Penn, Penn was worried because the land had no Atlantic coastline. Ships sailing from the port of Philadelphia had to go down the Delaware River to reach the ocean, and the river sometimes froze in winter. Penn asked the Duke of York to sell him the area we now call Delaware, which did have an Atlantic coastline. The Duke agreed. However, the Swedish, Dutch, and Finnish colonists who already lived in the area did not like the idea of being controlled by Pennsylvania. They wanted to make laws for themselves. So in 1702, Penn allowed Delaware to create its own lawmaking assembly.

## Stop and Check

COLLABORATE

**Talk** In what ways did government in Pennsylvania support people's rights and freedoms? In what way did it fail to support them? Discuss your views with a partner.

By the 1700s, Philadelphia had become a busy port and one of the largest cities in the English colonies.

# Life in the Middle Colonies

The English claimed the Middle Colonies, but the people who settled there came from many places besides England. The diversity of backgrounds and religions helped make the Middle Colonies unique. Only a few colonists were wealthy landowners and traders. Many were shopkeepers, craft workers, and small farmers. They worked hard, but there were great opportunities. Farming was difficult, with land to clear and weather to worry about. Yet even small farmers could prosper in the Middle Colonies.

Many endured difficulties hoping for a brighter future. In the cities, young boys often signed up as apprentices, or trainees learning a craft. They had to promise to work for several years with the master training them. To get to America, some people signed indenture agreements. They promised to work as servants for a certain number of years in exchange for having the cost of their trip to America paid. At the end of that period, they usually got a piece of land, a suit of clothes, or a set of tools—and their freedom. Enslaved Africans found it harder and harder to become free. However, the movement to end slavery was growing.

In addition to economic advantages, many people came to the colonies for religious reasons. Some, like Quakers, Jews, and Mennonites, came to the colonies to practice their religion more freely. Others were attracted to new religious movements. In 1739, George Whitefield, an English preacher, returned to the colonies to lead a Protestant movement known as the First Great Awakening, because it awakened strong religious feelings. Traveling through the colonies, Whitefield preached to huge crowds of people from many different backgrounds. He called for better treatment of enslaved Africans, yet he was also in favor of slavery.

George Whitefield's dramatic sermons drew large crowds.

Preachers were not the only public speakers that colonists went to hear. Political speeches were also well attended. And by the 1700s, printers were distributing newspapers that often contained political news—and criticism. *The New York Gazette*, New York's first newspaper, began publication in 1725. It was put out by a master printer that William Penn originally brought to Pennsylvania to print religious materials.

**Colonists attending a political discussion**

Words were central to the life of Philadelphia's most famous resident, Benjamin Franklin. Franklin opened his Philadelphia print shop in 1728. He married a woman who ran a bookshop. In 1731, he helped found America's first library. A year later, he began publishing *Poor Richard's Almanack*, a magazine famous for its proverbs, or wise sayings—such as "There are no gains without pains" and "Well done is better than well said." Franklin also wrote many other works, including his autobiography.

## Did You Know?

Ben Franklin was also a scientist and an inventor. You may have heard about his experiment with a kite in a lightning storm, which helped us understand how electricity works. Franklin was also the first person to use the terms "battery," "conductor," "positive charge," and "negative charge."

**Connect to Science** Do Internet research to find out one thing that Benjamin Franklin invented.

## Stop and Check

COLLABORATE

**Talk** What do the details about Benjamin Franklin show about life in the Middle Colonies? Discuss your ideas with a classmate.

TEXT: Franklin, Bejamin. Poor Richard's Almanack. Philadelphia: self-published at the New York Printing Office, 1732-1758.; PHOTO: (t)McGraw-Hill Education, (c, b)North Wind Picture Archives/Alamy

InfoGraphic

# The Triangular Trade and Slavery

## England, Africa, and the Americas

*Triangular trade* is the term used to describe the trade routes between England, Africa, and the Americas during the 1700s. Shipowners wanted their ships to carry cargo on every voyage so that they could cover the costs of travel. The triangular trade was designed for traders to sell products and pick up cargo at each stop. In the first stage, ships from England left bound for West Africa. The ships carried goods, such as guns, cloth, ironware, and rum, all made in England. Upon reaching the African coast, these goods were traded for African men, women, and children kidnapped by slave traders or purchased from African chiefs.

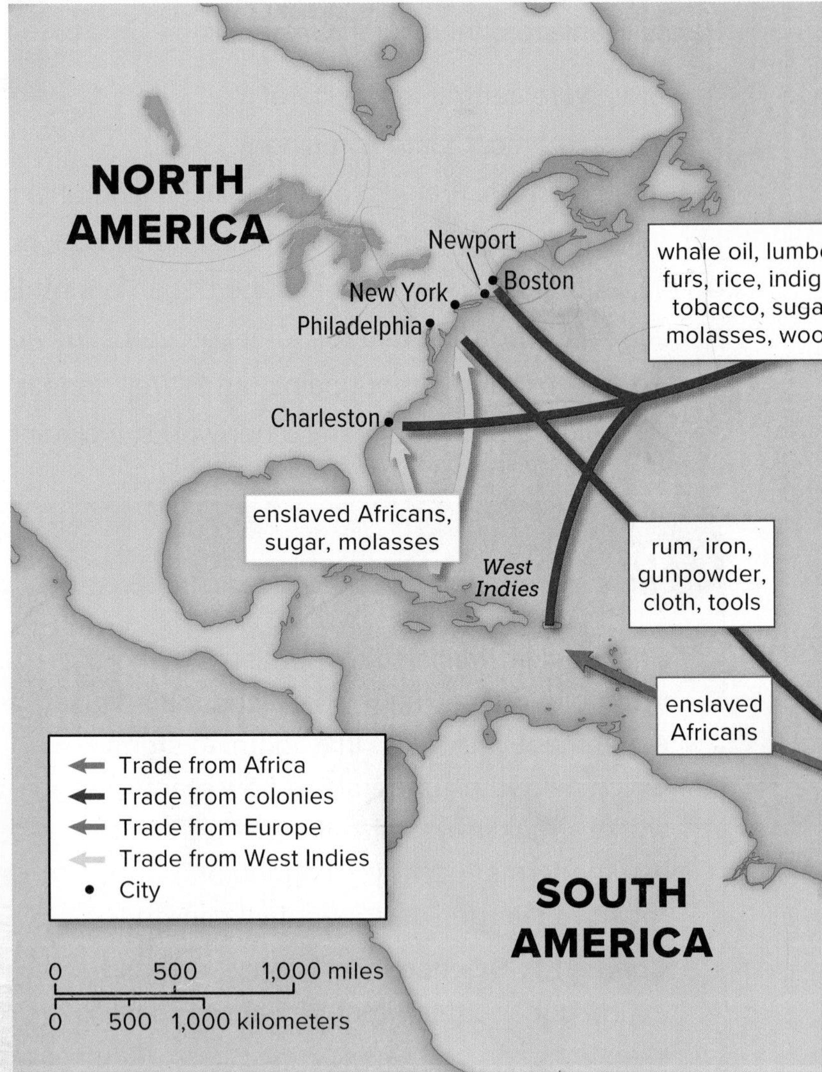


(bkgd spread) McGraw-Hill Education/Jill Braaten

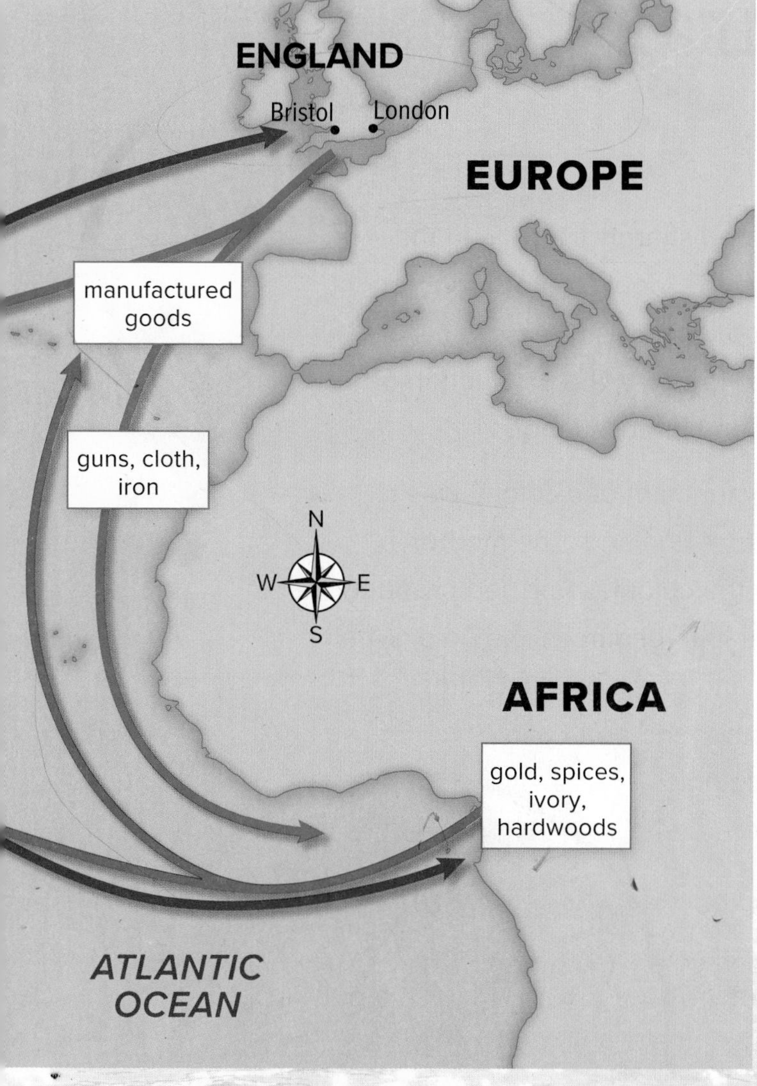


In the second stage, European traders bought enslaved Africans. Family members were separated. Traders held enslaved people until a ship appeared. Traders then sold the enslaved people to a European captain. The captain went through the long process of filling the ship.

When the ship was filled, the "Middle Passage"—the journey to the Caribbean Islands or North America—began. The journey was horrific. Many Africans died. Some committed suicide.

Many of the enslaved people were taken to the Americas and sold at auctions to the highest bidder. Others were taken to Europe. In the third stage, traders used money from the sale of enslaved people to buy sugar, cotton, and tobacco, which were shipped back to England for sale.

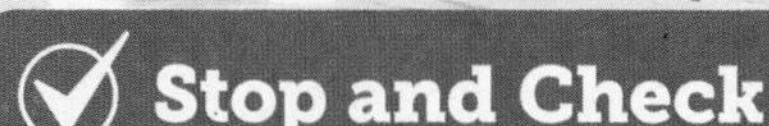

## Stop and Check

COLLABORATE

**Talk** Why do you think people called the journey from Africa to the Americas the "Middle Passage"?

Lesson 5

# How Did Economics Impact People in the Southern Colonies?

## An Agricultural Economy

Life in the rural southern colonies differed sharply from life in the colonies to the north. The South provided the ideal **environment** for crops like rice, cotton, tobacco, and indigo. This was due to its rich soil, high humidity, and long growing season. However, the production of these crops required large areas of land and intense labor.

During the colonial period, the primary function of a colony was to produce raw goods for the mother country—England. The mother country would then, in turn, ship back to the colonies finished products. The original thirteen colonies lacked valuable resources like gold. What they could offer were agricultural goods and forest products. For northern colonies, this initially meant lumber and non-cash crops, such as wheat. For the southern colonies, it meant cash crops like tobacco and rice.

As the colonies grew, the demand for domestic goods grew faster than Britain could keep up with. In response, the northern colonies began producing more valuable finished goods such as furniture, iron, and ships. Meanwhile, Southerners became more adept at producing cash crops. In time, finding the labor needed to produce crops like rice and tobacco became a difficult problem for the southern colonies.

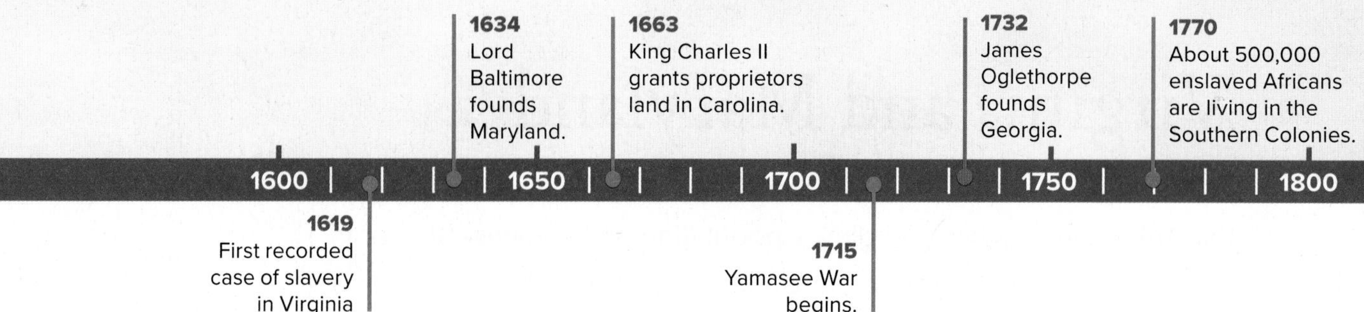

1600
1619
First recorded case of slavery in Virginia

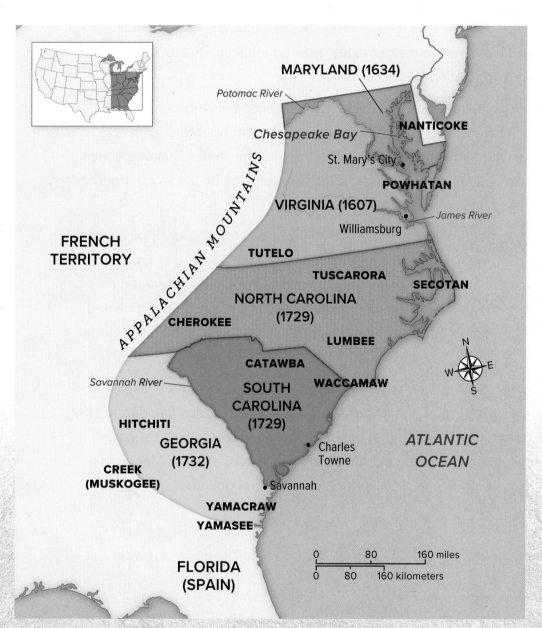


James Oglethorpe founds Georgia.
1750
1770
About 500,000 enslaved Africans are living in the Southern Colonies.
1800

MARYLAND (1634)
Potomac River
Chesapeake Bay
NANTICOKE
St. Mary's City
POWHATAN
VIRGINIA (1607)
James River
Williamsburg
FRENCH TERRITORY
APPALACHIAN MOUNTAINS
TUTELO
TUSCARORA
SECOTAN
NORTH CAROLINA (1729)
CHEROKEE
LUMBEE
CATAWBA
Savannah River
SOUTH CAROLINA (1729)
WACCAMAW
HITCHITI
GEORGIA (1732)
CREEK (MUSKOGEE)
Charles Towne
ATLANTIC OCEAN
Savannah
YAMACRAW
YAMASEE
FLORIDA (SPAIN)
0 80 160 miles
0 80 160 kilometers
N E S W

Lord Baltimore founds Maryland.
1650
1663
King Charles II grants proprietors land in Carolina.
1700
1715
Yamasee War begins.

Colonists in the Southern Colonies lived alongside many Native American peoples.

# Virginia and Maryland

Starting with the Jamestown settlement, Virginia was the first colony in the American South. As Virginia's population grew, new settlements appeared west and north of the James River. This rich land was called the Tidewater. The Tidewater, a 75-mile-wide strip of Virginia's coast, often flooded. Despite the presence of salt water, the land is fertile. Settlers were able to make money growing tobacco. By 1700, the colony's population was 70,000.

In Virginia, the Church of England, also called the Anglican Church, was the established church of the colony. An established church is the official church of a nation or state. In Virginia, this meant that everyone had to pay a tax to the Anglican Church, even if he or she worshipped in another church.

In contrast to Virginia, Maryland was founded for religious reasons. In 1632, George Calvert, Lord Baltimore of England, decided to create a community especially for Roman Catholics. King Charles I granted Calvert land north of Virginia on which to start a colony. Calvert named the new colony "Maryland" in honor of the king's wife, Queen Henrietta Maria.

George Calvert died before he could visit the colony. As a result, his son Cecilius became the second Lord Baltimore. Cecilius decided to stay in England to make sure that the king continued to support a separate colony of Maryland. He sent his brother Leonard Calvert to Maryland in his place. Lord Leonard Calvert became the first governor of Maryland.

**A tobacco field**

In 1634, Leonard Calvert, along with about 300 colonists, arrived at St. Clement's Island in Maryland. Calvert bought a village from the Yoacomoco, a group of Native Americans. The village became known as St. Mary's City. Calvert promised to trade fairly with the Yoacomoco and to protect them from their enemies.

On the land that the Yoacomoco cleared, the Maryland colonists and enslaved persons planted corn and tobacco. As the colony grew, Maryland colonists, like those in Virginia, discovered the profitability of selling tobacco to England. By the late 1600s, plantations—large farms that grow one crop—lined many of the creeks and rivers of Maryland. Chesapeake Bay had a harbor that was deep enough for large ships to use. This made it easy to transport goods to other colonies and to England.

Most of the settlers who came to Maryland from England were Catholic. Many of Maryland's other settlers, however, came from Virginia and were members of the Church of England. Soon, Anglicans in Maryland outnumbered the Catholics. This meant that Catholics might have faced persecution. Fortunately, Maryland's charter—the Maryland Toleration Act, passed in 1649—protected them. This protection did not extend to Jews or to all Christians, but it was a significant stepping stone toward religious freedom in the colonies.

George Calvert, Lord Baltimore

## Stop and Check

COLLABORATE

**Talk** Why did the people of Virginia and Maryland grow tobacco?

**Find Details** As you read add additional information to the graphic organizer on page 123 in your Inquiry Journal.

# The Carolinas and Georgia

England kept adding to its North American colonies. The new king, Charles II, set his sights on land south of Virginia. In 1663, he gave a charter to eight **proprietors**. Seven years later, they founded their first settlement, the port city of Charles Towne.

From the beginning, Carolina had two regions. In the southern part, Charles Towne's natural harbor, warm climate, and natural resources made it a center for agriculture and trade. The southern part of Carolina also had large areas of low, marshy land—ideal for growing rice. Wealthy colonists built plantations outside the city. There they grew tobacco, rice, and indigo—a plant used to make blue dye.

Colonists who settled in northern Carolina grew tobacco and sold forest products, such as timber and tar. The economy in northern Carolina grew slowly due primarily to the lack of a good harbor, which made trade difficult. By 1729, the differences between colonial life in the north and in the south resulted in the colony's splitting into North Carolina and South Carolina.

For years, the Tuscarora had lived in northern Carolina's Coastal Plain. They were an agricultural people, related to the Iroquois. The colonists had a habit of cheating the Tuscarora in trade deals and moving in on their land. Tensions erupted in 1711 when Chief Hancock, a Tuscarora leader, killed a local surveyor. A surveyor is someone who determines land boundaries. The chief believed the surveyor had stolen Tuscarora land when he measured boundaries. The Tuscarora then attacked settlements in the disputed area, named New Bern, killing more than 130 people. The colony's government sent troops to attack the Tuscarora and forced them to surrender in 1713. Similarly, conflicts arose with the Yamasee, a group that had once been an ally to South Carolina. The Yamasee claimed the colonists owed them money. With a large army, the Yamasee attacked colonists in 1716. With help from the Cherokee, however, the colonists eventually defeated the Yamasee in 1717.

A rice field

Georgia, the last of the thirteen colonies created by the British, was founded in 1732. James Oglethorpe, a respected British general and member of the English Parliament, planned to use Georgia as a home for debtors. In England, debtors (people who owe money they can't repay) were sent to prison, often with their entire families. Oglethorpe thought that instead of wasting away in prison, debtors would be better off trying to make a fresh start for themselves as colonists.

James Oglethorpe

But it was Oglethorpe's military experience, rather than his plan for dealing with debtors, that most interested King George II. The King worried about an invasion of South Carolina by the Spaniards from Florida or by the French from Louisiana. When Oglethorpe suggested that the new colony could help protect South Carolina, the King listened and granted Oglethorpe his charter. In November of 1732, a group of 114 men, women, and children left London bound for the newest English colony in America. It was called Georgia after King George II.

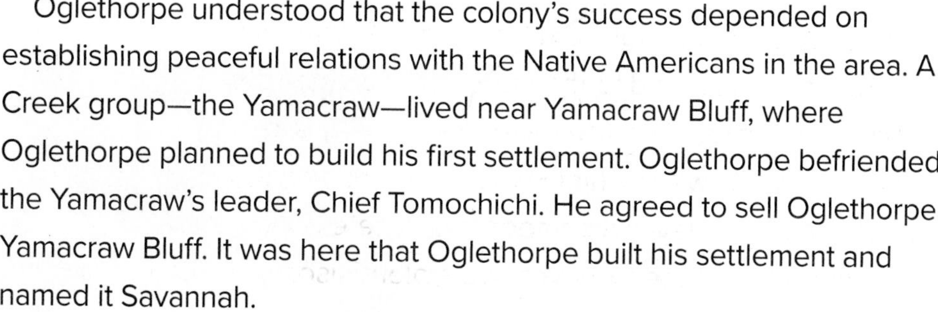

Oglethorpe understood that the colony's success depended on establishing peaceful relations with the Native Americans in the area. A Creek group—the Yamacraw—lived near Yamacraw Bluff, where Oglethorpe planned to build his first settlement. Oglethorpe befriended the Yamacraw's leader, Chief Tomochichi. He agreed to sell Oglethorpe Yamacraw Bluff. It was here that Oglethorpe built his settlement and named it Savannah.

Initially, Georgia's growth was slow. Oglethorpe's plan to settle Georgia with English debtors failed because few debtors took up the offer. In the beginning, colonists grew corn and tobacco. Later, rice and indigo became important crops.

## Stop and Check

**Write** How did land features affect the economies and populations of North and South Carolina?

**Find Details** As you read, add additional information to the graphic organizer on page 123 in your Inquiry Journal.

# Life in the Southern Colonies

Most Southern colonists lived on small farms with their families. Southern colonists who had once been indentured servants often ended up owning smaller farms. Every family member worked to keep the farm running. Religion was an important part of colonists' lives. Because colonists spent most of their time working, they often combined work with play. An entire community, for example, would get together to build houses for newly married people. Colonists held plowing and corn-husking competitions. At quilting bees, neighbors sewed together pieces of cloth to make a bedspread. When they were not helping their parents, children played with simple toys, such as balls, dolls, marbles, kites, and jump ropes. In the evening, families often read books aloud, played music, or sang together.

Those who owned plantations, especially large plantations, lived a wealthy lifestyle. They mainly used enslaved Africans along with some hired workers to keep the plantation running. Large plantation owners had great influence on government. Their view that the economy of the South would suffer without enslaved people was widely accepted in the region.

Large plantations were like small villages. Plantations often had a mill, a blacksmith, and a carpenter's shop. The planter's family lived in the center of the plantation, in a section called "the big house." Most plantations of the 1700s, however, were much smaller than the one shown in the picture, with the average planter owning about 20 enslaved people. Male family members helped the planter manage the land and crops. The women helped manage the household. Most children on plantations were educated at home.

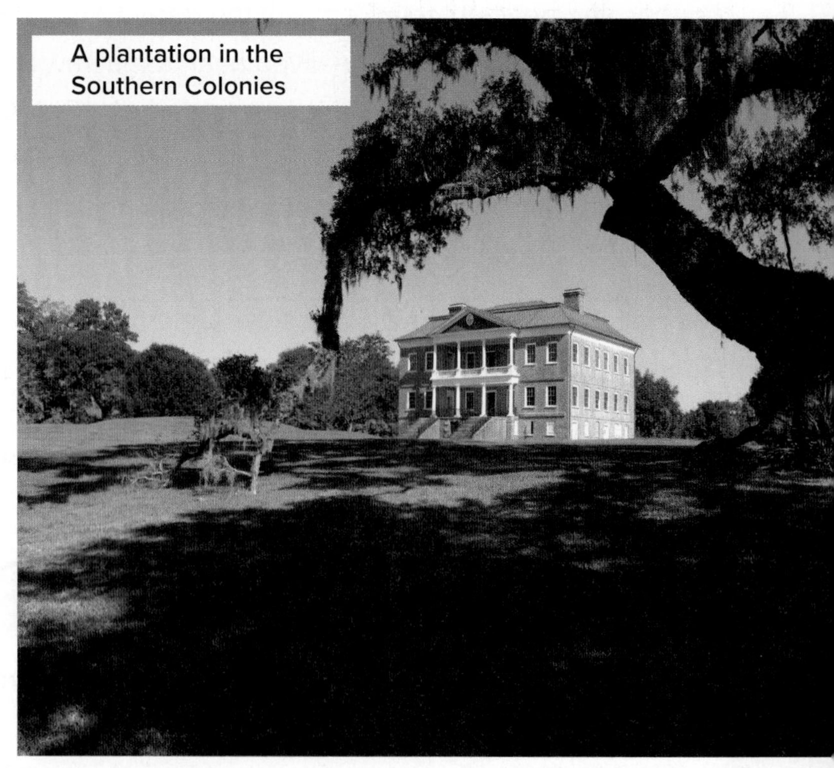
A plantation in the Southern Colonies

By 1750, enslaved people had been living in the Southern Colonies for more than a hundred years. Although many enslaved people worked on small farms, most worked on large plantations.

In contrast to plantation owners, enslaved people lived in small, poorly made cabins near the crop fields. The work on plantations started at sunrise and ended at sundown. The overseer was the man hired by the plantation owner to oversee, or manage, work in the fields. The overseer told enslaved people what to do. The overseer also harshly punished people.

Cabin for enslaved people

Enslaved people on Southern tobacco plantations did the backbreaking work of planting tobacco, caring for it, and then harvesting it. In South Carolina, enslaved people often had to move tons of dirt to build rice fields and irrigation canals. To help overcome the harshness of their lives, enslaved people often turned to family. On Sundays, usually the only day of the week they did not work, some enslaved parents could visit their children who had been sold away from them. However, this was only if the children lived on neighboring plantations. When families were together, they told stories and sang songs that mainly taught about values and beliefs. The stories about Africa gave children a sense of a different past. Sadly, these enslaved families were not officially recognized under the law.

Not all African Americans in the Southern Colonies were enslaved. About five percent were free. Some had been freed, while others had escaped. Some bought their freedom by working paid jobs. Free African Americans lived in cities and towns. They also lived in the backcountry—the eastern foothills of the Appalachian Mountains. There, many lived in friendship with local Native Americans.

## Stop and Check

COLLABORATE

**Talk** How did the economy of the Southern Colonies affect the lives of the various people living there?

**Find Details** As you read, add additional information to the graphic organizer on page 123 in your Inquiry Journal.

# An Inhumane System

The type of work assigned to enslaved people depended on the economy of the colony in which they lived. In the North, many of the enslaved people worked in New England's busy shipyards. In Rhode Island and New York, enslaved people did farm work. It was rare for a Northerner to own more than one enslaved person. Northern farms were small, and it was not profitable to use large numbers of enslaved people there.

Southern farms, on the other hand, were often huge and grew cash crops. The major cash crop of the Southern Colonies in the 1600s was tobacco. Both rice and tobacco required many workers to plant, tend, and harvest the crop. Most Southern plantations had about 20 enslaved people. South Carolina was unusual. By 1720, enslaved people made up more than half of the population of the colony.

**An auction block for enslaved people**

Education Images/Universal Images Group/Getty Images

The possibility of enslaved people rebelling was a constant fear for colonial leaders. Leaders in states with large enslaved populations were especially concerned. In part to ease those worries, colonies and later states wrote laws defining the status of enslaved people and the rights of their owners. These laws were called slave codes. The purpose of the slave codes was to place harsh restrictions on enslaved people and give owners absolute power over them. The slave codes varied from colony to colony. Most prevented the enslaved people from learning to read and write. Most states also prevented them from leaving the plantation without permission, testifying in court, or gathering together without a white person being present.

Enslaved people had been kidnapped, forced to work, separated from their families, and punished harshly. They resisted their situation by slowing their work, running away, and on occasion rebelling violently.

Despite the hardships they suffered through, enslaved people managed to build a culture. They orally passed down African traditions, introduced African words into the English language, and told stories to their children to teach them about life. They also created many work songs and spirituals that are still sung to this day.

## PRIMARY SOURCE

## In Their Words... Enslaved Africans

Enslaved people working in the fields often sang work songs to relieve their boredom and to take their minds off their exhaustion. These songs sometimes had a "call and response" structure, in which one person sang a verse and the others responded with a chorus. Many lyrics featured Christian themes and dialect, or language that is specific to a region or group of people. The songs often focused on the peace and relief that a person could find in the afterlife.

### Here are lyrics for two songs sung by enslaved people in the South:

**I Don't Feel Weary**

*Chorus*

I don't feel weary and noways tired,
O glory hallelujah

*Verses*

Just let me in the kingdom
While the world is all on fire
O glory hallelujah

Going to live with God forever
While the world is all on fire
O glory hallelujah

And keep the ark a-moving
While the world is all on fire
O glory hallelujah

**In the Mansions Above**

*Chorus*

Good Lord, in the mansions above,
Good Lord, in the mansions above,
My Lord, I hope to meet my Jesus
In the mansions above.

*Verses*

If you get to heaven before I do,
tell my Jesus I'm a-comin' too,
To the mansions above.

My Lord, I've had many trials here below;
My Lord, I hope to meet you
In the mansions above.

Fight on, my brother, for the mansions above,
For I hope to meet my Jesus there
In the mansions above.

TEXT: Slave Songs of the United States, compiled by William Francis Allen, Charles Pickard Ware, and Lucy McKim Garrison, 59. New York: A. Simpson & Company, 1867.; PHOTO: McGraw-Hill Education

### Stop and Check

**Write** How did the colony where enslaved people lived affect the kind of work they had to do?

**Find Details** As you read, add additional information to the graphic organizer on page 123 in your Inquiry Journal.

# Life in Africa Before the 16th Century

Long before the slave trade, western Africa was home to a variety of cultures and contained communities both big and small. There were great empires, such as Ghana, Mali, and Songhai. Gold from Mali helped Europe's economy grow in the 13th and 14th centuries A.D. and was a major reason why European explorers would later travel to the region. However, much of western Africa did not have major states ruled by monarchs.

Many peoples, such as the Igbo and Yoruba, had smaller and more democratic societies. Igbo and Yoruba often lived in compounds made up of extended family. A larger village or town might develop from a cluster of family compounds. Towns were more frequent in Yoruba society. Often, a community would be governed by a council of elders or an elected chief. Kinship, or family ties, also impacted who was chosen to lead. In many traditional communities, an important religious practice was communicating with ancestors who had the power to speak to the gods. These ancestors provided access to spiritual guidance and power.

The people in these societies focused on farming, herding animals, and exchanging goods in nearby markets. Among the Yoruba people, men would be responsible for farming while women would sell goods in the marketplace. The Yoruba were also skilled artisans. Their art included ivory and wood carvings, leatherwork, and casts of heads and masks made from molten metal.

Mediterranean Sea
Red Sea
ATLANTIC OCEAN
INDIAN OCEAN
N
W
E
S
Northern Africa
Western Africa
Central Africa
Eastern Africa
Southern Africa
0 1,000 2,000 miles
0 1,000 2,000 kilometers

**The United Nations has identified five major subregions of the African continent.**

**This Yoruba artifact was created by pouring molten copper into a mold.**

Some of the continent's oldest and greatest empires emerged in western Africa. During a period of economic decline in Europe, a long line of kings ruled over the kingdom of Ghana. Ghana's economy depended on trading its gold to the Berber people for salt. Around the 8th century A.D., the growth of Muslim trade networks brought wealth and Islamic influence to the region. Many people converted from traditional African faiths to Islam. In the 13th century, a leader named Sundiata Keita founded the kingdom of Mali. The kingdom would eventually grow to include the powerful trading centers of Gao and Timbuktu. The last major empire in the region was the Songhai kingdom, although there were other smaller kingdoms over the centuries.

**The Great Mosque of Djenné in Mali is an earthen monument originally constructed in the 13th or 14th century.**

People from these kingdoms produced unique art and architecture and founded one of the world's greatest centers of learning, Timbuktu. Many buildings in the region were constructed from sun-dried mud bricks and clay. The Great Mosque in Djenné, Mali, is the largest free-standing earthen building in the world. Many buildings in Timbuktu were made in the same manner and have been given special protections by world organizations in order to preserve them for future generations.

During the Middle Ages, people traveled from all over the world to trade and learn in the city of Timbuktu. At the time, one quarter of the city's 100,000 inhabitants were scholars. Many of these scholars studied at the University of Sankore, one of the world's earliest universities. The subjects studied there included law, mathematics, astronomy, medicine, and Islamic theology. People have worked to preserve the academic texts from the city's past. However, thousands of texts were destroyed as a result of war from 2012 to 2013.

## Stop and Check

**Think** Compare what someone's life might be like if he or she lived in Timbuktu versus in an Igbo compound. How might that person make a living in each location?

# Map and Globe Skills

## The Thirteen Colonies: Then and Now

The United States has steadily grown in population since the Constitution was ratified in 1788. Historians estimate that around four million people lived in the United States in 1790. In 2015, the nation had a population over 320 million. The maps in this section will allow you to investigate some of the changes that have occurred in the two centuries since the writing of the Constitution.

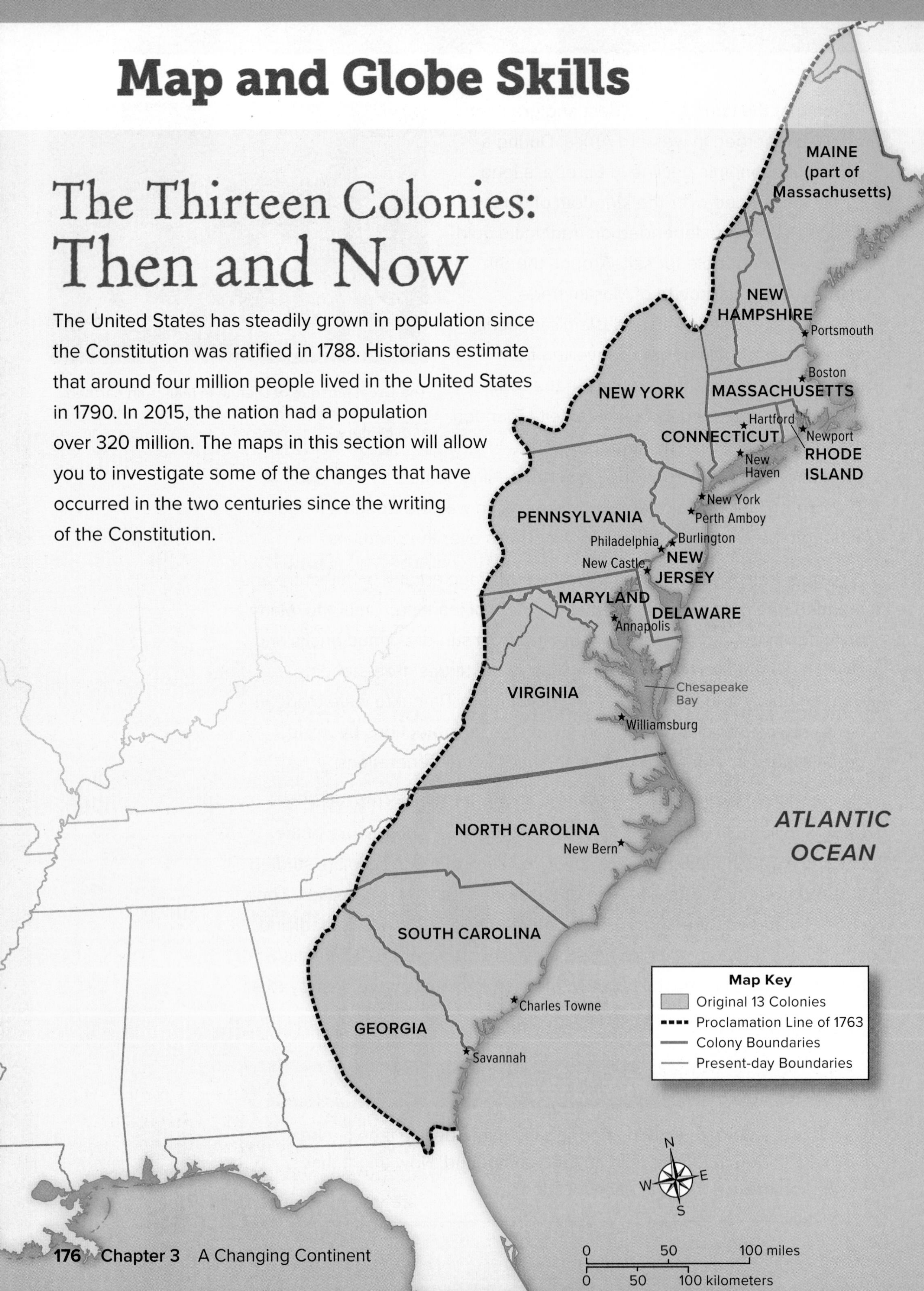

## Connecticut
**1790 Population:** 237,946
**2015 Population:** 3,590,886
★ **Capital:** Hartford

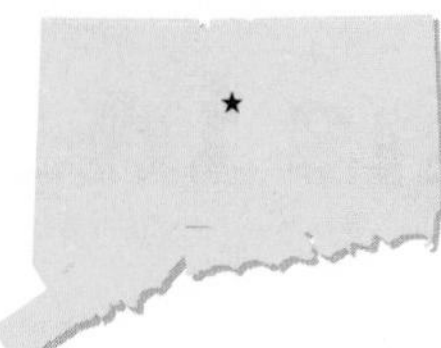

## Delaware
**1790 Population:** 59,096
**2015 Population:** 945,934
★ **Capital:** Dover

## Georgia
**1790 Population:** 82,548
**2015 Population:** 10,214,860
★ **Capital:** Atlanta

## Maryland
1790 Population: 319,728
2015 Population: 6,006,401
★ **Capital:** Annapolis

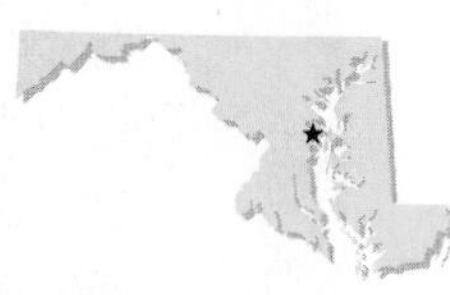

## Massachusetts
1790 Population: 378,787
2015 Population: 6,794,422
★ **Capital:** Boston

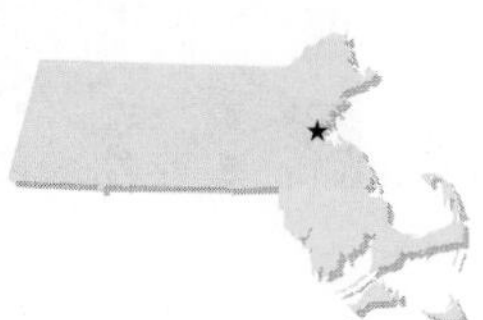

## New Hampshire
1790 Population: 141,885
2015 Population: 1,330,608
★ **Capital:** Concord

## New Jersey
1790 Population: 184,139
2015 Population: 8,958,013
★ **Capital:** Trenton

## New York
1790 Population: 340,120
2015 Population: 19,795,791
★ **Capital:** Albany

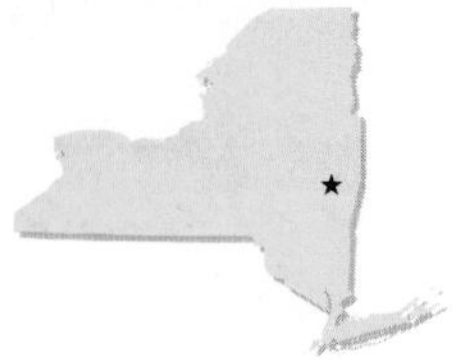

## North Carolina
1790 Population: 393,751
2015 Population: 10,042,802
★ **Capital:** Raleigh

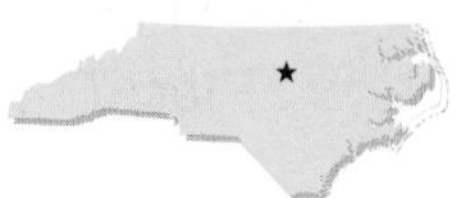

## Pennsylvania
1790 Population: 434,373
2015 Population: 12,802,503
★ **Capital:** Harrisburg

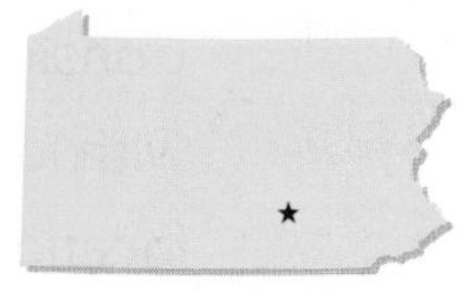

## Rhode Island
1790 Population: 68,825
2015 Population: 1,056,298
★ **Capital:** Providence

## South Carolina
1790 Population: 249,073
2015 Population: 4,896,146
★ **Capital:** Columbia

## Virginia
1790 Population: 747,610
2015 Population: 8,382,993
★ **Capital:** Richmond

### Stop and Check

**Think** Using the Thirteen Colonies map and the information for each state, note which states have different capitals than they had in 1788. What reasons might a state have for moving its capital?

# Connections in Action!

## Back to the EQ

**Think** about the Chapter EQ, **"What Is the Impact of People Settling in a New Place?"**

- **Talk** with a partner about what you learned in the chapter. Choose two settlements to compare and contrast. Consider each settlement's relations with local Native Americans, its location, its economy, and its form of government.
- Which settlement was more successful and in what ways? What do you think led to its success?
- **Share** your ideas with the class. Then have a discussion about the different types of settlements and governments in early America.

# More to Explore

## How Can You Make an IMPACT?

### Compare and Contrast

Work as a group to organize your notes about each early North American settlement. To help you discuss the settlements, fill in a five-column chart with the headings Origin, Parent Country, Relations with Native Americans, Successes, and Failures.

### Write an Encyclopedia Entry

Use your research to write an encyclopedia entry about one early North American settlement. Include the story of its founding, information about its relations with local Native Americans, and facts and statistics about its population, economy, location, and so on.

### Word Play

Using the words from the chapter Word Bank, create lists of synonyms, or words that have the same or nearly the same meaning. For example, synonyms for *assembly* may include *council* and *congregation*. Keep your list handy and add to it as you read the next chapters.

THE IMPACT TODAY

# Why Is the Western Hemisphere So Diverse?

## Cultures and Languages of the Americas

The languages of North and South America are closely related to those of the early explorers and settlers. People in most of Latin America and the Caribbean speak Spanish because of the Spanish conquistadors. People in Brazil speak Portuguese because Portugal held Brazil as a colony until it became independent.

Canada's official languages are English and French. Canada is part of the Commonwealth, a collection of nations that were once part of the British Empire. People in the province of Quebec speak French because the region was settled by French fur trappers. Most of the people in the United States speak English, though the nation has no official language. Spanish is common as well. According to the U.S. Census Bureau, over 350 languages are spoken in the United States today, reflecting the influences of explorers, Native Americans, enslaved Africans, and immigrants.

Although most of the people in the Americas speak a European language, they often do not speak it the same way. The many accents of American English are distinct from those used in the United Kingdom. French speakers from Quebec, Louisiana, and Paris might not understand some of one another's words. The dialects of Spanish in Latin America are unique from those in Spain.

### WHAT IS THE IMPACT TODAY?

**Talk** An ever-more-connected world and our diverse society make having the ability to speak more than one language a useful skill. Talk to your classmates to see what languages can be spoken in your class. Are there any languages you would like to learn in the future? Why?

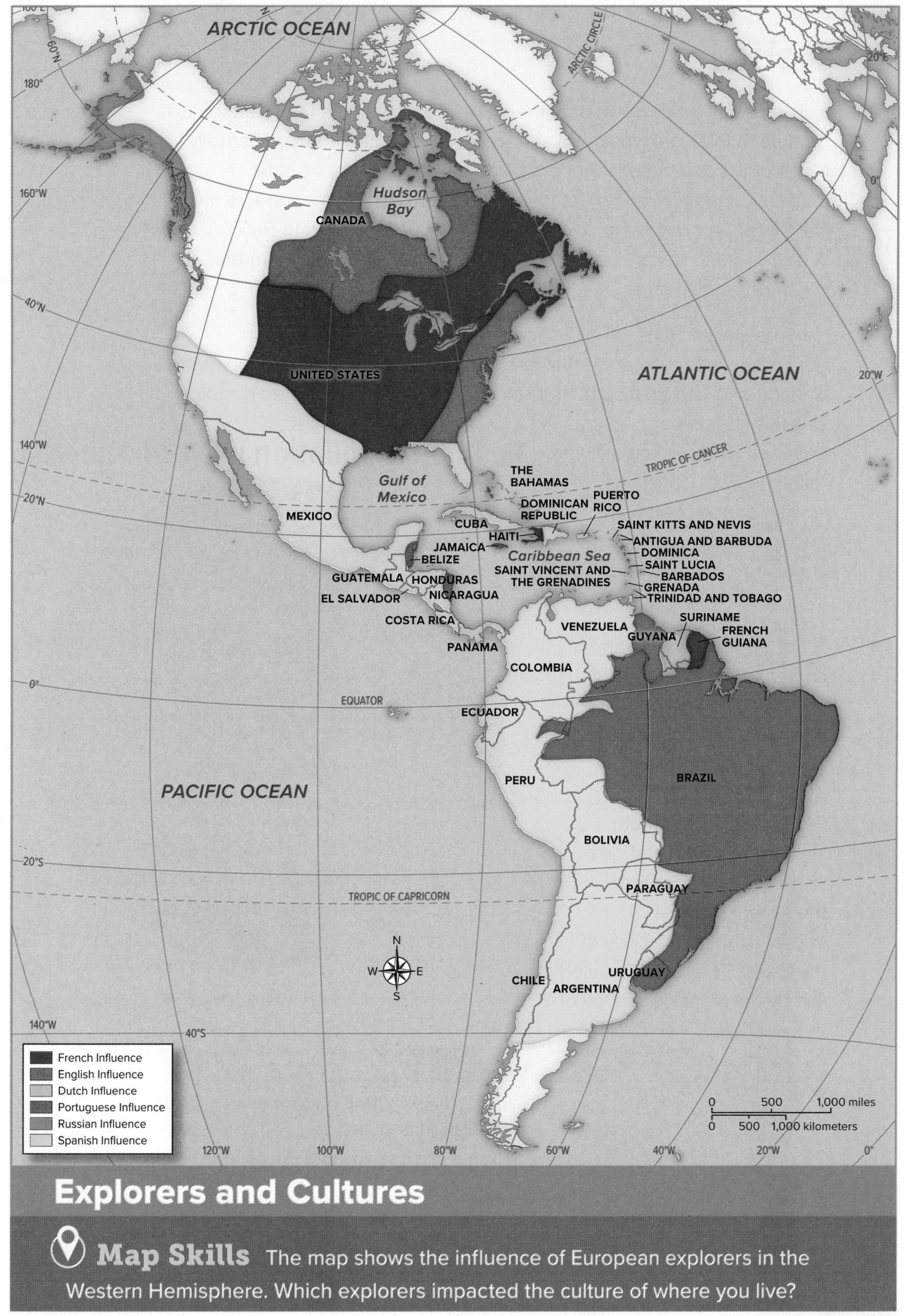


## Explorers and Cultures

**Map Skills** The map shows the influence of European explorers in the Western Hemisphere. Which explorers impacted the culture of where you live?

# Religion

Europeans brought not only their languages but also their religions. Spain and Portugal were, and still are, predominately Roman Catholic. Much of the Americas is therefore Roman Catholic. As of 2010, 39 percent of the world's Catholics come from Latin America and the Caribbean. Among them is Pope Francis I, who was born in Buenos Aires, Argentina, and became pope in 2013. He is the first pope from the Western Hemisphere.

In the United States, the First Amendment of the Constitution guarantees citizens freedom to choose any religion or no religion at all. Canada and Mexico also guarantee religious freedom to their people. Diversity exists both between religions and within religions, with Christians, Jewish people, Muslims, and people of other faiths choosing different ways to practice their faiths.

Often, when a religion comes to a new people, it will pick up some of their traditions and adapt them. The Catholic holidays of All Saints' Day and All Souls' Day, for example, incorporated celebrations that originally honored the Aztec goddess Mictecacihuatl, the Lady of the Dead. The result is called Día de los Muertos, or Day of the Dead. Mexican families honor the memories of deceased family members in this celebration.

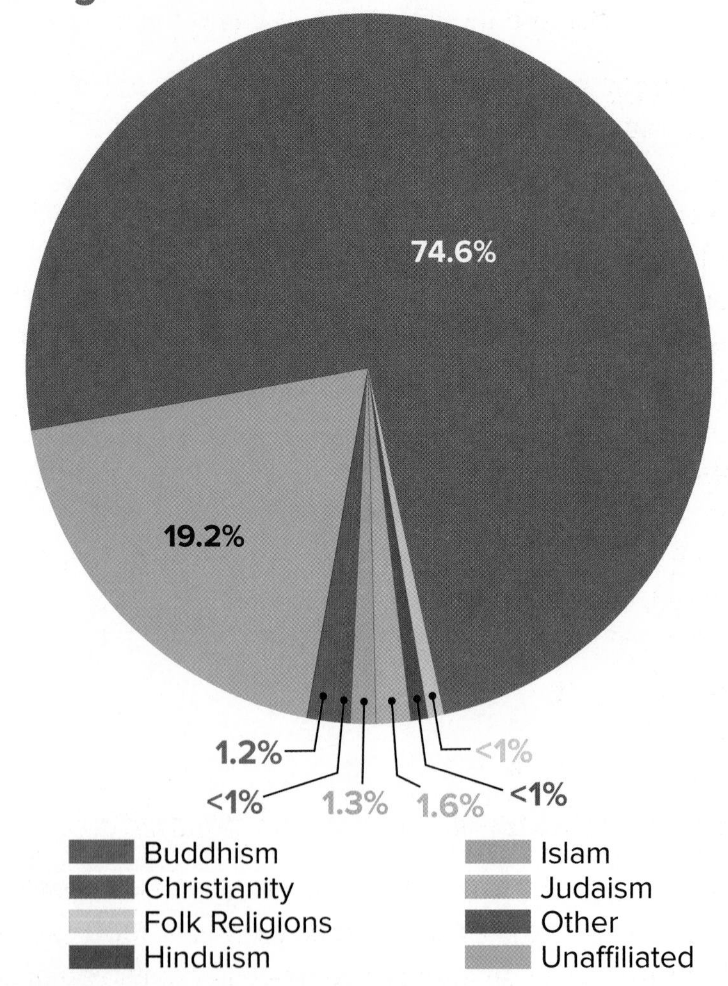

Religious Composition of North America

# Other Cultural Contributions

Culture extends beyond language and religion to foods, music, art, traditions, holidays, and other expressions of different peoples that make them unique. These expressions of culture often have both roots in the past and wide branches into many different types of communities today.

For example, the cooking technique we call barbeque originated with the Taíno people of the Caribbean before the age of explorers. The Taíno people called the wooden structure they used to smoke meat "barbacoa." Spanish conquistadors brought barbacoa to the mainland, where it took hold with populations both indigenous and colonial. English colonists introduced the idea of adding sauces. Today, we enjoy many types of barbeque as it has been adapted in different regions of our country and world.

Along with the barbecue, people may eat potato salad, which was invented in Germany after the Spanish introduced Europe to South American potatoes. Perhaps corn, originally cultivated by Native Americans, will also be served. No party would be complete without music, with many popular modern music forms influenced by jazz and blues, styles created by African Americans using a mixture of African and European elements. As night falls, families might gather to watch fireworks, invented by the Chinese. To exercise the next day, someone might practice Indian yoga or Afro-Brazilian capoeira. Indeed, almost every aspect of daily life is a fusion of multiple cultures.

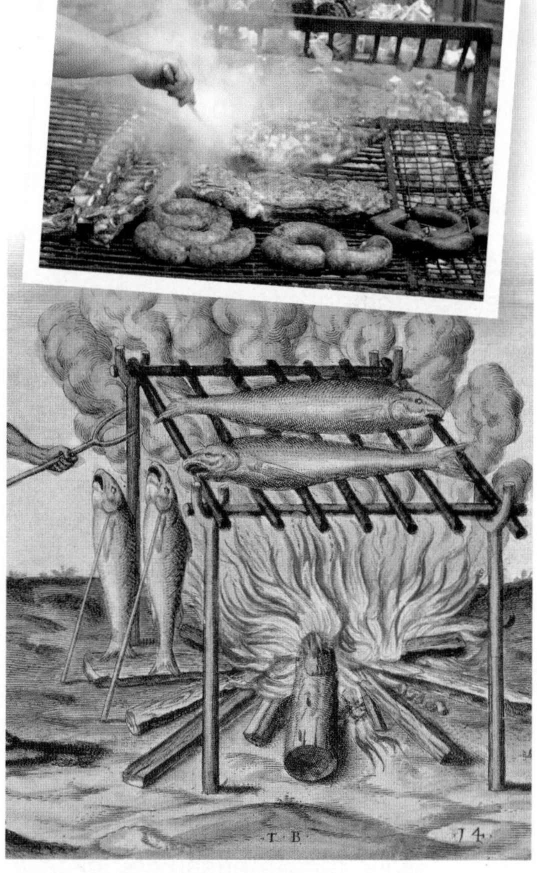


Depiction of Taíno Barbacoa

## WHAT IS THE IMPACT TODAY?

COLLABORATE

**Discuss** Think of habits, traditions, arts, foods, or other products of culture that come from diversity and combining of cultures.

How would your life be different if that cultural product did not exist? What enjoyable activities might you no longer be able to do?

(t)McGraw-Hill Education, (c)Shutterstock/rocharibeiro, (b)DEA/G. DAGLI ORTI/De Agostini/Getty Images

# The Road to War

## Why Would a Nation Want to Become Independent?

In this chapter, you'll read about the conflicts that arose between the American colonies and Great Britain. You'll learn about how colonists were divided between wanting independence and wanting reconciliation with Great Britain, and you'll discover what ultimately led them down the road to war.

## **Step into the Time** Chronological Thinking

Look at the time line. What was happening in other parts of the world while the American colonists were beginning to rebel against British rule?

**Americas**

**1754** The French and Indian War begins.

**1763** Treaty of Paris ends the French and Indian War.

**1763** Proclamation of 1763 sets aside land west of the Appalachians for Native Americans.

1730 — 1740 — 1750 — 1760

**World Events**

**1735** Qianlong becomes emperor of China.

**1736** Safavid Empire ends in Persia (modern-day Iran).

**1740–1741** Cold weather and poor harvests kill more than a third of the population in Ireland.

**1760** George III becomes ruler of Great Britain.

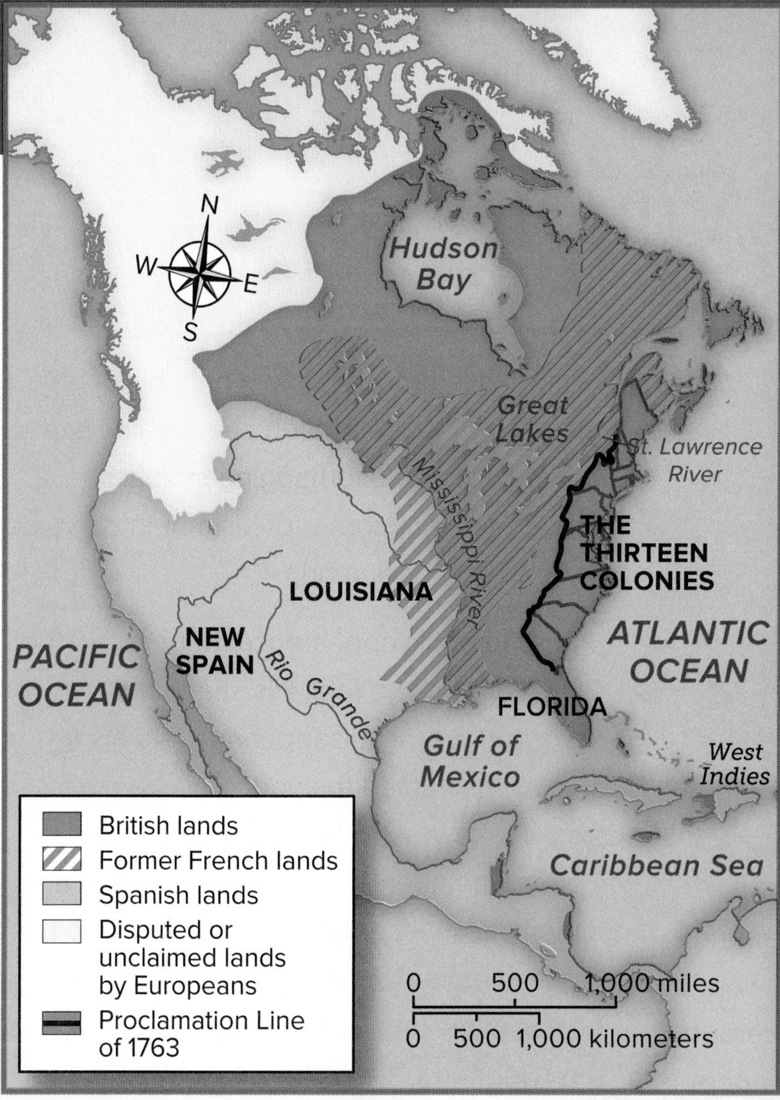

## North America after the French and Indian War, 1763



### Step into the Place

1. What areas were under French control before the French and Indian War?
2. What happened to that territory as a result of the French and Indian War?

**1765** Parliament passes the Stamp Act and the Quartering Act.

**1767** Parliament passes the Townshend Acts.

**1769–1770** British captain James Cook explores Australia and New Zealand.

**1770**

**1772** Samuel Adams forms the first Committee of Correspondence.

**1773** Colonists protest the Tea Act with the Boston Tea Party.

**1774** Joseph Priestley of Great Britain becomes the first scientist to publish a description of the chemical element oxygen.

**1774** The First Continental Congress meets.

**1775**

# Connect Through Literature

*excerpt from*

## Duel in the Wilderness

by Karin Clafford Farley

*Governor Dinwiddie of Virginia summons a young George Washington to the Capitol Building in Williamsburg to discuss an important mission to the Ohio River Valley.*

George stood at attention while the secretary introduced him. Then, extending his right leg forward as was the custom, he bowed deeply to the Governor and the Council members.

Robert Dinwiddie, the royal lieutenant governor, sat in a carved wood and cane armchair topped with a crown at the far end of the large oval table. The table itself was covered with a brightly woven turkey carpet littered with quill pens, inkwells, and papers. Only eight members of the twelve-member Council were present. They sat in identical chairs, except for the crown, on either side of the table. George stood alone at the open end. No one smiled or attempted to put George at ease, not even his friend, Colonel William Fairfax.

George fixed his eyes on the Governor; they never wavered. His muscles never twitched. His mouth, set in a firm, thin line, never quivered, except once. As George looked at the Governor, he could not help seeing him as a fat, melting candle. His red face drooped down onto his double chins which met his fallen chest which had slipped onto his overhanging stomach. George felt one corner of his mouth curve up as he fought back a grin.

In spite of his appearance, Robert Dinwiddie was no fool. His sharp blue eyes narrowed, almost disappearing into his fat face as he studied the young man before him. "Major Washington, I have informed the Council members of your offer to act as a diplomatic messenger to carry a letter to the French commander and learn by what right he has come into His Majesty's lands beyond the Allegheny Mountains on the River Ohio," he said in a thick Scottish accent.

Before Governor Dinwiddie could say more, one of the elderly Council members struggled to his feet. "Your Honour, I must protest! When you said the Major here was a younger brother of the late Major Lawrence Washington, I did not realize how much younger. Why, he is but a boy! How can you think of sending him on such a delicate mission to the French? We need a man of experience! Mature judgment! I'll wager he has not yet reached his majority. He would have to ask his mother's permission to go!"

The council room inside the Virginia Capitol Building in Williamsburg

Laughter broke out around the table. Burning under such cruel joking at his expense, George felt his control over his fiery temper slip away from him, and he did not care. Anger flashed in his eyes. He knew he should not speak while standing at attention, but the words were out before he could stop them. "I turned twenty-one early this year, Sir!"

His protest went unheeded as another councillor joined in. "Your Honour, I agree. I did not realize when we confirmed your appointment of Mr. Washington to replace his late brother as adjutant that he was not nearer in age and experience to the three other adjutants of the dominion's militia."

This time George caught a shake of the head and a warning look from his friend, Colonel William Fairfax. He struggled to control his temper by clamping his teeth over the inside of his lower lip until he tasted blood.

Robert Dinwiddie answered their protests. "Gentlemen, you know I have offered this mission to several other older, more qualified men. They have all found reasons to decline it. The Major here is a military man. We need a military man to spy—ah—er—assess the French buildup of forces in the Ohio country."

Colonel Fairfax interrupted. "Gentlemen, I have known Major Washington for many years. His brother Lawrence was my son-in-law. George is like a second son to me. Since the age of fifteen, he has earned his own way as a licensed surveyor for this colony and has the reputation for being one of the most skillful. He has traveled many times to the frontier in the course of his work. He is used to the hard, out-of-doors life."

"But has he ever crossed the mountains to Logstown or Murdering Town?" someone shouted out.

(bkgd)McGraw-Hill Education, (inset)Daniel Ladd/Alamy Stock Photo

Colonel Fairfax answered by asking his own question. "Who has crossed the mountains? That is a dark and mysterious land to us. The Indian tribes have allowed some traders in; men who are useful to them. Sometimes we have coaxed a few of the Indians to the edge of the wilderness to give them presents, to assure them we are their brothers. But no high official of the government has gone beyond the mountains. Not from this colony nor any other that I know of. Now this fine young man, one of our own Virginia militia adjutants, has volunteered to undertake this critical task, and you question, Sir? Could you endure the hardships of such a journey, Sir? Certainly I could not. His youth is what recommends him most. I say we engage him."

But the councillor was not to be put off. "Last year, His Honour tried to send a letter to the French by Trader William Trent, a man of long experience in the wilderness. Even Trent was afraid to go north of Logstown toward Lake Erie where the French are known to be. Traders have been taken prisoner or killed, their goods taken, and they themselves sent to gaol in Canada. Every day more Indians ally themselves to the French, who reward them for killing Englishmen. If Major Washington is like a son to you, how can you suggest he make a journey from which he has so little hope of returning?"

Gaol[1] in cold Canada? The very thought made George shiver. No, no, he told himself, he would be a diplomat, not a trader. English traders might be imprisoned, but not diplomats. At this very moment, William Keppel, Earl of Albemarle and the official royal governor of Virginia, was the English ambassador to the French court. Yet he could not take such heart about the Indians being rewarded for killing Englishmen. A vivid memory crowded his mind. He was on a surveying trip on the upper Potomac River and he stopped for the night at Trader Thomas Cresap's outpost. While there, he met an Iroquois war party, friendly to Cresap, returning up the Warrior's Path from a raid on the Cherokees. All night long they danced to their pounding drums and the rattle of gourds. Five years had passed, but George could feel his excitement as if it were yesterday.

Colonel Fairfax continued to speak to the Council. "I have great trust in Major Washington, as does my esteemed cousin, Lord Fairfax. Major Washington is a great favorite of his lordship's."

---

[1] *Gaol* is the British spelling of the word *jail*.

At the mention of Thomas, Lord Fairfax, to whose grandfather King Charles I had granted the largest tract of land in Virginia, the entire Shenandoah Valley, all discussion among the Council members abruptly ended. His lordship rarely left Greenwood, his estate in the remote Shenandoah Valley. But he made his power as the wealthiest man and highest ranking nobleman in the colony felt through his kinsman, Colonel William Fairfax.

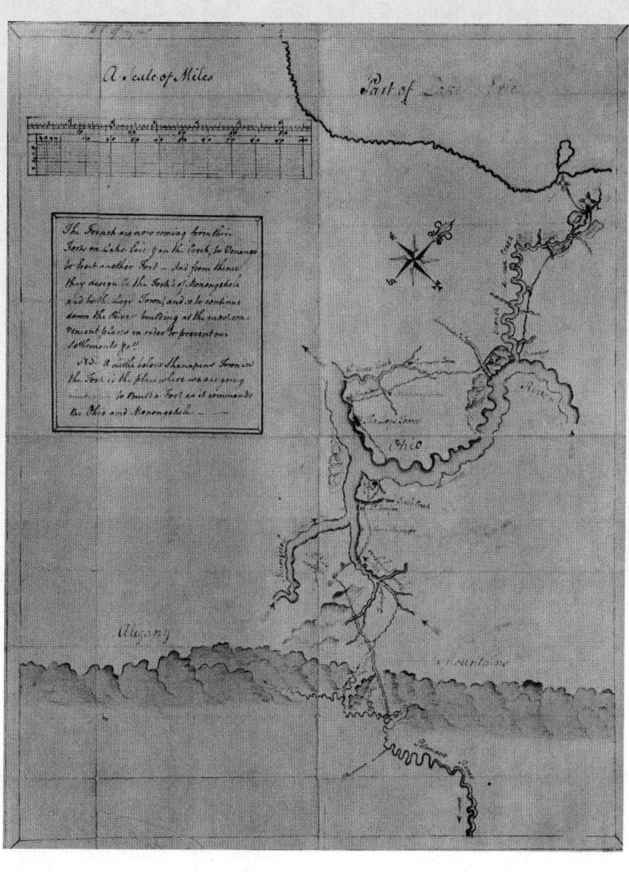


Washington drew this map during his mission to the Ohio River Valley.

Governor Dinwiddie drew attention back to himself. He did not look at the Council members. Instead, he studied George intently. "Just so there is no misunderstanding, do you know what I am asking?"

George made no effort to reply. His eyes remained fixed on the Governor's face, and he tried not to blink.

"To deliver this letter we would send in the King's name, you would have to cross the Alleghenies to Venango or heaven knows where to find the French commander. You would be gone at least a month, for there are no roads beyond Winchester, as you know. Snow and rain will be coming to the high country. And if you do make contact with the French, they no doubt will smile in your face, shrug their shoulders in that confounded Gallic way they have, send me a charming letter in return, and have one of their agents put a knife in your back some dark night. That is the mission we speak of. Do you still wish to volunteer?"

## Think About It

1. Why are the Council members unsure about Washington at the beginning?
2. What are three reasons why Washington is a good candidate for the mission?
3. Explain Colonel Fairfax's motivation for defending Washington.

George could feel the eyes of Queen Anne boring into his back from her portrait hanging on the wall behind him. "I am ready, Sir, to serve faithfully my King and country in any way I can."

# People You Should Know

## James Logan

The son of Chief Shikellamy of the Oneida people, James Logan was a respected figure in the Pennsylvania colony. His good relationship with the white settlers in the area of the Ohio River Valley lasted until 1774. At that time, a trader murdered Logan's family during the Yellow Creek Massacre. This treachery sparked the conflict that came to be called Lord Dunmore's War between the Native Americans and European settlers. Later, he helped the British army during the American Revolution.

## Sarah Bradlee Fulton

Called "Mother of the Boston Tea Party," Sarah Bradlee Fulton used her own kitchen as a meeting place for the men who dumped tea into Boston Harbor on December 16, 1773. She and other "Daughters of Liberty" showed similar resistance to the British throughout the revolution that was to come. She organized women to nurse wounded soldiers after the Battle of Bunker Hill and acted as a courier, crossing enemy lines and risking her own life during the Revolutionary War.

## William Pitt, the Elder

## Chief Pontiac

A British leader, William Pitt was a mastermind of Great Britain's strategy in the Seven Years' War, which included the French and Indian War. Pitt convinced Parliament to put him in charge, to give him almost unlimited resources, and to let him completely restructure the British military in order to win the conflict. His strategies worked, and Great Britain won the war. They also left Britain with tremendous debt that Britain wanted the colonists to help pay for. Later, Pitt spoke out against Britain's taxing the colonists without allowing them to be represented in Parliament.

A chief of the Ottawa people of the Great Lakes region, Pontiac forged an alliance to beat back the British in the conflict known as Pontiac's War (1763–1766). His alliance included almost all of the Native American tribes between Lake Superior and the lower Mississippi. His strategy was fairly successful at first, but years of fighting took their toll. Pontiac signed a peace treaty with the British in 1766.

# What Caused the Conflict Between Great Britain, France, and Native Americans?

## Conflict in the Ohio River Valley

In the early 1700s, England and France were each creating colonial empires in North America. England, which became Great Britain in 1707, established thirteen colonies between the Atlantic Coast and the Appalachian Mountains. These British colonies had a large, growing population and a vigorous economy based on farming and trade. The colonies of New France consisted of two areas: what is now Canada and also Louisiana in the Mississippi River Valley. New France was far larger than the British colonies in total land area but much smaller in population. Most colonists in New France were involved in the fur trade.

By the mid-1700s, the British and French colonists were coming into conflict. The French fur traders wanted to preserve the forested wilderness as it was. As the British colonists wanted more land for farming, the French feared that British farmers would cut down the trees, ruining the **habitat** of fur-bearing animals.

1750 | 1755 | 1760 | 1765 | 1770 | 1775

**1754**
War breaks out between British and French settlers in the upper Ohio River Valley.

**1759**
A British victory at the Battle of Quebec is a turning point in the war.

**1763**
The Treaty of Paris ends the French and Indian War.

**1763–1764**
Ottawa leader Chief Pontiac leads resistance to the British.

**1766**
Pontiac and the British agree to a peace treaty.

**In 1757, the Oneida, Seneca, and other native groups crossed Lake Champlain to aid the French.**



Native American groups were drawn into this struggle. They wanted to protect their ways of life. As a result, they became allies with either the French or the British. The Algonquin and Huron (also called Wyandot) groups sided with the French. These Native Americans also wanted to preserve the forested wilderness and forest animals from British settlers. In addition, the French had aided the Algonquin and Huron in their struggles with their traditional enemies, the Iroquois Confederacy. The Iroquois sided with the British because they were angry at the French for helping their enemies.

The focus of the struggle between the French and the British, and their Native American allies, was the upper Ohio River Valley. In firm control of the territories of New France, French settlers had spread southward into the Great Lakes region. They established a major outpost there at Detroit in 1701. By the 1750s, farmers and traders from the British colonies of Virginia and Pennsylvania had begun to cross the Appalachian Mountains, moving into the lands beyond. To halt this advance, the French built a line of forts from Lake Erie to western Pennsylvania. The British saw the forts as a threat and decided to try to drive the French out.

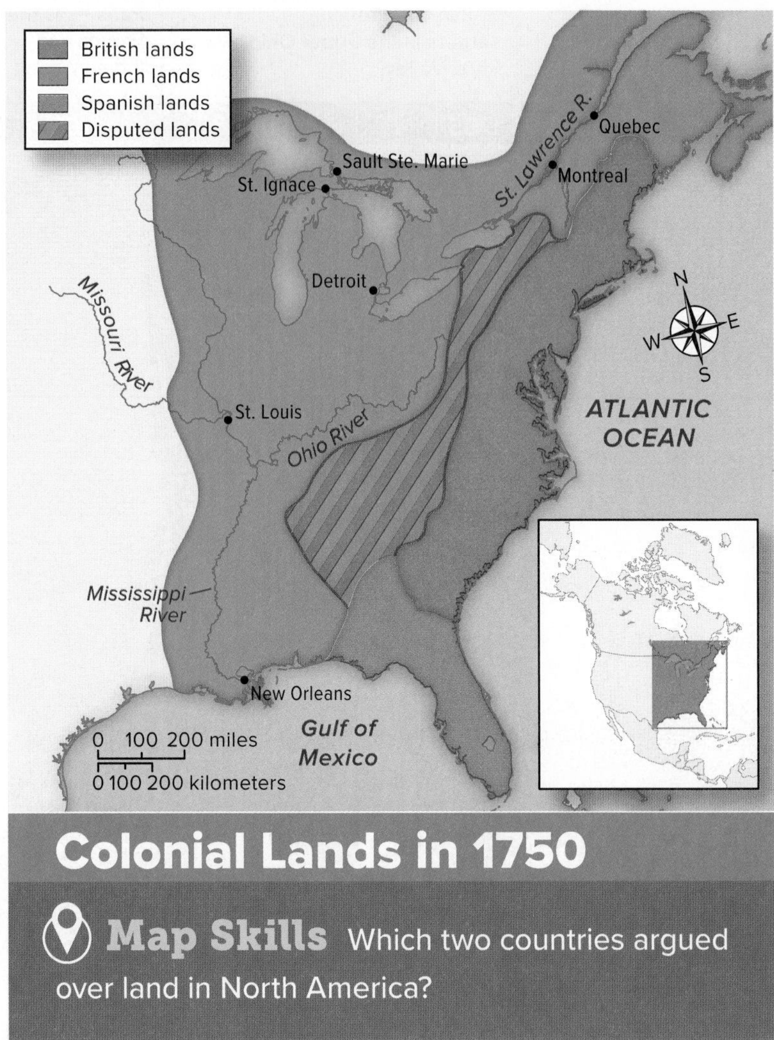


## Colonial Lands in 1750

**Map Skills** Which two countries argued over land in North America?

### Stop and Check

**Think** How did France's choice of allies among Native Americans cause the Iroquois to become allies of the British?

**Find Details** As you read, add additional information to the graphic organizer on page 143 in your Inquiry Journal.

# The Battle at Fort Duquesne

Robert Dinwiddie was the lieutenant governor of the British colony of Virginia. He wanted to convince the British government in London of the seriousness of the French threat in the Ohio Valley. So, in early 1754, Dinwiddie sent 22-year-old George Washington with a small force to strengthen a British **outpost** at the site of what is now the city of Pittsburgh. As Washington neared the fort, he discovered that French troops had already seized it and renamed it Fort Duquesne (doo KAIN).

Washington quickly built a temporary post in the area and named it Fort Necessity. From this base, Washington's troops launched a successful attack against the French on May 28, 1754. But the French counterattacked on July 3, forcing Washington to surrender. He and his men were allowed to return to Virginia, and the French destroyed Fort Necessity. The French and Indian War had begun.

Back in Virginia, Washington found his defeat had not harmed his reputation. The colonial government thanked him for his efforts, and he was named head of Virginia's militia on the frontier. Washington remarked in a letter to his brother, "I have heard the bullets whistle; and believe me, there is something charming in the sound."

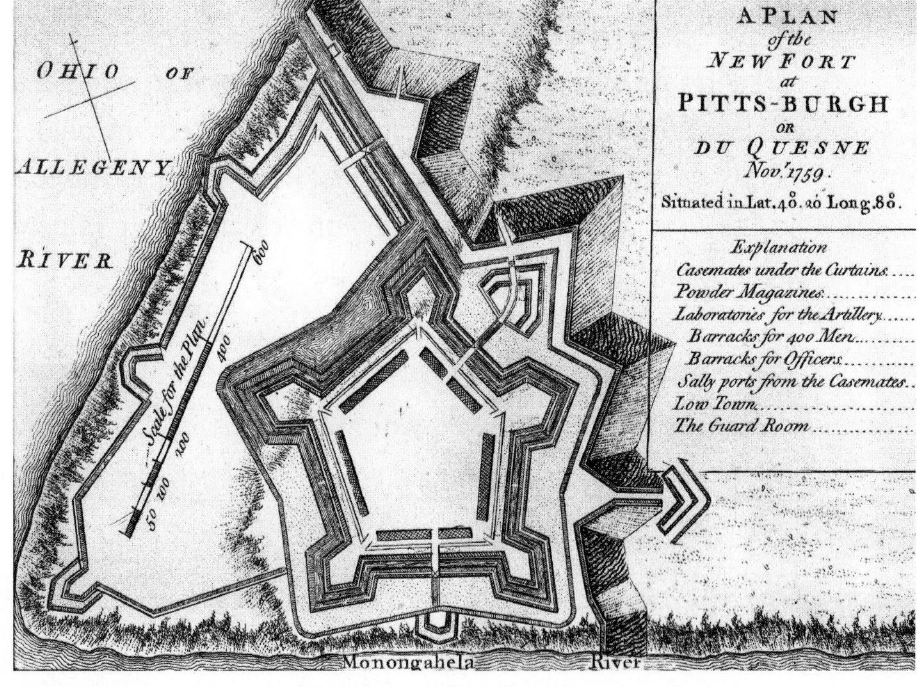


An early map of Fort Duquesne, later renamed Fort Pitt

 **Stop and Check**

COLLABORATE

**Talk** How did Washington's expedition into the Ohio Valley support Robert Dinwiddie's views about the French? Discuss your opinion with a partner.

# The French Gain the Upper Hand

The early phase of the war was marked by French victories. Their Native American allies taught the French how to make surprise attacks from behind trees and rocks. By contrast, British troops, who marched into battle in formation, were easy targets. Such British tactics resulted in disaster in 1755 when General Edward Braddock led another group of British troops against Fort Duquesne. Colonel George Washington rode alongside Braddock. On July 9, the French and their allies ambushed the British forces in the wilderness. British losses were severe. Some 900 of their 1,400 troops were killed or wounded, including nearly all the officers. Braddock himself was fatally wounded. Now in command, Washington was able to lead the remaining British forces to safety.

The French continued to be victorious. In 1756, their commander Louis-Joseph de Montcalm led a force of French soldiers and Native Americans in the capture of an important British post, Fort Oswego, in the Great Lakes region. Montcalm reported that he had taken 1,600 prisoners and seized 100 cannon, six armed vessels, and a two-year supply of food. "All this cost us only 30 men killed and wounded," he said. Montcalm's victory gave the French full control of Lake Ontario. The following year, he captured another British post, Fort William Henry, which was near present-day Lake George, New York.

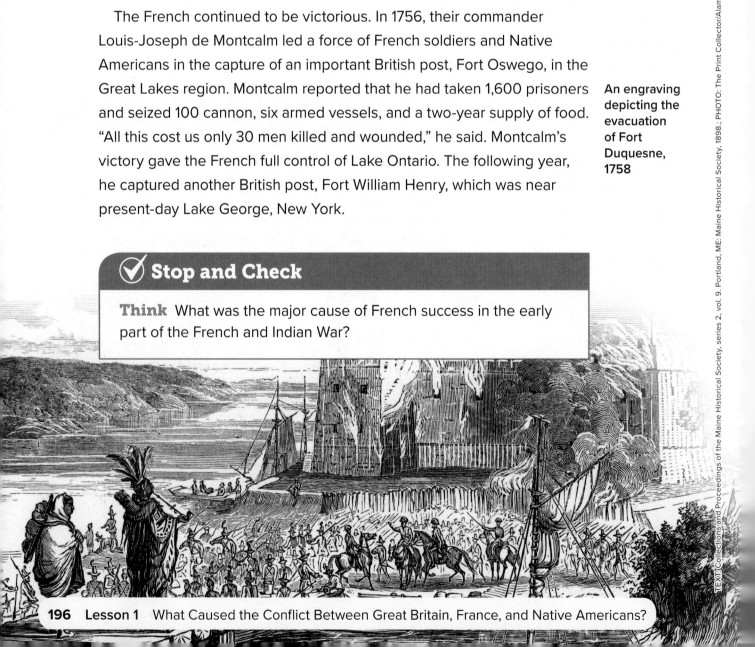

## Stop and Check

**Think** What was the major cause of French success in the early part of the French and Indian War?

**An engraving depicting the evacuation of Fort Duquesne, 1758**

# The Turning Point

News of French victories shocked the British colonies. The colonists begged the British Prime Minister, William Pitt, for more help. Pitt believed that the war in North America was critical to the overall struggle between Great Britain and France. The two nations were also at war in Europe. Pitt convinced the British government to pour more money, troops, and other supplies into the conflict. In addition, the British navy blockaded ports in New France, cutting off shipments of food and other supplies to French colonists. Finally, both British soldiers and American colonial militias became skilled in fighting the way Native Americans did in the wilderness. All of these factors changed the course of the war.

In 1758, British troops defeated the French at Louisbourg, Nova Scotia. Several months later, Colonel John Bradstreet led the British to victory over the French in a battle at Fort Frontenac on Lake Ontario. In November, the British finally retook Fort Duquesne. They renamed it Fort Pitt in honor of the British prime minister. In 1759, Sir William Johnson forced the French to surrender Fort Niagara. British General Jeffery Amherst then defeated the French at Fort Ticonderoga near Lake Champlain in upstate New York.

## Then and Now

The city of Pittsburgh, Pennsylvania, was built around Fort Pitt. The land where Fort Pitt used to be is now a public park, though the brick outline of the old fort is still intact. The site is also home to the Fort Pitt Museum, which presents the story of western Pennsylvania's essential role in the French and Indian War as well as the American Revolution.

**Fort Pitt in 1758 (background) and Fort Pitt Block House today (top-right)**

The climax of the war came in June 1759 when the British moved against the French stronghold at Quebec. The city of Quebec is located on steep cliffs above the St. Lawrence River. Both the river's strong currents and the fortress's cannon protected it. A British assault at the end of July failed. British commander James Wolfe decided on a daring plan—a surprise attack.

During the early hours of September 13, 1759, Wolfe landed an advance force in darkness. These soldiers climbed the steep cliffs and captured a French outpost. By morning, Wolfe's entire force was assembled on the Plains of Abraham outside the city. Like Wolfe, French commander Montcalm also decided to take a risk. He attacked immediately instead of waiting for reinforcements. The two armies both numbered about 4,500 men. However, Wolfe's troops were professional soldiers, while Montcalm's were volunteers. The battlefield was not forested wilderness, but open country. The careful musket fire of Wolfe's troops halted the advance of the French and then caused them to retreat. Both Montcalm and Wolfe were fatally wounded in the battle.

On September 18, the French surrendered Quebec City. A year later, the French surrendered their last stronghold, Montreal. The British now controlled New France.

## Stop and Check

COLLABORATE

**Talk** What kinds of advantages did the land around Quebec provide to both the French and the British?

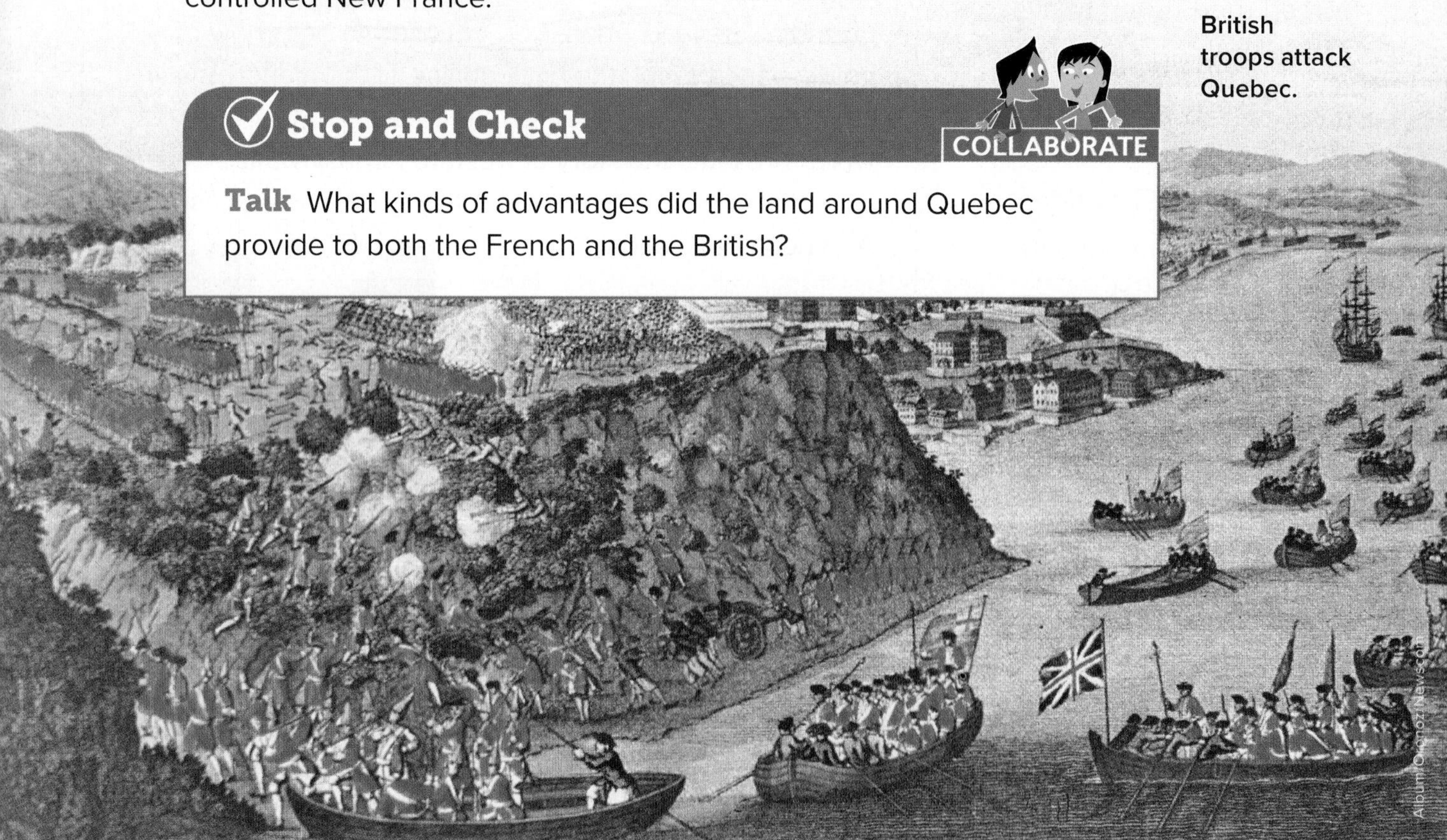

British troops attack Quebec.

# Outcomes and Aftermath

The French tried to retake Quebec in 1762 but failed. In Europe, meanwhile, Great Britain and France continued their war. Spain aided the French and, in return, France agreed to give Spain much of the Louisiana Territory. By 1763, the French were ready to negotiate a peace treaty with Great Britain. The Treaty of Paris was signed on February 10, 1763.

In October 1763, news of the Treaty of Paris reached North America. The defeated French could no longer aid Native Americans in their resistance to British settlers. However, Great Britain wanted to keep down the cost of defending its American colonies. To stop British settlements in the Ohio River Valley, British King George III issued the Proclamation of 1763. This official order set aside all British land west of the Appalachian Mountains for Native Americans. This decision satisfied the native peoples but angered American colonists hungry for land.

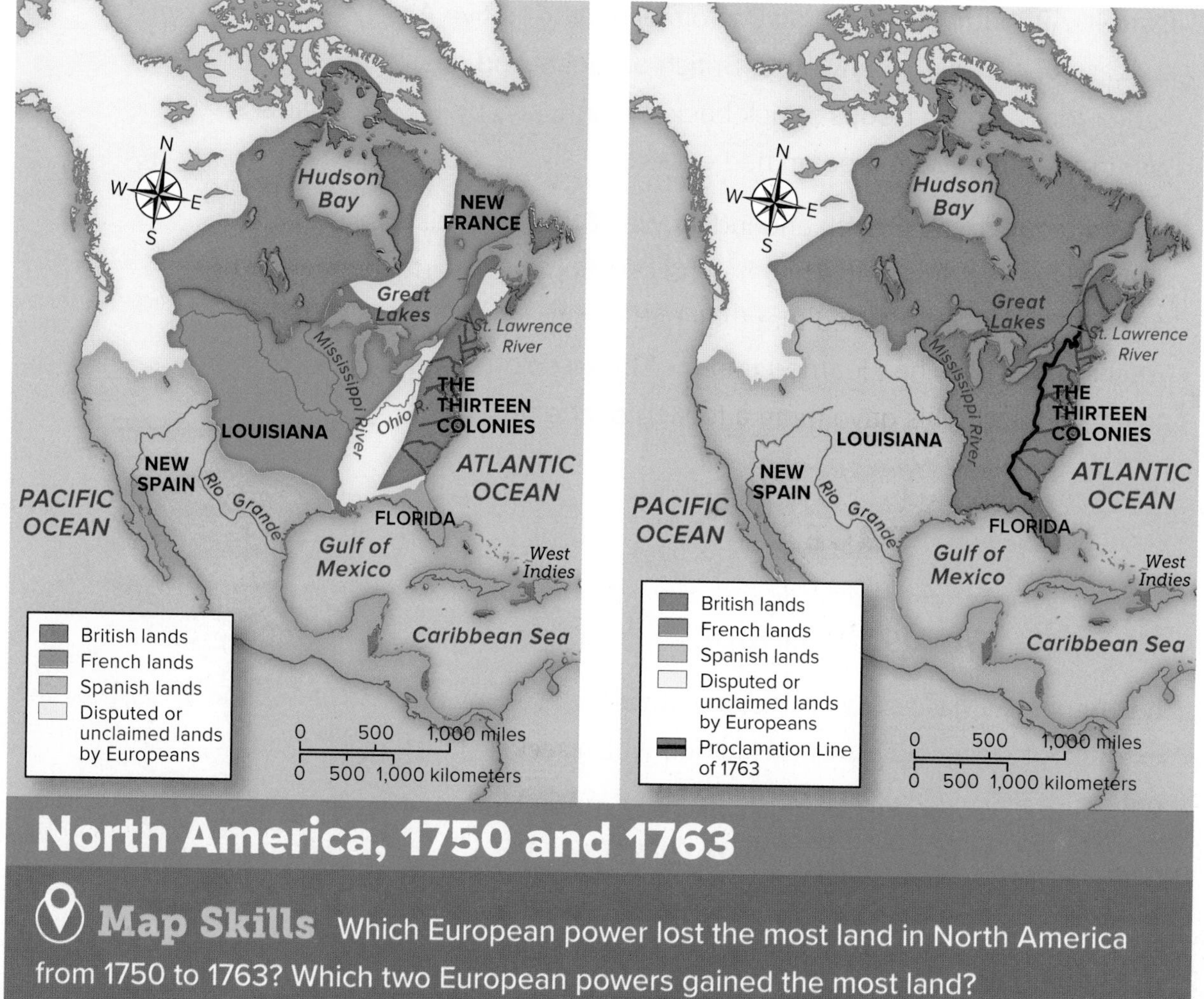


## North America, 1750 and 1763

**Map Skills** Which European power lost the most land in North America from 1750 to 1763? Which two European powers gained the most land?

By 1760, although the British were defeating the French in North America, their control over the lands was not firm. Some of the Native American allies of the French decided to resist British rule. The most important leader of this resistance was Pontiac. He was a member of the Ottawa, an Algonquin-speaking group whose homeland was in what is now northern Michigan and parts of Canada. As French outposts in Ottawa territory were surrendered to the British, Pontiac agreed not to attack British troops if they treated him with respect. His experience with the British convinced Pontiac, however, that they were a threat. Soon, settlers would follow these troops, Pontiac correctly believed. The settlers would want to turn Ottawa hunting grounds into farms.

In 1762, Pontiac organized almost every Native American group from Lake Superior to the lower Mississippi River Valley. The plan, which Pontiac announced in early 1763, was for each group to attack the nearest British outpost. Then, all the Native Americans would combine in a general attack on the British settlements. Pontiac himself was to attack Detroit. Although his attack on Detroit failed, the Native Americans were successful in seizing many other British outposts and destroying frontier settlements. British troops struck back, though, and by 1764 Pontiac's War in the Great Lakes region had ended.

As a result of the French and Indian War, British colonists saw themselves in a new way. They had helped fight a powerful enemy and had won. They also proved that they had strong leaders, such as George Washington. They had learned that the British colonies could unite in a common effort. This gave them a feeling of strength.

**PRIMARY SOURCE**

## In Their Words... Pontiac

**It is important for us, my brothers, that we exterminate from our lands this nation which seeks only to destroy us. You see as well as I that we can no longer supply our needs, as we have done from our brothers, the French.**

—from a speech by Pontiac to the Ottawa people in May 1763

TEXT: Pontiac. 5 May 1763. Quoted in Michigan Society of the Colonial Wars, M. Agnes Burton, ed., Journal of Pontiac's Conspiracy, 1763 (Detroit, MI: Clarence Monroe Burton, 1912), 38.; PHOTO: North Wind Picture Archives/Alamy

The colonists also saw their relationship with Great Britain in a new light. They were angry with the British government for the Proclamation of 1763. Many colonists ignored the order and continued to cross the Appalachians to settle in the lands reserved for Native Americans. The colonists knew that they could rely very little on British protection from Native American attacks. In the end, the effect of the French and Indian War would be to unite the colonists in opposition to British government policy. Soon, this would lead them to fight for their own independence.

George Washington leads an attack on a French encampment.

**PRIMARY SOURCE**

## In Their Words... George Washington

The Virginia troops showed a good deal of bravery, and were nearly all killed; for I believe, out of three companies that were there, scarcely thirty men are left alive. ... I luckily escaped without a wound, though I had four bullets through my coat, and two horses shot under me.

—from George Washington's letter to his mother about Braddock's defeat, July 18, 1755

 **Stop and Check**

COLLABORATE

**Talk** Why didn't the British colonists obey the Proclamation of 1763? Were they right or wrong to disobey it?

TEXT: Washington, George. George Washington to his mother, Mary Ball, 14 July 1755. In Some Old Historic Landmarks of Virginia and Maryland..., by W.H. Snowden, p. 121. Alexandria, VA: G.H. Ramey & Sons, 1904.;
PHOTO: (t)McGraw-Hill Education, (b)North Wind Picture Archives/Alamy

# What Were the Views of the Patriots, the Loyalists, and the British?

## New Taxes

Great Britain's 1763 victory in the French and Indian War came at a great cost. The war doubled Britain's debt, which reached 122 million pounds in 1763. Adding to the cost were the British troops left behind to protect the colonies from further conflict. King George III, who had been on the throne for only three years, struggled to find ways to pay the massive debt.

George III was a young king determined to make his mark as a strong ruler. He surrounded himself with advisors who agreed he should rule the colonies with a firm hand. British citizens already paid high taxes. The advisors argued that it was only fair to tax colonists to help pay for Britain's protection during and after the war.

Parliament, the British legislature, passed the Sugar Act in 1764. It forced the colonists to pay a tax on all sugar products. An older British tax on sugar products already existed, but the British government had never enforced it. With the new Sugar Act, any colonist who refused to pay was arrested and fined. However, the Sugar Act did not bring in enough money to make a significant impact on Britain's debt.

**1763 February** Treaty of Paris ends the French and Indian War.

**1763 October** Proclamation of 1763 sets aside land west of the Appalachians for Native Americans.

**1764** Parliament passes the Sugar Act.

**1765** Parliament passes the Stamp Act.

62 | 1763 | 1764 | 1765

In the 1760s and 1770s, the British Parliament passed tax laws that made many colonists unhappy.

One year later, Parliament passed the Stamp Act. It forced colonists to buy stamps for all printed documents. This included everyday paper products such as letters, newspapers, pamphlets, and even playing cards.

Many colonists were furious. They disagreed with Britain's **imposing** the tax on them. Colonists complained that Parliament passed the new tax laws without colonists' consent, or agreement. One strong opponent of the tax laws was Samuel Adams of Massachusetts. Adams sent protest letters to newspapers and addressed delegates from the colony's assembly. In one letter, he stated, "If our trade may be taxed, why not our lands? Why not . . . everything we possess or use?"

A British stamp used on printed documents

## Chart Skills

GDP is the Gross Domestic Product, the total value of all goods and services a country produces in a year. When a country owes more in debt than it produces in a year, it can take a long time for the country to pay down its debt.

**The Growth of Britain's Debt**

| Year | British Debt as a Percentage of GDP |
|---|---|
| 1700 | 23 |
| 1710 | 34 |
| 1720 | 83 |
| 1730 | 76 |
| 1740 | 68 |
| 1750 | 107 |
| 1760 | 132 |
| 1770 | 126 |

Source: ukpublicspending.co.uk

## Stop and Check

COLLABORATE

**Talk** How did Britain plan on paying the war debt?

**Find Details** As you read, add additional information to the graphic organizer on page 151 in your Inquiry Journal.

# The Colonies Respond

Colonists were still British citizens. Since the British government had spent money to protect these citizens, Parliament believed that the colonists should pay their fair share for the French and Indian War in the form of taxes. Many colonists saw the Stamp Act as taxation without representation. That meant they were forced to pay taxes approved by officials they had not elected. Colonists who demanded that Americans have more control of their government were known as Patriots.

Before these tax laws, only colonial legislatures had taxed colonists. Colonists had accepted those taxes because they had elected the officials. These officials, they argued, were the only ones who should be allowed to tax goods. To make matters worse, the new tax money collected from the colonists went to Britain instead of the colonial governments.

Every colony protested the new tax law. In Boston, some colonists formed a group to protest the Stamp Act. They called themselves the Sons of Liberty. Samuel Adams actively participated in this group. The Sons of Liberty met under an elm tree that Adams called "The Liberty Tree." As tensions continued between the colonies and Great Britain, many Patriots began talking about breaking away from Great Britain and becoming independent.

**Colonists protesting in the streets**

Not all colonists were Patriots, however. A third of all colonists remained loyal to King George III. These people were called Loyalists. Many of them were wealthy, but others were ordinary people. Some business leaders were Loyalists. Philadelphia merchant Thomas Clifford complained that independence would "assuredly prove unprofitable." Many Loyalists wished to remain British citizens or were fearful that independence would lead to chaos.

In October 1765, representatives from nine colonies met in New York City and formed the Stamp Act Congress. The representatives declared that Parliament had no right to tax the colonists, since colonists were not allowed to vote for members of Parliament. These laws, they argued, were against British legal traditions.

Parliament created more conflict by ignoring colonists' concerns. On November 1, the Stamp Act took effect. In turn, angry colonists staged a **boycott.** Boycotting means refusing to do business with—or to buy goods from—a person, group, or country. Colonists refused to use the new stamps.

This teapot was made for sale in the colonies to celebrate the cancellation of the Stamp Act.

Smithsonian National Museum of American History, Kenneth E. Behring Center

Colonial women joined the protest. They formed a group called the "Daughters of Liberty." They made a kind of cloth known as "homespun" and found other ways to replace British goods with homemade items.

Colonists refused to purchase British goods, such as tea. The boycott began to hurt British merchants. Because of the boycott, Parliament in 1766 voted to cancel the Stamp Act.

**Stop and Check**

COLLABORATE

**Talk** Why were colonists' different types of protests effective?

# Views From a Patriot and a Loyalist

Colonists who demanded that Americans have more control of their government were known as Patriots. Colonists who wanted to remain loyal to the British government were called Loyalists. The following quotations show the points of view of George Mason, a Patriot, and Joseph Galloway, a Loyalist.

"We claim nothing but the liberty and privileges of Englishmen, in the same degree, as if we had still continued among our brethren in Great Britain: these rights have not been forfeited by any act of ours, we can not be deprived of them without our consent, but by violence and injustice."

—George Mason, letter to the Committee of Merchants in London, June 6, 1766

George Mason

Joseph Galloway

"The protection of America has, in no small degree, contributed to this burden of the mother country. To the large sums of money that have been expended from the English treasury and the parental care of a British Parliament, we in a great measure owe our present freedom. . . ."

—Americanus (pseudonym for Joseph Galloway), letter to the *New York Gazette*, 15 August 1765, reprinted two weeks later in the *Pennsylvania Journal* (29 August 1765)

**What Do You Think?** Whose argument do you think is more convincing? Why?

TEXT: (t)Mason, George. George Mason to the Committee of Merchants in London, 6 June 1766. In The Life of George Mason, 1725-1792, Volume 1, ed. Kate Mason Rowland, no. 3. New York: G.P. Putnam's Sons, 1892., (b)Galloway, Joseph. "Americanus." Letter to The New-York Gazette, 15 August 1765.; PHOTO: (t)McGraw-Hill Education, (c)Bettmann/Getty Images

# The Townshend Acts

Parliament gave in to colonial pressure when it **repealed** the Stamp Act in 1766, but the break from taxes did not last long. In 1767, Parliament found another way to raise taxes. It passed the Townshend Acts, which were named for the treasurer of the British government, Charles Townshend. Parliament believed colonists would be more accepting of a tax on factory-made goods imported from Great Britain. These included common imports such as tea, paper, glass, lead, and paint. Again, colonists were angry. They demanded Britain cancel the Townshend Acts. They also organized a boycott of the newly taxed items as well as any colonial businesses that continued to sell or use taxed goods.

**Goods Taxed Under the Townshend Acts**

tea
paper
glass
lead
paint

After the passage of the Townshend Acts, a Pennsylvania farmer named John Dickinson began writing a series of letters to the people of Great Britain. Although he was a Patriot, Dickinson was against independence and argued in favor of peaceful protest of Britain's taxes. Some other Patriots agreed with him. In fact, there were many among the British, Patriots, and Loyalists who did not wish to go to war. But in the coming years, relations between the colonists and Great Britain would become only more tense.

Britain feared the boycotts could lead to violence, and so they acted on these fears. Britain sent troops to Boston, which was the center of colonial protests. What happened next would push the two sides even closer to war.

## Stop and Check

**Think** Based on what you have read about colonists' protests, do you think Britain was justified in sending troops to Boston?

Colonial boycotts affected the economy in Britain as well as in the colonies.

## Around the World

### How Did the Boycott Hurt Britain's Economy?

The French and Indian War had left Britain not only with debt but also with an economic **recession**. Colonists' boycott of British goods weakened trade in a struggling British economy. British businesses and factories suffered losses from fewer products being exported to the colonies. So, like the colonists, British merchants began organizing to pressure Parliament to end the Stamp Act. Parliament took the merchants' concerns more seriously than the colonists' concerns. It canceled the Stamp Act.

**What Do You Think?** What was similar about colonists' and British merchants' organizing efforts? What was different about them?

# What Increased Tensions Between Great Britain and the Colonists?

## The Boston Massacre

Tensions were high between colonists and British soldiers in Boston in early 1770. The people of Boston were not happy with the increase in the number of British soldiers in the city. Because of the Quartering Act, some residents were forced to allow British officers to stay in their homes. On March 5, the conflict turned deadly. Historians debate the specific details, but all accounts begin the same way.

A group of colonists gathered at the Customs House, where taxes on imported goods were paid to Great Britain. British soldiers arrived. An exchange of angry words and insults quickly turned physical. The colonists hurled snowballs and ice at the soldiers. Some of the soldiers lost control and fired their **muskets** into the crowd. Five colonists were killed as a result of these actions. Among them was Crispus Attucks, a man who had escaped from slavery.

The incident became known as the Boston Massacre. Samuel Adams and the Sons of Liberty used the event as fuel to add to the growing movement for colonial self-government.

**1765**
Parliament passes the Stamp Act and the Quartering Act.

**1767**
Parliament passes the Townshend Acts.

**1772**
Samuel Adams forms the first Committee of Correspondence.

**1773**
Parliament passes the Tea Act.

**1774**
The First Continental Congress meets.

1760 | 1765 | 1770 | 1775

The conflict between the colonists and the British troops turned deadly in Boston in early 1770.

traveler1116/iStock/Getty Images

Biography

# *Samuel Adams* AND THE COMMITTEES OF CORRESPONDENCE

A portrait of Samuel Adams

Samuel Adams was a key figure in the colonists' quest for freedom. He was among the founders of the Sons of Liberty, a group that was organized to protest the Stamp Act. It continued to speak out against British rule. Anti-British feeling spread slowly throughout the colonies. Adams realized that the colonists needed a way to communicate. Having previously written letters to newspapers to protest the Stamp Act, Adams knew that the fastest and most reliable way to communicate was through letters. In 1772, he formed a 21-person committee to communicate the Patriots' plans and progress. He adapted this idea from a committee that was formed in 1764 to protest new British rules about currency and customs.

By forming the committee, Adams—and other Sons of Liberty—could stay up-to-date with the events in the colonies. Thus, the Committee of Correspondence was born. Within a few months, more than 80 similar Committees of Correspondence formed throughout the colonies. A few years later, a volunteer rider for the Boston Committee of Correspondence would also make history. His name was Paul Revere.

Samuel Adams continued to be an influential figure during the Revolutionary War and in the early republic. In 1776, he signed the Declaration of Independence. Later, he was elected governor of Massachusetts. During his time in government, he fought for the rights of boys and girls to receive free and equal education.

**Stop and Check**

COLLABORATE

**Talk** What did Samuel Adams do to show his opposition to the way Britain was ruling the colonies? How did his actions help the colonists?

**Find Details** As you read, add new information to the graphic organizer on page 159 in your Inquiry Journal.

# The Boston Tea Party

Some of the colonists' protests worked. Parliament repealed the Townshend Acts. However, it also passed the Tea Act in 1773. The Tea Act gave the British East India Company the exclusive right to sell tea in the colonies without paying export taxes. This allowed the company to sell its tea at a price cheaper than that of other merchants' tea. Colonial tea merchants could no longer compete. Further, colonists still had to pay taxes when they bought the tea. This upset Samuel Adams, the Sons of Liberty, and other colonists for two reasons. First, it was another tax that they had not voted to approve. Second, it hurt local businesses because it gave a British company a **monopoly** on tea.

In late November 1773, three ships from the East India Company landed in Boston Harbor. Some Boston residents decided to protest the Tea Act by refusing to let the ships unload their cargo. Governor Thomas Hutchinson wanted to honor the new law and decided that the ships were to remain in the harbor until the tea was sold.

The angry colonists threw British tea into Boston Harbor.

The Sons of Liberty broke open 342 tea chests.

A few weeks later, on the night of December 16, 1773, the Sons of Liberty took action. About 50 members, some dressed as Mohawk Native Americans, boarded the ships. They broke open the tea chests and dumped the contents of the chests into the harbor. This act of **vandalism** became known as the Boston Tea Party. Similar protests happened in New York and in Annapolis, Maryland, but only the city of Boston would face immediate consequences.

Parliament wanted to punish the colonists for their actions. It closed Boston Harbor until the colonists paid for the tea they had destroyed. It also banned town meetings and sent more soldiers to live in the city. This series of acts was known as the Coercive Acts. The Patriots called them the Intolerable Acts, because they found the actions hard to tolerate, or live with. Instead of breaking the protestors' spirits, these acts unified the anti-British colonists in their struggle. Representatives from the colonies decided to meet to discuss what to do next. Their meeting would be called the First Continental Congress.

## Stop and Check

COLLABORATE

**Talk** How did the passage of laws after the Boston Tea Party motivate the colonists to take action?

Cayman/Alamy

# The First Continental Congress

Attendees of the First Continental Congress met at Carpenters' Hall in Philadelphia.

On September 5, 1774, representatives from the colonies met in Philadelphia to discuss the Coercive Acts. Their goal was to plan a response to these laws. Fifty-six men represented 12 of the 13 colonies. Each colony was granted one vote. After rejecting a plan to **reconcile** with the British government, the First Continental Congress decided to write a petition, or written request, to King George III. In the document, members of the congress outlined complaints about the way the British government had been treating them. They reminded the king of their status as British citizens. They demanded that they be given the same rights—including the right to representation—that were granted to other British citizens. Then they asked the king to repeal the Coercive Acts and other laws they felt were unfair to the colonists. Lastly, they proposed an end to trade with Britain until their demands were met.

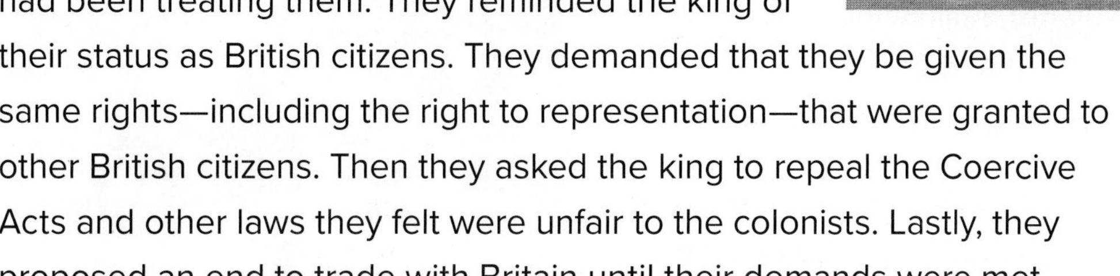

**PRIMARY SOURCE**

## In Their Words... The First Continental Congress

The foundation of English liberty, and of all free government, is a right in the people to participate in their legislative council: and as the English colonists are not represented, and from their local and other circumstances, cannot properly be represented in the British parliament, they are entitled to a free and exclusive power of legislation in their several provincial legislatures, where their right of representation can alone be preserved, in all cases of taxation and internal polity, subject only to the negative of their sovereign, in such manner as has been heretofore used and accustomed.

—from the *Declaration of Rights and Grievances,* October 14, 1774

**Stop and Check**

**Think** How does having a common goal unite a large group of people?

TEXT: Declaration and Resolves of the First Continental Congress, Res. 4, October 14, 1774. Documents Illustrative of the Formation of the Union of the American States. Government Printing Office, 1927. House Document No. 398. Selected, Arranged and Indexed by Charles C. Tansill.; PHOTO: (t)McGraw-Hill Education, (b)Zack Frank/Shutterstock.com

# Connections in Action!

## Back to the EQ

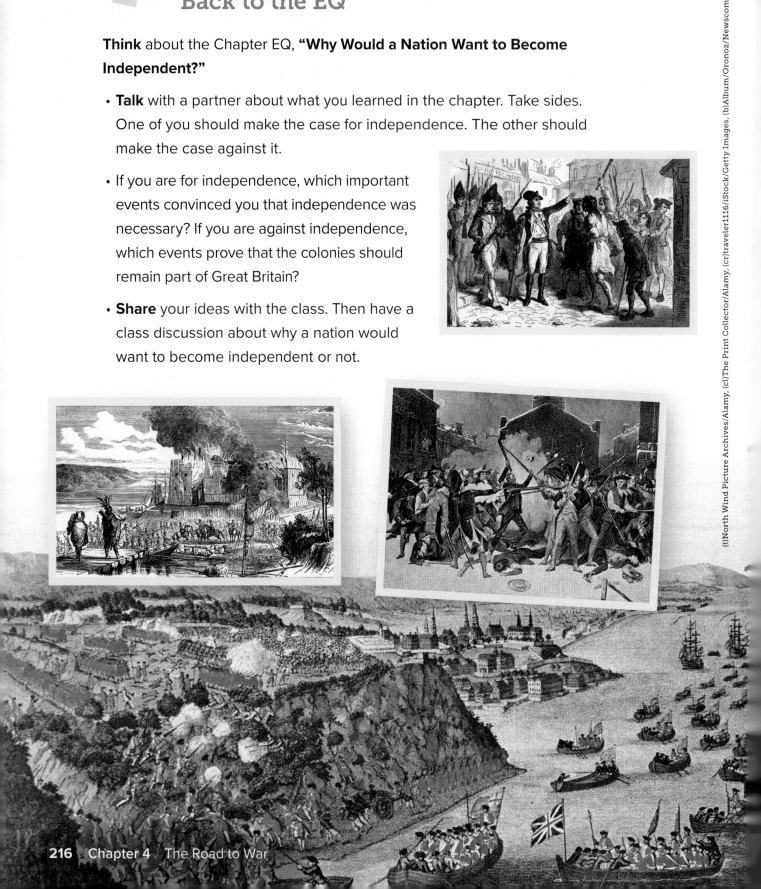

**Think** about the Chapter EQ, **"Why Would a Nation Want to Become Independent?"**

- **Talk** with a partner about what you learned in the chapter. Take sides. One of you should make the case for independence. The other should make the case against it.
- If you are for independence, which important events convinced you that independence was necessary? If you are against independence, which events prove that the colonies should remain part of Great Britain?
- **Share** your ideas with the class. Then have a class discussion about why a nation would want to become independent or not.

(t)North Wind Picture Archives/Alamy, (cl)The Print Collector/Alamy, (cr)traveler1116/iStock/Getty Images, (b)Album/Oronoz/Newscom

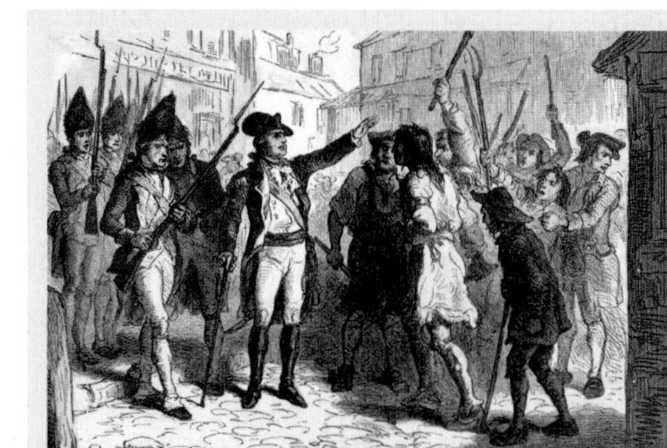

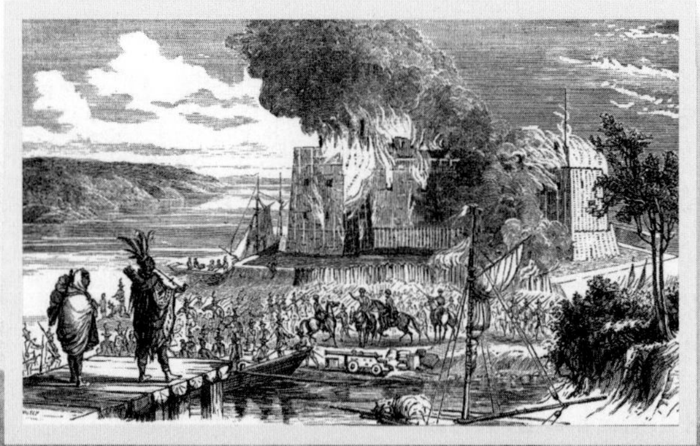

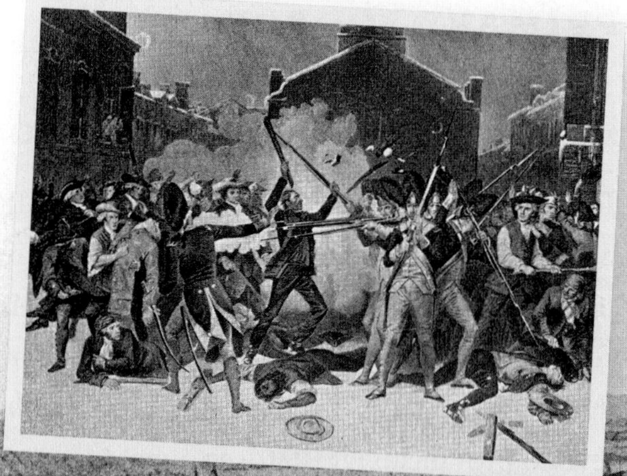

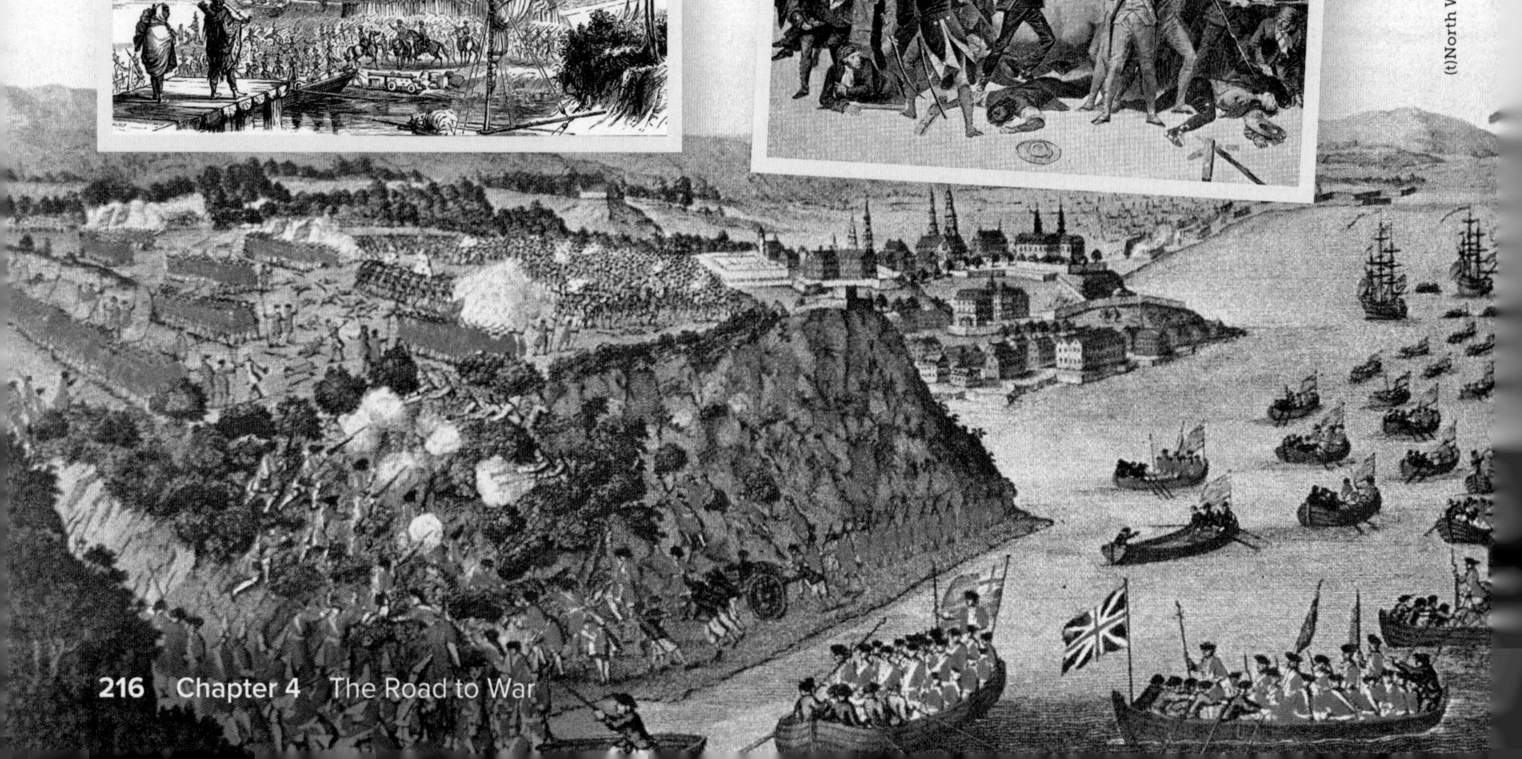

# More to Explore
## How Can You Make an IMPACT?

### Television Interview
Work with a partner. One of you will play the part of someone who witnessed the Boston Tea Party. The other will play a television interviewer. Together, develop questions that give your viewers answers about *who was involved*, as well as *where, when, why,* and *how* the Boston Tea Party happened. Act out the interview for your class.

### Letter to the Editor
Imagine you are a colonist in New England. Write a letter to the editor of your local newspaper about how Parliament's taxes affect your daily life. Your letter should persuade readers to take some kind of action. Use evidence from the text to support your claims.

### Word Play
Choose three words from the chapter Word Bank. Write a short story in which each of the terms is a key word. Keep in mind that you can use different forms of a word as needed to fit your story—for example, *vandal* in place of *vandalism* and *boycotted* instead of *boycott*.

THE IMPACT TODAY

# Why Do People Pay Taxes?

## Taxing and Spending

Taxes, spending, and representation played key roles in why colonists revolted against the British in the American Revolution. So, how does government tax, spend, and impact the economy today?

Every level of government—federal, state, and local—sets a budget or plan for how to collect and spend money. Governments collect most of their money from taxes. But they also collect fees for everything from parking on a public road to a museum ticket to a dog license.

The federal government collects taxes such as individual income taxes, payroll taxes, and corporate income taxes. State and local governments collect income taxes, property taxes, sales taxes, and other taxes.

People can use coins, credit cards, and smart phones to pay for parking.

### 2017 U.S. Federal Government Taxes Collected

For every $100 collected in revenue, about...

= **$3.3 trillion** in revenue collected!

**$48** came from individual income taxes.

**$35** came from payroll taxes.

**$9** came from corporate income taxes.

**$8** came from other taxes and fees.

Source: Congressional Budget Office

(t)J Dennis/Shutterstock, (c, b)©McGraw-Hill Education

The federal government spends money on many things, including national defense, Social Security, healthcare, and other services that impact the entire nation. Each year, the federal government spends in the trillions of dollars!

Source: Congressional Budget Office

States fund projects and services such as public schools, transportation, public safety, and courts. Your local government typically spends money on police and fire protection, parks and recreation, garbage removal, water and sewer services, and fixing roads.

At every level of government, tax dollars help fuel government-provided services we use every day. Every time someone rides a bike down the road, watches a news story about a fire, visits a national park, or goes to a public school, a person sees his or her tax dollars at work.

## WHAT IS THE IMPACT TODAY?

**Talk** Pick one government service you or your family members use. Suppose a person or business provided the service instead of the government.

How would the service be paid for? How might the service change? Are there some things that only governments can do?

# Debating Choices

As with a personal budget, government budgets involve choices about how to collect and spend money. On the federal level, the president and Congress work together to prepare and approve the budget. On the state level, your governor and state legislature decide. Locally, your town's council and mayor make budget decisions.

A budget surplus occurs when the government collects more than it spends. A budget deficit happens when governments spend more than they collect. In this case, the government needs to borrow money. Just like individuals, governments need to pay back the money with interest, an extra charge to pay for borrowing.

## Chart Skills

The chart shows a sample of yearly surpluses or deficits from the past 30 years, in dollars. Deficits are shown in orange type. An estimate* is provided for 2020.

What do you notice about deficits and surpluses over this time period?

**U.S. Federal Government Budget**

| Year | Surplus or Deficit |
|---|---|
| 1990 | −221 Billion |
| 1995 | −164 Billion |
| 2000 | 236 Billion |
| 2005 | −318 Billion |
| 2010 | −1.3 Trillion (1,300 Billion) |
| 2015 | −438 Billion |
| 2020* | −987 Billion |

Source: U.S. Office of Management and Budget

Citizens can impact government tax-and-spending choices by lobbying their representatives, protesting in public, and voting for candidates who reflect their economic ideas and values. Debates over spending and taxes can become challenging. Governments can even shut down and stop providing some services until representatives agree on a budget.

# Growing the Economy

Alexander Hamilton

The nation's first secretary of the treasury, Alexander Hamilton, believed in a strong government role in the economy. He fought for spending on roads, bridges, and power supplies to help trade and businesses. He proposed a tariff, or tax on goods imported from other countries, to pay for this and other economic investments. Hamilton's ideas helped transform the U.S. into a global economic leader.

Today, governments at all levels invest in projects, people, and ideas to help the economy grow. In addition to transportation and the power grid, governments invest in medical research, education, and even exploring space to help the economy. And the federal government still applies tariffs at times on foreign goods to help companies that make the same goods in America. Foreign countries often retaliate with tariffs on American goods.

Governments also give tax incentives, or breaks, to businesses to help grow the economy. States and cities often compete with one another with lower business taxes to get corporations to build factories and headquarters in their area. Governments must weigh the cost of tax breaks. Offering tax breaks reduces tax revenue but may lead to more jobs.

## WHAT IS THE IMPACT TODAY?

COLLABORATE

**Talk** A town council has $100,000 remaining in its budget. It can afford to build a new playground or provide a tax break to a company to build a new grocery store in its town. Each costs $75,000.

What would you choose to do if you were on the council? Why? Is there another solution?

# The American Revolution

## What Does the Revolutionary Era Tell Us About Our Nation Today?

In this chapter, you'll read about important events and people in the American Revolution. You'll think about why these events and people are important, the impact they had during the Revolution, and how the Revolution still impacts our nation today.

## Step into the Time Chronological Thinking

Look at the time line. What was going on in the rest of the world during the same years as the American Revolution?

**Americas**

**1775** Revolutionary War begins at Lexington and Concord in Massachusetts.
George Washington becomes the leader of the Continental Army.

**1776** Continental Congress signs the Declaration of Independence.

**1777** Continental Army wins the Battle of Saratoga.

**1778** French and American governments sign the Treaty of Alliance.

1775 — 1776 — 1777 — 1778

**World Events**

**1776** Wolfgang Amadeus Mozart's Serenade No. 7 is first performed in Salzburg, Austria.

**1778** Tây Sơn Dynasty is established in Vietnam.

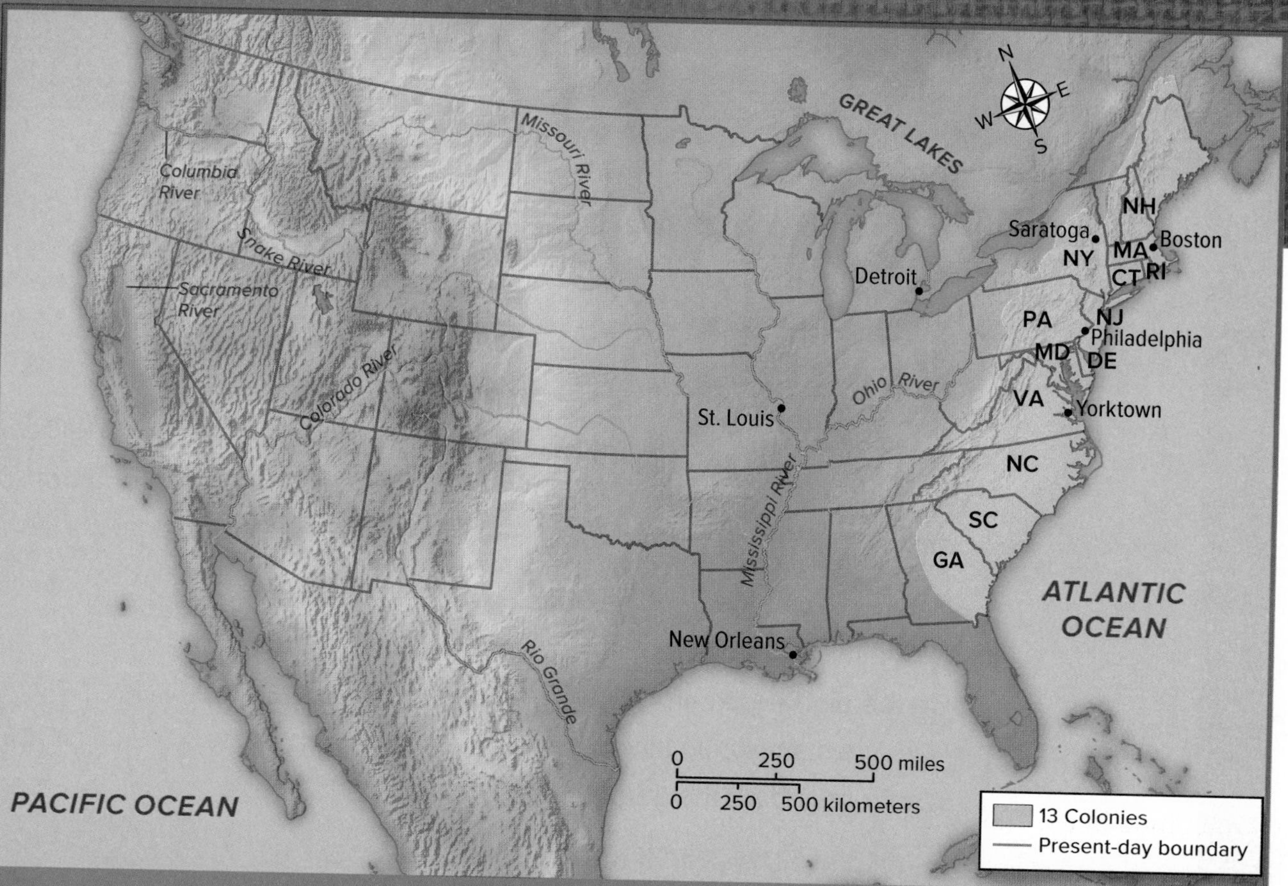

PACIFIC OCEAN

ATLANTIC OCEAN

GREAT LAKES

Columbia River
Snake River
Sacramento River
Colorado River
Missouri River
Ohio River
Mississippi River
Rio Grande

NH
MA
Boston
Saratoga
NY
CT
RI
Detroit
PA
NJ
Philadelphia
MD
DE
VA
Yorktown
St. Louis
NC
SC
GA
New Orleans

N
E
S
W

0 250 500 miles
0 250 500 kilometers

13 Colonies
Present-day boundary

## The Original Thirteen British Colonies

### Step into the Place

1. Which of the cities or settlements identified on the map are not located in one of the original Thirteen Colonies?
2. Find Yorktown, Virginia, and Saratoga, New York, on the map. Use the time line to find out what important events happened in these two cities during the American Revolution.

**1779**
British army shifts focus to Southern states.

**1780**
Hundreds are killed during the Gordon Riots in London.

**1781**
Continental Army defeats British at Yorktown, Virginia.

**1781**
Sir William Herschel discovers the planet Uranus.

**1782**
The city of Bangkok is founded as the capital of Siam.

**1783**
Peace of Paris formally ends Revolutionary War.

**1783**
Laki volcano erupts and causes famine in Iceland.

1779 1780 1781 1782 1783

# Connect Through Literature

## Selections from
# Paul Revere's Ride

By Henry Wadsworth Longfellow

*Paul Revere was a Patriot who, along with Samuel Prescott and William Dawes, rode from Boston to Lexington and Concord to warn of a British attack. This poem written 100 years later, celebrated that famous ride.*

Listen, my children, and you shall hear
Of the midnight ride of Paul Revere,
On the eighteenth of April, in Seventy-five;
Hardly a man is now alive
Who remembers that famous day and year.

He said to his friend, "If the British march
By land or sea from the town to-night,
Hang a lantern aloft in the belfry arch
Of the North Church tower as a signal light,—
One, if by land, and two, if by sea;
And I on the opposite shore will be,
Ready to ride and spread the alarm
Through every Middlesex village
and farm, For the country folk to be up and to arm."
Then he said, "Good night!" and with muffled oar
Silently rowed to the Charlestown shore . . .

You know the rest. In the books you have read,
How the British Regulars fired and fled,—
How the farmers gave them ball for ball,
From behind each fence and farmyard wall,
Chasing the Red Coats down the lane,
Then crossing the fields to emerge again
Under the trees at the turn of the road,
And only pausing to fire and load.

So through the night rode Paul Revere;
And so through the night went his cry of alarm
To every Middlesex village and farm,—
A cry of defiance and not of fear,
A voice in the darkness, a knock at the door,
And a word that shall echo forevermore!
For, borne on the night-wind of the Past,
Through all our history, to the last,
In the hour of darkness and peril and need,
The people will waken and listen to hear
The hurrying hoof beats of that steed,
And the midnight message of Paul Revere.

## Think About It

1. What was the purpose of Paul Revere's ride?
2. How do you think a poem helps people remember Paul Revere's story differently than an informative article in a book would?
3. Longfellow describes Revere's warning as "a cry of defiance and not fear." How is a "cry of defiance" different from a "cry of fear"?

# People You Should Know

## John Hancock

John Hancock, from Boston, Massachusetts, was an important Patriot during the American Revolution. Hancock was a very wealthy man, and he used his money to support the revolution. He was the president of the Second Continental Congress, and he also served twice as the governor of Massachusetts. As president of the Continental Congress, he was the first person to sign the Declaration of Independence.

## Peter Salem

Peter Salem was an African American soldier in the American Revolution. He was born into slavery in 1750. In 1775, he was freed by his owner so he could serve in the militia. Peter Salem fought in the Battle of Concord. He also fought at the battles of Bunker Hill and Saratoga. Salem spent nearly five years fighting for the freedom of the American colonies. He is buried in Framingham, Massachusetts. In 1882, the town erected a monument to Peter Salem and declared June 17 Peter Salem Day.

## Mercy Otis Warren

Mercy Otis Warren was born in Massachusetts in 1728. She is considered the first American woman to write primarily for a public audience, rather than herself. She wrote about politics and what was happening in the American colonies. During the American Revolution, she was an adviser to many political leaders, including Patrick Henry, George Washington, Thomas Jefferson, and John Adams. Mercy Otis Warren's writings had an important effect on the shaping of our nation.

## Haym Salomon

Haym Salomon, a Jewish American businessman, was a strong supporter of the American Revolution. He realized that a major obstacle to the success of the United States would be its lack of money. He stepped in to arrange loans and funding from France. When that wasn't enough, he lent huge amounts of his own money to keep the revolution alive. He also gave money to founding fathers, such as Thomas Jefferson, to ensure those men could continue to do their important work. By the end of the war, Salomon was completely broke, but the young nation did not repay him.

(t)McGraw-Hill Education, (bl)Everett Historical/Shutterstock.com, (br)The National Archives and Records Administration

# Lesson 1 How Did the American Revolution Start?

## The Battles of Lexington and Concord

By 1775, the colonists were tired of British taxes and oppression. After some violent encounters with British troops, the colonists began stockpiling arms and gunpowder in Lexington and Concord, two towns near Boston, Massachusetts.

### Paul Revere Rides

On April 18, 1775, British General Thomas Gage ordered 700 soldiers from Boston to seize and destroy colonial war supplies and to arrest patriot leaders Samuel Adams and John Hancock. Gage's plan was to make a surprise attack on Lexington and Concord, so he gave his troops orders not to allow any colonists to leave Boston that night.

Little did General Gage know that a small group of patriots had learned of his plan to attack the two towns. Under cover of night, Paul Revere, William Dawes, and Samuel Prescott set out to warn the people in the area. Revere arrived at Lexington around midnight. When a guard for Adams and Hancock asked him not to make so much noise, Revere told him, "You'll have noise enough before long. The regulars [British troops] are coming!"

Paul Revere set out at night to warn of Britain's plan to attack Lexington and Concord.

**December 1773**
Boston Tea Party dumps tea into Boston Harbor.

**April 1775**
Fighting begins at Lexington.

**May 1775**
Second Continental Congress meets in Philadelphia.

**June 1775**
Battle of Bunker Hill

73 | 1774 | 1775

**An engraving of the Battle of Lexington**

## Battle at Lexington

When the British troops reached Lexington, Captain John Parker was waiting with the local **militia**. Massachusetts relied on the militia and other volunteer soldiers called the minutemen when emergency troops were needed. John Robins, one of the colonial militiamen, described the sight of the British advancing: "There appeared a number of the King's troops . . . at the distance of about sixty or seventy yards from us . . . and on a quick pace toward us. . . ."

TEXT: Robins, John. "Affidavit No. 5, Lexington, April 24, 1775." Depositions Concerning Lexington and Concord. In Journals of the Continental Congress, 1774-1789, Thursday May 11, 1775.; PHOTO: Library of Congress Prints & Photographs Division [LC-DIG-pga-00995]

## The First Shots

Captain Parker's orders to the militia were very simple, "Don't fire unless fired upon, but if they mean to have a war, let it begin here."

As the distance between the two groups grew smaller, someone in one of the groups fired a shot. To this day, no one knows which side fired first, but other shots quickly followed. Even though the battle lasted only a few minutes, eight militiamen were killed. The British succeeded in taking Lexington and marched on to Concord.

## Arriving in Concord

Doctor Samuel Prescott, one of the men working with Paul Revere, had warned Concord of the impending attack. The townspeople moved most of the arms and gunpowder to nearby towns. When the British arrived, they found only the few supplies the townspeople of Concord had not had time to hide.

By now the church bells were ringing loudly to alert the local farmers of the British attack. The Concord **rebels** turned on the British troops. Minutemen, local farmers, and townspeople fired at the British troops from behind fences, houses, and trees.

The British troops were forced to retreat back to Boston, 18 miles away. By the time they reached safety, more than 90 British soldiers had been killed and 174 were wounded. With these two battles, the war for American independence had begun!

The British heard that the Americans were holding large amounts of weapons at Concord.

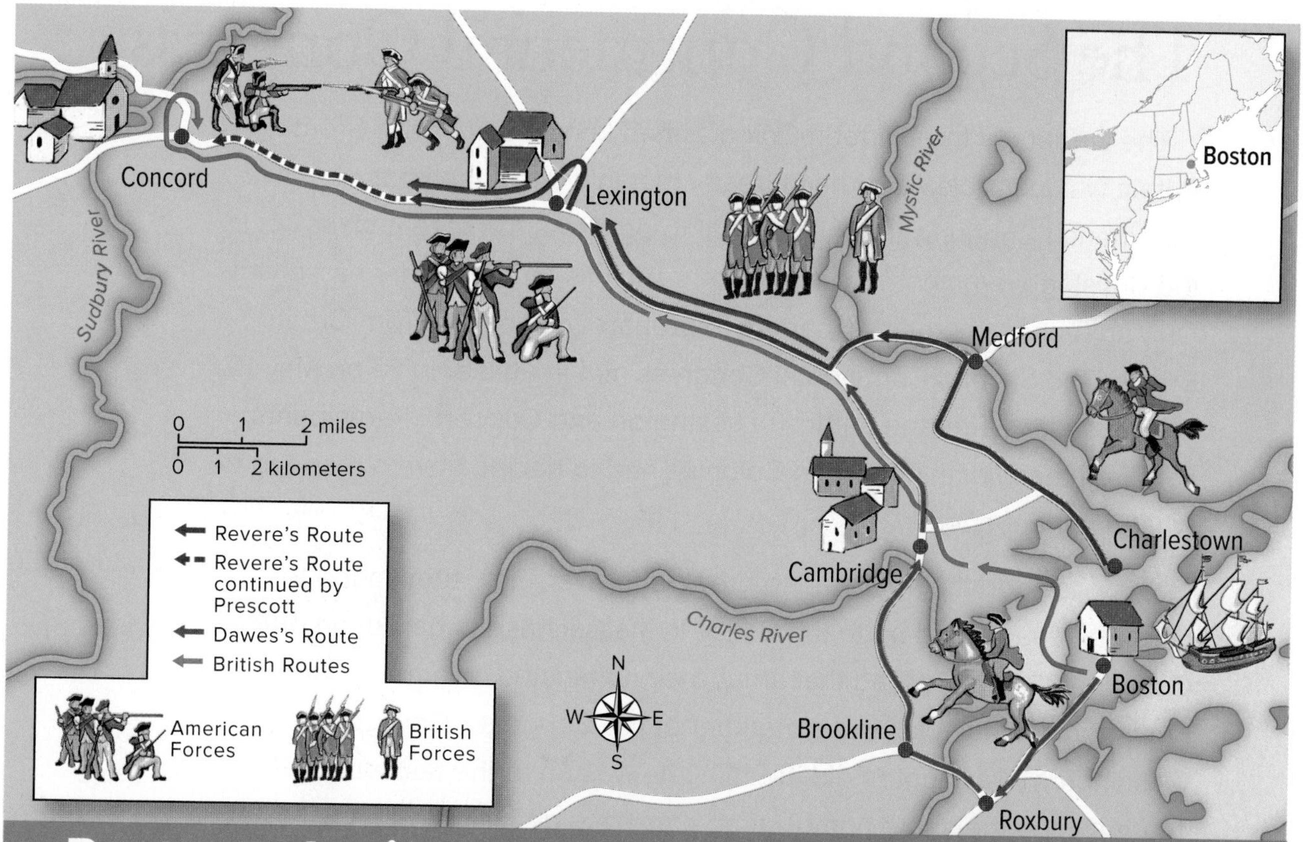

## Routes to Lexington and Concord

**Map Skills** Working with a partner, use the information provided on the map to determine who traveled the greatest distance to get to Lexington: Paul Revere, William Dawes, or the British. Use the scale to determine how many miles each traveled.

### Stop and Check

**Perspectives** Why is it important that some colonists found out about the British plans ahead of time?

**Find Details** As you read, add additional information to the graphic organizer on page 175 in your Inquiry Journal.

# The Second Continental Congress

The leaders of the Thirteen Colonies had known a war with Great Britain was possible. They had already met in 1774, in the First Continental Congress, to decide what to do about the recent taxes set by the British government. Great speakers such as Patrick Henry had given fiery speeches to urge the leaders to prepare to separate from Great Britain. The Second Continental Congress met in Philadelphia on May 10, 1775, just days after the battles of Lexington and Concord. Participants sent from each of the Thirteen Colonies had to decide how to respond to what had happened.

They decided that they had to prepare for war. First, they made the militia that had stood up to the British in Massachusetts part of an official Continental army. To lead that army, they nominated a veteran of the French and Indian War and a member of the Congress: George Washington. Washington did not think he was up to the task of commanding the entire army, but he agreed to do his best.

*Congress Voting Independence* by Robert Pine and Edward Savage

(b)taviphoto/iStockphoto/Getty Images, (inset)ClassicStock.com/SuperStock

**PRIMARY SOURCE**

## In Their Words... George Washington

Though I am truly sensible of the high Honor done me in this Appointment, yet I feel great distress, from a consciousness that my abilities and Military experience may not be equal to the extensive and important Trust: However, as the Congress desire it I will enter upon the momentous duty, and exert every power I Possess In their service and for the Support of the glorious Cause.

—address to the Continental Congress, June 16, 1775

The Second Continental Congress was not just a single meeting. It began as a series of meetings during the spring and summer of 1775. Besides establishing a Continental Army, the members also elected a president—John Hancock—and drafted the Olive Branch Petition. This was an attempt to resolve the conflicts between the colonies and Great Britain. However, King George III refused to receive the Congress's peace offering.

As Great Britain's grip on the colonies weakened, the Continental Congress became the unofficial government. The war was far from over, but the colonists were learning how to govern themselves. The members would continue to meet throughout the war and even afterwards to make important decisions for the Thirteen Colonies.

### Stop and Check

COLLABORATE

**Connect to Now** Is the Second Continental Congress anything like our government today? Using what you know, discuss with a partner how the Second Continental Congress is similar or different.

TEXT: "Washington Accepts his Appointment as Commander of Continental Army." Journals of the Continental Congress, vol. 2. June 16, 1775.; PHOTO: (t)McGraw-Hill Education, (b)Yale University Art Gallery

InfoGraphic

# Soldiers of the American Revolution

## The Minutemen

The citizen soldiers in the local militia didn't have uniforms. Instead, they wore their own clothes. Because the minutemen were the first ones to arrive for battle, many of the colonies made an effort to arm them with muskets and other supplies. Minutemen had the advantage over British troops of being familiar with frontier hunting and knowing what the local land was like.

### Hat

Since minutemen provided their own clothing, they wore whatever hat they owned. Styles varied greatly among the minutemen.

### Waistcoat and Coat

A sleeveless and collarless waistcoat was worn over a man's shirt. Waistcoats were usually made of linen or wool. Men wore a coat over the waistcoat. These overcoats were usually made of heavy linen or wool.

### Musket

A good soldier could load and fire his musket three times per minute. Muskets weren't very accurate and didn't work well in wet weather.

### Breeches

Knee breeches were common in the 18th century. These came just below the knee and were closed with ties or buttons. Breeches were made of leather, wool, or linen.

## The Redcoats

The British redcoats were all issued uniforms and muskets. Because battlefields of the 18th century could be smoky and confusing, the soldiers wore red. This way, British soldiers wouldn't have trouble separating friend from foe. The redcoats had the advantages of military training and better equipment over the colonial minutemen.

**Hat**

Hats identified which regiment a soldier belonged to.

**Musket**

The British Short Land Pattern musket was standard issue. Soldiers would affix a bayonet, or attachable blade, to the musket's muzzle for close combat.

**Buttons**

There could be as many as three dozen buttons on a soldier's uniform. Buttons often had the name of the soldier's regiment inscribed on them. Buttons had to be polished regularly.

**Facings**

These visible linings along the edges of the soldier's coat were colored to show the regiment he belonged to.

### Stop and Check

**Perspectives** Based on what you have just read about British and colonial fighters, who do you think had the advantage in battle? Discuss your opinion with a partner.

# The Battle of (Not) Bunker Hill

On June 18, 1775, James Warren, a Boston colonist, explained the conflict in Boston to his wife, Mercy Otis Warren, "It is impossible to describe the confusion in this place, women and children flying into the country, armed men going to the field, and wounded men . . . fill the streets."

British general Thomas Gage decided to occupy the hills around Boston. Word about the British plan spread quickly. Colonel William Prescott and General Israel Putnam led one thousand colonial troops to hills north of Boston, across the Charles River. The original plan was to fortify Bunker Hill, which means to build earthen walls around it. This way, the colonists could fire cannons at the British troops stationed across the Charles River in Boston. Instead, the colonists decided to protect Breed's Hill, which was closer to the river. The colonists worked all night to build a fort for protection.

## The Battle Begins

British troops crossed the Charles River by boat and marched up Breed's Hill. The militia and civilians, or ordinary citizens, waited, hidden behind the walls they had built. The colonists did not have much ammunition, or musket balls and gunpowder. Officers told them not to waste ammunition by firing at British soldiers who were too far away. Historians say that either Colonel Prescott or General Israel Putnam said, "Don't shoot until you see the whites of their eyes."

### Then and Now

A 221-foot granite obelisk in Charlestown, Massachusetts, commemorates the Battle of Bunker Hill. The cornerstone was placed in 1825 on the fiftieth anniversary of the battle by the Marquis de Lafayette, a hero of the American Revolution. The monument was completed in 1842.

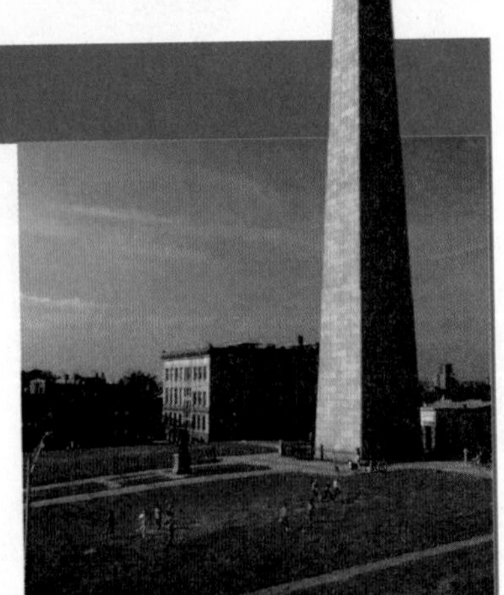

## A British Victory

Twice, the British charged up the hill only to be stopped by the militia. Both times they were forced down by gunfire. After a third try, the British overwhelmed the colonists. The British won the battle, but the victory was costly. More than a thousand soldiers were killed or wounded. Although the battle occurred on Breed's Hill, it became known as the Battle of Bunker Hill. Great Britain was one of the most powerful nations on Earth, but winning a war against the colonists would not be easy.

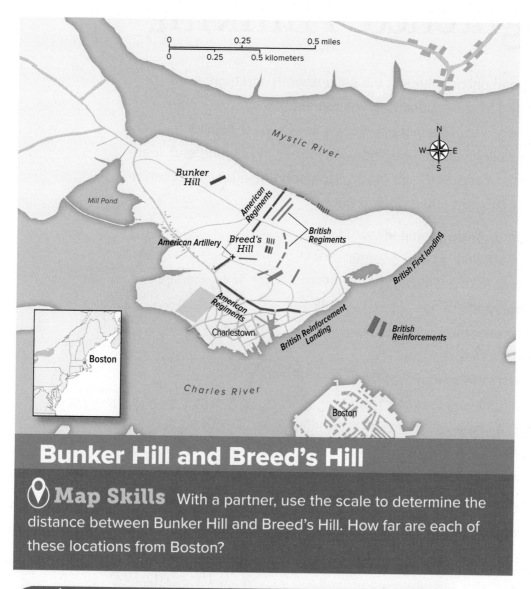



### Bunker Hill and Breed's Hill

**Map Skills** With a partner, use the scale to determine the distance between Bunker Hill and Breed's Hill. How far are each of these locations from Boston?

### Stop and Check

**Perspectives** How might the large number of casualties have changed the way the British viewed the colonists?

# Lesson 2 Why Is the Declaration of Independence Still Important Today?

## Enlightened Thinking

Many European philosophers in the seventeenth and eighteenth centuries wanted to understand how reason and knowledge could improve people's lives. This movement was known as the Enlightenment. Thinkers such as John Locke and Thomas Hobbes in England and Jean-Jacques Rousseau (roo-SOH) in France also used these ideas to change the way people thought about government.

Before this time, most people in Europe believed that kings and queens had a divine right to rule. This right allowed the **monarchs** to rule with absolute power over their subjects. As Enlightenment ideas spread, however, people began to believe that the main duty of government was to protect its citizens. In return, the people would give their consent to be governed by a ruler. This idea is called the *social contract*.

The Enlightenment greatly influenced the Americans who wrote the Declaration of Independence. The idea of the social contract is particularly important in the Declaration.

Jean-Jacques Rousseau

1775 | 1776 | 1777

**April 1775**
Battles of Lexington and Concord

**January 1776**
Thomas Paine publishes *Common Sense.*

**May 1776**
Second Continental Congress begins meeting again.

**July 1776**
Congress agrees on Declaration of Independence.

**August 1776**
Members of Congress begin to sign Declaration of Independence.

**The Committee of Five was appointed to draft the Declaration of Independence.**

(bkgd)McGraw-Hill Education, (c)©Comstock Images/Alamy, (inset)Library of Congress Prints and Photographs Division [LC-USZC2-2243]

# Common Sense

Thomas Paine was living in London when he met Benjamin Franklin. Franklin advised Paine to emigrate to North America to build a new life there. When Paine arrived in Philadelphia in November 1774, the colonies were edging toward revolution. He got a job as the editor of *Pennsylvania Magazine*.

After fighting broke out in Lexington and Concord, Paine wrote a 50-page pamphlet titled *Common Sense*. He published it in January 1776. He argued that government should be a social contract, as other Enlightenment thinkers had suggested. Paine also believed that the colonies had lived through so much tyranny that there could be no **reconciliation** with Great Britain. Paine put his argument into such simple language that ordinary people easily understood his ideas. His powerful pamphlet got many colonists talking about independence.

**PRIMARY SOURCE**

## In Their Words... Thomas Paine

**. . . and that the *elected* might never form to themselves an interest separate from the *electors*, prudence will point out the propriety of having elections often; because as the *elected* might by that means return and mix again with the general body of the *electors* in a few months, their fidelity to the public will be secured by the prudent reflection of not making a rod for themselves. And as this frequent interchange will establish a common interest with every part of the community, they will mutually and naturally support each other, and on this (not on the unmeaning name of king), depends the *strength of government, and the happiness of the governed.***

—from *Common Sense*, published in January 1776

TEXT: Paine, Thomas. Common Sense. Philadelphia: W. & T. Bradford, February 14, 1776.; PHOTO: Courtesy National Gallery of Art, Washington

# Writing the Declaration

In June 1776, Richard Henry Lee of Virginia told the Second Continental Congress, "These United colonies are, and of a right, ought to be, free and independent States." The Congress nominated five members to outline the colonies' reasons for wanting independence from Great Britain. The members of the committee were John Adams of Massachusetts, Benjamin Franklin of Pennsylvania, Robert Livingston of New York, Roger Sherman of Connecticut, and Thomas Jefferson of Virginia.

The committee chose Jefferson to write the first draft. He wrote for two weeks. Then Franklin and Adams made minor changes before presenting the Declaration to the full Congress on June 28, 1776. The other members of the Congress argued about the wording of the document. One of the most controversial issues was language Jefferson had included about the evils of slavery. Representatives from the Southern Colonies, whose economies depended on slavery, wanted that language removed. John Adams later said, "I knew his southern brethren would never . . . [allow the section] to pass in Congress." Jefferson ultimately agreed to take out the section, and the Southern members gave their approval, leading to Congress voting in favor of the Declaration.

Thomas Jefferson was born in Virginia.

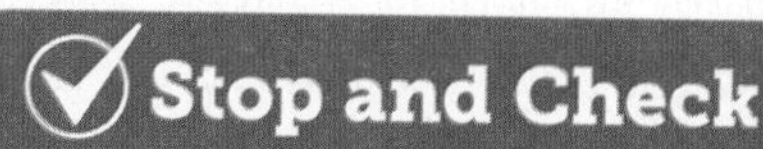

## Stop and Check

COLLABORATE

**Talk** What prompted Congress to remove the language about slavery from the Declaration of Independence?

**Find Details** As you read, add new information to the graphic organizer on page 183 in your Inquiry Journal.

# Signing the Declaration

After two days of debating the details of the Declaration, the members passed the final version on July 4, 1776. Word spread. The document was reprinted in newspapers and posted in meetinghouses and churches. On August 2, the members began to sign the Declaration. John Hancock, the president of the Congress, signed first. The rest of the 56 members signed beneath his signature. Each man knew he was risking his life and his property by putting his name on the Declaration. But the signers believed so strongly in independence that they took the risk. They could only hope that the colonists' Continental Army would be strong enough to beat the British.

**John Hancock was the first delegate to sign the Declaration of Independence.**

## Citizenship

### A Call for Unity

The members knew that signing the Declaration of Independence would be viewed by the British government as an act of treason. This meant each man who signed put his life at risk. The members needed to be unified as they bravely met this danger. After signing, Ben Franklin is believed to have remarked, "We must all hang together, or assuredly we shall all hang separately."

Even though not every member of the Second Continental Congress wanted the colonies to gain independence from Great Britain, they did indeed "all hang together." John Dickinson argued that the colonies should reconcile with Great Britain. He refused to sign. After Congress passed the Declaration, however, Dickinson showed his support for the new nation by joining the Pennsylvania militia. He did this even though he had disagreed with the other delegates on the question of independence.

TEXT: Benjamin Franklin. 1776. First quoted in Jared Sparks, The Works of Benjamin Franklin, vol. 1 (Boston: Hilliard Gray, and Company, 1840), 408.; PHOTO: Library of Congress Prints and Photographs Division [LC-USZC2-2711]

# Structure of the Declaration

IN CONGRESS, JULY 4, 1776.

The unanimous Declaration of the thirteen united States of America,

**Preamble**

The first paragraph is the inspirational introduction to the document.

**List of Grievances**

This list of 27 complaints against King George III outlines why the colonists want their independence from Great Britain.

**Declaration of Independence**

The concluding paragraph states in firm terms that the colonies are declaring themselves free and independent from Great Britain.

## Stop and Check

**Think** Why was it important to list 27 reasons the colonists wanted to be free from King George III and Great Britain?

# Does the Declaration Still Matter?

More than 240 years after the Declaration of Independence was signed, it still inspires people in the United States and around the world to believe in the ideal of self-government. Part of the document's success is a result of how well Jefferson made his case. The document argues that freedom belongs to everyone and no tyrant deserves the right to rule.

Though the words are still powerful today, some of their meanings have changed. For example, our understanding of the important phrase "all men are created equal" has grown to include women, African Americans, Native Americans, and people of all other backgrounds.

The phrase "Life, Liberty, and the pursuit of Happiness" is often used today, too. It means that all people have natural rights, or rights they are born with. No government can take these rights away.

Another key phrase from the Preamble argues that a government derives its power from the "consent of the governed." This idea, taken from John Locke, describes the social contract that continues to exist between a ruler and the people: Each gains power from the other.

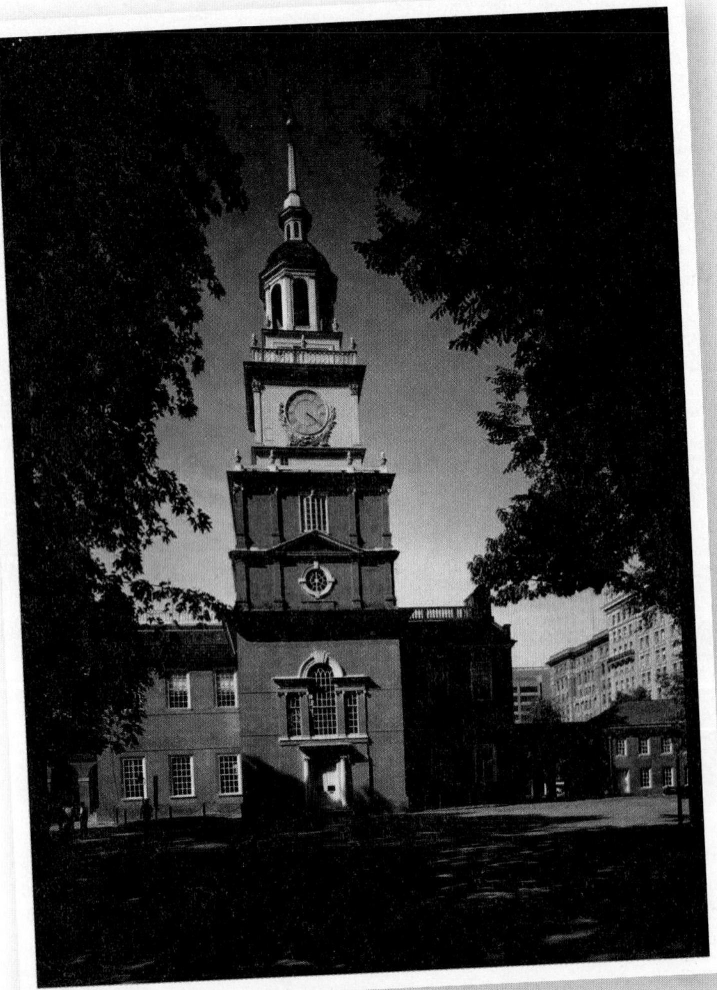

**Independence Hall in Philadelphia, Pennsylvania, site of the Second Continental Congress**

The statement "It is their right, it is their duty, to throw off such government" argues that the colonies are justified in their revolution. Because King George III was considered a tyrant, the Declaration states that it is the right and, more importantly, the duty of the colonists to "throw off" his rule over them.

What about the rest of the British people? The Declaration states that they will be considered "Enemies in War, in Peace Friends." This means that if the British continue to fight, the Americans will fight back. If they make peace, the Americans will be their friends.

**PRIMARY SOURCE**

## In Their Words... Thomas Jefferson

**We hold these truths to be self-evident, that all men are created equal, that they are endowed by their Creator with certain unalienable Rights, that among these are Life, Liberty and the pursuit of Happiness.–That to secure these rights, Governments are instituted among Men, deriving their just powers from the consent of the governed, . . .**

—from the Preamble to the Declaration of Independence

## Stop and Check

**Talk** Why has the meaning of the phrase "all men are created equal" changed over the years?

# Philadelphia, Pennsylvania

Philadelphia was more than just a meeting place for the drafters of the Declaration of Independence. In 1777, Philadelphia was the largest city in North America. It was centrally located among the new American states. This location made it a good place to hold meetings that included leaders from each state. In the city today, you can still tour Philadelphia's past.

**Liberty Bell**

The Liberty Bell originally hung in the belfry of Independence Hall. It now resides in its own building nearby. The bell was rung for the First Continental Congress and the Battles of Lexington and Concord. On July 8, 1776, the bell was rung before the public reading of the Declaration of Independence.

**Elfreth's Alley**

Near Independence Hall is Elfreth's Alley, the oldest street in the country. People have lived and worked in Elfreth's Alley since 1702.

**Franklin Court**

Visitors can view many objects that once belonged to Benjamin Franklin in Franklin Court. The area includes a working print shop as well as a post office once run by Franklin, who was America's first Postmaster General.

**Betsy Ross House**

According to legend, Betsy Ross made the first United States flag after a visit from George Washington in June 1776. During this visit, Ross showed Washington a 5-pointed star made from a folded square of cloth with a single cut of the scissors.

## Stop and Check

**Talk** Why was Philadelphia an ideal place for the Second Continental Congress to meet?

**What Do You Think?** Why is the Declaration of Independence still important today?

# Lesson 3 What Were the Defining Moments of the War?

## Strengths and Weaknesses of the Two Sides

The American Revolution presented challenges for both the British and the Americans. Neither side was prepared to fight a war that would last eight years. They would often have shortages of equipment, soldiers, and the money to pay for both. While a wealthy and powerful nation like Britain would seem to have a great advantage, both sides had their strengths and weaknesses.

The war was very expensive for Britain. All soldiers and supplies had to be sent by ship across the Atlantic Ocean. Britain financed the war by raising taxes on citizens living in Britain. Many British people disagreed with the war because they did not want higher taxes.

The American army received its funding from the Second Continental Congress. Congress, however, often did not have enough money to pay soldiers or buy supplies or food for them. As a result, it was difficult to keep men from deserting, or leaving the army. Some people, known as **profiteers**, took advantage of the poor wartime economy to hoard goods and sell them at high prices. However, the war had tremendous support from civilians in the colonies. To help with the war effort, civilians made musket balls and blankets. They gathered food and supplies to send to the front.

**April 1775**
Battles of Lexington and Concord

**July 1776**
Congress agrees on Declaration of Independence.

**January 1777**
After a series of losses in New York, George Washington's Continental Army triumphs over British twice in New Jersey.

1775 | 1776 | 1777 | 1778 | 1779

**1777–1778**
Washington's Continental Army endures a brutal winter at Valley Forge in Pennsylvania.

**February 1778**
Americans and French sign Treaty of Alliance.

**October 1777**
British suffer a major defeat at the Battle of Saratoga.

**French ships (on the left) battle the British Navy during the Revolutionary War. France's entry into the war on the American side was a defining moment of the war.**

The British had more soldiers, including Native Americans and paid German **mercenaries**, or people who fight for money. The British soldiers were also better trained and armed than the American soldiers. However, the British soldiers were trained to fight only in open battlefields. Americans were more familiar with the land where they lived. The Americans took advantage of this British weakness to surprise the British in different kinds of terrain such as the swamps of the south and the forests of the north. The Americans' more plain-looking clothes helped them blend into the landscape, while the British soldiers' red coats made them easy targets.

Ultimately, the British failed to recognize both their own weaknesses and the Americans' strengths. One of their biggest mistakes was underestimating the Americans' willingness to risk everything to win their independence.

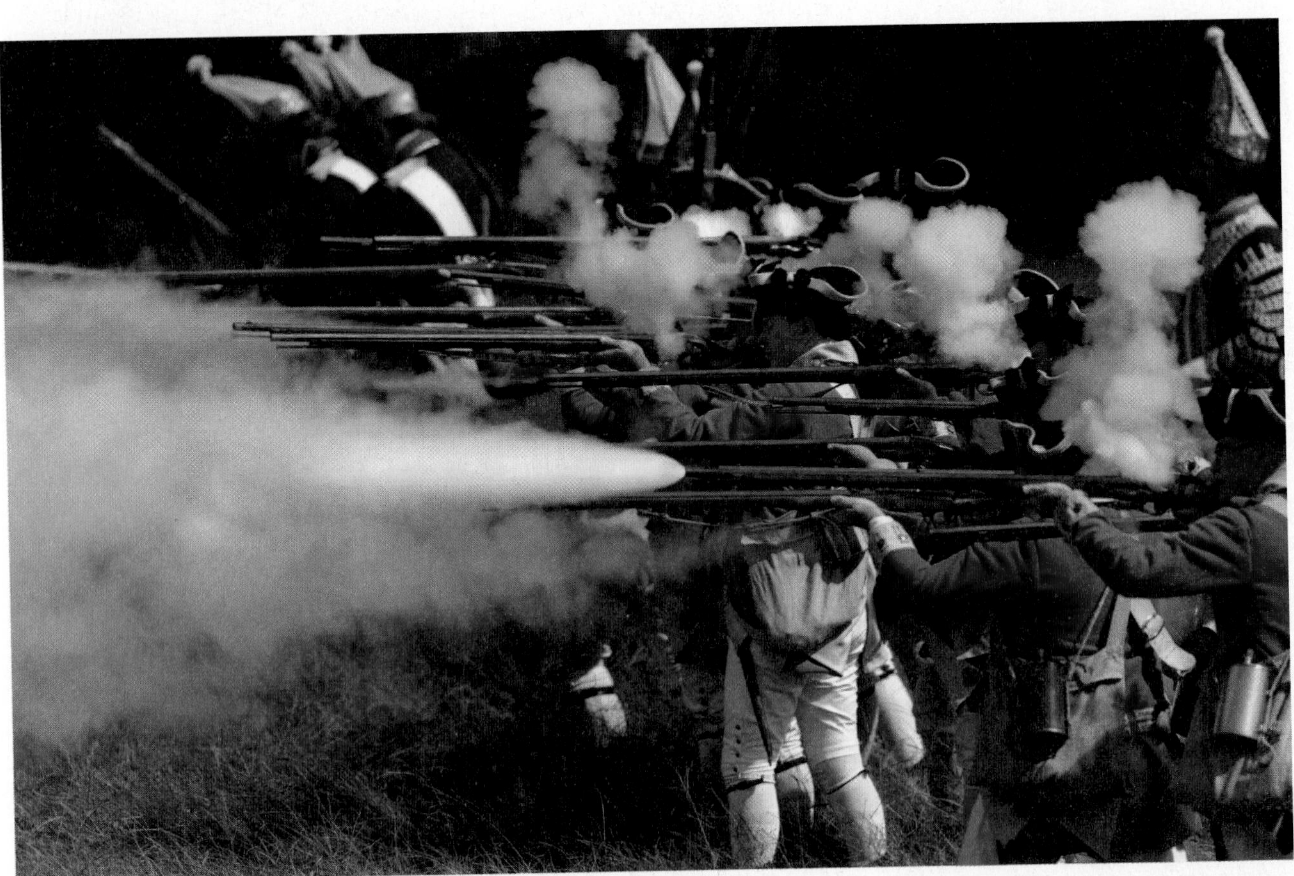

Michael Melford/National Geographic/Getty Images

**British soldiers were trained to fight only in open battlefields. Their red coats made them easy targets.**

# Washington on the Offensive

After the Battles of Lexington and Concord and the signing of the Declaration of Independence, the Americans suffered some major setbacks. The Continental Army lost important battles in New York State. By the middle of 1776, George Washington's soldiers had been driven into Pennsylvania.

Washington needed victories to boost his soldiers' morale. He was concerned that many would leave his army and go home when their term of service ran out. On Christmas night, 1776, he led 2,400 soldiers across the Delaware River from Pennsylvania into New Jersey.

The army reached Trenton at dawn and attacked at once, surprising and defeating German mercenaries who were fighting for the British. A few days later, Washington won another victory when his soldiers left their campfires burning near Trenton so the British would not be aware that they had snuck away to attack Princeton successfully. It became clear that the Americans had a chance of winning the war after all.

**Stop and Check**

**Talk** How did Washington prove in 1776 and 1777 that he was capable of defeating the British troops?

**Find Details** As you read, add new information to the graphic organizer on page 191 in your Inquiry Journal.

Commander-in-Chief George Washington led the Continental Army.

# The Battle of Saratoga

In 1777, the British decided to try to capture the Hudson River Valley, cutting off New York and New Jersey from the states in New England. British General John Burgoyne believed this would fatally weaken the American army. His army invaded the valley from its base in Canada.

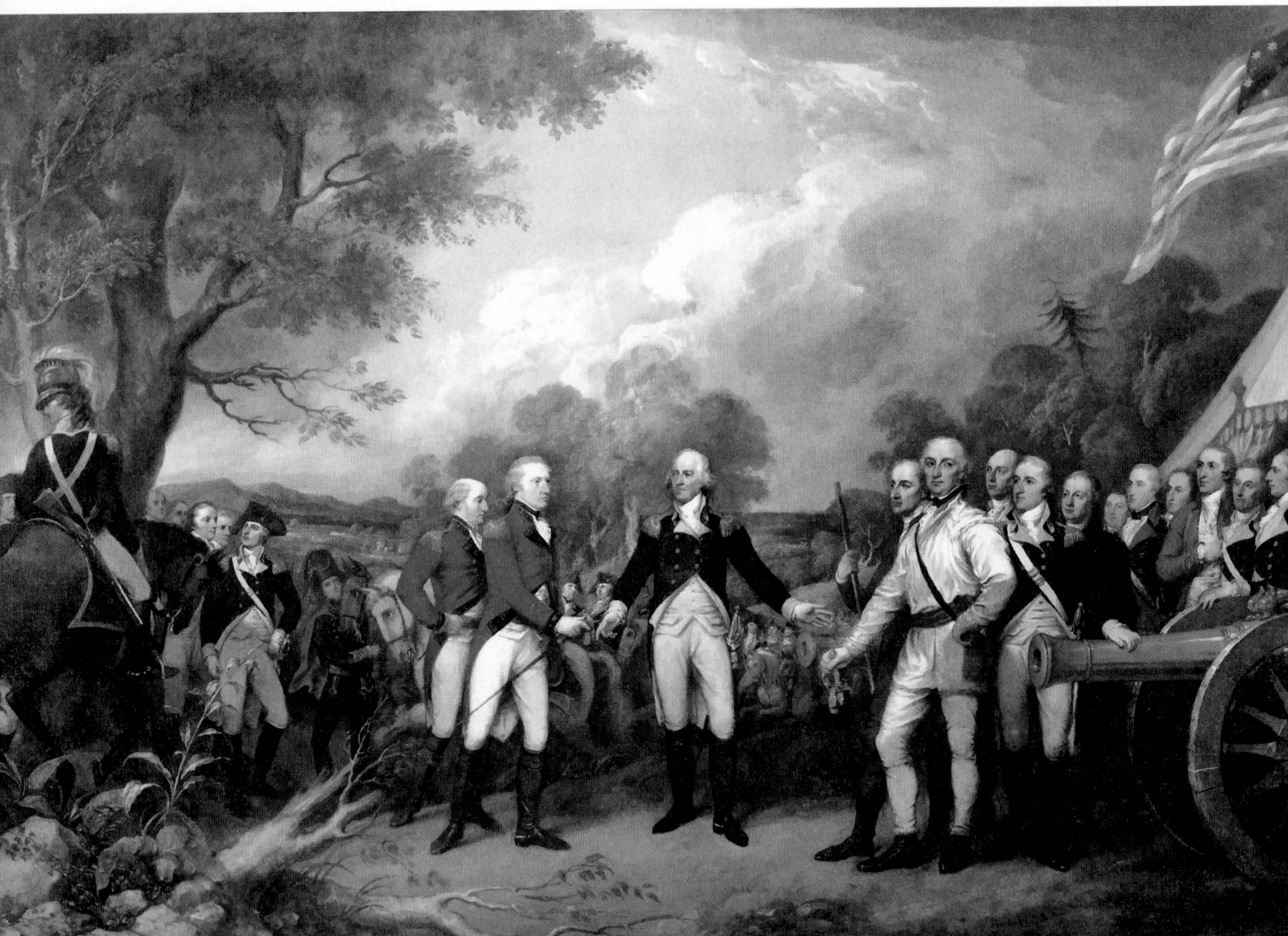

**British General Burgoyne surrenders at Saratoga, New York.**

Part of Burgoyne's plan depended on help from Mohawk and Iroquois scouts. Burgoyne's army became bogged down in terrain made difficult by forests and swamps. The Mohawk and Iroquois began to lose confidence in British promises that they could prevent more colonists from taking their lands. As the scouts drifted away, Burgoyne had no information about where the Americans were or what they were doing.

The Americans, on the other hand, were prepared. General Thomas Gates planned an attack on British forces near Saratoga, New York. The American fighting force was three times the size of that of the British. Gates also sent expert riflemen to attack British troops as they moved through New York. By the time the British forces reached Saratoga, they had been badly weakened.

Even though his troops were weakened and outnumbered, Burgoyne was sure he could still defeat the Americans. He chose to attack at Freeman's Farm near Saratoga. Before the British could attack, however, a Polish engineer named Tadeusz Kościuszko (tah-DEH-oosh kohsh-CHOOSH-koh) helped the Americans fortify the walls around Freeman's Farm and the surrounding roads. Kościuszko helped protect the Americans and their supply lines from the British attack in this first Battle of Saratoga. General Gates was also able to obtain fresh troops to strengthen his lines of defense against the British.

## Then and Now

The battlefields of Saratoga are now part of a National Park. When you visit, you can go on a self-guided tour. You can see a monument, a 155-foot tall obelisk to the American victory. You can also take a walk through Victory Woods, the site of General Burgoyne's last encampment before surrendering.

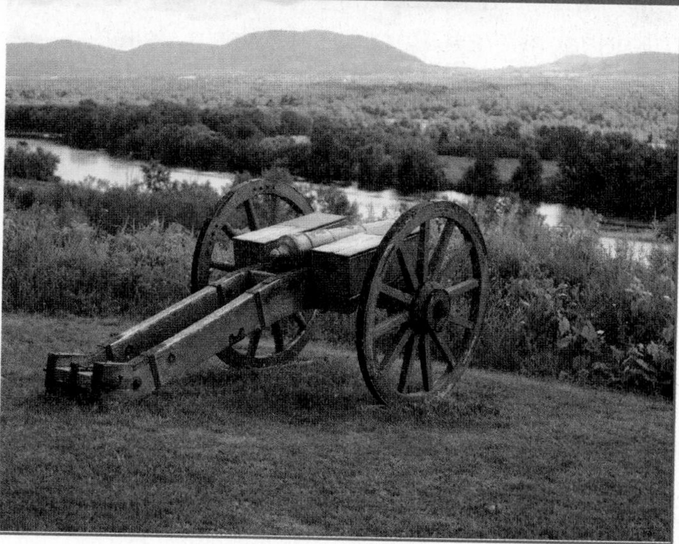

Throughout September 1777, American riflemen who were hidden in the hillsides shot at any British soldier who tried to fetch water from the Hudson River. This further weakened the British troops. On October 7, American General Benedict Arnold's forces drove back a portion of Burgoyne's soldiers who had been scouting the area to gain information. This battle became known as the Second Battle of Saratoga.

By mid-October, Burgoyne's troops were greatly reduced in number. As a result of the Americans' preparedness, the British were cut off from receiving more supplies. They were running out of food. Finally, after two more months of fighting, Burgoyne decided to surrender to Gates on October 17. The victory at Saratoga changed the direction of the war.

## Biography

### Tadeusz Kościuszko

Born in Poland, Tadeusz Kościuszko emigrated to the United States in 1776. He immediately joined the American fight for independence. Because he was a skilled engineer, Kościuszko was asked to help fortify the meeting place of the Continental Congress. In 1777, he joined General Gates in upstate New York. There, he helped fortify Freeman's Farm and the American supply lines. He went on to prove his bravery and cleverness at several more battles during the war before being promoted to the rank of brigadier general. After the Revolution, he was granted American citizenship.

The Miriam and Ira D. Wallach Division of Art, Prints and Photographs: Print Collection, Emmet Collection of Manuscripts Etc. Relating to American History. The New York Public Library

## Stop and Check

**Think** Why did it matter that the American forces were able to fortify Freeman's Farm and the surrounding roads before the British attacked?

# A Turning Point

The Americans' victory at the two Battles of Saratoga proved to the rest of the world that the Americans were capable of defeating the British. In 1777 and 1778, Benjamin Franklin, who was then the American Ambassador to France, worked with French officials to create the Treaty of Alliance. As a result of this treaty, France sent troops, warships, and supplies to the United States.

Individual Europeans agreed to come to the aid of the United States, too. Baron Friedrich von Steuben of Prussia helped to train American soldiers to fight together. Casimir Pulaski of Poland trained soldiers to fight on horseback and became a general. He gave his life in battle for American independence. The Marquis de Lafayette of France became a valuable member of Washington's staff. He would prove his worth at the Battle of Yorktown.

Casimir Pulaski

Since it was allied with France, Spain also joined America's struggle with Great Britain. In 1779, the governor of the Spanish territory of Louisiana closed the port of New Orleans to British ships and opened it to American ships. Spain also made loans to support the American war effort. Spanish Colonel Bernárdo de Galvez led a force to fight the British in the South.

 **Stop and Check**

**Talk** Why was the Battle of Saratoga a turning point in the Revolutionary War?

# Winter at Valley Forge

Despite the great victory at Saratoga, the Continental Army elsewhere suffered a number of defeats, including two near Philadelphia in late 1777. Washington's 11,000 men set up camp that winter at Valley Forge, Pennsylvania. The site seemed easy to defend, should the British attack. It was also close to good roads, which would allow the army to get supplies.

**American soldiers suffered during the brutal winter at Valley Forge.**

Bettmann/Getty Images

That winter, however, was a time of cold, hunger, and loneliness for the Patriot soldiers. Often the only food was "fire cakes," which were made of a paste of flour and water baked hard over a campfire. Many soldiers gave up and went home. At least 2,500 died of diseases that winter, including smallpox, typhoid, and influenza. Those who lived faced frostbite and starvation. The Marquis de Lafayette later wrote, "The unfortunate soldiers were in need of everything; they had neither coats, hats, shirts, nor shoes, their feet and legs froze."

Washington begged the Continental Congress and the state governors for supplies. He described the terrible sufferings of his army. His letters were answered with promises, but very little help arrived.

Washington held his army together with little but the force of his own leadership. He used the time at Valley Forge wisely, however. Groups of 100 soldiers took turns training with Baron von Steuben. Then each trainee taught another 100 men what he had learned. By the spring, more money became available due to the alliance with France. While Washington's troops came to Valley Forge a barefoot, ragged band, they marched away in 1778 as professional soldiers.

### Stop and Check

**Talk** What happened to the soldiers of the Continental Army at Valley Forge?

**What Do You Think?** How did the talents of individual Europeans like von Steuben, Pulaski, and Kościuszko strengthen the cause of American Independence?

TEXT: Marie Joseph Paul Yves Roch Gilbert Du Motier marquis de Lafayette. Memoirs, Correspondence and Manuscripts of General Lafayette, Volume 1. New York: Saunders and Otley, 1837.; PHOTO: McGraw-Hill Education

# What Was It Like to Live During the Revolution?

## Women of the Revolution

The Revolutionary War impacted the lives of more than just the soldiers and generals waging war. The Revolutionary War changed the lives of every civilian in the colonies.

American women supported the war in many ways. Mercy Otis Warren and Hannah Winthrop recorded and wrote letters about the events of the Revolution so everyone knew what was happening. Phillis Wheatley, a freed African American, wrote poetry that inspired many people. Other women tended farms or minded shops while their husbands were away fighting in the army.

Some women followed their husbands to war and did whatever they could to help. Earning the nickname "Molly Pitcher," Mary Ludwig Hays carried pitchers of water to men on the battlefield. Legend has it that she took her husband's place at a cannon when he became too exhausted to fight during the Battle of Monmouth in 1778.

Molly Pitcher helps load a cannon at a battle in New Jersey.

Still other women remained loyal to the British crown. Either for religious reasons, or because their families' businesses depended on British trade, Loyalist men and women wanted reconciliation with Great Britain. Some of them even worked actively against the revolution.

There were also women who worked actively to help create the new United States. Abigail Adams exchanged many letters with her husband, John, in which they discussed important issues facing the Continental Congress. Abigail asked her husband to remember women's rights as he helped to create the new government.

**PRIMARY SOURCE**

## In Their Words... Abigail Adams

I long to hear that you have declared an independency—and by the way in the new Code of Laws which I suppose it will be necessary for you to make I desire you would Remember the Ladies, and be more generous and favorable to them than your ancestors. Do not put such unlimited power into the hands of the Husbands. Remember all Men would be tyrants if they could. If particular care and attention is not paid to the Ladies we are determined to foment a Rebellion, and will not hold ourselves bound by any Laws in which we have no voice, or Representation. That your Sex are Naturally Tyrannical is a Truth so thoroughly established as to admit of no dispute, but such of you as wish to be happy willingly give up the harsh title of Master for the more tender and endearing one of Friend. Why then, not put it out of the power of the vicious and the Lawless to use us with cruelty and indignity with impunity.

—from a letter to John Adams, March 31, 1776

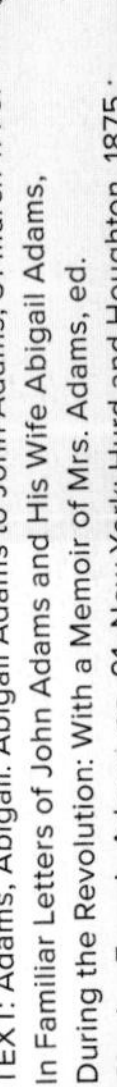

TEXT: Adams, Abigail. Abigail Adams to John Adams, 31 March 1776. In Familiar Letters of John Adams and His Wife Abigail Adams, During the Revolution: With a Memoir of Mrs. Adams, ed.

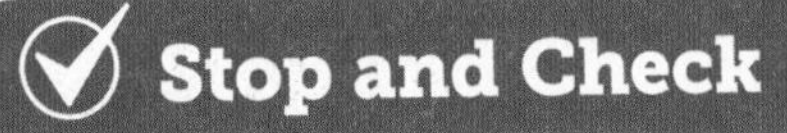

**Stop and Check** COLLABORATE

**Talk** Why did Abigail Adams ask John Adams to "remember the ladies"?

# The Secret War

Life during the Revolutionary War was filled with divisions and intrigue. Many Loyalists spied on the Patriots for the British. Some who helped the British made it appear that they were instead helping the Patriot cause. Benedict Arnold was an American general who eventually turned **traitor**. He gave important information about a planned invasion of Canada to the British. He later fled to England, but people started calling any traitor a "Benedict Arnold" because of his treachery.

The Patriot side had its own spies. Nathan Hale was attempting to spy on the British in 1776 when he was captured. He was hanged without a trial. Reportedly, his famous last words were "I only regret that I have but one life to lose for my country."

One of the most successful American spies was James Armistead, a man born into slavery. He volunteered to spy for General Lafayette, managing to become a servant to the British general Cornwallis. Armistead smuggled important information to Lafayette, which helped the Continental Army win the Battle of Yorktown. After the war, Lafayette helped Armistead win his freedom.

Nathan Hale was put to death for being a Patriot spy.

## Stop and Check

COLLABORATE

**Think** With a partner, discuss why people call someone who betrays them a "Benedict Arnold."

**Find Details** As you read, add new information to the graphic organizer on page 199 in your Inquiry Journal.

# African Americans Join the Cause

This man is dressed as a soldier of the First Rhode Island Regiment.

The words "all men are created equal" in the Declaration of Independence gave hope to enslaved Africans. Many supported the revolution because they believed those famous words might one day apply to them.

In all, about 5,000 African American soldiers served in the Continental Army. The First Rhode Island Regiment, formed in 1778, consisted mainly of African Americans. These included men freed from slavery in exchange for their service. Another African American freed from slavery in exchange for fighting was Peter Salem. He lived in Massachusetts and fought in the Battles of Concord and Bunker Hill.

African Americans also served in the Continental Navy. A 14-year-old free African American named James Forten was captured in 1781 during his service as a powder boy. The British offered him his freedom, but he turned down the offer saying, "No, I'm a prisoner for my country and I'll never be a traitor to her." He was held for seven months as a prisoner of war.

TEXT: James Forten to Sir John Beasley,1781. Quoted in Julie Winch, A Gentleman of Color: The Life of James Forten (Oxford University Press, 2002), 46.; PHOTO: Mario Tama/Getty Images News/Getty Images

# Native Americans Choose Sides

During the Revolutionary War, Native Americans had to decide whom to support. As the colonies grew bigger, they began to take more and more land from the Native Americans. The British promised to protect Native Americans' land from the Americans who wanted to settle there. Most of the Iroquois Confederacy, led by Chief Joseph Brant, sided with the British. The Oneida and Tuscarora supported the American cause.

Brant's Native American loyalists fighting for the British attacked American settlements in New York's Mohawk Valley. They also provided scouts to help the British troops. The Iroquois eventually lost faith in the British and stopped participating in the war.

However, Americans would continue to regard Native Americans as enemies. As a result, many Americans felt no guilt about taking more lands from native peoples after the war.

**Stop and Check** COLLABORATE

**Talk** Why did many Native Americans at first side with the British during the Revolutionary War?

Why did many African Americans choose to fight with the colonists?

**Iroquois chief Joseph Brant supported the British army during the war.**

# The Hardships of War

Wartime Shortages
Paper Dollars Equaling One-Dollar Coin, 1777–1781


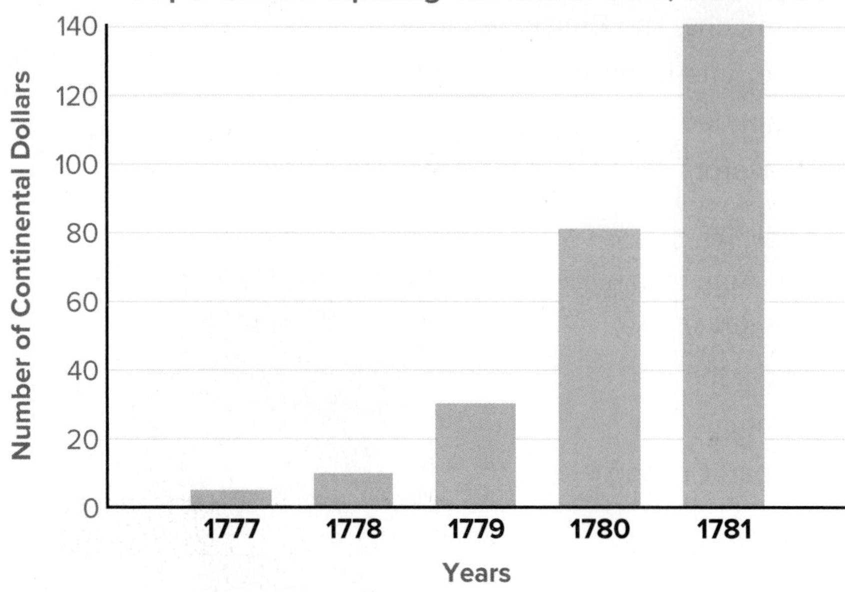


**The amount of paper Continental dollars needed to equal a one-dollar coin rose dramatically during the Revolutionary War.**

Congress had trouble paying for the war. To afford expensive supplies, they began to print more and more dollars, called "Continentals." They printed so many Continentals, however, that the money began to lose value due to **inflation**. Soon the bills were nearly worthless. A pair of shoes that had cost a few Continental dollars at the start of the war cost 5,000 Continental dollars by the end.

Because their money lost almost all of its value, people had trouble buying the food and supplies they needed. Even for the wealthy, goods that had once been imported from Great Britain were now hard to find. These shortages led people to hoard food, clothes, and other goods. Some people hoarded to try to support their families. Others did it to make money by charging high prices to others. Laws were passed against profiteering, but the laws were difficult to enforce.

**Talk** What problems did inflation cause?

**What Do You Think?** What would it have been like to live during the American Revolution?

# Are Women and African Americans of the Revolution Overlooked?

Work with a partner. Design a monument that honors the contributions of women or African Americans during the war. Consider what your monument should look like.

- Make an outline of the ways women and African Americans contributed to the war.
- Who were some individuals you learned about, and how do they represent the larger groups?
- Think about other monuments you have seen, and think about how your monument could compare with them.

Draw or make a model of your monument.

Present your monument to the class. Explain what you have learned about how women and African Americans helped the war effort.

**James Armistead, who was an enslaved African, risked his life to spy for the colonists.**

**Deborah Sampson disguised herself as a man so she could join the Continental Army.**

# What Did the Colonists Gain by Winning the War?

## The War Moves South

By 1779, the American Continental Army had turned back British attacks in the north and the west. British leaders decided to focus on the Southern Colonies. The Southern Colonies had higher proportions of Loyalists, and the British hoped to have their help in defeating the Americans once and for all. General Charles Cornwallis became the leader of British troops in the South in 1780.

Congress had very little money and almost no supplies for forces in the Southern Colonies. Between 1778 and 1781, the British won battles against American General Nathanael Greene at Savannah, Georgia, and at Charles Towne and Camden in South Carolina. At first it seemed as if Cornwallis's plans were working. However, the colonists' greater knowledge of the land they were fighting for proved to be an advantage.

***The Dawn of Peace: Morning of the Surrender of Yorktown*** **by A. Gilchrist Campbell**

**June 1779**
Spain declares war on Great Britain.

**May 1780**
General Charles Cornwallis becomes British commander in the South.

**September 1783**
Peace of Paris ends American Revolution.

1775 | 1780 | 1785

**October 1781**
British are defeated at Yorktown, Virginia.

The Continental Army managed to surprise the British in several raids led by Captain Francis Marion. Marion was called "The Swamp Fox" because his small force of raiders attacked the British unexpectedly and then retreated into the swamps of South Carolina.

Cornwallis pursued the Continental Army through the Carolina backcountry. When the two armies met in March 1781 at Guilford Court House, in North Carolina, Cornwallis lost one-fourth of his men. He declared it a victory because Greene's troops had left the battlefield. The loss, however, crippled the British forces. When word of the battle reached England, Charles James Fox declared in Parliament that "Another such victory would destroy the British army."

Because of the heavy losses, Cornwallis knew his men needed to rest and resupply. He fled north to Virginia to await ships from British headquarters in New York City. This movement would present George Washington with an opportunity.

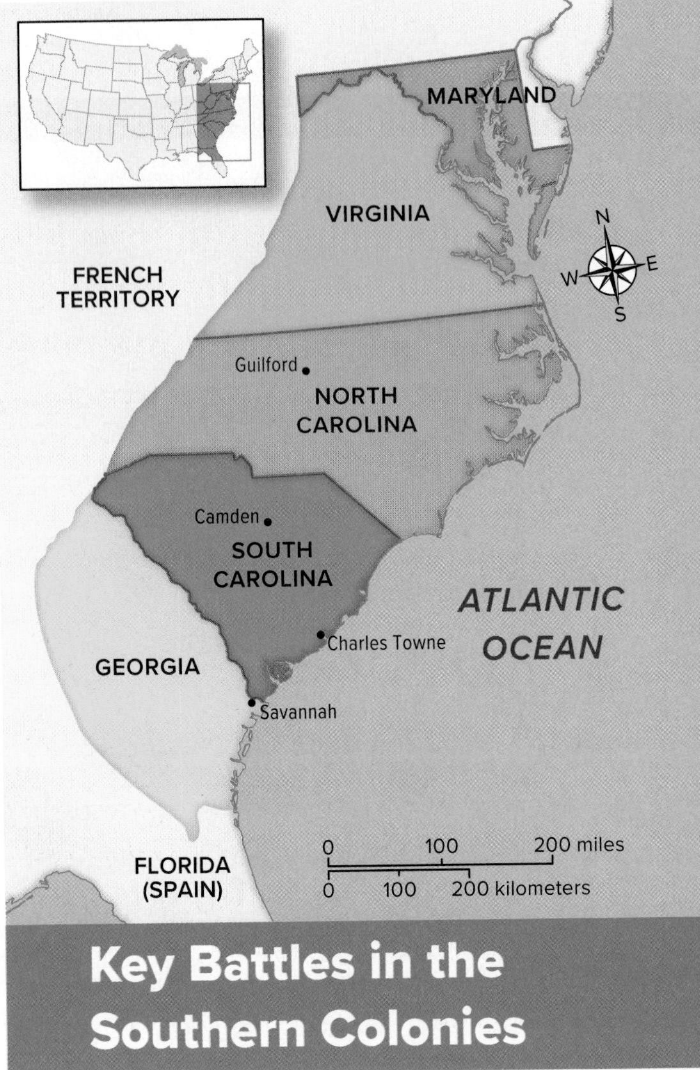


## Key Battles in the Southern Colonies

### Stop and Check

**Talk** Why was it important that Cornwallis lost so many men as a result of his victory at the Battle of Guilford Court House?

**Find Details** As you read, add new information to the graphic organizer on page 207 in your Inquiry Journal.

Charles James Fox to the British House of Commons. 1781. Quoted in Henry Lee and Robert Edward Lee, Memoirs of the War in the Southern Department of the United States (New York: University Publishing Company, 1869), 286.

# The Battle of Yorktown

George Washington had put the Marquis de Lafayette in charge of a troop of soldiers in Virginia. When Cornwallis marched north to Virginia, Lafayette wrote to Washington, "Were I to fight a battle, I should be cut to pieces. . . . I am not strong enough even to get beaten."

Lafayette did have an important secret weapon, however. James Armistead, who was enslaved in Virginia, volunteered to spy for Lafayette. From a position as Cornwallis's servant, he passed information about Cornwallis's plans and weaknesses.

From the intelligence Armistead provided, Lafayette formed a plan to **blockade** Chesapeake Bay. This prevented Cornwallis from resupplying his troops. Armistead told Cornwallis that the Americans planned to attack New York City, tricking Cornwallis into believing his army was safe at Yorktown.

Meanwhile, Washington's troops and a French army moved quickly and secretly to Yorktown to join Lafayette. By the time Cornwallis realized what had happened, he was surrounded by a force more than twice the size of his own.

**French general Jean de Rochambeau, with George Washington, gives orders for the attack on Yorktown.**

The British battled the Americans and French at Yorktown for nearly three weeks. American cannons fired into the British camp. Outside the city, American and French troops blocked Cornwallis and his men from any possible escape. Meanwhile, French ships' blockade of Chesapeake Bay continued to prevent Cornwallis from getting any fresh supplies or troops.

Earlier that month, French naval forces resisted a British fleet that would have supplied Cornwallis with reinforcements. Another British fleet set out to rescue the troops at Yorktown on October 17, but it was too late. On October 19, Cornwallis surrendered to Washington.

## Did You Know?

George Washington and the Comte de Rochambeau, a French general, were in New York when word came that Cornwallis had fled to Virginia. Washington wrote to Lafayette, telling him to keep Cornwallis there. Washington left a few men in New York and began a rapid march south to join Lafayette. After marching his men to Maryland, Washington met up with a French fleet of ships at Chesapeake Bay. The ships carried the American and French troops south to Williamsburg, Virginia. From there, Washington's troops joined Lafayette's and surrounded Cornwallis at Yorktown.

Marquis de Lafayette

## Stop and Check

**Talk** Why did Washington move quickly from New York to Virginia?

# Battle Map of Yorktown

Washington and Lafayette created a plan that trapped Cornwallis on the Yorktown peninsula. A combination of French ships and French and American soldiers kept Cornwallis from getting new supplies.

French ships carried French and American troops south to Williamsburg, Virginia.

Washington's troops met Lafayette's troops to surround the British.

A blockade of French ships prevented the British from getting supplies.

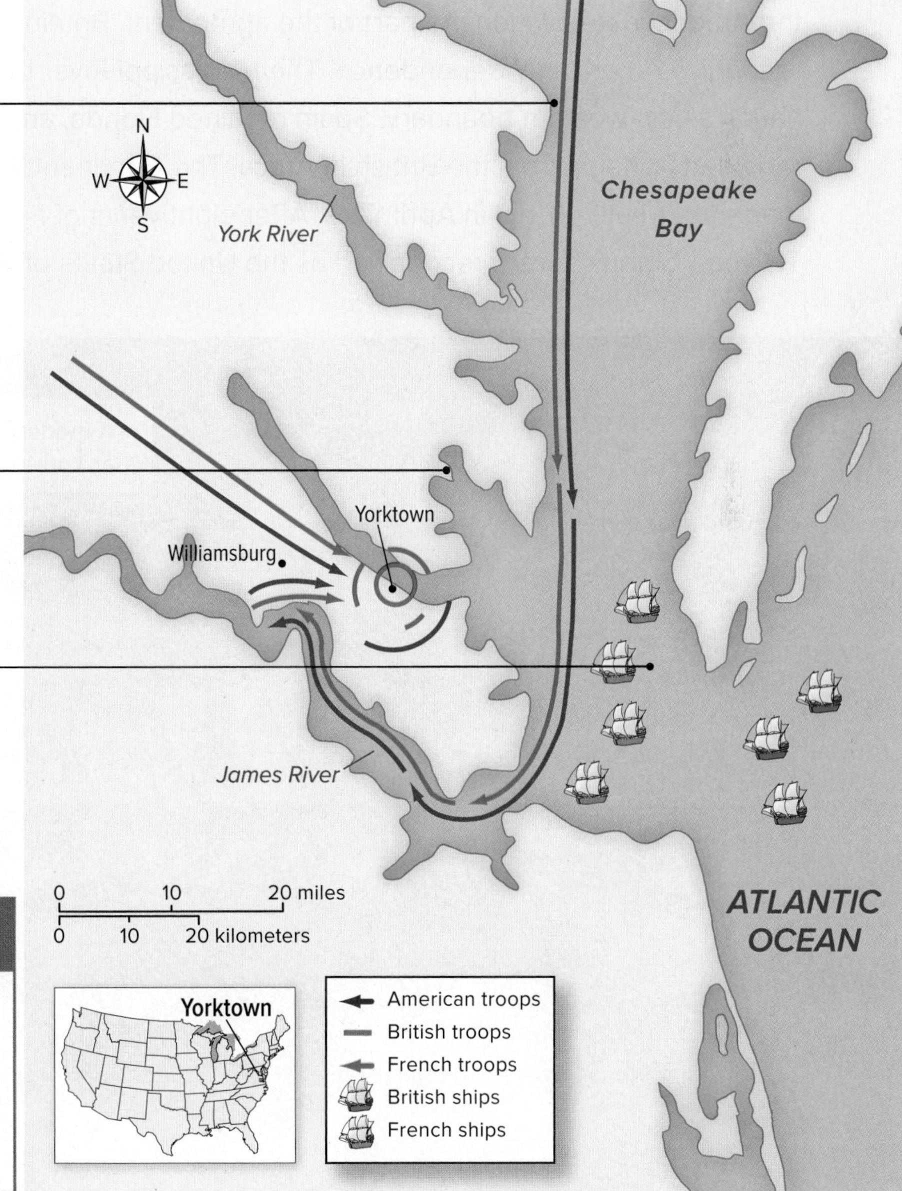


### Stop and Check

**Think** How was Yorktown's location on a peninsula important to Washington's plan?

# Ending the War

The Battle of Yorktown marked the end of the main British resistance to American independence. There were still British troops in several cities and on the frontier, but the cost of the war had gotten so high that the British people were opposed to supporting the war with their taxes.

The slow process of ending the war began as Britain agreed to **negotiate** a treaty with the United States and its allies, France and Spain. The peace talks took place in Paris. John Adams, Benjamin Franklin, and John Jay were on hand to negotiate for the United States.

The Peace of Paris, as it came to be called, was the treaty that ended the American Revolution. As part of the agreement, Britain had to recognize American independence. The Mississippi River became the nation's new western boundary. Spain regained Florida, and France regained Senegal from the British in Africa. The Continental Congress made the treaty official in April 1783. After eight years of fighting, the Thirteen Colonies were recognized as the United States of America.

A modern reenactment of the battle at Yorktown, Virginia

Nancy Carter/North Wind Picture Archives

John Adams (seated, left), and John Jay (standing, right) signed the Peace of Paris for the United States.

**PRIMARY SOURCE**

## Peace of Paris, Article I

His Britannic Majesty acknowledges the said United States, viz. New-Hampshire, Massachusetts-Bay, Rhode-Island and Providence Plantations, Connecticut, New-York, New-Jersey, Pennsylvania, Delaware, Maryland, Virginia, North-Carolina, South-Carolina, and Georgia, to be free, sovereign and independent States; that he treats with them as such; and for himself, his heirs and successors, relinquishes all claims to the government, property and territorial rights of the same, and every part thereof.

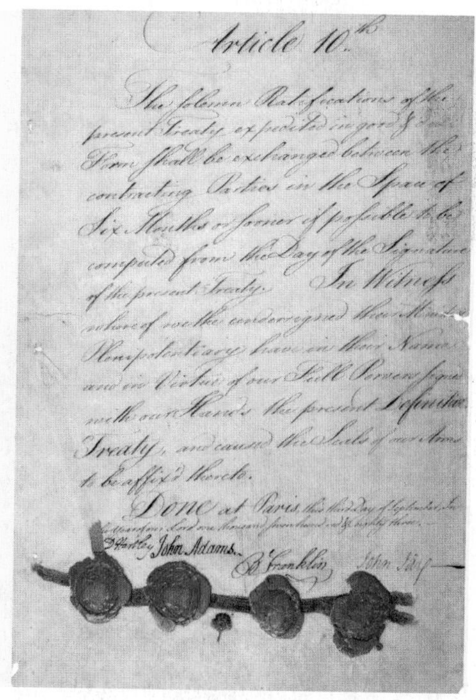

Article 10th

The solemn Ratifications of the present Treaty expedited in good & due Form shall be exchanged between the contracting Parties in the Space of Six Months or sooner if possible to be computed from the Day of the Signature of the present Treaty. In Witness whereof we the undersigned their Ministers Plenipotentiary have in their Name and in Virtue of our Full Powers signed with our Hands the present Definitive Treaty, and caused the Seals of our Arms to be affixed thereto.

Done at Paris this third Day of September in the year of our Lord one thousand seven hundred & eighty three.

Hartley John Adams. B Franklin John Jay

## Stop and Check

COLLABORATE

**Talk** What agreements were part of the Peace of Paris?

TEXT: Treaties and Other International Acts of the United States of America. Edited by Hunter Miller, Volume 2 Documents 1-40 : 1776-1818. Washington: Government Printing Office, 1931.;
PHOTO: (bkgd)McGraw-Hill Education, (t)Kean Collection/Archive Photos/Getty Images, (b)National Archives and Records Administration (299805)

# No Victory for Some

After the war ended, the 40,000 Loyalists left in the country had to decide what to do. Some moved to Canada, which was still controlled by the British. Others remained in the United States. They tried to make the best of life there, but many were forced to give up their homes and property.

Enslaved people had hoped the end of the war would mean the end of slavery. To create a united government, however, the Congress agreed to allow slavery to continue in return for the support of Southern States.

Native Americans—including the Mohawk and Iroquois—who had sided with the British found that more and more Americans settled on Native American lands. The Americans saw the native peoples as enemies because of the Iroquois alliance with the British. Eventually, the Mohawk and Iroquois signed a peace agreement with the United States.

It would still take many years before the phrase "all men are created equal" could truly include all people in the United States.

Those African Americans who were free at the end of the Revolutionary War also met with disappointments. They found themselves receiving unequal treatment in many forms. One free African American in Massachusetts, Prince Hall, collected signatures for a petition protesting one form of this discrimination.

**PRIMARY SOURCE**

## In Their Words... Prince Hall

. . . we are of the humble opinion that we have the right to enjoy the privileges of free men. But that we do not will appear in many instances, and we beg leave to mention one out of many, and that is of the education of our children which now receive no benefit from the free schools in the town of Boston, which we think is a great grievance, as by woeful experience we now feel the want of a common education. We, therefore, must fear for our rising offspring to see them in ignorance in a land of gospel light when there is provision made for them as well as others and yet can't enjoy them, and for not other reason can be given this they are black.

—from a petition presented to the Massachusetts state legislature, October 1787

**Stop and Check**

**Talk** What happened to Loyalists after the war?

**What Do You Think?** Did everyone in the United States gain his or her independence as a result of the war?

TEXT: Hall, Prince. "Petition for Equal Educational Facilities," (October 17, 1787). Quoted in Herbert Aptheker, ed., A Documentary History of the Negro People in the United States: From Colonial Times through the Civil War, Volume 1. (New York: Citadel Press, 1951), 19–20.; PHOTO: McGraw-Hill Education

# Connections in Action!

## Back to the EQ

**Think** about the Chapter EQ, **"What Does the Revolutionary Era Tell Us About Our Nation Today?"**

- **Talk** with a partner about the people and events that you read about in this chapter. Consider ways that they contributed to the cause of freedom from Great Britain.
- How do these people and events continue to influence our nation today?
- **Share** your ideas with the class.

(bkgd)Yale University Art Gallery, (tl)Library of Congress Prints & Photographs Division [LC-DIG-pga-00995], (bl)Library of Congress

# More to Explore

## How Can You Make an IMPACT?

### Debate in Action

The colonists were divided about whether or not to go to war with Great Britain. If you were a colonist, which side would you have supported? Why?

### Take a Stand

Choose a person from this chapter who you think was one of the most important figures in the American Revolution. Make a list of the reasons you think that way. Use evidence from the text to support your opinion. Get together with a partner or small group and talk about your choice. Be prepared to defend your thinking!

### Word Play

Choose three words from the chapter Word Bank. For each of those words, find two words that have the same base word. Write the definition for each base word. For example, for the word *revolutionary*, you could use *revolt* and *revolution*. Get together with a partner and switch word lists. Take turns using each new word in a sentence.

THE IMPACT TODAY

# How Do Citizens Make Their Views Heard?

## Why Vote?

The people of the Thirteen Colonies fought a war to get a government that would hear their voices. Of course, citizens cannot fight a war every time they want a pothole fixed or a new park in their neighborhood. The primary way that citizens have a say in their government's decisions is through voting. America has a representative democracy, or a republic. Citizens entrust elected officials to make decisions on their behalf.

The most well-known elected official in the United States is the president. The presidential election is an event of enormous importance. It is important to pay attention to the smaller elections too. Legislators actually create the laws and are elected to represent smaller groups of people. It is usually easier to contact and express views to a senator or representative than the president. Legislators also have the power to define the districts where people live and vote. Sometimes legislators shape these districts in ways that give one political party an advantage. This unfair practice is called gerrymandering.

State and local positions are also very important. Offices such as sheriff, mayor, and state senator are likely to have a greater effect on an individual's daily life. People can also have a say in specific issues. People can vote directly for a decision in ballot initiatives or referendums.

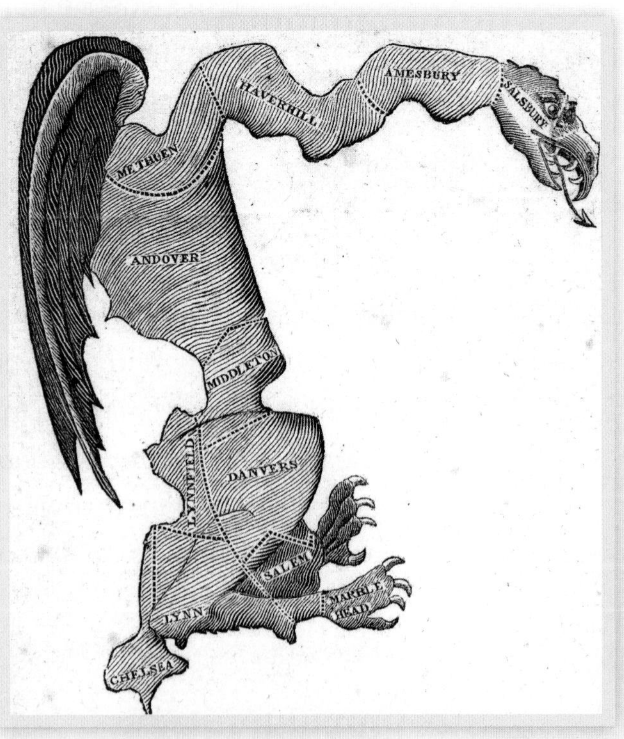

This unfairly drawn district originally was said to look like a salamander. This political cartoon added claws, wings, and scary teeth to call it a "Gerrymander."

# Staying Informed

Politicians are regular people. They can make mistakes, be unaware of the issues, or even be corrupt. Frequent elections allow voters the chance to replace officials who have failed to make decisions in the best interest of the people they represent. However, elections don't matter if voters do not keep themselves informed. Citizens need to watch their leaders to ensure they are making moral and intelligent decisions that serve the interests of the people they represent.

**Even though people must be 18 years old to vote, young people should still stay informed about what leaders are doing.**

News organizations are the primary way people receive information about what the government is doing. Through newspapers, TV, radio, and the Internet, voters are able to learn about important issues and what elected officials are doing to solve these issues. To make sure the government cannot force news organizations to lie or hide information, the Constitution of the United States of America guarantees freedom of the press. Unfortunately, personal beliefs or even corruption may lead journalists or political leaders to present misleading or even false stories. People can combat misinformation by paying attention to multiple news sources and by using critical thinking to make up their minds.

Informed citizens are empowered citizens. Voters should use what they know to decide which candidates will best represent their views and fight for their needs. Informed citizens can also teach elected officials about issues they may have missed or misunderstood.

## WHAT IS THE IMPACT TODAY?

COLLABORATE

**Talk** Think about all the different ways you can stay informed about issues in your school, city, state, country, and world.

Where do you get information to stay informed? What and who are your sources of information? Discuss and compare your sources with a partner.

# Being a Good Citizen

Citizenship comes not only with rights but responsibilities. Citizens should respect authority by supporting and defending the Constitution and obeying laws. Sometimes, a law will seem unfair. Instead of breaking the law, try to understand its purpose or work to change the law.

Citizens should participate in government. All citizens who are eligible to vote should make use of that right. Citizens must also pay taxes on time and honestly. Tax money helps to improve society and benefits everyone. Courts may also call upon citizens to serve on juries. Finally, a good citizen should be willing to join the armed forces or otherwise assist in defending the country if the need arises.

Most importantly, citizens should help one another. The United States of America draws strength from its citizens' diversity of backgrounds, beliefs, and views. A citizen should stay informed and help inform others but should also respect other people's right to disagree. A good citizen should stand up for the rights of others as well as his or her own. Volunteering to improve the community is also the responsibility of a good citizen.

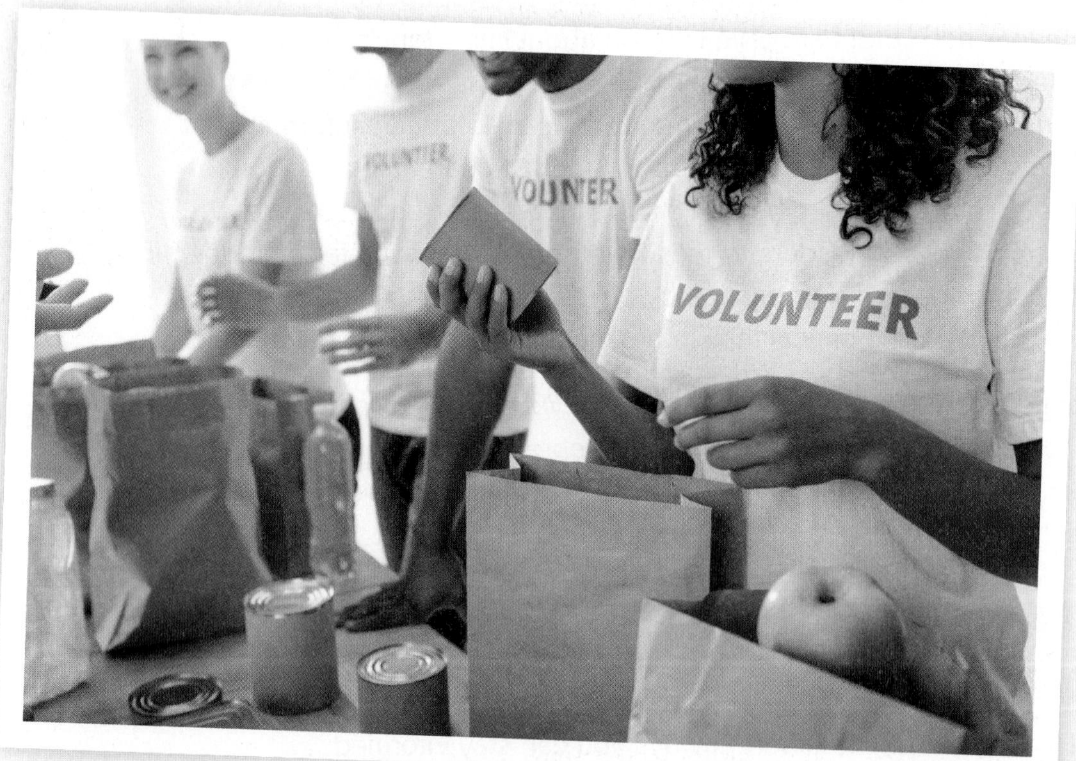


Helping improve the community is an important part of citizenship.

LightField Studios/Shutterstock

# Making a Difference

Americans who are too young to vote can still make their voices heard. Anyone can call or write to a government official to voice his or her concerns. A person can also attend a town hall meeting to publicly speak with legislators and other officials.

A petition is another way to send a message to the government. To create a petition, a person or group makes a written statement explaining a problem they want the government to address. Next, the petition maker will gather signatures to show how many people support the petition. The petition is then presented to government officials as proof of the importance of the issue.

The First Amendment protects the freedom to petition the government. It also protects the right to peaceably assemble, or protest. When citizens feel they are being ignored, marching in the streets may be the only way to bring attention to the issues that are meaningful to them. The Civil Rights Movement in the mid-20th century showed the effectiveness of peaceful public demonstrations in causing political change.

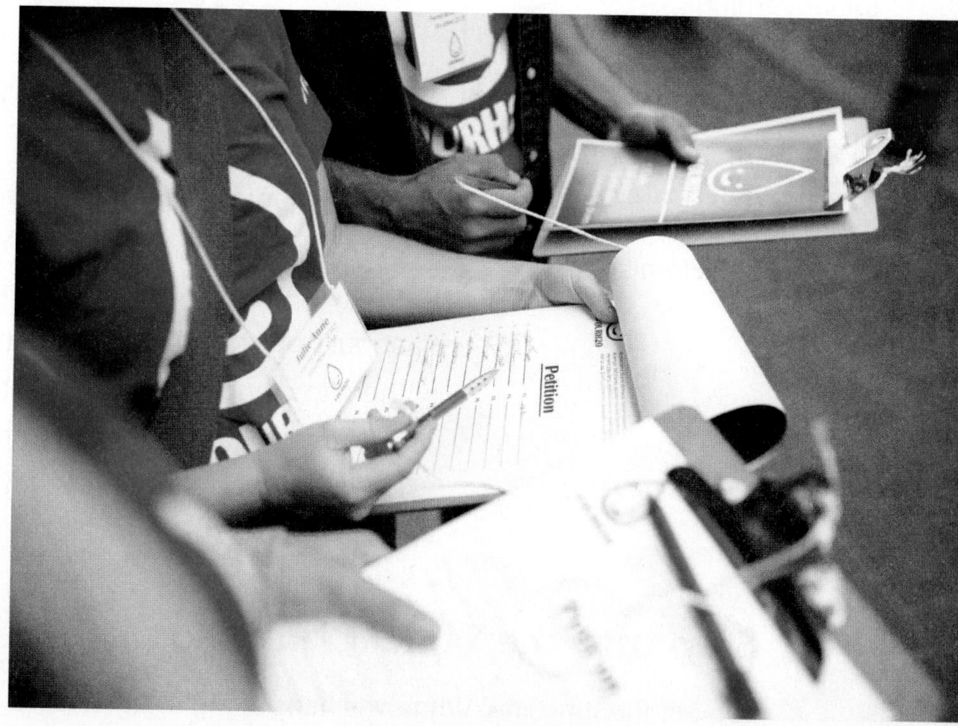




## WHAT IS THE IMPACT TODAY?

COLLABORATE

**Talk** People of all ages can make a difference, from their neighborhood or school to their state, country, or internationally.

How can you and your friends make a difference and be good citizens? Discuss different things you can do, big or small.

# Forming a New Government

## How Does the Constitution Help Us Understand What It Means to Be an American?

In this chapter, you'll read about how the United States Constitution was developed. You'll learn about the people who created a stronger national government, their opinions about how it should be run, and the pressures that drove them to compromise on important issues. You'll examine how the Constitution has changed over the course of U.S. history to protect the rights of all people.

## Step into the Time Chronological Thinking

Look at the time line. What was happening in other parts of the world while the United States Constitution was being developed?

**Americas**

**1776** Declaration of Independence is signed; Congress creates Articles of Confederation.

**1777** United States starts operating under Articles of Confederation.

**1781** Articles of Confederation is ratified by all 13 states.

1775 — 1780

**World Events**

**1778** Captain James Cook becomes first European to visit Hawaiian Islands.

**1779** War breaks out in South Africa between Dutch settlers and the Xhosa people.

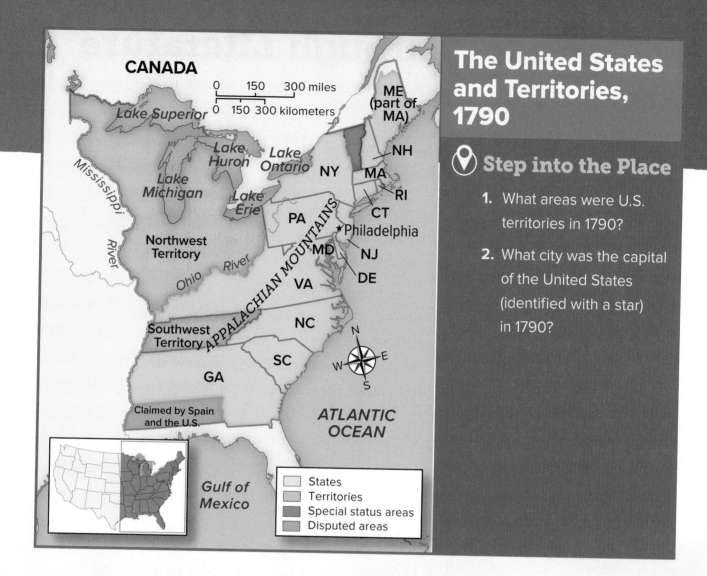

## The United States and Territories, 1790

### Step into the Place

1. What areas were U.S. territories in 1790?
2. What city was the capital of the United States (identified with a star) in 1790?

Once the Constitutional Convention agreed on the Constitution, at least nine states had to agree to it too. One by one, the 13 states signed the document and officially became part of the United States, beginning with Delaware and ending with Rhode Island. Gradually, new states joined the Union, but it took 169 years for the United States to look as it does today.

1783
Crimea becomes Russian territory following conflict with the Ottoman Empire.
1787
Mozart's opera *Don Giovanni* premieres in Prague.
1789
The French Revolution begins.
1789
Antoine-Laurent Lavoisier develops a way to organize chemical elements, beginning the study of modern chemistry.

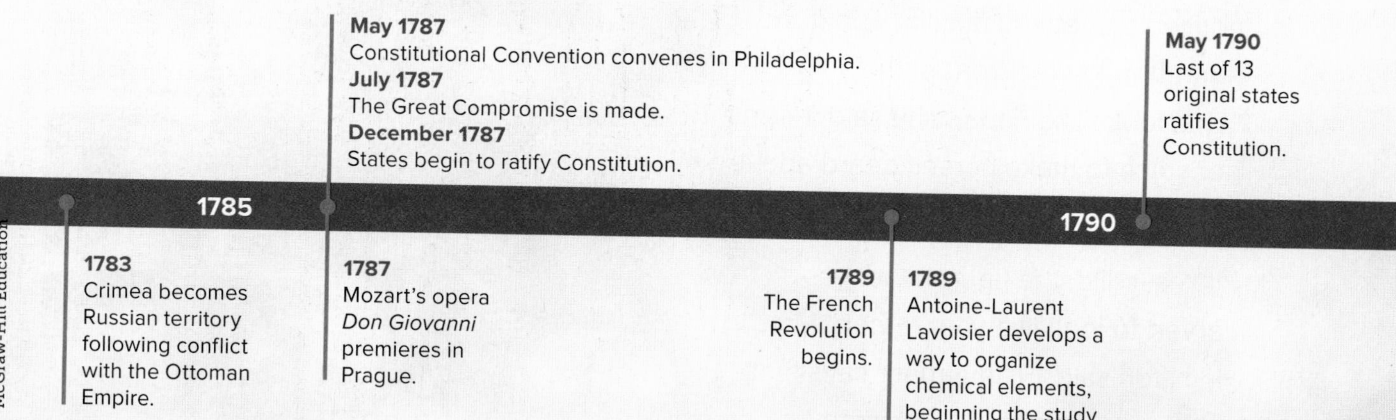

May 1787
Constitutional Convention convenes in Philadelphia.
July 1787
The Great Compromise is made.
December 1787
States begin to ratify Constitution.
May 1790
Last of 13 original states ratifies Constitution.
1785

# Connect Through Literature

## A Ship Called the Hamilton

by Virginia Calkins

It was July 23, 1788, and New York City was having a big parade. The Constitution of the United States had finally been ratified by ten states, and the people of New York wanted to celebrate.

Caught up in the excitement were Philip, Angelica, and Alexander, the natural children of Alexander and Betsy Hamilton. Fanny Antil, the orphan whom the Hamiltons had adopted, was excited, too. Baby James was only four months old, a bit too young to understand. The children waited impatiently for the parade to begin. Suddenly they heard the boom of a cannon. That was the starting signal.

A group of trumpeters led the parade. Then came artillerymen pulling a large cannon. Suddenly Philip exclaimed, "Look, everybody!" Coming toward them was a huge float pulled by ten white horses. The float was a replica of a ship, a thirty-two-gun frigate. It had been constructed by shipbuilders and was twenty-seven feet long, large enough for a crew of thirty plus their officers.

As the float came closer, Angelica noticed something familiar about the figurehead at the front of the ship. "That looks like Papa," she said, raising her voice to make herself heard above the cheers of the crowd.

"Yes, child, the figurehead was carved to look like your father," Mrs. Hamilton said. "The banner says that the ship is named the *Hamilton*."

Philip gave her a puzzled look. "Why did they name it after Father?" he asked.

"The people of New York are grateful to your father for the work he has done for the Constitution," his mother replied. "Remember when he was in Philadelphia last summer?"

Philip nodded. He remembered well.

"He was helping to write the Constitution then," Mrs. Hamilton said. "And remember last winter when he stayed up late night after night writing *The Federalist Papers*? Your father, Mr. Madison, and Mr. Jay wrote those papers to help people understand the Constitution and urge them to support it."

"I wish Father was here," Philip said with a sigh.

"I wish he was, too," his mother replied. "But your father is needed in Poughkeepsie. The State of New York is having a convention to decide whether it will ratify the Constitution, and your father is a delegate."

"Here comes another ship," little Alexander shouted.

This ship was made by sail makers and named the New Constitution. A carved figure of Alexander Hamilton stood on its deck, with papers representing the new Constitution in his right hand and the Articles of Confederation in his left. This was to indicate the change from the Articles of Confederation to the Constitution.

More floats followed. Angelica and Fanny liked the one that featured a beautiful garland of artificial flowers. Three of the flowers were drooping, and Mrs. Hamilton explained that they represented the three states (including New York) that had not yet ratified the Constitution.

The parade continued, with marching bands, tradesmen and merchants, doctors, professors, and public officials. Ten law students carried the ten state ratifications. Three officials carried the new Constitution. More than five thousand people participated in the parade.

When it was over and the Hamiltons turned toward home, Philip declared, "That was wonderful! I hope Father comes home soon so I can tell him all about it."

Eighty miles away in Poughkeepsie, Alexander Hamilton was fighting for ratification. When the convention had begun on June 17, only nineteen of the sixty-five delegates favored ratification. The leaders of the opposition were Governor George Clinton, who was the chairman of the convention, and Melancton Smith, a great debater. Hamilton believed that it was extremely important that New York join the Union. Besides being centrally located geographically, it also was a center of trade and commerce. How could he win over his opponents?

First he persuaded the delegates to debate the Constitution clause by clause, thus taking up time until he heard from New Hampshire or Virginia. At that point eight states had ratified; another would mean that the Constitution would go into effect, with or without New York. Hamilton hoped that another ratification would convince some of the delegates to switch sides.

When an Antifederalist introduced an amendment to make U.S. senators subject to recall by their state legislatures, Hamilton jumped up to object. He insisted that the Senate must be a stable body, not subject to the whims of state legislatures. As the debate dragged on, Hamilton waited anxiously for word from his friends.

Suddenly he heard hoof beats. An express rider brought news that on June 21 New Hampshire had ratified the Constitution. The United States of America had been born!

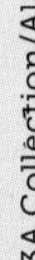

Still the Antifederalists would not give in. Governor Clinton suggested fifty-five amendments. He was willing to enter the Union on the condition that New York could withdraw if these amendments failed to pass within a reasonable time. Hamilton could not agree to this.

On July 2, a messenger arrived from James Madison. Virginia had ratified! With this large state in the Union, it would be difficult for New York to stand alone.

Word reached Poughkeepsie about the parade being planned in New York City. There were rumors that the city might secede from the state if the convention failed to ratify. On July 23, Melancton Smith and his men switched sides. The next day there was a move for conditional ratification. Hamilton read a letter from Madison to the delegates that said New York could not enter the Union "conditionally." Finally, on July 26, New York ratified the Constitution with a recommendation for a Bill of Rights and other amendments. The vote was 30 to 27.

Alexander Hamilton returned to his family a tired but happy man. Proudly, he showed the ratification document to Betsy and the children. The children were impressed, but they really wanted to tell their father about the parade.

"It was tremendous," Philip related. "There was a ship called the *Hamilton*."

His father picked up the ratification papers and moved toward the door. "I must bring this document to the Continental Congress at the City Hall," he said. "But I will return soon, and you can tell me about the parade. I want to hear everything, particularly about that ship called the *Hamilton*!"

## Think About It

1. Why was a parade held in New York City on July 23, 1788?
2. What was Alexander Hamilton's tactic to get New York state to ratify the constitution?
3. What are two pieces of evidence that show that New York City was in favor of ratifying the Constitution, even if the rest of the state was not?

# People You Should Know

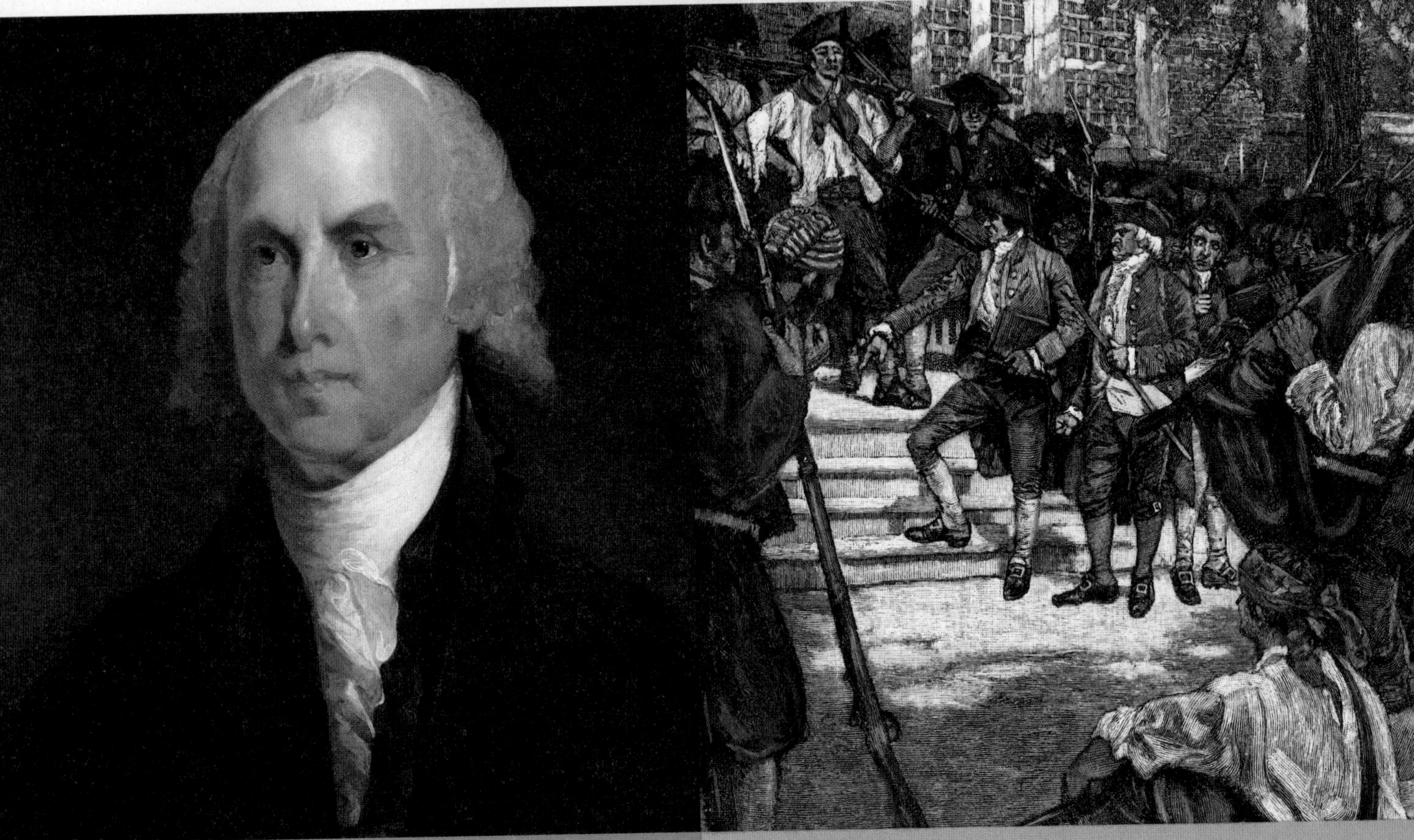

## James Madison

Known as the Father of the Constitution, James Madison created policies during the Constitutional Convention that shaped much of the U.S. Government as we know it today. After the convention, he worked with Alexander Hamilton and John Jay to promote ratification of the Constitution in a series of essays called *The Federalist Papers.* As a member of Congress, he supported adding to the Constitution ten amendments, which would later be known as the Bill of Rights. In 1808, he was elected the fourth president of the United States.

## Daniel Shays

A decorated veteran of the Revolutionary War, Daniel Shays later held local office in his native Massachusetts. When the economy declined during the years after the war, many people lost their homes and property. Shays led a group of people who protested this treatment. The short-lived but violent revolt came to be called Shays's Rebellion. Shays was arrested and sentenced to death, but eventually he was granted a pardon.

## George Mason

Though a respected member of Virginia society, George Mason had never been very interested in holding public office. When the Constitutional Convention convened in 1787, however, he accepted a post as one of Virginia's delegates. He argued for adding a bill of rights to the Constitution, protecting individual freedoms. The U.S. Bill of Rights was based partly on Virginia's state bill of rights, which Mason had written. He also argued against slavery and compromises that allowed slavery to continue in the new nation. Yet Mason owned enslaved people himself and never freed them.

## Martin Luther King Jr.

Even after the Emancipation Proclamation and the Civil War ended slavery in the United States, African Americans living in the South were still not free. They were separated from white people in public places, and they were treated with injustice and prejudice. In the 1950s and 1960s, Martin Luther King Jr. helped African Americans gain important civil and economic rights with his focus on peaceful protest and his inspiring messages. In one such speech, called the "I Have a Dream" speech, he envisioned a time when all people would live together in peace.

# What Was the Articles of Confederation and Why Did It Fail?

## One Nation or Thirteen States?

The **Articles** of Confederation was the first written document to establish a United States government. The Second Continental Congress began writing the Articles of Confederation in 1776 and approved it in 1777. However, it was not ratified by all 13 states until 1781. Its writers imagined a nation unlike European countries. They promised a "firm league of friendship" in which each state was guaranteed its "freedom and independence."

The Articles granted new powers to the national government. It created a Confederation Congress to govern the country. The Congress created departments of finance, foreign affairs, war, and the post office. The Congress also signed a peace treaty with Great Britain, formally ending the Revolutionary War.

The Articles allowed the states to continue to run their own governments independently. States retained the right to print their own money. States also had the authority to tax while the Confederation Congress did not. By 1786, many of the thirteen states had written their own constitutions that challenged the authority of the Articles of Confederation. Meanwhile, the Confederation Congress passed laws controlling the growth of the new country.

1776
Declaration of Independence signed; Second Continental Congress creates Articles of Confederation.
1781
Articles ratified by all 13 states
1787
Northwest Ordinance is passed; Constitutional Convention begins.
1770
1780
1790
1777
The United States starts operating under the Articles.
1786–1787
Shays's Rebellion

Daniel Shays leads farmers in a rebellion against the government of Massachusetts.

# The Northwest Ordinance

Congress organized the settlement of the Northwest Territory under the Articles of Confederation. This territory included land north of the Ohio River and east of the Mississippi River. The government would later divide the Northwest Territory into the states of Ohio, Indiana, Illinois, Michigan, Wisconsin, and Minnesota.

Congress **issued** the Northwest Ordinance to help organize the territory. The law defined a strict structure for the settlements. Areas with small populations could vote on legislators. Regions with at least 60,000 adults could register for statehood.

The Northwest Territory was divided into rectangular townships. Each township included 36 sections. Large companies bought much of the land in the townships. The companies sold smaller portions to settlers for a profit. Arthur St. Clair ran the Ohio Company. The company owned 1.5 million acres of the Northwest Territory. He became the first governor of the Northwest Territory.

In 1783, Congress ruled that, after the Revolutionary War, Native Americans no longer held the right to land in the Northwest Territory. The U.S. government began to treat the native peoples as conquered nations. Congress sent soldiers to the territory to remove Native Americans by force.

One army officer reported that settlers regularly attacked and killed groups of Native Americans without government support. To defend themselves, the Miami, Shawnee, and Delaware peoples formed a military alliance. In 1791, Miami chief Little Turtle led an attack on Arthur St. Clair's troops. Nine hundred of the U.S. troops were killed. It was the worst defeat suffered by U.S. soldiers in the history of war against Native Americans. Little Turtle died in one of the battles that followed, but the Native Americans' resistance forced the U.S. government to negotiate peace agreements.

The Northwest Ordinance declared that "neither slavery nor involuntary servitude" was allowed in the Northwest Territory. In the mid-1780s, however, most states outside of the territory still permitted white people to own enslaved people. Even free African Americans had many fewer rights than whites.

One right free African Americans did have was the right to worship in their own churches. Richard Allen founded the first fully independent African American church in Philadelphia in 1794, the African Methodist Episcopal (A.M.E.) Church. Communities of African American worshippers would go on to build A.M.E. churches across the United States.

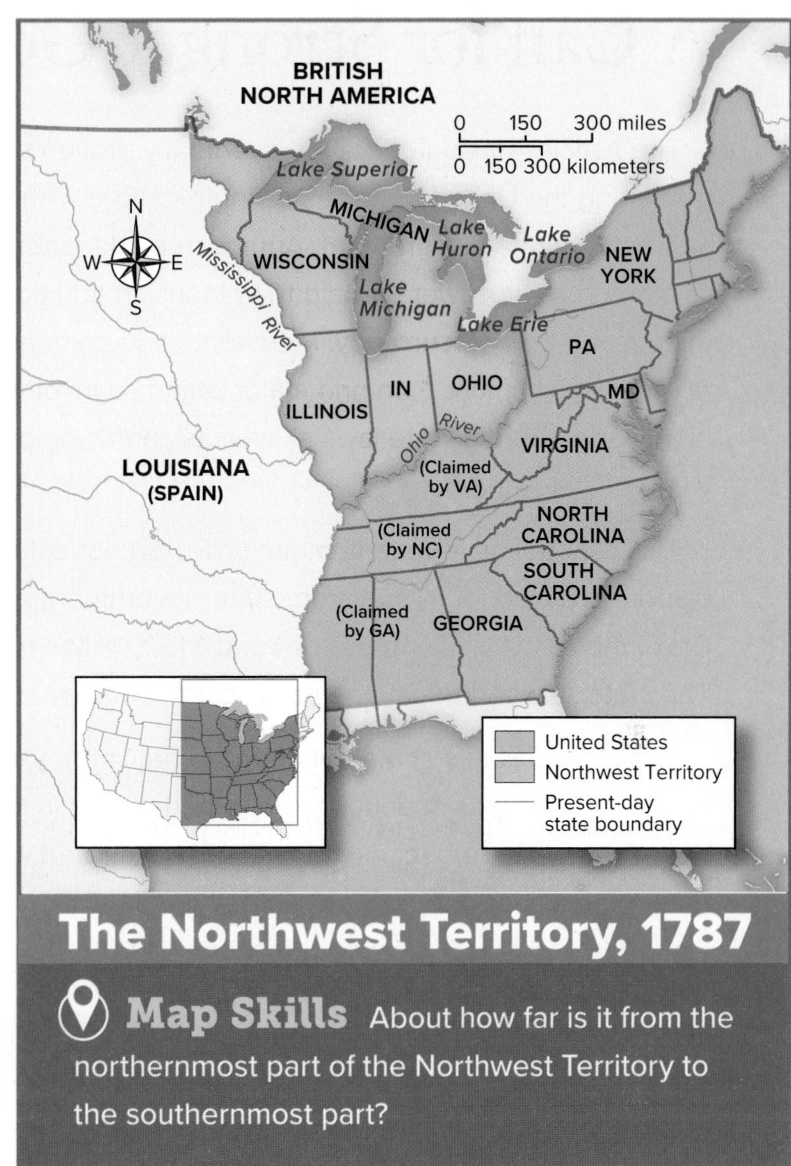


## The Northwest Territory, 1787

**Map Skills** About how far is it from the northernmost part of the Northwest Territory to the southernmost part?

## Stop and Check

COLLABORATE

**Talk** If you were living in one of the original thirteen colonies, would you consider moving to the Northwest Territory? Working with a partner, discuss the pros and cons of settling in the territory.

**Find Details** As you read, add additional information to the graphic organizer on page 227 in your Inquiry Journal.

# A Call for Stronger Government

The Articles of Confederation eventually proved to be weak in governing the United States as a single nation. Without the backing of a strong national government, American banks often found it difficult to make sure borrowers repaid their loans. In addition, each state maintained its own **currency**. Merchants and companies struggled to do business in more than one state. Doing so involved understanding highly complicated state laws as well as confusing differences in the value of states' money.

The national government, meanwhile, did not collect taxes. Instead, Congress asked for money from state governments. After the Revolutionary War, Congress needed $15.7 million to pay its debts. The states agreed to pay the national government only $2.4 million.

The United States could not afford to pay money owed to some of the military officials and leaders who had fought in the Revolutionary War. These people became increasingly frustrated with the government's lack of power over the states.

## Did You Know?

The U.S. government first issued print money during the Revolutionary War. These bills, called Continental Currency, helped pay for the war against the British. Realizing this, the British government printed counterfeit bills and passed them out in the United States. They succeeded in weakening the U.S. government by lowering the worth of the Continental Currency. This was the first example of paper-money counterfeiting as a form of economic warfare.

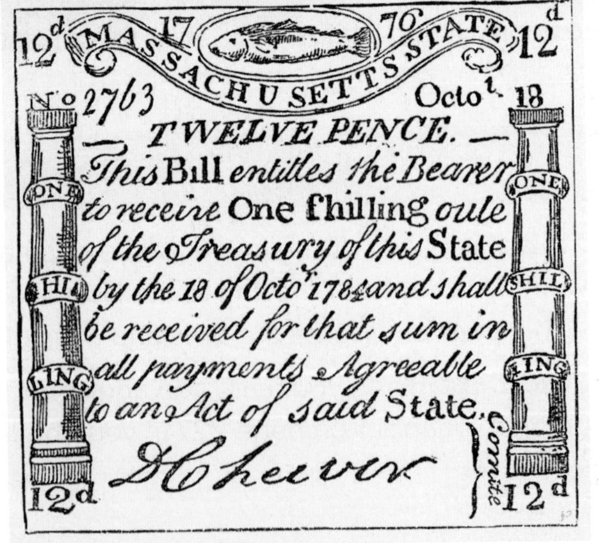


Paper money issued by the state of Massachusetts

In the 1780s, the national government's money problems led to violent conflict. Merchants in Boston decided to require that their bills be paid in gold and silver. They thought that the Massachusetts currency was too unstable. When farmers in western Massachusetts could not produce the necessary gold and silver coins to pay off their debts, they were jailed in large numbers.

The imprisoned farmers appealed to the Massachusetts legislature to help them pay their debts. The members of the legislature, however, were mostly lawyers and merchants who paid little attention to the farmers' requests. The legislators voted to raise taxes. This decision further burdened poor farmers.

The angry farmers had just recently experienced the power of revolt in the Revolutionary War. In 1786, they blocked the entrances of several county courthouses to stop the legal processes required to take the indebted farmers' land. Rebels attacked jails and released farmers who had been imprisoned. Daniel Shays, a Revolutionary War captain who was now a struggling farmer, led the rebels.

Daniel Shays and his supporters protested high taxes.



A group of Shays's men attacked a state arsenal—a building where weapons are stored—in 1787. A local militia defeated Shays's forces as they attempted to seize the weapons. Four men died and 20 more were wounded. Shays's Rebellion persisted nonetheless.

As the rebels continued to cause havoc in the state, the governor of Massachusetts, John Hancock, sent more than 4,000 troops to stop the rebellion. Badly outnumbered, most of Shays's men fled. The Massachusetts government captured and sentenced fifteen rebels to death. Two of the accused were executed, while Hancock pardoned the rest. Daniel Shays left Massachusetts for New York, where he returned to farming.

In the end, the Massachusetts government easily stopped Shays's Rebellion. The event nonetheless cast doubt over the Articles of Confederation. Wealthy Americans wanted a government that could protect their property against rebellions. Farmers needed a government that could print money and make laws on trade. The writers of the Articles had tried to avoid creating another overbearing national government, such as the British Parliament, which had passed laws without consulting with the American colonies. As a result, the states did not always think of themselves as a united country.

The nation's early leaders began to make plans to change. They wanted to act fast to avoid more rebellions. Members of Congress met to discuss how best to strengthen the Articles of Confederation. Eventually, they decided to hold a conference to change the document by which the nation was governed. Henry Lee, Jr., a friend of George Washington, explained the need for a change.

**PRIMARY SOURCE**

## In Their Words... Henry Lee, Jr.

**The period seems to be fast approaching when the people of these United States must determine to establish a permanent capable government or submit to the horrors of anarchy. . . . The decay of their commerce leaves the lower order unemployed, idleness in this body, and the intriguing exertions of another class whose desperate fortunes are remediable only by the ruin of society.**

—from a letter to George Washington, September 8, 1786

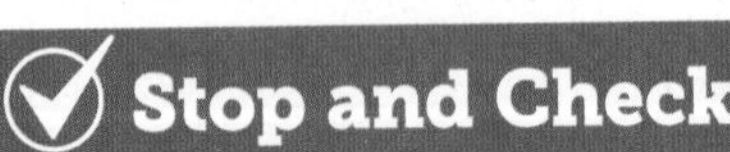

COLLABORATE

**Talk** How did the weaknesses of the Articles of Confederation lead to Shays's Rebellion?

Henry Lee, Jr. to George Washington, 8 September 1786. Founders Online, National Archives.

# Views on Rebellion

Thomas Jefferson and Samuel Adams—two of the signers of the Declaration of Independence—had widely different opinions regarding Shays's Rebellion. Read the following quotations from both men and consider their views in the context of what you have just read.

**Thomas Jefferson**

"I hold it that a little rebellion now and then is a good thing, and as necessary in the political world as storms in the **physical**. . . ."

**Samuel Adams**

"The man who dares to rebel against the laws of a republic ought to suffer death."

## Stop and Check

**You Decide** Working with a partner, choose to support either Adams or Jefferson in the debate over rebellion. Then partner with another pair of students who chose to support the opposite position. Take turns arguing each side, making sure to use specific details from the lesson to support your position.

**What Do You Think?** Why would Adams, who rebelled against Britain, oppose a rebellion against the U.S. government?

TEXT: (l)Thomas Jefferson to James Madison, Paris, January 30, 1787. The Thomas Jefferson Papers Series 1. General Correspondence. 1651-1827. Library of Congress., (r)Adams, Samuel. 1787. Quoted in Republic: A Monthly Magazine, Devoted to the Dissemination of Political Information, Vol. 4 (Washington, D.C.: The Republic Publishing Company, 1875), 185.; PHOTO: (bkgd)McGraw-Hill Education, (l)Stocktrek Images/Getty Images, (r)Library of Congress Prints & Photographs Division [LC-USZ62-102271]

# How Does the Constitution Set Up Our Government Framework?

## The Constitutional Convention

Shays's Rebellion showed that there was much dissatisfaction with the Articles of Confederation. On February 21, 1787, the Confederation Congress decided to gather **delegates** to discuss changing the Articles. This convention of delegates would take place at the Pennsylvania State House in Philadelphia. Invitations were sent to the states. All but Rhode Island sent delegates to the Constitutional Convention. Members of the Continental Congress were not the only delegates at the convention. The delegates also included Revolutionary War veterans, governors, lawyers, plantation owners, merchants, and other influential people. In total, fifty-five men took part in the convention, which began on May 25, 1787. They met in secret so that the delegates could speak freely and suggest ideas that might have hurt their reputations if the ideas became known. The doors were locked and the windows were covered. Although the convention's purpose was to fix the Articles of Confederation, the delegates soon began to write a new constitution for a new government.

1787
1788
1789
1790
February 1787
Confederation Congress calls for the rewriting of the Articles of Confederation.
July 1787
The Great Compromise is made.
June 1788
New Hampshire ratifies the Constitution, making it the law of the land.
May 1787
Constitutional Convention begins.
December 1787
Delaware is the first state to ratify the Constitution.
May 1790
Rhode Island becomes the last of the original 13 colonies to ratify the Constitution.
CONSTITUTION
OF THE
UNITED STATES OF AMERICA

The U.S. Constitution on display at the National Archives

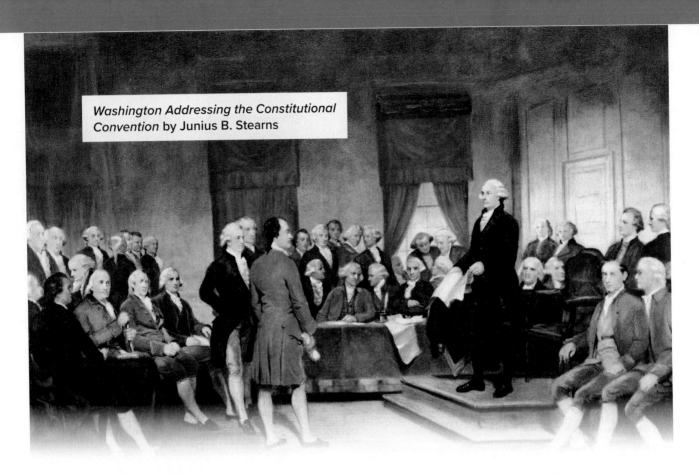

*Washington Addressing the Constitutional Convention* by Junius B. Stearns

# Conflicts and Compromises

George Washington was elected to lead the convention, but James Madison of Virginia did most of the work on the actual writing of the Constitution. Madison was largely responsible for convincing the other delegates to abandon the idea of fixing the Articles of Confederation. Madison wanted to start over and create a stronger national government. On May 29, 1787, Virginia governor Edmund Randolph proposed a plan of government designed by Madison and called the Virginia Plan.

The Virginia Plan called for a two-part legislature to make the laws. The members of the first part, or lower house, were to be elected by voters. The members of the second part, or upper house, were to be chosen by the members of the lower house. The lower house would also select a president as well as judges for a national court. In the Virginia Plan, Congress had the ability to veto state laws and even take over a state's government. The number of legislators in the houses would be calculated based on the number of people in each state.

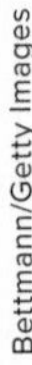

James Madison championed the Virginia Plan.

Some delegates had problems with the Virginia Plan. Under it, Congress would consist mainly of delegates from the states with the most people. These states would have more say in making laws and choosing officials. They could even take control of the governments of the smaller states. New Jersey delegate William Paterson offered an alternative. His New Jersey Plan also had a legislature to write laws. Its legislature would have only one house, and each state would have only one delegate. This way, every state would have an equal say.

This plan was opposed by the larger states. They asked why a small state should have the same power as a large state. If the government of a nation was not controlled by the majority of its people, then how could the government be a democracy? Furthermore, these delegates saw the plan as being too similar to the Articles of Confederation.

William Paterson created the New Jersey Plan.

The New Jersey Plan did answer some of the problems in the Articles, however. The national government would have some control over trade and would be able to raise money through import and stamp duties. There would also be an executive position created to control the military. Nonetheless, these measures weren't enough to convince the other delegates. They believed the New Jersey Plan would fail just as the Articles of Confederation had.

## InfoGraphic

# A Comparison of the Three Plans

### New Jersey Plan

- Appealed to smaller states
- Had a one-part legislature
- Each state would get one representative in the legislature.

### Virginia Plan

- Appealed to larger states
- Had a two-part legislature – a lower house would be elected by voters; an upper house would be elected by the lower house
- The number of representatives in the houses would be based on the number of people in each state.

### Great Compromise

- Has a two-part legislature
- The number of delegates in the House of Representatives would be determined by the population of each state.
- The Senate would have two delegates from each state.
- A law would not be approved until it passed through both the House of Representatives and the Senate.

So who was right? Both sides had fair points. *Democracy* means that laws should be agreed on by the majority of people, not by a small group of rulers. But states with small populations shouldn't be powerless against larger states. The argument continued for a month before Connecticut delegate Roger Sherman proposed the Great Compromise.

The Great Compromise combined the two plans. It called for a legislature with two houses. In one house, the House of Representatives, the population of a state would determine how many delegates the state would get. Here, the larger states had more power. In the other house, the Senate, each state would have two delegates. This would give the smaller states protection from the larger states. In order for a law to be approved, it would have to pass through both the House of Representatives and the Senate. In other words, a law would have to be supported by both a majority of the people and a majority of the states. The Great Compromise was adopted on July 16, 1787.

In addition to the Great Compromise, there was the Three-Fifths Compromise. Many of the delegates at the Constitutional Convention owned plantations with enslaved people. Should these people be counted as part of the population? Counting them would give states with slavery more representatives. However, enslaved people were denied by law any political power of their own, so those extra votes would go to the slaveholders. Without those extra votes, there was a good chance that Congress would outlaw slavery. The Southern states refused to join the new government unless they could be sure that Congress couldn't end slavery. Thus, the delegates decided that enslaved people would be counted, but for less than free persons. For every five enslaved people counted, three people would be added to the population count when determining representatives. The Southern states also agreed to stop future trading with other countries for enslaved people in 1808. However, people already enslaved, and their children, were to remain enslaved.

## Stop and Check

**Think** Which parts of the Great Compromise came from the Virginia Plan? Which part came from the New Jersey Plan?

**Find Details** As you read, add additional information to the graphic organizer on page 235 in your Inquiry Journal.

**What Do You Think?** Do you think the plan outlined in the Great Compromise was the best choice? Why or why not?

# The New Government

The Pennsylvania State House, now known as Independence Hall, where the U.S. Constitution was signed on September 17, 1787

After nearly four months of work, the delegates of the Constitutional Convention completed and signed the new U.S. Constitution. The document begins with a one-sentence Preamble, or introduction, that explains the purpose of the Constitution. The Preamble reflects the primary belief of the Founders of this country: A government is meant to serve its people. The government has to be effective enough to help people but organized in a way to prevent it from oppressing them. The delegates believed that a national government should have only as much power as the people allow it to have. To prevent the government from becoming too strong, the Constitution created a federal system in which the powers of government are divided. There is division of powers between state and national government, and there is also division of powers among the three branches of the national government.

The thirteen colonies rebelled against Great Britain because the British government had too much power and the colonies had too little. The Articles of Confederation failed because the states had too much power and the national government had too little. This time, the Framers of the Constitution wanted to get the balance of power just right.

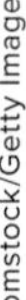

Both the state and the national governments can make laws and collect taxes. State governments, however, determine matters such as marriage age, driving age, and much of what is taught in public schools. State and local governments are also in charge of services like most police and fire protection, public libraries, and public transportation. What people need or want from a government can vary from person to person, city to city, and state to state. The Founders thought it best to have many everyday duties handled by state and local governments. The average person can access these government bodies more easily. They also can shift more easily to suit the unique needs of their area.

Meanwhile, the national government is divided into three branches: the legislative branch, the executive branch, and the judicial branch. Each branch has its own set of powers and duties, and no branch can do the job of another. Not only that, each branch has powers and weaknesses compared with the other branches. This system of checks and balances ensures that no individual or group becomes too powerful.

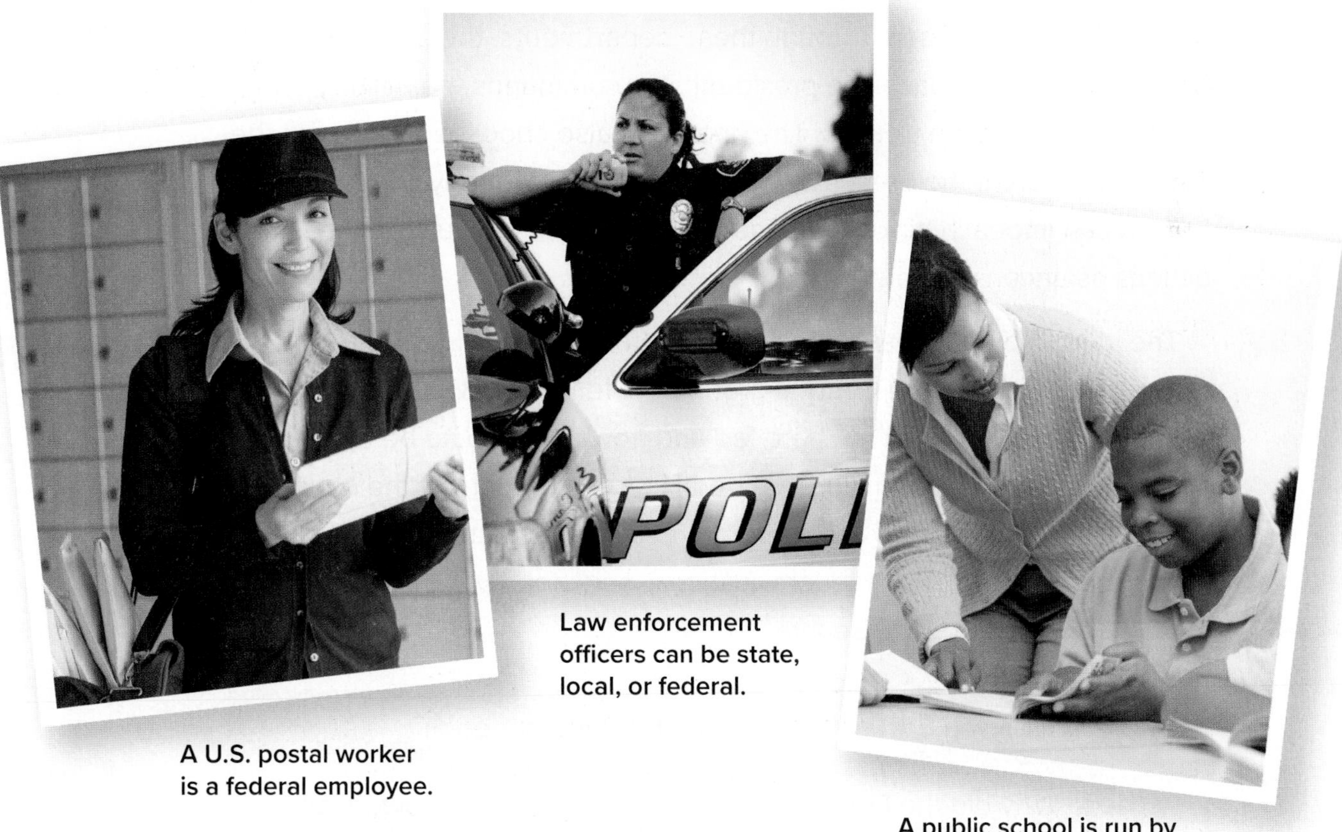


A U.S. postal worker is a federal employee.

Law enforcement officers can be state, local, or federal.

A public school is run by the state and local governments.

The legislative branch is in charge of making laws. It consists of Congress, which has two houses. In the House of Representatives, each state has a number of representatives that is based on how many people live in the state. The representatives serve for two-year **terms**, and then they have to be re-elected if they want to stay. The other house, the Senate, has two senators for every state. Senators serve six-year terms, and they also can be re-elected. The members of Congress write **bills**, and a bill must be approved by both houses to be passed. The bills passed by Congress must be approved by the executive branch to become laws. If a bill is not approved by the executive branch, it can still become a law if a large majority of Congress approves it. Laws can be ruled unconstitutional by the judicial branch.

The executive branch carries out the law. The highest position is the President of the United States, but the executive branch also includes the vice president and the cabinet, which is composed of the leaders of various government departments. These departments include the Department of State, the Department of Defense, and the Department of Justice. The department heads are chosen by the president but must be approved by the Senate. Through these departments, the executive branch enforces the law. The president also commands the military and has the ability to sign treaties. The president also chooses justices for the Supreme Court. If the president fails to do the job properly, the legislative branch can impeach him or her. The judicial branch can rule presidential actions as unconstitutional.

The judicial branch makes decisions on how laws are interpreted. It consists of the Supreme Court, a group of nine justices who make decisions about whether laws are fair and how they should be applied. The judicial branch also includes federal judges throughout the country. Unlike the legislative and executive branches, most justices of the judicial branch serve for life. Each federal justice is selected by the president and must be approved by the Senate.

## Stop and Check

**Think** Why did the Founders want the government's powers and duties separated?

InfoGraphic

# Checks and Balances

## Executive Branch

President (elected)

- Enforces laws
- Is Commander-in-Chief of the military
- Signs or vetoes laws
- Nominates judges

## Legislative Branch

Congress (elected)

- Can override veto
- Passes laws
- Approves spending and taxes
- Can impeach judges and the president
- Approves treaties

## Judicial Branch

Supreme Court and other federal courts (appointed)

- Interpret laws
- Can rule whether actions or laws passed are constitutional

### Stop and Check

**Think** Give two examples of checks by the legislative branch.

(bkgd)McGraw-Hill Education, (t)iStockphoto/Getty Images, (bl)Dwight Nadig/Getty Images, (br)Hisham F. Ibrahim/Getty Images

# Economic Aspects of the Constitution

One of the weaknesses of the national government under the Articles of Confederation was its lack of power in economic matters. An important part of the new Constitution was granting additional powers to Congress so that it could have some control of the U.S. economy. Under the Constitution, Congress could create and collect taxes and similar fees and borrow money if needed. This way, the government was finally able to pay some of its outstanding debts from the Revolutionary War.

On another economic matter, states would no longer be able to make their own currency. Congress now had the power to coin, or create, money. The whole nation would now use a single currency. This made it much easier for people from different states to do business across state lines. Congress also became responsible for overseeing trade with other nations, including Native American groups.

Congress did not have total control of the economy, though. It wasn't allowed to pass certain types of taxes. Nor could it tax trade between states or do anything else that would favor one state over another. Any money that Congress received had to be appropriated, or set aside for a specific purpose. That money could not be spent on anything else. These rules were intended to ensure the fairness of the U.S. economy so that many people had a chance to prosper.

**PRIMARY SOURCE**

## In Their Words... The Constitution

**Article I Section 8. Powers Granted to Congress**

1. The Congress shall have power to lay and collect taxes, duties, imposts and excises, to pay the debts and provide for the common defense and general welfare of the United States; but all duties, imposts, and excises shall be uniform throughout the United States;

2. To borrow money on the credit of the United States;

3. To regulate commerce with foreign nations, and among the several states, and with the Indian tribes;

4. To establish a uniform rule of naturalization, and uniform laws on the subject of bankruptcies throughout the United States;

5. To coin money, regulate the value thereof, and of foreign coin, and fix the standard of weights and measures;

6. To provide for the punishment of counterfeiting the securities and current coin of the United States;

7. To establish post offices and post roads . . .

### Stop and Check

COLLABORATE

**Talk** Reread the excerpt of the Constitution above. Why is it important that these duties are performed at the national level rather than at the state level?

**Find Details** Complete the graphic organizer on page 235 in your Inquiry Journal using information you have gathered.

**What Do You Think?** What was the most important improvement the Constitution had over the Articles of Confederation?

# How Do the Constitution and the Bill of Rights Impact Citizens?

## The Debate Over Ratification

The states had to ratify, or officially approve, the Constitution for it to become law. The two sides of the constitutional debate went to work to earn the support of the people of the United States. The Federalists defended the Constitution. Their ranks included George Washington, James Madison, and Alexander Hamilton. The Antifederalists opposed the Constitution. Antifederalists such as Samuel Adams, George Mason, and Patrick Henry thought that with the Constitution states lost too much power to the national government. Both the Federalists and Antifederalists wrote papers in defense of their positions.

The Federalists insisted that the Constitution would unify the states. They wanted to divide power between different parts of the federal government. They hoped to avoid giving too much power to any one person. James Madison, Alexander Hamilton, and John Jay made the case for Federalism in a series of 85 essays called *The Federalist Papers*. They wrote anonymously under the pen name "Publius." From 1787 to 1788, the essays appeared in several New York newspapers. Their authors reasoned that the Constitution would maintain order in the nation. "If men were angels," Madison wrote, "no government would be necessary."

**1791**
Bill of Rights ratified

**1865**
Thirteenth Amendment ratified

**1868**
Fourteenth Amendment ratified

**1870**
Fifteenth Amendment ratified

**1920**
Nineteenth Amendment ratified

**1961**
Twenty-Third Amendment ratified

**1964**
Twenty-Fourth Amendment ratified

**1971**
Twenty-Sixth Amendment ratified

1750 | 1800 | 1850 | 1900 | 1950 | 2000

Tetra Images/Shutterstock.com

Women did not receive the constitutional right to vote in national elections until 1920.

Antifederalists objected to the Constitution by pointing to its limited ability to protect Americans' liberties. In his essay "Objections to This Constitution of Government," George Mason attacked the document. He argued, "There is no declaration of any kind, for preserving the liberty of the **press**, or the trial by **jury** in civil cases; nor against the danger of standing armies in time of peace."

Nine out of thirteen states' votes were required to pass the Constitution. Delaware, New Jersey, and Pennsylvania first ratified the Constitution in December of 1787. New Hampshire gave the decisive ninth vote to accept the Constitution in 1788.

Some worried that the remaining states would prevent the Constitution from being enforced. New York and Virginia were the two largest states in the country. Many of their leaders refused to support the Constitution as written. In Massachusetts, Elbridge Gerry had argued against the Constitution. He felt that "a free people," not the government, "are the proper guardians of their rights and liberties." Massachusetts Antifederalists demanded that the Constitution be revised to clearly indicate the rights of citizens.

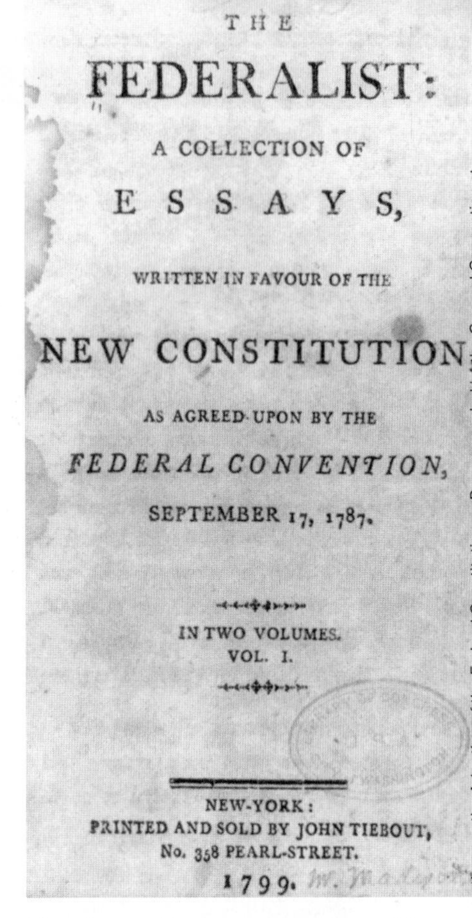

THE

FEDERALIST:

A COLLECTION OF

ESSAYS,

WRITTEN IN FAVOUR OF THE

NEW CONSTITUTION,

AS AGREED UPON BY THE

*FEDERAL CONVENTION,*

SEPTEMBER 17, 1787.

IN TWO VOLUMES.
VOL. I.

NEW-YORK:
PRINTED AND SOLD BY JOHN TIEBOUT,
No. 358 PEARL-STREET.
1799.

***The Federalist Papers*** **appeared in New York newspapers from 1787 to 1788.**

PRIMARY SOURCE

## In Their Words... Patrick Henry

Show me that age and country where the rights and liberties of the people were placed on the sole chance of their rulers being good men without a consequent loss of liberty! I say that the loss of that dearest privilege has ever followed, with absolute certainty, every such mad attempt.

—from a speech at the Virginia Constitution Ratifying Convention, 1788

James Madison, a Federalist, agreed to propose a Bill of Rights to Congress. The Bill of Rights included liberties that the Antifederalists believed the Constitution would not guarantee Americans. Madison promised to argue on behalf of the bill if the Antifederalists ratified the Constitution.

The agreement worked. Virginia and New York ratified the Constitution in 1788. The House of Representatives received the Bill of Rights in June 1789. North Carolina and Rhode Island then became the final states to ratify the Constitution.

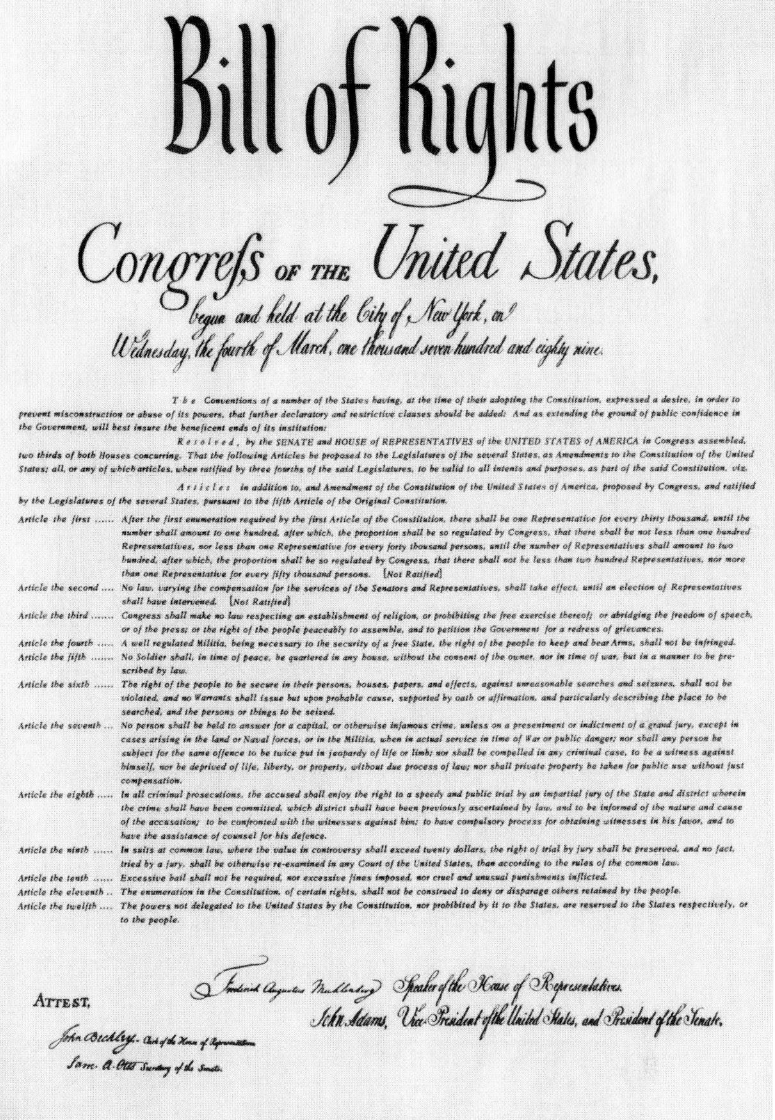

# Bill of Rights

Congress of the United States,
begun and held at the City of New York, on
Wednesday, the fourth of March, one thousand seven hundred and eighty nine.

The Conventions of a number of the States having, at the time of their adopting the Constitution, expressed a desire, in order to prevent misconstruction or abuse of its powers, that further declaratory and restrictive clauses should be added: And as extending the ground of public confidence in the Government, will best insure the beneficent ends of its institution:

Resolved, by the SENATE and HOUSE of REPRESENTATIVES of the UNITED STATES of AMERICA in Congress assembled, two thirds of both Houses concurring, That the following Articles be proposed to the Legislatures of the several States, as Amendments to the Constitution of the United States; all, or any of which articles, when ratified by three fourths of the said Legislatures, to be valid to all intents and purposes, as part of the said Constitution, viz.

Articles in addition to, and Amendment of the Constitution of the United States of America, proposed by Congress, and ratified by the Legislatures of the several States, pursuant to the fifth Article of the Original Constitution.

Article the first ...... After the first enumeration required by the first Article of the Constitution, there shall be one Representative for every thirty thousand, until the number shall amount to one hundred, after which, the proportion shall be so regulated by Congress, that there shall be not less than one hundred Representatives, nor less than one Representative for every forty thousand persons, until the number of Representatives shall amount to two hundred, after which, the proportion shall be so regulated by Congress, that there shall not be less than two hundred Representatives, nor more than one Representative for every fifty thousand persons. [Not Ratified]

Article the second .... No law, varying the compensation for the services of the Senators and Representatives, shall take effect, until an election of Representatives shall have intervened. [Not Ratified]

Article the third ....... Congress shall make no law respecting an establishment of religion, or prohibiting the free exercise thereof; or abridging the freedom of speech, or of the press; or the right of the people peaceably to assemble, and to petition the Government for a redress of grievances.

Article the fourth ..... A well regulated Militia, being necessary to the security of a free State, the right of the people to keep and bear Arms, shall not be infringed.

Article the fifth ....... No Soldier shall, in time of peace, be quartered in any house, without the consent of the owner, nor in time of war, but in a manner to be prescribed by law.

Article the sixth ...... The right of the people to be secure in their persons, houses, papers, and effects, against unreasonable searches and seizures, shall not be violated, and no Warrants shall issue but upon probable cause, supported by oath or affirmation, and particularly describing the place to be searched, and the persons or things to be seized.

Article the seventh ... No person shall be held to answer for a capital, or otherwise infamous crime, unless on a presentment or indictment of a grand jury, except in cases arising in the land or Naval forces, or in the Militia, when in actual service in time of War or public danger; nor shall any person be subject for the same offence to be twice put in jeopardy of life or limb; nor shall be compelled in any criminal case, to be a witness against himself, nor be deprived of life, liberty, or property, without due process of law; nor shall private property be taken for public use without just compensation.

Article the eighth ..... In all criminal prosecutions, the accused shall enjoy the right to a speedy and public trial by an impartial jury of the State and district wherein the crime shall have been committed, which district shall have been previously ascertained by law, and to be informed of the nature and cause of the accusation; to be confronted with the witnesses against him; to have compulsory process for obtaining witnesses in his favor, and to have the assistance of counsel for his defence.

Article the ninth ...... In suits at common law, where the value in controversy shall exceed twenty dollars, the right of trial by jury shall be preserved, and no fact, tried by a jury, shall be otherwise re-examined in any Court of the United States, than according to the rules of the common law.

Article the tenth ...... Excessive bail shall not be required, nor excessive fines imposed, nor cruel and unusual punishments inflicted.

Article the eleventh .. The enumeration in the Constitution, of certain rights, shall not be construed to deny or disparage others retained by the people.

Article the twelfth .... The powers not delegated to the United States by the Constitution, nor prohibited by it to the States, are reserved to the States respectively, or to the people.

Frederick Augustus Muhlenberg Speaker of the House of Representatives.
John Adams, Vice-President of the United States, and President of the Senate.

ATTEST,
John Beckley, Clerk of the House of Representatives.
Sam. A. Otis Secretary of the Senate.

Many Antifederalists would not support the Constitution without a Bill of Rights.

## Stop and Check

**Perspectives** Why did the Federalists continue to seek approval from all remaining states after the Constitution was ratified?

**Find Details** As you read, add additional information to the graphic organizer on page 243 in your Inquiry Journal.

(t)McGraw-Hill Education, (b)iStockphoto.com/leezsnow

# The Bill of Rights

In 1789, James Madison approached Congress with the first draft of a list of constitutional **amendments**. Congress chose 12 of these amendments to send to the states for approval. State leaders picked 10 of the amendments to ratify. Congress added the amendments, called the Bill of Rights, to the Constitution in December 1791.

Previously, government leaders had written documents defining the rights of their citizens. The British government signed a bill of rights in 1689. Several American states already had their own bills of rights by 1790. James Madison based his amendments partly on Virginia's bill of rights. Madison's rival, the Antifederalist George Mason, had written this document in 1776. Like many of the Constitution's framers, James Madison owned enslaved people who did not benefit from the rights defined in these amendments.

The Bill of Rights was ratified after the main text of the Constitution, but that does not make the section any less important. The rights outlined in the Bill of Rights define many aspects of life in the United States. The Bill of Rights sets limits on the U.S. government and protects the basic rights of all U.S. citizens.

Included in the Bill of Rights is freedom of speech, which includes the right to protest.

National Archives and Records Administration (NWDNS-306-SSM-4A-35-6)

The first part of the Bill of Rights secures individual rights. The First Amendment protects five freedoms: freedom of religion, freedom of speech, freedom of the press, freedom of assembly, and freedom to petition.

The Second Amendment protects the right "to keep and bear arms." The Supreme Court's interpretation of the amendment sets two constitutional rules. First, states can maintain militias. And second, the government may pass some laws to control, but not prevent, the use of firearms. The Third Amendment makes it unconstitutional for the government to force people to house soldiers.

The Fourth through Eighth Amendments guarantee the right to "due process." Due process of the law requires the government to follow a set of procedures when taking legal action against citizens. Due process is important in limiting the power of government. The amendments name specific actions that the government cannot take against its people.

The Ninth Amendment states that the rights of Americans extend beyond what is recorded in the Constitution. In the Tenth Amendment, the Constitution reserves all rights not provided to the federal government to be left for the states and the people.

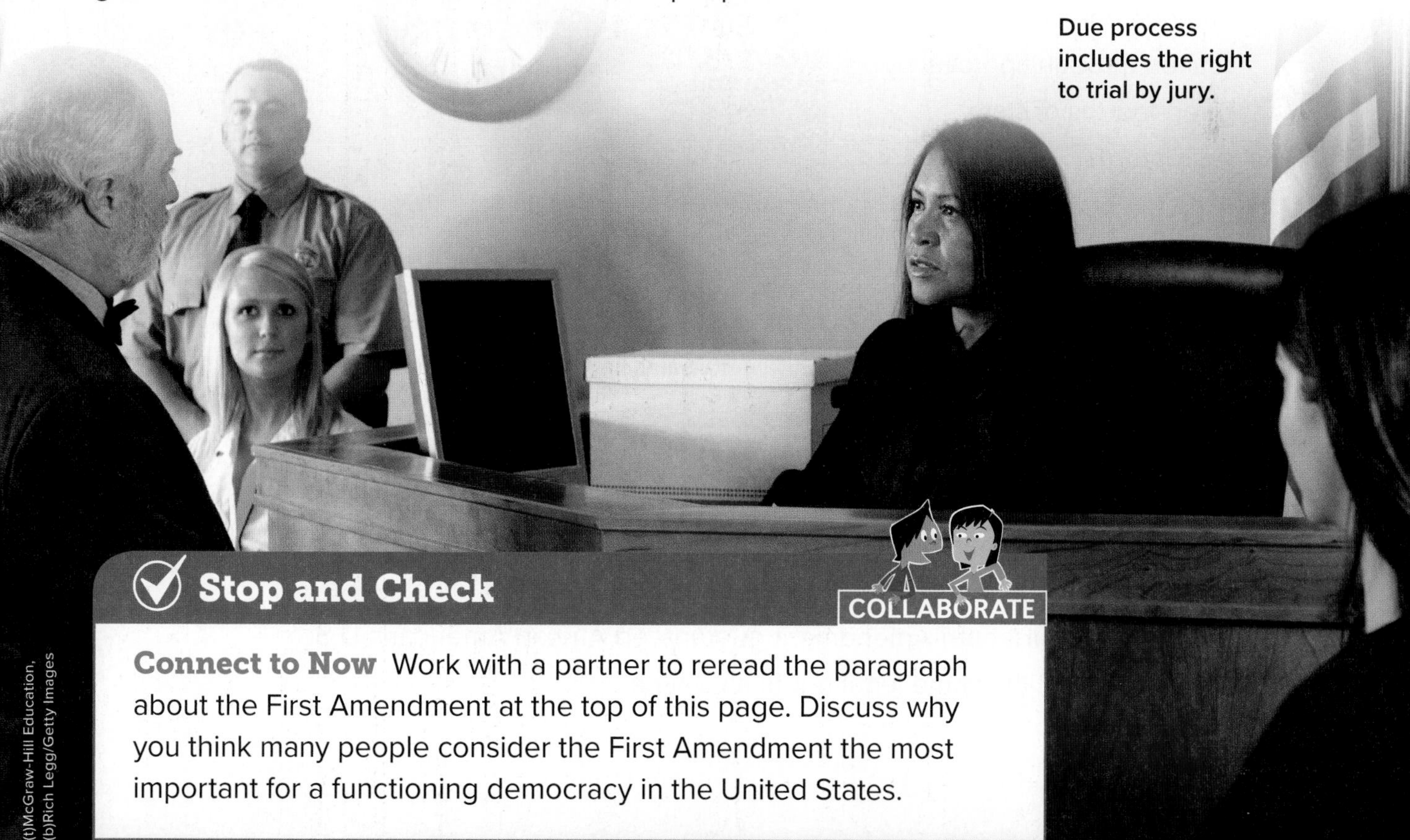

Due process includes the right to trial by jury.

## Stop and Check

COLLABORATE

**Connect to Now** Work with a partner to reread the paragraph about the First Amendment at the top of this page. Discuss why you think many people consider the First Amendment the most important for a functioning democracy in the United States.

# Amendments and Expanding Rights

The Bill of Rights introduced the first ten amendments to the Constitution. Seventeen more amendments have since been added. The Constitution's writers knew that the constitutional system needed flexibility. They wrote Article Five of the Constitution to define a process for amending the Constitution.

To become a part of the Constitution, an amendment must go through proposal and ratification. There are two ways to propose an amendment and two ways to ratify it.

Amendments may be proposed with the support of two-thirds of Congress. Alternatively, an amendment can be proposed if two-thirds of state legislatures call for a national convention. The amendment can then be ratified through approval by three-fourths of state legislatures.

Only white males had a voice in the new government.

Many of the seventeen amendments outside of the Bill of Rights expanded voting rights. In 1870, ratification of the Fifteenth Amendment allowed formerly enslaved African American men to vote. The Fifteenth Amendment would not be possible without the Thirteenth and Fourteenth Amendments. These amendments are sometimes called the Civil War amendments. The Thirteenth Amendment made slavery illegal. The Fourteenth Amendment guaranteed African Americans U.S. citizenship and the same legal rights as whites.

## Then and Now

### Voting Then

Until 1870, only white men could vote. Even after several amendments guaranteed voting rights for other groups such as women, nonwhite citizens were often discriminated against. In many cases, the government has tried to enforce the amendments by passing voter protection laws. For example, the Voting Rights Act of 1965 put into place specific rules that helped enforce the Fifteenth Amendment.

### Voting Now

Today, most United States citizens who are 18 years or older can vote. U.S. citizens living in other countries can submit their ballots by mail. Different states have different laws about whether people who have been convicted of certain crimes can vote. States also require varying types of registration and identification to vote on Election Day.

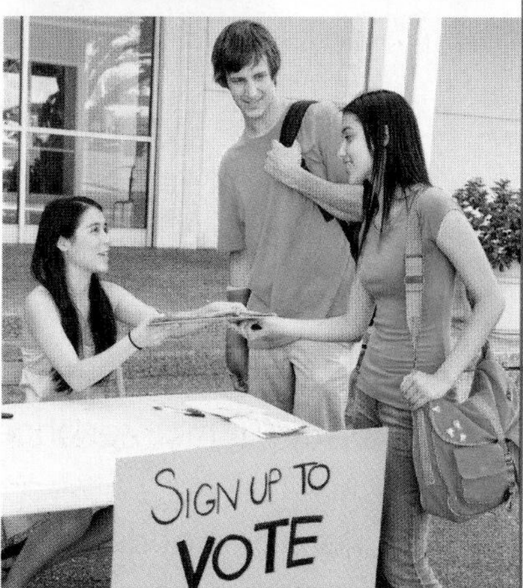


Protests for voting rights for women led to the ratification of the Nineteenth Amendment in 1920. The Twenty-Third Amendment gave residents of Washington, D.C., voting rights in 1961. Three years later, the practice of poll taxes was made illegal in the Twenty-Fourth Amendment. Poll taxes, or fees citizens had to pay to vote, had prevented many people from voting, especially African Americans in the South.

Until 1971, only citizens 21 and older could vote. Some Americans argued that if 18-year-olds could fight in wars, they should be allowed to vote. The Twenty-Sixth Amendment set the new voting age at 18.

## Stop and Check

**Connect to Now** Choose one of the amendments mentioned in the section. Write a law that would help enforce the amendment. How does your law help guarantee the liberties protected by the amendment?

(t)McGraw-Hill Education, (c)Library of Congress, Prints and Photographs Division (LC-USZ62-135533), (b)Yellow Dog Productions/Photodisc/Getty Images

# Civic Responsibilities

Citizens of the United States are responsible for participating in certain aspects of the government. William Tyler Page expressed these responsibilities in his 1917 patriotic statement "The American's Creed." He wrote that Americans had a duty "to love it, to support its Constitution, to obey its laws, to respect its flag, and to defend it against all enemies."

Obeying the law is a civic responsibility because it contributes to our safety. The government can also call on citizens to defend the nation. People can sometimes be required to join the military if the country is at war. People in the U.S. have a civic responsibility to pay taxes. State and federal governments use taxes for programs and projects that better the country. Roads, government buildings, and public schools rely on tax money for maintenance and improvements.

As a part of due process, the Sixth Amendment guarantees the right to a trial by jury. Americans must judge court cases as part of a jury. In many cases, the jury makes the final decision about whether someone is guilty or innocent. Without citizens' participation in juries, Americans could not be guaranteed their right to due process.

Citizens can help their government by exercising their voting rights.

One important way citizens can participate in politics is by expressing their opinions at local-government meetings.

## Participating in Politics

U.S. citizens have the right to vote. Participating in elections is not required, though. Our government depends on people exercising their right to vote. Citizens of the United States are responsible for guiding the direction of the country. Responsible citizens stay informed about the issues and candidates. Each person's vote influences the direction of government. Voting is one of the ways citizens make their voices heard.

Citizens participate in United States politics in other ways. Government leaders use information from citizens to act in the public interest. People can write, email, or call their elected officials. They can sign petitions to argue for change in government. Protesting and marching are other direct ways for citizens to express their support for or opposition to a political position.

Citizens can also contribute to the nation by volunteering. Volunteers often respond to civic issues that affect the health, safety, and liberties of people in the United States. Political campaigns also depend on volunteers to reach voters.

Finally, citizens may serve as public officials. Any citizen who fulfills basic requirements is eligible to run for office. Public officials help determine the course of the country.

### Stop and Check

COLLABORATE

**Perspectives** Work with a partner to reread the section on civic responsibilities. Talk about the quotation from "The American's Creed." What do you think about the duties mentioned in the Creed? What other responsibilities do you think are important for citizens in a country?

**What Do You Think?** Should Americans be required to vote?

# Connections in Action!

## Back to the EQ

**Think** about the Chapter EQ, **"How Does the Constitution Help Us Understand What It Means to Be an American?"**

- **Talk** with a partner about what you learned about in the chapter. Discuss what it means to be an American. Then identify how the Constitution supports that definition.
- Consider the Bill of Rights as well as later amendments that expanded rights to all citizens. Come to an agreement about which amendments were most important, and take notes about your conclusions.
- **Share** your ideas with the class. Then have a class discussion about how the Constitution helps us understand what it means to be an American.

THE
FEDERALIST:
A COLLECTION OF
ESSAYS,
WRITTEN IN FAVOUR OF THE
NEW CONSTITUTION,
AS AGREED UPON BY THE
FEDERAL CONVENTION,
SEPTEMBER 17, 1787.

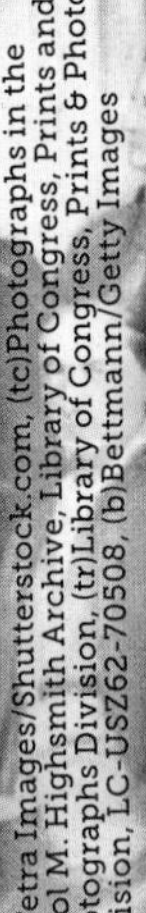

# More to Explore

## How Can You Make an IMPACT?

### Act Out Amendments

Choose an amendment to the Constitution. Identify the purpose of the amendment, the year it was ratified, and three to five details about its history. Present the amendment to your class, and listen as others present the amendments they have chosen. Discuss as a group how each amendment works together to create a unified Constitution.

### Letter to a Friend

Imagine you are one of the delegates at the Constitutional Convention. Write a letter to a friend from the delegate's point of view. The letter should be about an issue that was important to the delegate, such as the Bill of Rights, strong state governments, a strong national government, and so on. Use evidence from the text in your letter.

### Word Play

Choose three words from the chapter Word Bank. Define each word by drawing a picture that explains what the word is, describes it in context, or shows it in action.

# THE IMPACT TODAY

# How Does History Shape a Country's Government?

## History and Government of Canada

Like the United States, the Canadian government was shaped by the country's history. Canada remained a British colony for many years after the United States gained its independence from Great Britain. By 1855, after several revolts, British Parliament allowed many Canadian colonies to become self-governing colonies. Later, British Parliament passed the British North American Act, finally making Canada an independent nation on July 1, 1867. Until 1982, the act would serve as Canada's constitution.

The British North American Act gave the Canadian government a structure similar to that of the government of Great Britain. Both are constitutional monarchies led by the British monarch. The monarch's powers are mostly ceremonial. Like the United States, Canada has a legislative branch. It's called a parliament. The Parliament's two houses are called the Senate and the House of Commons. The party that wins the most seats in the House of Commons chooses the leader of the executive branch, the prime minister. Unlike the United States, Canadians do not directly vote for their top leader, the prime minister.

In 1960, Canada passed the Canadian Bill of Rights. Like the U.S. Bill of Rights, it protects the freedoms of religion, speech, and the press, and it guarantees legal rights to all citizens. However, the Canadian Bill of Rights only applied to federal laws and not laws of Canadian provinces, which are like our states. In 1982, Canada wrote a new constitution that included the Canadian Charter of Rights and Freedoms. The Charter has greater power than the Bill of Rights and applies to federal and provincial laws.

Canada's national capital is Ottawa, Ontario. This photograph shows the changing of the guard in front of the parliament building.

# History and Government of Mexico

Mexico was a colony of Spain from 1521 until 1821. But the struggle for Mexican independence began on September 16, 1810. A Catholic priest, Miguel Hidalgo y Costilla, called on Mexicans to revolt against Spain in a speech known as the *Grito de Dolores* or *Cry of Dolores,* given from his church in Dolores, Mexico. Hidalgo's revolt failed but inspired other Mexicans to continue the fight. Spain finally recognized Mexican independence on August 24, 1821. Today, Mexicans celebrate Independence Day on September 16.

Benito Juárez was president of Mexico in the mid-1800s. He reformed the legal system, created separation of church and state, and stopped an attempt by Europeans to gain control of Mexico.

During its early years, Mexico controlled land throughout much of what is now the western United States and Central America. Mexico lost more than half of its land to the United States in 1848 after the Mexican-American War.

In 1857, new Mexican leaders created a constitution that made the government a democracy, established freedom of speech, eliminated business monopolies, and separated church and state. This ignited years of conflict with people who wanted to preserve colonial values. Two civil wars and an unsuccessful attempt by France to install an emperor led to a period of instability that lasted until 1940.

Today, Mexico's government is a federal republic, just like the U.S. government. The president is elected by the people and can serve only one six-year term. The Mexican legislature consists of a Senate and a Chamber of Deputies. The country has a supreme court and numerous federal and regional courts. The latest constitution, created in 1917, guarantees personal freedom and civil liberties.

## WHAT IS THE IMPACT TODAY?

COLLABORATE

**Talk** How are the histories and governments of Canada and Mexico alike and different? What is one thing you like or do not like about each country's form of government?

# History and Government of Cuba

Spain conquered Cuba in 1514, brutally attacking the native peoples. In the late 1800s, Cubans grew tired of their corrupt Spanish rulers and high taxes. José Martí, a poet, began a revolt in 1895. With help from the United States, the Cubans forced Spain to abandon the island by 1898. Cuba became fully independent on May 20, 1902.

Cuba's governments from 1902 to the 1950s were often run by corrupt, military-backed rulers. Foreign investors controlled much of the land and economy. Most Cubans were poor. In the 1950s, a Cuban lawyer named Fidel Castro organized revolts against then dictator Fulgencio Batista. On January 1, 1959, Batista and his followers fled the country, and Castro set up a new government. Cubans celebrate January 1 as Liberation Day.

The government seized control of foreign property and businesses in Cuba and formed an alliance with the Soviet Union, leading to tensions with the United States. Today, Cuba's government is controlled by one party, the Communist Party of Cuba. Cuba's constitution, adopted in 1976, gave the government complete control of the economy, including decisions on investment, prices, and income. This type of economy is called a **command economy**. The constitution and later amendments also guarantee free healthcare, education, and other rights.

People vote for a legislative body called the National Assembly of People's Power. But choice of who can run for office is heavily controlled. In 2018 elections, the Communist Party received every vote. This Assembly selects a Council of State, judges, and the Cuban president. Fidel Castro and his brother Raúl ran the country from 1959 to 2018. The Council of State, the Cuban president, and his or her chosen cabinet make laws and decisions that heavily influence and direct Cuban daily life.

**La Plaza de la Revolución in Havana, Cuba, is a square that pays tribute to the Cuban Revolution of the 1950s, which brought Fidel Castro to power.**

Chris Cheadle/age fotostock

# History and Government of Brazil

Brazil has the next-largest population in the Western Hemisphere after the United States. Brazil was a colony of Portugal from 1533 to 1822. For most of the 1800s, Brazil's form of government was a constitutional monarchy led by an emperor. The last emperor and monarch, Pedro II, was forced to leave in 1889.

Juscelino Kubitschek served as president of Brazil in the late 1950s. He was typical of Brazil's strong presidents of the 1900s. He built a new national capital in Brasilia in the center of the country.

Like many other Latin American countries, Brazil had only limited democracy for most of the 1900s. Many people in these nations wanted stability to prevent other countries from taking control of them. Strong leaders and weak legislatures became common. As long as the economy grew, opposition to leaders was limited. A government in which one leader has total power is called a **dictatorship**.

Until the 1930s, only wealthy landowners could vote in Brazil. When the rest of the population got the right to vote, there was a long struggle for power. Presidents often suspended the constitution so that they could try to develop the economy more quickly. They created large petroleum and steel industries and built roads and power plants. But they also limited personal freedom, with the help of the military. Beginning in the 1980s, the government of Brazil became more balanced. Presidents shared power with the legislature. A new constitution in 1988 limited the president's powers and the military's role in government. It also allowed for more personal freedoms.

The Brazilian National Congress has two parts, a Federal Senate and a Chamber of Deputies. The Congress has power over the federal budget and approves treaties. Congress can override a presidential veto with a majority vote. The executive branch is led by a president and cabinet. The judicial branch has two parts. One consists of state and federal courts. The other has courts that deal with labor, military, and voting issues. Above these two parts is a Supreme Court.

## WHAT IS THE IMPACT TODAY?

COLLABORATE

**Talk** How are the histories and governments of Canada, Mexico, Brazil, and Cuba alike and different? Name at least one thing each country shares and one thing that makes the country and its government unique. Which type of government do you like best?

# A Growing Nation

**Lesson 1**
Early Leaders and Decisions

**Lesson 2**
Advancements in Technology and Transportation

**Lesson 3**
People of the Young Republic

**Lesson 4**
Westward Expansion

**Lesson 5**
Conflicts and Compromises

**The IMPACT Today**
Economics and Personal Finance

## What Do the Early Years of the United States Reveal About the Character of the Nation?

In this chapter, you'll read about how early leaders, conflicts, and a growing population led to major changes within the United States. You'll read about how important inventions changed the way of life for many Americans and allowed them to expand their own horizons by traveling west. You'll learn about the consequences of this westward movement for native peoples. You'll also explore the conflicts and compromises over slavery.

## Step into the Time Chronological Thinking

Look at the time line. What was happening in other parts of the world while the United States was growing and changing?

**Americas**

**1788** The U.S. Constitution becomes law.

**1789** George Washington becomes the first president.

**1793** Eli Whitney invents the cotton gin.

**1803** President Thomas Jefferson makes Louisiana Purchase.

**1812–1815** The War of 1812

**1819** Simón Bolívar liberates New Granada in South America.

1780 | 1790 | 1800 | 1810 | 1820

**World Events**

**1796** English physician Edward Jenner develops smallpox vaccine.

**1800** Alessandro Volta of Italy creates the first electric battery.

**1806** The British take control of Cape Colony in South Africa.

**1815** Napoleon is defeated at Battle of Waterloo in Belgium.

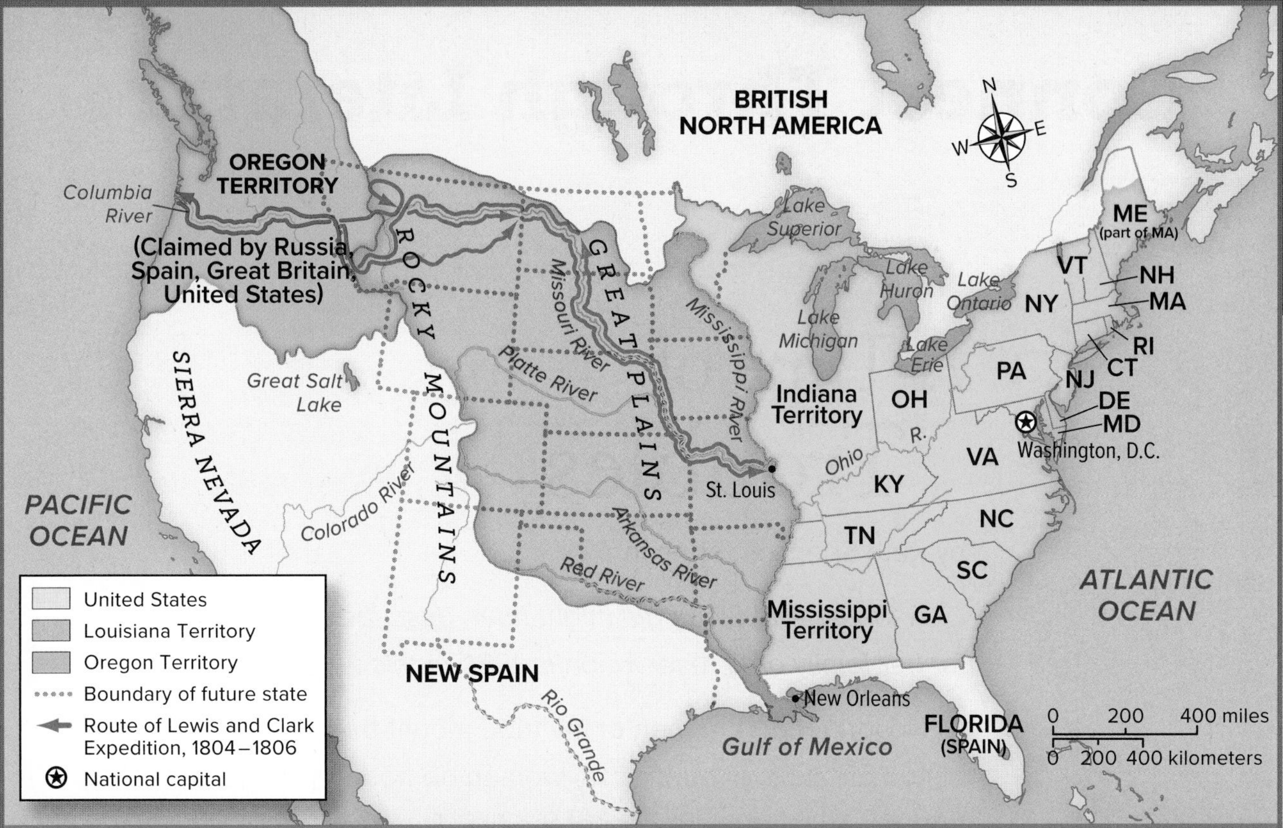

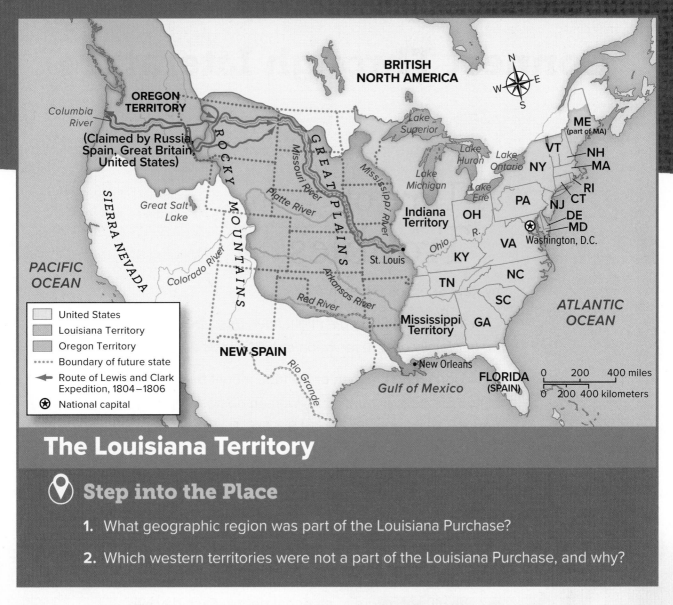

# The Louisiana Territory

## Step into the Place

1. What geographic region was part of the Louisiana Purchase?
2. Which western territories were not a part of the Louisiana Purchase, and why?

In the years immediately following the American Revolution, the new nation added several new states, including Vermont, Kentucky, and Tennessee. The biggest addition to the nation's territory came in 1803, however, with the purchase of the Louisiana Territory from France by President Thomas Jefferson.

20 — 1830 — 1840 — 1850 — 1860

- **1821** Mexico wins independence from Spain.
- **1824** Beethoven writes his Ninth Symphony.
- **1826** The first photograph is taken.
- **1830** Indian Removal Act is passed.
- **1837** Victoria becomes queen of England.
- **1839** First Opium War between Great Britain and China begins.
- **1845** The Great Famine (Irish Potato Famine) begins.
- **1846-1847** The Mexican War
- **1848-1849** California Gold Rush
- **1852** *Uncle Tom's Cabin* is published.
- **1857** Supreme Court decides Dred Scott case.
- **1859** The French seize the city of Saigon in Vietnam.

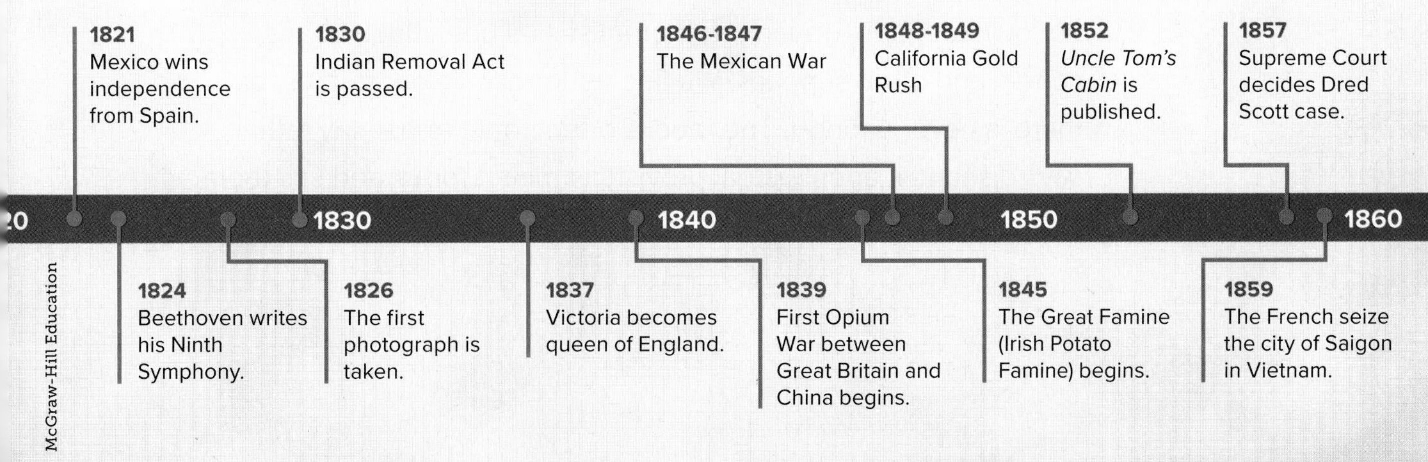

# Connect Through Literature

## A Time of Troubles

by Ruth Spencer Johnson

*A 13-year-old Sioux girl might have described what life was like for her family on a reservation in 1880 in this way:*

No longer do the men of my tribe mount their horses and ride out on great bison hunts. The women do not prepare feasts of fresh bison meat roasted over the fire. The enormous herds are gone, and so are the days when we traveled freely, setting up our tepee camps wherever the bison led us. The white men say we must learn to farm instead of hunt. They insist we become "civilized" and adopt their ways. Our tribe must stay on this reservation, which is a small part of the land we used to roam.

Before the reservation, my people rose with the sun, ready to use the gifts of nature to meet our needs. Each day was a challenge, but we were free. Now we must depend on the white man's promise to feed and clothe us, but the government has not kept its word.

The Great Father pledged to give us cattle, tools, and seeds for farming, as well as blankets and cloth. While we learn to grow our own food, the government promises us beef, flour, beans, coffee, and other supplies. We line up to receive our rations, but there is never enough. The food is often not fit to eat. My father says dishonest agents steal provisions meant for us and sell them for a profit.

Like my father, the men of our tribe were once proud hunters providing us with meat and skins from bison, elk, and other animals. They were warriors, ready to protect their families at a moment's notice. When we moved to the reservation, they had to give up their weapons and learn to plow. But farming takes fertile land and good weather, and we have neither. Settlers take the best land, and drought and hot summer winds kill many of the crops. We have not been able to raise enough food, and now we are starving.

As always, my mother and the other women cook, clean, and raise children. The home is a woman's responsibility, but without fresh bison hides, Mother cannot repair our tepee or make a new one. Government officials insist we dress like white settlers, so we must now sew our garments from thin cloth instead of animal skins. Without our warm bison robes and deerskin clothing, we are always cold in the winter winds.

**Sioux (Lakota) Native Americans resting at camp**

As if cold and hunger aren't enough to deal with, our people have been sick. We have little resistance to white men's diseases, and many people die—especially children. Officials have forbidden our medicine men from using traditional ways to treat the sick, so they must act in secret. We children are busy doing chores and helping our parents, but we try to find a little time to play so we can forget our troubles for a while. Boys pretend to be warriors and hunters. Girls play with their dolls, and we all like to play ball and stick games. In the evening, we gather around our grandparents to hear them tell stories about their youth. They have so much wisdom to pass on to us!

Churches have set up schools on the reservation to teach us English and try to turn us into Christians. The teachers cut our hair short and give us new names. They want us to learn to live like them and hope we will help our parents give up the ancient ceremonies and customs. But when we go home after school, most of us still speak our own language and follow our traditional ways.

Some of my friends have been sent to boarding schools where they must live year-round. The white men think children are more likely to change if they are separated from their families for long periods. Students who return to their families after years at boarding school often feel like they no longer belong with their own people. This is a sad thing because we place a high value on family. My tribe has struggled since we were forced onto the reservation. Some of our people want to learn the white man's ways, thinking that's the only path to survival. A few men have even become policemen and help enforce the reservation laws. But many people cling to tradition, and this has created conflict. The reservation officials do not allow us to mourn our dead or celebrate the seasons in the traditional ways.

Flandreau Indian School choir, South Dakota, early 1900s



Still, some things have not changed. The Sioux will always love the earth and all its creatures. We treasure our children and respect our elders. We try to follow the right path in life, and we ask the Great Spirit to give us strength and wisdom.

Many of us long for the old days and desperately hope for a way off the reservation. You can hear our yearning in the songs we sing around the fire on cold nights. Oh, Great Spirit, please hear our cries!

## Think About It

1. What has changed for the Sioux girl and her family?
2. How does life on the reservation compare with the life the Sioux led before?
3. How do the Sioux maintain their way of life despite the hardships of the reservation?

# People You Should Know

## Frederick Douglass

Frederick Douglass was a brilliant writer and speaker. He spoke out against slavery and helped convince people that slavery was a great injustice. Douglass was born into slavery. As a boy, he was taught to read and write. Then his owner decided education would make him unfit to be enslaved, so Douglass had to continue his education in secret. After several attempts, Douglass escaped slavery. He began to write and lecture about slavery. He later purchased his freedom and started his own newspaper. His autobiography *Life and Times of Frederick Douglass* became a classic of American Literature. Douglass became the first African American to hold a high rank in the U.S. government.

## Dolley Madison

First Lady Dolley Madison is best remembered for her actions during the War of 1812. As the British neared Washington D.C., Madison realized that the brand new White House would be a tempting target. She managed to find a wagon, had it loaded with fine china and other valuable objects, and sent it off for safekeeping at the Bank of Maryland. Just before she was forced to leave, she convinced her staff to break the frame on the famous portrait of George Washington by Gilbert Stuart so that the painting could be removed. Her quick thinking saved important pieces of U.S. history and culture from the fire that later burned down the mansion.

## Sacagawea

When she was about 12 years old, Sacagawea (also spelled Sacajawea and Sakakawea) was kidnapped by the Hidatsa people from her Shoshone family. A few years later, a French-Canadian fur trader named Toussaint Charbonneau purchased her. She later became his wife. Soon after, Meriwether Lewis and William Clark hired Charbonneau as a guide and interpreter for their expedition to explore the Louisiana Purchase. When they realized they would need someone who also spoke Shoshone, however, they agreed to bring Sacagawea along. She was pregnant at the time, and she gave birth on the trail to a son, Jean Baptiste. She lent her knowledge of languages and landmarks to the expedition, helping to make it a success.

## Tecumseh

Shawnee chief Tecumseh was a respected leader in the Ohio River Valley. A gifted and inspiring orator, he crafted an alliance between several groups of Native Americans to try to stop white expansion. He used this alliance to help the British fight the Americans during the War of 1812. Tecumseh helped the British win several important battles before the Americans defeated him in Canada. Tecumseh's death at the Battle of the Thames in 1813 signaled the end of Native American resistance to U.S. settlement of the Ohio River Valley.

# How Did Early Decisions Shape the Nation?

## A New Government Is Launched

In 1789, George Washington became the first President of the United States sworn in under the new Constitution. The Constitution had merely outlined how the new government would operate. Now the new President and Congress would have to fill in all the details.

Congress created three departments to help President Washington govern and set **policy**. The Department of Treasury managed the nation's finances. The Department of State dealt with foreign relations. The Department of War (now called the Department of Defense) handled military matters. To head these departments, President Washington appointed three talented people: Alexander Hamilton as Secretary of the Treasury, Thomas Jefferson as Secretary of State, and Henry Knox as Secretary of War. Washington also appointed Edmund Randolph as Attorney General, or the main lawyer for the federal government. Randolph would join Hamilton, Jefferson, and Knox in the nation's first Cabinet, or group of top presidential advisers.

**1800** U.S. capital moves to Washington, D.C.

**1803** President Thomas Jefferson makes Louisiana Purchase.

**1804** Lewis and Clark Expedition begins.

**1814** British burn Washington, D.C., during War of 1812.

**1823** President James Monroe issues Monroe Doctrine.

'90 | 1800 | 1810 | 1820

**1789** George Washington becomes president.

Library of Congress, Prints and Photographs Division (LC-USZC4-12011)

George Washington at his second inauguration at Congress Hall in Philadelphia, March 4, 1793

All of these changes to help the government work also made it bigger. So in 1790, President Washington signed a law to establish a new national capital called the District of Columbia. The President hired Pierre L'Enfant, a French engineer, to design the city and later replaced him with Andrew Ellicott, who kept much of L'Enfant's grand plan. Working with Ellicott was Benjamin Banneker, a free-born African American, who helped lay out the city. Banneker was one of the first African Americans appointed by a President to work for the federal government.

**Benjamin Banneker**

The years of George Washington's presidency saw a rise in political tension. Washington had chosen his Cabinet to provide a variety of opinions. Alexander Hamilton and Thomas Jefferson had very different views of what the new nation should be like. Hamilton thought the United States should have a strong central government and an economy that emphasized commerce and industry. Jefferson thought a strong central government would lead to corruption. He preferred a more agricultural nation with a weak federal government and more political power for the states. In general, President Washington agreed with Hamilton's economic proposals. He believed they were vital to the foundation of the new nation's economy.

After two terms in office, George Washington decided to leave the presidency. He wished to retire from public life and establish that the president was not a monarch. By then, the division in his Cabinet had led to the beginning of the nation's first political parties. John Adams, Washington's vice president, shared Hamilton's views, and they helped to form what became known as the Federalist Party. James Madison and many other Southern politicians shared Jefferson's views in what became known as the Democratic-Republican Party. In the election of 1796 to succeed Washington, John Adams ran against Thomas Jefferson and won. Four years later, Adams ran against Jefferson again and lost.

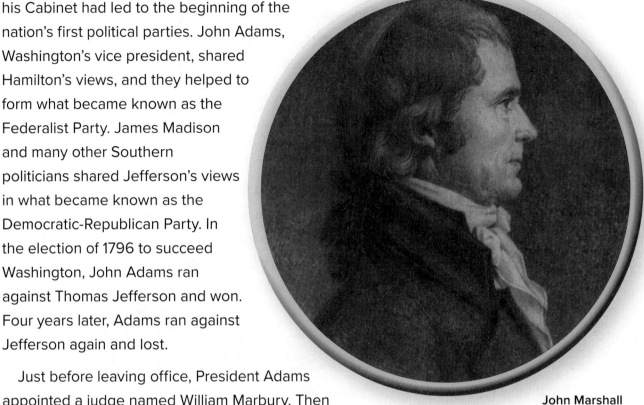

John Marshall

Just before leaving office, President Adams appointed a judge named William Marbury. Then James Madison, Secretary of State for President Jefferson, refused to give Marbury his official papers, even though a section of the Judiciary Act of 1789 passed by Congress said he should. At a famous hearing of the U.S. Supreme Court, Chief Justice John Marshall ruled that this section of the Judiciary Act was **unconstitutional**, or against the guidelines included in the U.S. Constitution. The case, *Marbury* v. *Madison*, is very important. It established the principle that the Supreme Court can review laws passed by Congress and, if necessary, declare them unconstitutional.

## Stop and Check

COLLABORATE

**Talk** What government divisions, positions, and other "firsts" were established during George Washington's presidency?

**Find Details** As you read, add additional information to the graphic organizer on page 259 in your Inquiry Journal.

# A Nation Expands

In 1789, George Washington signed a new Northwest Ordinance. It made clear that the rules for settling territory, established in the previous ordinance, were still in effect under the new Constitution. One part of the ordinance banned slavery north of the Ohio River. However, settlers from the South brought enslaved people into Kentucky and Tennessee. Even in the northern territories, African Americans had a difficult time. Laws were passed to keep African Americans out of some states. These same states forced free African Americans already there to show papers proving they were free.

Native Americans did not recognize the right of U.S. citizens to purchase land in the new territories. As newcomers poured in, tensions mounted. Violence between native peoples and new settlers led President Washington to send the army to Ohio three times during his presidency. The Native Americans would eventually be forced to give up most of Ohio.

COLLABORATE

**Talk** Why do you think settlers were able to bring enslaved people into the new territory even though it was against the law?

General Harmar defeated by Miamis, 1790

# The Louisiana Purchase

During the 1790s, control of the port of New Orleans had passed from France to Spain, and back to France again. While the United States had a deal with Spain to use the river and port, President Jefferson was worried that the French could close the river and port to U.S. commerce. So he sent Robert Livingston, U.S. Minister to France, and future President James Monroe, a special ambassador, to meet with the French and offer to buy New Orleans.

The American flag is raised in New Orleans after the city became part of the United States as a result of the Louisiana Purchase.

France and Great Britain were involved in a series of conflicts. France needed money for its military. The French also realized that they could not protect Louisiana if the British attacked from Canada. So the French government made a surprising offer: France would sell not just New Orleans but the entire Louisiana colony to the United States.

The deal was an excellent one for Jefferson—530 million acres of land for 15 million dollars. That's about 3.5 cents an acre. Still, making the purchase was a hard decision for the president. For years, he had argued for a federal government with limited power. Having the federal government buy new territory was not a power spelled out in the Constitution. Nevertheless, Jefferson decided that he could not pass up such a good opportunity for the nation.

President Jefferson officially announced the Louisiana Purchase on July 4, 1803. The Louisiana Territory became part of the United States, doubling the size of the nation. As in the past, these land exchanges involved European nations, and the United States would mostly ignore the claims of Native Americans already living on the land. This would bring conflict in future decades, when more and more settlers came west to mine and farm the land.

Meanwhile, to most U.S. citizens living east of the Mississippi River, the land that the nation had purchased was largely unknown territory. Jefferson himself had been fascinated by the West and its potential for some time. Even before the Louisiana Purchase, Jefferson had asked Congress for money to fund an expedition to explore the western part of the continent and seek a route to the Pacific Ocean. Those plans took on new significance after the Louisiana Purchase.

To lead the expedition, Jefferson chose his personal secretary, Meriwether Lewis, an army captain with experience on the frontier. Lewis then asked William Clark, an army friend, to share his command. Calling their group the Corps of Discovery, Lewis, Clark, and more than thirty others set out from a camp near St. Louis on May 14, 1804. Among them were John Ordway, a New Hampshire soldier who was in charge of supplies during the journey, and an enslaved man named York.

**PRIMARY SOURCE**

## In Their Words... The Louisiana Purchase

**The inhabitants of the ceded territory shall be incorporated in the Union of the United States and admitted as soon as possible according to the principles of the federal Constitution to the enjoyment of all these rights, advantages and immunities of citizens of the United States, and in the mean time they shall be maintained and protected in the free enjoyment of their liberty, property and the Religion which they profess.**

—from the Louisiana Purchase, Article III

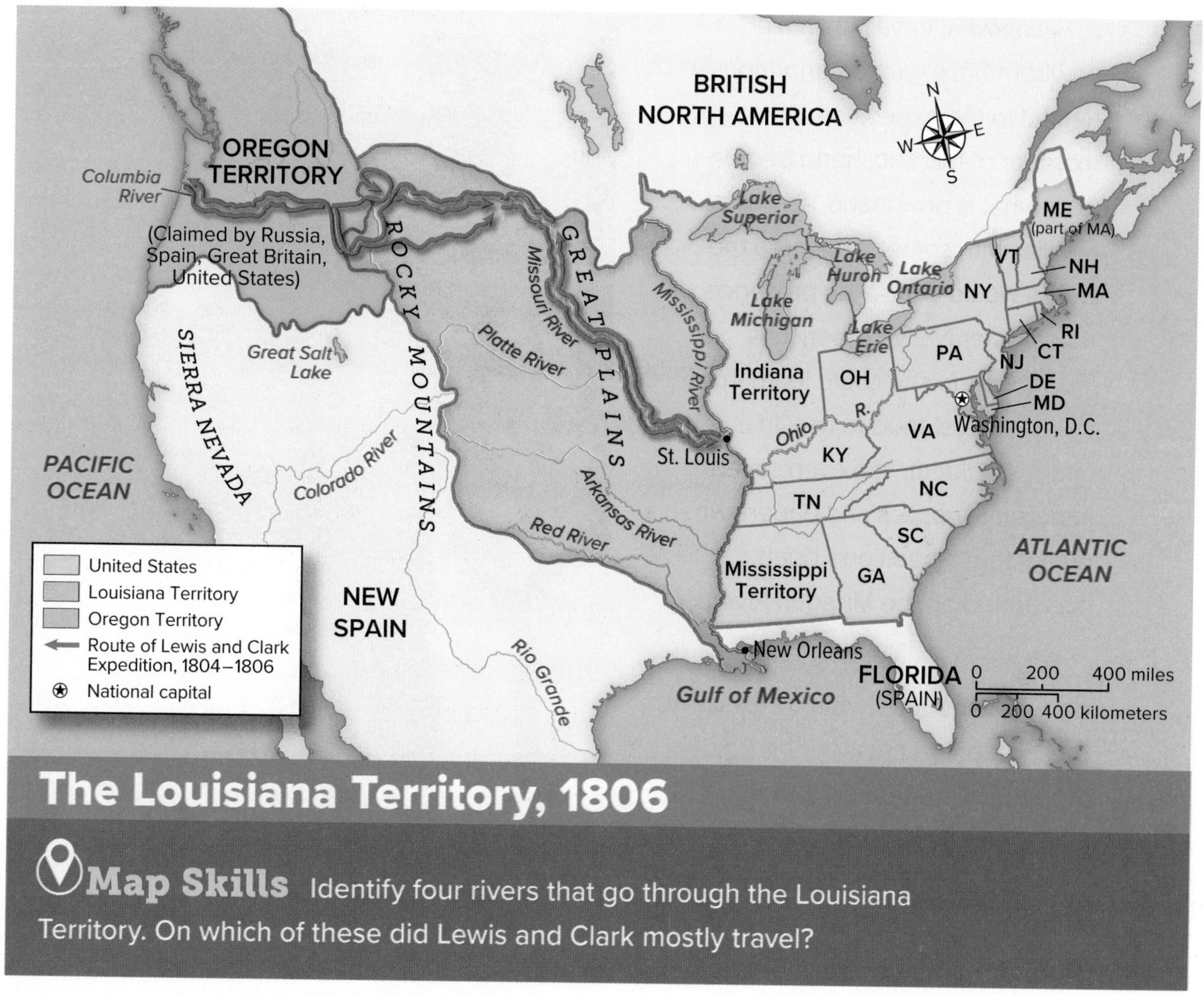


## The Louisiana Territory, 1806

**Map Skills** Identify four rivers that go through the Louisiana Territory. On which of these did Lewis and Clark mostly travel?

The Corps traveled west on the Missouri River, meeting with many native tribes, including the Oto, the Missouri, and the Teton and Yankton Sioux. In late October of 1804, near Mandan and Hidatsa villages in what is now North Dakota, the explorers established a winter camp that they called Fort Mandan. Not long afterward, Lewis and Clark hired a French-Canadian fur trapper named Toussaint Charbonneau and his Native American wife, Sacajawea, to serve as interpreters and guides for the rest of the trip.

Sacajawea, traveling with a newborn baby, proved enormously helpful to the expedition. As a member of the Shoshone people from what is now Idaho, she was familiar with some of the area the Corps would cross. Her presence made other Native Americans friendlier, and she could learn from them the best trails to use. In a famous incident, she even saved important supplies and papers when one of the expedition's boats overturned on the Missouri River.

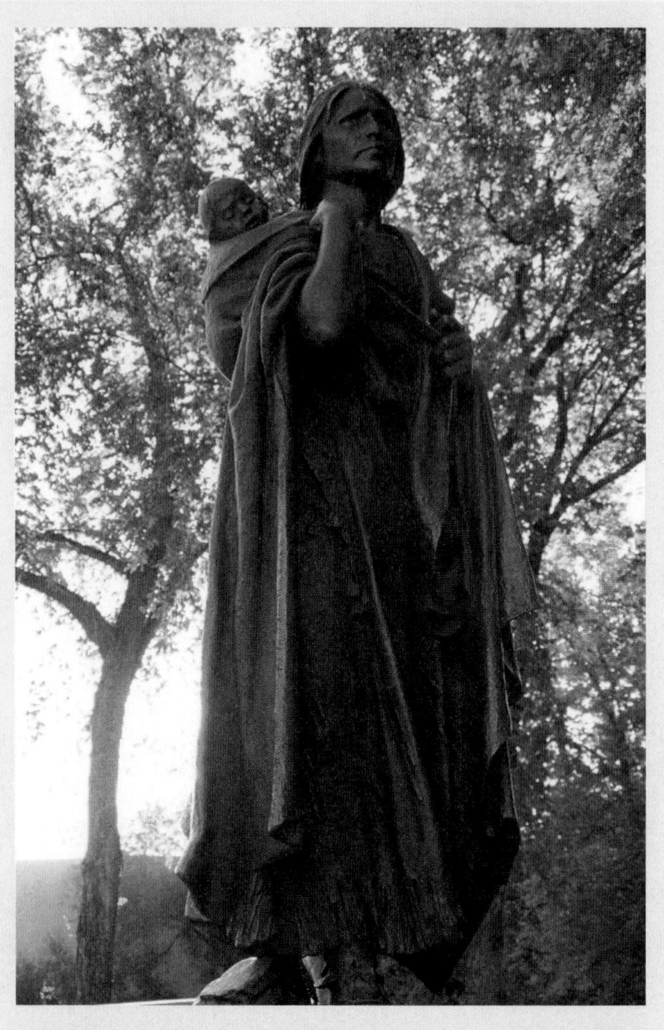

**Sacajawea, shown in the statue with her newborn baby, is also honored on a one-dollar coin.**

Traveling on water when possible and land when necessary, the expedition crossed the Rocky Mountains, continued to the Columbia River, and then went down it to the Pacific Ocean. There the Corps camped for another winter before traveling back east, reaching St. Louis on September 23, 1806. Having completed a journey of about 8,000 miles, Lewis and Clark were treated as national heroes.

Lewis and Clark's Corps of Discovery was not the only group to explore the Louisiana Territory. In 1805, President Jefferson sent army lieutenant Zebulon Pike to search for the source of the Mississippi River. He did not find it. A year later, Pike was sent to explore the southwestern portion of the Louisiana Purchase. There he tried and failed to climb the mountain peak now named in his honor.

## Stop and Check

COLLABORATE

**Talk** Why did Jefferson purchase the Louisiana Territory? What role did Sacajawea play in helping to explore it?

# The War of 1812

Britain and France were at war when James Madison was elected president in 1808. The United States tried to stay neutral and trade with both sides. Neither side liked that policy. Each kept trying to block the United States from trading with its enemy. British actions, however, made that nation very unpopular with the United States.

The British stopped U.S. ships, claiming they were searching for British sailors who had deserted. Then they took American sailors off the ships, claiming they were British, and forced them to serve in the British navy. This policy, called impressment, made people in the United States furious. Many also thought the British in Canada were purposely causing Native Americans unrest in the Northwest Territories with the hope of getting back land they had lost to the United States. In Congress, pro-war politicians, or "war hawks," demanded U.S. action. President Madison came to agree with them. And so, with Congress eager for war and the president in agreement, the War of 1812 began.

U.S. attacks on Canada were unsuccessful, although one attack resulted in the burning of legislative buildings in the town of York. A British attack from Canada was also repelled in the Battle of Lake Erie in 1813. The next year, British troops landed in Maryland and successfully attacked Washington, D.C. The entire government had to flee the capital. Evacuating the White House, First Lady Dolley Madison managed to save important government papers. White House employees saved a famous portrait of George Washington. The British destroyed the White House and badly damaged the Capitol, which had been under construction.

**PRIMARY SOURCE**

## In Their Words... Dolley Madison

I have pressed as many Cabinet papers into trunks as to fill one carriage; our private property must be sacrificed, as it is impossible to procure [get] wagons for its transportation. I am determined not to go myself until I see Mr. Madison safe.

—from Dolley Madison's Letter to Her Sister, August 23, 1814

TEXT: Dolley Madison to her sister, Anna Cutts, August 23, 1814. In Dolly Madison, by Maud Wilder Goodwin, pp. 173–175. New York: C. Scribner's Sons, 1896.; PHOTO: McGraw-Hill Education

This print gives a British artist's impression of what the 1814 burning of Washington, D.C., might have looked like.

The British attempt to attack Baltimore was less successful. Francis Scott Key, an American lawyer and poet held captive on a British ship in Baltimore Harbor, watched the British attack Fort McHenry there. The next morning, the American flag was still flying over the fort. Key was so moved that he wrote a poem that later became the words to the U.S. national anthem, "The Star-Spangled Banner."

Finally, British and U.S. diplomats met in Europe and signed the Treaty of Ghent to end the war. Neither side won or lost, but Britain abandoned its efforts to establish a Native American state in the Northwest. Native Americans in the Northwest Territory suffered the most losses in the War of 1812. The United States defeated them and forced them to sign away lands with no interference from the British.

The Federalist Party, which had opposed the war, now nearly vanished from the political scene. With just one effective political party and a strong sense of national unity and purpose, the period following the War of 1812 is often called the Era of Good Feelings. The president most associated with this era is James Monroe, who won the election of 1816 with the support of retiring President Madison and was reelected with little opposition four years later.

## Stop and Check

**Think** What were the causes of the War of 1812?

# The Monroe Doctrine

Starting in 1810, many colonies in Latin America began declaring their independence from the European countries that had colonized them. The United States generally supported these efforts and worried that European nations would try to reestablish colonial rule. In an 1823 speech to Congress, President Monroe laid out U.S. policy on such behavior. That policy came to be called the Monroe Doctrine. It would become the single most influential piece of foreign policy in U.S. history. The doctrine had these main points:

- The United States would not involve itself in European politics.
- The United States recognized current European colonies in the Americas.
- Except for the colonies existing at the time, the United States expected Europe to stay out of North and South America and would regard any interference there as a hostile act that could lead to war.

James Monroe

Read the two different points of view about the Monroe Doctrine. Then answer the questions that follow.

| Pro-Monroe Doctrine View | Anti-Monroe Doctrine View |
|---|---|
| The Monroe Doctrine shows that the United States wanted to protect its neighbors in the Americas and wanted them to be free and independent nations. | The Monroe Doctrine shows that the United States thought of itself as the main power in the Americas and wanted to control its neighbors without any competition. |

## Think About It

1. Think about the conflicts that led up to the Monroe Doctrine. What earlier events or conflicts might have caused the United States to be wary of European powers in North America?

2. Research times when the United States has used the Monroe Doctrine, such as the Spanish American War or the Cuban Missile Crisis. Was the United States justified in its actions?

3. Do you agree with either of the points of view above? Why or why not? Can you think of a point of view different from both of these?

# How Did Advancements in Technology and Transportation Shape the Nation?

## New Technology Paves the Way

In the years after the American Revolution, another revolution was taking place. It wasn't a revolution in government or politics, but it did greatly change the way people lived. Before, almost everything was made by hand. But beginning in the late 1700s, machines were invented that could more quickly do the same work that people were doing. New technology also changed how people traveled and how they sent messages over long distances. This great shift to a society that relied on machines to make and do things is known as the Industrial Revolution.

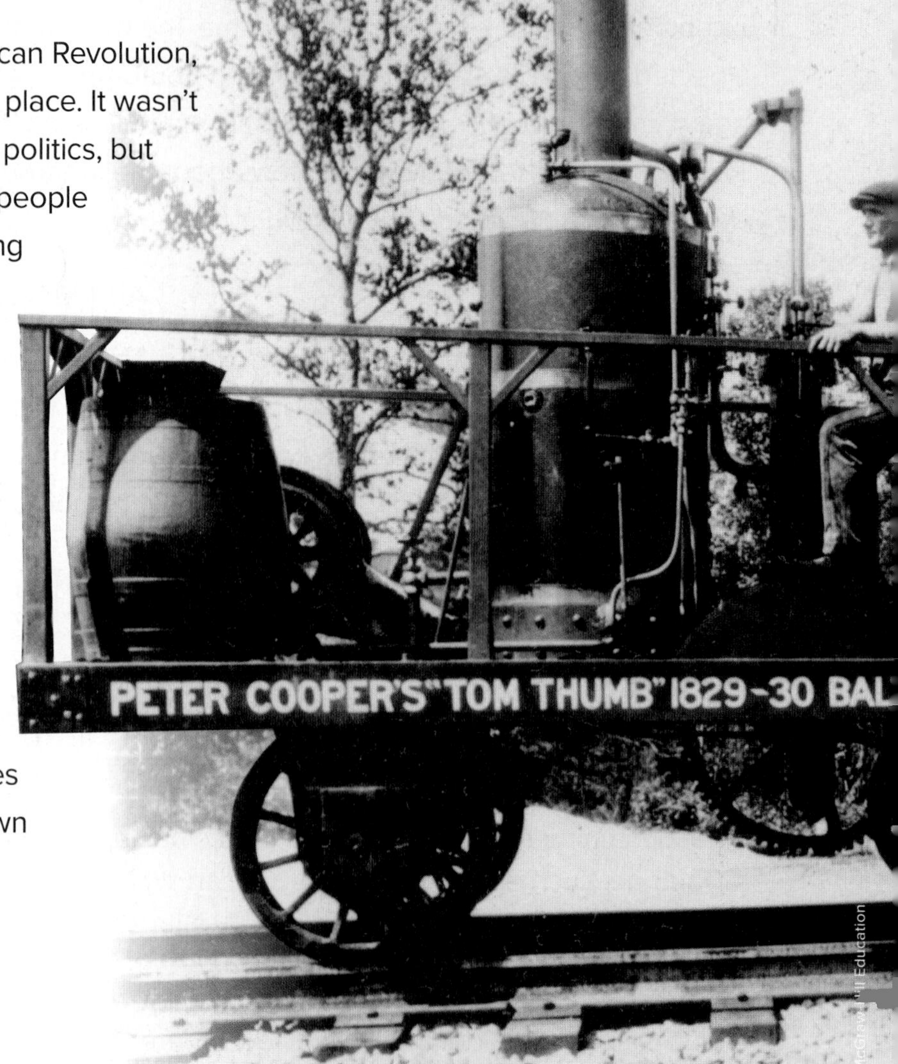

**1790** Samuel Slater builds the first factory in the U.S.

**1793** Eli Whitney invents the cotton gin.

**1807** Robert Fulton builds a practical steamboat.

**1811** Construction begins on the National Road.

**1825** The Erie Canal opens.

**1830** B & O Railroad begins using *Tom Thumb*, the first U.S. steam locomotive.

**1844** The first U.S. telegraph lines begin operating.

1790 | 1800 | 1810 | 1820 | 1830 | 1840

The Industrial Revolution began in Britain. For years, the British tried to keep secret how they used moving water in streams and rivers to power machines. Then a man named Samuel Slater, who had worked in a British factory with water-powered machines, moved to the United States and brought those secrets with him. Slater built the first factory on U.S. soil in Pawtucket, Rhode Island, in 1790. Like most other early factories, Slater's was a textile mill, a factory producing cloth or other woven fabrics.

Vintage Images/Alamy

The *Tom Thumb* was the first American-built steam locomotive to travel by railroad.

Twenty years later, a Boston merchant named Francis Cabot Lowell went to Britain to learn about new developments in its factories. In 1813, he built his own factory on the Charles River in Waltham, Massachusetts. It had a large power **loom** for weaving and all the equipment for making cloth under one roof. Lowell died soon after starting the factory. But his partners decided to expand. They built several mills on the Merrimack River and a town for their workers, which they called Lowell. Many of those workers were immigrants from other nations. They also hired young women from farms all over New England; these women became known as the Lowell Mill Girls.

**Cotton mill workers spun cotton into thread and wove thread into cloth.**

Lowell, Massachusetts, was the first of many U.S. mill towns. These towns needed to be on rivers or streams with moving water to power the machinery. The towns were especially common in New England. The region had many rapidly flowing rivers. Its rocky soil and short growing season made it hard to earn a lot of money from farming. This is why farmers were glad to have their daughters working in the mills. The chief products of the mills were cotton cloth and woolen fabric. Wool came from sheep. Cotton came from plants that needed a warm climate to grow. In the United States, it was grown mainly in the South.

While visiting a cotton plantation, a New Englander named Eli Whitney saw that common green-seed cotton was very hard to clean because the seeds stuck to the fiber. He began working on a machine to separate the seeds from the fiber. That machine, the cotton gin, revolutionized Southern agriculture. It made growing cotton so profitable that most plantation owners made it their main crop. Growing cotton still required much labor, however. As cotton plantations grew larger, more and more enslaved people were put to work in the cotton fields. By 1850, there were five times as many enslaved people in the United States as there had been in 1790.

North Wind Picture Archives

The use of the cotton gin was not the only big change in agriculture. For thousands of years, farmers had cut down their crops using a hand-held tool called a scythe. The slow process limited the number of crops farmers could harvest. Then, in 1831, a farmer's son named Cyrus McCormick invented a horse-drawn reaping machine that could harvest crops much faster. Farmers using the McCormick reaper could plant many more acres of crops. Planting itself was made easier by another invention, the mechanical plow. This device dug up the soil so seeds could be planted. Charles Newbold, a New Jersey blacksmith, invented the first cast iron plow in 1797. Another blacksmith, John Deere, improved the plow in 1837 by using steel blades. Steel was stronger than the iron previously used.

Many other inventions changed the way people made or did things. In 1845, Elias Howe, who had once worked in a machine shop in Lowell, created the first practical sewing machine. Also in the 1840s, Charles Goodyear developed a way to make rubber withstand heat and cold without cracking. The process, called vulcanization, made rubber the useful material it is today.

In 1803, Eli Whitney, inventor of the cotton gin, was hired to make 10,000 guns for the U.S. Army. Whitney realized that the job would go much faster if he could produce, for all guns, large quantities of parts that were exactly the same. This would allow the parts to be assembled more quickly. Whitney's idea of **interchangeable** parts affected far more industries than just the one that made guns. Clocks, furniture—in fact, just about anything built in factories—could be made more quickly and cheaply by using interchangeable parts.

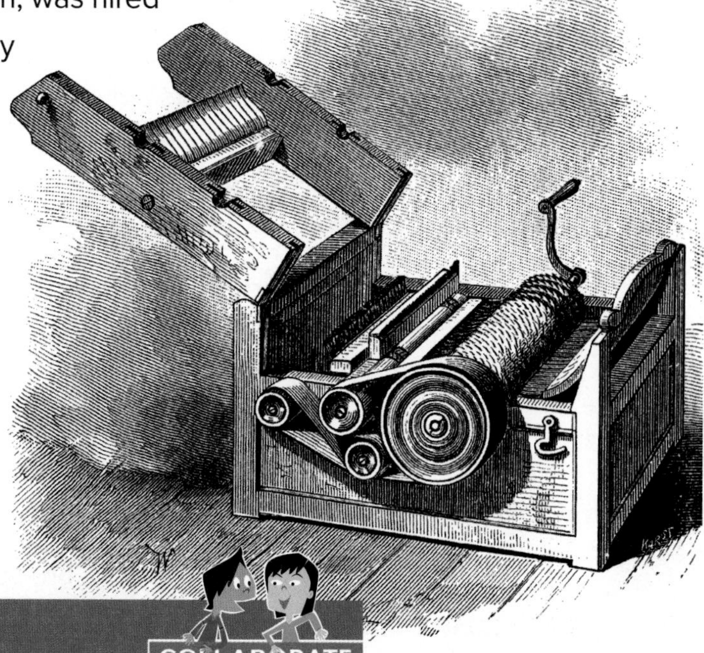

**The cotton gin, invented by Eli Whitney, separated seeds from cotton fiber much more quickly and easily than could be done by hand.**

## Stop and Check

COLLABORATE

**Talk** What effects, both good and bad, did the cotton gin have on the Southern economy? Why was Eli Whitney's development of interchangeable parts so important?

**Find Details** As you read, add additional information to the graphic organizer on page 267 in your Inquiry Journal.

# New Forms of Transportation

In 1800, there were four main ways to travel: on foot, on horseback, by water, or in horse-drawn vehicles such as stagecoaches. All were very slow. Private roads, which charged tolls, were better maintained than public roads. Both types of roads, however, grew muddy when it rained, and they developed potholes. Yet roads were needed to unify the expanding nation. In 1806, Congress voted to fund a road connecting the East and the Midwest. By the early 1830s, the National Road carried many carts and stagecoaches along a route that extended from Maryland to Illinois. Parts of the road were among the first U.S. roadways made of macadam, a newly developed paving material using crushed gravel.

In 1800, the easiest way to ship goods was by water, but waterways did not always connect. One way to solve this problem was to build artificial waterways called canals to make the connections. In 1817, New York Governor DeWitt Clinton began a project to build a canal connecting the Hudson River in the eastern part of the state with Lake Erie on New York's western border. Critics called the expensive project Clinton's Ditch. It was complicated because the land was higher at one end than the other. Engineers solved this problem by building locks, which worked like elevators to lift and lower boats in the water. When the Erie Canal finally opened in 1825, Clinton's critics were proved wrong. An instant success, the canal let people ship goods much more quickly and cheaply. Soon people in the United States began building other canals.

**Steamboats on the Hudson River**

ISAAC NEWTON

FRANCIS SKIDDY

Yale University Art Gallery

The steam engine, one of the most important inventions of the Industrial Revolution, could be used to run many kinds of equipment. In 1807, Robert Fulton showed the world that a steam engine could be used to run a boat. His steamboat took about a day and a half to travel up the Hudson River from New York City to Albany, New York—a distance of about 150 miles. Before the steamboat, the same trip took much longer. Fulton's steamboat was not the first one ever invented, but it was the first to prove successful. Soon many different kinds of steamboats were traveling the nation's waterways. They were especially important for quickly moving goods against the direction of a river's current—for example, north on the Mississippi River.

Steam power was also the source of another form of transportation, the train. For centuries, people had recognized that running carts on rails instead of bumpy dirt roads made the ride smoother. However, early vehicles on rails were pulled by animals. Now engineers began experimenting with iron locomotives, engines that ran on rails and were powered by steam. The first locomotives were built in Britain. As the design improved, the locomotive was used to pull cars behind it in a new form of transportation—the train. It was nicknamed the Iron Horse. The rails on which trains ran were called "rail roads," and so were the companies that ran them. In 1828, the first U.S. railroad company, the Baltimore & Ohio (B & O) Railroad, was formed. Many more would follow.

Trains were much faster than other types of transportation at the time. Even the earliest trains cut down on travel time by about half. A trip from New York to Washington, D.C. that took four days by stagecoach only took two days by train. This meant that trains helped unite the large, spread-out nation that the United States was becoming.

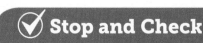

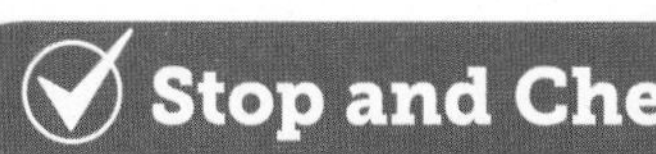

COLLABORATE

**Talk** Why were trains particularly helpful in uniting the nation?

# Advancements in Communication

When George Washington became President in 1789, the United States had about 75 post offices. That number grew as the nation grew. Mail traveled by horse, stagecoach, boat, and eventually train. As transportation improved, so did communication, since messages could be carried more quickly. Nevertheless, the messages still had to be carried.

An important new invention changed the way Americans communicated. In the 1830s, a group of inventors including Samuel F. B. Morse developed a device called a telegraph that could send messages by using electrical signals over a wire. Morse and his fellow inventor Alfred Vail also developed a code—called Morse Code—to give meaning to the electrical signals. The code used different sequences of short and long signals to represent letters. Workers used the coded letters to spell out the words of a message. Morse demonstrated the telegraph to members of Congress, who awarded him $30,000 to set up a telegraph line between Baltimore, Maryland, and Washington, D.C. On May 24, 1844, Morse tapped out his first long-distance message on the telegraph, "What hath God wrought?"

By pressing down on a key, the telegraph operator could send electrical messages in Morse code.

Over the next few years, telegraph poles went up across the United States, with telegraph wires strung between them. A person would go to a telegraph office and pay to send a message to another office in a distant location. The message would usually move across the wires and reach its destination in minutes. Like the new forms of transportation, this rapid new form of communication helped tie the nation together.

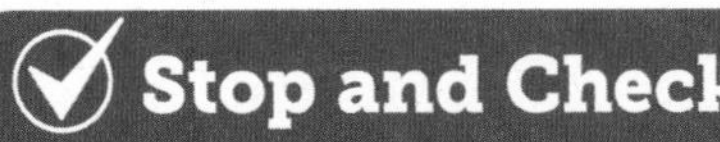

## Stop and Check

**Talk** How was the telegraph different from the type of long-distance communication people had used before?

TEXT: Samuel Morse to Alfred Vail, Baltimore, May 1844. From Edward Lind Morse. National Museum of American History; PHOTO: ©Comstock Images/Alamy

# The Growth of Cities

The Industrial Revolution turned towns into cities and made existing cities much larger. Factory jobs paid better than farm labor did. So factories lured people away from farms to cities and towns. They also drew immigrants to the United States, mostly from Canada and Europe. In 1820, only about 700,000 people lived in all the cities of the United States. By 1840, the population of cities was nearly 1.8 million.

New forms of transportation also led to the growth of cities. Steamboat traffic helped make river ports, like Cincinnati and St. Louis, much busier. The Erie Canal in upstate New York spurred the growth of Albany at its eastern end, Buffalo at its western end, and Syracuse and Rochester in between. It also made New York City an even greater center of shipping and trade.

Like boat traffic, the growth of railroads also led to the growth of cities. Atlanta, Georgia, began its existence as the junction, or meeting point, between the Georgia Railroad and the Western & Atlantic Railroad. Indianapolis, Indiana, had fewer than 8,000 residents in 1847. Then the Indianapolis & Madison Railroad came to town. The city's population quickly doubled. As the railroads moved farther west, Chicago, Illinois, emerged as the great railroad center of the nation. Chicago had fewer than 5,000 residents in 1840. Twenty years later, it had well over 100,000.

In the 1800s, many immigrants lived in large cities such as New York City.

**Stop and Check**

COLLABORATE

**Talk** What were two reasons for the growth of cities?

# Who Were the People Living in the Early United States?

## The First Pioneers

The American Revolution had created a new nation, but there were still many Americans without land. About one out of five Americans lived in poverty, or without enough money for proper food or supplies. Without land, people were unlikely to improve their lives. Between 1790 and 1820, the population of the United States grew, from about 4 million to nearly 10 million. Most Americans were farmers. They needed large families to do the many chores a farm required. When farmers died, their land was divided among their children. Even a large farm might not provide enough land for all of the children. Some people moved to cities, but others looked to the lands in the West. For poor people, these lands offered a chance to build a new life.

After the British gave up its western lands in 1783, settlers rushed into western Georgia, Pennsylvania, New York, and beyond. Some of this area later became the states of Kentucky, Tennessee, and Ohio. A person who is the first to enter a new land or region is called a pioneer. Even though we call the white settlers who moved into the area west of the Appalachians pioneers, they were not the first people in these lands. This area had been inhabited by Native Americans for centuries.

In 1769, a trader named John Findley chose an experienced explorer, Daniel Boone, to help him find an inland trail from North Carolina to Kentucky. They found a natural passage through the Appalachian Mountains, which they called the Cumberland Gap. When they crossed the Cumberland Gap into Kentucky, they found a land of rich soil. Boone and his friends wanted to make money from this new land. In 1775, Boone and 30 other pioneers began to improve the trails between the Carolinas and the West.

**1794** Battle of Fallen Timbers

**1795** Treaty of Greenville

**1811–1813** Tecumseh's War

**1812–1815** War of 1812

**1845–1849** The Great Famine (Irish Potato Famine)

70 | 1780 | 1790 | 1800 | 1810 | 1820 | 1830 | 1840 | 1850

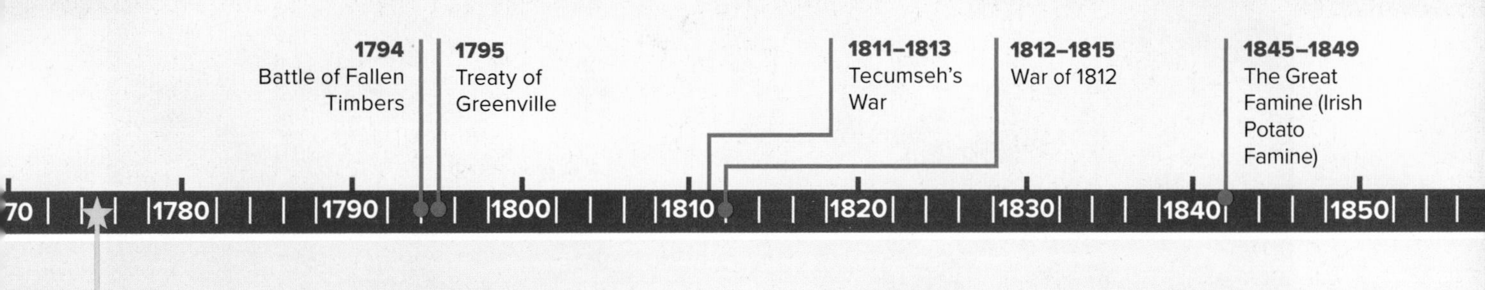

**1775** Daniel Boone travels through the Cumberland Gap.

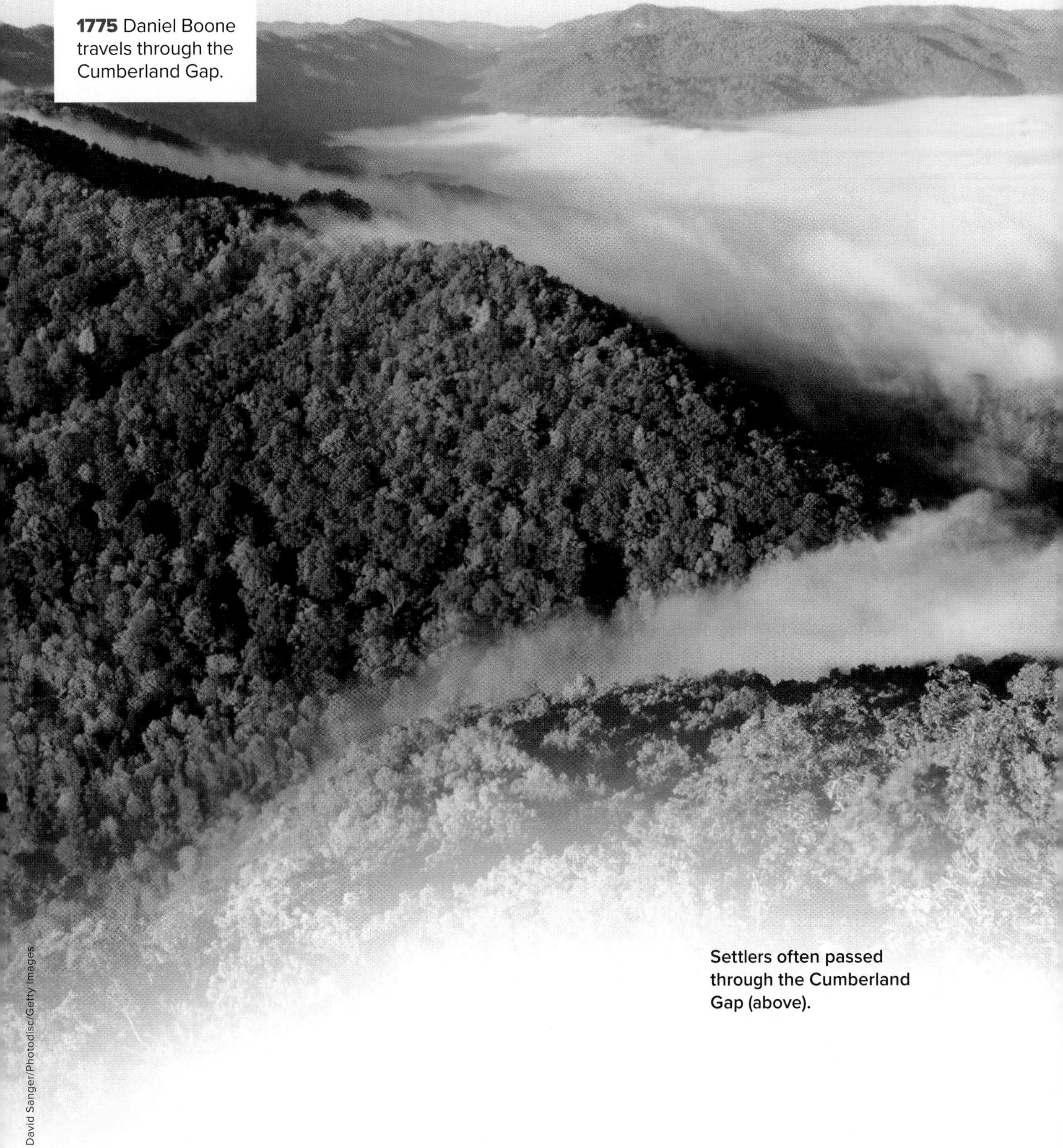

Settlers often passed through the Cumberland Gap (above).

David Sanger/Photodisc/Getty Images

Daniel Boone leading settlers through the Cumberland Gap in 1775

Daniel Boone was the most famous of the American pioneers of this era. His father had come from Great Britain and settled in Pennsylvania. Boone was born in 1734. Young Boone learned to survive on the unsettled lands around his home. When Boone was 16, his family moved to North Carolina. Boone married Rebecca Bryan in 1756 and tried farming, but he preferred life on the frontier.

Boone had a sense of humor. He is believed to have once said, "I have never been lost, but I will admit to being confused for several weeks."

In 1775, Boone founded Boonesborough, Kentucky. In 1776, during the Revolutionary War, he and his men were captured by Shawnee people and taken to a British military post. Boone gained the trust of the Shawnee and learned of a British plan to attack Boonesborough. He escaped in time to save the town. After exploring Tennessee and Kentucky in the early 1770s, Boone and his family moved to what is now Missouri in 1799. Daniel Boone died in 1820.

 **Stop and Check**

COLLABORATE

**Talk** What were some of the reasons people in the early United States moved farther west?

# Native Americans in the Early Republic

The greatest threat to Native Americans during this period was white settlers. For more than 150 years, Native Americans had seen settlers stream west and into their territory. This threatened their land and their way of life.

In 1787, Congress passed the Northwest Ordinance. The law was intended to outline how the western territories should be governed and the rules for becoming a state. It did, however, include a promise that Native American lands and territories would never be taken away from them. But that promise was not kept.

In 1794, eight Native American groups joined together to drive invading settlers out of their land in what is today Ohio. They were defeated by the United States Army at the Battle of Fallen Timbers in northwestern Ohio.

The next year, these Native Americans had to accept the Treaty of Greenville. The treaty forced them to give up most of their land in the Ohio Territory. However, some Native Americans would continue to resist the settlers.

**PRIMARY SOURCE**

## In Their Words... The Treaty of Greenville

And in consideration of the peace now established . . . the said Indian tribes do hereby cede and relinquish forever, all their claims to the lands lying eastwardly and southwardly of the general boundary line now described: and these lands, or any part of them, shall never hereafter be made a cause or pretense, on the part of said tribes, or any of them, of war or injury to the United States, or any people thereof.

—from The Treaty of Greenville, August 3, 1795

TEXT: A Treaty of Peace between the United States of America and the Tribes of Indians..., art. 3." In The Public Statutes at Large of the United States of America, Vol. 7, edited by Richard Peters, 49. Boston: Charles C. Little and James Brown, 1848.; PHOTO: McGraw-Hill Education

One of the Native Americans who remained in Ohio and had not signed the Treaty of Greenville was Tecumseh of the Shawnee people. Tecumseh spoke to his people of native pride and hoped that native peoples could reclaim some of their lost territory in what are now Ohio and Indiana. Tecumseh founded his own community in Indiana. Tecumseh tried to unite all western native peoples to fight against invading settlers. William Henry Harrison, who was the governor of the Indiana Territory, became alarmed at Tecumseh's growing power. In 1811, Harrison attacked and destroyed Tecumseh's community. Tecumseh and the Shawnees were among the Native American groups who sided with the British in the War of 1812. Native peoples hoped that a British victory would stop the invasion of U.S. settlers into their territories. Tecumseh was eventually killed in 1813 while fighting for the British.

**PRIMARY SOURCE**

## In Their Words... Tecumseh

You ought to know what you are doing to the Indians. . . . It is a very bad thing and we do not like it. . . . No groups among us have the right to sell, even to one another, and surely not to outsiders who want it all, and will not do with less. . . . Sell a country! Why not sell the air, the clouds, and the Great Sea, as well as the earth? Did not the Great Spirit make them all for the use of his children?

—a passage from Tecumseh's speech to Governor William Henry Harrison, Indiana Territory, 1810

TECUMSEH.

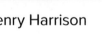

### Stop and Check

COLLABORATE

**Talk** What about Tecumseh made William Henry Harrison alarmed?

**Find Details** As you read, add additional information to the graphic organizer on page 275 in your Inquiry Journal.

TEXT: Tecumseh. In a speech to William Henry Harrison. Vincennes, Indiana Territory. 12 August 1810.; PHOTO: chpaquette/iStock/Getty Images

# African Americans in the Early United States

In the late 1700s, feelings about slavery began to change in the United States. The economies, cultures, and attitudes of the North and South grew increasingly different.

Large cities and new factories were growing quickly in the North. Immigrants flooded the United States to fill factory jobs. By 1804 all northern states had outlawed slavery or approved gradual emancipation. Slavery may have been illegal north of the Ohio River, but free African Americans faced discrimination there. Ohio, Indiana, and Illinois passed laws requiring African Americans to show papers proving they were free.

In the South, the economy had not changed much. The plantation was still the main way of life. On large farms, hundreds of enslaved people worked without pay. There were very few free African Americans in the region. Some white Southerners worked on small farms, and not all had enslaved people. However, the plantation owners were the wealthiest and had the most political power.

As the United States expanded west, many wondered if slavery would expand as well. In 1819 Missouri applied for statehood as a slave state, a state in which slavery is allowed. At the time, the nation had a balance of 11 slave states and 11 free states in which slavery was not allowed. Letting Missouri enter the Union as a slave state would give slave states more votes in the U.S. Senate.

**An antique sketch of enslaved people laboring in a cotton field**

## The Missouri Compromise, 1820

**Map Skills** Working with a partner, use the information provided in the key to determine which states made up the larger area of the United States—slave states or free states.

Congress argued over Missouri for a year. In 1820, Senator Henry Clay from Kentucky came up with the Missouri Compromise. Under this plan, Missouri was added as a slave state. Maine, which had been part of Massachusetts, became a free state. The compromise stated that, in the future, slavery would not be allowed in any states north of Missouri's southern border.

This compromise was only a temporary solution. As the United States continued to expand, new compromises and decisions had to be made.

### Stop and Check

**Write** How was life for African Americans in the South different from those in the North?

# A Nation of Immigrants

In the mid-1800s, the **composition** of the U.S. population began to change dramatically. More immigrants came to the United States between 1845 and 1860 than ever before. Many Europeans came to find work. Some Chinese came in the 1840s to seek fortunes. Later, they worked on the railroads. The Irish, however, left their homeland for a very different reason.

In the mid-1800s, many people in Ireland were forced by British property owners to plant and eat potatoes, and little else. Most of the livestock and food the Irish raised went to England or was sold to pay high rents. Depending on only one crop proved disastrous. Starting in late 1845, potatoes throughout Ireland did not grow because of a plant disease involving a fungus. The results were devastating. About 2.5 million people starved to death. Between late 1845 and 1861, a million Irish people immigrated to the United States to escape starvation.

Immigrants often found work at docks along the East Coast.

The 1820s and 1830s is often called the Canal Age. It was during this period that the construction of several major canals filled the transportation needs of the young country. One of the largest such projects was the construction of the Erie Canal. Irish, German, and English immigrants did most of the backbreaking work required to build these canals. The work was difficult and often dangerous. Many of the workers died from accidents and disease. Later, when the canal work was done, some immigrants settled in towns and cities along the canal. Others decided to seek their fortunes by traveling west.

## Around the World

### Irish Potato Famine Causes

- British control of Ireland results in poor Irish farmers giving or selling to Britain most of their crops.
- As a result, most of Ireland's poor depended almost exclusively on the potato for food.
- In late 1845, a blight—a destructive disease caused by a fungus—attacked Ireland's potatoes, and most of the crop was ruined.
- Ireland's poor lacked the money to purchase the food their farms produced.

**A disease that destroyed potato crops in Ireland in the late 1840s had a massive impact on the United States.**

### Irish Potato Famine Effects

- Famine occurred among Ireland's poor.
- About 2.5 million people starved to death.
- Between 1846 and 1861, a million Irish people immigrated to the United States.

### Stop and Check

COLLABORATE

**Talk** What was difficult about working on the Erie Canal?

# Fighting for Women's Education

Benjamin Rush (1746–1813) is perhaps best known for his political activities during the American Revolution, which included signing the Declaration of Independence. He is also known for his career as a doctor, a professor of chemistry, and a political leader. Somewhat overlooked, however, are the various causes to which he devoted himself. One of these causes was the education of women.

Colonial America did not offer many educational opportunities to women. It was widely believed that there was no need to educate women beyond the very basics of reading, writing, and math. The Young Ladies' Academy of Philadelphia was founded in 1787 and sponsored and supervised by many of Philadelphia's male religious and political leaders, including Benjamin Rush. The academy offered its female students a wide variety of courses, including writing, English grammar, mathematics, geography, chemistry, and natural philosophy.

Benjamin Rush led the way in educational reform for women because he believed that such reform was good for the country. Rush gave many speeches on the importance of women's education. Rush believed that all children, including girls, should be rigorously educated. Rush believed that people who did not support the education of women had "little minds." His hope was that education would help students become good citizens, create national character, and unite the country.

Benjamin Rush

## Stop and Check

**Think** Imagine you are in a position to devote yourself to a cause, as Benjamin Rush did. What would the cause be? What would you do to benefit the cause?

(t)McGraw-Hill Education, (b)The Miriam and Ira D. Wallach Division of Art, Prints and Photographs: Print Collection, Emmet Collection of Manuscripts Etc. Relating to American History. The New York Public Library

## Map and Globe Skills

# The United States, 1821

By the time of the Missouri Compromise, the United States had changed significantly. A nation that had begun with thirteen states now had twenty-four. The United States had covered about 860,000 square miles in 1790. By the 1820 census, the area was roughly 1.7 million square miles, about double its original size. The population had grown from about 3.9 million people to about 9.6 million.

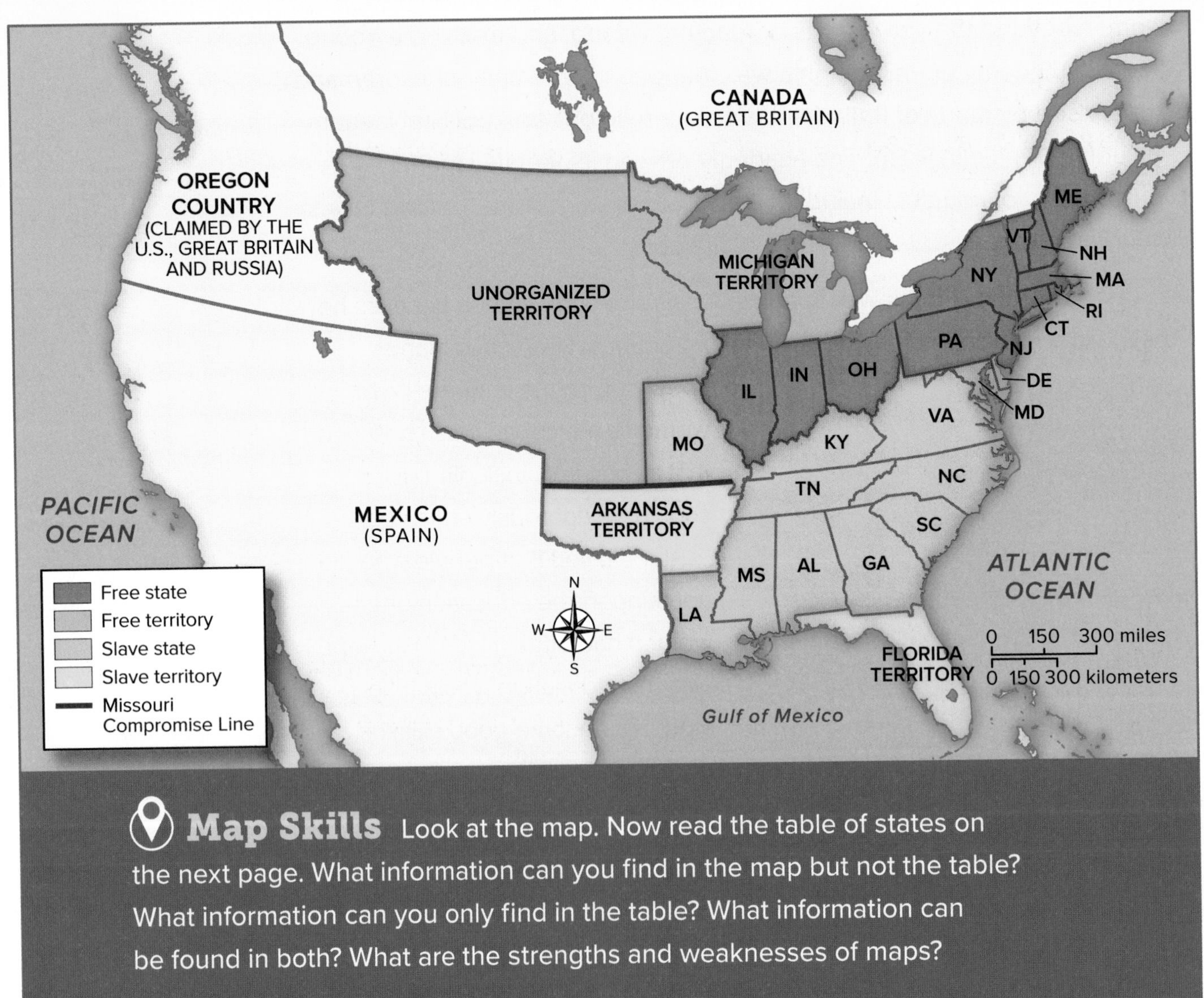


**Map Skills** Look at the map. Now read the table of states on the next page. What information can you find in the map but not the table? What information can you only find in the table? What information can be found in both? What are the strengths and weaknesses of maps?

## Alabama
**1820 Population:** 127,901
**2015 Population:** 4,858,979
★ **Capital:** Montgomery

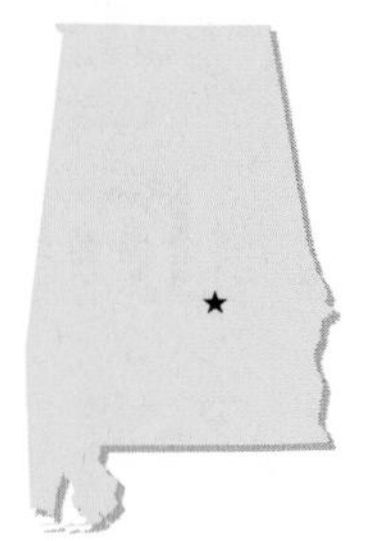

## Illinois
**1820 Population:** 55,211
**2015 Population:** 12,859,995
★ **Capital:** Springfield

## Indiana
**1820 Population:** 147,178
**2015 Population:** 6,619,680
★ **Capital:** Indianapolis

## Kentucky
**1820 Population:** 564,317
**2015 Population:** 4,425,092
★ **Capital:** Frankfort

## Louisiana
**1820 Population:** 153,407
**2015 Population:** 4,670,724
★ **Capital:** Baton Rouge

## Maine
**1820 Population:** 298,335
**2015 Population:** 1,329,328
★ **Capital:** Augusta

## Mississippi
**1820 Population:** 75,448
**2015 Population:** 2,992,333
★ **Capital:** Jackson

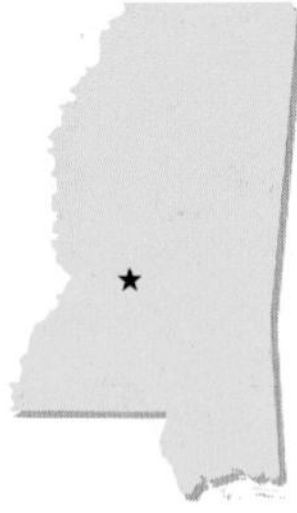

## Missouri
**1820 Population:** 66,586
**2015 Population:** 6,083,672
★ **Capital:** Jefferson City

## Ohio
**1820 Population:** 581,434
**2015 Population:** 11,613,423
★ **Capital:** Columbus

## Tennessee
**1820 Population:** 422,813
**2015 Population:** 6,600,299
★ **Capital:** Nashville

## Vermont
**1820 Population:** 235,764
**2015 Population:** 626,042
★ **Capital:** Montpelier

# Lesson 4 How Did Westward Expansion Impact People Living in the United States?

## Trails to the West

The first European settlers to travel west were fur traders who used Native American trails and lived in the wilderness. The Native Americans in the area often helped these "mountain men" survive. By the 1830s, there was less demand for furs, and the number of traders declined. New settlers consisted mainly of families who traveled in groups of wagons led by experienced guides. Their destination was the rich farmland of the Oregon Territory. It was said that these settlers had "Oregon Fever," because of their desire to start new lives in the far West.

Since 1818, Great Britain and the United States had shared a claim to the Oregon Territory. After 1840, however, U.S. citizens began to believe their country should extend all the way from the Atlantic Ocean to the Pacific Ocean. This idea, called **Manifest Destiny**, led U.S. President James K. Polk to negotiate the Oregon Treaty with Great Britain. The two nations agreed to extend the United States-Canada border at the 49th parallel of latitude all the way to the Pacific Ocean.

U.S. citizens also began moving to Mexican territories that included what are now the states of California, New Mexico, and Texas. In the late 1840s, news of gold being discovered at Sutter's Mill drew 80,000 people to California. This flood of fortune hunters to California is known as the Gold Rush.

**1820s**
"Mountain men" appear in Rockies.

**1830**
Indian Removal Act is passed.

**1838**
Cherokee are forced to relocate.

**1841**
First wagon train on Oregon Trail

**1846**
Oregon Treaty divides United States and Canada at the 49th parallel.

**1848**
Treaty of Guadalupe Hidalgo is signed.

1820 | 1830 | 1840 | 1850

Everett Collection/Shutterstock.com

Depiction of settlers on a trail, traveling westward

0 200 400 miles
0 200 400 kilometers
CANADA
Trail
Present-day boundary
City
Fort
Mountain pass
Columbia River
Ft. Walla Walla
Ft. Vancouver
Oregon Trail
Bozeman Trail
Ft. Hall
Ft. Boise
Snake R.
Mississippi River
Ft. Laramie
California Trail
Donner Pass
South Pass
Mormon Trail
Sacramento
San Francisco
Salt Lake City
Ft. Bridger
Nauvoo
Omaha
Sutter's Fort
Beckwourth Pass
Platte River
Oregon Trail
St. Louis
Old Spanish Trail
River
Santa Fe Trail
Independence
Colorado
Los Angeles
Santa Fe
El Camino Real (to Mexico)
Red River
El Paso
MEXICO
PACIFIC OCEAN
Rio Grande
Gulf of Mexico
120°W
110°W
N
W
E
S

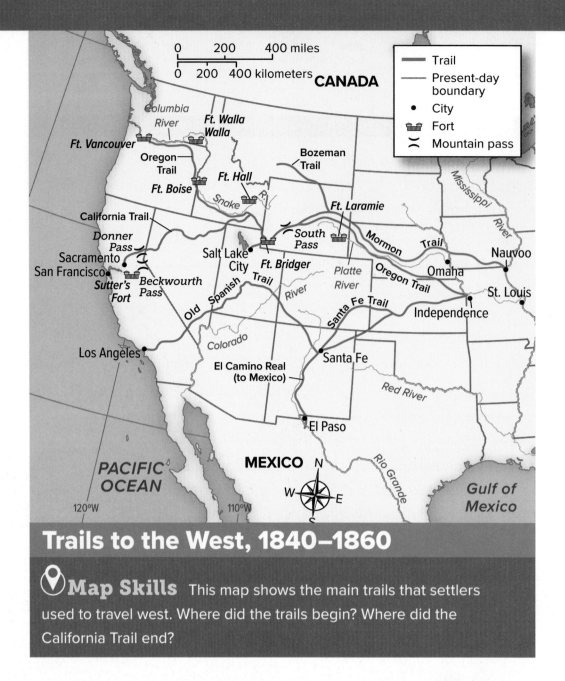

## Trails to the West, 1840–1860

**Map Skills** This map shows the main trails that settlers used to travel west. Where did the trails begin? Where did the California Trail end?

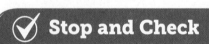

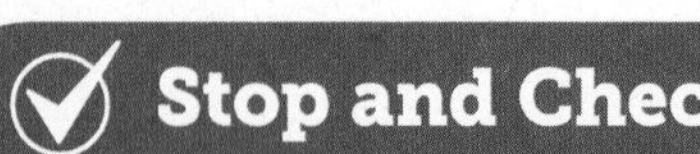

**Talk** Why did "Oregon Fever" cause settlers to move west?

**Find Details** As you read, add new information to the graphic organizer on page 283 in your Inquiry Journal.

**What Do You Think?** Would you have been willing to leave your livelihood in the East to stake your claim to land in the West? Why?

# Life on the Wagon Train

Life on the trails was challenging but exciting. On the Oregon Trail, settlers had to travel for six months across about 2,000 miles of wilderness. Many families traveled in groups of wagons called wagon trains. These families were able to provide protection for one another.

Most wagon trains consisted of wagons called "prairie schooners" because their white covers looked like a ship's sails from a distance. This type of wagon was usually pulled by a team of oxen. The wagon had to carry everything the family would need for the journey and for its new home. The supplies included tools, weapons, food, seeds for planting, books, cooking utensils, spare wagon parts, medicine, and clothes.

Each member of the family had jobs to do on the journey. Men drove the wagon and were responsible for repairing it. They also hunted for food and protected their families. Women cooked and cleaned, set up camp, and were responsible for managing their families' supplies. They also cared for and taught their children. Children helped out where they could and collected "buffalo chips," manure that was used as fuel for campfires.

A wagon train traveling west with the Rocky Mountains in the background

PRIMARY SOURCE

## In Their Words... Sarah Byrd

We came from I-O-WAY in 1848. That's a long time ago, ain't it? Joe Watt was captain of our train. Bein' so little, I don't remember how many was in the train, but I've heard 'em say it was a big one. Every night when we camped the wagons was pulled in a circle an' hooked together with chains an' oxen yokes. The folks camped inside that circle, an' close along-side was the [livestock], an' a guard was set up for the night.

Yes, it must have ban an awful job cookin'. I was too little to do anything. 'Course they had to cook on the open fire, an' on the plains, most o' the time there was nothin' to burn but buffalo chips. I guess they got use to it, but I wouldn't like to.

—from an interview of Byrd recalling her journey to Oregon, February 28, 1939

Along the trail, conditions could be difficult. The settlers had to face dangerous thunderstorms, floods, snow and ice, rocky terrain, and deep rivers. Disease was also a danger, as settlers lacked access to good medical care. Each obstacle put the people and their precious supplies in danger.

The dangers didn't stop people from using the trails, however. By 1861, about 300,000 people had traveled the Oregon Trail to the West.

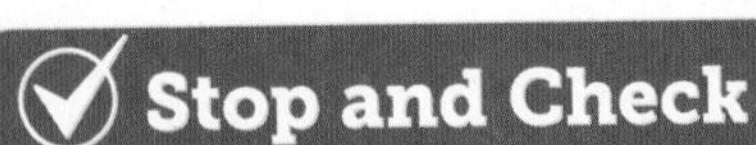

COLLABORATE

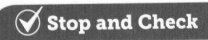

**Talk** What were the benefits and drawbacks of moving west?

Sarah L. Byrd, interview by Sara B. Wrenn, March 1, 1939, Portland, Oregon. Library of Congress, Manuscript Division, WPA Federal Writers' Project Collection, Folklore Project, Life Histories, 1936-39, MSS55715: BOX A729.

# The Age of Jackson

As the United States expanded westward, the government began to include members of Congress who gave a voice to the needs and opinions of western settlers. In 1824, only about 360,000 American citizens voted. Then new laws allowed all white men age 21 or older to vote. Before then, only wealthy male landowners could vote. Four years later, the number of voters increased more than 200 percent to about 1.2 million. This **surge** of new voters—farmers, frontier settlers, and city workers—helped elect a "common man," Andrew Jackson, as president in 1828. Born on the frontier, Jackson was a farmer-politician with no college education or public-speaking skills. He had fought in the Revolutionary War at the age of 13 and later became a popular general during the War of 1812. This "man of the people" went on to become one of the most powerful and controversial presidents in U.S. history.

**Chief Justice John Marshall swears in Andrew Jackson as president.**

Jackson's actions as president ignited much conflict. Opponents accused Jackson of trying to take away Congress's power. He vetoed much legislation, preventing Congress from passing the laws it wanted.

One major conflict arose in South Carolina. When Congress passed a new federal tax on imported goods in 1832, South Carolina politicians threatened to leave the Union. Because Southern states had few local industries, they relied on imported products. The new tax would make these products very expensive. Jackson responded to South Carolina's threat by sending troops and warships to force the state to pay the tax. The action enraged citizens, who compared the move to Britain's attempts to enforce new taxes on colonists in the 1700s.

## InfoGraphic

### Political Cartoons

Through political cartoons, artists express their opinions on current news, people, and events. Cartoons usually exaggerate details in a humorous or ridiculous way to make a statement. To identify the artist's opinion, look closely at the title, labels, and details of the cartoon. How do you think this artist felt about Jackson's actions as president?

**Subject**
Andrew Jackson

**Symbol**
King's clothing stands for Jackson's power

**Detail**
Jackson holds the veto in his hand

**Detail**
Jackson tramples on the Constitution

**Title**

*King Andrew the First* (artist unknown)

Another controversial action by Jackson concerned the Second Bank of the United States, which helped to manage the nation's money supply. Convinced that the charter of the Bank of the United States was unconstitutional, Jackson removed all of the federal government's money from the bank in 1836. He ordered that the money be transferred to state and local banks. There were no regulations in place to monitor these banks, however. Many of them made unwise investments in land. When the economy weakened in 1837, the invested money could not be recovered.

The "man of the people" had caused a major economic crisis, putting many working people he claimed to represent in difficult times.

### Stop and Check

**Think** How was Jackson's leadership different from that of the presidents before him?

**Find Details** As you read, add additional information to the graphic organizer on page 283 in your Inquiry Journal.

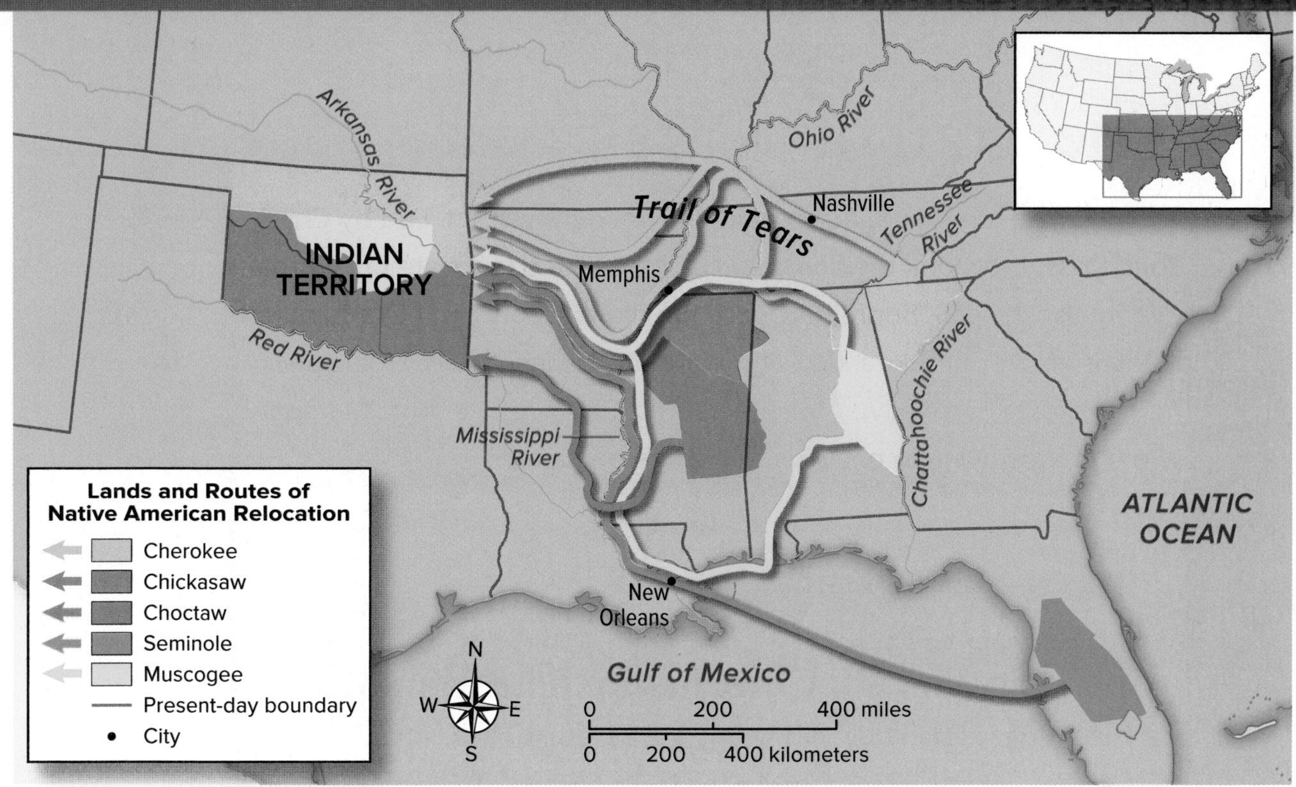


# The Indian Removal Act

In the early 1800s, Native Americans in the Southeast were protected by the treaties signed with the U.S. government. The treaties guaranteed their right to their homeland and protection from settlers. Native American communities flourished with their own schools and local governments. Life alongside settlers was peaceful until settlers began demanding more land. Settlers' demands for land increased when gold was discovered on Cherokee lands in Georgia. Conflict grew worse.

As a general, Andrew Jackson had fought several campaigns against Native Americans. He believed that Native Americans threatened the expansion of the United States. He supported violating the treaties to free up more land for white settlers. He believed that moving Native Americans to land west of the Mississippi River would end the threat.

In 1830, Congress passed the Indian Removal Act and Andrew Jackson signed it into law. This law forced Native Americans to leave their homelands so settlers could live there. The act allowed the U.S. government to relocate Native Americans to "Indian Territory," in parts of what is now Oklahoma.

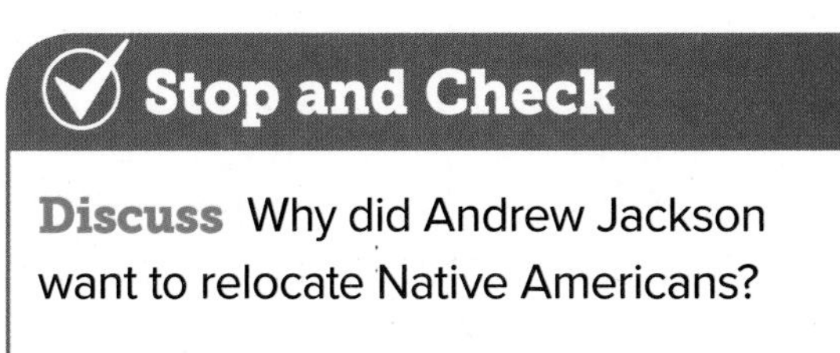

# The Trail of Tears

The Cherokee fought against the Indian Removal Act. Led by Chief John Ross, they took their case to court and sued the state of Georgia. Eventually, the U.S. Supreme Court, the highest court in the land, ruled in favor of the Cherokee, determining that "the laws of Georgia can have no force" on Native American lands. Chief Justice John Marshall wrote the following to explain the Court's opinion.

**PRIMARY SOURCE**

## In Their Words... Chief Justice John Marshall

Treaties have been duly ratified by the Senate of the United States of America, and by which treaties the United States of America acknowledge the said Cherokee Nation to be a sovereign nation, authorized to govern themselves, and all persons who have settled within their territory, free from any right of legislative interference by the several states composing the United States of America in reference to acts done within their own territory, and by which treaties the whole of the territory now occupied by the Cherokee Nation on the east of the Mississippi has been solemnly guarantied to them, all of which treaties are existing treaties at this day, and in full force . . .

—from *Worcester* v. *Georgia* ruling, 1831

President Jackson ignored that ruling, however. He ordered soldiers to force the Cherokee off the lands they legally owned. In 1838, General Winfield Scott led about 7,000 federal troops onto Cherokee lands in northwest Georgia and neighboring areas. He told the Cherokee that they were surrounded, escape was impossible, and force would be used if they did not comply. The soldiers then burned the Cherokee's homes and forced them to travel 800 miles into Indian Territory.

**PRIMARY SOURCE**

### In Their Words... Chief John Ross

We are overwhelmed! Our hearts are sickened, our utterance is paralyzed, when we reflect on the condition in which we are placed, by the audacious practices of unprincipled men. . . . In truth, our cause is your own; it is the cause of liberty and of justice; it is based upon your own principles, which we have learned from yourselves; for we have gloried to count your Washington and your Jefferson our great teachers . . .

—from a letter to the U.S. Congress, 1836

Of the approximately 15,000 Cherokee forced to leave their homes, about 2,000 died in camps waiting for the move to begin. During the one-year march, another 2,000 Cherokee died from disease, starvation, and severe weather conditions. The Cherokee called this forced march "the place where they cried." In English, it became known as the Trail of Tears.

### Stop and Check

**Think** How did President Jackson and Congress force the removal of the Cherokee from their own land?

# The Seminole Wars

Andrew Jackson had a long history of interfering with the rights of Native Americans, starting when he was a general in the U.S. military. It was then that he first became involved in wars between the U.S. military and the Seminole people of Florida.

In the first Seminole War in 1817, General Jackson led forces in an invasion of Seminole land to recapture runaway enslaved people that the Seminole had welcomed. U.S. soldiers burned down the towns in this region.

When Jackson became president, he again attempted to relocate the Seminole in Florida and take over their land. Settlers and Jackson sought to enforce the Indian Removal Act in Florida. Some of the Seminole formed an army under the leadership of Chief Osceola and fought against U.S. troops. When the U.S. Army approached Osceola, claiming to come in peace, they took him prisoner. He later died in prison. Even so, the Seminole continued fighting to remain in Florida. By the end of the Seminole Wars, U.S. soldiers had removed 3,000 Seminole from their Florida homes and killed 1,500 more.

Chief Osceola

## Stop and Check

COLLABORATE

**Talk** What similarities were there between the Trail of Tears and the Seminole Wars?

# A War with Mexico

By 1835, more than 25,000 Americans, including 2,000 enslaved people, had moved to Mexico's Texas province. But, the Americans did not want to accept Mexico's conditions for the land—becoming Mexican citizens, taking up Catholicism, and following Mexico's laws which included a ban on slavery.

In December 1835, 500 Americans, including Stephen Austin, attacked San Antonio. They took control of the Alamo, a Spanish mission that the Mexican Army had turned into a fort. On March 2, 1836, the Americans declared their independence and established the Republic of Texas. Four days later, Mexican General Antonio López de Santa Anna recaptured the Alamo, killing every American inside. A month later, inspired by the battle cry, "Remember the Alamo!", Texas General Sam Houston attacked and defeated a large Mexican force at San Jacinto. The Republic of Texas stood. In 1845, the U.S. Congress voted to accept Texas into the Union.

The Alamo

U.S. President James K. Polk also wanted to buy California and other Mexican territories. Mexico said no. Finally, a disagreement between the United States and Mexico over Texas's border led to war. In 1847, U.S. troops attacked Mexico City, and the Mexican government agreed to end the war. Both nations signed the Treaty of Guadalupe Hidalgo in 1848. Mexico would sell 320 million acres of land to the United States, and the Rio Grande was recognized as Texas's southern border. The future states of California, Nevada, and Utah, and parts of Arizona, New Mexico, Colorado, and Wyoming were also part of the deal. In 1854, the Gadsden Purchase added 29,670 square miles to this area and created the existing southern border of the United States.

**Stop and Check**

**Think** What factors contributed to war between the United States and Mexico?

# What Conflicts and Compromises Shaped the North and South?

## The Political Balance in 1848

As the United States expanded westward, so too did the problem of slavery. By 1804, states north of Maryland had either abolished slavery or voted for gradual emancipation. The states of the North did not want slavery to expand to new territories, and the states of the South did. Senator Henry Clay came up with the Missouri Compromise in 1820. The Compromise sought to maintain a balance between free and slave states. The Missouri Compromise line was drawn across the country's map, lining up with the southern border of Missouri at the latitude line of 36°30′ (36 degrees 30 minutes). Missouri was allowed to become a slave state, but any territory north of that line was considered free.

Maine, a free state, and Missouri, a slave state, entered the Union as the 23rd and 24th states. In 1836, Arkansas became a state. Since it was below the Missouri Compromise line, it allowed slavery. Michigan was allowed to join as a free state in 1837. Florida and Texas gained statehood in 1845 as slave states. They were followed by the free states Iowa, in 1846, and Wisconsin, in 1848.

The Missouri Compromise did not solve the problem of slavery. It merely delayed conflict between the North and the South. The peace was eventually broken by another peace: the end of the Mexican War. In 1848, the United States gained territory that included what would become Arizona, California, Colorado, Nevada, New Mexico, and Utah. Much of this territory was south of the Compromise line and could become slave states. This potential imbalance added urgency to the debate about slavery.

**1850**
Compromise of 1850 is passed.

**1852**
*Uncle Tom's Cabin* is published.

**1854**
Kansas-Nebraska Act is passed.

**1857**
Dred Scott case is decided.

1848 | 1850 | 1852 | 1854 | 1856 | 1858

Henry Clay was known for the compromises he proposed in Congress.

# Economies of the North and the South

The system of slavery was not the only difference between the North and the South. By the mid-1800s, the two regions had developed very different economies.

The states in the Southern United States were agricultural. The South's main source of wealth, as in colonial times, was cash crops. By the mid-1800s, cotton had replaced tobacco as the most commonly grown crop, but large plantations still held economic and political power in the South just as they had in the past. Plantation owners sold cotton and other goods to the North and Europe and bought manufactured goods from them. The South did little of its own manufacturing.

The North was more industrialized than the South. The Northern economy was more dependent on factories, which used paid labor. The pay was often very low by today's standards, but it was high enough that immigrants came to America seeking work. The North also invested more of its money in setting up transportation and communication networks by building railroads, canals, and telegraph lines. People, products, and ideas could all travel much more rapidly and easily in the North than in the South. In addition, the North had more large cities than the South did.

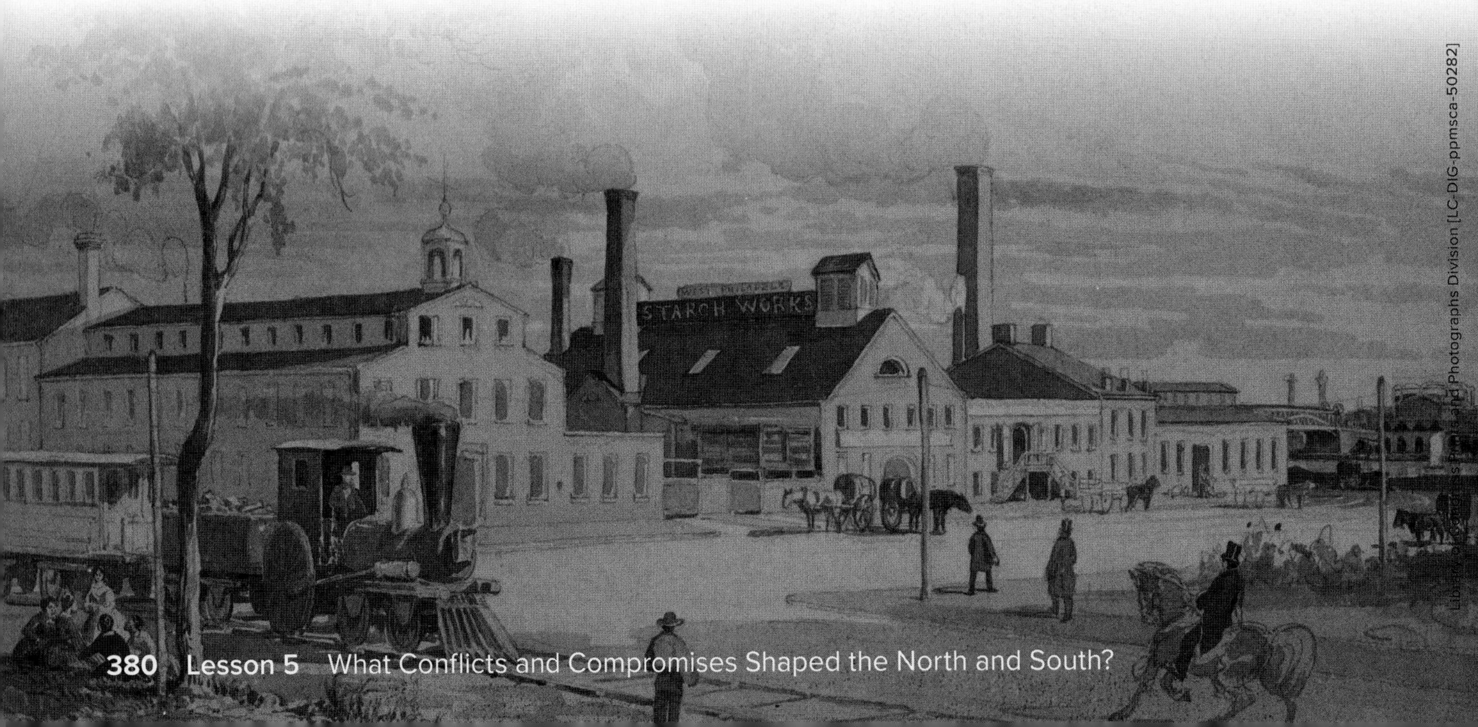

# Views on Tariffs

The U.S. Constitution grants Congress the power to create taxes and similar fees. This includes tariffs, or taxes on imported goods. In 1828 and 1832, the U.S. government created controversial tariffs. Since the Northern economy relied more on manufacturing than the South did, people in the North favored tariffs on manufactured goods that were imported. A tariff would protect Northern manufacturers from European competitors. The South did very little manufacturing, but it bought many goods from Europe. These tariffs did not benefit the South. They only made products more expensive for Southerners.

The Constitution states that "all Duties, Imposts and Excises shall be uniform throughout the United States." The tariffs of 1828 and 1832 applied to all states, but they helped the North more than the South. The South claimed that this made the tariffs unconstitutional. Vice President John C. Calhoun, whose home state of South Carolina was hurt by the tariffs, began to rally support for the idea of states' rights. Supporters of states' rights believe that a state's authority should override the authority of the federal government. Calhoun convinced South Carolina to adopt the Ordinance of Nullification. This declared that the state would not pay the tariffs. The other Southern states did not support South Carolina, and Congress passed the Force Bill, threatening to use the military to collect tariffs. South Carolina dropped the Ordinance of Nullification.

The Nullification Crisis showed that the North and the South had different views of states' rights. Calhoun and other Southerners believed that this was a threat to slavery. If the North outlawed slavery for the whole country, the South would have to either obey or try to form its own nation.

**Stop and Check**

COLLABORATE

**Talk** How did the lifestyles and views of Northerners and Southerners differ before the Civil War?

**Find Details** As you read, add new information to the graphic organizer on page 291 in your Inquiry Journal.

# Opposition to Slavery

In the 18th century, many people in the North believed that slavery was morally wrong and should be ended. They were called **abolitionists**. The abolition movement was not strong enough to outlaw slavery when the Constitution was written, but it grew in strength over time. By 1804, every state north of Maryland had abolished slavery or approved gradual emancipation. In 1807, the United States made it illegal to bring any more people captured for slavery into the country. In the years leading up to the Civil War, the abolitionists became a powerful political force.

Many groups united under the cause of abolition. Quakers and other religious groups opposed slavery for moral reasons. Others simply wanted to protect Northern businesses from the possibility of slavery-fueled Southern manufacturing. Many abolitionists recognized the humanity of the enslaved people. William Lloyd Garrison published the anti-slavery newspaper *The Liberator* and in 1833 founded the American Anti-Slavery Society. It connected two thousand smaller, local anti-slavery societies. Not surprisingly, many of the most dedicated abolitionists were free or formerly enslaved African Americans.

Isabella Baumfree was born into slavery in New York in the 1790s. Throughout her childhood, she was bought and sold many times, and some of her masters were very cruel. In the 1820s, she was given her freedom. She believed God was calling her to fight for abolition and women's rights, and she became a preacher and public speaker known as Sojourner Truth. (*Sojourner* is another word for *traveler*.) She traveled across the Midwest to tell the truth about slavery. Her story, *The Narrative of Sojourner Truth: A Northern Slave*, helped fund her travels. Truth was six feet tall, had a powerful voice, and spoke with passion. Her forceful personality brought her into contact with other abolitionist leaders. One of these was Frederick Douglass.

**Sojourner Truth traveled across much of the North to speak out against slavery.**

Frederick Douglass was also born into slavery in Maryland. The wife of one slave owner taught him to read, even though it was against state law. He eventually escaped and became an abolitionist speaker. His autobiography, *Life and Times of Frederick Douglass,* is an American classic and one of the best historical accounts of slavery. His story convinced many people that slavery was inexcusably evil. He later began his own newspaper, *The North Star.* Douglass believed that simply convincing people that slavery was wrong was not enough. He urged abolitionists to enter politics to force an end to slavery through law.

**PRIMARY SOURCE**

## In Their Words... Frederick Douglass

**What, to the American slave, is your 4th of July? I answer; a day that reveals to him, more than all other days in the year, the gross injustice and cruelty to which he is the constant victim.**

—from an 1852 speech on the Declaration of Independence

Another writer who influenced the abolition movement was Harriet Beecher Stowe. While living in Cincinnati, Ohio, she could see the cruelty enslaved people endured in Kentucky, just across the border. She learned about life in slave states from escapees, friends, and her own visits. Stowe was inspired to write the novel *Uncle Tom's Cabin* in 1852. In its first year, the novel sold more than 300,000 copies. Readers were moved by the story of an enslaved family torn apart across different plantations. The book also described other abusive treatment of enslaved people. *Uncle Tom's Cabin* greatly increased support in the North for abolition.

**Stop and Check**

**Think** Why would writing a book and giving speeches be effective strategies for promoting the abolitionist movement?

TEXT: Foner, Philip S. The Life and Writings of Frederick Douglass, Volume 2: Pre-Civil War Decade 1850-1860.International Publishers Co., Inc.: New York, 1950.; PHOTO: (t)McGraw-Hill Education, (b)Library of Congress Prints and Photographs Division [LC-DIG-ds-07422]

# The Underground Railroad

While many Americans spoke and wrote against slavery, some took more direct action. Many African Americans escaped slavery through the Underground Railroad. This was a secret network of sympathetic people who helped enslaved "people" find their way to freedom. However, it was neither underground nor a railroad. People called it "underground" because it was hidden, and it was a "railroad" because it was a network of "lines," or routes, with "stations" or safe houses. The people who guided **fugitives** along the Underground Railroad were called "conductors."

Harriet Tubman helped many people escape to the North.

The most famous conductor was Harriet Tubman, but before that she was a passenger. Like many other African American abolitionists, Tubman was born into slavery. She escaped when she was about 30. After she reached the free state of Pennsylvania, she risked her freedom and life to go back into the South to help more enslaved "people" escape. Enslaved people would spread messages about her by singing songs with hidden meanings. Harriet Tubman worked in secret, so historians are not sure of the exact number of people she helped escape. However, it is believed that Harriet Tubman made about 13 trips back to the South and helped about 70 people escape from slavery.

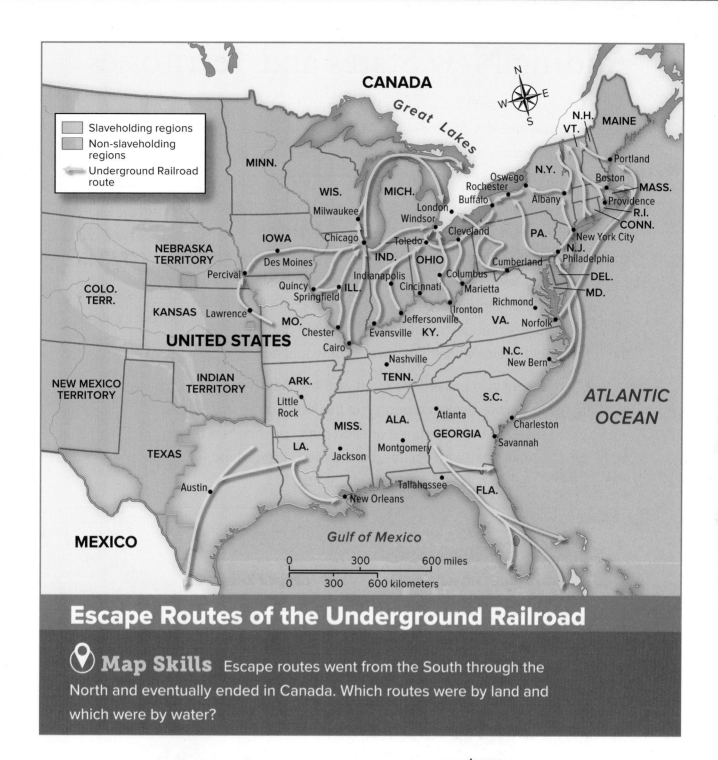

## Escape Routes of the Underground Railroad

**Map Skills** Escape routes went from the South through the North and eventually ended in Canada. Which routes were by land and which were by water?

## Stop and Check

**Draw** Imagine you are a conductor on the Underground Railroad. Draw a simple map and plan a route to guide a group of escaped enslaved people. Consider geography and the need to rest or hide. Explain to a partner how you chose the route.

# Adding New States and Territories

The U.S. government tried to keep the country together by keeping the number of free and slave states equal. California wanted to enter as a free state, tipping the balance to 16 free versus 15 slave states. The South feared this would lead to banning slavery in the entire country.

Henry Clay, the senator who came up with the Missouri Compromise, once again devised a solution, the Compromise of 1850. This compromise had complicated details. To appease anti-slavery groups, California was admitted as a free state, and although slavery would still be allowed in Washington, D.C., slave trading became illegal there. To satisfy pro-slavery groups, the people of the Utah and New Mexico territories could decide if their state would or would not allow slavery.

The government also passed the Fugitive Slave Act. This act made it illegal to help runaway enslaved people in the North or South. People who helped fugitives could be fined or even put in prison. As a result, many African Americans who escaped using the Underground Railroad decided to keep going until they reached Canada.

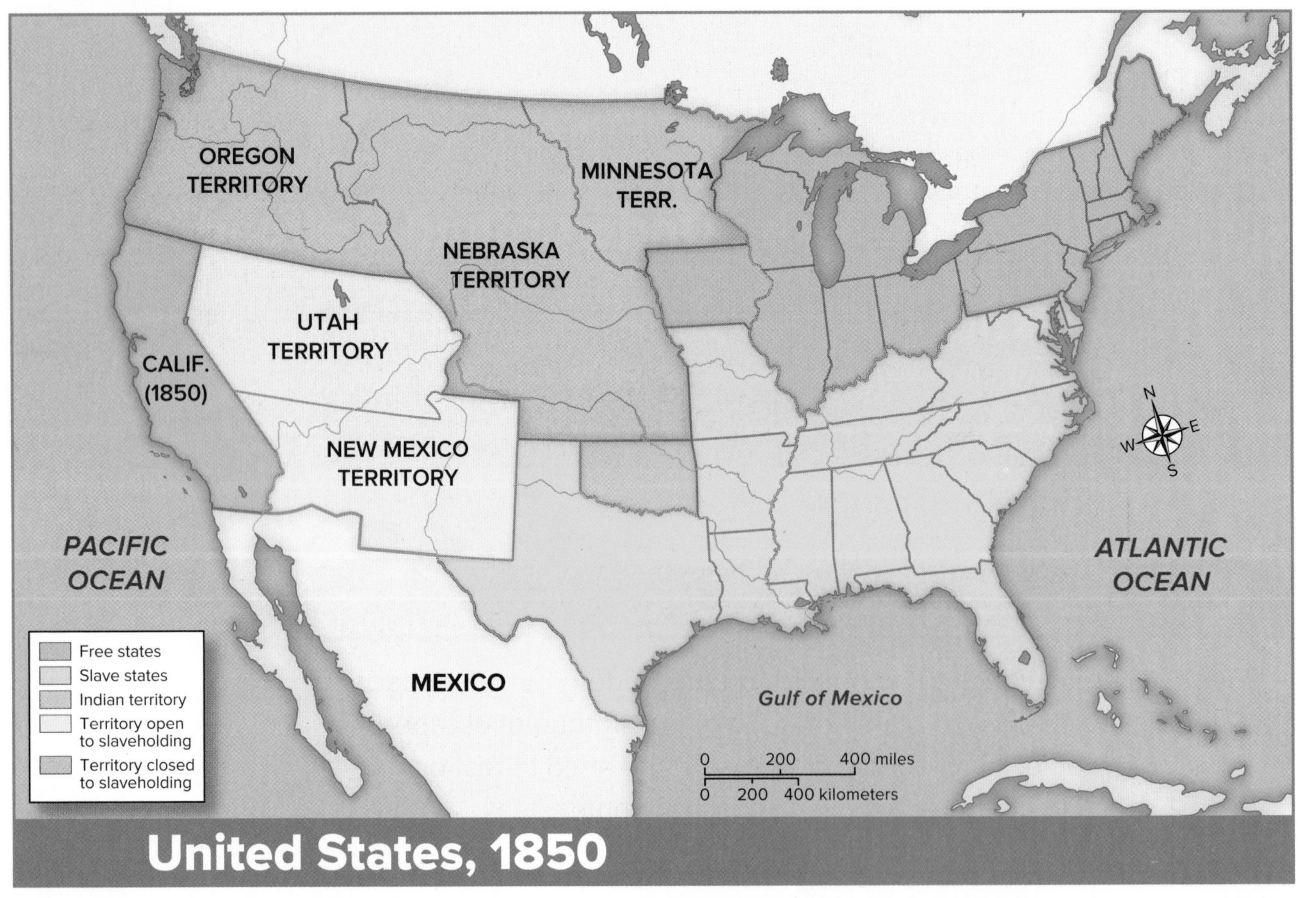


United States, 1850

At first, it appeared that Senator Clay, the Great Compromiser, had succeeded again in preventing conflict. This peace was short-lived. In 1854, Senator Stephen Douglas from Illinois introduced the Kansas-Nebraska Act. The Kansas-Nebraska Act allowed residents of those states the chance to decide if their state would be free or if it would allow slavery.

The Kansas-Nebraska Act caused unforeseen problems. "Border ruffians," people from neighboring states, quickly moved into Kansas to give more votes to the side they supported. Some of these settlers brought weapons to try to scare away people from the other side. The territory was called "Bleeding Kansas" because of the violent clashes that occurred off and on over the next several years. The stage was set for an even larger conflict over slavery.

WASHINGTON TERR.
OREGON TERRITORY
NEBRASKA TERRITORY
MINNESOTA TERR.
UTAH TERRITORY
KANSAS TERRITORY
NEW MEXICO TERRITORY
PACIFIC OCEAN
ATLANTIC OCEAN
MEXICO
Gulf of Mexico
N S E W
0 200 400 miles
0 200 400 kilometers

Free states
Slave states
Indian territory
Territory open to slaveholding
Territory closed to slaveholding

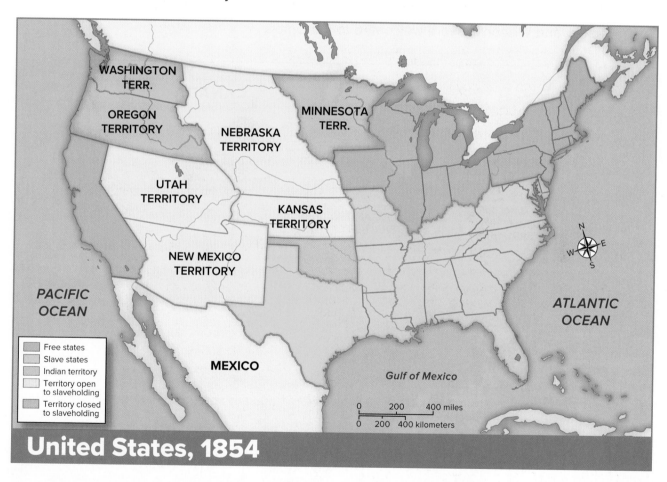

## United States, 1854

## Stop and Check

COLLABORATE

**Talk** Why did letting residents choose if a state would be free or allow slavery cause problems?

## Map and Globe Skills

# The States and Territories, 1850

Throughout the 1800s, the United States continued to grow and change. As the nation's population grew, so did the number of states and territories. The Treaty of Guadalupe Hidalgo, which ended the Mexican War, greatly expanded the nation's boundaries. Furthermore, between the years of 1821 and 1850, Arkansas, California, Michigan, Florida, Iowa, Texas, and Wisconsin were welcomed to the Union.

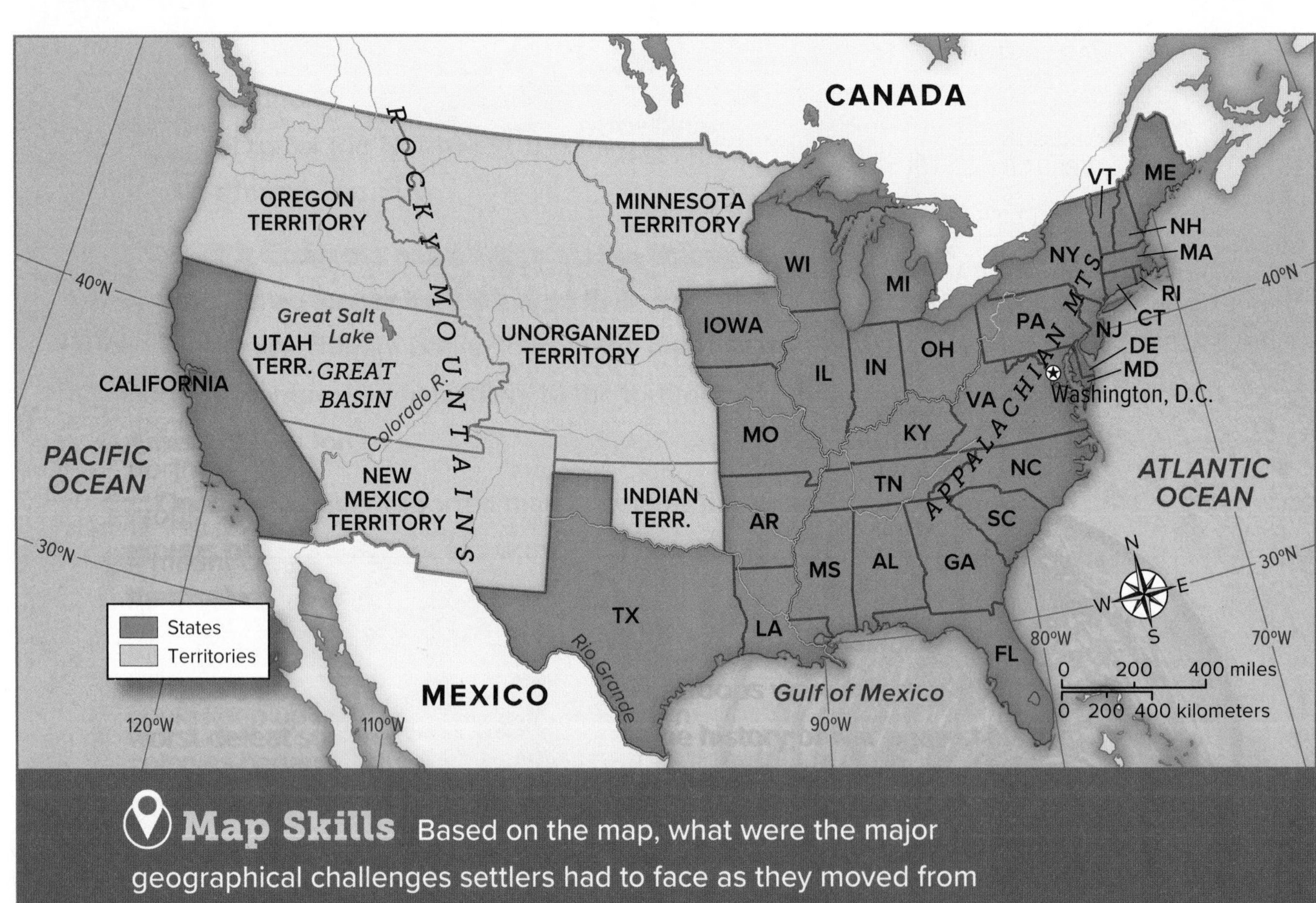


**Map Skills** Based on the map, what were the major geographical challenges settlers had to face as they moved from the East Coast toward California?

## Arkansas

**Population in 1850:** 209,897
**Population in 2015:** 2,978,204
★ **Capital:** Little Rock

## California

**Population in 1850:** 92,597
**Population in 2015:** 39,144,818
★ **Capital:** Sacramento

## Florida

**Population in 1850:** 87,445
**Population in 2015:** 20,271,272
★ **Capital:** Tallahassee

## Iowa

**Population in 1850:** 192,214
**Population in 2015:** 3,123,899
★ **Capital:** Des Moines

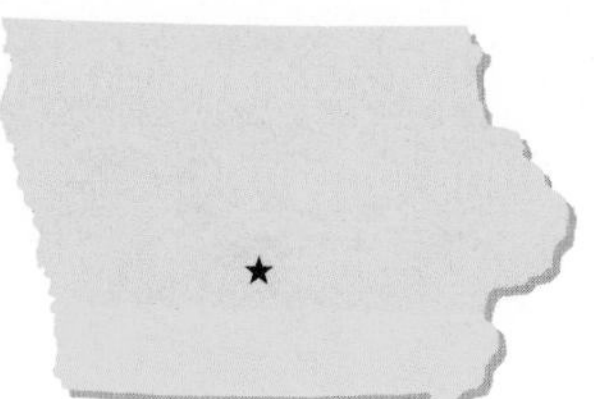

## Michigan

**Population in 1850:** 397,654
**Population in 2015:** 9,922,576
★ **Capital:** Lansing

## Texas

**Population in 1850:** 212,592
**Population in 2015:** 27,469,114
★ **Capital:** Austin

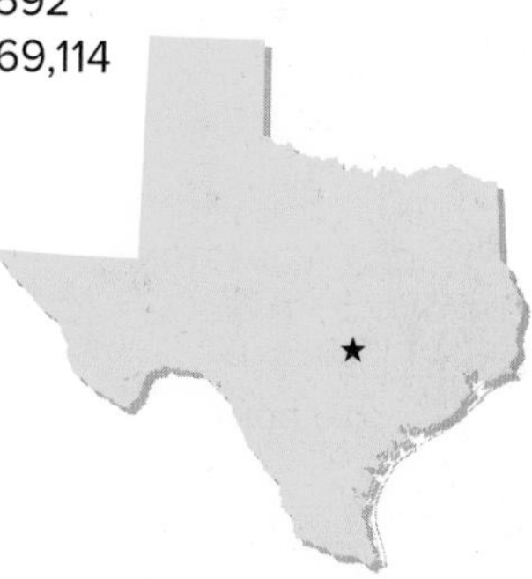

## Wisconsin

**Population in 1850:** 305,391
**Population in 2015:** 5,771,337
★ **Capital:** Madison

# The States Adopted After 1850

Since 1850, nineteen more states have joined the United States. The most recent additions, Alaska and Hawaii, achieved statehood in 1959. This means that no new state has joined the Union in nearly 60 years. However, citizens have begun statehood movements in Washington, D.C., and Puerto Rico.

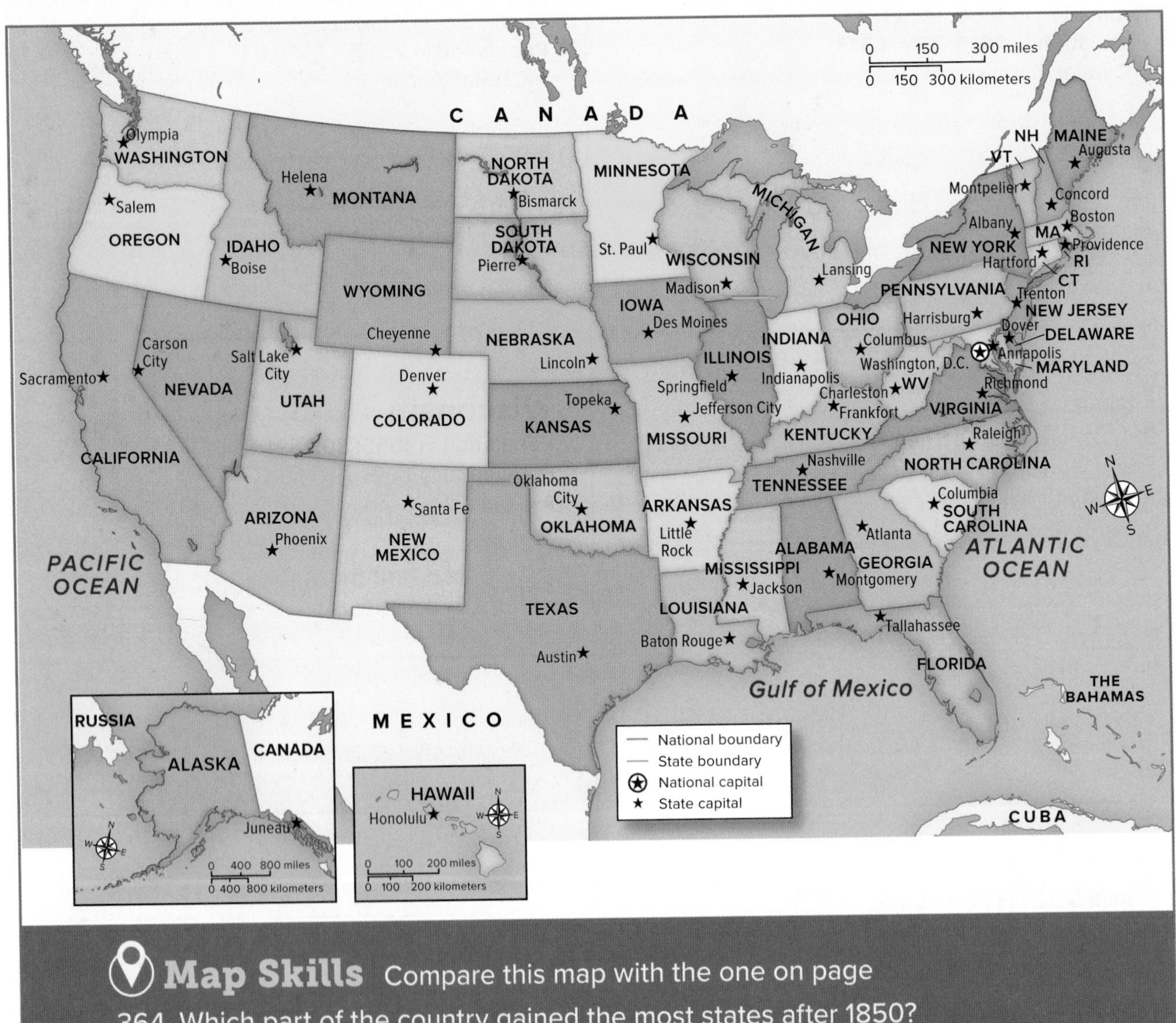


**Map Skills** Compare this map with the one on page 364. Which part of the country gained the most states after 1850? Which two new states share no borders with the other 48?

## Alaska

**Population in 1900:** 63,592
**Population in 2015:** 738,432
★ **Capital:** Juneau

## Arizona

**Population in 1900:** 122,931
**Population in 2015:** 6,828,065
★ **Capital:** Phoenix

## Colorado

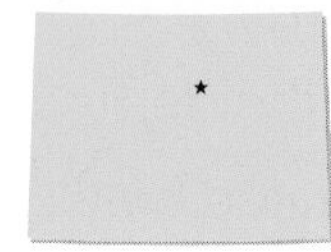

**Population in 1900:** 539,700
**Population in 2015:** 5,456,574
★ **Capital:** Denver

## Hawaii

**Population in 1900:** 154,001
**Population in 2015:** 1,431,603
★ **Capital:** Honolulu

## Idaho

**Population in 1900:** 161,772
**Population in 2015:** 1,654,930
★ **Capital:** Boise

## Kansas

**Population in 1900:** 1,470,495
**Population in 2015:** 2,911,641
★ **Capital:** Topeka

## Minnesota

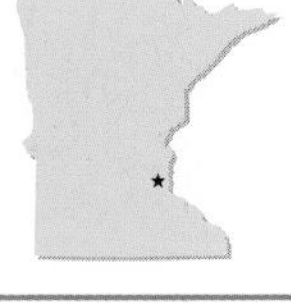

**Population in 1900:** 1,751,394
**Population in 2015:** 5,489,594
★ **Capital:** St. Paul

## Montana

**Population in 1900:** 243,329
**Population in 2015:** 1,032,949
★ **Capital:** Helena

## Nebraska

**Population in 1900:** 1,066,300
**Population in 2015:** 1,896,190
★ **Capital:** Lincoln

## Nevada

**Population in 1900:** 42,335
**Population in 2015:** 2,890,845
★ **Capital:** Carson City

## New Mexico

**Population in 1900:** 195,310
**Population in 2015:** 2,085,109
★ **Capital:** Santa Fe

## North Dakota

**Population in 1900:** 319,146
**Population in 2015:** 756,927
★ **Capital:** Bismarck

## Oklahoma

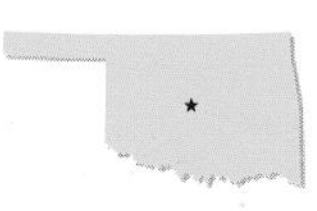

**Population in 1900:** 790,391
**Population in 2015:** 3,911,338
★ **Capital:** Oklahoma City

## Oregon

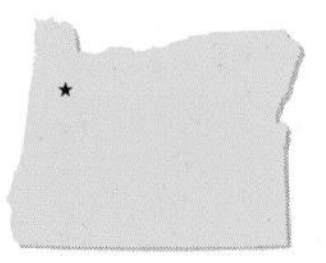

**Population in 1900:** 413,536
**Population in 2015:** 4,028,977
★ **Capital:** Salem

## South Dakota

**Population in 1900:** 401,570
**Population in 2015:** 858,469
★ **Capital:** Pierre

## Utah

**Population in 1900:** 276,749
**Population in 2015:** 2,995,919
★ **Capital:** Salt Lake City

## Washington

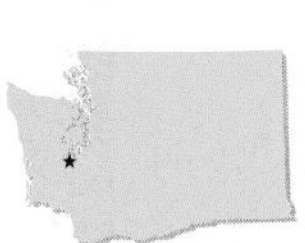

**Population in 1900:** 518,103
**Population in 2015:** 7,170,351
★ **Capital:** Olympia

## West Virginia

**Population in 1900:** 958,800
**Population in 2015:** 1,844,128
★ **Capital:** Charleston

## Wyoming

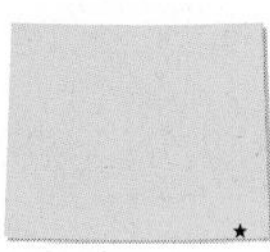

**Population in 1900:** 92,531
**Population in 2015:** 586,107
★ **Capital:** Cheyenne

# Connections in Action!

## Back to the EQ

**Think** about the Chapter EQ, **"What Do the Early Years of the United States Reveal About the Character of the Nation?"**

- **Talk** with a partner about what you learned from the chapter. Discuss what early innovations and the desire to move west say about the character of the United States.
- **Think** about how the nation changed. What was it like to travel there? Why were people interested in taking risks to establish new lives there? Who benefited from expansion? Who suffered from it? Does this suffering reflect poorly on the character of our nation?
- **Share** your ideas; then have a discussion about the positive and negative characteristics of the United States that emerged during this period of growth.

ISAAC NEWTON

FRANCIS SKIDDY

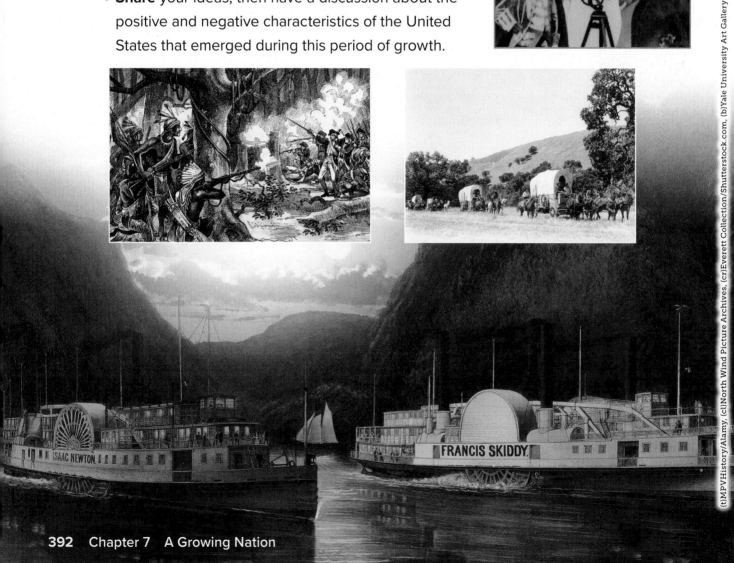

(t)MPVHistory/Alamy, (cl)North Wind Picture Archives, (cr)Everett Collection/Shutterstock.com, (b)Yale University Art Gallery

# More to Explore

## How Can You Make an IMPACT?

### Write a Song

Work with a partner or small group to write a song that captures the spirit of the early United States. You can write any kind of song, even a kind that wasn't invented at the time, such as hip hop, rock, or a show tune.

### Perform Your Song

Perform your song by presenting it to your class or recording it and posting it to your class website or blog. Work together to practice it before performing it. Listen respectfully to other groups' songs.

### Word Play

Choose five words from the chapter Word Bank. Make a list of words in the same family by adding prefixes and suffixes or by changing the tense or part of speech of the word; for example: *composition, compose, composer, composite, composure.* Use a dictionary to confirm whether the words you are creating are actual words.

# THE IMPACT TODAY

# How Do Economics And Finances Affect People's Decisions?

## Basics of Our Economy

When you go to the store, do you ever wonder how prices are determined? Why does a candy bar cost less than a sandwich? Why can't sale prices be used every day? Why do we have to pay for things in the first place? All of this is explained by economics, the social science that studies how people produce, distribute, and consume goods and services. These factors interact in complex and often surprising ways.

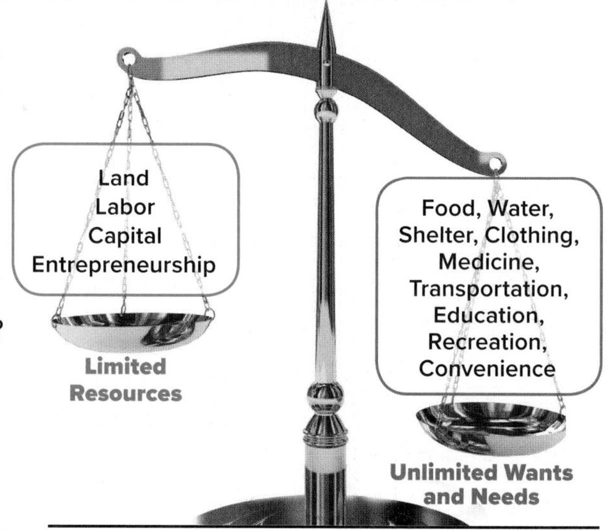


**The wants and needs of consumers are infinite, but the ability to produce is finite. This creates scarcity.**

To understand any economy, big or small, you must start by understanding basic principles. An economy is ultimately a result of consumption. Humans, like other living things, need to consume. We need food, water, air, shelter, space, and other things. In addition to needs, we have wants. For example, we want to be entertained and we want to have luxury items. Some needs and wants are freely available, like air and sunlight. Others require effort.

If you wanted to make a wool sweater, it would require resources and labor. First, you would need a lamb. That would be your resource. You would need to provide food, water, protection, and other needs until the lamb grew into a sheep. Then you would shear the sheep to get wool. Next, you would spin the wool into yarn and knit it into a sweater. This process would be labor. Labor and resources are limited. A worker eventually needs to rest, and a sheep can produce only so much wool. But because the needs and wants of consumers are unlimited, and resources and the ability to produce are limited, the result is scarcity.

(t)Adam Gault/Getty Images, (b)alexsl/Getty Images

The division of labor can reduce scarcity. It would take a lot of time and energy for each person who wants a wool sweater to raise a sheep, shear wool, spin yarn, and knit a sweater. It's easier if the work is divided among specialists. If a shepherd raises and shears three sheep, a worker with a spinning wheel can use that wool to make three times as much yarn. Then, a knitter can make three sweaters, one for each person. The shepherd wouldn't need a spinning wheel, the person doing the spinning wouldn't need to know how to knit, and the knitter wouldn't need any sheep. The three people reduce the total amount of labor, equipment, training, and resources required, and everyone still gets a sweater.

Goods are products that people make for you to buy, like the electronics in this factory.

Although division of labor increases production, it also complicates the economy. The person with the spinning wheel needs wool to make yarn, but he or she can't give yarn to the shepherd in exchange for wool. The shepherd has little use for yarn. Should the shepherd wait until he or she gets a sweater before giving the person with the spinning wheel more yarn, or will the promise of a sweater be good enough? What if the knitter decides to just take the yarn and leave town? This is why money has replaced bartering, or trading, in modern societies. As long as everyone agrees that money has value, it can be exchanged instantly to anyone for any good or service.

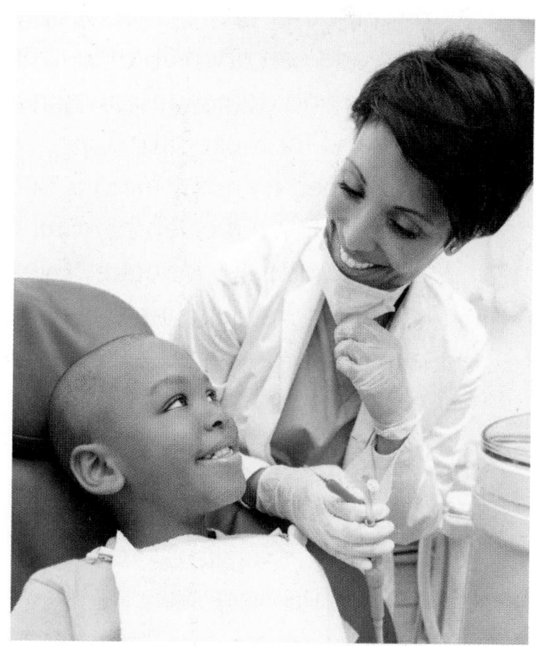

Services are actions you can pay someone to perform, like a dental checkup.

## WHAT IS THE IMPACT TODAY?

**Talk** Where does scarcity come from? What does scarcity create?

(t)McGraw-Hill Education, (c)Kim Steele/Getty Images, (b)wavebreakmedia/Shutterstock

# Deciding Value

Who decides how much money a good or service is worth? The answer is everyone. Price is largely determined by supply and demand. Supply is how much of the product is currently available. A smaller supply usually creates a higher price. Gold is worth more than copper because gold is rarer than copper. Supply is determined not only by how much of a resource exists but also by how much work is put into making it. Remember, the amount of work a person can do is limited. The more time-consuming and difficult a product is to create, the less of it a person can make in a lifetime. A car is made of fairly inexpensive metals, plastics, and other materials. However, the amount of work it takes to shape and assemble these materials results in a higher price tag. Rare materials and difficult production result in a small supply, which creates a high price.

High demand, on the other hand, results in a high price. Demand is how much consumers want or need a product. Food is always in demand because all people need to eat. A book about unicycle repair, on the other hand, is really only interesting to people who ride unicycles. Demand can often change. During the winter, demand for hot chocolate is high and demand for lemonade is low. When summer comes, the demand for these products becomes reversed. Demand can be influenced by many factors, such as environment, fashion, and technology. If a celebrity wears a certain type of hat, demand for that hat could suddenly skyrocket. Even though the hat is made of inexpensive materials, its value increases because more people want it. Similarly, if an expensive device turns out to be dangerous to its user, demand will plummet and so will its price.

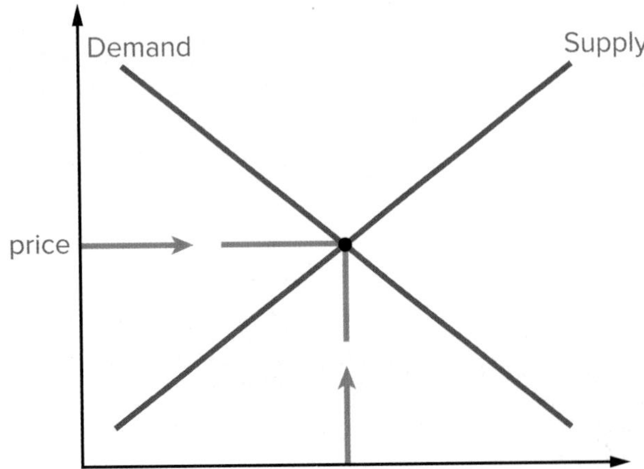


**A product's price is determined by supply and demand. The intersection where the two meet will be the final price in the market.**

# Entrepreneurs

Part of America's economic strength comes from the role that entrepreneurs play in the economy. An entrepreneur is a "risk-taker" who uses or combines resources in a new or different way in hopes of making a profit. An entrepreneur has almost complete control over what his or her business makes, sells, or does. The government limits entrepreneurs only to ensure things like workplace safety and fair wages.

Entrepreneurs help an economy grow and adapt rapidly by making new or better goods and services for consumers. Entrepreneurs also compete with one another to earn the dollars that consumers spend. This competition usually benefits society as a whole. Businesses that sell similar products will each try to make their own product cheaper, better, or both so that they can outsell their competitors. Every business is looking for ways to create goods and services that are better and more efficient. With so many entrepreneurs working to introduce more and better products, the entire country benefits.

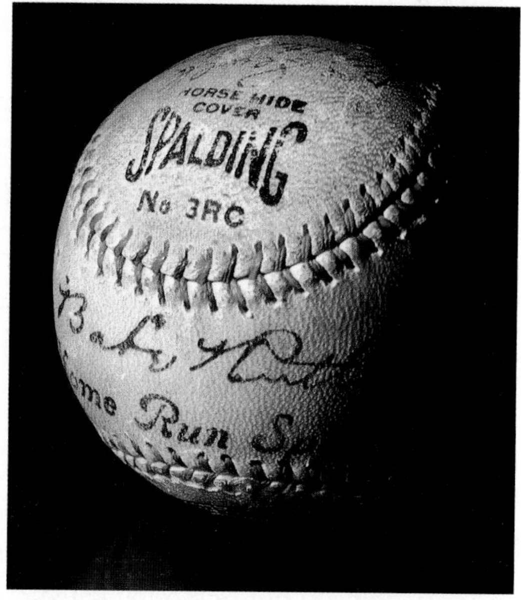


A baseball autographed by a famous player will have a low supply and a high demand. This will create a high price.

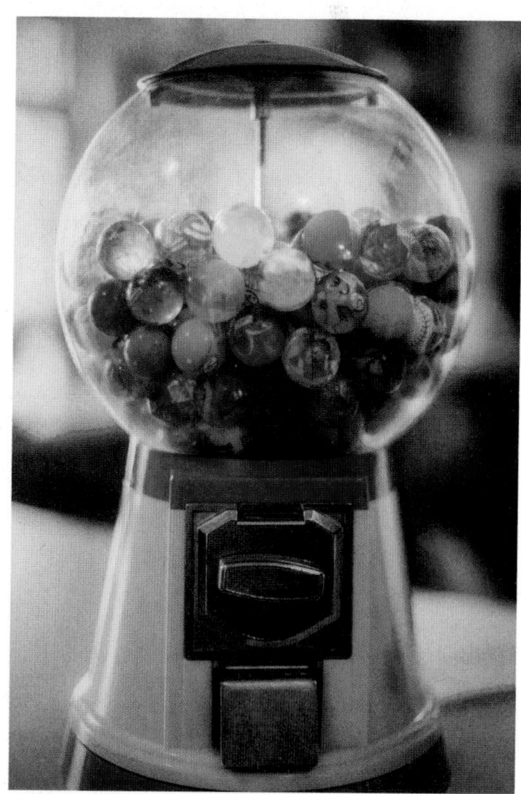

A small rubber bouncy ball will have a high supply and a low demand. This will create a low price.

## WHAT IS THE IMPACT TODAY?

COLLABORATE

**Talk** Make a list of your own examples of things that are in high supply and low demand and things that are in low supply and high demand. Tell how supply and demand might affect the price of each item.

# To Buy or Not to Buy

Entrepreneurs are important, but no business can survive without consumers. With so many goods and services available, it can be hard for a consumer to choose how to spend his or her hard-earned money. A careless person can run out of money very quickly.

When considering how to spend money, it is important to make a budget. First, determine how much money you have available. Next, consider your wants and needs. Things you need to buy, like food, clothing, and shelter, are top priority. You must set aside money for necessary expenses first. Whatever is left over can be used for things you want. By keeping track of how much you are able to spend, you can make sure you won't run out of money. Another way to ensure you won't run out of money is to save extra money. Choosing to keep the money for later can help you if something unexpected happens.

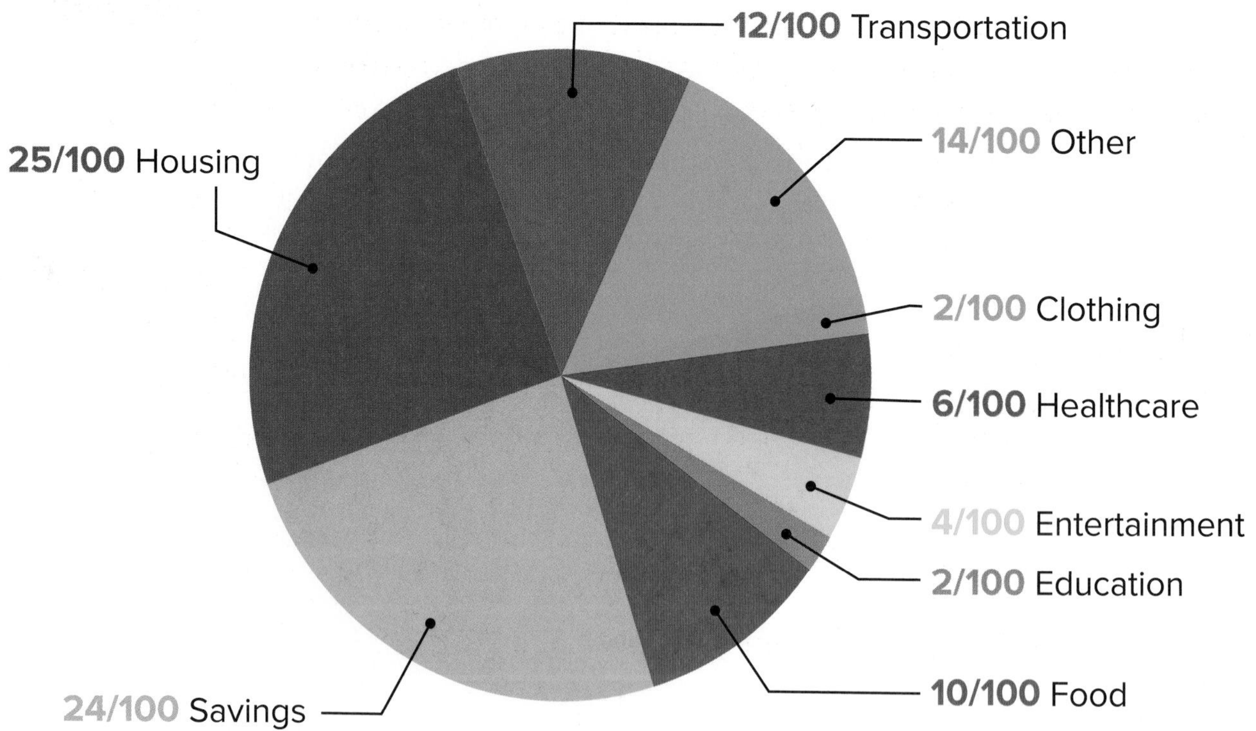


A typical household's budget

A good way to save money is by putting it in a bank. When you put your money in a savings account at a bank, you are actually allowing the bank to use your money. In exchange, the bank gives you a positive incentive, or reward, called interest. The money in your bank account increases by a small percentage over time. This way, when you get your money back, you will also get back the interest. People may also borrow money from a bank. When a bank loans money, they charge interest. You have to pay back the money, plus a small percentage that grows over time. This negative incentive encourages you to pay back the loan quickly. Taking a loan from a bank is a good way to get money for an expensive purchase such as a car or a house, but paying back a loan can be difficult. As a result, it is important to think carefully before choosing to take a loan.

**What are the costs and benefits of saving money?**

Your money can also grow through investments. Entrepreneurs often need capital, or money and resources, to start a business. If you give them capital, in exchange you can receive part of their profits. A person who invests can make a lot of money if the business succeeds. This is a powerful positive incentive. Investing has an equally powerful negative incentive, though. If a business fails, the capital you invested may be lost. Consequently, people often pay attention to supply and demand to help predict if a business will succeed or fail.

You can also invest the money in yourself by improving your skills and knowledge. Just like the prices of products, a worker's wages are influenced by supply and demand. Doctors, for example, usually have high wages because they are in short supply while being high in demand. That is, the number of people with advanced knowledge and skills in medicine is small, while the need for medical professionals is high. Spending money on your own education to learn useful skills can allow you to choose a career with higher wages. Over time, it is likely you will earn more money than you initially spent.

## WHAT IS THE IMPACT TODAY?

**Talk** If you won $5,000 in a contest, how would you use the money? What are the potential risks and benefits of your choices?

# The Civil War and Reconstruction

## What Was the Effect of the Civil War on U.S. Society?

In this chapter, you will read about important events and people in the Civil War. You will think about why these events and people are important. You will discover the impact they had during the Civil War and Reconstruction. You will also consider how the events that happened during this time period still impact our nation today.

## Step into the Time Chronological Thinking

Look at the time line. What was going on in the rest of the world during the same years as the Civil War and Reconstruction?

**Americas**

**1858** Abraham Lincoln and Stephen Douglas debate the issue of slavery.

**1859** Anti-slavery forces raid Harpers Ferry, Virginia.

**1860** The Confederate States of America is formed.

**1861** The Civil War begins.

1857 | 1858 | 1859 | 1860 | 1861

**World Events**

**1859** Charles Dickens publishes *A Tale of Two Cities.*

**1861** Building of the Paris Opéra begins.

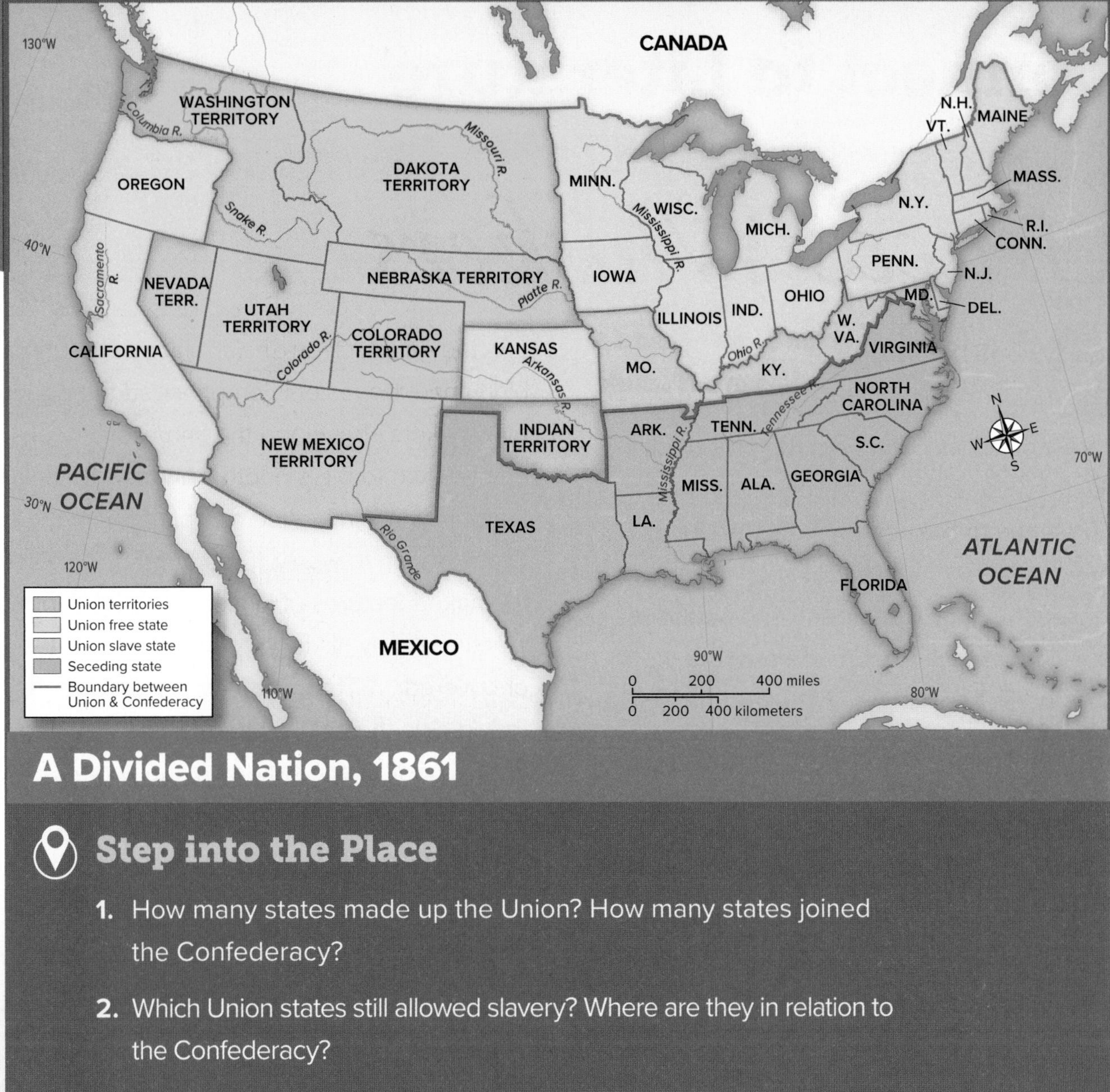


## A Divided Nation, 1861

### Step into the Place

1. How many states made up the Union? How many states joined the Confederacy?
2. Which Union states still allowed slavery? Where are they in relation to the Confederacy?

**1862** | **1863** | **1864** | **1865** | **1866**

**1863**
The Emancipation Proclamation is enacted.

**1865**
The Civil War ends.

Reconstruction of the South begins.

**1865**
English mountaineer Edward Whymper climbs the Matterhorn.

**1866**
Swedish scientist Alfred Bernhard Nobel invents dynamite.

# Connect to Literature

## *Grace's Whiskers*

By K. C. Tessendorf

By the fall of 1860, it looked as though Abraham Lincoln might win the presidential election. However, the slaveholding South threatened to break away from the Union if that happened. Anti-Lincoln spokesmen sensed that they were losing and began to turn vicious—even in a rural New York classroom:

"Faugh! I say that Old Abe . . . no, I mean Old *Ape* is so ugly that even the devil is afraid of him," ranted eleven-year-old Willy Jessup with a wink to his allies.

"Oh, what a terrible, cruel lie to say about our next president!" Classmate Grace Bedell's cheeks flushed with anger. "Willy, your mouth ought to be scrubbed with lye soap. Apologize!"

"All right—I'll take it back. Because he looks more like a baboon!"

But valiant Grace was defending her hero blindly, for she had never seen a picture of Abraham Lincoln. Shortly afterward, her father brought home a colorful poster from a campaign rally. Grace was upset when she saw what Lincoln looked like. The artist had drawn a split rail fence around the faces of Abraham Lincoln and his vice-presidential running mate, Senator Hannibal Hamlin.

In the gaunt, clean-shaven face of Lincoln, high cheekbones only emphasized the deep eye sockets above and the shrunken cheeks below. Next to the smooth fullness of Hamlin's features, Lincoln looked downright homely. Grace began to worry. If too many people saw the naked features of Lincoln, he might not be elected. If only his face could be remodeled or covered . . . That was it—whiskers! Surely they'd hide the hollow cheeks. The next day after school, Grace sat down and wrote a letter to Abraham Lincoln, telling him that he could improve his appearance by growing a beard. Realizing how bold she was, Grace nervously misspelled "Chautauqua," wrote "A B" because she had not seen "Abe" in print, and even left out a few words.

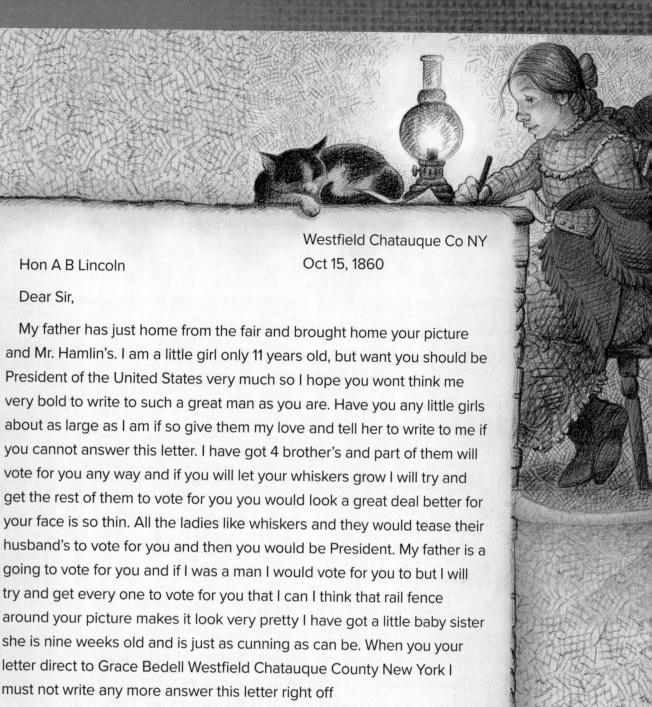

Westfield Chatauque Co NY
Oct 15, 1860

Hon A B Lincoln

Dear Sir,

My father has just home from the fair and brought home your picture and Mr. Hamlin's. I am a little girl only 11 years old, but want you should be President of the United States very much so I hope you wont think me very bold to write to such a great man as you are. Have you any little girls about as large as I am if so give them my love and tell her to write to me if you cannot answer this letter. I have got 4 brother's and part of them will vote for you any way and if you will let your whiskers grow I will try and get the rest of them to vote for you you would look a great deal better for your face is so thin. All the ladies like whiskers and they would tease their husband's to vote for you and then you would be President. My father is a going to vote for you and if I was a man I would vote for you to but I will try and get every one to vote for you that I can I think that rail fence around your picture makes it look very pretty I have got a little baby sister she is nine weeks old and is just as cunning as can be. When you your letter direct to Grace Bedell Westfield Chatauque County New York I must not write any more answer this letter right off

Good bye

Grace Bedell

She addressed the envelope to Hon. Abraham Lincoln, Esq., Springfield, Illinois. Then she stuck on a penny stamp and hurried to the post office, handing her letter to the clerk just as he was closing the wicket for the day.

Abraham Lincoln's campaign office occupied a large room staffed only by Lincoln and two secretaries. The candidate was available to any visitors who came to wish him well, offer advice, or ask for a government job.

The postman delivered a great pile of mail each day, including letters from people who did not wish him well. The secretaries answered the important letters in longhand, ignoring those that were filled with hate. Lincoln had little time to write letters himself, but he read as many as he could, and his staff informed him of the contents of the rest. Grace's letter probably came into Lincoln's possession right away. A ray of sunshine would be welcome, especially after a letter demanding a job or a grim note warning that a rifle bullet would stop him before he ever reached the White House. Grace's appeal touched Lincoln so much that he immediately wrote a reply in his own hand.

Meanwhile, although she didn't really expect an answer, hope directed Grace's footsteps to the post office each day after school. One afternoon the postmaster himself approached her with an envelope marked Private. The return address was that of A. Lincoln, Springfield, Illinois! The postmaster was brimming with curiosity, but Grace did not stay to satisfy it. She darted outside and ran home to tell her family the incredible news. Eagerly she read:

Private Springfield, Ill.
Oct 19. 1860

Miss. Grace Bedell

My dear little Miss.

Your very agreeable letter of the 15th is received— I regret the necessity of saying I have no daughters— I have three sons—one seventeen, one nine, and one seven, years of age— They, with their mother, constitute my whole family— As to the whiskers, having never worn any, do you not think people would call it a piece of silly affection if I were to begin it now?

Your very sincere well-wisher

A. Lincoln.

Grace read her precious letter each night in bed until Lincoln won the election. Believing he would not grow a beard, she didn't respond to Lincoln's question, as she might have done. Yet in Springfield in early December, Lincoln told his barber, "Billy, let's give them a chance to grow."

And when the rail journey east to his inauguration was scheduled, the little town of Westfield was surprised to learn that Lincoln's train would halt there briefly. "I'll bet Old Abe's making a special stop here just see you, Gracie," people teased. Her older sisters promised to take her with them. A neighbor made a bouquet of yellow paper roses for Grace to carry just in case. When the train arrived, Grace stood on the platform, her heart thumping. Then he said crisply, "I have a little correspondent in this place, and if she is present, will she please come forward?" People near Lincoln raised their voices.

"Who is it? What is her name?"

"Grace Bedell."

A sister's boyfriend first led, then carried Grace through the crowd. Smiling, Abraham Lincoln stepped down onto the station platform. He shook hands with Grace and bent to kiss her. Tongue-tied, she raised a hand to touch the scratchy beard brushing against her face. Lincoln pointed at his full-grown adornment and said, "You see I let these whiskers grow for you, Grace." Face flaming with embarrassment, Grace ran away. She was home before she noticed that she still grasped the battered rose bouquet, most of its petals now missing. President Lincoln continued on to Washington, D.C., where he began the grave task of preserving the Union during the Civil War. During those difficult years, his whiskers made him seem more fatherly, presidential. And that is how we best remember him. When she grew up, Grace moved out to frontier Kansas. Sixty years later, as an eighty-year-old grandmother, Grace heard from a collector who had bought her Lincoln letter. Amid all the wartime papers, he told her, the president had kept her letter in a special place. She remembered: "As he bent down to kiss me, he seemed so very kind but looked very sad."

## Think About It

1. Why did Grace's neighbor give her a bouquet of paper flowers?
2. Why was Grace embarrassed when President Lincoln spoke to her?
3. Do you think Lincoln's whiskers had an impact on how people viewed him?

# People You Should Know

## Robert Smalls

Robert Smalls was born into slavery in 1839. During the Civil War, Smalls escaped the South and became a naval hero for the Union. As an enslaved man, Smalls worked on a steamship that carried guns and ammunition for the Confederacy. He and other African Americans on board seized control of the ship. They brought it to the Union Army. Smalls worked with Union forces and became the first African American ship captain in U.S. service.

## Clara Barton

Clara Barton was born in Massachusetts in 1821. Barton was working in the U.S. Patent Office in Washington, D.C., when the Civil War began. She soon volunteered to help the troops. Barton organized and delivered medicine and medical supplies. Soon after, she started serving as a nurse and earned the nickname "Angel of the Battlefield." After the war, Barton continued to offer aid to soldiers and founded the American Red Cross in 1881.

## Harriet Tubman

Harriet Tubman escaped slavery when she ran away to Philadelphia in 1849. She returned the next year to help some relatives escape. Tubman began working as a conductor on the Underground Railroad. She helped hundreds of enslaved people find freedom. During the Civil War, she used her knowledge of the Southern landscape to lead Union troops into Confederate territory. She also worked as a spy, delivering valuable information to Union leaders.

## Ulysses S. Grant

Ulysses S. Grant left his hometown in Ohio and enrolled in the United States Military Academy at West Point, New York, in 1839. Grant fought in the Mexican War but eventually resigned from the military. He returned to the military at the onset of the Civil War. Grant helped train new recruits. He went on to become a general in the Union Army. Grant accepted General Robert E. Lee's surrender to end the Civil War. Later, he would be elected the 18th president of the United States.

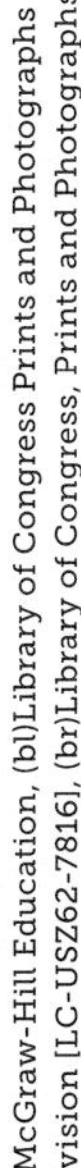

# What Tensions About Slavery Caused the Civil War?

## The Lincoln-Douglas Debates

In 1858, the race for one of Illinois's seats in the United States Senate drew national attention. One candidate was the current senator, Stephen A. Douglas, a popular Democrat. His challenger was Abraham Lincoln, a little-known Republican and former member of the U.S. House of Representatives. Before the election, Lincoln and Douglas participated in a series of seven debates, or public discussions. One key topic was slavery. The candidates held different positions.

Douglas refused to speak out against slavery. He believed in **popular sovereignty**, or allowing the people in each territory to decide on the issue of slavery themselves. This position supported the spread of slavery if the people voted in favor of it. Lincoln clearly showed that he was opposed to the spread of slavery. During a speech he gave after accepting the Republican nomination for senator, Lincoln said, "This government cannot endure permanently half-slave and half-free." Lincoln knew that the country needed to find a solution to remain united.

Lincoln impressed many people with his debating skills, but he lost the election. At the time, members of the state legislature chose the winner. There were more Democrats in the Illinois state legislature than there were Republicans, so Douglas won. Nevertheless, Lincoln did gain something valuable in the election. He earned a national reputation that encouraged Republicans to choose him as their candidate in the next presidential election.

TEXT: Abraham Lincoln. "House Divided Speech." Illinois Republican State Convention. Springfield, IL. June 16, 1858. Gilder Lehrman Collection #: GLC02533.; PHOTO: McGraw-Hill Education

**1858**
Lincoln debates Douglas.

**1859**
John Brown leads raid on Harpers Ferry.

**1860**
South Carolina is the first state to secede from Union.

**1860**
Abraham Lincoln is elected president.

**1861**
Fort Sumter is attacked.

| 1857 | 1858 | 1859 | 1860 | 1861 | 1862 |
|---|---|---|---|---|---|

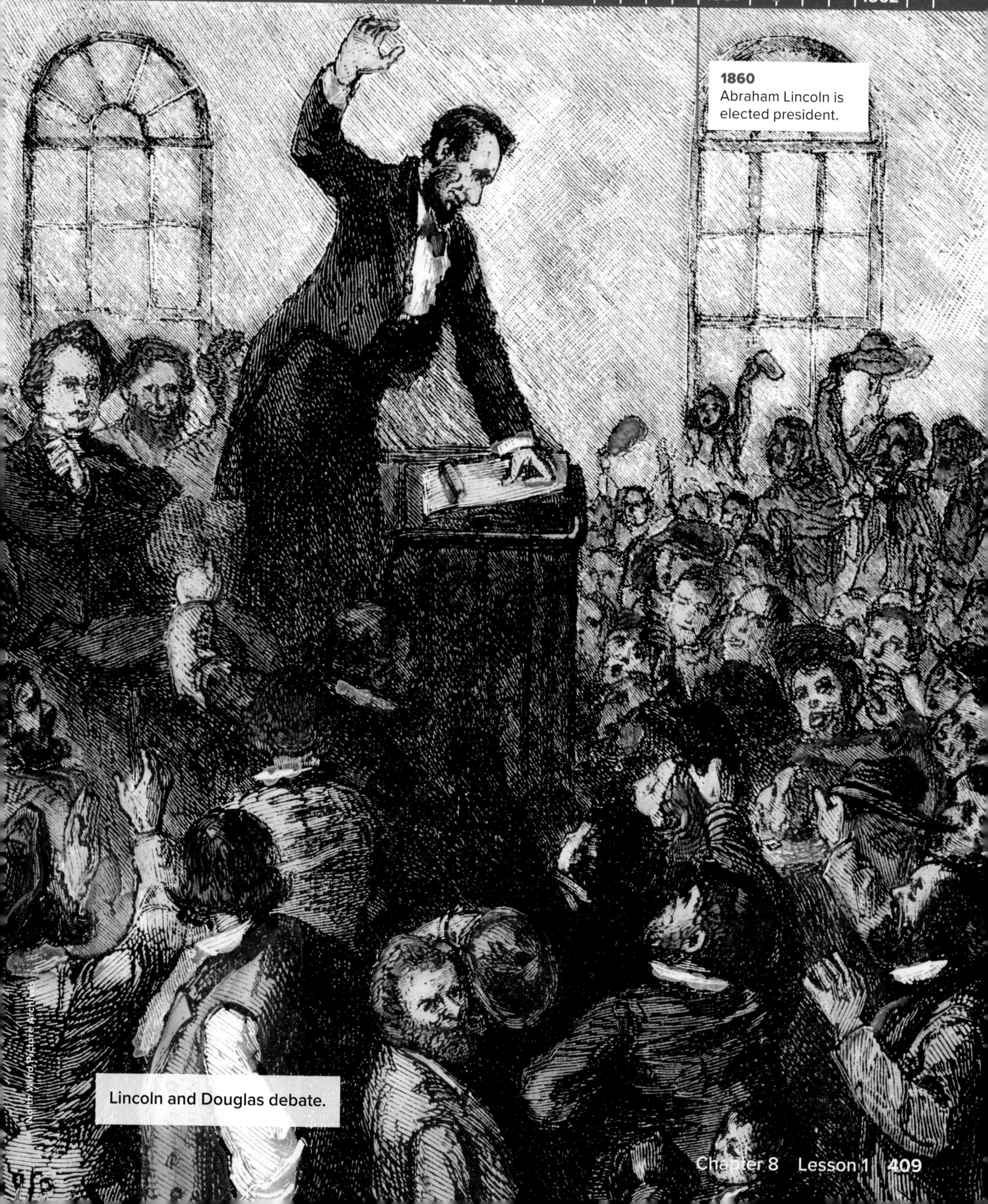

Lincoln and Douglas debate.

North Wind Picture Archives

# The Anti-Slavery Movement Becomes Violent

Across the nation, tensions rose over the issue of slavery. Some citizens began to take action. Violence broke out in Kansas in 1856. Northern abolitionists clashed with Southerners who believed slavery should be allowed in the territory. Some settlers who supported slavery burned the city of Lawrence, Kansas, to the ground. Abolitionist John Brown and his sons killed five Southerners three days later. The violence from "Bleeding Kansas" spilled over the territory's borders.

John Brown continued to fight back against slavery however he could. In 1859, Brown led an attack against a U.S. Army arsenal in Harpers Ferry, Virginia (now a part of West Virginia). The arsenal housed a large number of rifles and other weapons. Brown's plan was to arm enslaved people in a revolt against plantation owners. On October 16, Brown and a small group of followers successfully took control of the arsenal. The enslaved people nearby did not join him or start a revolt. Two days later, troops under the command of Colonel Robert E. Lee regained control of the arsenal. Brown was caught, convicted of treason, and hanged for his crimes. Southerners worried that more attacks would follow.

**Stop and Check**

COLLABORATE

**Think** With a partner, discuss the causes and effects of John Brown's actions.

**Find Details** As you read, add new information to the graphic organizer on page 311 in your Inquiry Journal.

# John Brown: Hero or Villain?

People had different views of John Brown. Some people saw him as a hero in the cause to abolish slavery. Others found his tactics too violent. Read the following quotations below and consider their different points of view.

*The Last Moments of John Brown*
**by Thomas Hovenden**

**PRIMARY SOURCE**

*"His zeal in the cause of freedom was infinitely superior to mine. Mine was as the taper light; his was as the burning sun. Mine was bounded by time; his stretched away to the silent shores of eternity. I could speak for the slave; John Brown could fight for the slave. I could live for the slave; John Brown could die for the slave."*

—**Frederick Douglass**, "John Brown: An Address," Harpers Ferry, West Virginia, May 30, 1881, reprinted in *The Colored Orator,* 1891.

*"Grim-visaged war, civil commotion, pillage and death, disunion and universal desolation thronged through the mind of John Brown. To him law was nothing, the Union was nothing, the peace and welfare of the country were nothing, the lives of the citizens of Virginia were nothing. Though a red sea of blood rolled before him, yet he lifted up his hand and cried, 'Forward.'"*

—**Daniel W. Voorhees**, *Addresses of Hon. Daniel W. Voorhees, of Indiana,* Richmond, Virginia, 1861.

**What Do You Think?** Look at the picture above. What do you think is the artist's opinion of John Brown? Do you think he would more likely agree with Douglass or Voorhees?

TEXT: (l)"John Brown: An Address by Frederick Douglass." Fourteenth Anniversary of Storer College, Harper's Ferry, WV, May 30, 1881. Dover, NH: Morning Star Job Printing House, 1881. Copy in John Brown Pamphlets, Vol. 5, Boyd B. Stutler Collection, West Virginia State Archives., (r)Daniel W. Voorhees. "Defense of John E. Cook." Charles Town, VA, 8 November 1859. In Forty Years of Oratory, ed. Harriet Cecilia Voorhees, et. al., vol. 2. Indianapolis: The Bowen-Merrill Company, 1898.; PHOTO: (t)McGraw-Hill Education, (b)The Metropolitan Museum of Art, New York, Gift of Mr. and Mrs. Carl Stoeckel, 1897

# The Election of 1860

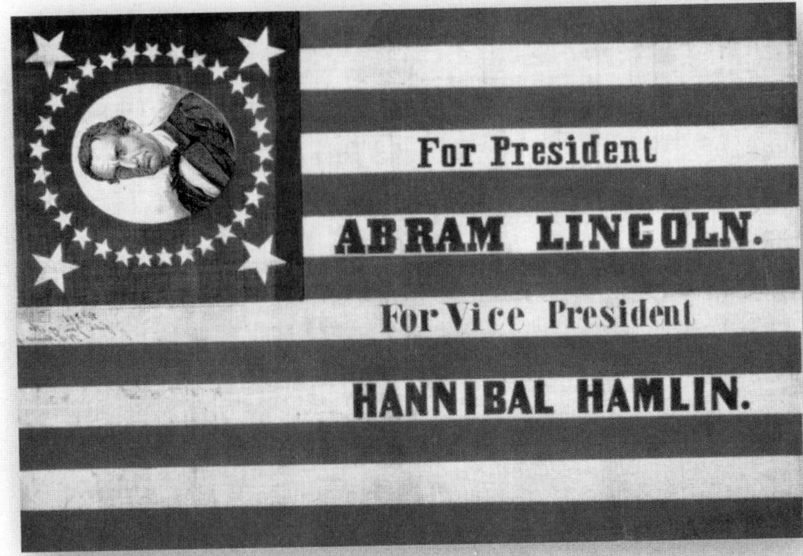


Senator Hannibal Hamlin of Maine was Lincoln's running mate.

Two years after their race for an Illinois Senate seat, Republican Abraham Lincoln and Democrat Stephen A. Douglas faced each other in another election. Both men were nominated for president of the United States in 1860. Also nominated were Southern Democrat John C. Breckinridge and John Bell, a candidate for the Constitutional Union party. Once again slavery was a key issue, and the candidates were divided on the issue. Only Lincoln took a strong stand against the spread of slavery into new territories.

Even though it was a national election, the candidates found support within different regions of the country. Lincoln and Douglas battled in the North. Breckinridge and Bell sought support in the South where Lincoln was not on ballots. On Election Day, Lincoln won nearly 40 percent of the popular vote and 180 electoral college votes out of 303. This was enough to earn Lincoln the presidency, even though he failed to win the support of any Southern states.

**Votes in the Electoral College**

**1860 Presidential Election Results**

| Candidate | Political Party | Electoral Votes |
|---|---|---|
| Abraham Lincoln | Republican | 180 |
| John C. Breckinridge | Southern Democrat | 72 |
| John Bell | Constitutional Union | 39 |
| Stephen A. Douglas | Democrat | 12 |

OR 3, CA 4, MN 4, IA 4, WI 5, MI 6, IL 11, IN 13, OH 23, MO 9, KY 12, TN 12, AR 4, TX 4, LA 6, MS 7, AL 9, GA 10, SC 8, NC 10, VA 15, FL 3, PA 27, NY 35, VT 5, NH 5, ME 8, MA 13, RI 4, CT 6, NJ 7*, DE 3, MD 8

- Lincoln (Republican)
- Breckinridge (Southern Democratic)
- Bell (Constitutional Union)
- Douglas (Democratic)
- Mixed
- Territories

* Four electors in New Jersey voted for Lincoln and three voted for Douglas.

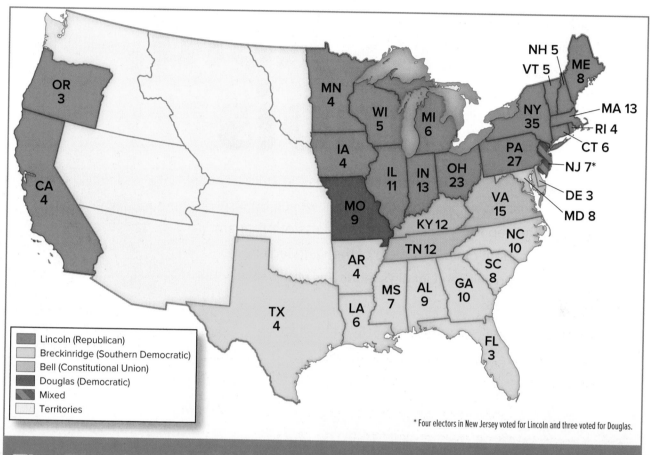

## The Election of 1860

**Map Skills** The numbers in the map represent how many electoral votes each state had. States with larger populations have more electoral votes. Why is it significant that Lincoln was popular with voters in the North?

### Stop and Check

**Think** What do these election results reveal about the state of the country in 1860?

# Springfield, Illinois

**Springfield** is located in central Illinois. It is the state's capital. It was not the first city to hold that title, however. Springfield became the capital in 1837 due to the efforts of Abraham Lincoln and eight other members of the state legislature. Today, you can still see Lincoln's legacy as you walk through the city's streets.

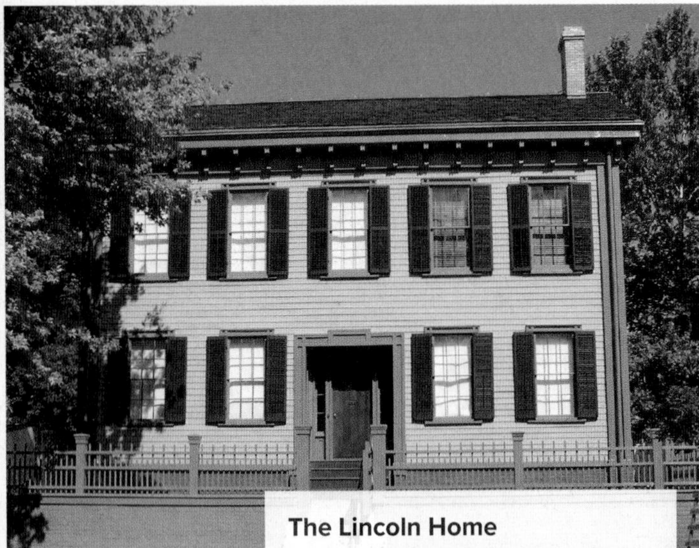

**The Lincoln Home**
Lincoln and his wife, Mary Todd, bought this house on the corner of Eighth and Jackson Streets in 1844. Three of their boys were born in the home. As their family grew, so did their house. The Lincolns remodeled, expanding the second story in 1856.

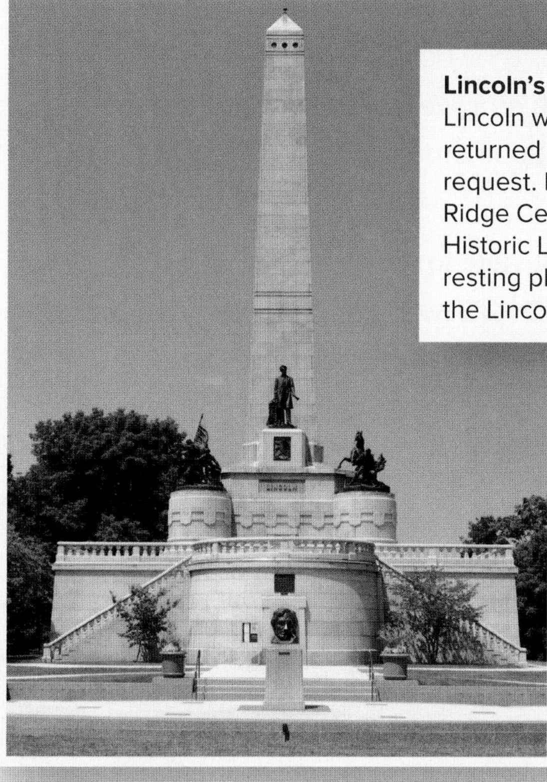

**Lincoln's Tomb**
Lincoln was assassinated in 1865. His body was returned to Springfield at Mary Todd Lincoln's request. Lincoln's 117-foot-tall tomb at the Oak Ridge Cemetery has been made a National Historic Landmark. This site is also the final resting place of Mary Todd Lincoln and three of the Lincolns' sons. It remains open to visitors.

**The Lincoln Presidential Library and Museum**
The Abraham Lincoln Presidential Library and Museum opened in 2005. It quickly became one of the most visited presidential libraries in the country. It holds 12 million books, documents, and artifacts. Among them are original copies of the Emancipation Proclamation and the Gettysburg Address. Visitors view exhibits and artifacts as they learn about Lincoln's life, family, career, and legacy.

**The Old State Capitol Building**
Located on Sixth Street, this building was the seat of state government from 1839 to 1876. Lincoln worked in the Capitol during his last term in the Illinois House of Representatives. It was also the site of his famous "House Divided" speech which included the quote, "A house divided against itself cannot stand." His law office still stands across the street.

## Stop and Check

COLLABORATE

**Talk** Why would Springfield want to preserve buildings that were important in Lincoln's life? What does that say about him?

# The South Secedes

Southern leaders worried about states' rights. They believed that each state had the right to decide on key issues, such as slavery. Lincoln was elected president on November 6, 1860. Many Southerners believed that Lincoln would try to end slavery.

In December, South Carolina became the first state to **secede**. This poster was printed only 15 minutes after the South Carolina legislature voted to secede from the Union. When first copies were handed out, the crowds of people in South Carolina cheered.

Mississippi, Florida, Alabama, Georgia, Louisiana, and Texas followed in the months before Lincoln's inauguration. The Confederate States of America, or Confederacy, was founded in February 1861.

As a new nation, they needed to establish a federal government, write new laws, print new money, and build a military. Citizens of this new Confederacy declared Richmond, Virginia, as their capital. They elected Jefferson Davis as president of the Confederacy.

Less than 100 years after the Declaration of Independence was signed, the nation was broken.

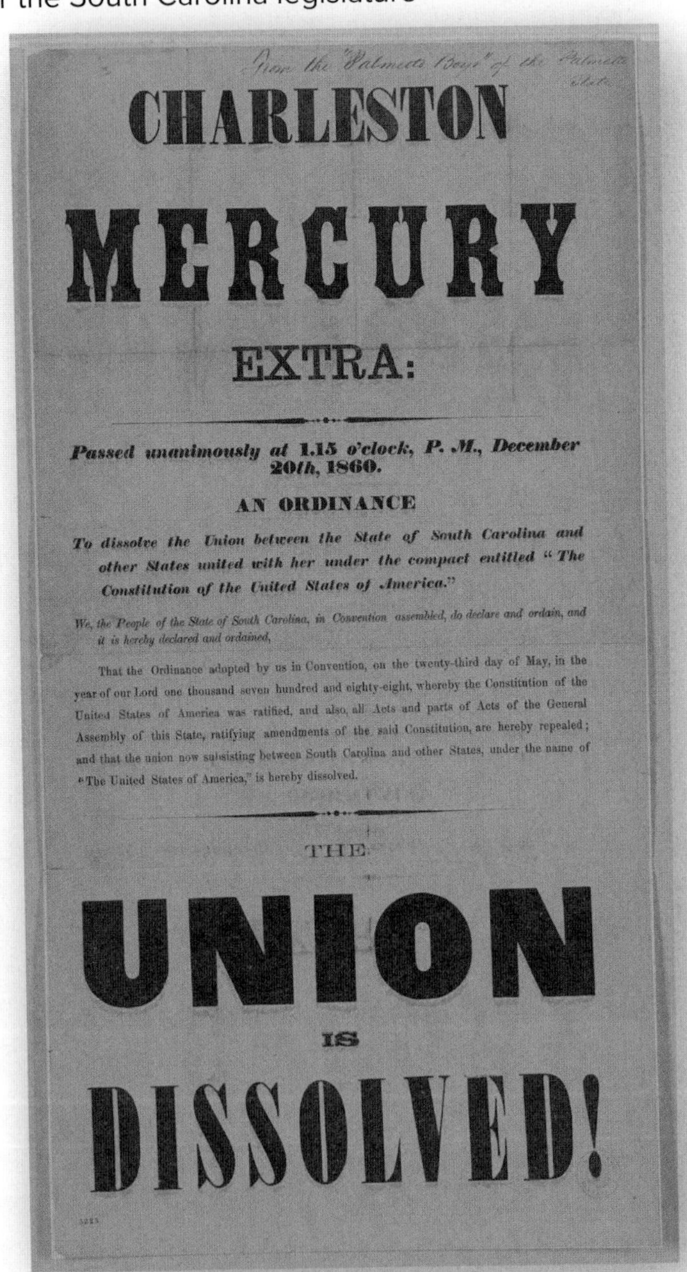

CHARLESTON

MERCURY

EXTRA:

*Passed unanimously at 1.15 o'clock, P. M., December 20th, 1860.*

AN ORDINANCE

*To dissolve the Union between the State of South Carolina and other States united with her under the compact entitled "The Constitution of the United States of America."*

*We, the People of the State of South Carolina, in Convention assembled, do declare and ordain, and it is hereby declared and ordained,*

That the Ordinance adopted by us in Convention, on the twenty-third day of May, in the year of our Lord one thousand seven hundred and eighty-eight, whereby the Constitution of the United States of America was ratified, and also, all Acts and parts of Acts of the General Assembly of this State, ratifying amendments of the said Constitution, are hereby repealed; and that the union now subsisting between South Carolina and other States, under the name of "The United States of America," is hereby dissolved.

THE

UNION

IS

DISSOLVED!

This poster was printed only 15 minutes after the South Carolina legislature voted to secede from the Union.

West Virginia separated from Virginia in 1861 and was admitted to the Union in 1863.

In February 1861, delegates met in Alabama to form the Confederate States of America.

South Carolina was the first state to secede from the Union.

Union territories
Union free state
Union slave state
Slave state seceding before siege at Ft. Sumter, April 1861
Slave state seceding after siege at Ft. Sumter, April 1861
Boundary between Union & Confederacy

## Secession of Southern States, 1861

**Map Skills** Look at the map. Locate the capitals of the Union and the Confederacy. Locate South Carolina. What do you notice about the states that left the Union first? What do you notice about the states that left the Union later?

Lincoln, in his inaugural address on March 4, 1861, stated he had no interest in ending slavery in Southern states. He said the expansion of slavery was the only major dispute. He cited the Constitution when saying that secession was unlawful. He argued it was his duty to maintain the Union. He called for a non-violent solution and said that force would not be used by the government unless the South attacked first.

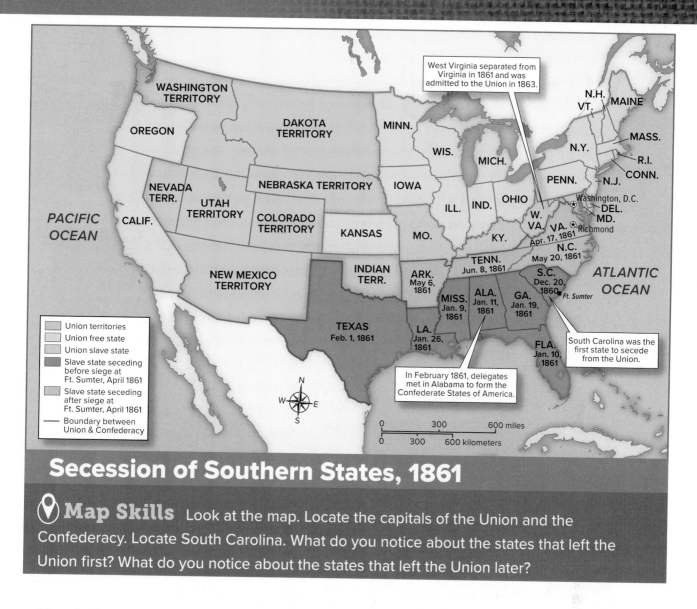


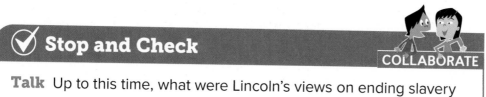

### Stop and Check

**Talk** Up to this time, what were Lincoln's views on ending slavery in the South and extending slavery to new states? Why did the Southern states secede before Lincoln's inauguration?

# War Begins!

Soon after its creation, the Confederacy began to take action against the Union. In the spring of 1861, Confederate troops seized several U.S. Army forts in the South. They surrounded Fort Sumter in the Charleston Harbor in South Carolina and demanded that the Union troops inside surrender. The troops were running out of supplies. President Lincoln had a choice to make. He could either ask the troops to leave or he could send them supplies. He worried that sending supplies could be seen as an act of war, but the troops needed help. After consulting with his advisers, Lincoln decided to send supplies. Before the supplies arrived, however, the Confederate forces fired upon Fort Sumter on April 12, 1861. The Union troops soon surrendered.

This flag was flown at Fort Sumter when it was attacked on April 12, 1861.

Three days after the attack on Fort Sumter, Lincoln called for 75,000 volunteers from the state militias to help stop the Southern rebellion. As a result, Virginia, Arkansas, North Carolina, and Tennessee seceded from the Union and joined the Confederacy. The Civil War had begun.

Fort Sumter stands on a man-made island near Charleston, South Carolina.

## PRIMARY SOURCE

### In Their Words... Maj. Robert Anderson

Having defended Fort Sumter for thirty four hours until the quarters were entirely burned the main gates destroyed by fire. The gorge walls seriously injured. The magazine surrounded by flames and its door closed from the effects of heat. Four barrells and three cartridges of powder only being available and no provisions remaining but pork. I accepted terms of evacuation offered by General Beauregard. . . .

—from the telegram sent to Secretary of War Simon Cameron.

S.S.BALTIC.OFF SANDY HOOK APR.EIGHTEENTH.TEN THIRTY A.M. .VIA NEW YORK. . HON.S.CAMERON. SECY.WAR. WASHN. HAVING DEFENDED FORT SUMTER FOR THIRTY FOUR HOURS. UNTIL THE QUARTERS WERE ENTIRELY BURNED THE MAIN GATES DESTROYED BY FIRE.THE GORGE WALLS SERIOUSLY INJURED.THE MAGAZINE SURROUNDED BY FLAMES AND ITS DOOR CLOSED FROM THE EFFECTS OF HEAT .FOUR BARRELLS AND THREE CARTRIDGES OF POWDER ONLY BEING AVAILABLE AND NO PROVISIONS REMAINING BUT PORK.I ACCEPTED TERMS OF EVACUATION OFFERED BY GENERAL BEAUREGARD BEING ON SAME OFFERED BY HIM ON THE ELEVENTH INST.PRIOR TO THE COMMENCEMENT OF HOSTILITIES AND MARCHED OUT OF THE FORT SUNDAY AFTERNOON THE FOURTEENTH INST.WITH COLORS FLYING AND DRUMS BEATING.BRINGING AWAY COMPANY AND PRIVATE PROPERTY AND SALUTING MY FLAG WITH FIFTY GUNS. ROBERT ANDERSON.MAJOR FIRST ARTILLERY.COMMANDING.

The telegram sent from the Army officer in charge of Fort Sumter, announcing their surrender to Confederate troops.

### Stop and Check

COLLABORATE

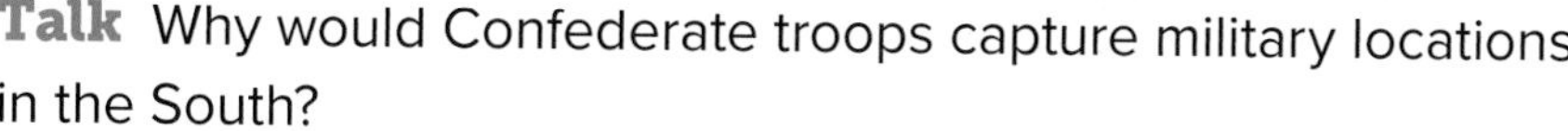

**Talk** Why would Confederate troops capture military locations in the South?

## What Do You Think?

What was the most important event that led to the outbreak of the Civil War?

# How Did Each Side Plan on Winning the Civil War?

## The Battle of Bull Run

Two and a half months after the firing on Fort Sumter, Union and Confederate forces met in battle near Manassas, Virginia. It was July of 1861. Both sides believed it would be a short war.

Brigadier General Irvin McDowell led Union troops toward the Confederate capital of Richmond, Virginia. Confederate troops led by General Pierre G. T. Beauregard stopped the Union soldiers near a small stream called Bull Run. Union troops snuck past the Confederate soldiers and crossed the stream, but the Confederate "rebels" mounted a strong defense. Among them were troops led by General Thomas J. Jackson. He earned the nickname "Stonewall" for firmly holding a hill as Union soldiers attacked.

Confederate reinforcements arrived in the afternoon and pushed the Union soldiers back across the stream. Exhausted and afraid, the Union troops began to retreat. As a result, the Union lost the battle. This defeat shocked the North.

**1861**
Union calls for volunteers to fight.

**1861**
Battle of Bull Run

**1862**
Battle of Shiloh

1860 | 1861 | 1862 | 1863

**1862**
Battle of the *Monitor* and the *Merrimack*

*The Battle of Bull Run*, lithograph by Kurz & Allison, 1889

# The Strategy of Each Side

When the war began, each side believed it had a strong **strategy** for winning. A strategy is a plan for achieving a goal over a period of time. A nation's war strategy is a plan for using the nation's resources to support its military goals. Each army or navy wants to have as many advantages as possible when it meets its enemy in combat.

## The Union Strategy

The Union's commanding general, Winfield Scott, developed the Union strategy, which a newspaper cartoonist referred to as "the Anaconda Plan." An anaconda is a snake known for squeezing its prey to death. The Union plan was to cut the Confederacy off from outside supplies on which it depended. The plan required a blockade of Southern ports and control of the Mississippi River. This would effectively squeeze the life out of the South by blocking supplies from getting in.

This strategy had a good chance of success. Most Northern farms produced food. In contrast, most Southern farms produced tobacco and cotton—crops that cannot be eaten. That meant that the South relied on imported food. Cutting off its supply would starve its citizens. A blockade would also make it difficult for the South to export its crops and receive shipments of weapons and resources from other countries.

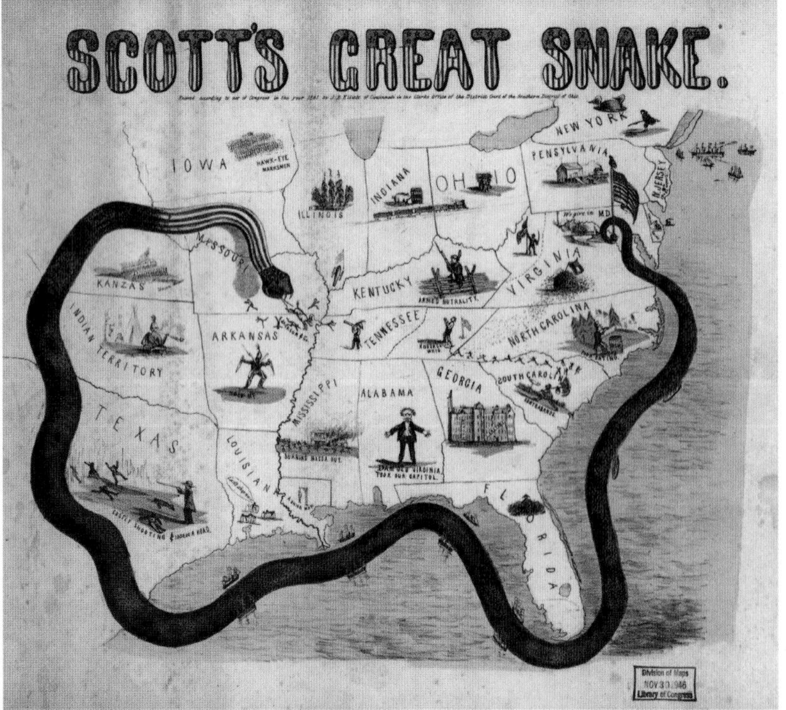


This map shows General Scott's strategy to win the war.

Library of Congress, Geography and Map Division [G3701.S5 1861 .E4 CW 11]

## The Confederate Strategy

The priority of President Jefferson Davis and his generals was to defend the Confederacy. The Confederate strategy for winning was to use its home-field advantage, meaning its knowledge of the Southern landscape. When the war began, the Confederacy called up more volunteers (400,000) than the Union was legally able to do (75,000). With a strong defense, the Confederacy planned to win battle after battle and make the Union give up.

The Confederacy had fewer factories than the North, so it looked for help from other countries. Its wealth from trade in cotton and tobacco provided resources for buying weapons from other countries. President Davis asked for help from Great Britain and France, but those countries were reluctant to get involved in a foreign war. They did not want to damage their own trade.

### Biography

Native Virginian Robert E. Lee (1807–1870) commanded the Army of Northern Virginia for most of the Civil War. When war broke out, President Lincoln offered him command of a new Union army, but Lee refused. Although he opposed secession, he was loyal to his home state.

Robert E. Lee

### Stop and Check

**Draw** Think about how the map with the snake illustrates the Union strategy. Draw a picture that illustrates the Confederate strategy.

**Find Details** As you read, add new information to the graphic organizer on page 319 in your Inquiry Journal. Read the InfoGraphic on pages 424–425 to compare the sides' resources.

# RESOURCES of The Union & The Confederacy

= major battle

Flag of the United States

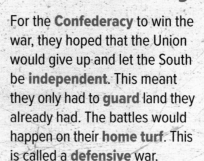

Flag of the Confederate States

## The Union

Abraham Lincoln

For the **Union** to win the war, they had to **force** the South to **surrender** and come back to the Union. This meant they had to **invade** southern land. They were fighting on **unfamiliar territory.** The North was on the **offensive.**

## The Confederacy

For the **Confederacy** to win the war, they hoped that the Union would give up and let the South be **independent**. This meant they only had to **guard** land they already had. The battles would happen on their **home turf**. This is called a **defensive** war.

Jefferson Davis

## Population

**21.5 million** | **9 million**

including

**.5 million** | **3.5 million**

**enslaved people**

Total Forces on the Battlefield

**2,672,341 soldiers**

**750,000 to 1,227,890 soldiers**

Confederate numbers are not exact because military records were incomplete or destroyed.

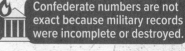

# Finance and Industry

**$263,000,000**
in bank deposits and coined money

**$74,000,000**
in bank deposits and coined money

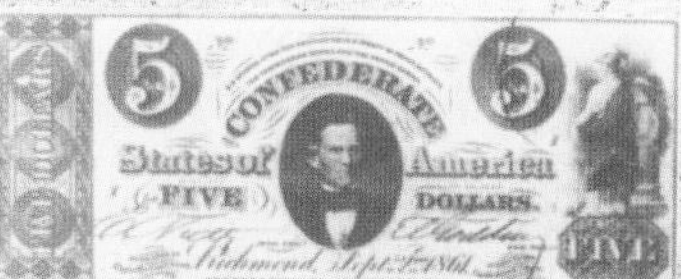


The **Confederacy:**

- grew two-thirds of the **world's** cotton supply
- had few textile factories
- relied on farming economy

The **Union:**

- had many textile factories
- made farm machinery
- made railroad supplies

**110,000 factories** **21,000 factories**

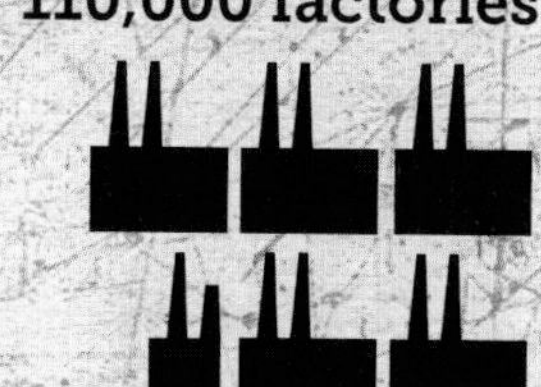

**20,000 miles of railroad** **9,000 miles of railroad**

## Agriculture

The Union had twice as many horses, too!
**3.4 million** vs. **1.7 million**

**106 million**
acres of farmland in use

**57 million**
acres of farmland in use

Northern farming became more mechanized. Southern agriculture remained labor intensive.

WHEAT
**100 million bushels**
20 million bushels

RICE
**225 million bushels**
Not much at all!

CORN
**550 million bushels**
250 million bushels

(tl)Library of Congress Prints and Photographs Division [LC-DIG-ds-11256], (tr)Library of Congress Prints and Photographs Division [LC-USZ62-93587], (cl)Library of Congress Prints and Photographs Division [LC-DIG-cwpb-01858], (cr)Library of Congress Prints and Photographs Division [LC-USZ62-51072], (b)Photo courtesy of USDA Natural Resources Conservation Service

# The Battle of Shiloh

The Union had difficulties in early battles in the East, but it achieved early successes farther west. Union General Ulysses S. Grant led western troops to Pittsburg Landing on the Tennessee River in early April 1862. He planned to attack two major Confederate railroad lines nearby. Grant's army set up several camps. Some were around a log church called the Shiloh Meeting House.

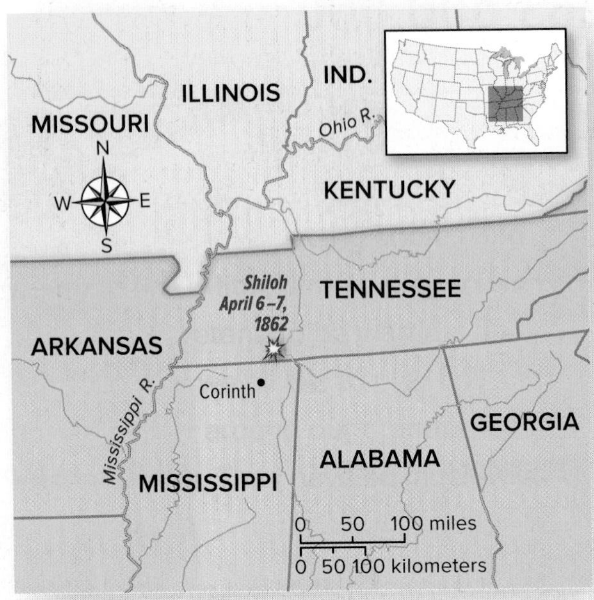


**Shiloh was part of the war's Western Theater, or area of conflict.**

A veteran of the Black Hawk War and the Mexican War, General Albert Sidney Johnston, led Confederate troops in a surprise attack on Grant's army on April 6. Confederate soldiers poured out of the woods and engaged Union troops around the church. Soldiers on both sides were inexperienced, and fighting became confused and uncoordinated. General Johnston was shot and killed. The battle stopped at nightfall. Union reinforcements arrived during the night, and on the next morning the Confederates retreated from the battlefield.

**PRIMARY SOURCE**

## In Their Words... Henry Morton Stanley, Confederate soldier

We drew nearer to the firing, and soon a sharper rattling of musketry was heard. "That is the enemy waking up," we said. Within a few minutes, there was another explosive burst of musketry, the air was pierced by many missiles, which hummed and pinged sharply by our ears, pattered through the tree-tops and brought twigs and leaves down on us. "Those are bullets," [another soldier] whispered with awe.

—from Stanley, Henry M., *The Autobiography of Henry M. Stanley* (1909)

Stanley, Henry Morton. The Autobiography of Sir Henry Morton Stanley. Edited by Dorothy Stanley. Boston: Houghton Mifflin Company, 1909.

*The Battle of Shiloh* by Henry Alexander Ogden

Unlike the Battle of Bull Run nine months earlier, Union troops outnumbered Confederate troops at Shiloh. However, both sides suffered much higher **casualties**. At Bull Run, roughly 5,000 soldiers were killed, wounded, captured, or missing. At Shiloh, this number was more than 23,000. At least 1,700 soldiers died on each side. More than 11,000 Union soldiers and almost 9,000 Confederate soldiers were wounded, captured, or missing. The Battle of Shiloh caused both sides to realize the war would be longer and bloodier than they had first expected.

## Stop and Check

COLLABORATE

**Talk** Why did the Battle of Shiloh persuade both sides that the Civil War would be long, desperate, and costly?

# Technology and the War

Both sides developed and refined technology. They communicated with telegraphs and transported troops and supplies with railroads. They fought with guns, cannons, ironclad ships, torpedo boats, and submarines.

The Confederate submarine the CSS *H. L. Hunley* tried to break the Union blockade. It sank the USS *Housatonic* near Charleston, South Carolina, but shortly afterward, the submarine sank. There were no survivors.

Railroads were vital for moving people and supplies. The Union had more than twice as much track as the Confederacy, plus at least one factory ready to produce locomotives.

Armies used the telegraph to report on battles and communicate information about enemy troops. For example, the Union used telegraphs to communicate observations from hot-air balloons. Both sides flew these "spy" balloons and used signal flags to send messages as well. Early aircraft carriers launched balloons along coasts and into rivers.

**Ironclads** were ships covered in armor. On March 8, 1862, the Confederate ironclad CSS *Virginia* badly damaged a Union fleet near Newport News, Virginia. To protect the rest of their fleet, the Union sent its ironclad *Monitor* to attack the *Virginia*. The battle took place on March 9, 1862. The *Monitor* was successful in defending the Union ships, but both sides felt victorious because neither ironclad ship was sunk. The battle is often called the "Battle of the *Monitor* and the *Merrimack*" because the *Virginia* was originally called the *Merrimack*. The battle marked the end of the era of wooden battleships.

**The Confederate submarine CSS *H. L. Hunley***

PRIMARY SOURCE

## In Their Own Words . . .
### Lieutenant Samuel Dana Green, USS *Monitor*

The fight was over now and we were victorious. . . . As we ran long side the *Minnesota*, Secretary Fox hailed us, and told us we had fought the greatest Naval battle on record and behaved as gallantly as men could. . . . The next morning at 8 o'clock we got underweigh, and stood through our fleet. Cheer after cheer went up from the Frigates and small craft for the glorious little *Monitor* and happy indeed did we all feel.

—from copy of letter written by the late Lieutenant Samuel Dana Green, U. S. Navy

The first battle of ironclad ships

**Stop and Check**

COLLABORATE

**Talk** How have the innovations that were used in the Civil War been updated for modern times?

**What Do You Think?** How did the Union and the Confederacy each plan on winning the war?

TEXT: Post, Lydia Minturn, ed. Soldiers' Letters from the Camp, Battle-Field and Prison. New York: Bunce & Huntington, 1865.; PHOTO: (t)McGraw-Hill Education, (b)Library of Congress Prints & Photographs Division [C-DIG-ppmsca-31277]

# What Was It Like to Live During the Civil War?

## Civil War Soldiers

In some ways, the Union soldiers and the Confederate soldiers who met on the battlefield in the Civil War were similar. Both groups were eager to join the army at the start of the war. Most soldiers on each side were under the age of 30. Teenage boys were part of each army, too. Some worked as drummer boys, but others lied about their age so they could **enlist** as soldiers. Many Union and Confederate soldiers worked as farmers before the war, but each side included men from a variety of occupations. Both the Union forces and the Confederate forces also included men who were not born in the United States.

Despite these similarities, the Union and Confederate troops found themselves on opposite sides of a brutal conflict. The Union soldiers wore blue uniforms, while the Confederates wore mainly gray, especially later in the war. The Union forces called the Southern forces "Rebels," and the Confederates called the troops from the North "Yankees." The Union and Confederate troops had different strengths. The Southerners had more experience in shooting, hunting, and riding. They also had a strong military background, with seven of the nation's eight military schools located in the South. The Union troops had less experience but more funding. They also had better access to supplies, since 80 percent of the nation's factories were located in the North.

**April 1862**
The Confederacy issues draft.

**March 1863**
The Union issues draft.

**April 1863**
Richmond bread riots occur.

1861 | 1862 | 1863 | 1864

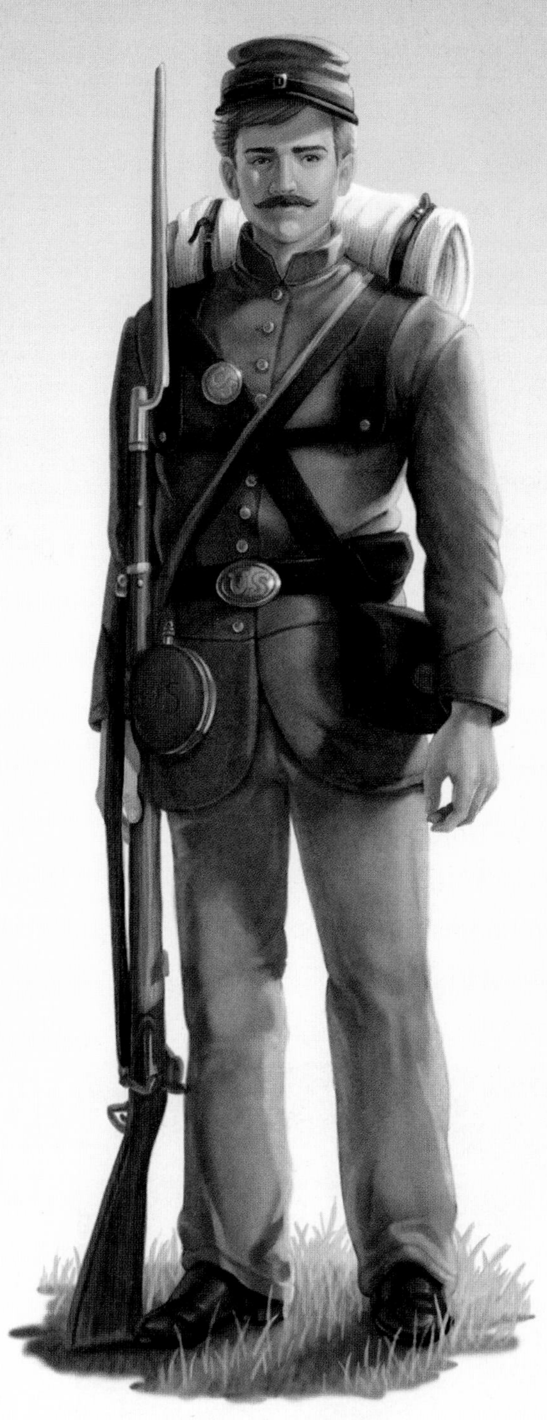

A Union soldier and a Confederate soldier

Events in Kansas reflected the split loyalties of the nation.

# Choosing Sides

Geography determined loyalties for many soldiers in the Civil War. Most Northerners fought for the Union, and most Southerners fought for the Confederacy. For others, choosing sides was difficult. This choice was especially difficult in the border states. The border states were Delaware, Kentucky, Maryland, Missouri, and West Virginia. These states allowed slavery and did not support Lincoln in the Election of 1860. Even so, they did not secede from the Union with the other slave states.

Officially, the border states remained part of the Union. However, men from border states enlisted in both sides of the conflict. This split some families and communities apart. Brothers fought against brothers. Fathers fought against their sons. Neighbors fought against neighbors.

## Did You Know

Conflict over choosing sides even affected the president's family. Lincoln's wife, Mary Todd Lincoln, was from Kentucky. When war broke out and people were deciding which side to fight for, some people in her family chose to fight for the Confederacy. Critics from the North questioned the first lady's loyalty to the Union. Southerners considered her a traitor.

# Native Americans in the Civil War

Native Americans fought on both sides of the Civil War. Some, such as the Delaware people, stayed loyal to the Union. Others, such as the Cherokee, joined the Confederacy because some members of the Cherokee Nation were slaveholders. Native American groups hoped that participating in the war would encourage positive relationships with the government. Tragically, unfair treatment of Native Americans continued both during and after the war.

No matter which side they chose during the war, Native Americans came out on the losing end. The war claimed many lives. The Cherokee, for example, lost thousands of members. Groups that signed treaties with the Confederates found that their agreements were not honored. Furthermore, the Union punished those tribes that had joined the Confederacy by relocating them or even with executions.

John Ross, Chief of the Cherokee

Native American groups loyal to the Union didn't fare much better. The Delaware people, for example, had already been relocated from the east coast to Kansas. Then after the war, they lost even this land and were forced to move into present-day Oklahoma.

John Ross was the chief of the Cherokee during the Civil War. As the war progressed, some Cherokee felt that they should side with the Union. Ross wrote letters to Abraham Lincoln to explain the Cherokee Nation's new position and to ask the Union president for support. He asked for "ample Military Protection for life and property" along with "a recognition by the [government] of the obligations of existing Treaties."

## Stop and Check

COLLABORATE

**Talk** What did Native Americans hope to gain by fighting in the Civil War?

**Find Details** As you read, add new information to the graphic organizer on page 327 in your Inquiry Journal.

# The Reality of War

In the early days of the war, men were eager to prove their patriotism by joining the Union or Confederate forces. Many believed the conflict would be resolved within a few short months, so volunteers did not hesitate to enlist. Life in military camps quickly spoiled their dreams of easily won glory.

On average, soldiers fought only one day a month or less, so most of their time was spent at camp. Food was bad and sometimes even harmful. Diseases spread easily due to unsanitary living conditions. In fact, twice as many soldiers died from disease than were killed on the battlefields. Soldiers struggled with boredom and sought ways to fill their time. Many spent hours writing letters to their loved ones, sharing their feelings and details about the hardships of war.

Union and Confederate soldiers alike were afraid that their bodies would not be able to be identified if they fell during battle. Neither army included identification tags in their uniforms, so many soldiers would write their names on a scrap of paper and pin it to their clothing.

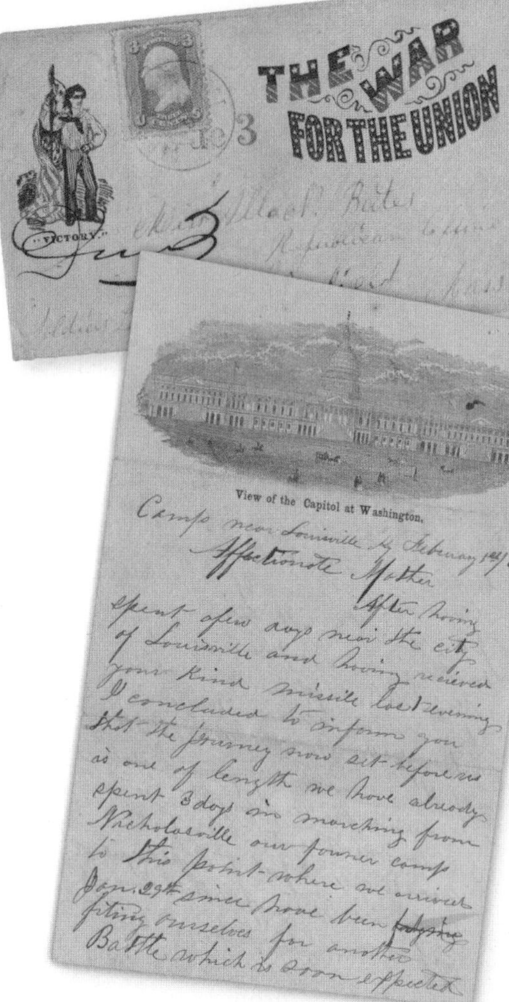


Camp near Louisville 4 February 18[illegible]
Affectionate Mother
After having spent a few days near the city of Louisville and having received your kind missile last evening I concluded to inform you that the journey now set before us is one of length we have already spent 3 days in marching from Nicholasville our former camp to this point where we arrived Jan. 29th since have been fitting ourselves for another Battle which is soon expected

Soldiers on both sides wrote letters home.

Civil War doctor kit

As the war dragged on, losses grew, and fewer men were willing to volunteer. Both sides issued a **draft**, or selection of men who were required to serve in the military. On April 16, 1862, the Confederate Congress passed a law at the request of President Jefferson Davis. The law extended the enlistment of current soldiers by three years and required all white male citizens between the ages of 18 and 35 in Southern states to enlist for a minimum of three years. Within a year, the Union called for its own draft. The Enrollment Act of 1863 required all male citizens between the ages of 20 and 45, including immigrants who planned to become citizens, to join the Union forces.

Both the Union and Confederacy made exceptions that allowed some men to avoid enlisting in the military. The Confederacy passed a law in October of 1862 that allowed slaveholders with twenty or more enslaved people to avoid the draft. Many Southerners resented the law, believing it favored wealthy slaveholders. Similarly, in the Union the Enrollment Act of 1863 gave wealthy Northern men the option to avoid the draft. A man could avoid the draft by paying $300 to another man to serve for him. This option led to riots in Northern cities, since most citizens couldn't afford to avoid the draft.

**PRIMARY SOURCE**

### In Their Words... Confederate Private Alexander Hunter

We went hungry, for six days not a morsel of bread or meat had gone in our stomachs—and our menu consisted of apple; and corn. We toasted, we burned, we stewed, we boiled, we roasted these two together, and singly, until there was not a man whose form had not caved in, . . . Our under-clothes were foul and hanging in strips, our socks worn out, and half of the men were bare-footed, many were lame and were sent to the rear. . . . Many became ill from exposure and starvation, and were left on the road.

—from a letter dated September 21, 1862

## Stop and Check

**Talk** As the war dragged on, why do you think fewer men were willing to volunteer? Discuss your answer with a partner.

InfoGraphic

# Life in a Civil War Camp

What was life like if you were a soldier during the Civil War? Some days were spent on the battlefield, but most of your days would be spent in camp. Troops were often on the move, so their means of shelter had to move with them. Soldiers mostly slept in open tents called "shelter halfs." Soldiers slept on tarred or rubberized blankets. Wool blankets were used for warmth.

## Food

Troops carried basic rations with them while they marched. Union soldiers' standard meals included hardtack, which was a hard, flavorless cracker or biscuit. Foraging, or searching for food in the countryside, was also common. Permanent camps had regular cooks, but healthy ingredients were scarce.

## Disease

Soldiers spent most of their days in close contact with each other. Outdoor living made it hard to stay clean. Lice and diseases—like measles, chickenpox, and dysentery—spread quickly from soldier to soldier.

## Activities

Soldiers completed drills to keep their skills sharp. In their free time, they enjoyed playing cards, sports, and other games. Soldiers also spent many hours sharing songs and writing letters home.

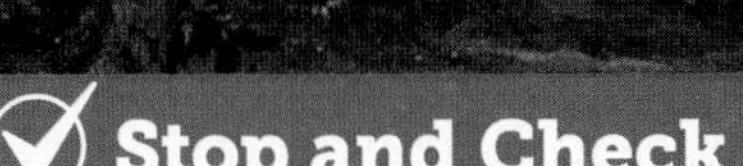


**Think** How do you think conditions in the camp affected the soldiers over the course of the war?

# The War Effort

Civilians on both sides worked hard to support the war effort. Women worked in factories, ran shops, and labored on farms. Resources were stretched thin as each side tried to support the troops' needs. Because the Union controlled most of the railroads and coastal ports, food became scarce in the South. Prices rose to ten times higher than they were in 1861. On April 2, 1863, in Richmond, Virginia, a group of more than 100 women demanded that the governor, John Letcher, find a solution to the food shortage. He failed to help. Hundreds of armed civilians joined the crowd, and a riot began. They looted the government food storehouses and nearby shops, shouting "Bread or Blood!" Letcher and Jefferson Davis threatened to respond with force, and the women went home.

***Frank Leslie's Illustrated Newspaper*** **printed this drawing of the Richmond Bread Riots on May 23, 1863.**

American women also worked as professional nurses for the first time during the Civil War. Clara Barton was one such woman. Barton served as a battlefield nurse, taking care of the wounded. She also founded the American Red Cross in 1881. Nurses took care of troops outside of the battlefield, as well. Schools, churches, and homes were turned into makeshift hospitals because most of the country lacked any healthcare system. Women who volunteered at these hospitals often treated Union and Confederate soldiers alike.

**Female volunteers treated patients on the battlefield and in makeshift hospitals.**

Some women wanted to join the fight. There were two ways women became involved in active duty. Women were barred from enlisting, but some disguised themselves as men and became soldiers. For example, Frances Clayton served with the Fourth Missouri Artillery and was wounded twice in battle. Other women served as spies. Rose O'Neal Greenhow and Belle Boyd worked as Confederate spies. These women sent messages about the Union's plans to the Confederate army. Greenhow also helped the Confederacy gain financial support in Europe. Harriet Tubman, well-known abolitionist and conductor on the Underground Railroad, was a spy for the Union and even helped lead soldiers through the South.

Frances Clayton disguised herself as a man to fight for the Union.



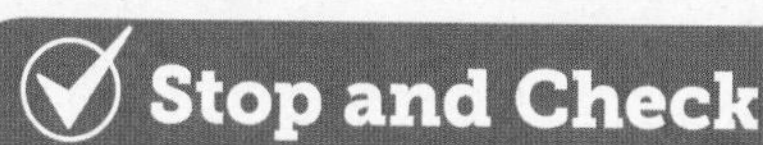

## Stop and Check

**Talk** How did women support the war effort?

**Find Details** As you read, add new information to the graphic organizer on page 327 in your Inquiry Journal.

# The African American Experience

Life for African Americans during the Civil War varied depending on their location. African Americans in the South were enslaved. Slaveholders volunteered enslaved people to serve as cooks or manual laborers in camps. Enslaved people were also forced to help build the Confederate railroad. In the North, African Americans faced discrimination because a federal law from 1792 barred them from enlisting. Lincoln and his advisers worried that allowing free African Americans to enlist in the Union army would cause the border states, where slavery was still legal, to secede. Frederick Douglass played an important role in helping convince Lincoln to allow African Americans to serve. After Lincoln issued the Emancipation Proclamation on January 1, 1863, African American men were allowed to enlist in the Union forces.

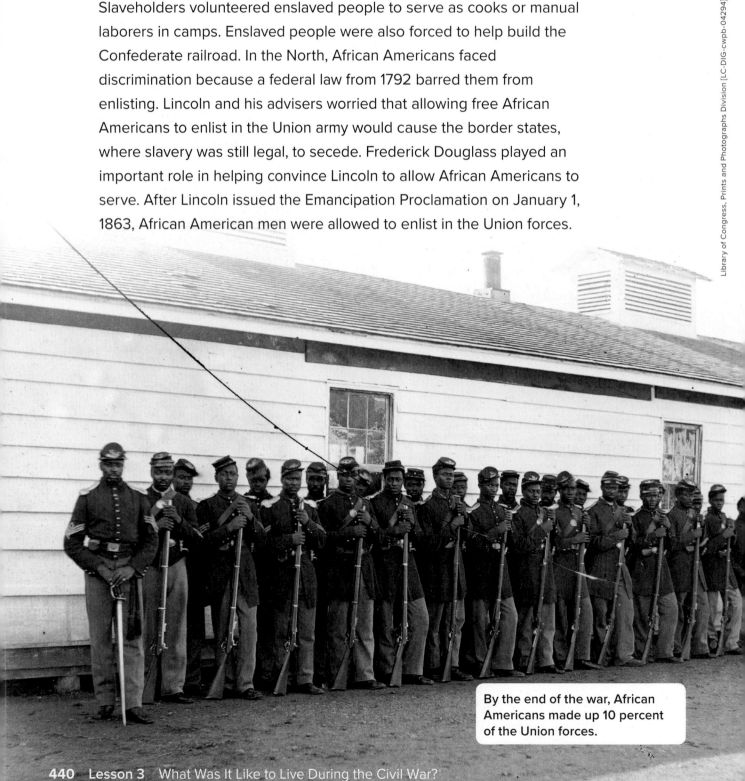

By the end of the war, African Americans made up 10 percent of the Union forces.

PRIMARY SOURCE

## In Their Words... John W. Fields, an enslaved man from Kentucky

At the beginning of the Civil War I was still at this place as a slave. It looked at the first of the war as if the South would win, as most of the big battles were won by the South. This was because we slaves stayed at home and tended the farm and kept their families.

To eliminate the solid support of the South, the Emancipation Act was passed, freeing all slaves. . . . I did not realize that I was free until 1864. I immediately resolved to run away and join the Union Army and so my brother and I went to Owensburg, Kentucky, and tried to join. My brother was taken, but I was refused as being too young. I tried at Evansville, Terre Haute, and Indianapolis but was unable to get in. I then tried to find work and was finally hired by a man at $7.00 a month. That was my first independent job.

—from an interview conducted on September 17, 1937, *Born in Slavery: Slave Narratives from the Federal Writers' Project, 1936 to 1938*

### Stop and Check

**Talk** What challenges did African Americans face during the Civil War?

**What Do You Think?** If you had lived during the Civil War, how would you have responded to the problems that people faced?

TEXT: Miller, Cecil C. "Interview with John W. Fields, Ex-Slave of Civil War Period." Lafayette, IN, 17 September 1937. In Slave Narratives. Vol. 5, Indiana Narratives. Washington, D.C., 1941. Library of Congress, Federal Writer's Project, United States Work Projects Administration (USWPA).; PHOTO: (t)McGraw-Hill Education, (b)Library of Congress, Federal Writer's Project, United States Work Projects Administration [WPA Slave Narrative Project: Container, A924, vol. 5]

# How Did Key Moments Lead to the End of the Civil War?

## The Battle of Antietam

In the fall of 1862, a series of Confederate victories in the east put General Robert E. Lee in a position to invade Union territory. Lee hoped that a Southern victory might give the Confederacy the status it needed to be recognized as a nation by European countries. Such recognition could restore the foreign market for the South's cotton.

Lee moved his tired but confident troops northward toward Maryland. Unfortunately for Lee, one of his officers lost a copy of the battle plans. A Union officer found the plans and alerted the Union commander, General George McClelland. McClelland prepared a major attack. Lee learned of the lost plans and had time to organize some of his forces for battle. The Union army was slow to get into position for the attack near Antietam Creek in western Maryland.

The Battle of Antietam began on September 17, 1862. The Union unleashed a massive offensive that nearly succeeded in breaking the Confederate lines. The battle is considered a strategic Union victory. Confederate forces had to retreat to Virginia afterwards. But the defeat could have been much worse for Lee and his soldiers if the Union had attacked sooner.

In the end, the Battle of Antietam was the bloodiest single day of combat in American military history. On the Union side, the number of killed or wounded soldiers exceeded 11,000, and Confederate casualties were more than 9,000.

**September 1862**
Battle of Antietam

**July 1863**
Battle of Gettysburg

**April 1865**
Lee surrenders to Grant at Appomattox Court House.

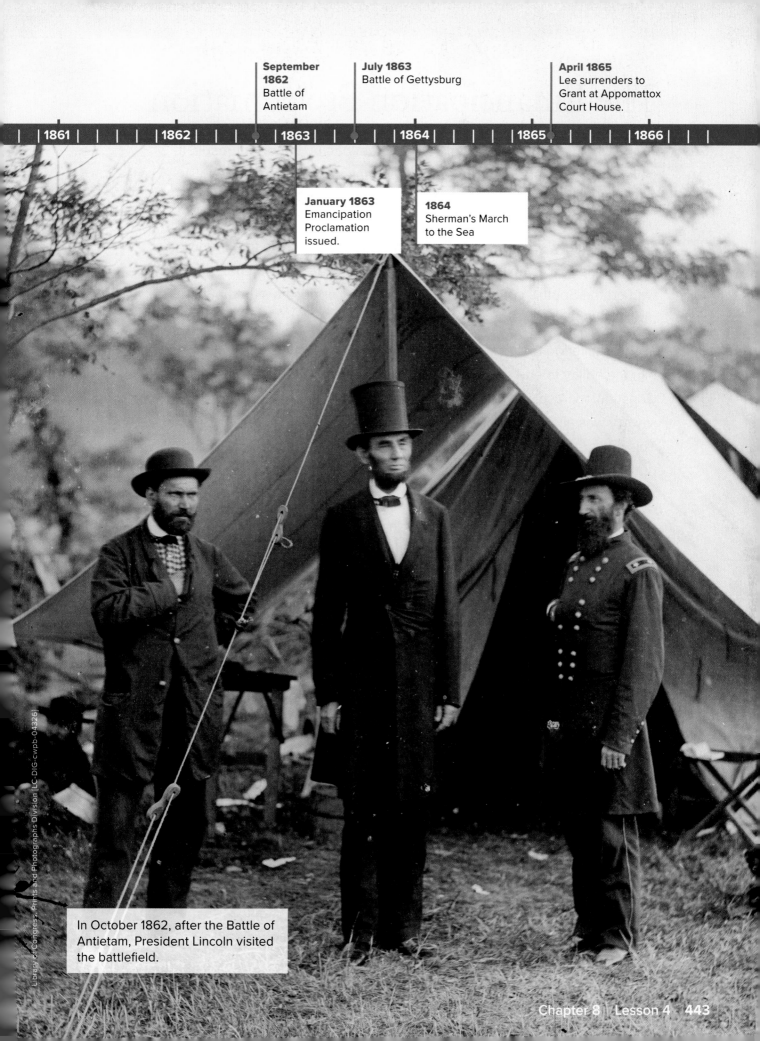

| 1861 | 1862 | 1863 | 1864 | 1865 | 1866 |

**January 1863**
Emancipation Proclamation issued.

**1864**
Sherman's March to the Sea

In October 1862, after the Battle of Antietam, President Lincoln visited the battlefield.

# The Emancipation Proclamation

The Union victory at the Battle of Antietam had an important result. It gave President Lincoln the opportunity to make the focus of the war about ending slavery. The abolitionist movement was putting pressure on him to end slavery. Taking a stand against slavery would also give the Union a military advantage. Anti-slavery nations like Britain and France would be less likely to support the South. As much as these countries wanted the South's cotton, they did not want to oppose a side that had taken a clear stand against slavery.

The challenge that Lincoln faced was that the Constitution did not give him the ability to end slavery. Lincoln did not want to go against the Constitution. Also, he did not want to lose the border states where slavery was allowed. So, he used one power allowed in the Constitution. This power let the United States seize the property of an enemy nation during war. Since the South considered enslaved people to be property, the Union could set them free.

The Emancipation Proclamation declared that all enslaved people in the Confederacy would be considered free as of January 1, 1863. It did not apply to the enslaved people in the border states since they were part of the Union. However, it was clear that if the Union won the war, all slavery would end in the United States.

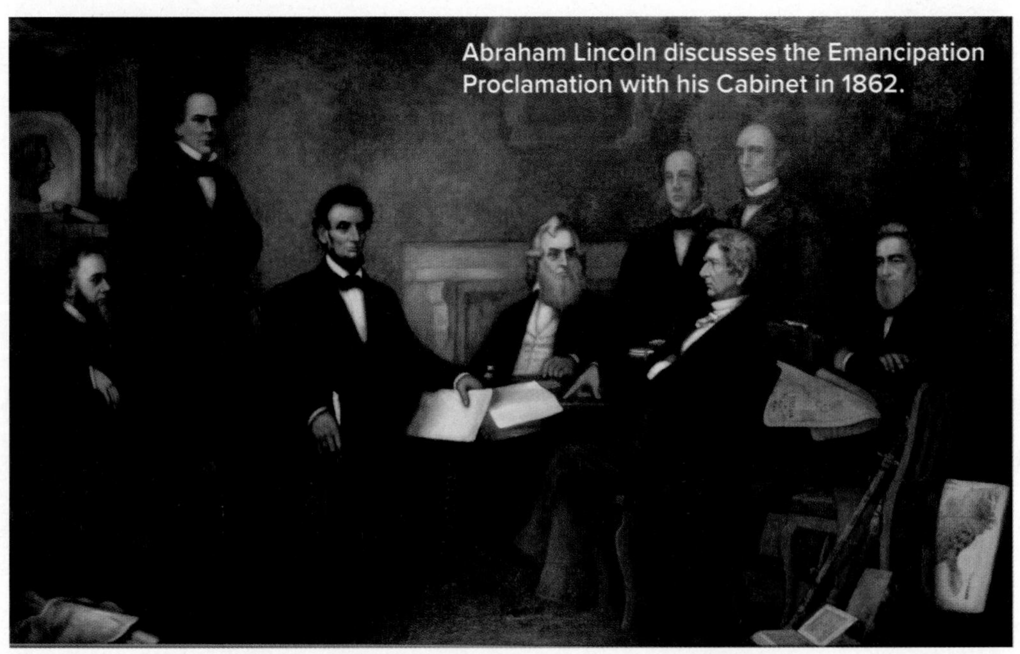

Abraham Lincoln discusses the Emancipation Proclamation with his Cabinet in 1862.

PRIMARY SOURCE

## In Their Words... Abraham Lincoln

That on the first day of January, in the year of our Lord one thousand eight hundred and sixty three, all persons held as slaves within any State or designated part of a State, the people whereof shall then be in rebellion against the United States, shall be then, thenceforward, and forever free; . . .

And I further declare and make known, that such persons of suitable condition, will be received into the armed service of the United States to garrison forts, positions, stations, and other places, and to man vessels of all sorts in said service.

And Upon this act, sincerely believed to be an act of justice, warranted by the Constitution, upon military necessity, I invoke the considerate judgment of mankind, and the gracious favor of Almighty God.

—from the Emancipation Proclamation, final draft

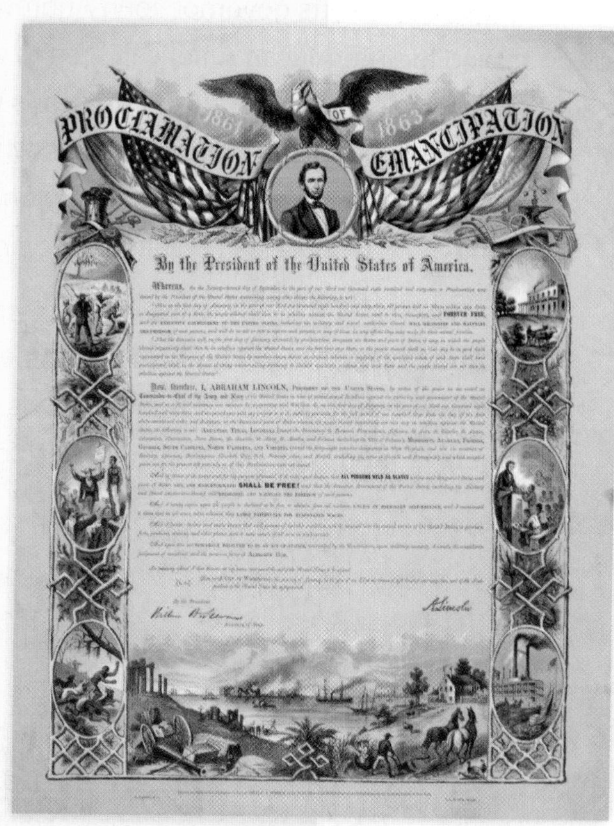

## Stop and Check

COLLABORATE

**Talk** How do you think different groups reacted to the Emancipation Proclamation?

**Find Details** As you read, add new information to the graphic organizer on page 335 in your Inquiry Journal.

TEXT: Lincoln, Abraham. "Emancipation Proclamation." Washington, D.C., January 1, 1863. Library of Congress, Rare Book and Special Collections Division, Alfred Whital Stern Collection of Lincolniana.;
PHOTO: (t)McGraw-Hill Education, (b)Library of Congress Prints & Photographs Division [LC-DIG-pga-04067]

# The 54th Massachusetts Volunteer Regiment

After President Lincoln issued the Emancipation Proclamation, the Union began to allow African Americans to join the army. African Americans were eager to join the fight. The Massachusetts 54th Volunteer Infantry Regiment was their first opportunity to do so. Members included two sons of Frederick Douglass.

Massachusetts governor John Andrew created some controversy when he called for free African American men to volunteer for the regiment. Some white people doubted that African Americans were capable of performing well as soldiers. For officers, Andrews chose white men, mostly abolitionists. These included the commanding officer, Colonel Robert Gould Shaw. As time passed, some African American privates were promoted to officer status based on good performance as soldiers.

By May 1863 the 54th Massachusetts was ready to go. The soldiers paraded through the streets of Boston. Crowds came to see this ground-breaking group of brave men. The regiment then left for the front lines.

A recruitment poster for freed African Americans

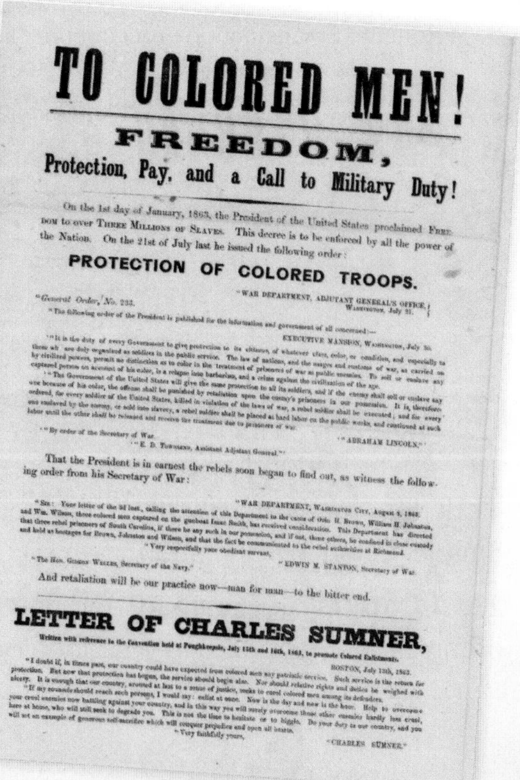

TO COLORED MEN!

FREEDOM,

Protection, Pay, and a Call to Military Duty!

On the 1st day of January, 1863, the President of the United States proclaimed FREEDOM to over THREE MILLIONS OF SLAVES. This decree is to be enforced by all the power of the Nation. On the 21st of July last he issued the following order:

PROTECTION OF COLORED TROOPS.

"ABRAHAM LINCOLN."

That the President is in earnest the rebels soon began to find out, as witness the following order from his Secretary of War:

"EDWIN M. STANTON, Secretary of War.

And retaliation will be our practice now—man for man—to the bitter end.

LETTER OF CHARLES SUMNER,

"CHARLES SUMNER."

African American Civil War Memorial

(l)NPS Photo, (r)National Archives and Records Administration [1497351]

The Union Army was trying to capture the key Confederate port of Charleston in South Carolina. The 54th Massachusetts volunteered to lead an attack on an important fort outside the city, Fort Wagner.

Despite heavy losses, the Massachusetts regiment managed to fight its way into the fort. Colonel Shaw was killed leading the charge. The regiment bravely held the fort for as long as it could. When Confederate reinforcements arrived, the Union soldiers had to retreat.

The courage shown by the troops at Fort Wagner made it clear that African American troops could fight just as well as white troops. In fact, Sergeant William H. Carney became the first African American to earn the Medal of Honor, the highest award issued by the military. By the end of the war, nearly 200,000 African Americans had joined the Union Army.

## Stop and Check

**Think** Why was it important for African Americans to be a part of the Union Army?

The 54th Massachusetts Infantry Regiment leading the attack on Fort Wagner in South Carolina in 1863

# The Turning Point of the War

Just as in 1862, major victories in Virginia gave Robert E. Lee the confidence to invade the North again in 1863. The Confederates marched through Maryland and entered Pennsylvania. Despite Lee's confidence, his soldiers were in desperate need of fresh supplies to replace worn out items such as shoes. Confederate soldiers looked for supplies anywhere they could. When one patrol entered the small farming village of Gettysburg looking for shoes, they encountered Union troops. Anticipating a battle, both sides rushed huge numbers of troops into the area. The Union took up a defensive position in hills near the village.

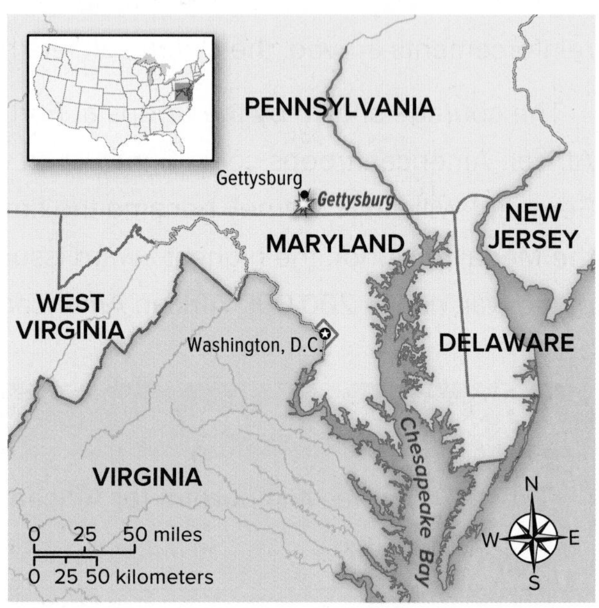


Of the war's major battles, Gettysburg took place the farthest north.

The Battle of Gettysburg was fought over the course of several days, July 1–3, 1863. Neither side could claim an easy victory. The Confederate troops repeatedly launched massive assaults against the Union forces. The Union, however, had plenty of reserve troops to answer the attacks.

The battle climaxed with what came to be known as "Pickett's Charge." On the third day of the fighting, General Lee ordered General George Pickett to charge the middle of the Union formation. Confederate soldiers formed lines about a mile wide and half a mile deep. More than 12,000 rebel soldiers ran almost one mile across an open field. More than 6,000 soldiers were killed or wounded by cannon and rifle fire from the Union army. Lee was forced to retreat on July 4.

Gettysburg would be the largest battle of the war. In all, about 51,000 soldiers were killed or wounded in the Battle of Gettysburg. This was the most of any battle ever fought in North America. The Confederacy lost such a large number of troops that it was never again able to invade the North. The Confederates' chances of winning the war took a severe blow.

## Stop and Check

**Think** Why was the Battle of Gettysburg the turning point of the war?

The Battle of Gettysburg resulted in huge losses on both sides.

# The Gettysburg Address

In November 1863, several months after the Battle of Gettysburg, President Lincoln traveled to the site of the battle. He participated in a ceremony to dedicate a cemetery there. The featured speaker, former senator Edward Everett, spoke for two hours describing the famous battle and soldiers' many acts of courage.

By contrast, Lincoln spoke for only three minutes. He started the speech by saying, "Four score and seven years ago our fathers brought forth on this continent, a new nation, conceived in Liberty, and dedicated to the proposition that all men are created equal." Lincoln then said that the people of the Union should honor the dead soldiers by continuing the war and reuniting the nation. He concluded by saying "government of the people, by the people, and for the people shall not perish from this earth."

**The Gettysburg Address is considered one of the greatest speeches in American history.**

TEXT: Lincoln, Abraham. "Hay Draft of the Gettysburg Address." Dedication of the Soldiers' National Cemetery, Gettysburg, PA, November 19, 1863. John Hay Papers, Manuscript Division, Library of Congress, Digital ID # cw0127p1.; PHOTO: Everett Historical/Shutterstock

# The Battle of Vicksburg

In July 1863, at the same time as the victory at Gettysburg, the Union won another big victory. The Confederacy had only one fort remaining along the Mississippi River, at Vicksburg, Mississippi. If the Union could gain control of this fort, it would have complete control of the river. Texas and other states west of the Mississippi would be cut off from the rest of the Confederate states, badly disrupting supply lines.

**On July 4, 1863, Confederate forces surrendered Vicksburg after a long siege.**

Taking Vicksburg was no easy task, for the fort had huge guns that could easily sink ships passing by along the Mississippi River. But Union General Ulysses S. Grant was up to the challenge.

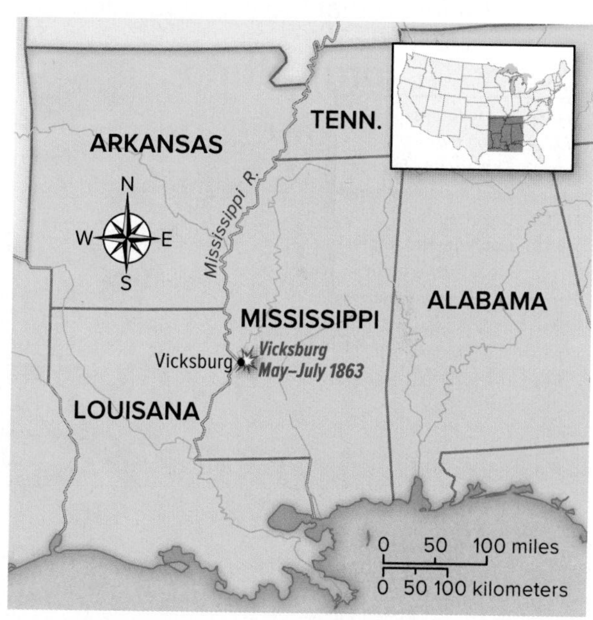


Approaching Vicksburg, Grant tried to attack the fort directly. But the Confederate forces had dug trenches and other elaborate defenses, and Grant suffered heavy losses. Instead of a direct attack, he then laid **siege** to the fort. To do this Grant's troops surrounded the area, cutting off outside supplies and support to the fort. On July 4, the half-starved Confederate forces surrendered.

The Battle of Vicksburg had achieved a key step in the Anaconda Plan. Now the Union controlled the entire Mississippi River. Impressed with Grant's military genius, Lincoln brought Grant to Washington, D.C., and made him commander of all Union armies.

## Stop and Check

COLLABORATE

**Talk** Which Union victory do you think was more important, the Battle of Gettysburg or the Battle of Vicksburg?

# The End of the War

With Grant now in the East, General William Tecumseh Sherman was put in charge of the Union armies farther west. After Vicksburg, the next Union target was Atlanta, Georgia—one of the South's largest cities and a key railroad junction. To get to Atlanta, General Sherman's troops had to overcome months of stubborn resistance by Confederate forces. Finally, in September 1864, Sherman captured and burned Atlanta.

From Atlanta, Sherman sent his troops on a "March to the Sea" through Georgia to Savannah, a key Confederate port along the Atlantic Ocean. He told his soldiers to destroy anything of value to the enemy. The 60,000 troops traveled about 300 miles, cutting a 60-mile-wide path of destruction. They terrorized the residents and sent waves of fear across the South. They burned crops and buildings. They destroyed railroads and factories. They even killed horses, cows, mules, and pigs. Sherman believed that the North needed to break the South's fighting spirit.

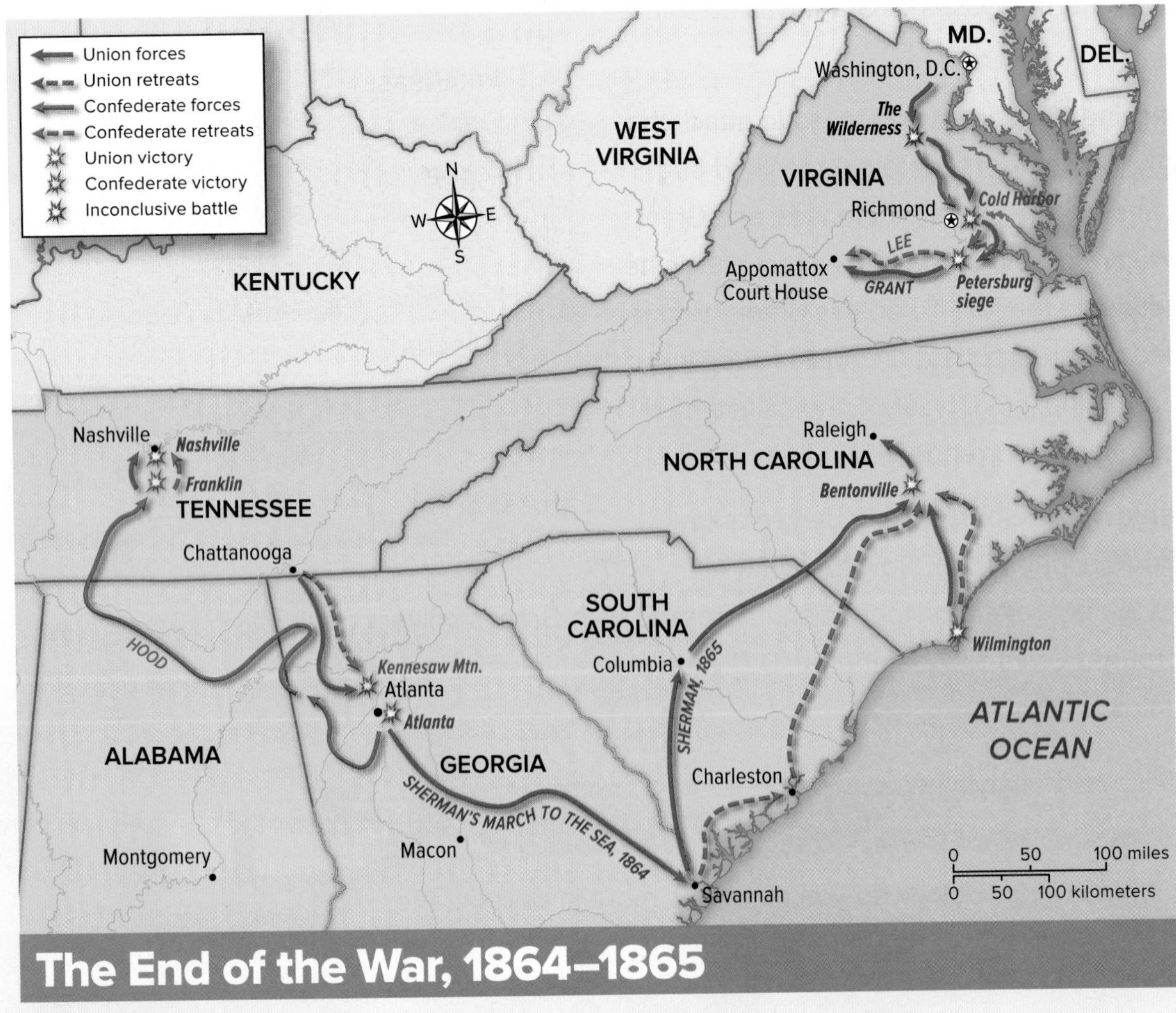


The End of the War, 1864–1865

## Battles in the East

Confederate general Robert E. Lee, *right*, surrenders to Union general Ulysses S. Grant, *left*, in April 1865.

In Virginia, General Grant used his larger army and better supplies to try to grind down the Confederate forces of Robert E. Lee. Union forces fought to surround Lee's army outside the Confederate capital of Richmond, Virginia. Lee again showed great skill as a general. He fought a clever defensive war. In the region surrounding Richmond, Lee's troops continually dug trenches from which they could defend against Union attacks.

Grant stopped attacking and laid siege to the key railroad center of Petersburg outside Richmond in June 1864. Lee had to defend Petersburg to keep his supply lines open. For months Grant slowly tightened the pressure on Lee's supplies. The Confederate troops became weak from hunger and illness.

## Surrender at Appomattox

In April 1865, Union forces took control of the last road and railroad connecting Lee's army to its supplies. Lee had to march his troops out of Petersburg to the west. The Union then cut off Lee's escape route, and Grant moved a mass of troops to confront the Confederates.

With his troops trapped with no reinforcements or supplies, Lee realized that he was out of options. Lee surrendered to Grant on April 9, 1865, at Appomattox Courthouse in Virginia. Grant offered generous terms. Lee's troops could keep their horses to help with farm work. They would not be charged with treason. Finally, the Civil War was over. The government and historians estimate that between 620,000-750,000 died and about 475,000 were wounded in the war.

### Stop and Check

COLLABORATE

**Write** What challenges did Robert E. Lee's troops face during the final battles of the war?

**What Do You Think?** What key events led to the end of the Civil War?

# What Challenges Did the United States Face After the Civil War?

## After the War

The Presidential Election of 1864 fell during the final months of the Civil War. Even though the Union was doing well, Lincoln feared that the long, bloody war would affect his chances of winning the election. Nevertheless, he won easily, with the support of nearly every state in the Union. As Lincoln prepared for his second term in office, he focused on reuniting the country. He wanted to forgive, not punish, the South. This goal was clear in his second inaugural address. In the speech, he called for "malice toward none" and "charity for all." General Robert E. Lee surrendered the largest Confederate army on April 9, 1865, and other large parts of the Confederate army surrendered in the weeks that followed.

Lincoln would not live long enough to enjoy peace after the war's end. On April 14, 1865, less than a week after Lee's surrender, Lincoln was assassinated. Lincoln was enjoying a play at Ford's Theater in Washington, D.C., when John Wilkes Booth, an actor and strong supporter of the South, snuck into his private box. Booth fired a single shot. He then jumped onto the stage, shouted the South was avenged, and then fled. Lincoln died the following day, and Vice President Andrew Johnson was sworn in as president. Lincoln's death shocked the nation.

TEXT: Abraham Lincoln. "Second Inaugural Address." Washington, D.C. March 4, 1865. Library of Congress, Manuscript Division, Abraham Lincoln Papers.; PHOTO: (t)McGraw-Hill Education

1865
Abraham Lincoln is assassinated.
1868
The Fourteenth Amendment is ratified.
1877
Reconstruction ends.
1860
1865
1870
1875
1880
1865
The Thirteenth Amendment is ratified.
1870
The Fifteenth Amendment is ratified.
Library of Congress Prints and Photographs Division

*The Assassination of President Lincoln by* Currier and Ives

# Rebuilding the South

After the war ended, there was a lot of work to be done. The work of rebuilding the South was called Reconstruction. Southern states had to rejoin the Union. New state governments needed to be established under new leaders who would work to unite the country after the war. The status of newly freed African Americans needed to be decided. Now that agriculture in the South could no longer rely on slavery, the economy needed to be rebuilt. The entire country would again use American currency. Confederate money was now worthless.

The physical damage in the South was widespread. General Sherman's troops had destroyed everything in their path as they cut their way through Georgia and then South Carolina. Most of the war's battles had taken place on Southern land. Buildings, farms, schools, and even entire cities needed to be rebuilt.

After the war, many Southern cities were in ruins.

Library of Congress Prints and Photographs Division [LC-DIG-cwpb-02660]

For Reconstruction to work, people in government would have to work together to make decisions. President Lincoln had established some plans with Congress for rebuilding the South. Lincoln hoped to focus on healing. He also wanted to help African Americans in the South. After Lincoln's assassination, President Andrew Johnson was put in charge of Reconstruction. He had his own ideas about how the nation should rebuild. In the wake of Lincoln's death, President Andrew Johnson and Congress clashed over how Reconstruction would happen.

# Reconstruction Plans

Congress wanted to help newly freed African Americans. The Radical Republicans were a powerful anti-slavery group within Congress who wanted equal rights for African Americans. Lincoln agreed with them on this issue and signed a law that created the Freedmen's Bureau. This organization provided food, clothing, housing, legal aid, and medical aid to African Americans. Poor whites in the South also received some benefits.

As the new president, Johnson did not support the Freedmen's Bureau. He and Congress also disagreed about the requirements to let Southern states back in the Union. Congress wanted to be harsher on the Southern states. Johnson **pardoned** white Southerners who pledged loyalty to the United States, except Confederate leaders. He decided that the Southern states could decide most of their own laws as they created new state governments. As a result, many states in the South passed laws called "black codes," which placed restrictions on African Americans. Johnson's refusal to stop such codes angered the Radical Republicans.

After two years of fighting with Johnson for control of Reconstruction, Congress passed the first Reconstruction Act in 1867. This act divided the South into five districts. The districts would remain under federal military control. Federal troops would occupy the South throughout the Reconstruction Era. Before the states could be fully readmitted to the Union, they had to form new state governments. They also had to write new state constitutions that outlawed slavery.

The Freedmen's Bureau opened 4,000 schools in the South.

**Stop and Check**

COLLABORATE

**Talk** Why do you think African Americans of the time needed help from the Freedmen's Bureau?

Citizenship

# Civil War Amendments

Constitutional amendments were an important part of Congress's plan to reunite the nation. Congress wanted to fix the Constitution so that slavery would never again be allowed in the United States. Congress wanted to make sure African Americans had all the rights of citizenship.

The Thirteenth Amendment was passed on February 1, 1865, before the end of the war and Lincoln's death. This amendment abolished slavery in the United States. The amendment officially became part of the Constitution on December 6, 1865, after it had been ratified by the required three-fourths of states, or 27 of 36 states at the time. With the ratification of this amendment, millions of former enslaved people were now free under the law.

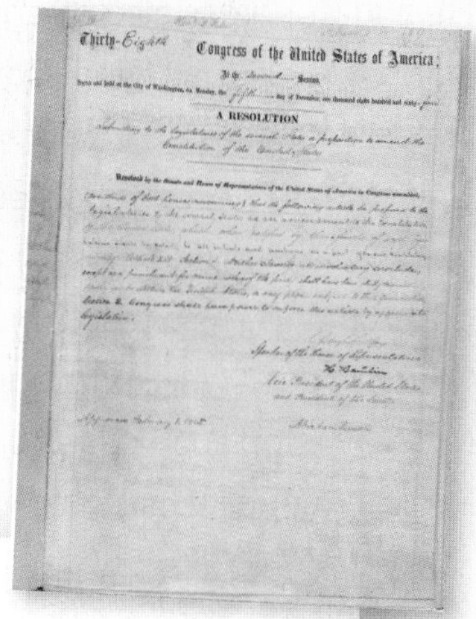
Thirty-Eighth Congress of the United States of America;

A RESOLUTION

**PRIMARY SOURCE**

## In Their Words... The Thirteenth Amendment

Neither slavery nor involuntary servitude, except as a punishment for crime whereof the party shall have been duly convicted, shall exist within the United States, or any place subject to their jurisdiction.

—from The Thirteenth Amendment to the Constitution, 1865

The Fourteenth Amendment followed in 1868. It gave full citizenship rights to African Americans and granted them the same legal status as white citizens. It also protected naturalized citizens, or people born in other countries who had already been legally granted citizenship. Citizenship was not extended to include Native Americans at this time. The Fourteenth Amendment guaranteed all citizens equal protection under the law.

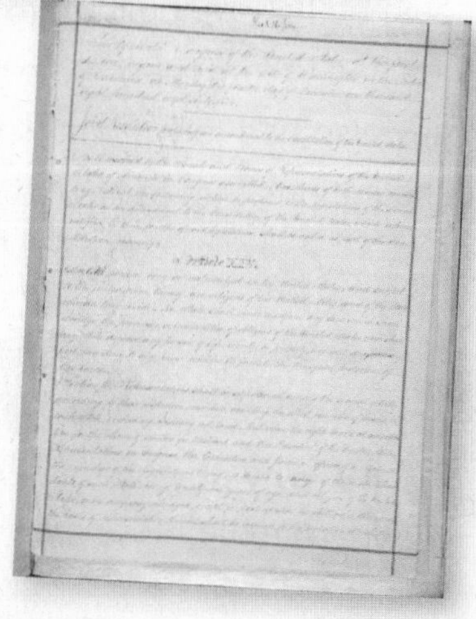

**The Thirteenth, Fourteenth, and Fifteenth Amendments were ratified during Reconstruction.**

**PRIMARY SOURCE**

## In Their Words... The Fourteenth Amendment

All persons born or naturalized in the United States, and subject to the jurisdiction thereof, are citizens of the United States and of the State wherein they reside. No State shall make or enforce any law which shall abridge the privileges or immunities of citizens of the United States; nor shall any State deprive any person of life, liberty, or property, without due process of law; nor deny to any person within its jurisdiction the equal protection of the laws.

—from The Fourteenth Amendment to the Constitution, 1868

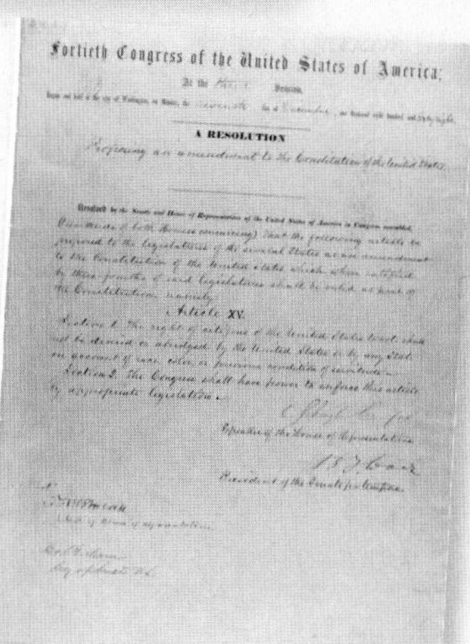
Fortieth Congress of the United States of America;

A RESOLUTION

Article XV.

Suffrage, or the right to vote, was not part of the Fourteenth Amendment. Congress wanted to secure this right for African American men. The Fifteenth Amendment made it illegal for any state to deny a man the right to vote based on race. This amendment was ratified in 1870. While this amendment made it possible for African American men to vote, it did not grant women the same right.

**PRIMARY SOURCE**

## In Their Words... The Fifteenth Amendment

The right of citizens of the United States to vote shall not be denied or abridged by the United States or by any State on account of race, color, or previous condition of servitude.

—from The Fifteenth Amendment to the Constitution, 1870

Americans have a responsibility to stand up for their own rights and for the rights of others. Reread the previous quotations from each Constitutional amendment and consider how they expanded the rights of freed African Americans.

### Stop and Check

COLLABORATE

**Talk** Why were Constitutional amendments necessary to ensure equal rights for African Americans?

TEXT: (t)U.S. Costitution, amend. 14, sec. 1. Passed by Congress June 13, 1866. Ratified July 9, 1868., (b)U.S. Costitution, amend. 15, sec. 1. Passed by Congress February 26, 1869. Ratified February 3, 1870.;
PHOTO: (t)McGraw-Hill Education, (b)National Archives and Records Administration

The first African Americans elected to Congress represented Mississippi, Alabama, South Carolina, Florida, and Georgia.



# A Step Toward Progress for African Americans

The Thirteenth, Fourteenth, and Fifteenth Amendments had some immediate positive effects on the lives of African Americans. For the first time in the nation's history, all African Americans were free and recognized as citizens. They could own land and get paid for their work.

African American men received the right to vote with the Fifteenth Amendment. In addition to voting in elections, African Americans started running for public office in large numbers. More than 600 African Americans were elected to state legislatures during Reconstruction. Another 16 were elected to the U.S. Congress. In 1870, Hiram R. Revels of Mississippi became the first African American senator, followed by Blanche K. Bruce, in 1874.

Education began to improve for African Americans as well. Before the Civil War, many Southern states had passed laws that made it illegal to teach enslaved people to read. During Reconstruction, enrollment in schools increased literacy rates among the African American population. New schools were founded for African Americans, including colleges and universities.

# The Continuing Struggle

Not everyone was in favor of the advancements of African Americans. Although African Americans were free and had new rights under the Constitution, it did not mean that everyone saw them as equals. Many white Southerners resented Reconstruction. They did not want to pay higher taxes to support new schools. They were also against African Americans holding public office. Some white Southerners turned to violence. They threatened African Americans to discourage them from voting or owning property. They raided African Americans' homes and committed murders.

African Americans also faced resistance when seeking employment. Many ended up working on farms belonging to the same people who had enslaved them. Plantation owners needed people to work their lands but lacked cash. African Americans often did not want to work directly for wages from those that had enslaved them. So, landowners allowed African Americans and poor whites to use small plots of their land in exchange for a share of the crops that were produced. This system was known as **sharecropping**.

Sharecropping gave African Americans and poor whites the opportunity to find work. But it required them to pay the landowner a share of the crops plus money for farm supplies from crops they sold. After paying the landowner what they owed, sharecroppers had very little money left over. Sometimes they earned less than they owed. Many struggled with poverty and fell into debt. Under this system, sharecroppers could not even afford to leave their jobs. All too often, sharecropping was a system that benefited the landowners and punished the sharecroppers.

## Stop and Check

COLLABORATE

**Talk** Why was sharecropping an unfair system?

**Find Details** As you read, add new information to the graphic organizer on page 343 in your Inquiry Journal.

# Reconstruction Ends

Former Union General Ulysses S. Grant was elected president in 1868. Grant approved Congress's continued plans for Reconstruction. This included a series of acts to stop racist groups from interfering with African Americans' ability to vote, run for office, or enjoy equal protection under the law. Many Southerners were tired of federal troops occupying their region. Northerners and the federal government were also getting weary of funding the Reconstruction efforts in the South. Many people were losing interest in this cause, even though reforms were incomplete.

Grant easily won reelection in 1872, but the next presidential election was a much closer contest. Democrat Samuel J. Tilden won the popular vote. The electoral vote was extremely close, and in several Southern states votes were disputed. His opponent, Republican Rutherford B. Hayes, promised to remove all Union troops from the South in exchange for electoral votes. Hayes won the election and kept his promise. Reconstruction ended in 1877.

By this time, all Southern states had been readmitted to the Union under new state governments and constitutions. Once the Union troops left, the Southern states passed a series of laws that made segregation, or the separation of people due to race, legal in the South. Under these laws, African Americans could not go to the same schools, use the same public transportation, or dine at the same restaurants as whites. Segregation led to unequal and unfair treatment of African Americans.

African American men voting in an election in Washington, D.C., during Reconstruction

CANADA

WASHINGTON TERRITORY
OREGON
MONTANA TERRITORY
IDAHO TERRITORY
WYOMING TERRITORY
DAKOTA TERRITORY
MINN.
WISCONSIN
MICHIGAN
NEW YORK
NEW HAMPSHIRE
VERMONT
MAINE
MASSACHUSETTS
RHODE ISLAND
CONNECTICUT
NEW JERSEY
DELAWARE
MARYLAND
PENN.
OHIO
IND.
ILLINOIS
IOWA
NEBRASKA 1867
NEVADA
UTAH TERRITORY
COLORADO 1876
CALIFORNIA
KANSAS
MISSOURI
KENTUCKY
W. VA.
VIRGINIA 1870
NORTH CAROLINA 1868
TENNESSEE 1868
SOUTH CAROLINA 1868
ARKANSAS 1868
INDIAN TERRITORY
ARIZONA TERRITORY
NEW MEXICO TERRITORY
TEXAS 1870
LA. 1868
MISS. 1870
ALA. 1868
GEORGIA 1870
FLORIDA 1868
PACIFIC OCEAN
ATLANTIC OCEAN
MEXICO
Gulf of Mexico
N E S W
0 200 400 miles
0 200 400 kilometers

1876 Date admitted or readmitted to Union

States of the Confederacy

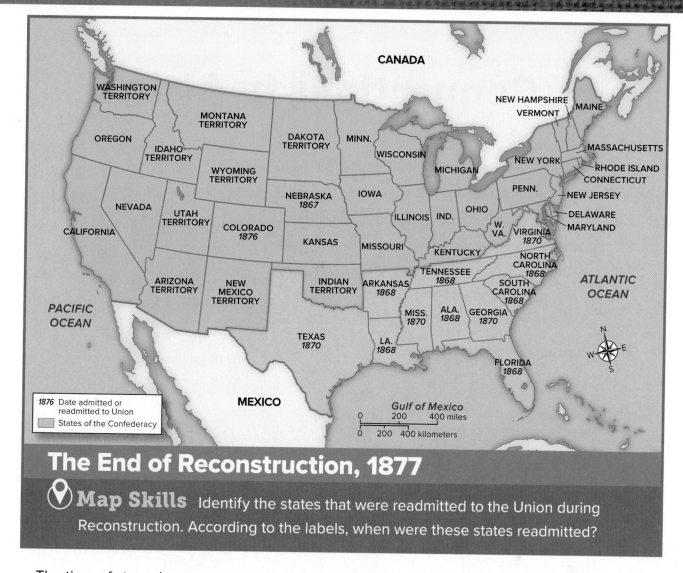

## The End of Reconstruction, 1877

**Map Skills** Identify the states that were readmitted to the Union during Reconstruction. According to the labels, when were these states readmitted?

The time of struggle was not over for African Americans. It would be many years before the progress begun during Reconstruction would be continued by a new generation of Americans.

Before the Civil War, Frederick Douglass said, "With no struggle there is no progress." This phrase rings true for all eras of history. The United States has faced many challenges, including civil war and segregation, and has endured. Lessons from our history still need to be learned. By learning from the past, Americans move closer to a more perfect Union.

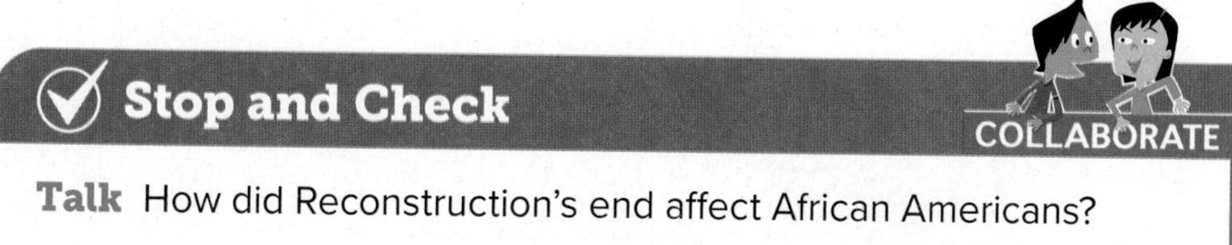


**Talk** How did Reconstruction's end affect African Americans?

**What Do You Think?** In your opinion, was Reconstruction a success or failure?

# Connections in Action!

## Back to the EQ

**Think** about the chapter Essential Question, **"What Was the Effect of the Civil War on U.S. Society?"**

- **Talk** with a partner about what you learned from the chapter. Discuss what happened in the years before, during, and after the Civil War. How did some events lead directly to others?
- **Think** about how the nation changed in structure and in attitudes during and after the war. What were the most important changes? Why?
- **Share** your ideas with the class. Then have a class discussion about how the events of the Civil War and Reconstruction have had a lasting effect on U.S. society.

# More to Explore

## How Can You Make an IMPACT?

### Write a Narrative

Write a narrative that explores the major events surrounding the Civil War. Remember to include scenes, descriptions, characters, and dialogue. You may choose to write from the point of view of the Union or the Confederate States. You should try to include a combination of perspectives.

### Share Your Narratives

Exchange narratives with your classmates. Read one another's work and have a discussion about what you thought was interesting in each other's narratives. Discuss what you learned about the Union or Confederate perspectives while writing your narrative.

### Crossword Puzzle

Create a crossword puzzle and write clues for each word in the chapter Word Bank. Exchange puzzles with a partner. Solve your partner's puzzle.

THE IMPACT TODAY

# How Have Young People in Modern Times Fought for a Better Life?

## Young People in the Civil Rights Movement

The Civil War ended slavery and resulted in amendments that were supposed to eliminate racial inequality in the United States. However, African Americans continued to experience discrimination throughout the country. In the 1950s, a movement arose that challenged racial discrimination. Young people played a critical role in these challenges.

Jim Crow laws created segregation, and African Americans were not allowed to enter many public places. This included schools that were attended by white children. The National Association for the Advancement of Colored People (NAACP) argued that the separate schools created for African American children did not provide the same quality of education that schools for white children did. NAACP lawyers filed a lawsuit in Topeka, Kansas, on behalf of 13 families. One of the families included an 11-year-old girl named Linda Brown and her father, Oliver. The case came to be known as *Brown* versus *Board of Education of Topeka*.

The U.S. Supreme Court agreed to rule on the Topeka case along with several related cases in 1954. The court gave a unanimous ruling in favor of the NAACP's argument. Segregated school districts across the country had to change their rules and allow a mix of races in their schools. This process is known as desegregation. Some communities resisted desegregation. African American students bravely faced this resistance in order to gain equal access to education.

**School children faced resistance in the struggle for school desegregation.**

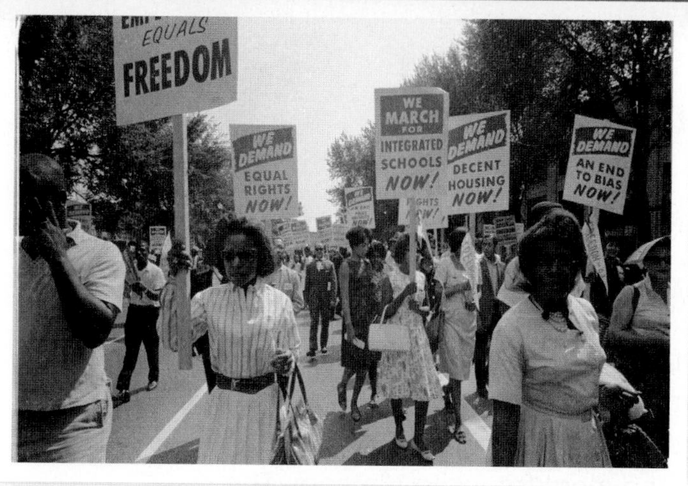


Efforts of Freedom Riders and college students protesting segregation led to massive protests for civil rights, such as the 1963 March on Washington.

Another way that young people participated in the Civil Rights Movement involved restaurants. Some department stores had lunch counters where people could order meals. In many states, Jim Crow laws forbid African Americans from being served at lunch counters. On February 1, 1960, four African American college students sat down at a segregated lunch counter in Greensboro, North Carolina, and tried to order coffee. The white service staff ignored them. The protests soon spread to lunch counters across the South. Some white people jeered at the students and poured ketchup and sugar on their heads. People who supported the protesters stopped shopping at the stores. After several months, the stores began to desegregate their lunch counters.

Some civil rights activists took great risks to end segregation. Among these were the Freedom Riders. An organization called the Congress of Racial Equality (CORE) organized the Freedom Riders. CORE wanted to integrate bus and railroad stations. The Supreme Court ruled in 1960 that segregation could not exist in stations that handled buses and trains traveling from state to state. The Freedom Riders wanted to make sure the Supreme Court ruling was followed. The group included people of all races. Many were college students. In the early 1960s, busloads of Freedom Riders repeatedly came from the North and traveled across the South. Some of the buses were attacked by mobs. In a few cases, Freedom Riders were murdered. The Freedom Riders inspired others to oppose segregation.

## WHAT IS THE IMPACT TODAY?

COLLABORATE

**Talk** Think about the various ways that young people participated in the Civil Rights Movement. How would the United States be different today if there had been no Civil Rights Movement? Support your answer using text evidence.

# Other Youth Movements of the 1960s

## Protests Against the Vietnam War

Another major protest movement of the 1960s involved the Vietnam War. The United States had become involved in the war to try to stop the spread of communism in Southeast Asia. Beginning in 1965, the U.S. government began sending more and more troops to Vietnam. The government used a draft to expand the size of U.S. military forces. In a draft, a government randomly chooses people to join the armed services. Those people who refuse to serve are put in jail. Young men had to register for the draft when they turned 18.

Young people opposed the Vietnam War for reasons other than just the draft. Some believed that the South Vietnam government was corrupt. The United States was supporting this government against communists, which included both the North Vietnamese army and southern rebels called Viet Cong. Still other U.S. opponents of the war thought too many Vietnamese civilians were being killed and injured in the war. Television broadcasts of war damage and casualties contributed to this feeling.

These opponents organized large protests in the late 1960s and early 1970s. For example, nearly 500,000 people marched against the war in November 1969 in Washington, D.C. Most of the protestors were young people, including college students. Public opposition to the war grew after four students were killed by National Guard troops during a protest at Kent State University in Ohio in 1970. The United States eventually removed its troops from Vietnam in 1973.

**Many young people in the United States protested during the late 1960s and early 1970s against U.S. involvement in the Vietnam War.**

# Protests for Voting Rights and Environmental Protection

During World War II, the minimum age for the U.S. military draft was lowered to 18. At that time Americans had to be at least 21 years old to vote. People began to ask why people who were old enough to be drafted were not old enough to vote. People under 21 who wanted to vote began using the slogan "Old enough to fight, old enough to vote."

This issue resurfaced during the Vietnam War. People who were under 21 and unhappy about the draft resented not being able to vote. The widespread anti-war protests spilled over into a movement to lower the voting age. Several states had already lowered their voting ages, but protesters demanded legislation that would lower the age in all 50 states. Public pressure led Congress to pass an amendment to the Constitution, and by July 1971 enough states had ratified it for the 26th Amendment to take effect.

Protesters rally during the first Earth Day. They are holding brooms to urge the government to clean up the environment.

Around the same time, young people were marching for another important cause: the environment. Interest in protecting the environment had received a boost in 1962 when Rachel Carson published *Silent Spring*. This book explained how pesticides were polluting water. More people began to protest for environmental action when a massive oil spill along the California coast in 1969 killed hundreds of birds. This led Senator Gaylord Nelson to organize the first Earth Day in 1970. Twenty million people engaged in protests on April 22, including thousands of events on college campuses.

Environmental action led to the passage of the Clean Air Act in 1970, the creation of the Environmental Protection Agency (EPA) in 1971, and the passage of the Clean Water Act in 1972. The level of air and water pollution steadily decreased in the United States in the years that followed.

## WHAT IS THE IMPACT TODAY?

COLLABORATE

**Talk** How were protests against the Vietnam War and protests for an 18-year-old voting age related?

What caused interest in environmental issues to increase during the 1960s?

# Young People Organize for Change Today

Young people continue to protest for their beliefs just as they did in the Civil Rights Movement and the anti-war movement. In the 1960s, television reports about the Vietnam War and its protests made an impact. Today, electronic media is making an impact. Protesters are creating campaigns that combine technology and social media with traditional protest methods, such as marches.

In 2018, students from Marjory Stoneman Douglas High School in Parkland, Florida, launched a protest movement after a violent, gun-related incident at their school. The students began their campaign by appearing on network news programs to tell about their experiences. They then set up an office and came up with a name for their movement, Never Again. They created online videos, social media accounts, and a website to tell their side of the story and raise funds.

Using social media and the money they raised, the group organized what they called the March for Our Lives in March 2018 in Washington D.C. They called for school safety primarily through additional gun control measures including bans on certain guns. The march drew about 800,000 participants and inspired marches by young people across the nation.

Not all Stoneman Douglas students held the same viewpoints. Some favored solutions that focused on enhanced school security and more modest gun control measures. Students from different sides engaged in debates both in television appearances and on social media, showing that young people can set an example for a healthy democracy.

**High school students all over the country, including in Houston, Texas, participated in the March for Our Lives protest.**

Michelmond/Alamy Stock Photo

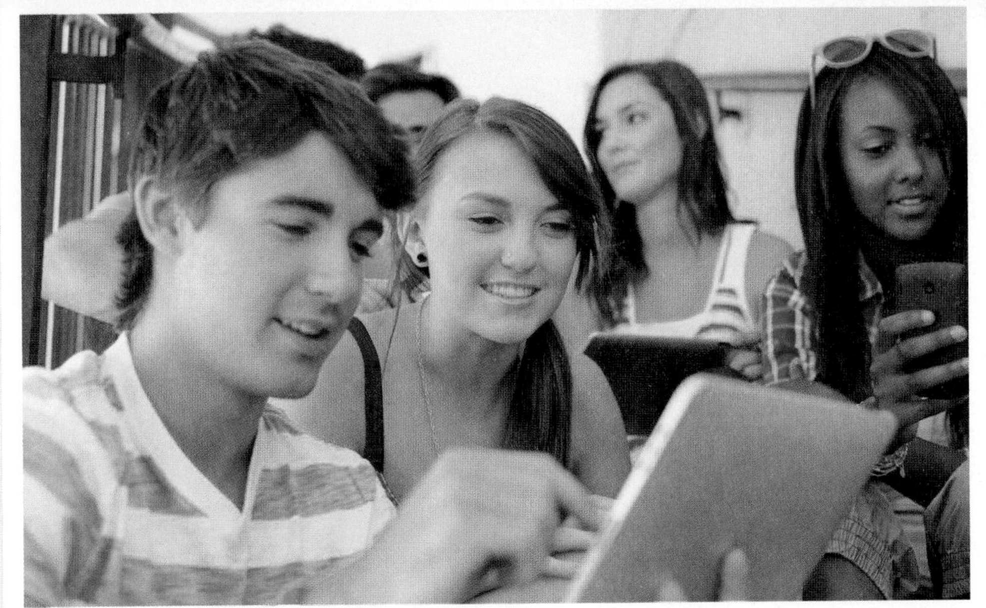

The internet and social media have made it easier for young people to be social activists. They are able to share concerns about current events and issues more quickly and more widely than in the past.

This use of technology to find solutions for social problems has been growing among young people. Many teenagers have created websites to promote tolerance and to work against stereotypes. Young people have used social media to warn about the dangers of bullying and to provide support for each other. Children in war-torn countries have shared their experiences online for the world to see.

These online efforts to combat racism, intolerance, bullying, and war have made a big impact in the real world. Community events, workshops, and entire organizations have grown out of these websites and social media campaigns.

Online media will continue to play a major role in student activism in the years to come. With the amount of time that young people spend on their devices, social media is one of the most efficient tools for voicing concerns about issues.

Other young people have taken action is recent years offline, including starting community gardens to feed the hungry, starting a lemonade stand to raise money for cancer research, inventing a device to detect lead in water, and much more. Young people show that it is possible to bring about change in one's community, nation, and around the world.



## WHAT IS THE **IMPACT** TODAY?

**COLLABORATE**

**Talk** What types of technology and media do you use? How do you think you could use that media to promote an issue that is important to you?

# Reference Sources

The Reference Section has many parts, each with a different type of information. Use this section to explore people, places, and events as you investigate and take action.

# Presidents of the United States

**1. George Washington** (1732–1799)
Years in Office: 1789–1797
Vice President: John Adams
Home State: Virginia
Political Party: Federalist
First Lady: Martha Dandridge Washington

**2. John Adams** (1735–1826)
Years in Office: 1797–1801
Vice President: Thomas Jefferson
Home State: Massachusetts
Political Party: Federalist
First Lady: Abigail Smith Adams

**3. Thomas Jefferson** (1743–1826)
Years in Office: 1801–1809
Vice President: Aaron Burr 1801–1805; George Clinton 1805–1809
Home State: Virginia
Political Party: Democratic-Republican
First Lady: (none)

**4. James Madison** (1751–1836)
Years in Office: 1809–1817
Vice President: George Clinton 1809–1812, died; Elbridge Gerry 1813–1814, died
Home State: Virginia
Political Party: Democratic-Republican
First Lady: Dolley Payne Madison

**5. James Monroe** (1758–1831)
Years in Office: 1817–1825
Vice President: Daniel D. Tompkins
Home State: Virginia
Political Party: Democratic-Republican
First Lady: Elizabeth Kortright Monroe

**6. John Quincy Adams** (1767–1848)
Years in Office: 1825–1829
Vice President: John C. Calhoun
Home State: Massachusetts
Political Party: Democratic-Republican
First Lady: Louisa Johnson Adams

**7. Andrew Jackson** (1767–1845)
Years in Office: 1829–1837
Vice President: John C. Calhoun 1829–1832 resigned; Martin Van Buren 1833–1837
Home State: Tennessee
Political Party: Democrat
First Lady: (none)

**8. Martin Van Buren** (1782–1862)
Years in Office: 1837–1841
Vice President: Richard M. Johnson
Home State: New York
Political Party: Democrat
First Lady: (none)

**9. William Henry Harrison** (1773–1841)
Years in Office: 1841 (one month); died in office
Vice President: John Tyler
Home State: Ohio
Political Party: Whig
First Lady: Anna Symmes Harrison

**10. John Tyler** (1790–1862)
Years in Office: 1841–1845
Vice President: (none)
Home State: Virginia
Political Party: Whig
First Lady: Letitia Christian Tyler, died 1842; Julia Gardiner Tyler

**11. James K. Polk** (1795–1849)
Years in Office: 1845–1849
Vice President: George M. Dallas
Home State: Tennessee
Political Party: Democrat
First Lady: Sarah Childress Polk

**12. Zachary Taylor** (1784–1850)
Years in Office: 1849–1850 (died in office)
Vice President: Millard Fillmore
Home State: Kentucky
Political Party: Whig
First Lady: Margaret Smith Taylor

**13. Millard Fillmore** (1800–1874)
Years in Office: 1850–1853
Vice President: (none)
Home State: New York
Political Party: Whig
First Lady: Abigail Powers Fillmore

**14. Franklin Pierce** (1804–1869)
Years in Office: 1853–1857
Vice President: William R. King, died 1853
Home State: New Hampshire
Political Party: Democrat
First Lady: Jane Appleton Pierce

**15. James Buchanan** (1791–1868)
Years in Office: 1857–1861
Vice President: John C. Breckinridge
Home State: Pennsylvania
Political Party: Democrat
First Lady: (none)

**16. Abraham Lincoln** (1809–1865)
Years in Office: 1861–1865 (assassinated)
Vice President: Hannibal Hamlin 1861–1865; Andrew Johnson 1865
Home State: Illinois
Political Party: Republican
First Lady: Mary Todd Lincoln

**17. Andrew Johnson** (1808–1875)
Years in Office: 1865–1869
Vice President: (none)
Home State: Tennessee
Political Party: Democrat
First Lady: Eliza McCardle Johnson

**18. Ulysses S. Grant** (1822–1885)
Years in Office: 1869–1877
Vice President: Schuyler Colfax 1869–1873; Henry Wilson 1873–1875, died
Home State: Illinois
Political Party: Republican
First Lady: Julia Dent Grant

**19. Rutherford B. Hayes** (1822–1893)
Years in Office: 1877–1881
Vice President: William A. Wheeler
Home State: Ohio
Political Party: Republican
First Lady: Lucy Webb Hayes

**20. James A. Garfield** (1831–1881)
Years in Office: 1881 (assassinated)
Vice President: Chester A. Arthur
Home State: Ohio
Political Party: Republican
First Lady: Lucretia Rudolph Garfield

**21. Chester A. Arthur** (1829–1886)
Years in Office: 1881–1885
Vice President: (none)
Home State: New York
Political Party: Republican
First Lady: (none)

**22. Grover Cleveland** (1837–1908)
Years in Office: 1885–1889
Vice President: Thomas A. Hendricks
Home State: New York
Political Party: Democrat
First Lady: Frances Folsom Cleveland

**23. Benjamin Harrison** (1833–1901)
Years in Office: 1889–1893
Vice President: Levi P. Morton
Home State: Indiana
Political Party: Republican
First Lady: Caroline Scott Harrison, died 1892

**24. Grover Cleveland** (1837–1908)
Years in Office: 1893–1897
Vice President: Adlai E. Stevenson
Home State: New York
Political Party: Democrat
First Lady: Frances Folsom Cleveland

**25. William McKinley** (1843–1901)
Years in Office: 1897–1901 (assassinated)
Vice President: Garret A. Hobart 1897–1899, died; Theodore Roosevelt 1901
Home State: Ohio
Political Party: Republican
First Lady: Ida Saxton McKinley

**26. Theodore Roosevelt** (1858–1919)
Years in Office: 1901–1909
Vice President: Charles W. Fairbanks 1905–1909
Home State: New York
Political Party: Republican
First Lady: Edith Carow Roosevelt

**27. William Howard Taft** (1857–1930)
Years in Office: 1909–1913
Vice President: James S. Sherman 1909–1912, died
Home State: Ohio
Political Party: Republican
First Lady: Helen Herron Taft

**28. Woodrow Wilson** (1856–1924)
Years in Office: 1913–1921
Vice President: Thomas R. Marshall
Home State: New Jersey
Political Party: Democrat
First Lady: Ellen Louise Axson Wilson, died 1914; Edith Bolling Galt Wilson

**29. Warren G. Harding** (1865–1923)
Years in Office: 1921–1923 (died in office)
Vice President: Calvin Coolidge
Home State: Ohio
Political Party: Republican
First Lady: Florence King Harding

**30. Calvin Coolidge** (1872–1933)
Years in Office: 1923–1929
Vice President: Charles G. Dawes 1925–1929
Home State: Massachusetts
Political Party: Republican
First Lady: Grace Goodhue Coolidge

**31. Herbert C. Hoover** (1874–1964)
Years in Office: 1929–1933
Vice President: Charles Curtis
Home State: California
Political Party: Republican
First Lady: Lou Henry Hoover

**32. Franklin D. Roosevelt** (1882–1945)
Years in Office: 1933–1945 (died in office)
Vice President: John Nance Garner 1933–1941; Henry Wallace 1941–1945; Harry S. Truman 1945
Home State: New York
Political Party: Democrat
First Lady: Anna Eleanor Roosevelt

**33. Harry S. Truman** (1884–1972)
Years in Office: 1945–1953
Vice President: Alben W. Barkley (1949–1953)
Home State: Missouri
Political Party: Democrat
First Lady: Elizabeth (Bess) Wallace Truman

(flag)Daniel Kaesler/EyeEm/GettyImages, (presidents)White House Collection/White House Historical Association

**34. Dwight D. Eisenhower** (1890–1969)
Years in Office: 1953–1961
Vice President: Richard M. Nixon
Home State: Kansas
Political Party: Republican
First Lady: Marie (Mamie) Doud Eisenhower

**35. John F. Kennedy** (1917–1963)
Years in Office: 1961–1963 (assassinated)
Vice President: Lyndon B. Johnson
Home State: Massachusetts
Political Party: Democrat
First Lady: Jacqueline Bouvier Kennedy

**36. Lyndon Baines Johnson** (1908–1973)
Years in Office: 1963–1969
Vice President: Hubert H. Humphrey
Home State: Texas
Political Party: Democrat
First Lady: Claudia (Lady Bird) Taylor Johnson

**37. Richard M. Nixon** (1913–1994)
Years in Office: 1969–1974 (resigned)
Vice President Spiro T. Agnew 1969–1973, resigned; Gerald R. Ford 1973–1974
Home State: California
Political Party: Republican
First Lady: Thelma (Pat) Ryan Nixon

**38. Gerald R. Ford** (1913–2006)
Years in Office: 1974–1977
Vice President: Nelson A. Rockefeller
Home State: Michigan
Political Party: Republican
First Lady: Elizabeth (Betty) Bloomer Ford

**39. James (Jimmy) Carter** (1924– )
Years in Office: 1977–1981
Vice President: Walter F. Mondale
Home State: Georgia
Political Party: Democrat
First Lady: Rosalynn Smith Carter

**40. Ronald W. Reagan** (1911–2004)
Years in Office: 1981–1989
Vice President: George H. W. Bush
Home State: California
Political Party: Republican
First Lady: Nancy Davis Reagan

**41. George H. W. Bush** (1924– )
Years in Office: 1989–1993
Vice President: J. Danforth (Dan) Quayle
Home State: Texas
Political Party: Republican
First Lady: Barbara Pierce Bush

**42. William Jefferson Clinton** (1946– )
Years in Office: 1993–2001
Vice President: Albert Gore, Jr.
Home State: Arkansas
Political Party: Democrat
First Lady: Hillary Rodham Clinton

**43. George W. Bush** (1946– )
Years in Office: 2001–2009
Vice President: Richard Cheney
Home State: Texas
Political Party: Republican
First Lady: Laura Welch Bush

**44. Barack H. Obama** (1961– )
Years in Office: 2009–2017
Vice President: Joseph (Joe) Biden
Home State: Illinois
Political Party: Democrat
First Lady : Michelle LaVaughn Robinson Obama

**45. Donald John Trump** (1946– )
Years in: Office 2017 –
Vice President: Michael Richard (Mike) Pence
Home State: New York
Political Party: Republican
First Lady: Melania Knavs Trump

(t)McGraw-Hill Education, (presidents 34-43)White House Historical Association, (presidents 44, 45)Whitehouse.gov

# The Themes of Geography

To show how our world is connected, some geographers have divided the study of geography into five different themes. The themes are location, place, region, movement, and human interaction. Understanding these themes of geography will help you understand historical events.

## Location

In geography, location means a place on Earth's surface. A location can be defined in different ways. One way is by street name and number. You write a location when you address a letter. Places can also be located by a set of numbers. These numbers refer to a geographical grid system called latitude and longitude.

## Place

Each place on Earth has physical features such as rivers, mountains, or valleys. Its different features make each place unique. A mountain peak, for example, has very different features from an ocean beach. Most places also have human characteristics. These include population densities, major cities, or languages and religions. Descriptions of most places are combinations of both their human and physical features.

## Region

A region is bigger than a place or a location. Regions cover large areas of land that share physical or human characteristics. The Mountain States of America, for example, share a dry climate and high mountains. The Middle West is known for its farms.

## Movement

Throughout history, wars, economic troubles, or climate changes have caused people to move from one place to another. As people moved, they often made changes to a place. Geographers study why these movements occurred. They also look at how movement changed the culture and physical landscape of an area.

## Human Interaction

Geographers are interested in how the environment influences people. Hot areas, for example, draw people to the beach. Cold areas draw people to the ski slopes. Geographers also study how people interact with, or affect, their environment. This human interaction determines how land is used for recreation, housing, and industry.

# Dictionary of Geographic Words

1 CANAL A channel built to carry water for irrigation or transportation

2 CANYON A deep, narrow valley with steep sides

3 COAST The land along an ocean

4 DAM A wall built across a river, creating a lake that stores water

5 DELTA Land made of soil left behind as a river drains into a larger body of water

6 DESERT A dry environment with few plants and animals

7 GLACIER A huge sheet of ice that moves slowly across the land

8 GULF Part of an ocean that extends into the land; larger than a bay

9 HARBOR A sheltered place along a coast where boats dock safely

10 HILL A rounded, raised landform; not as high as a mountain

11 ISLAND A body of land completely surrounded by water

12 LAKE A body of water completely surrounded by land

13 MOUNTAIN A high landform with steep sides; higher than a hill

14 MOUNTAIN PASS A narrow gap through a mountain range

15 MOUNTAIN RANGE A row or chain of mountains

16 MOUTH The place where a river empties into a larger body of water

17 OASIS A fertile area in a desert that is watered by a spring

18 OCEAN A large body of salt water; oceans cover much of Earth's surface

19 PEAK The top of a mountain

20 PENINSULA A body of land nearly surrounded by water

21 PLAIN A large area of nearly flat land

22 PLATEAU A high, flat area that rises steeply above the surrounding land

23 PORT A city where ships load and unload goods

24 RESERVOIR A natural or artificial lake used to store water

25 RIVER A stream of water that flows across the land and empties into another body of water

26 RIVER BASIN All the land that is drained by a river and its tributaries

27 SOURCE The starting point of a river

28 TRIBUTARY A smaller river that flows into a larger river

29 VALLEY An area of low land between hills or mountains

30 VOLCANO An opening in Earth's surface through which hot rock and ash are forced out

# United States: Political

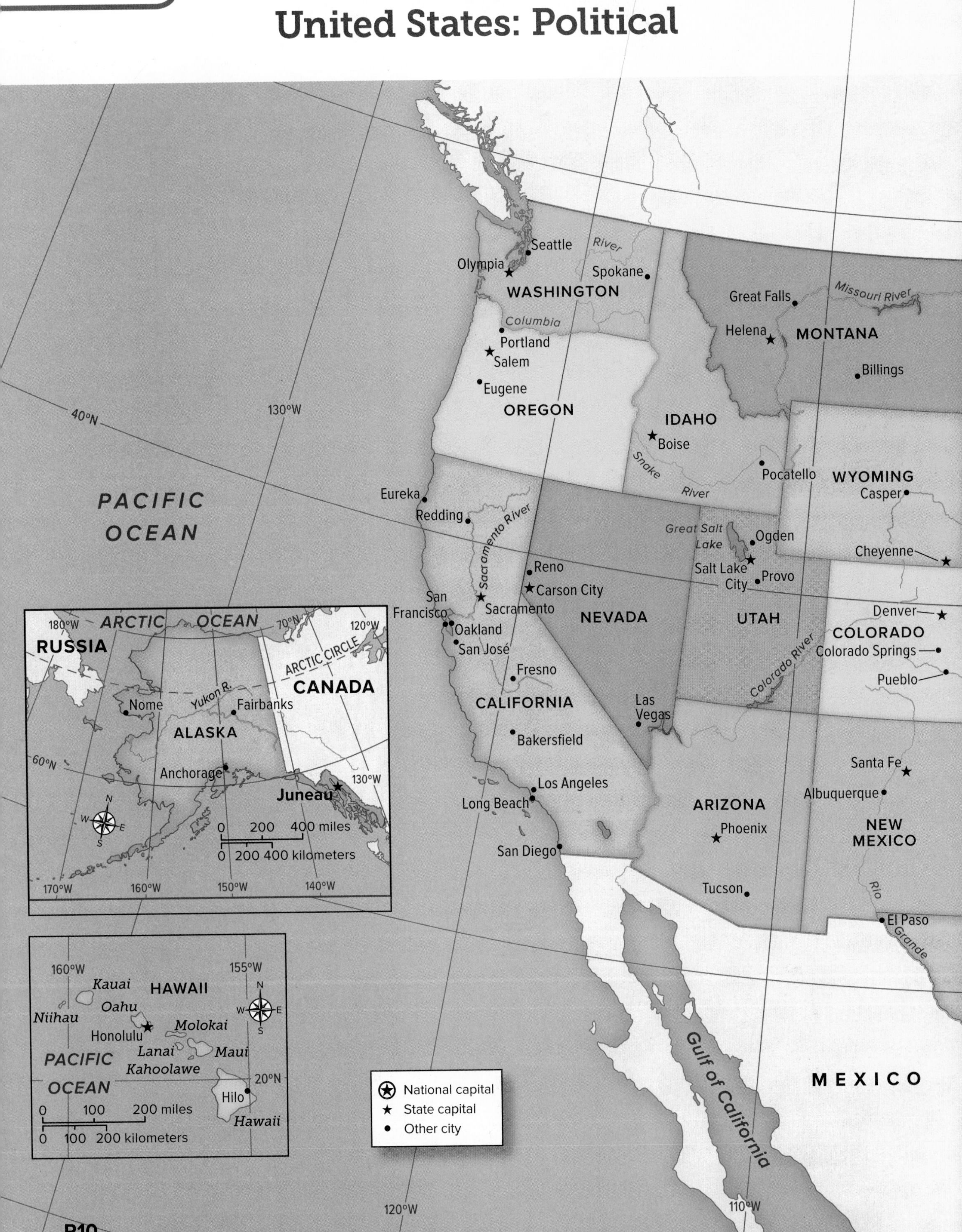
PACIFIC OCEAN
WASHINGTON
Seattle
Olympia
Spokane
River
Columbia
OREGON
Portland
Salem
Eugene
IDAHO
Boise
Snake River
Pocatello
MONTANA
Great Falls
Missouri River
Helena
Billings
WYOMING
Casper
Cheyenne
Eureka
Redding
Sacramento River
Reno
Carson City
San Francisco
Sacramento
Oakland
San José
NEVADA
Great Salt Lake
Ogden
Salt Lake City
Provo
UTAH
Denver
COLORADO
Colorado Springs
Pueblo
Colorado River
Fresno
CALIFORNIA
Las Vegas
Bakersfield
Los Angeles
Long Beach
San Diego
ARIZONA
Phoenix
Tucson
Santa Fe
Albuquerque
NEW MEXICO
El Paso
Rio Grande
Gulf of California
MEXICO
40°N
130°W
120°W
110°W
RUSSIA
ARCTIC OCEAN
ARCTIC CIRCLE
CANADA
Yukon R.
Nome
Fairbanks
ALASKA
Anchorage
Juneau
180°W
70°N
120°W
60°N
130°W
170°W
160°W
150°W
140°W
0 200 400 miles
0 200 400 kilometers
HAWAII
Kauai
Niihau
Oahu
Honolulu
Molokai
Lanai
Maui
Kahoolawe
Hilo
Hawaii
PACIFIC OCEAN
160°W
155°W
20°N
0 100 200 miles
0 100 200 kilometers
National capital
State capital
Other city

CANADA
NORTH DAKOTA
Grand Forks
Fargo
Bismarck
SOUTH DAKOTA
Pierre
Sioux Falls
MINNESOTA
Duluth
St. Paul
Minneapolis
Lake Superior
WISCONSIN
Green Bay
Milwaukee
Madison
MICHIGAN
Lake Michigan
Grand Rapids
Lansing
Detroit
Lake Huron
Lake Ontario
Lake Erie
NEBRASKA
Omaha
Lincoln
Platte River
Missouri River
IOWA
Cedar Rapids
Des Moines
Davenport
ILLINOIS
Chicago
Gary
Springfield
INDIANA
Indianapolis
Evansville
OHIO
Toledo
Cleveland
Columbus
Cincinnati
Ohio River
KANSAS
Topeka
Wichita
Kansas City
Kansas City
MISSOURI
St. Louis
Jefferson City
KENTUCKY
Frankfort
Louisville
TENNESSEE
Nashville
Memphis
Knoxville
Tennessee River
Mississippi River
OKLAHOMA
Oklahoma City
Tulsa
Arkansas River
Red River
ARKANSAS
Fort Smith
Little Rock
TEXAS
Dallas
Fort Worth
Austin
Houston
San Antonio
Laredo
Corpus Christi
Brazos River
Colorado River
LOUISIANA
Shreveport
Baton Rouge
New Orleans
MISSISSIPPI
Jackson
Biloxi
ALABAMA
Birmingham
Montgomery
Mobile
GEORGIA
Atlanta
Columbus
Savannah
FLORIDA
Tallahassee
Jacksonville
Orlando
Tampa
Miami
SOUTH CAROLINA
Columbia
Charleston
NORTH CAROLINA
Raleigh
Charlotte
VIRGINIA
Richmond
Norfolk
WEST VIRGINIA
Charleston
Washington, D.C.
MARYLAND
Baltimore
Annapolis
DELAWARE
Dover
PENNSYLVANIA
Pittsburgh
Harrisburg
Philadelphia
NEW JERSEY
Trenton
Newark
NEW YORK
New York
Buffalo
Albany
CONNECTICUT
Hartford
RHODE ISLAND
Providence
MASSACHUSETTS
Boston
VERMONT
Montpelier
NEW HAMPSHIRE
Concord
MAINE
Augusta
Portland
ATLANTIC OCEAN
Gulf of Mexico
THE BAHAMAS
50°N
40°N
30°N
70°W
80°W
90°W
N
S
E
W
0
200
400 miles
0
200
400 kilometers
McGraw-Hill Education

# United States: Physical

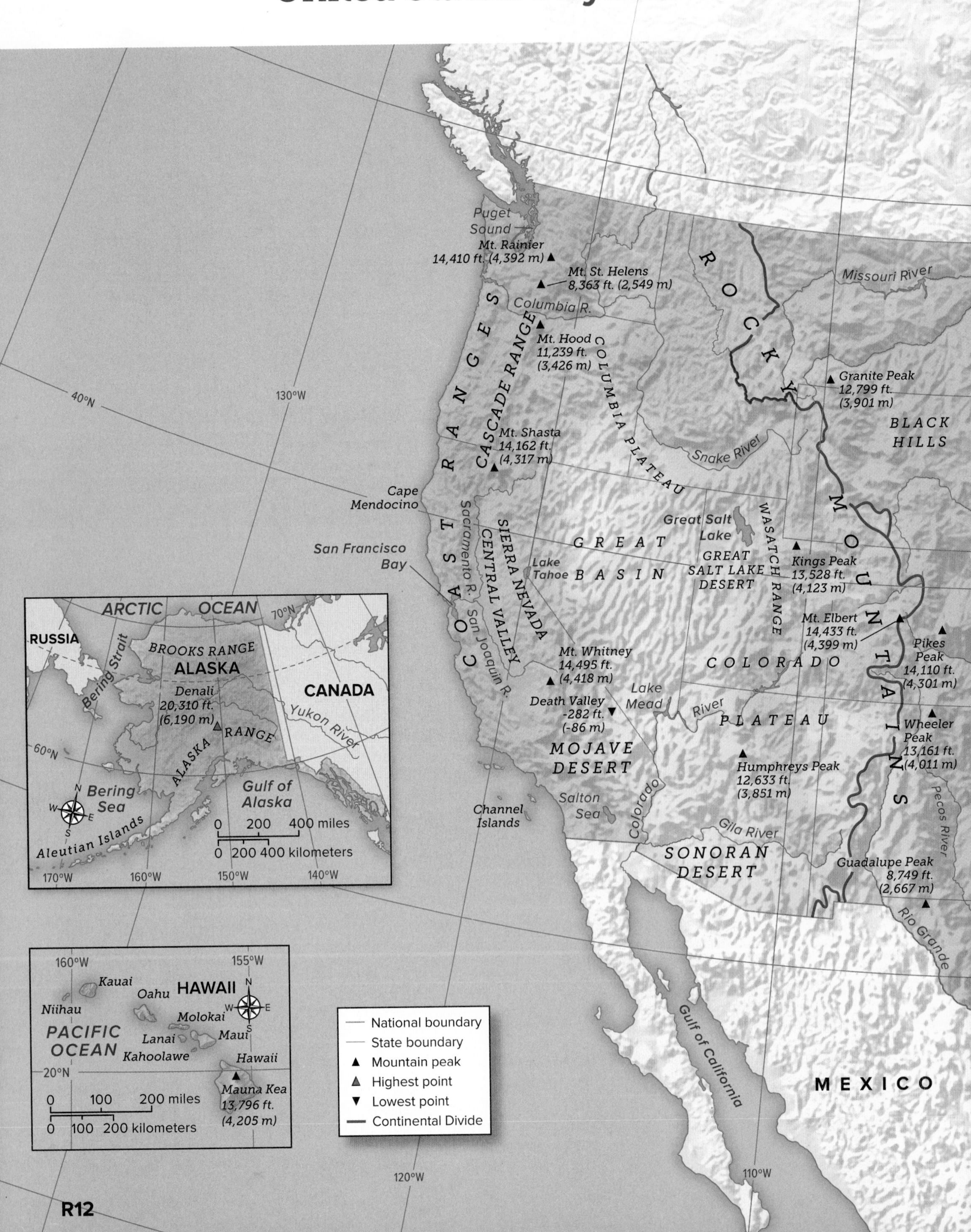

Puget Sound
Mt. Rainier 14,410 ft. (4,392 m)
Mt. St. Helens 8,363 ft. (2,549 m)
Columbia R.
Mt. Hood 11,239 ft. (3,426 m)
CASCADE RANGE
COLUMBIA PLATEAU
Mt. Shasta 14,162 ft. (4,317 m)
COAST RANGES
ROCKY MOUNTAINS
Missouri River
Granite Peak 12,799 ft. (3,901 m)
BLACK HILLS
Snake River
Cape Mendocino
San Francisco Bay
Sacramento R.
CENTRAL VALLEY
SIERRA NEVADA
Lake Tahoe
GREAT BASIN
Great Salt Lake
GREAT SALT LAKE DESERT
WASATCH RANGE
Kings Peak 13,528 ft. (4,123 m)
Mt. Elbert 14,433 ft. (4,399 m)
Pikes Peak 14,110 ft. (4,301 m)
San Joaquin R.
Mt. Whitney 14,495 ft. (4,418 m)
Death Valley -282 ft. (-86 m)
Lake Mead
COLORADO PLATEAU
River
Wheeler Peak 13,161 ft. (4,011 m)
MOJAVE DESERT
Humphreys Peak 12,633 ft. (3,851 m)
Salton Sea
Colorado
Channel Islands
Gila River
SONORAN DESERT
Pecos River
Guadalupe Peak 8,749 ft. (2,667 m)
Rio Grande
Gulf of California
MEXICO
40°N
130°W
120°W
110°W
ARCTIC OCEAN
70°N
RUSSIA
BROOKS RANGE
ALASKA
Bering Strait
Denali 20,310 ft. (6,190 m)
CANADA
Yukon River
ALASKA RANGE
60°N
Bering Sea
Gulf of Alaska
Aleutian Islands
0 200 400 miles
0 200 400 kilometers
170°W
160°W
150°W
140°W
160°W
155°W
Kauai
Oahu
HAWAII
Niihau
Molokai
PACIFIC OCEAN
Lanai
Maui
Kahoolawe
Hawaii
20°N
Mauna Kea 13,796 ft. (4,205 m)
0 100 200 miles
0 100 200 kilometers
National boundary
State boundary
Mountain peak
Highest point
Lowest point
Continental Divide

CANADA
0
200
400 miles
0
200
400 kilometers
GREAT LAKES
Lake Superior
MESABI RANGE
Lake Michigan
Lake Huron
Lake Ontario
Lake Erie
St. Lawrence River
WHITE MTS.
Mt. Washington 6,288 ft. (1,917 m)
GREEN MTS.
ADIRONDACK MTS.
Cape Cod
Hudson R.
Susquehanna R.
40°N
Long Island
GREAT PLAINS
Mississippi River
Missouri River
Platte River
CENTRAL PLAINS
ALLEGHENY PLATEAU
ALLEGHENY MTS.
Delaware Bay
Ohio River
Wabash River
Potomac River
Chesapeake Bay
APPALACHIAN MOUNTAINS
PIEDMONT
ATLANTIC COASTAL PLAIN
Cape Hatteras
Arkansas River
INTERIOR PLAINS
OZARK PLATEAU
Mt. Mitchell 6,684 ft. (2,037 m)
Tennessee River
Savannah River
Mississippi River
OUACHITA MOUNTAINS
Red River
ATLANTIC OCEAN
Alabama River
Chattahoochee River
Brazos River
30°N
Colorado River
GULF COASTAL PLAIN
WARDS PLATEAU
Mobile Bay
Mississippi River Delta
Galveston Bay
Lake Okeechobee
THE BAHAMAS
Gulf of Mexico
N
W
E
S
Florida Keys
Straits of Florida
90°W
80°W
McGraw-Hill Education

# World: Political

160°W
120°W
80°N
60°N
40°N
20°N
0° EQUATOR
20°S
40°S
60°S
ALASKA (U.S.)
CANADA
NORTH AMERICA
UNITED STATES
MIDWAY ISLANDS (U.S.)
BERMUDA (U.K.)
ATLANTIC OCEAN
TROPIC OF CANCER
HAWAII (U.S.)
See inset below
MEXICO
Caribbean Sea
GUYANA
PACIFIC OCEAN
VENEZUELA
SURINAME
GALAPAGOS ISLANDS (Ecuador)
COLOMBIA
ECUADOR
FRENCH GUIANA (France)
SOUTH AMERICA
AMERICAN SAMOA (U.S.)
SAMOA
COOK ISLANDS (N.Z.)
FRENCH POLYNESIA (France)
PERU
BRAZIL
BOLIVIA
TONGA
PITCAIRN ISLAND (U.K.)
TROPIC OF CAPRICORN
PARAGUAY
URUGUAY
CHILE
ARGENTINA
FALKLA ISLANDS
SOUTH GEOR SOUTH SAND ISLANDS
ANTARCTIC CIRCLE
80°W
120°W
160°W
90°W
80°W
70°W
60°W
Gulf of Mexico
FLORIDA (U.S.)
0 200 400 miles
0 200 400 kilometers
THE BAHAMAS
TROPIC OF CANCER
TURKS & CAICOS ISLANDS (U.K.)
ATLANTIC OCEAN
20°N
CUBA
PUERTO RICO (U.S.)
VIRGIN IS. (U.K.)
ST. KITTS & NEVIS
MEXICO
CAYMAN IS. (U.K.)
HAITI
DOMINICAN REPUBLIC
ANTIGUA & BARBUDA
BELIZE
VIRGIN IS. (U.S.)
GUADELOUPE (France)
JAMAICA
MONTSERRAT (U.K.)
GUATEMALA
DOMINICA
MARTINIQUE (France)
HONDURAS
N
Caribbean Sea
CURAÇAO (Netherlands)
BONAIRE (Netherlands)
ST. LUCIA
EL SALVADOR
W
E
S
ST. VINCENT & THE GRENADINES
BARBADOS
NICARAGUA
ARUBA (Netherlands)
GRENADA
TRINIDAD AND TOBAGO
10°N
COSTA RICA
PACIFIC OCEAN
PANAMA
VENEZUELA
COLOMBIA
GUYANA

ARCTIC OCEAN
0°
40°E
80°E
120°E
160°E
80°N
SVALBARD (Norway)
ARCTIC CIRCLE
ICELAND
See inset below
RUSSIA
EUROPE
KAZAKHSTAN
MONGOLIA
ASIA
GEORGIA
UZBEKISTAN
KYRGYZSTAN
ARMENIA
TURKMENISTAN
TAJIKISTAN
TURKEY
AZERBAIJAN
SYRIA
TUNISIA
LEBANON
IRAQ
AFGHANISTAN
IRAN
KUWAIT
QATAR
PAKISTAN
NEPAL
BHUTAN
CHINA
NORTH KOREA
SOUTH KOREA
JAPAN
PACIFIC OCEAN
TROPIC OF CANCER
40°N
20°N
MOROCCO
ALGERIA
LIBYA
EGYPT
ISRAEL
JORDAN
SAUDI ARABIA
BANGLADESH
TAIWAN
UNITED ARAB EMIRATES
OMAN
INDIA
MYANMAR (BURMA)
LAOS
NORTHERN MARIANA ISLANDS (U.S.)
WAKE ISLAND (U.S.)
MAURITANIA
MALI
NIGER
CHAD
SUDAN
ERITREA
YEMEN
THAILAND
VIETNAM
GUAM (U.S.)
MARSHALL ISLANDS
PHILIPPINES
BURKINA FASO
BENIN
NIGERIA
AFRICA
DJIBOUTI
GUINEA
GHANA
CENTRAL AFRICAN REPUBLIC
SOUTH SUDAN
ETHIOPIA
SRI LANKA
CAMBODIA
BRUNEI
PALAU
FEDERATED STATES OF MICRONESIA
LIBERIA
TOGO
CAMEROON
SOMALIA
MALDIVES
MALAYSIA
COTE D'IVOIRE
UGANDA
KENYA
EQUATOR
KIRIBATI
0°
SAO TOMÉ AND PRINCIPE
GABON
RWANDA
DEM. REPUBLIC OF THE CONGO
BURUNDI
EQUATORIAL GUINEA
TANZANIA
SEYCHELLES
INDONESIA
PAPUA NEW GUINEA
SOLOMON ISLANDS
CONGO
ANGOLA
COMOROS
INDIAN OCEAN
EAST TIMOR
TUVALU
ATLANTIC OCEAN
ZAMBIA
MALAWI
NAMIBIA
ZIMBABWE
MADAGASCAR
VANUATU
FIJI
BOTSWANA
MAURITIUS
TROPIC OF CAPRICORN
20°S
MOZAMBIQUE
REUNION (France)
NEW CALEDONIA (France)
AUSTRALIA
SOUTH AFRICA
SWAZILAND
LESOTHO
N
W
E
S
FRENCH SOUTHERN & ANTARCTIC LANDS (France)
40°S
NEW ZEALAND
0 1,000 2,000 miles
0 1,000 2,000 kilometers
40°E
80°E
120°E
160°E
60°S
ANTARCTIC CIRCLE
ANTARCTICA
80°S
10°E
20°E
30°E
40°E
50°E
60°N
FINLAND
RUSSIA
NORWAY
SWEDEN
0 200 400 miles
0 200 400 kilometers
ESTONIA
North Sea
DENMARK
Baltic Sea
LATVIA
LITHUANIA
IRELAND
UNITED KINGDOM
RUSSIA
BELARUS
50°N
NETHERLANDS
POLAND
BELGIUM
GERMANY
ATLANTIC OCEAN
LUXEMBOURG
CZECH REPUBLIC
UKRAINE
LIECHTENSTEIN
FRANCE
SLOVAKIA
SWITZERLAND
AUSTRIA
MOLDOVA
HUNGARY
RUSSIA
SLOVENIA
ROMANIA
CROATIA
MONACO
BOSNIA AND HERZEGOVINA
SERBIA
GEORGIA
Black Sea
ANDORRA
CORSICA (France)
BULGARIA
40°N
PORTUGAL
SPAIN
MONTENEGRO
KOSOVO
ITALY
MACEDONIA
SARDINIA (Italy)
ALBANIA
TURKEY
BALEARIC IS. (Spain)
GIBRALTAR (U.K.)
SICILY (Italy)
GREECE
MOROCCO
ALGERIA
TUNISIA
MALTA
CRETE (Gr.)
CYPRUS
SYRIA
LEBANON
Mediterranean Sea

# World: Physical

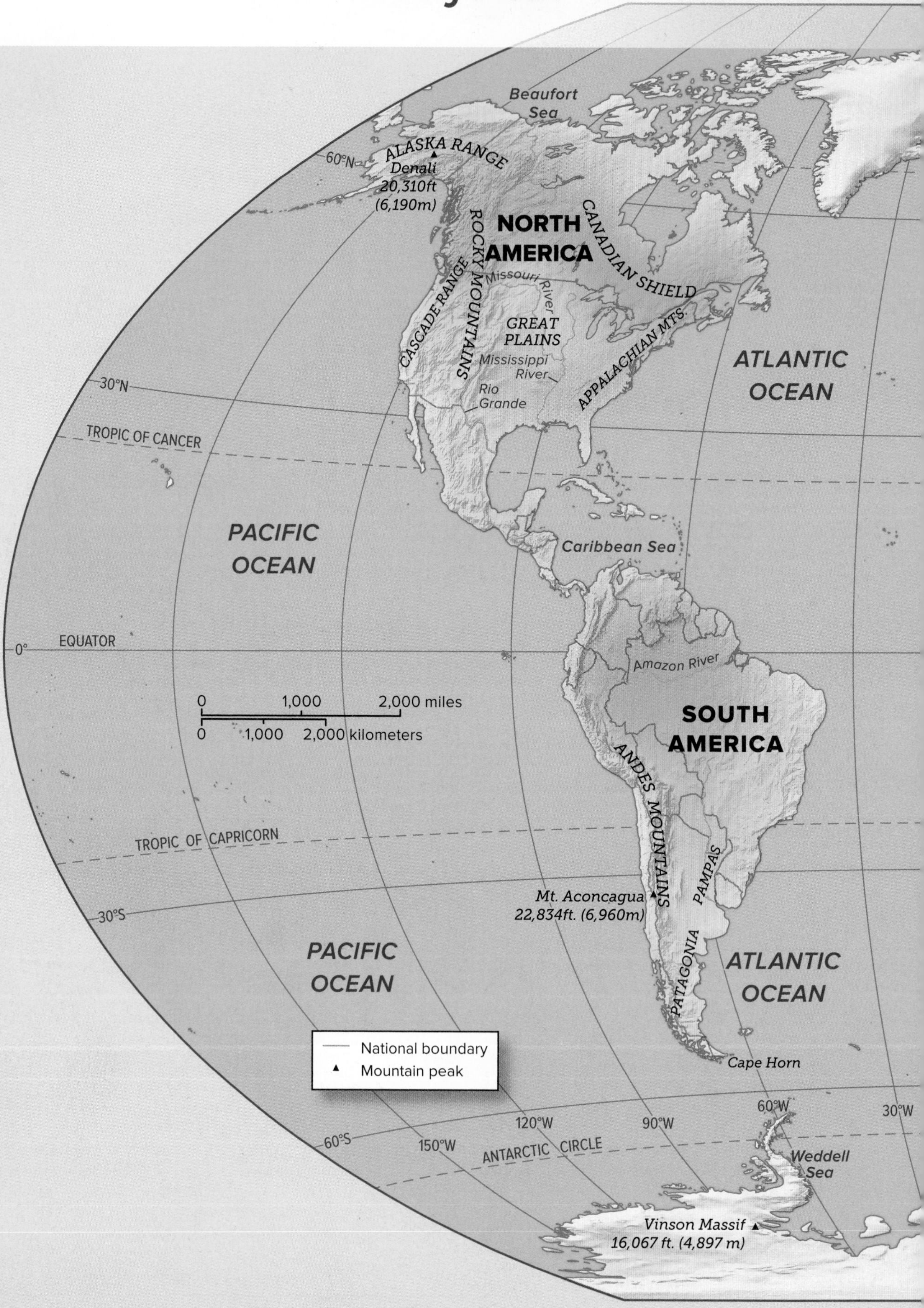

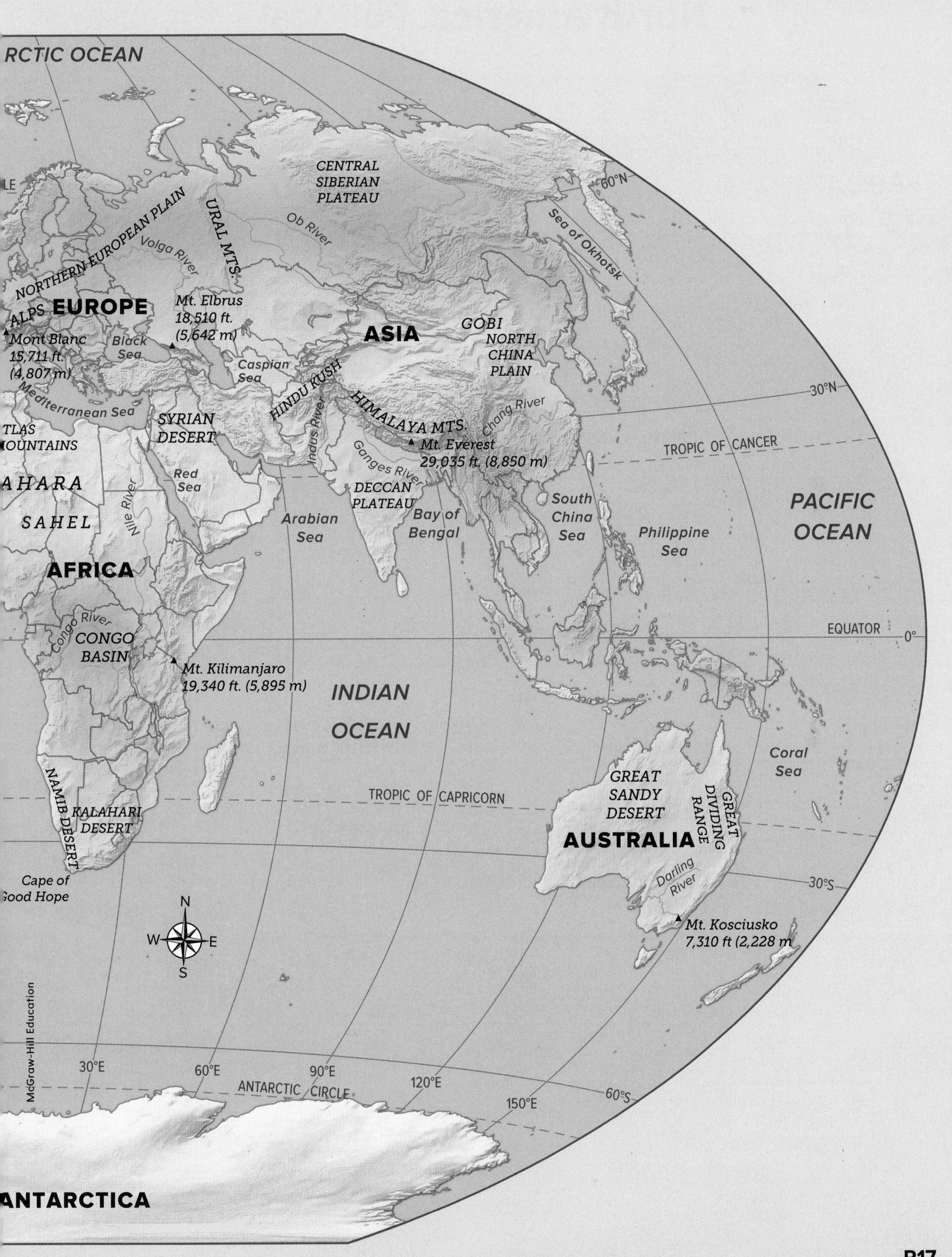
RCTIC OCEAN
CENTRAL SIBERIAN PLATEAU
60°N
Sea of Okhotsk
Ob River
URAL MTS.
NORTHERN EUROPEAN PLAIN
Volga River
ALPS
EUROPE
Mt. Elbrus 18,510 ft. (5,642 m)
Mont Blanc 15,711 ft. (4,807 m)
Black Sea
Caspian Sea
ASIA
GOBI
NORTH CHINA PLAIN
HINDU KUSH
HIMALAYA MTS.
Mediterranean Sea
SYRIAN DESERT
TLAS OUNTAINS
Indus River
Chang River
30°N
Mt. Everest 29,035 ft. (8,850 m)
TROPIC OF CANCER
Ganges River
AHARA
Red Sea
Nile River
DECCAN PLATEAU
SAHEL
Arabian Sea
Bay of Bengal
South China Sea
Philippine Sea
PACIFIC OCEAN
AFRICA
Congo River
CONGO BASIN
EQUATOR
0°
Mt. Kilimanjaro 19,340 ft. (5,895 m)
INDIAN OCEAN
Coral Sea
NAMIB DESERT
KALAHARI DESERT
TROPIC OF CAPRICORN
GREAT SANDY DESERT
GREAT DIVIDING RANGE
AUSTRALIA
Darling River
30°S
Cape of Good Hope
N
W
E
S
Mt. Kosciusko 7,310 ft (2,228 m
McGraw-Hill Education
30°E
60°E
90°E
120°E
150°E
ANTARCTIC CIRCLE
60°S
ANTARCTICA

# North America: Political

ARCTIC OCEAN
ASIA
Chukchi Sea
Bering Sea
Bering Strait
Alaska (U.S.)
Yukon River
Fairbanks
Anchorage
Beaufort Sea
Banks Island
Queen Elizabeth Islands
Parry Islands
Ellesmere Island
Greenland (Denmark)
ICELAND
Victoria Island
Baffin Island
Baffin Bay
Nuuk
Davis Strait
Iqaluit
Labrador Sea
Mackenzie River
Great Bear Lake
Yellowknife
Great Slave Lake
Gulf of Alaska
Juneau
Hudson Bay
Lake Athabasca
CANADA
Island of Newfoundland
Edmonton
Lake Winnipeg
Vancouver
Winnipeg
Quebec
Montreal
Ottawa
Seattle
Columbia R.
Snake River
Portland
Missouri River
Lake Superior
Lake Huron
Lake Ontario
Lake Michigan
Toronto
Boston
Minneapolis
Detroit
Lake Erie
New York
Philadelphia
Chicago
Great Salt Lake
Salt Lake City
UNITED STATES
Washington, D.C.
ATLANTIC OCEAN
San Francisco
Denver
Colorado River
Arkansas River
St. Louis
Ohio River
Tennessee River
Bermuda (U.K.)
Los Angeles
Phoenix
Red River
Mississippi R.
Atlanta
Dallas
Ciudad Juarez
Rio Grande
Houston
New Orleans
PACIFIC OCEAN
THE BAHAMAS
Nassau
Miami
Gulf of Mexico
Monterrey
Havana
CUBA
Puerto Rico (U.S.)
ANTIGUA AND BARBUDA
ST. KITTS AND NEVIS
St. John's
DOMINICAN REPUBLIC
HAITI
Port-au-Prince
Santo Domingo
MEXICO
Guadalajara
JAMAICA
Kingston
Roseau
DOMINICA
ST. LUCIA
ST. VINCENT & THE GRENADINES
GRENADA
TRINIDAD AND TOBAGO
Mexico City
BELIZE
Belmopan
GUATEMALA
Caribbean Sea
HONDURAS
Tegucigalpa
Guatemala City
San Salvador
NICARAGUA
EL SALVADOR
Managua
COSTA RICA
San José
PANAMA
Panama City
SOUTH AMERICA
National capital
Other city
N
S
E
W
0 300 600 miles
0 300 600 kilometers
80°N
70°N
60°N
50°N
40°N
30°N
20°N
10°N
0°
EQUATOR
180°
170°W
160°W
150°W
140°W
130°W
120°W
110°W
100°W
90°W
80°W
70°W
60°W
50°W
40°W
30°W
20°W
10°W
10°E
20°E

# North America: Physical

Greenland
Denmark
Labrador Sea
Hudson Bay
COAST MOUNTAINS
ROCKY MOUNTAINS
CANADIAN SHIELD
GREAT PLAINS
CANADA
Gulf of St. Lawrence
PACIFIC OCEAN
Great Lakes
Montréal
Toronto
New York
Philadelphia
Chicago
COASTAL RANGES
UNITED STATES
ATLANTIC OCEAN
APPALACHIAN MOUNTAINS
CENTRAL LOWLANDS
Los Angeles
COASTAL PLAIN
Baja Peninsula
SIERRA MADRE OCCIDENTAL
MEXICAN PLATEAU
SIERRA MADRE ORIENTAL
Houston
TROPIC OF CANCER
Gulf of Mexico
BAHAMAS
DOMINICAN REPUBLIC
Havana
CUBA
Greater Antilles
HAITI
Yucatan Peninsula
JAMAICA
Ecatepec
Mexico City
BELIZE
Caribbean Sea
MEXICO
N
W
E
S
GUATEMALA
HONDURAS
NICARAGUA
EL SALVADOR
COSTA RICA
PANAMA
30°W
40°W
50°W
60°W
70°W

# Europe: Political

ARCTIC OCEAN
ARCTIC CIRCLE
ATLANTIC OCEAN
North Sea
Baltic Sea
Bay of Biscay
Mediterranean Sea
Black Sea
AFRICA
ASIA
ICELAND
Reykjavik
Faroe Islands (Denmark)
Shetland Islands (U.K.)
IRELAND
Dublin
Belfast
UNITED KINGDOM
Glasgow
Edinburgh
Liverpool
London
NORWAY
Oslo
Bergen
SWEDEN
Stockholm
Göteborg
FINLAND
Helsinki
DENMARK
Copenhagen
ESTONIA
Tallinn
LATVIA
Riga
LITHUANIA
Vilnius
RUSSIA
BELARUS
Minsk
POLAND
Warsaw
Lodz
NETHERLANDS
Amsterdam
BELGIUM
Brussels
LUXEMBOURG
Luxembourg
GERMANY
Berlin
Hamburg
Cologne
Munich
Dresden
Rhine River
FRANCE
Paris
Nantes
Bordeaux
Marseille
Corsica (France)
MONACO
Monaco
ANDORRA
Andorra la Vella
SPAIN
Madrid
Bilbao
Valencia
Barcelona
Cartagena
Ebro River
Balearic Isands (Spain)
PORTUGAL
Lisbon
GIBRALTAR (U.K.)
SWITZERLAND
Bern
LIECHTENSTEIN
Vaduz
ITALY
Rome
Milan
Venice
Naples
Sardinia (Italy)
Sicily (Italy)
SAN MARINO
MALTA
Valletta
AUSTRIA
Vienna
CZECH REPUBLIC
Prague
SLOVAKIA
Bratislava
HUNGARY
Budapest
SLOVENIA
Ljubljana
CROATIA
Zagreb
BOSNIA AND HERZEGOVINA
Sarajevo
MONTENEGRO
Podgorica
SERBIA
Belgrade
KOSOVO
Priština
ALBANIA
Tirana
MACEDONIA
Skopje
GREECE
Athens
Crete (Greece)
BULGARIA
Sofia
ROMANIA
Bucharest
MOLDOVA
Chisinau
UKRAINE
Kiev
Kharkiv
Odessa
Dnieper River
RUSSIA
Moscow
St. Petersburg
Arkhangel'sk
Nizhniy Novgorod
Kazan
Samara
Saratov
Volgograd
Rostov
Volga River
National capital
Other city
N
S
E
W
70°N
60°N
50°N
40°N
20°W
10°W
0°
10°E
20°E
30°E
40°E
50°E
60°E

# Asia: Political

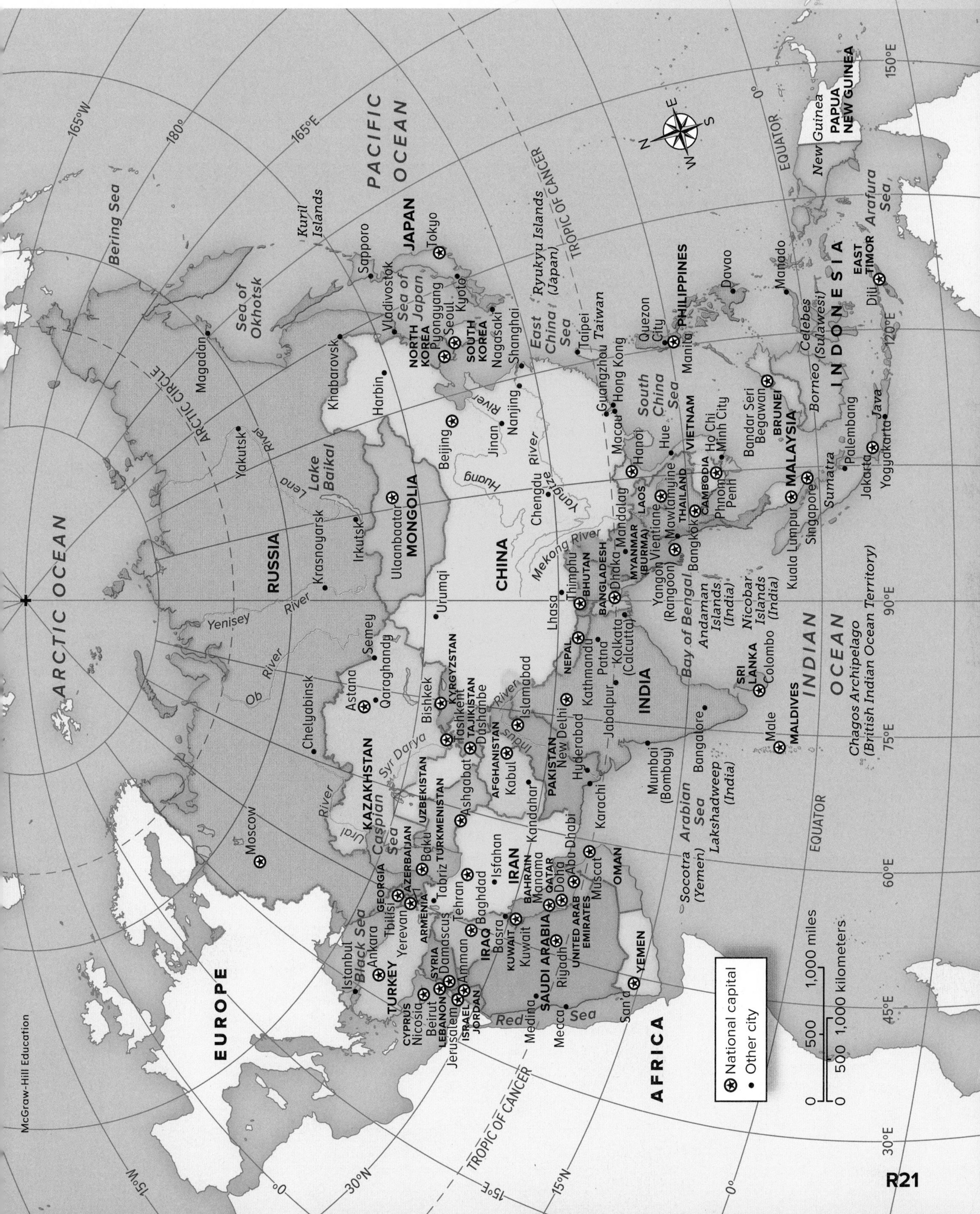

# Africa: Political

EUROPE
ASIA
Mediterranean Sea
Madeira Islands (Portugal)
Canary Islands (Spain)
Tangier
Rabat
Fez
Casablanca
MOROCCO
Marrakech
Algiers
Oran
Tunis
TUNISIA
Tripoli
Benghazi
Alexandria
Cairo
Laayoune
Western Sahara (Morocco)
ALGERIA
LIBYA
EGYPT
Nile R.
Red Sea
Aswan
Lake Nasser
TROPIC OF CANCER
MAURITANIA
Nouakchott
Senegal R.
MALI
Niger River
NIGER
CHAD
SUDAN
Port Sudan
Khartoum
ERITREA
Asmara
DJIBOUTI
Djibouti
Gulf of Aden
Dakar
SENEGAL
Banjul
GAMBIA
GUINEA-BISSAU
Bissau
GUINEA
Conakry
SIERRA LEONE
Freetown
Monrovia
LIBERIA
BURKINA FASO
Bamako
Ouagadougou
Niamey
Kano
N'Djamena
BENIN
NIGERIA
Abuja
GHANA
CÔTE D'IVOIRE
Yamoussoukro
TOGO
Accra
Lomé
Porto-Novo
Lagos
Benue River
Gulf of Guinea
Malabo
EQUATORIAL GUINEA
SÃO TOMÉ AND PRÍNCIPE
São Tomé
CAMEROON
Yaoundé
CENTRAL AFRICAN REPUBLIC
Bangui
SOUTH SUDAN
Juba
Addis Ababa
ETHIOPIA
SOMALIA
Mogadishu
UGANDA
Kampala
KENYA
Nairobi
RWANDA
Kigali
Lake Victoria
Bujumbura
BURUNDI
Kisangani
Libreville
GABON
CONGO
Brazzaville
Kinshasa
DEMOCRATIC REPUBLIC OF THE CONGO
Kananga
Lake Tanganyika
Dodoma
TANZANIA
Mombasa
Pemba Island
Zanzibar
Dar es Salaam
INDIAN OCEAN
SEYCHELLES
COMOROS
Moroni
Mayotte (France)
EQUATOR
ATLANTIC OCEAN
Cabinda (Angola)
Luanda
ANGOLA
MALAWI
Lake Malawi
Lilongwe
ZAMBIA
Lusaka
Zambezi River
MOZAMBIQUE
Harare
ZIMBABWE
MADAGASCAR
Antananarivo
NAMIBIA
Windhoek
BOTSWANA
Gaborone
Pretoria
Johannesburg
Maputo
SWAZILAND
Mbabane
Bloemfontein
Maseru
LESOTHO
Orange R.
Durban
SOUTH AFRICA
Cape Town
Port Elizabeth
Cape of Good Hope
TROPIC OF CAPRICORN
N
S
E
W
National capital
Other city
0 500 1,000 miles
0 500 1,000 kilometers
40°N
30°N
20°N
10°N
0°
10°S
20°S
30°S
20°W
10°W
0°
10°E
20°E
30°E
40°E
50°E

# South America: Political

Caribbean Sea
CENTRAL AMERICA
Barranquilla
Maracaibo
Valencia
Caracas
Lake Maracaibo
Orinoco River
VENEZUELA
Medellín
Magdalena River
Gulf of Panama
Bogotá
Cali
COLOMBIA
Georgetown
GUYANA
Paramaribo
SURINAME
Cayenne
FRENCH GUIANA (France)
ATLANTIC OCEAN
N
W
E
S
15°N
Quito
EQUATOR
0°
ECUADOR
Guayaquil
Iquitos
Negro River
Manaus
Amazon River
Belém
Equator
Tapajos River
Xingu River
Madeira River
Trujillo
PERU
Callao
Lima
Cuzco
BRAZIL
Recife
São Francisco River
Lake Titicaca
La Paz
Arequipa
15°S
BOLIVIA
Sucre
Salvador (Bahía)
Brasília
Paraguay River
Paraná River
Belo Horizonte
PARAGUAY
Antofagasta
TROPIC OF CAPRICORN
Asunción
São Paulo
Rio de Janeiro
Tucumán
CHILE
Uruguay River
Porto Alegre
Córdoba
Rosario
30°S
Valparaíso
Santiago
PACIFIC OCEAN
ARGENTINA
URUGUAY
Montevideo
Buenos Aires
Rio de la Plata
Concepción
Colorado River
ATLANTIC OCEAN
45°S
National capital
Other city
Falkland Islands (Islas Malvinas) (U.K.)
0 250 500 miles
0 250 500 kilometers
Strait of Magellan
Punta Arenas
105°W
90°W
75°W
60°W
45°W
30°W
South Georgia (U.K.)
McGraw-Hill Education

# Glossary

**abolitionist** a person who believed slavery was wrong and should be ended

**amendment** an addition to the Constitution

**article** a paragraph in a legal document

**assembly** a government legislature that represents the people of a particular place

**bill** a suggestion for a new law

**blockade** an obstacle preventing the movement of people or goods

**boycott** to refuse to do business or have contact with a person, group, company, country, or product

**cash crop** a plant that is grown for making money

**casualties** people killed or wounded during warfare

**cede** to give up something to someone else

**charter** a document granting someone ownership of something.

**claim** to declare that a place belongs to one's country upon arrival at the place

**colony** a territory settled by people from another place, usually far away

**commerce** the buying and selling of goods

**composition** the way in which something is put together

**conquest** victories by invading armies

**covenant** a contract; an agreement

**currency** the type of money used in a particular place

**delegate** a person who represents other people

**demand** the level of need for something

**dissension** disagreement between members of a group over an important issue

**diverse** containing many types of people or things

**draft** a picking of persons for required military service

**encomiendas** system of forced labor in Spanish colonies

**endeavor** to try hard to achieve a goal

**enlist** to enroll for military service

**environment** the setting in which something takes place

**fugitive** a person who flees or has escaped

## H

**habitat** an environment that is favorable to the survival of a species

**harvest** to take and gather such crops as wheat and corn for use

**hieroglyph** a type of ancient writing that uses pictures for words

**hunter-gatherer** an early human who lived by gathering wild plants and hunting animals

**imposing** putting in place by a government order

**inflation** increase in the cost of goods and services

**interchangeable** something that can be used in place of something else because it is identical

**ironclads** armored naval vessels

**issue** to give out or publish

**jury** a group of citizens that decides the outcome of a court case

**loom** a machine for making thread or yarn into cloth

## M

**Manifest Destiny** the belief that it was divine will for the United States to expand westward to the Pacific Ocean

**mercenary** soldier from a different country who is paid to fight in a war

**merchants** people who buy and sell goods

**mesa** a flat-topped hill with steep sides

**militia** a group of citizens organized for military service

**missionary** person on a religious mission, usually to convert others to Christianity

**monarch** a king or queen who rules a nation

**monopoly** complete control of something

**musket** a long gun similar to a rifle

**navigation** the art of guiding a boat, plane, or other transportation vehicle

**negotiate** to discuss and bargain for a solution

**oral history** spoken records, including stories, that have been passed from one generation to the next

**outpost** a fort or other military structure established away from the main army to help guard against surprise attacks

**pardon** to excuse an offense without a penalty

**physical** relating to material objects; having actual form

**policy** an official position on an issue

**popular sovereignty** allowing people in each territory to decide on an issue themselves

**potlatch** a special feast given by Native Americans of the Northwest Coast, in which the guests receive gifts

**prairie** flat or gently rolling land covered mostly with grasses and wildflowers

**press** the news media, including newspapers and magazines, websites, and TV and radio

**profiteer** people who take advantage of a poor economic situation, hoarding goods and selling them at high prices to make a large profit

**proprietor** a person with the legal right or title to something

## R

**rebel** person who defies authority

**recession** a temporary downturn in business activity

**reconcile** to become friendly again after a disagreement; to make peace with

**reconciliation** returning to the previous friendly condition of a relationship after a disagreement

**repeal** cancelation or withdrawal

**resistance** defense to diseases developed by the immune system

## S

**secede** to withdraw

**settlement** town created by people in an area previously uninhabited by that people

**sharecropping** farming land for the owner in return for a share of the value of the crop

**siege** the placing of an army around a city to force it to surrender

**slash-and-burn** a method of clearing land for farming by cutting and burning trees

**strategy** a careful plan or method

**surge** sudden increase

**term** the period of time during which an elected person is in office

**totem pole** a tall carved log used by Native Americans of the Northwest Coast to honor an important person or to mark a special event

**traitor** someone who betrays his or her country

**unconstitutional** an action or policy that goes against the Constitution of the United States

**vandalism** destruction of property

**warship** ships mounted with cannons or other large guns

# Index

This index lists many topics along with the pages in this book on which they are found. Page numbers after a *c* refer you to a chart or graph; after an *m*, a map; after a *p*, photographs; after a *ptg*, artwork; and after a *q*, a quotation.

## A

## D

## E

## M



## N